Basics of the
U.S. Health Care System

Third Edition

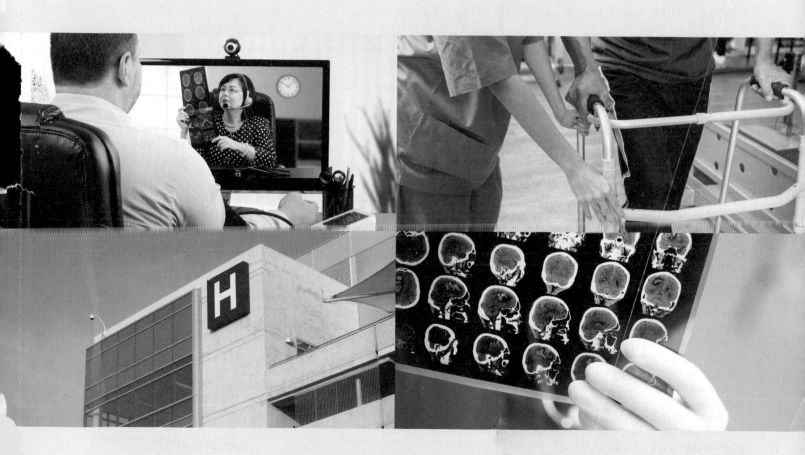

Nancy J. Niles, PhD, MPH, MS, MBA
Associate Professor, Rollins College, Winter Park, Florida

JONES & BARTLETT
LEARNING

World Headquarters
Jones & Bartlett Learning
5 Wall Street
Burlington, MA 01803
978-443-5000
info@jblearning.com
www.jblearning.com

Jones & Bartlett Learning books and products are available through most bookstores and online booksellers. To contact Jones & Bartlett Learning directly, call 800-832-0034, fax 978-443-8000, or visit our website, www.jblearning.com.

10300-7

Production Credits
VP, Executive Publisher: David D. Cella
Publisher: Michael Brown
Associate Editor: Lindsey Mawhiney
Associate Editor: Danielle Bessette
Production Manager: Carolyn Rogers Pershouse
Senior Vendor Manager: Tracey McCrea
Vendor Manager: Juna Abrams
Senior Marketing Manager: Sophie Fleck Teague
Manufacturing and Inventory Control Supervisor: Amy Bacus
Composition and Project Management: Integra Software Services Pvt. Ltd.

Cover Design: Kristin Parker
Rights & Media Specialist: Merideth Tumasz
Media Development Editor: Shannon Sheehan
Cover Images: Blood Pressure: © verbaska/Shutterstock; Walker: © Tyler Olson/Shutterstock; Hospital: © Steve Design/Shutterstock; MRI: © sfam_photo/Shutterstock
Printing and Binding: LSC Communications
Cover Printing: LSC Communications

Library of Congress Cataloging-in-Publication Data
Names: Niles, Nancy J., author.
Title: Basics of the U.S. health care system / Nancy Niles.
Description: Third edition. | Burlington, MA : Jones & Bartlett Learning, [2018] | Includes bibliographical references and index.
Identifiers: LCCN 2016045762 | ISBN 9781284102888(pbk.)
Subjects: | MESH: Delivery of Health Care | Insurance, Health | National Health Programs | United States
Classification: LCC RA445 | NLM W 84 AA1 | DDC 362.1--dc23 LC record available at
    https://lccn.loc.gov/2016045762

6048

Printed in the United States of America
20 19 18 17   10 9 8 7 6 5 4

Brief Contents

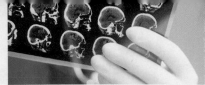

Hospital: © Steve Design/Shutterstock; Blood Pressure: © verbaska/Shutterstock; MRI: © stanj photo/Shutterstock

Contents

About the Author

Nancy J. Niles, PhD, MS, MBA, MPH, is in her 12th year of full-time undergraduate teaching. She is in her second year of teaching undergraduate and graduate healthcare management and administration courses at Rollins College in Winter Park, Florida. Prior to Rollins College, she taught 8 years of undergraduate business and healthcare management classes in the AACSB-accredited School of Management at Lander University in Greenwood, South Carolina, having spent 4 years teaching in the Department of Business Administration at Concord University in Athens, West Virginia. She became very interested in health issues as a result of spending two tours with the U.S. Peace Corps in Senegal, West Africa. She focused on community assessment and development, obtaining funding for business- and health-related projects. Her professional experience also includes directing the New York State lead poisoning prevention program and managing a small business development center in Myrtle Beach, South Carolina.

Her graduate education has focused on health policy and management. She received a master of public health from the Tulane School of Public Health in New Orleans, Louisiana, a master of management with a healthcare administration emphasis, and a master of business administration from the University of Maryland University College, and a doctorate from the University of Illinois at Urbana, Champaign in health policy.

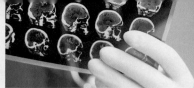

Acknowledgments

My mother, Joyce Robinson, continues to amaze me with her energy and I applaud her for her important work as a guardian ad litem for children in South Carolina. They are lucky to have her. I would also like to mention my childhood friends, Victoria Haskins McLaughlin, Maria Barrington Hummel, Shelley Teahan, and Susan Kalafut. Although I don't see them as much as I would like, I have wonderful memories of our adventures together in Albany, New York.

I would like to thank my husband, Donnie Niles, the love of my life, for his continued love and support. I would also like to thank Mike Brown at Jones & Bartlett Learning, who provided me with this opportunity to write my first textbook and now the third edition to my first effort. I also thank Danielle Bessette and Carmel Isaac who have been wonderful. I so appreciate their input into my projects.

Preface

I am very pleased to be updating this textbook because of the continued changes in the U.S. healthcare system as a result of the passage of the Affordable Care Act (ACA) in 2010. Fortunately, millions of individuals now have healthcare insurance as a result of the Act. Although the Act continues to be controversial, the Act has focused our healthcare delivery on patient centeredness and performance-based outcomes, which has improved the delivery of U.S. healthcare services. Preventable medical errors continue to be a problem but healthcare facilities are developing strategies to reduce these preventable errors.

I continue to review and update the student activities. I also included a section on a current events exercise. My students enjoy this type of exercise because they can apply the textbook information to a current healthcare event. The following is a summary of each chapter.

▶ Chapter 1

It is important as a healthcare consumer to understand the history of the U.S. healthcare delivery system, how it operates today, who participates in the system, what legal and ethical issues arise as a result of the system, and what problems continue to plague the healthcare system. We are all consumers of health care. Yet, in many instances, we are ignorant of what we are actually purchasing. If we were going to spend $1,000 on an appliance or a flat-screen television, many of us would research the product to determine if what we are purchasing is the best product for us. This same concept should be applied to purchasing healthcare services.

Increasing healthcare consumer awareness will protect you in both the personal and professional aspects of your life. You may decide to pursue a career in health care either as a provider or as an administrator. You may also decide to manage a business where you will have the responsibility of providing health care to your employees. And last, from a personal standpoint, you should have the knowledge from a consumer point of view so you can make informed decisions about what matters most—your health. The federal government agrees with this philosophy. The Affordable Care Act's health insurance marketplaces provide cost and service data so consumers can determine what is the best healthcare insurance to purchase and what services they will be receiving for that purchase. Recently, the Centers for Medicare and Medicaid Services (CMS) used its claim data to publish the hospital costs of the 100 most common treatments nationwide. The purpose of this effort is to provide data to consumers regarding healthcare costs because the costs vary considerably across the United States. This effort may also encourage pricing competition of healthcare services. The U.S. Department of Health and Human Services is providing funding to states to increase their healthcare pricing transparency

As the U.S. population's life expectancy continues to lengthen—increasing the "graying" of the population—the United States will be confronted with more chronic health issues because, as we age, more chronic health conditions develop. The U.S. healthcare system is one of the most expensive systems in the world. According to 2014 statistics, the United States spent $2.9 trillion or $9,255 per person on healthcare expenditures or 17.5% of its gross domestic product. The gross domestic product (GDP) is the total finished products or services that are produced in a country within a year. These statistics mean that over 17% of all of the products made within the borders of the United States within a year are healthcare related. Estimates indicate that healthcare spending will be 19.3% of the gross domestic product. The Gallup-Healthways Well-Being Index indicate that in 2014, the number of uninsured Americans has dropped to 16%. Among the states, Hawaii had the lowest percentage of uninsured individuals under age 65 in 2014 (2.5%), followed by Massachusetts (3.2%), Delaware (5.4%), and Iowa (6.4%). The District of Columbia also had a low insurance rate of 3.3%. Texas (21.5%), Oklahoma (21.5%), Alaska (21.2%), and Florida (18.8%) had the highest percentage of uninsured individuals under age 65 in 2014. The rates of uninsured individuals have dropped most among lower-income and black Americans. These drops have been attributed to the insurance mandate of the Affordable Care Act. The Institute of Medicine's (IOM) 1999 report indicated that nearly 100,000 citizens die each year as a result of medical errors. There have been more recent studies that indicate this estimate is much higher despite many quality improvement initiatives implemented over the years.

Although U.S. healthcare costs are very high, the United States does not offer healthcare coverage as a right of citizenship. The U.S. is the only major country that does not offer healthcare as a right. Most developed countries have a universal healthcare program, which means access to all citizens. Many of these systems are typically run by the federal government, have centralized health policy agencies, are financed through different forms of taxation, and payment of healthcare services are by a single payer—the government. France and the United Kingdom have been discussed as possible models for the United States to follow to improve access to health care, but these programs have problems and may not be the ultimate solution for the United States. However, because the United States does not offer any type of universal healthcare coverage, many citizens who are not eligible for government-sponsored programs are expected to provide the service for themselves through the purchase of health insurance or the purchase of actual services. Many citizens cannot afford these options, resulting in their not receiving routine medical care. The Patient Protection and Affordable Care Act of 2010 (PPACA), more commonly called the Affordable Care Act, has attempted to increase access to affordable healthcare. One of the mandates of the Act was the establishment of electronic health insurance marketplaces, which provide opportunities for consumers to search for affordable health insurance plans. There is also a mandate that individuals who do not have health insurance purchase health insurance if they can afford it or pay a fine. Both of these mandates have decreased the number of uninsured in the United States.

Despite U.S. healthcare expenditures, disease rates in the United States remain higher than those of many other developed countries because the United States has an expensive system that is available to only those who can afford it. Findings from a recent MetLife annual survey indicate that healthcare costs are worrying employees and their employers. Over 60% of employees are worried they will not be able to pay out-of- pocket expenses not covered by insurance. Employers are increasing the cost sharing of their employees for healthcare benefits because of the cost increases. Because the United States does not have universal health coverage, there are more health disparities across the nation. Persons living in poverty are more likely to be in poor health and less likely to use the healthcare system compared to those with incomes above the poverty line. If the United States offered universal health coverage, the per capita expenditures would be more evenly distributed and likely more effective. The major problem for the United States is that healthcare insurance is a major determinant of access to health care. Although there has been a decrease in the number of uninsured in the United States as a result of the individual mandate to purchase health insurance by the Affordable Care Act, there is still limited access to routine health care statistics. The infant mortality rate is often used to compare the health status of nations worldwide. Although our healthcare expenditures are very high, our infant mortality rates rank higher than many countries. Racial disparities in disease and death rates continue to be a concern. However, there has been a decline of 13% in infant mortality rates in the U.S. from 2000 to 2013. If you compare this statistic worldwide to comparable countries, their rates dropped during the same time period by 26%. The U.S. has more work to do regarding this issue. Both private and public participants in the U.S. health delivery system need to increase their collaboration to reduce these disease rates. Leaders need to continue to assess our healthcare system using the Iron Triangle to ensure there is a balance between access, cost, and quality.

▶ Chapter 2

The Patient Protection and Affordable Care Act (PPACA) or as it is commonly called, the Affordable Care Act (ACA), and its amendment, the Healthcare and Education Affordability Reconciliation Act of 2010, was signed into law on March 23, 2010, by President Barack Obama. The passage of this complex landmark legislation has been very controversial and continues to be contentious today.

There were national public protests and a huge division among the political parties regarding the components of the legislation. People, in general, agreed that the healthcare system needed some type of reform, but it was difficult to develop common recommendations that had majority support. Criticism focused in part on the increased role of government in implementing and monitoring the healthcare system. Proponents of healthcare reform reminded people that Medicare is a federal-government entitlement program because when individuals reach 65 years of age, they can receive their health insurance from this program. Millions of individuals are enrolled in Medicare. Medicaid is a state-established governmental public welfare insurance program based on income for millions of individuals, including children that provides health care for its enrollees.

However, regardless of these two programs, many critics felt that the federal government was forcing people to purchase health insurance. In fact, the ACA does require most individuals to obtain health insurance only if they can afford it. But with healthcare system expenditures comprising 17.9% of the U.S. gross domestic product and with millions of Americans not having access to health care, resulting in poor health indicators, the current administration's priority was to create mandated healthcare reform.

The Affordable Care Act has focused on primary care as the foundation for the U.S. healthcare system. The legislation has focused on 10 areas to improve the U.S. healthcare system, including quality, affordable, and efficient healthcare; public health and primary prevention of disease; healthcare workforce increases; community health; and increasing revenue provisions to pay for the reform. However, once the bill was signed, several states filed lawsuits. Several of these lawsuits argued that the act violates the U.S. Constitution because of the mandate of individual healthcare insurance coverage as well as that it infringes on states' rights with the expansion of Medicaid. The 2012 U.S. Supreme Court decision that upheld the constitutionality of the individual mandates should decrease the number of lawsuits. Despite these lawsuits, this legislation has clearly provided opportunities to increase consumer empowerment of the healthcare system by establishing the state American Health Benefit Exchanges, providing insurance to those individuals with preexisting conditions, eliminating lifetime and annual caps on health insurance payouts, improving the healthcare workforce, and providing databases so consumers can check the quality of their health care. The 10 titles of this comprehensive legislation are also focused on increasing the role of public health and primary care in the U.S. healthcare system and increasing accessibility to the system by providing affordable health care.

Although this legislation continues to be controversial, a system-wide effort needed to be implemented to curb rising healthcare costs although there have been reports that healthcare costs are increasing and consumers are paying higher cost sharing amounts.

There are five areas of health care that account for a large percentage of healthcare costs: hospital care, physician and clinician services, prescription drugs, nursing, and home healthcare expenditures. The legislation targets these areas by increasing quality assurance and providing a system of reimbursement tied to quality performance, providing accessibility to consumers regarding the quality of their health care, and increasing access to community health services. Also, the Affordable Care Act has focused on improving the U.S. public health system by increasing the accessibility to primary prevention services such as screenings and wellness visits at no cost. The ACA has mandated that healthcare providers make available certain services with no cost sharing to the healthcare consumer: 15 preventive services for adults, 22 preventive services for women, 25 preventive services for children, and 23 preventive services for Medicare enrollees. Revenue provisions are in place to offset some of the costs of this legislation. With continued controversy, it will be difficult to quickly assess the cost effectiveness and impact of this health reform on improving the health care of U.S. citizens. The President had to veto a repeal of the bill and the House of Representatives have a Task Force to craft an improved ACA. The next major issue is whether typical middle class Americans can afford the high deductibles and increased cost sharing for their healthcare.

▶ Chapter 3

The one commonality with all of the world's healthcare systems is that they all have consumers or users of their systems. Systems were developed to provide a service to their citizens. However, the U.S. healthcare system, unlike other systems in the world, does not provide healthcare access to all of its citizens. It is a very complex system that is comprised of many public and private components. Healthcare expenditures comprise approximately 17.5% of the gross domestic product (GDP). Health care is very expensive and most citizens do not have the money to pay for health care themselves. Individuals rely on health insurance to pay a large portion of their healthcare costs. Health insurance is predominantly offered by employers. The uninsured rate remains at an all-time low with 9.1% of under 65 uninsured as of the end of 2015 according to CDC.gov data. Generally, 2016 saw a rough increase of all the 2015 numbers. The government believes this is the result of the universal mandate for individual health insurance coverage.

In the United States, in order to provide healthcare services, there are several stakeholders or interested entities that participate in the industry. There are providers, of course, that consist of trained professionals such as physicians, nurses, dentists, and chiropractors. There are also inpatient and outpatient facilities; the payers such as the insurance companies, the government, and self-pay individuals; and the suppliers of products, such as pharmaceutical companies, medical equipment companies, and research and educational facilities. Each component plays an integral role in the healthcare industry. These different components further emphasize the complexity of the U.S. system. It is projected that between 2014 and 2024, nearly 10 million jobs will be added in the U.S. healthcare industry. The United States spends the highest proportion of its GDP on healthcare expenditures. The system is a combination of private and public resources. Since World War II, the United States has had a private fee-for-service system that has produced generous incomes for physicians and has been profitable for many participants in the healthcare industry. The healthcare industry operates like traditional business industries. Organizations designated as for profit need to make money in order to operate. The main goal of entities that are designated nonprofit is based on a particular social goal, but they also have to make money in order to continue their operations.

There are several major stakeholders that participate or have an interest in the industry. The stakeholders identified as participants in the healthcare industry include consumers, employers, healthcare and non-healthcare employers, healthcare providers, healthcare facilities, governments (federal, state, and local), insurance companies, educational and training institutions, professional associations that represent the different stakeholders, pharmaceutical companies, and research institutions. It is also important to mention the increasing prominence of alternative therapy medicine. Each role will be discussed briefly in this chapter.

It is important to assess the system from an international perspective. Comparing different statistics from the OECD is valuable to assess the health of the United States. Despite the amount of money spent on health care in the United States, the United States ranked lower on many measures than other countries that spend less on their healthcare systems. These statistics may point to the fact that other countries' healthcare systems are more effective than the U.S. system or that their citizens have healthier lifestyles, although obesity rates are increasing globally.

▶ Chapter 4

During the Depression and World War II the United States had no funds to start a universal healthcare program—an issue that had been discussed for years. As a result, a private-sector system was developed that did not provide healthcare services to all citizens. However, the government's role in providing healthcare coverage evolved to being a regulatory body to ensure that the elderly and poor were able to receive health care. The passage of the Social Security Act of 1935 and the establishment of the Medicaid and Medicare programs in 1965 mandated the government's increased role in providing healthcare coverage. Also, the State Children's Health Insurance Program (SCHIP), now the Children's Health Insurance Program, established in 1997 and reauthorized by the Affordable Care Act (ACA) through 2019, continues to expand the government's role in children's health care. The laws require states, upon enactment, to maintain current income eligibility levels for CHIP through September 30, 2019. In addition to the reauthorization of the CHIP program, the ACA increased governmental interaction with the healthcare system by developing several of the governmental initiatives that focus on increasing the ability of individuals to make informed decisions about their health care.

In these instances, the government increased accessibility to health care as well as provided financing for health care to certain targeted populations. The government plays an important role in the quality of the U.S. healthcare system. The federal government provides funding for state and local governmental programs. Federal healthcare regulations are implemented and enforced at the state and local levels. Funding is primarily distributed from the federal government to the state government, which then allocates funding to local health departments. Local health departments provide the majority of services for their constituents. More local health departments are working with local organizations such as schools and physicians to increase their ability to provide education and prevention services.

The DHS and FEMA now play an integral role in the management and oversight of catastrophic events, such as natural disasters, earthquakes, floods, pandemic diseases, and bioterrorism. The DHS and FEMA collaborate closely with the CDC to ensure that both the state and local health departments have a crisis management plan in place for these events. These attacks are often horrific and frightening with a tremendous loss of life, and as a result, the state and local health departments need to be more prepared to deal with catastrophic events. They are required to develop plans and be trained to deal effectively with many of these catastrophic issues. Finally, the Affordable Care Act has increased government involvement in the healthcare industry to promote access to a quality healthcare system. This chapter will focus on the different roles the federal, state, and local governments play in the U.S. healthcare system. This chapter will also highlight different governmental programs and regulations that focus on monitoring how health care is provided.

▶ Chapter 5

There are two important definitions of public health. In 1920, public health was defined by Charles Winslow as the science and art of preventing disease, prolonging life, and promoting physical health and efficiency through organized community efforts for the sanitation of the environment, control of community infections, and education of individuals regarding hygiene to ensure a standard of living for health maintenance. Sixty years later, the Institute of Medicine (IOM), in its 1988 *Future of Public Health* report, defined public health as an organized community effort to address public health by applying scientific and technical knowledge to promote health. Both definitions point to broad community efforts to promote health activities to protect the population's health status. The Affordable Care Act is also emphasizing the importance of prevention and wellness. The establishment of the Prevention and Public Health Fund has supported several community-based public health programs. To date, the Fund has invested in a broad range of evidence-based activities including community and clinical prevention initiatives; research, surveillance, and tracking; public health infrastructure; immunizations and screenings; tobacco prevention; and public health workforce and training. As of 2016, funding has been allocated to public health priorities including Alzheimer's disease prevention, chronic disease self-management, diabetes prevention, hospital promotion of breastfeeding, and lead poisoning prevention.

The development of public health is important to note as part of the basics of the U.S. healthcare system because its development was separate from the development of private medical practices. Public health specialists view health from a collectivist and preventative care viewpoint: to protect as many citizens as possible from health issues and to provide strategies to prevent health issues from occurring. The definitions cited in the previous paragraph emphasize this viewpoint. Public health concepts were in stark contrast to traditional medicine, which focused on the relationship between a provider and patient. Private practitioners held an individualistic viewpoint—people more often would be paying for their services from their health insurance or from their own pockets. Physicians would be providing their patients guidance on how to cure their diseases, not preventing disease. As a healthcare consumer, it is important to recognize the role that public health plays in our health care. If you are sick, you go to your physician for medical advice, which may mean receiving a prescription. However, there are often times that you may not go see your physician because you do not have health insurance or you do not feel that sick or you would like to change one of your lifestyle behaviors. Public health surrounds consumers with educational opportunities to change a health condition or behavior. You can visit the CDC's website, which provides information about different diseases and health conditions. You can also visit your local health department. CDC has become very proactive in developing successful social media campaigns regarding public health issues. Traditional medicine has also become entrenched in social media as well. These tools are an effective way to communicate with a society that is so connected with social media applications on a daily basis.

The concept of public health has been more publicized in the 21st century because of the terrorist attacks of 2001, the anthrax attacks in post offices, the natural disasters of Hurricane Katrina and Super storm Sandy, the Boston Marathon bombing, the Ebola and Zika virus epidemics and flooding in the Midwest. Funding has increased for public health activities because of these events. The concept of bioterrorism is now a reality. Because public health is now considered an integral component to battling terrorism and consequently a matter of national security, federal funding dramatically increased. This chapter will discuss the concept of health and healthcare delivery and the role of public health in delivering health care. The concepts of primary, secondary, and tertiary prevention and the role of public health in those delivery activities will be highlighted. Discussion will also focus on the origins of public health, the major role epidemiology plays in public health, the role of public health in disasters, core public health activities, the collaboration of public health and private medicine, and the importance of public health consumers.

▶ Chapter 6

Inpatient services are services that involve an overnight stay of a patient. Historically, the U.S. healthcare industry was based on the provision of inpatient services provided by hospitals and outpatient services provided by physicians. As our healthcare system evolved, hospitals became the mainstay of the healthcare system, offering primarily inpatient with limited outpatient services. Over the past two centuries, hospitals have evolved from serving the poor and homeless to providing the latest medical technology to serve the seriously ill and injured. Although their original focus was inpatient services, as a result of cost containment and consumer preferences, more outpatient services are now being offered by hospitals. Hospitals have evolved into medical centers that provide the most advanced service. Hospitals can be classified by who owns them, length of stay, and type of services provided. Inpatient services typically focus on acute care, which includes secondary and tertiary care levels that most likely require inpatient care. Inpatient care is very expensive and, throughout the years, has been targeted for cost-containment measures. Hospitals have begun offering more outpatient services that do not require an overnight stay and are less financially taxing on the healthcare system. U.S. healthcare expenditures have increased as part of the gross domestic product, and consequently, more cost-containment measures have evolved. Outpatient services have become more prevalent because they are less expensive and they are preferred by consumers.

Although hospitals admit 35 million individuals annually, the healthcare industry has recognized that outpatient services are a cost-effective method of providing quality health care and has therefore evolved into providing quality outpatient care. This type of service is the preferred method of receiving health care by the consumer. In 2015, there were over 900 million visits to doctor's offices, which is the traditional method of ambulatory care. However, as medicine has evolved and more procedures, such as surgeries, can be performed on an outpatient basis, different types of outpatient care have evolved. As discussed previously, there are more outpatient surgical centers, imaging centers, urgent and emergent care centers, and other services that used to be offered on an inpatient basis. There will continue to be an increase in outpatient services being offered. Technology will increase the quality and efficiency of health care for consumers. Telemedicine will also become a more widely used model for health care because of continued advances in technology. The implementation of patient electronic health record systems nationwide will be the impetus for the development of more electronic healthcare services. This chapter will discuss the evolution of outpatient and inpatient healthcare services in the United States.

▶ Chapter 7

The healthcare industry is the fastest growing industry in the U.S. economy, employing a workforce of nearly 20 million healthcare workers. Considering the aging of the U.S. population and the impact of the Affordable Care Act, it is expected that the healthcare industry will continue to experience strong job growth. Job growth in many healthcare sectors is outpacing that in other industries. When we think of healthcare providers, we automatically think of physicians and nurses. However, the healthcare industry is composed of many different health service professionals, including dentists, optometrists, psychologists, chiropractors, podiatrists, nonphysician practitioners (NPPs), administrators, and allied health professionals. It is important to identify allied health professionals because they provide a range of essential healthcare services that complement the services provided by physicians and nurses. This category of health professionals is an integral component of providing quality health.

Health care can occur in varied settings. Physicians have traditionally operated in their own practices but they also work in hospitals, mental health facilities, managed care organizations, and community health centers. They may also hold government positions or teach at a university. They could be employed by an insurance company. Health professionals, in general, may work at many different organizations, both for profit and nonprofit. Although the healthcare industry is one of the largest employers in the United States, there continue to be shortages of physicians in certain geographic areas of the country. Rural areas continue to suffer physician shortages, which limits consumer access to health care. There have been different incentive programs to encourage physicians to relocate to rural areas, but shortages still exist. In most states, only physicians, dentists, and a few other practitioners may serve patients directly without the authorization of another licensed independent health professional. Those categories authorized include chiropractic, optometry, psychotherapy, and podiatry. Some states authorize midwifery and physical therapy. There also continues to be a shortage of registered nurses nationwide, with the most need identified in the south and west. There is also a shortage of qualified nursing faculty to teach in nursing schools, which limits the number of students enrolled in registered nursing programs. The American Association of Colleges of Nursing (AACN) is discussing this issue with policy makers.

Healthcare personnel comprise one of the largest labor forces in the United States. This chapter provided an overview of the different types of employees in the healthcare industry. Some of them require many years of education; however, some of these positions can be attained upon completion of 1–2 year programs. The healthcare industry will continue to progress as U.S. trends in demographics, disease, and public health pattern change, and cost and efficiency issues, insurance issues, technological influences, and economic factors continue to evolve. More occupations and professions will develop as a result of these trends. The major trend that will impact the healthcare industry is the aging of the U.S. population. The BLS predicts that half of the next decades' fastest growing job categories will be in the healthcare industry. The Affordable Care Act will continue to have an impact on the positive growth for this industry. This chapter will provide a description of the different types of healthcare professionals and their role in providing care in the U.S. system

▶ Chapter 8

The percentage of the U.S. gross domestic product (GDP) devoted to healthcare expenditures has increased over the past several decades. In 2014, the United States spent $2.6 trillion on health care or 17.5% of the GDP, which is the highest percentage of its GDP in the world. The Centers for Medicare and Medicaid Services (CMS) predicts annual healthcare costs will be $4.64 trillion by 2024, which represents nearly 20% of the U.S. GDP.

As healthcare technology and research provide for more sophisticated and more expensive procedures, there will be an increase in healthcare expenses. Three areas account for over 60% of national healthcare expenditures: hospital care, physician and clinical services, and prescription drugs (Health spending explorer, 2016). Unlike countries that have universal healthcare systems, payment of healthcare services in the United States is derived from (1) out-of-pocket payments or cost sharing from patients who pay entirely or partially for services rendered; (2) health

insurance plans, such as indemnity plans or managed care organizations; (3) public or governmental funding such as Medicare, Medicaid, and other governmental programs; and (4) health savings accounts (HSAs). Much of the burden of healthcare expenditures has been borne by private sources—employers and their health insurance programs. Individuals may continue to pay their health insurance premiums through the Consolidated Omnibus Budget Reconciliation Act (COBRA) once they are unemployed, but most individuals cannot afford to pay the expensive premiums.

As a result of the passage of the Affordable Care Act (ACA) of 2010, the government has played a proactive role in developing a healthcare system that is more consumer oriented. The Act is requiring more employers to offer health insurance benefits and requiring individuals to purchase healthcare insurance if they can afford it from the health insurance marketplaces. The Act also requires health insurance plans to provide more information about their plans to their members so they can make informed decisions about their healthcare.

To understand the complexity of the U.S. healthcare system, this chapter will provide a breakdown of U.S. healthcare spending by source of funds, and the major private and public sources of funding for these expenditures. It is important to reemphasize that there are three parties involved in providing health care: the provider, the patient, and the fiscal intermediary such as a health insurance company or the government. Therefore, also included in the chapter is a description of how healthcare providers are reimbursed for their services and how reimbursement rates were developed for both private and public funds.

▶ Chapter 9

Managed care is a healthcare delivery system organized to manage cost, utilization, and quality. Managed care refers to the cost management of healthcare services by controlling who the consumer sees and how much the service costs. Managed care organizations (MCOs) were introduced 40 years ago, but became more entrenched in the healthcare system when the Health Maintenance Organization Act of 1973 was signed into law by President Nixon. Healthcare costs were spiraling out of control during that period. Encouraging the increase in the development of HMOs, the first widely used managed care model, would help to control the healthcare costs. MCOs' integration of the financial industry with the medical service industry resulted in controlling the reimbursement rate of services, which allowed MCOs more control over the health insurance portion of health care. Physicians were initially resistant to managed care models because they were threatened by loss of income. As the number of managed care models increased, physicians realized they had to accept this new form of healthcare delivery and, if they participated in a managed care organization, it was guaranteed income. Managed care health plans have become a standard option for consumers. Medicare Part C, which is commonly called Medicare Advantage, offers managed care options to their enrollees. Medicaid managed care provides for the delivery of Medicaid health benefits and additional services through contracted arrangements between state Medicaid agencies and MCOs that accept a set payment per member per month (capitation) for these services. Many employers offer managed care plans to their employees.

There also have been issues with how MCOs have reimbursed physicians. The issue with silent PPOs has financially hurt physicians. Physicians have also had problems with timely reimbursement from MCOs. There were issues with fraudulent reimbursement rates of out-of-network services, which resulted in members paying exorbitant out-of-pocket expenses. However, the American Medical Association has developed tools to assist physicians with managed care contracting and reimbursement processes. The Affordable Care Act mandate that insurance companies must spend 80–85% of their premium revenues on quality care or be penalized with fines, give rebates to their members, or both will be an incentive for MCOs to provide quality and affordable care. As healthcare continues to focus on providing quality care and cost reduction, having a database such as HEDIS can provide important information to both the healthcare providers and consumers. This chapter will discuss the evolution of managed care and why it developed, the different types of managed care, the MCO assessment measures used for cost control, issues regarding managed care, and how managed care has impacted the delivery of healthcare services.

▶ Chapter 10

The general term informatics refers to the science of computer application to data in different industries. Health or medical informatics is the science of computer application that supports clinical and research data in different areas of health care. It is a methodology of how the healthcare industry thinks about patients and how their treatments are defined and evolved. For example, imaging informatics applies computer technology to organs and tissue. Health information systems are systems that store, transmit, collect, and retrieve this data. The goal of health information technology (HIT) goal is to manage the health data that can be used by patients–consumers, insurance companies, healthcare providers, healthcare administrators, and any stakeholder that has an interest in health care.

HIT impacts every aspect of the healthcare industry. All of the stakeholders in the healthcare industry use HIT. Information technology (IT) has had a tremendous impact on the healthcare industry because it allows faster documentation of every transaction. When an industry focuses on saving lives, it is important that every activity has a written document that describes the activity. Computerization of documentation has increased the management efficiency and accuracy of healthcare data. The main focus of HIT is the national implementation of an electronic patient record. Both President Bush and President Obama have supported this initiative.

This is the foundation of many IT systems because it will enable different systems to share patient information, which will increase the quality and efficiency of health care. This chapter will discuss the history of IT, different applications of IT health care, and the status of electronic health records and barriers for its national implementation.

The healthcare industry has lagged behind other industries utilizing IT as a form of communicating important data. Despite that fact, there have been specific applications developed for HIT such as e-prescibing, telemedicine, ehealth, and specific applied technologies such as the PatientPoint, MelaFind optical scanner, the Phreesia Pad, Sapien heart valve, robotic checkups, Electronic Aspirin, Accuson P10, and the Piccolo xpress, which were discussed in this chapter. Healthcare organizations have recognized the importance of IT and have hired CIOs and CTOs to manage their data. However, healthcare consumers need to embrace an electronic patient record, which is the basis for the Microsoft Health Vault. This will enable patients to be treated effectively and efficiently nationally. The patient health record can be integrated into the electronic health records that are being utilized nationwide. Having the ability to access a patient's health information could assist in reducing medical errors. As a consumer, utilizing a tool like HealthVault could provide an opportunity to consolidate all medical information electronically so, if there are any medical problems, the information will be readily available. The major IT issue in healthcare is the need to establish the interoperability of EHRs systems nationwide. This communication between systems will enable patients to be treated more quickly because there will be immediate access to their most current medical information. Although the federal government has indicated this communication between systems needs is necessary to ensure the full success of electronic health records system, the progress continues to be slow.

▶ Chapter 11

The healthcare industry is one of the most heavily regulated industries in the United States. Those who provide, receive, pay for, and regulate healthcare services are affected by the law. To be an effective healthcare manager, it is important to understand basic legal and ethical principles that influence the work environment, including the legal relationship between the organization and the consumer—the healthcare provider and the patient. The basic concepts of law, both civil and criminal healthcare law, tort reform, employment-related legislation, safety in the workplace, and the legal relationship between the provider and the patient will be discussed in this chapter. I have included some examples of LGBT-related claims that EEOC views as unlawful sex discrimination, which I think is timely.

▶ Chapter 12

Legal standards are the minimal standard of action established for individuals in a society. Ethical standards are considered one level above a legal action because individuals make a choice based on what is the "right thing to do," not what is required by law. There are many interpretations of the concept of ethics. Ethics has been interpreted as the moral foundation for standards of conduct. The concept of ethical standards applies to actions that are hoped for and expected by individuals. Actions may be considered legal but not ethical. There are many definitions of ethics but, basically, ethics is concerned with what are right and wrong choices as perceived by society and individuals.

The concept of ethics is tightly woven throughout the healthcare industry. It has been dated back to Hippocrates, the father of medicine, in the 4th century BC, and evolved into the Hippocratic Oath, which is the foundation for the ethical guidelines for patient treatment by physicians. In 1847, the American Medical Association (AMA) published a *Code of Medical Ethics* that provided guidelines for the physician–provider relationship, emphasizing the duty to treat a patient. To this day, physicians' actions have followed codes of ethics that demand the "duty to treat".

Applying the concept of ethics to the healthcare industry has created two areas of ethics: medical ethics and bioethics. Medical ethics focuses on the decisions healthcare providers make concerning medical treatment of patients. Euthanasia or physician-assisted suicide would be an example of a medical ethics topic. Advance directives are orders that patients give to providers to ensure that, if they are terminally ill and incompetent to make a decision, certain measures will not be taken to prolong that patient's life. If advance directives are not provided, the ethical decision of when to withdraw treatment may be placed on the family and provider. These issues are legally defined, although there are ethical ramifications surrounding these decisions.

This chapter will focus primarily on bioethics. This field of study is concerned with the ethical implications of certain biologic and medical procedures and technologies, such as cloning; alternative reproductive methods, such as in vitro fertilization; organ transplants; genetic engineering; and care of the terminally ill. Additionally, the rapid advances in medicine in these areas raised questions about the influence of technology on the field of medicine.

It is important to understand the impact of ethics in different aspects of providing health care. Ethical dilemmas in health care are situations that test a provider's belief and what the provider should do professionally. Ethical dilemmas are often a conflict between personal and professional ethics. A healthcare ethical dilemma is a problem, situation, or opportunity that requires an individual, such as a healthcare provider, or an organization, such as a managed care practice, to choose an action that could be unethical. A decision-making model is presented that can help resolve ethical dilemmas in the healthcare field. This chapter will discuss ethical theories, codes of healthcare conduct, informed consent, confidentiality, special populations, research ethics, ethics in public health, end-of-life decisions, genetic testing and profiling, and biomedical ethics, which focuses on technology use and health care.

▶ Chapter 13

According to the World Health Organization, mental wellness or mental health is an integral and essential component of health. It is a state of well-being in which an individual can cope with normal stressors, can work productively, and is able to make a contribution to his or her community. Mental health behavioral disorders can be caused by biological, psychological, and personality factors. By 2020, behavioral health disorders will surpass all physiological diseases as a major cause of disability worldwide. Mental disorders are the leading cause of disability in the United States. Mental illnesses can impact individuals of any age, race, religion, or income. According to the Substance Abuse and Mental Health Services Administration's 2014 National Survey, an estimated 43.6 million (18.1%) Americans age 18 or older experienced some form of mental illness. In 2014, 20.2 million adults (8.4%) had a substance use disorder. Anxiety disorders are the most common type of mental disorders, followed by depressive disorders.

Different mental disorders are more likely to begin and occur at different stages in life and are thus more prevalent in certain age groups. Lifetime anxiety disorders generally have the earliest age of first onset, most commonly around age 6. Although mental health is a disease that requires medical care, its characteristics set it apart from traditional medical care. U.S. Surgeon General David Satcher released a landmark report in 1999 on mental health and illness, *Mental Health: A Report of the Surgeon General*. The Surgeon General's report on mental health defines mental disorders as conditions that alter thinking processes, moods, or behavior and result in dysfunction or stress. The condition can be psychological or biological in nature. The most common conditions include phobias, which are excessive fear of objects or activities; substance abuse; and affective disorders, which are emotional states such as depression. Severe mental illness includes schizophrenia, major depression, and psychosis. Obsessive-compulsive disorders (OCD), intellectual disabilities, Alzheimer's disease, and dementia are also considered mentally disabling conditions.

According to the report, mental health ranks second to heart disease as a limitation on health and productivity. People who have mental disorders often exhibit feelings of anxiety or may have hallucinations or feelings of sadness or fear that can limit normal functioning in their daily life. Because the causes or etiologies of mental health disorders are less defined and less understood compared to traditional medical problems, interventions are less developed than in other areas of medicine. This chapter will discuss the following topics: the history of the U.S. mental healthcare system, a background of healthcare professionals, mental healthcare law, insurance coverage for mental health, barriers to mental health care, the populations at risk for mental disorders, the types of mental health disorders as classified by the American Psychiatric Association's *Diagnostic and Statistical Manual of Mental Disorders (DSM)*, liability issues associated with mental health care, an analysis of the mental healthcare system, and guidelines and recommendations to improve U.S. mental health care. A section on family and caregivers is also included.

▶ Chapter 14

The U.S. healthcare system has long been recognized for providing state-of-the-art health care. It has also been recognized as the most expensive healthcare system in the world and the price tag is expected to increase. Despite offering two large public programs—Medicare and Medicaid for elderly, indigent, or disabled individuals—current statistics indicate that millions of individuals are uninsured, although the Affordable Care Act's individual mandate to purchase health insurance coverage has reduced those numbers.

The U.S. healthcare system continues to evolve. Technology will continue to have a huge impact on health care. Consumers have more information to make healthcare decisions because of information technology. Healthcare providers have more opportunities to utilize technology such as robotic surgery, e-prescribing, and clinical decision support systems that will assist them with diagnoses. The Green House Project is an exciting initiative that may transform how long-term care will be implemented. As our population becomes grayer, more citizens will want to live as independently as possible for a longer period of time, and the Green House Project is an excellent template for achieving this goal. All of these initiatives are exciting for the healthcare consumer. The implementation of an EHR, which will enable providers to share information about a patient's health history, will provide the consumer with the opportunity to obtain more cost-effective and efficient health care. The Veterans Administration hospitals use the EHR system. Duke University Health System also uses an

EHR system in North Carolina. There are hospitals, physician practices, and other healthcare organizations that utilize EHR systems across the country. Even though implementing the system nationally will be extremely expensive—costs have been estimated in the billions—it will eventually be a cost-saving measure for the United States. The Affordable Care Act has provided many incentives to improve the quality of and access to the U.S. healthcare system. The Center for Medicaid and Medicare Innovation has over 40 demonstration projects that focus on different types of financing models that are based on the performance of healthcare providers.

The discussion concerning different countries' healthcare systems indicate that all countries have problems with their healthcare systems. Establishing a universal healthcare system in the United States may not be the answer. There are aspects of each of these programs that could be integrated into the U.S. system. There are a surprising number of similarities. The major differences are in the area of the control the government places on pharmaceutical prices and health insurers. Some governments limit drug manufacturers' and insurers' profitability in order to increase

healthcare access to their citizens. The main difference between these three countries and the United States is in the willingness of individuals to pay more so all citizens can receive health care. That collectivistic attitude does not prevail in the United States and would be difficult to institute. However, the mandates for both business and individuals to purchase health insurance coverage through the establishment of state health insurance marketplaces should improve the overall health of the United States.

This chapter will compare the U.S. healthcare system and the healthcare systems of other countries and discuss whether universal healthcare coverage should be implemented in the United States. This chapter will also discuss trends that may positively impact the U.S. healthcare system, including the increased use of technology in prescribing medicine and providing health care, complementary and alternative medicine use, new nursing home models, accountable care organizations, and the universal-healthcare-coverage programs in Massachusetts and San Francisco, California. The Affordable Care Act (ACA) will also be discussed because of its major impact on the U.S. healthcare system.

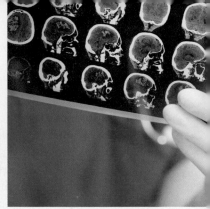

CHAPTER 1

History of the U.S. Healthcare System

LEARNING OBJECTIVES

The student will be able to:
- Describe five milestones of medicine and medical education and their importance to health care.
- Discuss five milestones of the hospital system and their importance to health care.
- Identify five milestones of public health and their importance to health care.
- Describe five milestones of health insurance and their importance to health care.
- Explain the difference between primary, secondary, and tertiary prevention.
- Explain the concept of the iron triangle as it applies to health care.

DID YOU KNOW THAT?

- When the practice of medicine first began, tradesmen such as barbers practiced medicine. They often used the same razor to cut hair as to perform surgery.
- In 2014, the United States spent 17.5% of the gross domestic product on healthcare spending, which is the highest in the world.
- As a result of the Affordable Care Act, the number of uninsured is projected to decline to 23 million by 2023.
- The Centers for Medicare and Medicaid Services predicts national health expenditures will account for over 19% of the U.S. gross domestic product.
- The United States is the only major country that does not have universal healthcare coverage.
- In 2002, the Joint Commission issued hospital standards requiring them to inform their patients if their results were not consistent with typical care results.

▶ Introduction

It is important as a healthcare consumer to understand the history of the U.S. healthcare delivery system, how it operates today, who participates in the system, what legal and ethical issues arise as a result of the system, and what problems continue to plague the healthcare system. We are all consumers of health care. Yet, in many instances, we are ignorant of what we are actually purchasing. If we were going to spend $1,000 on an appliance or a flat-screen television, many of us would research the product to determine if what we are purchasing is the best product for us. This same concept should be applied to purchasing healthcare services.

Increasing healthcare consumer awareness will protect you in both the personal and professional aspects of your life. You may decide to pursue a career in health care either as a provider or as an administrator. You may also decide to manage a business where you will have the responsibility of providing health care to your employees. And last, from a personal standpoint, you should have the knowledge from a consumer point of view so you can make informed decisions about what matters most—your health. The federal government agrees with this philosophy.

As the U.S. population's life expectancy continues to lengthen—increasing the **"graying" of the population**—the United States will be confronted with more chronic health issues because, as we age, more chronic health conditions develop. The U.S. healthcare system is one of the most expensive systems in the world. According to 2014 statistics, the United States spent $2.9 trillion or $9,255 per person on healthcare expenditures or 17.5% of its gross domestic product. The **gross domestic product (GDP)** is the total finished products or services that are produced in a country within a year. These statistics mean that over 17% of all of the products made within the borders of the United States within a year are healthcare related. Estimates indicate that healthcare spending will be 19.3% of the gross domestic product (CMS, 2016a). The Gallup-Healthways Well-Being Index indicate that in 2014, the number of uninsured Americans has dropped to 16%. Among the states, Hawaii had the lowest percentage of uninsured individuals under age 65 in 2014 (2.5%), followed by Massachusetts (3.2%), Delaware (5.4%), and Iowa (6.4%). The District of Columbia also had a low insurance rate of 3.3%. Texas (21.5%), Oklahoma (21.5%), Alaska (21.2%), and Florida (18.8%) had the highest percentage of uninsured individuals under age 65 in 2014 (Nation at a glance, 2015). The rates of uninsured individuals have dropped most among lower-income and black Americans. These drops have been attributed to the insurance mandate of the Affordable Care Act (Levy, 2015). The Institute of Medicine's (IOM) 1999 report indicated that nearly 100,000 citizens die each year as a result of medical errors. There have been more recent studies that indicate this estimate is much higher despite many quality improvement initiatives implemented over the years.

Although U.S. healthcare costs are very high, the United States does not offer healthcare coverage as a right of citizenship. The United States is the only major country that does not offer healthcare as a right. Most developed countries have a **universal healthcare program**, which means access to all citizens. Many of these systems are typically run by the federal government, have centralized health policy agencies, are financed through different forms of taxation, and payment of healthcare services are by a single payer—the government (Shi & Singh, 2008). France and the United Kingdom have been discussed as possible models for the United States to follow to improve access to health care, but these programs have problems and may not be the ultimate solution for the United States. However, because the United States does not offer any type of universal healthcare coverage, many citizens who are not eligible for government-sponsored programs are expected to provide the service for themselves through the purchase of health insurance or the purchase of actual services. Many citizens cannot afford these options, resulting in their not receiving routine medical care. The Affordable Care Act's health insurance marketplaces provide cost and service data so consumers can determine what is the best healthcare insurance to purchase and what services they will be receiving for that purchase. Recently, the Centers for Medicare and Medicaid Services (CMS) used its claim data to publish the hospital costs of the 100 most common treatments nationwide. The purpose of this effort is to provide data to consumers regarding healthcare costs because the costs vary considerably across the United States. This effort may also encourage pricing competition of healthcare services. The U.S. Department of Health and Human Services is providing funding to states to increase their healthcare pricing transparency (Bird, 2013). The **Patient Protection and Affordable Care Act of 2010 (PPACA)**, more commonly called the **Affordable Care Act**, has attempted to increase access to affordable healthcare. One of the mandates of the Act was the establishment of electronic health insurance marketplaces, which provide opportunities for consumers to search for affordable health insurance plans. There is also a mandate that individuals who do not have health insurance purchase health insurance if they can afford it or pay a fine. Both of these mandates have decreased the number of uninsured in the United States.

▶ Consumer Perspective on Health Care

What Is Health?

The World Health Organization (WHO) defines **health** as the state of complete physical, mental, and social well-being and not merely the absence of disease or infirmity (WHO, 1942). IOM defines health as a state of well-being and the capability to function in the face of changing circumstances. It is a positive concept emphasizing social and personal resources as well as physical capabilities (IOM, 1997). According to the Society for Academic Emergency Medicine (SAEM), health is a state of physical and mental well-being that facilitates the achievement of individual and societal goals (SAEM, 1992). All of these definitions focus on the impact an individual's health status has on his or her quality of life.

Health has several determinants or influences that impact the status of an individual's health. The individual lifestyle factors, such as exercise, diet and sexual activity are direct determinants of a person's health. Within the immediate environment of an individual, there are social and community networks external influences on health. In addition to the **social and community networks**, there are also the general **macroenvironmental conditions** of socioeconomic, cultural, and environmental conditions that impact health, such as education, work environment, living and working conditions, healthcare services, food production, job status, water and sanitation, and housing. These **determinants of health** tie into the activities of the U.S. healthcare delivery system and its impact on the determinants of an individual's health. These activities are often categorized as primary, secondary, and occasionally tertiary prevention (Determinants of Health, 2013). These concepts are vital to understanding the U.S. healthcare system because different components of the healthcare system focus on these different areas of health, which often results in lack of coordination between the different components.

Primary, Secondary, and Tertiary Prevention

According to the *American Heritage Dictionary* (2001), prevention is defined as "slowing down or stopping the course of an event." **Primary prevention** avoids the development of a disease. Promotion activities such as health education are primary prevention.

Other examples include smoking cessation programs, immunization programs, and educational programs for pregnancy and employee safety. State health departments often develop targeted, large education campaigns regarding a specific health issue in their area. **Secondary prevention** activities are focused on early disease detection, which prevents progression of the disease. Screening programs, such as high blood pressure testing, are examples of secondary prevention activities. Colonoscopies and mammograms are also examples of secondary prevention activities. Many local health departments implement secondary prevention activities. Tertiary prevention reduces the impact of an already established disease by minimizing disease-related complications. **Tertiary prevention** focuses on rehabilitation and monitoring of diseased individuals. A person with high blood pressure who is taking blood pressure medication is an example of tertiary prevention. A physician who writes a prescription for that blood pressure medication to control high blood pressure is an example of tertiary prevention. Traditional medicine focuses on tertiary prevention, although more primary care providers are encouraging and educating their patients on healthy behaviors (Centers for Disease Control and Prevention [CDC], 2007).

We, as healthcare consumers, would like to receive primary prevention to prevent disease. We would like to participate in secondary prevention activities such as screening for cholesterol or blood pressure because it helps us manage any health problems we may be experiencing and reduces the potential impact of a disease. And, we would like to also visit our physicians for tertiary measures so, if we do have a disease, it can be managed by taking a prescribed drug or some other type of treatment. From our perspective, these three areas of health should be better coordinated for the healthcare consumer so the United States will have a healthier population.

In order to understand the current healthcare delivery system and its issues, it is important to learn the history of the development of the U.S. healthcare system. Four major sectors of our healthcare system that have impacted our current system of operations will be discussed in this chapter: (1) the history of practicing medicine and the development of medical education, (2) the development of the hospital system, (3) the history of **public health**, and (4) the history of health insurance. In **TABLES 1-1** to **1-4**, several important milestones are listed by date and illustrate historic highlights of each system component. The list is by no means exhaustive, but provides an introduction to how each sector has evolved as part of the U.S. healthcare system.

TABLE 1-1 Milestones of Medicine and Medical Education 1700–2015

- 1700s: Training and apprenticeship under one physician was common until hospitals were founded in the mid-1700s. In 1765, the first medical school was established at the University of Pennsylvania.

- 1800s: Medical training was provided through internships with existing physicians who often were poorly trained themselves. In the United States, there were only four medical schools, which graduated only a handful of students. There was no formal tuition with no mandatory testing.

- 1847: The AMA was established as a membership organization for physicians to protect the interests of its members. It did not become powerful until the 1900s when it organized its physician members by county and state medical societies. The AMA wanted to ensure these local societies were protecting physicians' financial well-being. It also began to focus on standardizing medical education.

- 1900s–1930s: The medical profession was represented by general or family practitioners who operated in solo practices. A small percentage of physicians were women. Total expenditures for medical care were less than 4% of the gross domestic product.

- 1904: The AMA created the Council on Medical Education to establish standards for medical education.

- 1910: Formal medical education was attributed to Abraham Flexner, who wrote an evaluation of medical schools in the United States and Canada indicating many schools were substandard. The Flexner Report led to standardized admissions testing for students called the Medical College Admission Test (MCAT), which is still used as part of the admissions process today.

- 1930s: The healthcare industry was dominated by male physicians and hospitals. Relationships between patients and physicians were sacred. Payments for physician care were personal.

- 1940s–1960s: When group health insurance was offered, the relationship between patient and physician changed because of third-party payers (insurance). In the 1950s, federal grants supported medical school operations and teaching hospitals. In the 1960s, the Regional Medical Programs provided research grants and emphasized service innovation and provider networking. As a result of the Medicare and Medicaid enactment in 1965, the responsibilities of teaching faculty also included clinical responsibilities.

- 1970s–1990s: Patient care dollars surpassed research dollars as the largest source of medical school funding. During the 1980s, third-party payers reimbursed academic medical centers with no restrictions. In the 1990s with the advent of managed care, reimbursement was restricted.

- 2014: According to the 2014 Association of American Medical Colleges (AAMAC) annual survey, over 70% of medical schools have or will be implementing policies and programs to encourage primary care specialties for medical school students.

TABLE 1-2 Milestones of the Hospital and Healthcare Systems 1820–2015

- 1820s: Almshouses or poorhouses, the precursor of hospitals, were developed to serve primarily poor people. They provided food and shelter to the poor and consequently treated the ill. Pesthouses, operated by local governments, were used to quarantine people who had contagious diseases such as cholera. The first hospitals were built around areas such as New York City, Philadelphia, and Boston and were used often as a refuge for the poor. Dispensaries or pharmacies were established to provide free care to those who could not afford to pay and to dispense drugs to ambulatory patients.

- 1850s: A hospital system was finally developed but hospital conditions were deplorable because of unskilled providers. Hospitals were owned primarily by the physicians who practiced in them.

(continues)

TABLE 1-2 Milestones of the Hospital and Healthcare Systems 1820–2015	*(continued)*

- 1890s: Patients went to hospitals because they had no choice. More cohesiveness developed among providers because they had to rely on each other for referrals and access to hospitals, which gave them more professional power.

- 1920s: The development of medical technological advances increased the quality of medical training and specialization and the economic development of the United States. The establishment of hospitals became the symbol of the institutionalization of health care. In 1929, President Coolidge signed the Narcotic Control Act, which provided funding for construction of hospitals for patients with drug addictions.

- 1930s–1940s: Once physician-owned hospitals were now owned by church groups, larger facilities, and government at all levels.

- 1970–1980: The first Patient Bill of Rights was introduced to protect healthcare consumer representation in hospital care. In 1974, the National Health Planning and Resources Development Act required states to have certificate of need (CON) laws to qualify for federal funding.

- 1980–1990: According to the AHA, 87% of hospitals were offering ambulatory surgery. In 1985, the EMTALA was enacted, which required hospitals to screen and stabilize individuals coming into emergency rooms regardless of the consumers' ability to pay.

- 1990–2000s: As a result of the Balanced Budget Act cuts of 1997, the federal government authorized an outpatient Medicare reimbursement system.

- 1996: The medical specialty of hospitalists, who provide care once a patient is hospitalized, was created.

- 2002: The Joint Commission on the Accreditation of Healthcare Organizations (now The Joint Commission) issued standards to increase consumer awareness by requiring hospitals to inform patients if their healthcare results were not consistent with typical results.

- 2002: The CMS partnered with the AHRQ to develop and test the HCAHPS (Hospital Consumer Assessment of Healthcare, Providers and Systems Survey). Also known as the CAHPS survey, the HCAHPS is a 32-item survey for measuring patients' perception of their hospital experience.

- 2007: The Institute for Health Improvement launched the Triple Aim, which focuses on three goals: improving patient satisfaction, reducing health costs, and improving public health.

- 2011: In 1974, a federal law was passed that required all states to have certificate of need (CON) laws to ensure the state approved any capital expenditures associated with hospital/medical facilities' construction and expansion. The act was repealed in 1987 but as of 2014, 35 states still have some type of CON mechanism.

- 2011: The Affordable Care Act created the Centers for Medicare and Medicaid Services' Innovation Center for the purpose of testing "innovative payment and service delivery models to reduce program expenditures ... while preserving or enhancing the quality of care" for those individuals who receive Medicare, Medicaid, or Children's Health Insurance Program (CHIP) benefits.

- 2015: The Centers for Medicare and Medicaid Services posted its final rule that reduces Medicare payments to hospitals that have exceeded readmission limits of Medicare patients within 30 days.

TABLE 1-3 Milestones in Public Health 1700–2015

- 1700–1800: The United States was experiencing strong industrial growth. Long work hours in unsanitary conditions resulted in massive disease outbreaks. U.S. public health practices targeted reducing **epidemics**, or large patterns of disease in a population, that impacted the population. Some of the first public health departments were established in urban areas as a result of these epidemics.

(continues)

TABLE 1-3 Milestones in Public Health 1700–2015 *(continued)*

- 1800–1900: Three very important events occurred. In 1842, Britain's Edwin Chadwick produced the General Report on the Sanitary Condition of the Labouring Population of Great Britain, which is considered one of the most important documents of public health. This report stimulated a similar U.S. survey. In 1854, Britain's John Snow performed an analysis that determined contaminated water in London was the cause of a cholera epidemic. This discovery established a link between the environment and disease. In 1850, Lemuel Shattuck, based on Chadwick's report and Snow's activities, developed a state public health law that became the foundation for public health activities.

- 1900–1950: In 1920, Charles Winslow defined public health as a focus of preventing disease, prolonging life, and promoting physical health and efficiency through organized community efforts.

  During this period, most states had public health departments that focused on sanitary inspections, disease control, and health education. Throughout the years, **public health functions** included child immunization programs, health screenings in schools, community health services, substance abuse programs, and sexually transmitted disease control.

  In 1923, a vaccine for diphtheria and whooping cough was developed. In 1928, Alexander Fleming discovered penicillin. In 1933, the polio vaccine was developed. In 1946, the **National Mental Health Act (NMHA)** provided funding for research, prevention, and treatment of mental illness.

- 1950–1980: In 1950, cigarette smoke was identified as a cause of lung cancer.
  In 1952, Dr. Jonas Salk developed the polio vaccine.

  The **Poison Prevention Packaging Act of 1970** was enacted to prevent children from accidentally ingesting substances. Childproof caps were developed for use on all drugs. In 1980, the eradication of smallpox was announced.

- 1980–1990: The first recognized cases of AIDS occurred in the United States in the early 1980s.

  1988: The IOM Report defined *public health* as organized community efforts to address the public interest in health by applying scientific and technical knowledge and promote health. The first Healthy People Report (1987) was published and recommended a national prevention strategy.

- 1990–2000: In 1997, Oregon voters approved a referendum that allowed physicians to assist terminally ill, mentally competent patients to commit suicide. From 1998 to 2006, 292 patients exercised their rights under the law.

- 2000s: The second Healthy People Report was published in 2000. The terrorist attack on the United States on September 11, 2001, impacted and expanded the role of public health. The Public Health Security and Bioterrorism Preparedness and Response Act of 2002 provided grants to hospitals and public health organizations to prepare for bioterrorism as a result of September 11, 2001.

- 2010: The ACA was passed. Its major goal was to improve the nation's public health level. The third Healthy People Report was published.

- 2015: There has been an increase nationally of children who have not received vaccines due to parents' beliefs that vaccines are not safe. As a result, there have been measles outbreaks throughout the nation even though measles was considered eradicated decades ago.

TABLE 1-4 Milestones of the U.S. Health Insurance System 1800–2015

- 1800–1900: Insurance was purchased by individuals in the same way one would purchase car insurance. In 1847, the Massachusetts Health Insurance Co. of Boston was the first insurer to issue "sickness insurance." In 1853, a French mutual aid society established a prepaid hospital care plan in San Francisco, California. This plan resembles the modern health maintenance organization (HMO).

- 1900–1920: In 1913, the International Ladies Garment Workers began the first union-provided medical services. The National Convention of Insurance Commissioners drafted the first model for regulation of the health insurance industry.

(continues)

TABLE 1-4 Milestones of the U.S. Health Insurance System 1800–2015   *(continued)*

- 1920s: The blueprint for health insurance was established in 1929 when J. F. Kimball began a hospital insurance plan for school teachers at Baylor University Hospital in Texas. This initiative became the model for Blue Cross plans nationally. The Blue Cross plans were nonprofit and covered only hospital charges so as not to infringe on private physicians' income.

- 1930s: There were discussions regarding the development of a national health insurance program. However, the AMA opposed the move (Raffel & Raffel, 1994). With the Depression and U.S. participation in World War II, the funding required for this type of program was not available. In 1935, President Roosevelt signed the **Social Security Act (SSA)**, which created "old age insurance" to help those of retirement age. In 1936, Vassar College, in New York, was the first college to establish a medical insurance group policy for students.

- 1940s–1950s: The War Labor Board froze wages, forcing employers to offer health insurance to attract potential employees. In 1947, the Blue Cross Commission was established to create a national doctors network. By 1950, 57% of the population had hospital insurance.

- 1965: President Johnson signed the Medicare and Medicaid programs into law.

- 1970s–1980s: President Nixon signed the HMO Act, which was the predecessor of managed care. In 1982, Medicare proposed paying for hospice or end-of-life care. In 1982, diagnosis-related groups (DRGs) and prospective-payment guidelines were developed to control insurance reimbursement costs. In 1985, the Consolidated Omnibus Budget Reconciliation Act (COBRA) required employers to offer partially subsidized health coverage to terminated employees.

- 1990–2000: President Clinton's Health Security Act proposed a universal healthcare coverage plan, which was never passed. In 1993, the Family Medical Leave Act (FMLA) was enacted, which allowed employees up to 12 weeks of unpaid leave because of family illness. In 1996, the Health Insurance Portability and Accountability Act (HIPAA) was enacted, making it easier to carry health insurance when changing employment. It also increased the confidentiality of patient information. In 1997, the Balanced Budget Act (BBA) was enacted to control the growth of Medicare spending. It also established the State Children's Health Insurance Program (SCHIP).

- 2000: The SCHIP, now known as the Children's Health Insurance Program (CHIP), was implemented.

- 2000: The Medicare, Medicaid, and SCHIP Benefits Improvement and Protection Act provided some relief from the BBA by providing across-the-board program increases.

- 2003: The Medicare Prescription Drug, Improvement, and Modernization Act was passed, which created Medicare Part D, prescription plans for the elderly.

- 2006: Massachusetts mandated all state residents have health insurance by 2009.

- 2009: President Obama signed the **American Recovery and Reinvestment Act (ARRA)**, which protected health coverage for the unemployed by providing a 65% subsidy for COBRA coverage to make the premiums more affordable.

- 2010: The ACA was signed into law, making it illegal for insurance companies to rescind insurance on their sick beneficiaries. Consumers can also appeal coverage claim denials by the insurance companies. Insurance companies cannot impose lifetime limits on essential benefits.

- 2013: As of October 1, individuals could buy qualified health benefits plans from the Health Insurance Marketplaces. If an employer does not offer insurance, effective 2015, consumers can purchase it from the federal Health Insurance Marketplace. The federal government provided states with funding to expand their Medicaid programs to increase preventive services. MARGIN IS OFF

- 2015: The CMS posted its final rule that reduces Medicare payments to hospitals that readmit Medicare patients within 30 days after discharge. This rule is an attempt to focus hospital initiatives on quality care. The MARGIN IS OFF

Milestones of Medicine and Medical Education

The early practice of medicine did not require a major course of study, training, board exams, and licensing, as is required today. During this period, anyone who had the inclination to set up a physician practice could do so; oftentimes, clergy were also medical providers, as were tradesmen such as barbers. The red and white striped poles outside barber shops represented blood and bandages because the barbers were often also surgeons. They used the same blades to cut hair and to perform surgery (Starr, 1982). Because there were no restrictions, competition was very intense. In most cases, physicians did not possess any technical expertise; they relied mainly on common sense to make diagnoses (Stevens, 1971). During this period, there was no health insurance, so consumers decided when they would visit a physician and paid for their visits out of their own pockets. Often, physicians treated their patients in the patients' homes. During the late 1800s, the medical profession became more cohesive as more technically advanced services were delivered to patients. The establishment of the **American Medical Association (AMA)** in 1847 as a professional membership organization for physicians was a driving force for the concept of private practice in medicine. The AMA was also responsible for standardizing medical education (AMA, 2016a; Goodman & Musgrave, 1992).

In the early history of medical education, physicians gradually established large numbers of medical schools because they were inexpensive to operate, increased their prestige, and enhanced their income. Medical schools only required four or more physicians, a classroom, some discussion rooms, and legal authority to confer degrees. Physicians received the students' tuitions directly and operated the school from this influx of money. Many physicians would affiliate with established colleges to confer degrees. Because there were no entry restrictions, as more students entered medical schools, the existing internship program with physicians was dissolved and the Doctor of Medicine (MD) became the standard (Vault Career Intelligence, 2013). Although there were major issues with the quality of education provided because of the lack of educational requirements, medical school education became the gold standard for practicing medicine (Sultz & Young, 2006). The publication in 1910 of the *Flexner Report*, which evaluated medical schools in Canada and the United States, was responsible for forcing medical schools to develop curriculums and admission testing. These standards are still in existence today.

When the Medicare and Medicaid programs were enacted in 1965, Congress recognized that the federal government needed to support medical education, which resulted in ongoing federal funding to teaching hospitals to support medical resident programs. The responsibilities of teaching now included clinical duties. During the 1970s–1990s, patient care dollars exceeded research funding as the largest source of medical school support. Academic medical centers would be reimbursed without question by third-party payers. However, with the advent of managed care in the 1990s, reimbursement restrictions were implemented (Rich, Liebow, Srinivaan, Parish, Wollinscroft, Fein, & Blaser, 2002). With the passage of the ACA, which increased the need for primary care providers, more medical schools are focusing on primary care curriculum initiatives (AAMAC, 2016).

▶ Milestones of the Hospital System

In the early 19th century, **almshouses** or **poorhouses** were established to serve the indigent. They provided shelter while treating illness. Government-operated **pesthouses** segregated people who might otherwise spread their diseases. The framework of these institutions set up the conception of the hospital. Initially, wealthy people did not want to go to hospitals because the conditions were deplorable and the providers were not skilled, so hospitals, which were first built in urban areas, were used by the poor. During this period, many of the hospitals were owned by the physicians who practiced in them (Rosen, 1983).

In the early 20th century, with the establishment of a more standardized medical education, hospitals became more accepted across socioeconomic classes and became the symbol of medicine. With the establishment of the AMA, which protected the interests of providers, the physicians' reputation increased. During the 1930s and 1940s, the ownership of the hospitals changed from physician owned to church related and government operated (Starr, 1982).

In 1973, the first **Patient Bill of Rights** was established to protect healthcare consumers in hospitals. In 1974, a federal law was passed that required all states to have **certificate of need (CON)** laws to ensure the state approved any capital expenditures associated with hospital and medical facility construction and expansion. The Act was repealed in 1987, but as of 2014, 35 states still have some type of CON mechanism (National Conference of State Legislatures

[NCSL], 2016). The concept of CON was important because it encouraged state planning to ensure their medical system was based on need. In 1985, the **Emergency Medical Treatment and Active Labor Act (EMTALA)** was enacted to ensure that consumers were not refused treatment for an emergency. During this period, inpatient hospital use was typical; however, by the 1980s, many hospitals were offering outpatient or ambulatory surgery that continues into the 21st century. The Balanced Budget Act of 1997 authorized outpatient Medicare reimbursement to support these cost-saving measures (CDC, 2001). **Hospitalists**, created in 1996, are providers who focus exclusively on the care of patients when they are hospitalized. Creation of this new type of provider recognized the need of providing quality hospital care (American Hospital Association [AHA], 2016; Sultz & Young, 2006). In 2002, the Joint Commission on the Accreditation of Healthcare Organizations (now The **Joint Commission**) issued standards to increase consumer awareness by requiring hospitals to inform patients if their outcomes were not consistent with typical results (AHA, 2013). The CMS partnered with the AHRQ to develop and test the HCAHPS (Hospital Consumer Assessment of Healthcare, Providers and Systems Survey). Also known as the CAHPS survey, the HCAHPS is a 32-item survey for measuring patients' perception of their hospital experience. In May 2005, the National Quality Forum (NQF), an organization established to standardize health care quality measurement and reporting, formally endorsed the CAHPS® Hospital Survey. The NQF endorsement represents the consensus of many healthcare providers, consumer groups, professional associations, purchasers, federal agencies, and research and quality organizations. Since 2008, it has been nationally recognized as a standardized measurement for hospital comparisons (HCAHPS Fact Sheet, 2016).

In 2007, the Institute for Health Improvement launched the **Triple Aim**, which focused on the three goals of patient satisfaction, improving public health, and reducing healthcare costs (Zeroing in on Triple Aim, 2015).

In 2011, the ACA created the Centers for Medicare and Medicaid Services' Innovation Center for the purpose of developing innovative care and payment models. In 2015, the CMS also posted its final rule that reduces Medicare payments to hospitals that readmit Medicare patients within 30 days. This rule is an attempt to focus hospital initiatives on quality care (Rau, 2015)). As a result of this rule, many hospitals are focusing on the concept of quality improvement processes and performance-driven planning to ensure that these readmissions do not occur.

Hospitals are the foundation of our healthcare system. As our health insurance system evolved, the first type of health insurance was hospital insurance. As society's health needs increased, expansion of different medical facilities increased. There was more of a focus on ambulatory or outpatient services because first, we, as consumers, prefer outpatient services; and second, it is more cost effective. Although hospitals are still an integral part of our healthcare delivery system, the method of their delivery has changed. More hospitals have recognized the trend of outpatient services and have integrated those types of services in their delivery.

Milestones of Public Health

The development of public health is important to note because the process was separate from the development of private medical practices. Physicians were worried that governmental health departments could regulate how they practiced medicine, which could limit their income. Public health specialists also approached health from a collectivistic and preventive care viewpoint—to protect as many people as possible from health problems and to provide strategies to prevent health problems from occurring. Private practitioners held an individualistic viewpoint—citizens more often would be paying for physician services from their health insurance or from their own pockets and physicians would be providing them guidance on how to cure their diseases, not prevent them. The two contrasting viewpoints still exist today, but there have been efforts to coordinate and collaborate on additional traditional and public health activities.

During the 1700s into the 1800s, the concept of public health was born. In their reports, Edwin Chadwick, Dr. John Snow, and Lemuel Shattuck demonstrated a relationship between the environment and disease (Chadwick, 1842; Turnock, 1997). As a result of their work, public health laws were enacted and, by the 1900s, public health departments were focused on the environment and its relationship to disease outbreaks.

Disease control and health education were also integral components of public health departments. In 1916, the Johns Hopkins University, one of the most prestigious universities in the world, established the first public health school (Duke University Library, 2016). Winslow's definition of public health focuses on the prevention of disease, while the IOM defines public health as the organized community effort to protect the public by applying scientific knowledge (IOM, 1988; Winslow, 1920). These definitions are exemplified by the development of several vaccines for whooping cough, polio, smallpox, diphtheria, and the discovery of penicillin. All of these efforts focus on the protection of the public from disease.

The three most important public health achievements are (1) the recognition by the U.S. Surgeon General that tobacco use is a health hazard; (2) the development of many vaccines that that have eradicated some diseases and controlled the number of childhood diseases that exist; and (3) the development of early detection programs for high blood pressure and heart attacks and smoking cessation programs, which have dramatically reduced the number of deaths in this country (Novick, Morrow, & Mays, 2008).

Assessment, policy development, and assurance, core functions of public health, were developed based on the 1988 report, *The Future of Public Health*, which indicated there was an attrition of public health activities in protecting the community (IOM, 1988). There was poor collaboration between public health and private medicine, no strong mission statement and weak leadership, and politicized decision making. **Assessment** was recommended because it focused on the systematic continuous data collection of health issues, which would ensure that public health agencies were vigilant in protecting the public (IOM, 1988; Turnock, 1997). **Policy development** should also include planning at all health levels, not just federally. Federal agencies should support local health planning (IOM, 1988). **Assurance** focuses on evaluating any processes that have been put in place to ensure that the programs are being implemented appropriately. These core functions will ensure that public health remains focused on the community, has programs in place that are effective, and has an evaluation process in place to ensure that the programs do work (Turnock, 1997).

The **Healthy People 2000** report, which started in 1987, was created to implement a new national prevention strategy with three goals: increase life expectancy, reduce health disparities, and increase access to preventive services. Also, three categories of health promotion, health prevention, and preventive services were identified and surveillance activities were emphasized. *Healthy People 2000* provided a vision to reduce preventable disabilities and death. Target objectives were set to measure progress (CDC, 2016a).

The **Healthy People 2010** report was released in 2000. The report contained a health promotion and disease prevention focus to identify preventable threats to public health and to set goals to reduce the threats. Nearly 500 objectives within 28 focus areas were developed. Focus areas ranged from access to care, food safety, education, environmental health, to tobacco and substance abuse. An important component of *Healthy People 2010* is the development of an infrastructure to ensure public health services are provided. Infrastructure includes skilled labor, information technology, organizations, and research. In 2010, **Healthy People 2020** was released. It contains 1,200 objectives that focus on 42 topic areas. According to the **Centers for Disease Control and Prevention (CDC)**, a smaller set of *Healthy People 2020* objectives, called leading health indicators (LHIs), have been targeted to communicate high-priority health issues. Healthy People 2020 Progress Review webinars began in early 2013 and are scheduled to run through mid-2017 (CDC, 2016a). The goals for all of these reports are consistent with the definitions of public health in both Winslow's and the IOM's reports.

It is important to mention the impact on the scope of public health responsibilities of the terrorist attack on the United States on September 11, 2001; the anthrax attacks; the outbreak of global diseases such as severe acute respiratory syndrome (SARS); Ebola; the Zika virus; and the U.S. natural disaster of Hurricane Katrina. As a result of these major events, public health has expanded its area of responsibility. The terms "bioterrorism" and "disaster preparedness" have more frequently appeared in public health literature and have become part of strategic planning. The **Public Health Security and Bioterrorism Preparedness and Response Act of 2002** provided grants to hospitals and public health organizations to prepare for bioterrorism as a result of September 11, 2001 (CDC, 2009).

Public health is challenged by its very success because the public now takes public health measures for granted: Several successful vaccines targeted almost all childhood diseases, tobacco use has decreased significantly, accident prevention has increased, there are safer workplaces because of the Occupational Safety and Health Administration (OSHA), fluoride is added to the public water supply, and there is decreased mortality from heart attacks (Turnock, 1997). When major events like the Ebola crisis, *Escherichia coli* outbreaks, or the Zika epidemic occur, people immediately think that public health will automatically control these problems. The public may not realize how much effort, dedication, funding and research takes place to protect them.

▶ Milestones of the Health Insurance System

There are two key concepts in **group insurance**: "risk is transferred from the individual to the group and the group shares the cost of any covered losses incurred by its member" (Buchbinder & Shanks, 2007). Like life insurance or homeowner's insurance, **health insurance** was developed to provide protection should a covered individual experience an event that requires health care. In 1847, a Boston insurance company offered sickness insurance to consumers (Starr, 1982).

During the 19th century, large employers such as coal mining and railroad companies offered medical services to their employees by providing company doctors. Fees were taken from their pay to cover the service. In 1913, the International Ladies Garment Workers union began providing health insurance, which was negotiated as part of the contract (Duke University Library, 2016). During this period, there were several proposals for a national health insurance program but the efforts failed. The AMA was worried that any national health insurance would impact the financial security of its providers. The AMA persuaded the federal government to support private insurance efforts (Raffel & Raffel, 1994).

In 1929, a group hospital insurance plan was offered to teachers at a hospital in Texas. This became the foundation of the nonprofit Blue Cross plans. In order to placate the AMA, Blue Cross initially offered only hospital insurance in order to avoid infringement of physicians' incomes (Blue Cross Blue Shield Association [BCBS], 2007; Starr, 1982). In 1935, the Social Security Act was enacted; Social Security was considered "old age" insurance. During this period, there was continued discussion of a national health insurance program. But, because of the Depression and World War II, there was no funding for this program. The federal government felt that the Social Security Act was a sufficient program to protect consumers. These events were a catalyst for the development of a health insurance program that included private participation. Although a universal health coverage program was proposed during President Clinton's administration in the 1990s, it was never passed. In 2009, there has been a major public outcry at regional town hall meetings opposing any type of government universal healthcare coverage. In 2006, Massachusetts proposed mandatory health coverage for all residents, so it may be that universal health coverage would be a state-level initiative (KFF, 2013).

By the 1950s, nearly 60% of the population had hospital insurance (AHA, 2007). Disability insurance was attached to Social Security. In the 1960s, President Johnson signed into law **Medicare** and **Medicaid**, which assist elderly, disabled, and indigent individuals. President Nixon established the health maintenance organization (HMO), which focused on cost-effective measures for health delivery. Also, in the 1980s, diagnostic-related groups (DRGs) and prospective payment guidelines were established to provide guidelines for treatment. These DRGs were attached to appropriate insurance reimbursement categories for treatment. The **Consolidated Omnibus Budget Reconciliation Act (COBRA)** was passed to provide health insurance protection if an individual changes jobs. In 1993, the Family and Medical Leave Act (FMLA) was passed to protect an employee if there is a family illness. An employee can receive up to 12 weeks of unpaid leave and maintain his or her health insurance coverage during this period. The **Uniformed Services Employment and Reemployment Rights Act (USERRA)**, enacted in 1994, entitles individuals who leave for military service to return to their job. In 1996, the **Health Insurance Portability and Accountability Act (HIPAA)** was passed to provide stricter confidentiality regarding the health information of individuals. The Balanced Budget Act (BBA) of 1997 required massive program reductions for Medicare and authorized Medicare reimbursement for outpatient services (CMS, 2016b).

At the start of the 21st century, cost, access, and quality continue to be issues for U.S. health care. Employers continue to play an integral role in health insurance coverage. The largest public coverage program is Medicare, which covers 55 million people. In 2014, Medicare benefit payments totaled nearly $600 billion (Facts on Medicare, 2015). The State Children's Health Insurance Program (SCHIP), renamed CHIP, was implemented to ensure that children who are not Medicare eligible receive health care. The Medicare, Medicaid, and SCHIP Benefits Improvement and Protection Act provided some relief from the BBA of 1997 by restoring some funding to these consumer programs. In 2003, a consumer law, the **Medicare Prescription Drug, Improvement, and Modernization Act**, created a major overhaul of the Medicare system (CMS, 2016b). The Act created Medicare Part D, a prescription drug plan that became effective in 2006 and provides different prescription programs to the elderly, based on their prescription needs. In 2014, approximately $6 billion in Medicare benefits was spent on Medicare Part D (Facts on Medicare, 2015). The Act also renamed the Medicare cost plans to Medicare Advantage, which is a type of managed care program. Medicare contracts with private health insurance programs to provide services. This program, called Medicare Part C, provides both Medicare Parts A and B benefits. In 2014, approximately

$24 billion in Medicare benefit dollars were spent on the Medicare Part C plan (Facts on Medicare, 2015). In 2008, the **National Defense Authorization Act** expanded the FMLA to permit families of military service members to take a leave of absence if the spouse, parent, or child was called to active military service. The 2010 ACA required individuals to purchase health insurance by 2014. Despite these efforts, health insurance coverage continues to be an issue for the United States.

▶ Current System Operations

Government's Participation in Health Care

The U.S. government plays an important role in healthcare delivery. In the United States, three governmental levels participate in the healthcare system: federal, state, and local. The federal government provides a range of regulatory and funding mechanisms including Medicare and Medicaid, established in 1965 as federally funded programs to provide health access to the elderly (65 years or older) and the poor, respectively. Over the years, these programs have expanded to include individuals with disabilities. They also have developed programs for military personnel and veterans and their dependents.

Federal law, specifically EMTALA, ensures access to emergency services regardless of ability to pay (Regenstein, Mead, & Lara, 2007). The federal government determines a national healthcare budget, sets reimbursement rates, and also formulates standards for providers for eligible Medicare and Medicaid patients (Barton, 2003). The state level is responsible for regulatory and funding mechanisms but also provides healthcare programs as dictated by the federal government. The local or county level of government is responsible for implementing programs dictated by both the federal and the state levels.

The United States has several federal health regulatory agencies, including the CDC for public health, the **Food and Drug Administration (FDA)** for pharmaceutical controls, and the **Centers for Medicare & Medicaid Services (CMS)** for the indigent, disabled, and the elderly. The Joint Commission is a private organization that focuses on healthcare organizations' oversight, and the **Agency for Healthcare Research and Quality (AHRQ)** is the primary federal source for quality delivery of health services. The **Center for Mental Health Services (CMHS)**, in partnership with state health departments, leads national efforts to assess mental health delivery services. Although the federal government is to be commended because of the many agencies that focus on major healthcare issues, with multiple organizations there is often duplication of effort and miscommunication that result in inefficiencies (KFF, 2013). However, several regulations exist to protect patient rights. One of the first pieces of legislation was the **Sherman Antitrust Act of 1890** and ensuing legislation, which ensures fair competition in the marketplace for patients by prohibiting monopolies (Niles, 2013). Regulations such as HIPAA protect patient information; COBRA gives workers and families the right to continue healthcare coverage if they lose their job; the **Newborns' and Mothers' Health Protection Act (NMHPA)** of 1996 prevents health insurance companies from discharging a mother and child too early from the hospital; the **Women's Health and Cancer Rights Act (WHCRA)** of 1998 prevents discrimination against women who have cancer; the **Mental Health Parity Act (MHPA)** of 1996 and its 2008 amendment requires health insurance companies to provide fair coverage for mental health conditions; the **Genetic Information Nondiscrimination Act of 2008** prohibits U.S. insurance companies and employers from discriminating based on genetic test results; the **Lilly Ledbetter Fair Pay Act of 2009** provides protection for unlawful employment practices related to compensation discrimination; and finally, the **Affordable Care Act of 2010** focuses on increasing access to health care, improving the quality of healthcare delivery, and increasing the number of individuals who have health insurance. All of these regulations are considered **social regulations** because they were enacted to protect the healthcare consumer.

Private Participation in Health Care

The private sector focuses on the financial and delivery aspects of the system. Healthcare costs are paid by a health insurance plan, private or governmental, and the enrollee of the plan. Approximately 34% of 2014 healthcare expenditures were paid by private health insurance, insurance offered by a private insurance company such as Blue Cross; private **out-of-pocket expenses or payments**, funds paid by the individual, were 13.7%; and federal, state, and local governments paid 39%. Out-of-pocket payments are considered the individual's **cost share** of his or her healthcare costs. Approximately 83% of private health insurance premiums are paid for by the employer for the employee. This type of insurance is a type of **voluntary health insurance** set up by an individual's employer. The delivery of the services provided is through legal entities such as hospitals, clinics, physicians, and other medical providers (National Center for Health Statistics [NCHS], 2016). The different providers are an integral part of the medical care system and need to coordinate their care with the layers of the U.S. government. In order to ensure access to health care, communication is vital between public and private components of healthcare delivery.

▶ Assessing Your Healthcare System Using the Iron Triangle

Many healthcare systems are evaluated using the **Iron Triangle of Health Care**—a concept that focuses on the balance of three factors: quality, cost, and accessibility to health care (see **FIGURE 1-1**). This concept was created in 1994 by Dr. William Kissick (Kissick, 1994). If one factor is emphasized, such as cost reduction, it may create an inequality of quality and access because costs are being cut. Because lack of access is a problem in the United States, healthcare systems may focus on increasing access, which could increase costs. In order to assess the success of a healthcare delivery, it is vital that consumers analyze the balance between cost, access, and quality. Are you receiving quality care from your provider? Do you have easy access to your healthcare system? Is it costly to receive health care? Although the Iron Triangle is used by many experts in analyzing large healthcare delivery systems, as a healthcare consumer, you can also evaluate your

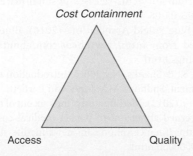

FIGURE 1-1 **The Iron Triangle of Health Care**

Reproduced from Kissick, William, MD, DR, PH, Medicine's Dilemmas, p. 3. New Haven, CT: Yale University Press, 1994. Reprinted by permission.

healthcare delivery system by using the Iron Triangle. An effective healthcare system should have a balance between the three components.

▶ Conclusion

Despite U.S. healthcare expenditures, disease rates in the United States remain higher than those of many other developed countries because the United States has an expensive system that is available to only those who can afford it (Regenstein, Mead, & Lara, 2007). Findings from a recent MetLife annual survey indicate that healthcare costs are worrying employees and their employers. Over 60% of employees are worried they will not be able to pay out-of-pocket expenses not covered by insurance. Employers are increasing the cost sharing of their employees for healthcare benefits because of the cost increases (Business Wire, 2013). Because the United States does not have universal health coverage, there are more health disparities across the nation. Persons living in poverty are more likely to be in poor health and less likely to use the healthcare system compared to those with incomes above the poverty line. If the United States offered universal health coverage, the per capita expenditures would be more evenly distributed and likely more effective. The major problem for the United States is that healthcare insurance is a major determinant of access to health care. Although there has been a decrease in the number of uninsured in the United States as a result of the individual mandate to purchase health insurance by the Affordable Care Act, there is still limited access to routine health care. statistic The infant mortality rate is often used to compare the health status of nations worldwide. Although our healthcare expenditures are very high, our infant mortality rates rank higher than those of many countries. Racial disparities in disease and death rates continue to be a concern. However, there has been a decline of 13% in infant mortality rates in the United States from 2000 to 2013. If you compare this statistic to comparable countries worldwide, their rates dropped during the same time period by 26%. The United States has more work to do regarding this issue (CDC, 2016b). Both private and public participants in the U.S. health delivery system need to increase their collaboration to reduce these disease rates. Leaders need to continue to assess our healthcare system using the Iron Triangle to ensure there is a balance between access, cost, and quality.

Wrap-Up

Vocabulary

Agency for Healthcare Research and Quality (AHRQ)
Almshouses
American Medical Association (AMA)
American Recovery and Reinvestment Act (ARRA)
Assessment
Assurance
Center for Mental Health Services (CMHS)
Centers for Disease Control and Prevention (CDC)
Centers for Medicare and Medicaid Services (CMS)
Certificate of need (CON)
Consolidated Omnibus Budget Reconciliation Act (COBRA)
Constitutional factors
Cost sharing
Determinants of health
Emergency Medical Treatment and Active Labor Act (EMTALA)
Employer health insurance
Epidemics
Family Medical Leave Act (FMLA)
Flexner Report
Food and Drug Administration (FDA)

Genetic Information Nondiscrimination Act of 2008
Graying of the population
Gross domestic product (GDP)
Group insurance
Health
Health insurance
Health Insurance Portability and Accountability Act (HIPAA)
Healthy People reports (2000, 2010, 2020)
Hospitalists
Iron Triangle of Health Care
Joint Commission
Lilly Ledbetter Fair Pay Act of 2009
Macroeconomic conditions
Medicaid
Medicare
Medicare Prescription Drug, Improvement, and Modernization Act
Mental Health Parity Act (MHPA)
National Defense Authorization Act
National Mental Health Act (NMHA)
Newborns' and Mothers' Health Protection Act (NMHPA)

Out-of-pocket payments or expenses
Patient Bill of Rights
Patient Protection and Affordable Care Act of 2010 (PPACA, or ACA)
Pesthouses
Poison Prevention Packaging Act of 1970
Policy development
Poorhouses
Primary prevention
Public health
Public health functions
Public Health Security and Bioterrorism Preparedness and Response Act of 2002
Secondary prevention
Sherman Antitrust Act of 1890
Social and community networks
Social regulations
Social Security Act (SSA)
Tertiary prevention
Triple Aim
Uniformed Services Employment and Reemployment Rights Act (USERRA)
Universal healthcare program
Voluntary health insurance
Women's Health and Cancer Rights Act (WHCRA)

References

American Heritage Dictionary. (4th ed.). (2001). New York: Bantam Dell.

American Hospital Association. (2007). Community accountability and transparency: Helping hospitals better serve their communities. Retrieved from http://www.aha.org/aha/content/2007/pdf/07accountability.pdf

American Medical Association. (2016a). Our history. Retrieved from http://www.ama-assn.org/ama/pub/about-ama/our-history.shtml

American Medical Association. (2016b). Reports of council on medical service. Retrieved from http://www.ama-assn.org/ama1/pub/upload/mm/38/i05cmspdf.pdf

Barton, P. (2003). *Understanding the U.S. health services system.* Chicago, IL: Health Administration Press.

Bird, J. (2013). CMS releases hospital price ranges of 100 most common treatments. Retrieved from http://www.fiercehealthfinance.com/story/cms-releases-hospital-price-comparison-data/2013-05-08

Blue Cross Blue Shield Association. (2016). Blue beginnings. Retrieved from http://www.bcbs.com/about/history/blue-beginnings.html

Buchbinder, S., & Shanks, N. (2007). Introduction to health care management. Sudbury, MA: Jones and Bartlett.

Business Wire. (2013). MetLife study finds six out of ten employees are concerned about out-of-pocket medical costs. Retrieved from http://finance.yahoo.com/news/metlife-study-finds-six-ten-130000050.html

Centers for Disease Control and Prevention. (2001). Trends in hospital emergency department utilization: United States, 1992–1999. Vital and Health Statistics, 13(150 revised).

Retrieved from http://www.cdc.gov/nchs/data/series/sr_13/sr13_150.pdf

Centers for Disease Control and Prevention. (2007). Skin cancer module: Practice exercises. Retrieved from http://www.cdc.gov/excite/skincancer/mod13.htm

Centers for Disease Control and Prevention. (2009). Selected federal legal authorities pertinent to public health emergencies. Retrieved from http://www.cdc.gov/phlp/docs/ph-emergencies.pdf

Centers for Disease Control and Prevention. (2016a). Healthy People 2020: Tobacco use. Retrieved from http://www.cdc.gov/tobacco/basic_information/healthy_people

Centers for Disease Control and Prevention. (2016b). NCHS data brief: Recent declines in infant mortality in the United States, 2005–2011. Retrieved from http://www.cdc.gov/nchs/data/databriefs/db120.htm

Centers for Medicare and Medicaid Services. (2016a). National health expenditure projections. Retrieved from http://www.cms.gov/Research-Statistics-Data-and-Systems/Statistics-Trends-and-Reports/NationalHealthExpendData/nationalHealthAccountsHistorical.html

Centers for Medicare and Medicaid Services. (2016b). HIPAA: General information. Retrieved from http://www.cms.hhs.gov/HIPAAGenInfo/01_Overview.asp

Chadwick, E. (1842). The sanitary conditions of the labouring class. London: W. Clowes.

Classen, D., Resar, R., Griffin, F., Federico, F., Frankel, T., Kimmel, N., James, B. (2011). Global Trigger Tool shows that adverse events in hospitals may be ten times greater than previously measured. *Health Affairs*, 30(4), 109.

Determinants of health. (2016). Retrieved from http://healthypeople.gov/2020/implement/assess.aspx

Duke University Library. (2016). Medicine and Madison Avenue. Timeline. Retrieved from http://library.duke.edu/digitalcollections/mma/timeline.html

Facts on Medicare spending and financing. (2015). Retrieved from http://kff.org/search/?s=Facts±on±Medicare±spending±and±financing+

Goodman, J.C., & Musgrave, G.L. (1992). *Patient power: Solving America's health care crisis*. Washington, DC: CATO Institute.

HCAHPS Fact Sheet. (2016). Retrieved from http://www.hcahpsonline.org/Facts.aspx

Health, United States, 2014. National Center for Health Statistics. Retrieved from http://www.cdc.gov/nchs/data/hus/hus14.pdf#highlights

Institute of Medicine. (1988). *The future of public health* (pp. 1–5). Washington, DC: National Academies Press.

Kissick, W. (1994). *Medicine's dilemmas*. New Haven and New London, CT: Yale University Press.

Kliff, S. (2012). Study: Fewer employers are offering health insurance. Retrieved from http://www.washingtonpost.com/blogs/wonkblog/post/study-fewer-employers-are-offering-health-insurance/2012/04/24/gIQAfGH6eT_print.html

Levy, J. (2015). U.S. uninsured rate continues to fall. Retrieved from http://www.gallup.com/poll/167798/uninsured-rate-continues-fall.aspx.

Ludmerer, K. (2004). The development of American medical education from the turn of the century to the era of managed care. *Clinical, Orthopaedics and Related Research*, 422: 256–262.

Nation at a glance: Uninsured Americans. (2016). Retrieved from http://www.cdc.gov/nchs/features/nation_jun2015/nation_at_a_glance_jun2015.htm

National Center for Health Statistics. (2014). *Health, United States, 2014. With special feature on socioeconomic status and health*. Washington, DC: U.S. Government Printing Office.

National Conference of State Legislatures. (2016). Certificate of need: State health laws and programs. Retrieved from http://www.ncsl.org/issues-research/health/con-certificate-of-need-state-laws.aspx

Niles, N. (2013). *Basic concepts of health care human resource management* (pp. 37–50). Sudbury, MA: Jones and Bartlett.

Novick, L., Morrow, C., & Mays, G. (2008). *Public health administration* (2nd ed., pp. 1–68). Sudbury, MA: Jones and Bartlett.

Raffel, M.W., & Raffel, N.K. (1994). *The U.S. health system: Origins and functions* (4th ed.). Albany, NY: Delmar Publishers.

Rau, J. (2015). 1,700 hospitals with quality bonuses from Medicare, but most will never collect. Retrieved from http://khn.org/news/1700-hospitals-win-quality-bonuses-from-medicare-but-most-will-never-collect/

Regenstein, M., Mead, M., & Lara, A. (2007). The heart of the matter: The relationship between communities, cardiovascular services and racial and ethnic gaps in care. *Managed Care Interface*, 20, 22–28.

Rich, E., Lebow, M., Srinivasan, M., Parish, D., Wollinscroft, J., Fein, O., & Blaser, R. (2002). Medicare financing of graduate medical education. *Journal of General Internal Medicine*, (17), 4;283–292.

Rosen, G. (1983). *The structure of American medical practice 1875–1941*. Philadelphia: University of Pennsylvania Press.

Starr, P. (1982). *The social transformation of American medicine*. Cambridge, MA: Basic Books.

Stevens, R. (1971). *American medicine and the public interest*. New Haven, CT: Yale University Press.

Sultz, H., & Young, K. (2006). *Health care USA: Understanding its organization and delivery* (5th ed.). Sudbury, MA: Jones and Bartlett.

Turnock, J. (1997). *Public health and how it works*. Gaithersburg, MD: Aspen Publishers, Inc.

Vault Career Intelligence. (2016). Home page. Retrieved from http://www.vault.com/wps/portal/usa

Winslow, C.E.A. (1920). *The untilled fields of public health* (pp. 30–35). New York: Health Service, New York Chapter of the American Red Cross.

Zeroing in on the Triple Aim. (2015). Retrieved from http://www.aha.org/content/15/brief-3aim.pdf.

▶ **Notes**

▶ Student Activity 1-1

In Your Own Words

Based on this chapter, please provide a definition of the following vocabulary words in your own words. DO NOT RECITE the text definition.

Group insurance:

_____

_____

Gross domestic product (GDP):

_____

_____

Pesthouses:

_____

_____

Voluntary health insurance:

_____

_____

Public health functions:

_____

_____

Primary prevention:

_____

_____

Secondary prevention:

_____

_____

Tertiary prevention:

_____

_____

Universal healthcare program:

_____

_____

_____

Epidemics:

_____

_____

_____

▶ Student Activity 1-2

Complete the following case scenarios based on the information provided in the chapter. Your answer must be **IN YOUR OWN WORDS.**

Real-Life Applications: Case Scenario One

Your mother knows that you are taking classes for your healthcare management degree. She just returned from a physician checkup and she was confused by the terminology they were using at the office. They mentioned several activities related to primary, secondary, and tertiary prevention.

Activity

Define each of the terms and provide examples of these types of prevention.

Responses

_____

_____

_____

_____

_____

_____

_____

_____

_____

_____

_____

_____

_____

_____

_____

_____

Case Scenario Two

You recently were promoted to assistant to the Chief Executive Officer of the Niles Hospital system.
The CEO is interested in building a hospital to expand the Niles healthcare system. She has asked you to investigate
the certificate of need (CON) process for this proposal.

Activity

Perform Internet research on the CON process and provide a report on the necessary steps to achieve this CON.

Responses

_____

_____

_____

_____

_____

_____

_____

_____

_____

_____

_____

_____

_____

_____

_____

_____

_____

Case Scenario Three

One of your friends had a very serious medical emergency and had to go to the hospital for treatment. She was very upset because upon her arrival, she was asked for her insurance card, which she did not have, and was transferred to another hospital quickly. You had learned there was a law that made this type of treatment by a hospital illegal. However, before telling your friend your opinion, you wanted to find out more about this law and whether it applied to her situation.

Activity

Perform Internet research on public health regulations and write up a report on whether you think the Emergency Medical Treatment and Active Labor Act (EMTALA) was applicable in this situation.

Responses

_____

_____

_____

_____

_____

_____

_____

_____

_____

_____

_____

_____

_____

_____

_____

_____

_____

_____

_____

_____

Case Scenario Four

As a public health student, you are interested in different public health initiatives the CDC has put forth over the years and whether they have been successful. You continue to hear the term "Healthy People reports." You are interested in the results of these reports.

Activity

Visit the CDC website and write a report on the Healthy People initiatives and whether or not you think they are successful initiatives.

Responses

_____

_____

_____

_____

_____

_____

_____

_____

_____

_____

_____

_____

_____

_____

_____

_____

_____

_____

_____

_____

_____

_____

▶ **Student Activity 1-3**

Internet Exercises

Write your answers in the space provided.

- ■   Visit each of the websites listed here.
- ■   Name the organization.
- ■   Locate their mission statement or statement of purpose on their website.
- ■   Provide a brief overview of the activities of the organization.
- ■   How do these organizations participate in the U.S. healthcare system?

Websites

http://www.ama-assn.org

Organization Name:

_____

_____

Mission Statement:

_____

_____

Overview of Activities:

_____

_____

_____

Importance of Organization to U.S. Health Care:

_____

_____

_____

http://www.cdc.gov

Organization Name:

_____

_____

Mission Statement:

_____

_____

_____

Overview of Activities:

_____

_____

_____

Importance of Organization to U.S. Health Care:

_____

_____

_____

http://www.cms.hhs.gov

Organization Name:

_____

_____

Mission Statement:

_____

_____

_____

Overview of Activities:

_____

_____

_____

Importance of Organization to U.S. Health Care:

_____

_____

_____

http://www.hhs.gov

Organization Name:

_____

_____

Mission Statement:

_____

_____

_____

Overview of Activities:

_____

_____

_____

Importance of Organization to U.S. Health Care:

_____

_____

_____

http://www.jointcommission.org

Organization Name:

_____

_____

Mission Statement:

_____

_____

_____

Overview of Activities:

_____

_____

_____

Importance of Organization to U.S. Health Care:

_____

_____

_____

http://www.ahrq.gov

Organization Name:

_____

_____

Mission Statement:

_____

_____

_____

Overview of Activities:

_____

_____

_____

Importance of Organization to U.S. Health Care:

_____

_____

_____

▸ **Student Activity 1-4**

Discussion Questions

The following are suggested discussion questions for this chapter.

1. What is the Flexner Report? How did it impact health care in the United States?

_____

_____

_____

_____

2. What are the Healthy People report initiatives? Describe three current initiatives to your classmates.

_____

_____

_____

_____

_____

3. Why was health insurance developed? What was Kaiser's role in this?

_____

_____

_____

_____

_____

4. Describe how the Iron Triangle can be used to assess health care. Give specific examples.

_____

_____

_____

_____

_____

_____

_____

_____

_____

5. What is the Patient Bill of Rights? Why was it developed? Have you ever seen the Patient Bill of Rights posted anywhere?

_____

_____

_____

_____

_____

_____

_____

6. Give five examples of public health activities in your personal or work environment.

_____

_____

_____

_____

_____

_____

_____

_____

▶ **Student Activity 1-5**

Current Events

Perform an Internet search and find a current events topic over the past three years that is related to this chapter. Provide a summary of the article and the link to the article and why the article relates to the chapter.

_____

_____

_____

_____

_____

_____

_____

_____

_____

_____

_____

_____

_____

_____

_____

_____

_____

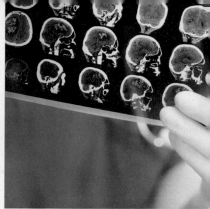

CHAPTER 2

Impact of the Affordable Care Act on Healthcare Services

▶ Introduction

The **Patient Protection and Affordable Care Act (PPACA)**, or as it is commonly called the **Affordable Care Act (ACA)**, and its amendment, the **Healthcare and Education Affordability Reconciliation Act of 2010**, were signed into law on March 23, 2010, by President Barack Obama. The goal of the act is to improve the accessibility and quality of the U.S. healthcare system. There are nearly 50 healthcare reform initiatives that are being implemented during 2010–2017 and beyond. The passage of this complex landmark legislation has been very controversial and continues to be contentious today.

There were national public protests and a huge division among the political parties regarding the components of the legislation. People, in general, agreed that the healthcare system needed some type of reform, but it was difficult to develop common recommendations that had majority support. Criticism focused in part on the increased role of government in implementing and monitoring the healthcare system. Proponents of healthcare reform reminded people that Medicare is a federal-government entitlement program because when individuals reach 65 years of age, they can receive their health insurance from this program. Millions of individuals are enrolled in Medicare. Medicaid is a state-established governmental public welfare insurance program based on income for millions of individuals, including children, that provides health care for its enrollees.

However, regardless of these two programs, many critics felt that the federal government was forcing people to purchase health insurance. In fact, the ACA does require most individuals to obtain health insurance only if they can afford it. But with healthcare system expenditures comprising 17.9% of the U.S. gross domestic product and with millions of Americans not having access to health care, resulting in poor health indicators, the current administration's priority was to create mandated healthcare reform.

▶ Legal Issues with the Affordable Care Act

The goal of the act is to improve the accessibility and quality of the U.S. healthcare system. There are nearly 50 healthcare reform initiatives that are being implemented over several years. As discussed earlier, the main bone of contention is the requirement of the act that U.S. citizens and legal residents must purchase health insurance or pay an annual fine for inaction. As a result of this mandate, over 20 states filed lawsuits, primarily questioning the constitutionality of this mandate. The second major contentious issue is whether Medicaid expansion requirements were constitutional because the federal government could withhold federal Medicaid funding to states that refuse to expand their Medicaid programs. Finally, the third contentious issue was requiring all businesses to offer health insurance coverage for contraception as part of their employee benefits. There was issues with this mandate because some religiously oriented businesses did not believe in certain components of the contraceptive mandate.

On June 28, 2012, the U.S. Supreme Court upheld the constitutionality of the ACA in a 5–4 ruling in the *Florida v. Sebelius* lawsuit regarding individual health insurance mandates and the *National Federation of Independent Businesses v. Sebelius* lawsuits filed regarding Medicaid expansion (ProCon.org, 2016a). However, the federal government could not withhold federal funding to states that refuse the Medicaid expansion because it could be considered coercion. As a result of this decision, the federal government was required to develop state incentives to accept the Medicaid expansion and to restrict the type of funding limitations to states that refuse the Medicaid expansions (Svendiman & Baumrucker, 2012).

On June 30, 2014, in the *Hobby Lobby* and *Conestoga vs. Sebelius* decisions, the Supreme Court ruled that the federal government cannot mandate that religious organizations provide, as part of their employee benefits, drugs or devices that end human life. Both Hobby Lobby and Conestoga Wood Specialties Corp. did not object to the entire contraceptive mandate but did object to that specific mandate.

On June 25, 2015, the Supreme Court ruled in favor of the Affordable Care Act. In *King v. Burwell*, by a vote of 6–3, the Supreme Court rejected a challenge brought on grounds that financial assistance should be given only to individuals who purchased health insurance via the federal marketplaces. The federal government argued that subsidies were available to all individuals who purchased health insurance via all marketplaces, both federal and state run.

The challengers were four residents of Virginia who did not want to purchase health insurance because they could not afford it. They resented the federal government mandate of requiring to purchase health insurance. They said they could not afford it but would have to purchase it, if the subsidies were available. If the subsidies ruling was overturned, there would have been 8 million individuals who would have lost their health insurance because they could not afford it otherwise (Ehrenfreund, 2015).

In January 2016, Congress enacted a repeal of the ACA's major provisions which the President vetoed. However, there has been a House of Representatives special task force assembled to develop a replacement for the ACA. Depending on the November 2016 elections that could impact what will occur with the ACA provisions.

On May 13, 2016, the Department of Health and Human Services issued final regulations on section 1557 of the ACA. The rule emphasizes that health care discrimination against LGBTQ individuals, particularly transgender and gender non-conforming people, is against federal law. Section 1557 provides protection based on race, color, national origin, sex, age, and disability. LGBT protection falls under sex discrimination. This rule applies to facilities that receive federal assistance, every federal program administered by the DHSS and programs under Title 1 of the ACA which includes hospitals, clinics, pharmacies, labs, and HIV testing sites nationally. This also includes most types of health insurance plans (Transgender, 2016).

▶ Major Provisions of the Affordable Care Act

TABLE 2-1 provides an updated summary of the over 40 major action items of the ACA (Centers for Medicare & Medicaid Services [CMS], 2013c). The key features of the law include rights and protection of healthcare consumers, insurance choice and insurance costs, benefits for those 65 and older, and employer requirements of providing healthcare benefits. The law itself is divided into 10 titles or areas of healthcare reform. This chapter will provide a summary of each title and an update on the implementation of these areas of healthcare reform. It is important to note that certain health insurance plans can be grandfathered plans which means they do not have to follow the rules and regulations of the ACA. These grandfathered plans are plans that were purchased before March 23, 2010. This means that on many old plans you can still be dropped from coverage for reasons other than fraud,

TABLE 2-1 Timeline for Affordable Care Act Regulations	
2010	Affordable Care Act Signed into Law
	States to Increase Medicaid Coverage
	One time $250 Rebate for Medicare Part D Donut Hole
	Target Healthcare Fraud
	Early Retiree Reinsurance Program (ERRP)
	Insurance for Preexisting Conditions
	Online Information for Healthcare Consumers at http://www.healthcare.gov
	Extend Age for Young Adults' Coverage to 26
	Prohibit Insurance from Dropping Coverage
	Appeal of Insurance Coverage Denials
	Eliminate Lifetime Limits on Insurance Coverage
	Regulate Annual Limits on Insurance Coverage
	Ban of Coverage Denial of Children with Preexisting Conditions
	Accountability of Insurance for High Rate Hikes

(continues)

TABLE 2-1 Timeline for Affordable Care Act Regulations *(continued)*

	Focus on Primary Health Workforce
	Establish State Consumer Assistance Programs
	Prevent Disease and Illness Initiatives
	Strengthen Community Health Centers
	Increased Payments for Rural Health
2011	Prescription Drug Discounts
	Free Preventive Care for Seniors
	Reduce Healthcare Premiums
	Strengthen Medicare Advantage
	Improve Quality and Efficiency of Health Care
	Improve Senior Care After Discharge from Hospital
	Innovation to Reduce Costs
	Increase Home and Community Health Services
2012	Encourage Integrated Healthcare Systems
	Decrease Health Disparities
	Reduce Administrative Costs
	Link Payment to Quality Care
2013	Increase Preventive Care Coverage
	Increase Medicaid Payments to Primary MDs
	Expanding Bundled Payments
	Open Enrollment in Health Insurance Marketplace effective October 1
2014	Start of Health Insurance Coverage through the Marketplace
	Promote Individual Responsibility
	Increase Access to Medicaid
	Eliminate Annual Limits of Insurance Coverage
	Increase of Small Business Health Insurance Tax Credit

(continues)

TABLE 2-1 Timeline for Affordable Care Act Regulations	*(continued)*
2015	Payment to Physicians Based on Quality Care
2017	Factors such as preexisting conditions, gender, health status, claims history, duration of coverage, and occupation can no longer be used by insurance companies to increase health insurance premiums.
	Members of Congress must shop on the health insurance marketplaces.
	Employers with 100 or fewer full-time equivalent employees can offer SHOP—Small Business Health Options plans. All new health plans must include the 10 essential health benefits.
	Premiums of new plans can be impacted by tobacco use, age, family size, geographic location, income, and type of plan. Individuals who have plans that have lost grandfathered status must sign up for a qualified health insurance plan.
2018	All healthcare plans must now offer preventive coverage.
	The Cadillac tax for higher coverage plans for employees will go into effect.
2020	The Medicare gap (donut hole) for prescription drugs will be eliminated.

Data from Centers for Medicare & Medicaid Services. Timeline of the health care law. Retrieved from https://www.healthcare.gov/timeline-of-the-health-care-law/#part=1 and http://obamacarefacts.com/health-care-timeline/.

be denied treatment for preexisting conditions, face annual and lifetime dollar limits and more. Americans with plans that lose grandfathered status will either have to switch to a new version of the plan or choose a different plan. In many cases Americans will be able to find a comparable plan on their State's health insurance marketplace and may even qualify for subsidies. The deadline for choosing a qualified plan is 2017.

Title 1–Affordability and Accessibility of Healthcare

The following are some of the major reforms that were implemented in 2010:

- Eliminate lifetime and unreasonable annual caps or limits on healthcare reimbursement with annual limitations prohibited by 2014.
- Provide assistance for the uninsured with preexisting conditions and prohibit denial of insurance coverage for preexisting conditions for children.
- Develop a temporary national high-risk pool for health insurance for individuals with preexisting conditions who have no insurance.
- Extend dependent coverage up to age 26.

- Establish www.healthcare.gov for consumers to access information about healthcare insurance.
- Create a reinsurance program for retirees who are not yet eligible for Medicare.

Discussion

In the past, health insurance companies would establish an annual or lifetime cap on reimbursement of consumers' healthcare insurance claims. This practice would be eliminated. Unlike the past, health insurance companies would also be prohibited from dropping individuals and children with certain conditions or not providing insurance to those individuals with preexisting conditions. This Pre-Existing Condition Insurance Plan (PCIP) provides new healthcare coverage options to individuals who have a preexisting condition and have had no insurance for the preceding six months. This served as a bridge to 2014, when all discrimination against preexisting conditions was prohibited.

Prior to the ACA, dependent coverage stopped at age 25. The act requires insurance companies to cover young adults on their parents' insurance until age 26, even if they are not living with their parents, are not declared dependents on their parents' taxes, or are no longer students. However, this would not apply to individuals who have employer-based coverage (U.S. Department of Labor, 2016).

In July 2010, the federal government established a web portal, www.healthcare.gov, to increase consumers' awareness about their eligibility for specific healthcare insurance company information and about governmental programs. This website was designed to provide information to the 36 states that opted not to create their own state exchanges. The website is an opportunity for individuals to sign up for health insurance plans. The projected date for open enrollment on healthcare.gov was October 1, 2013, with the legal requirement to sign up for 2014 healthcare coverage by December 15, 2013. However, serious technological problems occurred, which was very frustrating to those attempting to sign up for plans. Estimates indicated that only one percent of potential enrollees were able to enroll in plans during the first weeks of the website operation. The federal government did not anticipate the high volume on the website. There were also problems with the website's design. The federal government hired contactors to fix the website but problems continue to plague the website for several weeks during its initial launch. The poor implementation of the website was heavily criticized. U.S. Secretary of Health and Human Services Kathleen Sebelius was forced to resign in November 2014. Enrollment for 2015 was smoother. Open enrollment for 2016 began on November 1, 2015, and ended on January 31, 2016.

Also, a government temporary **reinsurance program** for employers who provide coverage to retirees over age 55 who are not yet eligible for Medicare will reimburse the employer 80% of the retiree claims of $50,000–$90,000. The act created a $5 billion program to provide financial assistance for employment-based plans to supply this coverage. This program was effective until January 2014, when the state-based Health Insurance Marketplaces were put in place and retirees not yet eligible for Medicare could buy their own insurance (U.S. General Accountability Office, 2016).

The following are selected major reforms that were implemented by 2014:

- Insurance companies were prohibited from setting insurance rates based on health status, medical condition, genetic information, or other related factors.
- Private health insurance coverage offered in the Marketplaces must offer the same **essential health benefits (EHBs)**.

- By October 1, 2013, states were required to establish the **Health Insurance Marketplaces**, where consumers can obtain information and buy health insurance. Open enrollment for health insurance also began on October 1, 2013, for health insurance that became effective January 1, 2014. Most individuals who were uninsured must have enrolled by January 1, 2014, in an insurance plan that has minimum essential healthcare coverage or pay an annual fee.
- In the past, there were issues with health insurance companies denying coverage based on health status or other conditions. Premiums now will be based on family type, geography, tobacco use, and age. In 2014–2016, only individuals and small-group employers were eligible to participate in the Marketplaces. In 2017, states can permit large group employers to participate. States may also organize regional exchanges. On May 8, 2013, the U.S. Department of Labor (DOL) issued guidance for employers regarding the requirement to notify employees of coverage options available through the exchanges (United Health Care, 2016). The ACA also established a summary of benefits and coverage (SBC), which offers consumers the opportunity to easily compare health insurance plans.
- **Consumer Operated and Oriented Plans (CO-OPs)**, which are member-run health organizations in all 50 states and must be consumer focused with profits targeted to lowering premiums and improving benefits, were established.
- The **Centers for Consumer Information and Insurance Oversight** awarded nearly $70 million in cooperative agreements to 105 organizations to provide assistance to insurance marketplaces.

Health insurance plans in the Marketplaces must offer at a minimum the following **essential health benefits**:

- Ambulatory patient services (outpatient care individuals receive without being admitted to a hospital)
- Emergency services
- Hospitalization (such as surgery)
- Maternity and newborn care (care before and after a baby is born)
- Mental health and substance-use disorder services, including behavioral health treatment (this includes counseling and psychotherapy)
- Prescription drugs

- Rehabilitative and habilitative services and devices (services and devices to help people with injuries, disabilities, or chronic conditions gain or recover mental and physical skills)
- Laboratory services
- Preventive and wellness services and chronic disease management
- Pediatric services (CMS, 2013d)

Health Insurance Marketplaces, run by the federal or state governments, are central locations for healthcare consumers to purchase health insurance coverage. They provide standardized information on the different types of health insurance coverage to suit consumer needs. Consumers complete an application to determine the types of coverage available to them, based on their need. Health insurance coverage is provided by private health insurance companies.

If individuals did not apply for health insurance coverage by March 31, 2014, which is when open enrollment ended, they were required to pay a fee and cannot obtain coverage until the next annual open enrollment. However, if a **life qualifying event** such as job change or geographic change occurred, they could be eligible to enroll at other times. The 2014 fee was 1% of the individual's yearly income or $95 per person, whichever was higher. The fee for an uninsured child was $47.50. The maximum amount a family would pay is $285. The fee increases every year. In 2016, it is 2.5% of income or $695, whichever is higher. Individuals who have very low income, participate in a religious sect that does not believe in health insurance, or are part of a federally recognized Indian tribe will not be charged a fee (CMS, 2016e).

The SBC was developed as a result of the ACA. This summary allows the consumer to compare the different types of benefits offered by health insurance companies. A consumer can compare price, benefits, and other features. This is required for all health insurance companies.

Recognizing that in some states only a small number of insurance companies offer coverage for individuals and small businesses, the Centers for Medicare and Medicaid Services (CMS) has awarded nearly $2 billion in loans to help create CO-OPs nationwide. As of December 2014, there were 24 CO-OP sponsors—consumer-run groups, membership associations, and other nonprofit organizations that will provide insurance coverage in designated geographic areas. They are now offering health plans through the Health Insurance Marketplace (CMS, 2016).

There are different types of plans that can be purchased on the marketplaces. **TABLE 2-2** outlines the different types of plans.

TABLE 2-2 How you and your plan share total costs of care		
Plan category	**The insurance company pays**	**You pay**
Bronze	60%	40%
Silver	70%	30%
Gold	80%	20%
Platinum	90%	10%

Source: http:www.healthcare.gov

Generally, the bronze levels have the lowest premiums but have the higher out of pocket expenses. The gold and platinum have the highest premiums but the lowest out of pocket expenses. When the healthcare consumer completes the marketplace application, information will be analyzed to determine if there are subsidies available based on income. A new 2016 feature allows the consumer to enter their prescription drugs and preferred providers to determine which plans will cover them (Understanding marketplace plans, 2016).

The Small Business Health Options (SHOP) was developed as part of the Marketplace to provide insurance plans from private insurance companies for businesses who have 100 or fewer employees. If the business has 25 or less employees, they may qualify for a health care tax credit for up to 50% of the premium costs.

The DHHS's Centers for Consumer Information and Insurance Oversight is responsible for the oversight of the health insurance provisions of the ACA. They will work with state governments to ensure the Marketplaces are being implemented properly. They will also help states with reviews of any unreasonable rate increases by insurance companies and other social regulations (CMS, 2016b). The Health Resources and Services Administration also awarded $150 million to 1200 community health centers to enroll uninsured individuals.

A controversial initiative is the Cadillac tax, effective 2018, that taxes generous health insurance plans that were typically negotiated by unions. This would force employers to offer less generous packages, which would limit health care spending over time. This has been a controversial mandate. Some economists who support the tax, indicate employees would be compensated by higher wages. The Cadillac tax would generate $91 billion in revenues over 10 years The arguments against the Cadillac tax indicate that it would impact lower income employees because employers would raise the employees cost sharing to offset the tax. This mandate could be repealed in the next administration (Altman, 2016)

Effective 2017, employers who have 100 or more full-time equivalent employees must offer them health insurance.

Enrollment Data for Marketplaces

The current enrollment numbers (as on February 2016) are roughly 12.7 million in the marketplace, and very roughly 20 million between the Marketplace, Medicaid expansion, young adults staying on their parents plan, and other coverage provisions. The uninsured rate remains at an all-time low with 9.1% of under 65 uninsured as of the end of 2015 according to CDC. Gov data. Generally, 2016 saw a rough increase of all the 2015 numbers (Obamacare enrollment, 2016).

A **public plan option** was also authorized to create a government-run health insurance agency that would compete with other health insurance companies. This would provide health insurance for individuals who could not afford private health insurance premiums. This program has not been implemented. However, in 2013, this type of program was reintroduced by the Senate as an amendment to the ACA. The purpose of these programs is to increase the number of consumers who have access to affordable health care.

Title II–The Role of Public Programs: Medicaid, CHIP, Medicare

- Medicaid eligibility has been expanded to cover lower incomes. The baseline is all individuals whose incomes are under 133% of the federal poverty level. States will receive matching funds to expand their Medicaid services, increasing accessibility to more consumers. As of 2016, 32 states had opted to expand their Medicaid programs. More states are expected to adopt the expansion because the federal government is willing to pay 100% of the state's costs through 2016 for the expansion.
- The Children's Health Insurance Program (CHIP) will be required to maintain income level eligibility through 2019.
- A new Medicaid benefit, Community First Choice, has been created to offer community services.
- In 2010, a onetime $250 rebate was given to Medicare Part D beneficiaries who entered the

coverage gap, also known as the "donut hole," in 2010. There are approximately 4 million seniors impacted by this financing gap.
- Medicare beneficiaries will receive an annual wellness visit with no cost sharing.

Discussion

Medicaid will expand to increase coverage for consumers who are not Medicare eligible. As discussed earlier, this mandate was contentious because states felt that the federal government was forcing them to expand their programs by withholding federal aid if states refused to expand. The federal government has limited the withholding mandate to certain newly eligible populations. It also simplifies enrollment for both individuals and families. The federal government will increase its payments to the states through 2019. Individuals will be able to enroll in these programs through the exchange and state websites. Community First Choice is an optional Medicaid benefit that focuses on community health services to Medicaid enrollees with disabilities. This will enable consumers to receive care at home or at community health centers rather than going to a hospital or another healthcare facility. This option became available on October 1, 2011, and provided a six percent increase in federal matching payments to states for expenditures related to this option. As of March 2016, eight states are utilizing this option (Medicaid. gov, 2016). These mandates will enable lower-income consumers and children to have access to health care at an affordable cost.

There was an issue with the Medicare Part D coverage gap, more commonly known as the donut hole for Medicare Part D. The coverage gap or donut hole starts after the beneficiary and the drug plan together have spent a designated amount for the covered drugs. The donut hole changes every year. For example, in 2016, once the beneficiary enters the coverage gap ($3,310), the individual must pay 45% of the plan's cost for covered brand drugs and 58% of the plan's cost for covered generic drugs until he or she reaches the end of the coverage gap ($4,850 in 2016); then a copayment for each covered drug is paid until the end of the year. Not all beneficiaries will reach the coverage gap because their drug costs are not that high. This increase in beneficiary out-of-pocket payments was very expensive for those enrolled and often resulted in individuals not obtaining necessary medication because of cost. Since the passage of the ACA, 6.6 million Medicare enrollees who were impacted by the donut hole have saved over $7 billion on prescription drugs, which averages $1,061 per beneficiary. In addition to the $250 rebate check, those impacted received discounts and increased coverage. They will continue to receive these benefits until the coverage gap is closed in 2020 (CMS, 2016a).

Title III—Improving the Quality and Efficiency of Health Care

- The **Independent Payment Advisory Board** was established to develop quality improvement proposals.
- The **Patient-Centered Outcomes Research Institute** was established.
- Ann **Independence at Home program** was created.

Discussion

Medicare payments will be linked to the quality of care. Long-term care hospitals, rehabilitation services, cancer hospitals, and hospice providers will participate in quality performance measures. A federal interagency **Working Group on Healthcare Quality** was established to develop national initiatives on quality performance. They collaborate with other federal agencies to implement the National Quality Strategy developed by the DHHS (AHRQ, 2016). Also, a new **Center for Medicare and Medicaid Innovation** will research different payment and delivery systems. Effective in 2012, hospital reimbursements were based on the hospital's percentage of preventable readmissions of Medicare beneficiary patients. The **Center for Medicare and Medicaid Innovation**'s goal is to support the development and testing of innovative healthcare payment and service delivery models. The center currently has several demonstration projects for payment and care models, including accountable care organizations, value-based purchasing, and coordinated and prevention care.

The 15-member Independent Payment Advisory Board will present to Congress proposals for cost savings and quality performance measures. This 15-member board, appointed by the President and confirmed by the Senate, will make recommendations to reduce Medicare spending, which will be implemented by the DHHS. This is the first time Congress has established a mechanism to set a cap on future Medicare spending (Moffitt, 2011).

The community health teams will increase access to community-based coordinated health care. Local healthcare providers will be encouraged to develop medication management services to assist with chronic

disease management. These measures increase the efficiency and effectiveness of Medicare. Also, there is a continued focus on community health activities that reduce the cost of healthcare services.

The Patient-Centered Outcomes Research Institute (PCORI) compares the outcomes of disease treatments. A nonprofit private organization established in 2010, the PCORI is responsible for providing assistance to physicians, patients, and policy makers in improving health outcomes and perform research that targets quality and efficiency of care. A trust fund has been established to pay for the PCORI's administration and research. According to its website, the PCORI facilitates more efficient research, which could significantly increase the amount of information available to healthcare decision makers and the speed at which it is generated. The PCORI has invested more than $250 million in the development of PCORnet: The National Patient-Centered Clinical Research Network. This network has partnerships in all 50 states. PCORnet established a functional research network of health information that is nationally representative and will significantly reduce the time and effort required to start studies and build the necessary infrastructure to conduct them. It will support a range of study designs, including large, simple clinical trials and studies that combine an experimental component, such as a randomized trial, with a complementary observational component. Because PCORnet enables studies to be conducted using real-time data drawn from the everyday healthcare experiences of people across the United States, it should increase the relevance of questions that can be studied and the usefulness of the study results. Research is focusing on prevalent health issues such as diabetes, obesity, breast cancer, hypertension, and heart disease (PCRI, 2016).

The Independence at Home program provides Medicare beneficiaries with at-home primary care and allocate any cost savings of this type of care to healthcare professionals who reduce hospital admissions and improve health outcomes (American Association of Nurse Practitioners, 2016). This three-year demonstration program, started in January 2012, assessed home health care for Medicare beneficiaries who are chronically ill. Medical care is administered by a team of providers and is available seven days per week around the clock. The goal of the program is to compare the cost of this type of care to hospital care of those Medicare beneficiaries who are chronically ill (Home Caregiver Services, 2016). According to the CMS, Independence at Home participants saved over $25 million in the demonstration's first performance year—an average of $3,070 per participating beneficiary—while delivering high-quality patient care in the home. The CMS awarded incentive payments of $11.7 million to nine participating practices that succeeded in reducing Medicare expenditures and met designated quality goals for the first year of the demonstration (CMS, 2016f).

Title IV–Prevention of Chronic Disease and Improving Public Health

- The **National Prevention, Health Promotion, and Public Health Council** (National Prevention Council) was established to develop a national health prevention strategy.
- To waive copayments or cost sharing for most preventive services, Medicare will cover 100% of the total cost.
- Medicaid must provide coverage to pregnant women for counseling and drug therapy for tobacco cessation and provide incentives for all enrollees who participate in healthy lifestyles.

Discussion

The National Prevention Council is an interagency council of 17 federal organizations chaired by the U.S. Surgeon General to promote health policies and assess infrastructures. The health priorities include tobacco-free living, drug and alcohol prevention programs, injury and violence-free living, active lifestyles for all ages, mental and sexual health, and healthy eating. The council's 2014 annual report included the following statistics:

1. Between 2012 and 2013, the number of tobacco-free college campuses increased by almost 70% from 774 to 1343;
2. By the end of 2013, over 6,500 U.S. schools had received a certification for promoting nutrition and physical activity;
3. The number of hospitals that promoted breastfeeding to new mothers tripled between 2008 and 2013;
4. Between 2012 and 2013, the national homeless rate dropped 7%, with an 8% drop in Veterans' homelessness; and
5. By 2012, 76% of U.S. school districts offered mental health or social services to students.

The **Prevention and Public Health Fund** was established to provide funding for public health programs. As of 2014, approximately $927 million was available to fund activities in 2015. A large portion of the funding was allocated to the Centers for Disease

Control and Prevention. Research indicates that these types of funding programs have the potential to improve health outcomes and reduce healthcare costs (American Public Health Association, 2016).

In addition, there will be no copayment for Medicare annual wellness visits and the development of a patient prevention program (discussed in Title II). Medicaid will also expand its coverage for prevention activities such as drug or tobacco cessation programs. There will be additional federal funding to Medicaid programs if they provide free immunizations or other clinical preventive services.

Title V–Healthcare Workforce

- The ACA established a **National Health Care Workforce Commission** to review healthcare workforce and projected needs. Funding was never appropriated for this initiative.
- The ACA developed programs to increase the supply of healthcare workers by training and education incentives.
- The ACA developed a **Primary Care Extension Program (PCEP)** to educate and provide assistance to primary care providers about preventive medicine. Funding was never provided for this program.

Discussion

A **National Health Care Workforce Commission** was developed to review workforce needs and make recommendations to the federal government to ensure that national policies are in alignment with consumer needs. As of January 2013, Congress had allocated $3 million for the commission, but funds were never appropriated and therefore the Commission has never met.

The PCEP was established to provide technical assistance to primary care providers about health promotion, chronic disease management, mental health, and preventive medicine. These initiatives are focused on prevention and health promotion. Family medicine groups have recommended annual funding of $120 million to administer the program. The PCEP would establish patient-centered medical homes by creating community-based health extension agents, whose role was to collaborate with local health agencies to identify community health priorities and determine the workforce needs for local areas. Because funding was not awarded, the AHRQ used existing appropriations to develop a pilot program in 2011. It was renamed IMPaCT, which stands for Infrastructure for Maintaining Primary Care Transformation. They provided funding for four projects from 2011 through 2013 in Oklahoma, North Carolina, Pennsylvania, and New Mexico. The states created a primary care team that would coordinate efforts between primary care and public health efforts. The grantees felt it was a success with reporting of healthier patient outcomes.

Title VI–Transparency and Program Integrity

■ The DHHS will publish standardized information on long-term care options for consumers so they can compare facilities.

■ A national system for direct patient access to employee background checks will be established.

■ A process to screen Medicare and Medicaid providers will be created.

■ The **Elder Justice Act**, intended to prevent and eliminate elder patient abuse, was enacted.

Discussion

As the U.S. population is graying, the number of individuals who live in assisted living and skilled nursing facilities at the end of their lives is increasing. There will be continued enrollment in both Medicare and Medicaid. These mandates focus on the importance of providing information about long-term facilities to consumers so they can select the appropriate facility for their relative. This title also focuses on providing additional information about the quality of the care given at long-term facilities. There is also a screening mechanism to ensure that these service providers are providing quality care.

The Elder Justice bill was introduced in the Senate in 2003 and contained landmark initiatives in the development of a national policy to prevent elder abuse and neglect, which continues to be a social issue. The Elder Justice Act was finally passed as part of the ACA. It targets abuse, neglect, and exploitation of the elderly. However, Congress did not award funding until 2012 for the activities associated with the act. In 2012, the DHHS transferred nearly $6 million in funding to implement Elder Justice Act activities in tribal organizations and programs in Texas, New York, Alaska, and California. Projects included forensic accountants to target elder financial abuse and screening tools to detect elder abuse. In 2013, $2 million was transferred to develop a reporting system for elder abuse. No funding was awarded in 2014. However, in 2015, the Elder Justice Act received $4 million in direct funding for the first time (Elder Justice Act, 2014).

Title VII–Improving Access to Innovative Medical Therapies

■ The existing section 340B of the Public Health Service Act of 1992 will be expanded so there will be more affordable drugs for children and underserved community residents.

Discussion

The 340B section expansion will allow more drug discounts for inpatient use at children's hospitals, cancer hospitals, critical care hospitals, and rural centers. This mandate increases drug affordability for patients who may need long-term care. Drug companies that participate in the Medicaid drug rebate program must sign pricing agreements for discounts on outpatient drugs purchased by qualified public health facilities (Mulcahey, Armstrong, Lewis, & Mattke, 2014).

Title VIII–Community Living Assistance Services and Supports

■ The **CLASS Independence Benefit Plan**, a self-funded long-term care insurance program for individuals with limited financial assistance, will be established.

Discussion

The CLASS Plan, effective January 1, 2011, enables consumers to purchase community living assistance.

Although supported by many community organizations, the Obama administration indicated it was not a viable program and the act was repealed on January 1, 2013 (The Arc, 2012).

Title IX–Revenue Provisions

■ Employers must report on the employee's annual W-2 form the value of the health insurance benefit coverage provided by the employer. An excise tax will be levied on expensive employer health insurance plans.

■ An annual flat fee is imposed on branded-prescription pharmaceutical companies and exporters, the medical device manufacturing industry, and health insurance providers, according to market share. Also, there is an excise tax on indoor tanning services.

■ Various provisions of the ACA affect **cafeteria plans** for healthcare benefits to employees, which enable them to select different benefits based on current lifestyle.

Discussion

The requirement for employers to inform their employees about the cost of the health insurance benefit as well as report the cost on W-2 forms emphasizes transparency. The employer must report it accurately because it will be reported on a federal form. In addition, a 40% excise tax will be placed on expensive employer-sponsored health plans.

Annual pharmaceutical fees or the branded prescription drug fees of approximately $2.5 billion will be applied to the drug manufacturing sector and are based on the market share of the U.S. drug market for branded prescription drugs. This is allocated across the industry sector with some exclusions. The fees began in 2011. The fee component, for example, was $2.5 billion in 2011 and $2.8 billion in 2012. The fee will steadily rise to $4.1 billion in 2018 and will be $2.8 billion a year thereafter. These fees will cost the industry approximately $85 billion over a decade (Office of the Inspector General, 2014). The same type of fee, initially $8 billion, was first applied to the health insurance industry in 2014. The fee will increase in years thereafter. It is important to note that these fees are nondeductible. A tax will be imposed on medical devices equal to 2.3% of the sales price and it is deductible. The fees and taxes will contribute to the operation of the healthcare reform mandates. Effective July 1, 2010, a 10% excise tax was imposed on indoor-tanning services.

A cafeteria plan is a type of employer-sponsored benefit plan that allows employees to select the type of benefits appropriate for their lifestyle. This plan could benefit both employers and employees because not all employees need the same type of benefits. Although cafeteria plans can be difficult to administer, they can be more cost effective because employees have different healthcare needs and may require less healthcare insurance coverage in some instances.

Title X–Strengthening Quality Affordable Care

- A **Physician Compare website** was developed.
- A **Nursing Home Compare website** was developed.
- The **Cures Acceleration Network** was developed.
- Permanent legal authority was provided for the **Indian Health Care Improvement Act (IHCIA)**, which provides health care to American Indians and Alaska Natives.

Discussion

The Physician Compare tool, part of the CMS website, has been established to help consumers with research about physicians who accept Medicare. It provides basic information about their address and contact information, education, languages spoken, gender, hospital affiliation, Medicare acceptance, and specialty (Medicare.gov, 2016a). A Nursing Home Compare tool, also located on the CMS website, was developed to enable consumers to research all nursing homes in the United States that are Medicare and Medicaid certified. A consumer can review facilities' inspection findings from the past three years. There are also Hospital, Home Health, and Dialysis Compare software tools (Medicare.gov, 2016b).

Also, the National Institutes of Health (NIH) is establishing the Cures Acceleration Network, a grants center to encourage research in the cure and treatment of diseases. All of these initiatives are targeting primary prevention, increasing consumer awareness of their health care, and providing incentives for disease research. The NIH may award grants annually up to $15 million to research these priority areas.

The Indian Healthcare Improvement Act, originally passed in 1979 but which had not been funded starting in 2000, was made permanent by the ACA. The improved act will authorize the establishment of comprehensive health services for American Indians and Alaskan Natives. The major goal of the act is to improve access and quality of care, including mental health services and alcohol and substance abuse programs to these targeted populations (U.S. Department of Health and Human Services, 2016).

▶ Conclusion

The Patient Protection and Affordable Care Act of 2010, or Affordable Care Act, and its amendment have focused on primary care as the foundation for the U.S. healthcare system (Goodson, 2010). The legislation has focused on 10 areas to improve the U.S. healthcare system, including quality, affordable, and efficient healthcare; public health and primary prevention of disease; healthcare workforce increases; community health; and increasing revenue provisions to pay for the reform. However, once the bill was signed, several states filed lawsuits. Several of these lawsuits argued that the act violates the U.S. Constitution because of the mandate of individual healthcare insurance coverage as well as that it infringes on states' rights with the expansion of Medicaid (Arts, 2010). The 2012 U.S. Supreme Court decision that upheld the constitutionality of the individual mandates should decrease the number of lawsuits. Despite these lawsuits, this legislation has clearly provided opportunities to increase consumer empowerment of the healthcare system by establishing the state American Health Benefit Exchanges, providing insurance to those individuals with preexisting conditions, eliminating lifetime and annual caps on health insurance payouts, improving the healthcare workforce, and providing databases so consumers can check the quality of their health care. The 10 titles of this comprehensive legislation are also focused on increasing the role of public health and primary care in the U.S. healthcare system and increasing accessibility to the system by providing affordable health care.

Although this legislation continues to be controversial, a system-wide effort needed to be implemented to curb rising healthcare costs, although there have been reports that healthcare costs are increasing and consumers are paying higher cost sharing amounts. There are five areas of health care that account for a large percentage of healthcare costs: hospital care, physician and clinician services, prescription drugs, nursing, and home healthcare expenditures (Longest & Darr, 2008). The legislation targets these areas by increasing quality assurance and providing a system of reimbursement tied to quality performance,

providing accessibility to consumers regarding the quality of their health care, and increasing access to community health services. Also, the Affordable Care Act has focused on improving the U.S. public health system by increasing the accessibility to primary prevention services such as screenings and wellness visits at no cost. The ACA has mandated that healthcare providers make available certain services with no cost sharing to the healthcare consumer: 15 preventive services for adults, 22 preventive services for women, 25 preventive services for children, and 23 preventive services for Medicare enrollees (Youdelman, 2013). Revenue provisions are in place to offset some of the costs of this legislation. With continued controversy, it will be difficult to quickly assess the cost effectiveness and impact of this health reform on improving the health care of U.S. citizens. The President had to veto a repeal of the bill, and the U.S. House of Representatives created a task force to craft an improved ACA. In light of the upcoming November 2016 presidential election, it is difficult to assess at this point whether the ACA will remain in place. Regardless of political views, many individuals now have access to health care because of the ACA. The next major issue is whether typical middle-class Americans can afford the high deductibles and increased cost sharing for their healthcare.

Wrap-Up

Vocabulary

Affordable Care Act (ACA)
Cafeteria plan
Center for Medicare and
   Medicaid Innovation
Centers for Consumer
   Information and Insurance
   Oversight
CLASS Independence Benefit
   Plan
Community First Choice
Consumer Operated and
   Oriented Plans (CO-OPs)
Cures Acceleration Network
Donut hole
Elder Justice Act
Essential Health Benefits (EHBs)
Health Insurance Marketplace

Healthcare and Education
   Affordability Reconciliation
   Act of 2010
Independence at Home
   program
Independent Payment Advisory
   Board
Indian Health Care Improvement
   Act (IHCIA)
Life qualifying event
National Health Care Workforce
   Commission
National Prevention, Health
   Promotion, and Public Health
   Council
Nursing Home Compare
   website

Patient-Centered Outcomes
   Research Institute
Patient Protection and Affordable
   Care Act (PPACA)
Physician Compare website
Prevention and Public Health
   Fund
Primary Care Extension Program
   (PCEP)
Public Plan Option
Reinsurance Program
Small Business Health Options
   Program (SHOP)
Summary of Benefits and
   Coverage (SBC)
Working Group on Healthcare
   Quality

References

Agency for Healthcare Research and Quality. (2012). National Strategy for Quality Improvement in Health Care: 2012 Annual Progress Report. Retrieved from http://www.ahrq.gov/workingforquality/nqs/nqs2012annlrpt.pdf

Allsup. (2010). Making the most of your Medicare coverage. Retrieved from http://www.allsup.com

Altman, D., (2015). Two substantive sides to debate over Obamacare's Cadillac tax. Retrieved from http://blogs.wsj.com/washwire/2015/10/02/two-substantive-sides-to-debate-over-Obamacare's-Cadillac-tax

American Association of Nurse Practitioners. (2010). Summary of new health reform law. Retrieved from http://www.aanp.org/NR

American Public Health Association. (2013, May). Get the facts: Prevention and Public Health Fund. Retrieved from http://www.apha.org/NR/rdonlyres/3060CA48-35E3-4F57-B1A5-CA1C1102090C/0/APHA_PPHF_factsheet_May2013.pdf

The Arc. (2012). Keeping the financing of long term services and supports a priority. Retrieved from http://insider.thearc.org/tag/community-living-assistance-services-and-supports-class

Arts, K. (2010). Legal challenges to health reform: An alliance for health reform toolkit. Retrieved from http://www.allhealth.org/publications/Uninsured/Legal_Challenges_to_New_Health_Reform_Law_97.pdf

Bihari, M. (2010). Understanding the Medicare Part D donut hole. Retrieved from http://healthinsurance.about.com/od/medicare/a/understanding_part_d.htm?p=1

Blancato, R. (2010). Elder Justice: A Congressional approach to a national problem. Retrieved from http://www.elderjusticecoalition.com/docs/Bob_Sept_speech.doc

Blancato, R. (2013). Health policy and promoting awareness: The Elder Justice Act. Power Point presentation, April 18, 2013, at Institute of Medicine. Retrieved from http://www.iom.edu/~/media/Files/Activity%20Files/Global/ViolenceForum/2013-APR-17/Presentations/02-14-Blancato.pdf

Centers for Medicare & Medicaid Services. (2016a). Details for title: On eve of Medicare anniversary, over 6.6 million seniors save over $7 billion on drugs. Retrieved from http://cms.gov/Newsroom/MediaReleaseDatabase/Press-Releases/2013-Press-Releases-Items/2013-07-29.html

Centers for Medicare & Medicaid Services. (2016b). Ensuring the Affordable Care Act serves the American people. Retrieved from http://w.cms.gov/cciio/index.html

Centers for Medicare & Medicaid Services. (2016c). Timeline of the health care law. Retrieved from http://www.healthcare.gov/timeline-of-the-health-care-law

Centers for Medicare & Medicaid Services. (2016d). What does marketplace health insurance cover? Retrieved from https://www.healthcare.gov/what-does-marketplace-health-insurance-cover

Centers for Medicare & Medicaid Services. (2016e). What if someone doesn't have health insurance coverage? Retrieved from https://www.healthcare.gov/what-if-someone-doesnt-have-health-coverage-in-2014

Center for Medicare & Medicaid Services. (2016f). Independence at Home programs. Retrieved from https://www.cms.gov/Newsroom/MediaReleaseDatabase/Press-releases/2015-Press-releases-items/2015-06-18.html

Center for Medicare & Medicaid Services. (2016g). Loan program helps support consumer-driven non-profit health insurers. Retrieved from http://www.cms.gov/CCIIO/Resources/Grants/new-loan-program.html

The Clinical Advisor. (2013). Family medicine group recommends funding Primary Care Extension Program.

Elder Justice Act. (Sept. 3, 2014). Congressional Research Service. Retrieved from https://www.fas.org/sgp/crs/misc/R43707.pdf

Ehrenfreund, M. (2015). A simple guide to today's important Supreme Court decision about Obamacare. Retrieved from http://www.washingtonpost.com/news/wonkblog/wp/2015/06/25/a-simple-guide-to-todays-important-supreme-court-decision-about-obamacare/#1

Goodson, J. (2010). Patient Protection and Affordable Care Act: Promise and peril for primary care. Retrieved from http://www.annals.org/content/early/2010/04/15/0003-4819-152-11-201006010-00249.full

Health Affairs. (2013). Health policy briefs: The co-op health insurance program. Retrieved from http://www.healthaffairs.org/healthpolicybriefs/brief.php?brief_id=87

Home Caregiver Services. (2012). Doctors making house calls coming back. Retrieved from http://www.homecaregiverservices.com/doctors-making-house-calls-coming-back

Longest, Jr., B., & Darr, K. (2008). *Managing health services organizations and systems.* Baltimore, MD: Health Professions Press.

Medicaid.gov. (2013). Community first choice. Retrieved from http://www.medicaid.gov/Medicaid-CHIP-Program-Information/By-Topics/Long-Term-Services-and-Support/Home-and-Community-Based-Services/Community-First-Choice-1915-k.html

Medicare.gov. (2016a). About physician compare. Retrieved from http://www.medicare.gov/find-a-doctor/staticpages/about/Physician-Compare-Information.aspx

Medicare.gov. (2016b). Nursing home compare, Retrieved from http://www.medicare.gov/nursinghomecompare

Moffitt, R. (2011). Obamacare and the Independent Payment Advisory Board: Falling short of real Medicare reform. Retrieved from

Mulcahey, A., Armstrong, C., Lewis, J., & Mattke, S. (2014). The 340B prescription drug discount program. Rand Corporation. Retrieved from http://www.rand.org

http://www.heritage.org/research/reports/2011/01/obamacare-and-the-independent-payment-advisory-board-falling-short-of-real-medicare-reform

Obamacare enrollment figures and sign up numbers quick facts. (2015). Retrieved from http://obamacarefacts.com/sign-ups/obamacare-enrollment-numbers/

Office of Inspector General. (2013). Early implementation of the consumer operated and oriented plan loan program. Retrieved from https://oig.hhs.gov/oei/reports/oei-01-12-00290.asp

Office of Inspector General. (2014). Memo regarding the branded prescription drug companies under the Affordable Care Act. Retrieved from https://oig.hhs.gov/oei/reports/oei-03-12-00560.pdf

PCRI. (2016). Retrieved from http://www.pcori.org/research-results/pcornet-national-patient-centered-clinical-research-network/clinical-data-and-0

ProCon.org. (2016a). Constitutional challenges to Obamacare: Patient Protection and Affordable Care Act (PPACA) in the courts. Retrieved from http://healthcarereform.procon.org/view.resource.php?resourceID=004134

ProCon.org. (2016b). Did you know? Retrieved from http://healthcarereform.procon.org/view.resource.php?resourceID=003726

Retrieved from http://www.clinicaladvisor.com/family-medicine -group-recommends-funding-primary-care-extension-program /article/286469

Silverman, E. (2012). What the Supreme Court ruling means to big pharma. Retrieved from http://www.forbes .com/sites/edsilverman/2012/06/28/what-the-supreme-court -ruling-means-for-pharma

Sullivan, S. (2012). First PCORI fees due July 31, 2013 for most health plans. Retrieved from http://www.erisaexchangeblog .com/2013/03/18/first-pcori-fees-due-july-31-2013-for-most -health-plans

Swendiman, K., & Baumrucker, E. (2012). Congressional Research Service Memorandum. Selected issues related to the effect of NFIB vs. Sebelius on the Medicaid expansion requirements in Section 201 of the Affordable Care Act. Retrieved from http ://www.ncsl.org/documents/health/aca_medicaid_expansion _memo_1.pdf

Transgender Law Center. (2016). Fact Sheet. Retrieved from https ://www.google.com/search?q=Transgender+Law+Center+&ie =utf-8&oe=utf-8#q=Transgender+Law+Center+Fact+Sheet+

Understanding marketplace plans. (2016). Retrieved from https ://www.healthcare.gov/choose-a-plan/plans-categories/

U.S. Department of Health and Human Services. (2016). Indian Healthcare Improvement Act made permanent (IHCIA). Retrieved from http://www.hhs.gov/news /press/2010pres/03/20100326a.html

U.S. Department of Labor. (2010). Young adults and the Affordable Care Act: Protecting young adults and eliminating burdens on families and businesses. Retrieved from http://www .dol.gov/ebsa/newsroom/fsdependentcoverage.html

U.S. Government Accountability Office (GAO). (2012a). Small employer health tax credit: Factors contributing to low use and complexity. Retrieved from http://www.gao.gov/products /GAO-12-549

United Health Care. (2013). Health benefit exchanges. Retrieved from http://www.uhc.com/united_for_reform_resource_center /health_reform_provisions/health_benefit_exchanges.htm

Wakefield, M. (2010). Remarks to the 35th National Primary Care Nurse Practitioner Symposium. Retrieved from http://www .hrsa.gov/about/news/speeches/2010/071610npsymposium. html

Youdelman, M. (2013). Health Advocate: Countdown to open enrollment 2013. Retrieved from http://healthlaw.org/images /stories/2013_09_Vol_17_Health_Advocate.pdf

▶ **Notes**

▶ Student Activity 2-1

In Your Own Words

Based on this chapter, please provide an explanation of the following concepts in your own words. DO NOT RECITE the text.

Cadillac tax:

_____

_____

Cafeteria plan:

_____

_____

Community First Choice:

_____

_____

Consumer Operated and Oriented Plan:

_____

_____

Elder Justice Act:

_____

_____

IMPaCT:

_____

_____

Independent Payment Advisory Board:

_____

_____

National Health Care Workforce Commission:

_____

_____

Nursing Home Compare website:

_____

_____

SHOP:

_____

_____

▸ # Student Activity 2-2

Complete the following case scenarios based on the information provided in the chapter. Your answer must be **IN YOUR OWN WORDS**.

Real-Life Applications: Case Scenario One

Your mother has a chronic healthcare condition that requires many visits to her healthcare provider. She recently changed jobs, which will require your family to move to a new state. She is also afraid that she will not receive healthcare insurance from her new company and is worried about finding a new provider to take care of her.

Activity

Explain to her about the new healthcare reform bill and how that will impact her situation.

Responses

_____

_____

_____

_____

_____

_____

_____

_____

_____

_____

_____

_____

_____

_____

_____

_____

_____

_____

Case Scenario Two

You have two elderly relatives who you think are not being treated well by their nursing home. You are not sure what to do. You speak to your parents about it and they suggest you research this issue. They know there are some mandates in the ACA regarding elderly care.

Activity

Perform research regarding the Elder Justice Act to determine if there are any solutions to this problem.

Responses

_____

_____

_____

_____

_____

_____

_____

_____

_____

_____

_____

_____

_____

_____

_____

_____

Case Scenario Three

Your mother is turning 55 and is being downsized from her job. She has yet to find another job. She has COBRA benefits for a certain period of time but is not sure what to do after. She is too young for Medicare.

Activity

Visit the www.healthcare.gov website to determine if there are any options for her to purchase health insurance.

Responses

_____

_____

_____

_____

_____

_____

_____

_____

_____

_____

_____

_____

_____

_____

_____

_____

_____

Case Scenario Four

You work for a healthcare facility that would like to apply for a grant to develop new ways to improve the quality of its health care.

Activity

Visit the Innovation Center on the www.cms.gov website. Develop a report on possible grants available for your healthcare facility.

Responses

_____

_____

_____

_____

_____

_____

_____

_____

_____

_____

_____

_____

_____

_____

_____

_____

_____

_____

▶ Student Activity 2-3

Internet Exercises

Write your answers in the space provided.

- ▪ Visit each of the websites listed here.
- ▪ Name the organization.
- ▪ Locate the organization's mission statement on its website.
- ▪ Provide a brief overview of the activities of the organization.
- ▪ How do these organizations participate in the U.S. healthcare system?

Websites

http://www.healthcare.gov

Organization Name:

_____

_____

Mission Statement:

_____

_____

Overview of Activities:

_____

_____

_____

Importance of Organization to U.S. Health Care:

_____

_____

_____

http://www.allhealth.org

Organization Name:

_____

_____

Mission Statement:

_____

_____

_____

Overview of Activities:

_____

_____

_____

Importance of Organization to U.S. Health Care:

_____

_____

_____

http://www.pnhp.org

Organization Name:

_____

_____

Mission Statement:

_____

_____

_____

Overview of Activities:

_____

_____

_____

Importance of Organization to U.S. Health Care:

_____

_____

_____

http://www.ahip.org

Organization Name:

_____

_____

Mission Statement:

_____

_____

_____

Overview of Activities:

_____

_____

_____

Importance of Organization to U.S. Health Care:

_____

_____

_____

http://www.hfma.org

Organization Name:

_____

_____

Mission Statement:

_____

_____

_____

Overview of Activities:

_____

_____

_____

Importance of Organization to U.S. Health Care:

_____

_____

http://www.acep.org

Organization Name:

_____

_____

Mission Statement:

_____

_____

_____

Overview of Activities:

_____

_____

_____

Importance of Organization to U.S. Health Care:

_____

_____

_____

▶ Student Activity 2-4

Discussion Questions

The following are suggested discussion questions for this chapter.

1. Select three initiatives of the Affordable Care Act in any of the 10 title areas that you think are important to improving our healthcare system. Defend your answer.

_____

_____

_____

_____

2. Do you think that the mandate for individual health insurance coverage is constitutional? Defend your answer.

_____

_____

_____

_____

_____

3. What do you think of the Nursing Home Compare website? Do you think the provides valuable information for consumers to support these important healthcare decisions?

_____

_____

_____

_____

_____

4. Discuss the new Patient Bill of Rights developed by the Affordable Care Act. and why.

_____

_____

_____

_____

_____

_____

_____

_____

5. What is a cafeteria plan? Do you think this is an effective way to provide health insurance benefits to employees? Perform an Internet search and locate a company that provides a cafeteria plan and report back to the discussion board on what the company offers.

_____

_____

_____

_____

_____

_____

_____

_____

▶ **Student Activity 2-5**

Current Events

Perform an Internet search and find a current events topic from the past three years that is related to this chapter. Provide a summary of the article and the link to the article and why the article relates to the chapter.

_____

_____

_____

_____

_____

_____

_____

_____

_____

_____

_____

_____

_____

_____

_____

_____

_____

_____

_____

_____

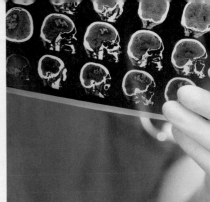

CHAPTER 3

Current Operations of the Healthcare System

LEARNING OBJECTIVES

The student will be able to:

- Identify the stakeholders of the U.S. healthcare system and their relationships with each other.
- Discuss the importance of healthcare statistics.
- Compare the United States to five other countries using different health statistics.
- List at least five current statistics regarding the U.S. healthcare system.
- Discuss complementary and alternative medicine and its role in health care.
- Define OECD and its importance to international health care.

DID YOU KNOW THAT?

- According to the Bureau of Labor Statistics, the projection for job growth in the healthcare industry over a 10-year period is 9.8 million jobs by 2024.
- Most healthcare workers have jobs that do not require a four-year college degree but health diagnostic and treatment providers are the most educated workers in the United States.
- Healthcare employment is found predominantly in large states such as California, New York, Texas, and Florida.
- Approximately 40% of U.S. adults use some form of nontraditional medicine.
- The healthcare industry and social assistance industry reported more work-related injuries than any other private industry.
- Life expectancy and infant mortality rates are an indication of the health of a population.

Introduction

The one commonality with all of the world's healthcare systems is that they all have consumers or users of their systems. Systems were developed to provide a service to their citizens. However, the U.S. healthcare system, unlike other systems in the world, does not provide healthcare access to all of its citizens. It is a very complex system that is comprised of many public and private components. Healthcare expenditures comprise approximately 17.5% of the **gross domestic product (GDP)**. Health care is very expensive and most citizens do not have the money to pay for health care themselves. Individuals rely on health insurance to pay a large portion of their healthcare costs. Health insurance is predominantly offered by employers. The uninsured rate remains at an all-time low with 9.1% of under 65 uninsured as of the end of 2015 according to CDC.Gov data. Generally, 2016 saw a rough increase of all the 2015 numbers. (Obamacare enrollment, 2016). The government believes this is the result of the universal mandate for individual health insurance coverage.

In the United States, in order to provide healthcare services, there are several **stakeholders** or interested entities that participate in the industry. There are providers, of course, that consist of trained professionals such as physicians, nurses, dentists, and chiropractors. There are also inpatient and outpatient facilities; the payers such as the insurance companies, the government, and self-pay individuals; and the suppliers of products, such as pharmaceutical companies, medical equipment companies, and research and educational facilities (Sultz & Young, 2006). Each component plays an integral role in the healthcare industry. These different components further emphasize the complexity of the U.S. system. The current operations of the delivery system and utilization statistics will be discussed in depth in this chapter. An international comparison of the U.S. healthcare system and select country systems will also be discussed in this chapter, which provides another aspect of analyzing the U.S. healthcare system.

Overview of the Current System Update

It is projected that between 2014 and 2024, nearly 10 million jobs will be added in the U.S. healthcare industry (Bureau of Labor Statistics [BLS], 2016a). The United States spends the highest proportion of GDP on healthcare expenditures of any country.

The system is a combination of private and public resources. Since World War II, the United States has had a private fee-for-service system that has produced generous incomes for physicians and has been profitable for many participants in the healthcare industry (Jonas, 2003). The healthcare industry operates like traditional business industries. Organizations designated as for profit need to make money in order to operate. The main goal of entities that are designated nonprofit is based on a particular social goal, but they also have to make money in order to continue their operations.

There are several major stakeholders that participate or have an interest in the industry. The stakeholders identified as participants in the healthcare industry include consumers, employers, healthcare and non-healthcare employers, healthcare providers, healthcare facilities, governments (federal, state, and local), insurance companies, educational and training institutions, professional associations that represent the different stakeholders, pharmaceutical companies, and research institutions. It is also important to mention the increasing prominence of alternative therapy medicine. Each role will be discussed briefly.

Major Stakeholders in the Healthcare Industry

Consumers

The main group of consumers is patients who need healthcare services from a physician, a hospital, or an outpatient facility. From an organizational perspective, the consumer is the most important stakeholder for an organization. The healthcare industry operates like a business. If a consumer has the means to pay out of pocket, from governmental sources, or from health insurance, the services will be provided. If an individual does not have the means to pay from any of these sources of funding, a service may not be provided. There is a principle of the U.S. healthcare system, **duty to treat**, which means that any person deserves basic care (Pointer et al., 2007). In some instances, healthcare providers will give care to someone who has no funding source and designate the care provided as a **charitable care or bad debt**, which means either the provider does not expect payment after the person's inability to pay has been determined or the efforts to secure the payment have failed (Smith, 2008). Businesses also take the same action. Many of them provide a community service or donate funds to a charitable cause, yet both traditional businesses and

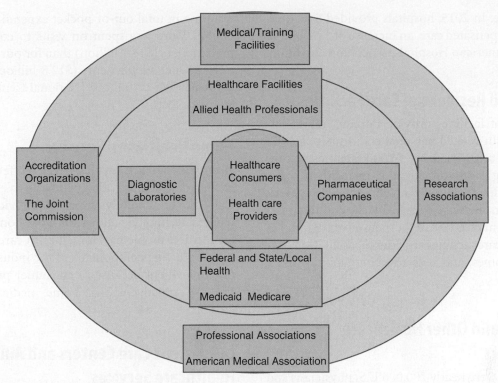

FIGURE 3-1 Healthcare Industry Stakeholders

healthcare organizations need to charge for their services in order to continue their operations.

There are also other consumer relationships in the healthcare industry. Consumers purchase drugs either from their provider or over the counter from pharmacies. The pharmaceutical companies market their products to physicians who in turn prescribe their products to their patients. The pharmaceutical companies also market their products to hospitals and outpatient facilities to encourage the use of their drugs in these facilities. Medical equipment companies also sell their products to facilities and individual providers.

Employers

Employers consist of both private and public employers. The healthcare industry is the largest U.S. employer. According to the **Bureau of Labor Statistics (BLS)**, there are several segments of the healthcare industry, including ambulatory healthcare services, hospitals, and nursing and **residential care facilities**. Ambulatory healthcare services are comprised of physicians, dentists, other health practitioners, outpatient care centers, medical and diagnostic laboratories, home healthcare services, and other ambulatory care. The hospital segment provides inpatient services primarily with outpatient as a secondary source. It provides general and surgical

care, psychiatric substance-abuse hospitals, and other specialty hospitals. Residential care facilities include nursing care, mental health, substance abuse and mental disabilities, community care for the elderly, and other residential care facilities (BLS, 2016b). Healthcare employment opportunities can be more easily found in large states such as California, New York, Texas, and Florida (BLS, 2016c). Employers outside the healthcare industry are also stakeholders because they provide a large percentage of health insurance coverage to individuals nationwide.

Hospitals

There are approximately 11,000 hospitals in the United States. Hospitals provide total medical care that ranges from diagnostic services to surgery and continuous nursing care. They traditionally provide inpatient care, although more hospital systems are also providing outpatient care. Some hospitals specialize in treatments for cancer, children's health, or mental health. It is important to note that hospitals are an integral component of the healthcare system. Many uninsured and underinsured individuals present themselves at emergency departments (EDs) across the country and use EDs as their primary care provider. In 2013, more than 136 million individuals presented themselves to the ED as their entry into health care. During times of public health crises, hospitals are the backbone of providing care. In 2015, hospitals provided $46.4 billion in uncompensated care, an increase of $7.1 billion from 2010 (American Hospital Association, 2016).

Nursing and Residential Care Facilities

These types of facilities provide nursing, rehabilitation, and health-related personal care to people who need ongoing care. There are 76,000 facilities nationwide. Nursing aides provide the majority of care. Residential care facilities provide around-the-clock social and personal care to the elderly, children, and others who cannot take care of themselves. Examples of residential care facilities are drug rehabilitation centers, group homes, and assisted-living facilities (BLS, 2016d).

Physicians and Other Healthcare Practitioners

In 2014, there were nearly 700,000 U.S. physicians and surgeons. In the past, physicians traditionally practiced solo, but more often physicians are practicing in a group practice to reduce administrative costs. In 2014, there were 151,000 dentists. The job outlook for both physicians and dentists is very positive due to the aging of the U.S. population. Other healthcare practitioners include chiropractors, optometrists, psychologists, therapists, and alternative medicine practitioners (BLS, 2016e).

Alternative health or **complementary and alternative medicine (CAM)** practitioners, who practice unconventional health therapies such as yoga, vitamin therapy, and spiritual healing, are being sought out by consumers, who have to pay out of pocket for these services because they are currently not covered by health insurance companies. However, chiropractors and acupuncturists who are also considered alternative medicine practitioners are more likely to be covered by health insurance companies. Recognizing consumer interest in this type of medicine, in 1998, the **National Center for Complementary and Alternative Medicine (NCCAM)** was established within the National Institutes of Health. Its purpose is to explore these types of practices in the context of rigorous science, train complementary and alternative researchers, and disseminate information. More medical schools are now offering some courses in alternative medicine.

According to the NCHS, an estimated 59 million persons aged 4 years and over had at least one expenditure for some type of complementary health approach, resulting in total out-of-pocket expenditures of $30.2 billion. More was spent on visits to complementary practitioners ($14.7 billion) than for purchases of natural product supplements ($12.8 billion) or self-care approaches ($2.7 billion) (National Center for Health Statistics, 2016).

Home Healthcare Services

Home healthcare services, which offer medical care in the home, are provided primarily to elderly, chronically ill, or mentally impaired individuals. Mobile medical technology allows for more home health care for medical problems. Home health care is one of the fastest growing components of the industry as a form of employment because of consumer preference and the cost effectiveness of home medical care (BLS, 2016f).

Outpatient Care Centers and Ambulatory Healthcare Services

Outpatient care centers include kidney dialysis centers, mental health and substance abuse clinics, and surgical and emergency centers. Ambulatory healthcare services include transport services, blood and organ banks, and smoking cessation programs (BLS, 2016g).

Laboratories

Medical and diagnostic laboratories provide support services to the medical profession. Workers may draw blood, take scans or X-rays, or perform other medical tests. This segment provides the fewest number of jobs in the industry (BLS, 2016h).

Government

As a result of the Medicare and Medicaid programs, the federal and state governments are the largest stakeholders in the U.S. healthcare system. The government at both levels is responsible for financing health care through these programs as well as playing the public provider role through state and local health departments. U.S. Department of Veterans Affairs medical facilities also provide services to those in the armed forces (Sultz & Young, 2006).

Insurance Companies

The insurance industry is also a major stakeholder in the healthcare industry. It is often blamed for the problems with the healthcare system because of the millions of underinsured and uninsured individuals. There have been many news reports highlighting the number of medical procedures that have been disproved for insurance coverage, the cost of health insurance coverage, etc. There are traditional indemnity plans such as **Blue Cross and Blue Shield**, but managed care, which is also considered an insurance plan, has become more popular for cost control. The Affordable Care Act has placed restrictions on what health insurance companies can do regarding reimbursement restrictions.

Educational and Training Organizations

Educational and training facilities such as medical schools, nursing schools, public health schools, and allied health programs play an important role in the U.S. healthcare industry because they are responsible for the education and training of healthcare employees. These institutions help formulate behaviors of the healthcare workforce.

Research Organizations

Governmental research organizations such as the National Institutes of Health (NIH) and the CDC not only provide regulatory guidance but also perform research activities to improve health care. However, there are also private research organizations, such as the **Robert Wood Johnson Foundation**, the **Pew Charitable Trusts**, and the **Commonwealth Fund**, that support research efforts through grants.

Professional Associations

Professional associations play an important role in healthcare policy. There are associations that represent physicians, nurses, hospitals, long-term care facilities, and so on. Most healthcare stakeholders are represented by a professional organization that guides them regarding their role in the healthcare industry. They also play a large role in governmental regulations because they often lobby at all governmental levels to protect their constituents. The following are examples of professional associations that represent some of the major stakeholder organizations in this industry.

- **American Hospital Association (AHA)**: The AHA is the most prominent association for all types of hospitals and healthcare networks. Founded in 1898, the AHA, which is a membership organization, provides education and lobbies for hospital representation in the political process at all governmental levels (AHA, 2016).
- **American Health Care Association (AHCA)**: Founded in 1949, the AHCA is a membership organization that represents nonprofit and for-profit nursing and assisted-living facilities, subacute-care providers, and facilities for developmentally disabled individuals. Their focus is to monitor and improve standards of nursing home facilities (AHCA, 2016).
- **American Association of Homes and Services for the Aging (AAHSA)**: The AAHSA, which is a membership organization, represents nonprofit adult day care services, home healthcare services, community services, senior housing, assisted-living facilities, continuing-care retirement communities, and nursing homes. It lobbies at all governmental levels regarding legislation that can impact the industry and provides technical assistance for these organizations (AAHSA, 2016).

Pharmaceutical Companies

A functioning healthcare system needs medications that are prescribed by a provider or purchased as an over-the-counter medicine from a pharmacy. The pharmaceutical industry is integral to the success of a healthcare system. Innovative drugs have improved people's quality of life. There has been an internal division within the pharmaceutical industry between the manufacturing of **brand name drugs** and generic or "me too" drugs. A **generic drug**, which does not have name recognition, is a less costly alternative to a brand name drug. The generic drug manufacturer must provide the same active ingredients as the brand name drugs; however, the manufacturing process is less costly to makers of generic drugs because they do not have to file for a patent. A generic drug has no patent protection and is sold at discounted prices (Zhong, 2012).

Brand name drugs such as Lipitor and Viagra are typically more expensive than generic drugs because such drugs might cost a pharmaceutical company more than $1 billion and take several years to develop. The Food and Drug Administration, which is responsible for approving drugs for human use, has traditionally upheld a very strict and lengthy approval process. However, recently, the FDA is removing red tape and speeding up the process for drugs that can help serious diseases. When a patent is awarded, a pharmaceutical company typically has 20 years' patent protection to develop a drug. However, because of the length of time it takes to determine the safety and effectiveness of a drug, once the drug is available for the public, the patent may be reduced several years (Mandal, 2014). Once that patent protection has ended, there are more opportunities for generic drug companies to control the market (Herper, 2013).

Like health insurance companies, the pharmaceutical industry is often vilified because of the cost of some prescribed medicines, which often precludes any consumers from purchasing these medications themselves without health insurance assistance. The industry's response is that it takes millions of dollars and years of research to develop an effective medicine and that is a major reason why some medicines cost so much. The pharmaceutical industry is represented by the **Pharmaceutical Research and Manufacturers of America (PhRMA)** (PhRMA, 2016).

Stakeholders' Environment

Working Conditions

Healthcare workers have many varied opportunities for workplace settings. Hospitals are a typical work environment, as are physician offices. As outpatient services have become more popular, healthcare professionals can work from their homes. Healthcare professionals can work in outpatient facilities, schools, laboratories, corporations, and other unconventional settings. They are exposed to serious health hazards, including contaminated blood, chemicals, drugs, and X-ray hazards. Depending on the job, there may be ergonomic issues due to lifting of patients and heavy equipment. This industry has one of the highest injury and illness rates. U.S. hospitals recorded nearly 58,000 work-related injuries and illnesses in 2013, amounting to 6.4 work-related injuries and illnesses for every 100 full-time employees: almost twice as high as the overall rate for private industry. In 2013, healthcare personnel reported seven times the national rate of musculoskeletal disorders compared with all other private sector workers. Nurse assistants and nurses have the highest injury rates of all occupations (OSHA, 2015).

Projected Outlook for Employment

The healthcare industry's employment outlook is positive. By 2024, there is a projection of an additional 22 million jobs. Growth will most likely be outside the inpatient hospital centers because cost containment is the major priority for health care. Health care will continue to grow for three major reasons: the aging of the U.S. population, advances in medical technology, and the increased focus on outpatient care.

Healthcare Statistics

U.S. Healthcare Utilization Statistics

The **National Center for Health Statistics (NCHS)**, which is part of the CDC, produces an annual reports on the health status of the United States. This publication, *Health, United States*, provides an overview of current data on healthcare utilization, resources, and expenditures. This publication examines all different aspects of the U.S. healthcare delivery system as well as assessing the health status of U.S. citizens. The following information is summarized from the 2015 publication.

U.S. Demographics and Healthcare

Life expectancy rates are an indication of the health of a designated population. Between 2004 and 2014, life expectancy at birth increased for females (1.1 years) to 81.4 years, white males (1.4 years) to 76.7 years, black females (2.3 years) to 78.4 years, and black males (3.1 years) to 72.5 years. Racial disparities exist in life expectancy at birth rates although they have narrowed. In 2014, the rate of white male life expectancy at birth was 4.2 years longer than that for black males, and the rate for white females was 3.0 years longer than that for black females. In 2014, Hispanic males (79.2 years) and females (84 years) had longer life expectancy rates than non-Hispanic white or non-Hispanic black males and females (CDC, 2016a).

Health Care Payers

Statistics from 2014 indicate that over 34% of personal health care expenses was paid by private health insurance, 23% was paid by Medicare, 17.4% by Medicaid, and nearly 1% was paid by consumers. The other 30% was paid by other types of programs and insurance. In 2014, the Medicare program had over 54 million enrollees with expenditures of nearly $613 billion an increase of $30 billion from 2013. The Medicare Part D drug program accounted for $78 billion up $8 billion from the previous year CDC (2016b).

U.S. and International Comparison of Health Statistics

Established in 1961, the **Organisation for Economic Cooperation and Development (OECD)** is a membership organization that provides comparable statistics of economic and social data worldwide and monitors trends of economic development. Currently 34 countries, including the United States, are members of this organization. Their budget is derived from the member countries; the United States contributes 25% of the budget. The OECD produces, on a continual basis, a health data set of the 34 member countries as well as candidate and key partner countries when possible (Brazil, China, Colombia, Costa Rica, India, Indonesia, Latvia, Lithuania, the Russian Federation, and South Africa) (Organisation for Economic Cooperation and Development [OECD], 2016). The following are highlights from the OECD health data (OECD, 2015).

Health indicators such as **infant mortality rates**, average life expectancy, and health risk behaviors are used to evaluate the health status of a population. Because the United States spends the highest **per capita** on health care in the world, it is expected that U.S. health indicators would rank superior to all other countries' healthcare indicators.

TABLE 3-1 OECD Country ISO Codes

Australia	AUS	Japan	JPN
Austria	AUT	Korea	KOR
Belgium	BEL	Luxembourg	LUX
Canada	CAN	Mexico	MEX
Chile	CHL	Netherlands	NLD
Czech Republic	CZE	New Zealand	NZL
Denmark	DNK	Norway	NOR
Estonia	EST	Poland	POL
Finland	FIN	Portugal	PRT
France	FRA	Slovak Republic	SVK
Germany	DEU	Slovenia	SVN
Greece	GRC	Spain	ESP
Hungary	HUN	Sweden	SWE
Iceland	ISL	Switzerland	CHE
Ireland	IRL	Turkey	TUR
Israel	ISR	United Kingdom	GBR
Italy	ITA	United States	USA

Partner country ISO codes			
Brazil	BRA	Indonesia	IDN
China	CHN	Latvia	LVA
Colombia	COL	Lithuania	LTU
Costa Rica	CRI	Russian Federation	RUS
India	IND	South Africa	ZAF

Health at a Glance 2015: OECD Indicators by OECD Publishing. Reproduced with permission of OECD Publishing via Copyright Clearance Center

Demographic Trends

The percentage of people in the United States over age 65 increased from 9% in 1960 to 15% in 2010 and is expected to double to 27% in 2050. The proportions will be large in Japan, Korea, and Spain, where, it is predicted, 40% of the population will be over 65 years old by 2050. The increase in the over-80 population share will increase dramatically. In 2010, the average in OECD countries was 4%, which will increase to 10% by 2050. These trends will place large strains on healthcare systems, particularly the long-term care sector (OECD, 2015).

Life Expectancy Rates

Current data trends indicated that OECD-country life expectancy rates are increasing, which can be attributed to improving health care services, lifestyle changes, and increased public health education. The 2013 average life expectancy in the OECD countries is 80.5 years. The U.S. average is 78.8 years. Spain and Switzerland have the highest life expectancy, more than 80 years. The lowest life expectancy rate is Mexico's, below 75 years. The gains in life expectancy in the United States have been less than in other OECD countries. For example, in 1970, the U.S. life expectancy was one year above the average of OECD countries; it is now more than one year below the OECD average. Possible reasons are the rates of uninsured individuals across the country, high obesity rates, and adverse living conditions due to poverty. Considering the high levels of U.S. healthcare spending, the life expectancy rates should be higher (OECD, 2015).

Life Expectancy at age 65

Life expectancy rates at age 65 have increased for both genders over the past 20 years in all OECD

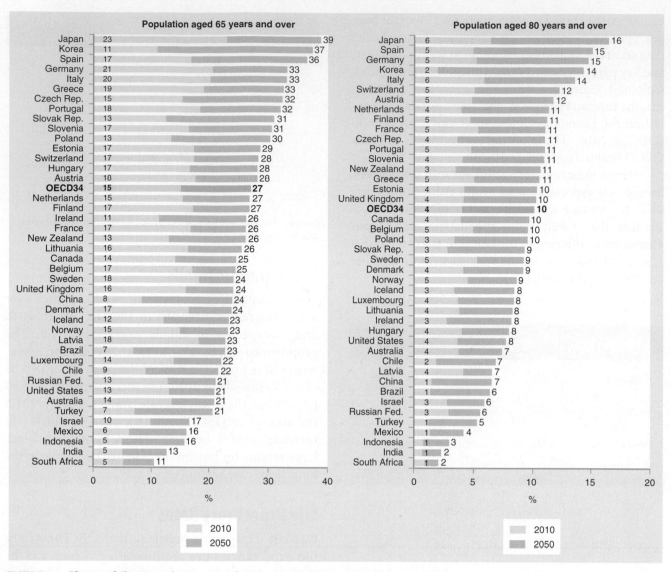

FIGURE 3-2 Share of the Population Aged over 65 and 80 Years, 2010 and 2050

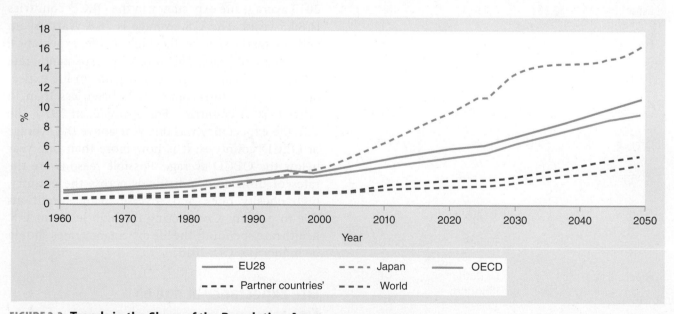

FIGURE 3-3 Trends in the Share of the Population Ages

countries: an increase of 5.5 years since 1970. Medical care advances and lifestyle changes have contributed to the age increase. In 2013, people over age 65 in OECD countries could expect to live 19.5 more years—21 years for women and 18 years for men. In the United States, the average life expectancy was slightly lower at 19.2 years. Life expectancy for women at age 80 was highest in France and Japan (11.5 years); for men at age 80, life expectancy was highest in Japan and Spain (9 years). In general, people with higher education tend to live longer and are healthier. It is also important to mention that even though people tend to live nearly 20 years longer post 65, those years may be issues with their health (OECD, 2015).

Life Expectancy by Gender and Educational Level

In all OECD countries, women's life expectancy rates are much higher than those of men. The 2013 average

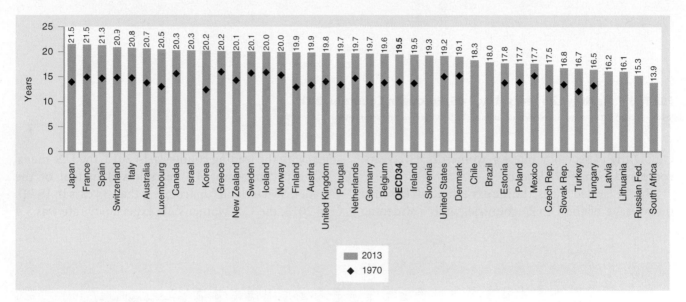

FIGURE 3-4 **Life Expectancy at Age 65, 1970 and 2013 (or Nearest Years)**

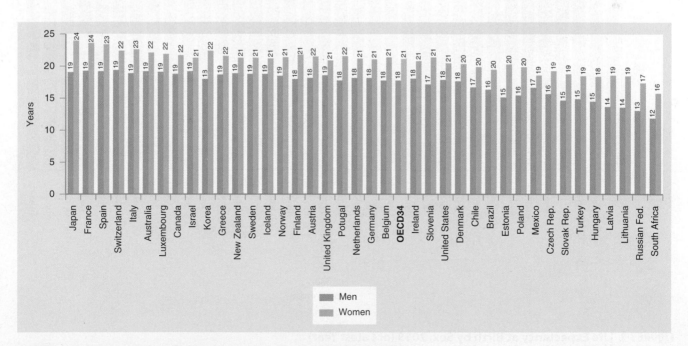

FIGURE 3-5 **Life Expectancy at Age 65 by Sex, 2013 (or Nearest Year)**

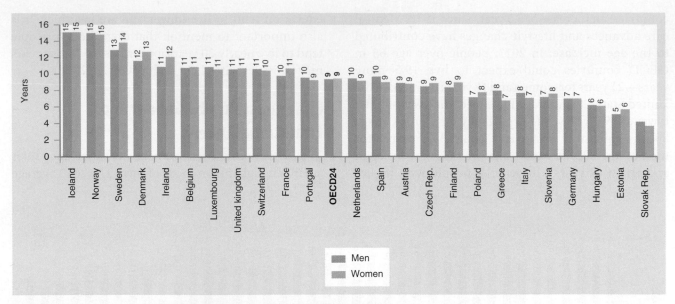

FIGURE 3-6 **Healthy Life Years at Age 65, European Countries, 2013**

Health at a Glance 2015: OECD Indicators by OECD Publishing. Reproduced with permission of OECD Publishing via Copyright Clearance Center

OECD life expectancy rate for women is 83.1 years, compared to men's 77.8 years.

In the United States, the life expectancy is less than the average of the OECD countries with a widening gap with the leading countries. In 2013, the U.S. mens' life expectancy was 4.3 years less than that of the leader, Switzerland (up from less than 3 years in 1970). In 2013, the U.S. women's life expectancy rate was 5.4

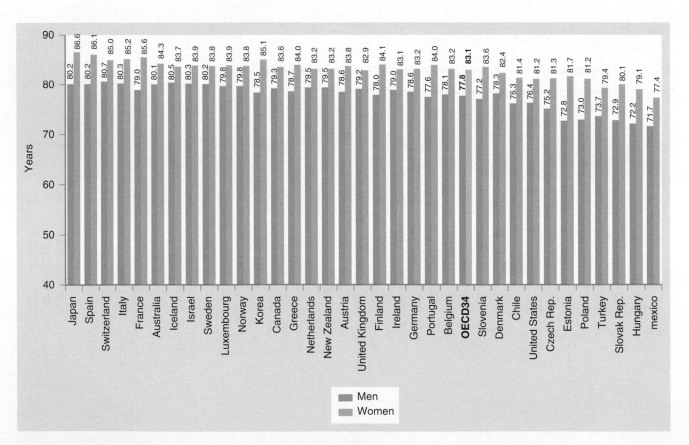

FIGURE 3-7 **Life Expectancy at Birth by Sex, 2013 (or Latest Year)**

Health at a Glance 2015. OECD Indicators by OECD Publishing. Reproduced with permission of OECD Publishing via Copyright Clearance Center

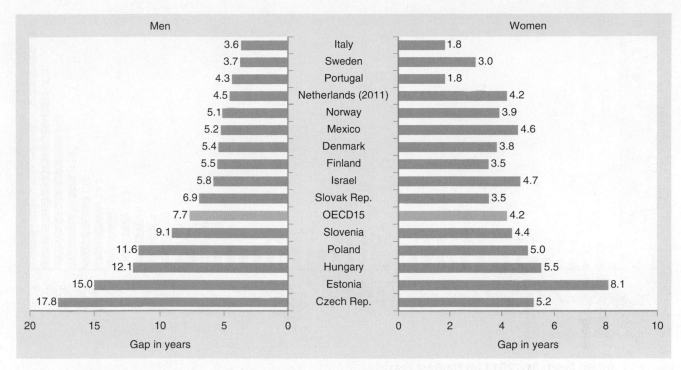

	Men		Women	

FIGURE 3-8 **Gap in Life Expectancy at Age 30 by Sex and Educational Level, 2012 (or Latest Year)**

years shorter than that of the leader, Japan (there was no gap in 1970). This gap may be due in part to our high obesity rates which are a significant risk factor for diseases (OECD, 2015).

According to OECD data, those individuals with the highest level of education live 6 years longer than those with the lowest level of education. There was an average gap of 8 years in educational levels in the men's life expectancy (OECD, 2015).

Infant Mortality

Infant mortality rates are measures of the number of children less than one year of age who die. The average 2013 OECD rate is 3.8. In 2013, there was little difference in infant mortality rates among most OECD countries, with the average less than 4 deaths per 1,000 live births. The lowest rates are found in Iceland, Slovenia, and Finland, at 1.3 and 1.7, respectively, for Slovenia and Finland. The highest rates are much higher than the OECD average of 3.8: Indonesia (24.5), South Africa (32.8), and India (41.4). The United States' reduction in infant mortality rate has been slower than that of other OECD countries. The U.S. rate, 5.0, is now higher than the OECD average. In the United States, there are large differences in infant mortality rates

among racial groups. Black women are more likely to give birth to low-birth-weight infants, and black infants' mortality rate is double that of white infants (NCHS, 2014).

Tobacco Use

According to the World Health Organization, tobacco use kills 6 million people annually, of whom 600,000 are killed from involuntary smoking or second-hand smoking (Tobacco, 2016). It is the largest preventable risk factor. In OECD countries, smoking rates vary widely. In the 34 OECD countries, 20% of the adult population smoked in 2013, although smoking rates in men are higher than women's rates in all OECD countries except Sweden and Iceland. The rates in Sweden, Iceland, Mexico, and Australia are less than 13% of the adult population. Smoking rates remain high in Greece for both males and females, and one in two men in Latvia and Indonesia smoke daily. However, smoking rates have declined in most OECD countries due to public health campaigns, smoke-free-environment policies, and increased taxation on tobacco products. The U.S. ranks 5th of the 34 countries rated regarding tobacco use which illustrates our national focus on tobacco free work environment and aggressive educational campaigns (OECD, 2015).

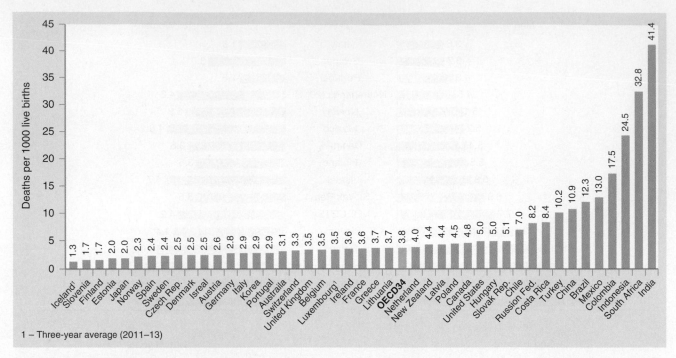

FIGURE 3-9 **Infant Mortality, 2013 (or Nearest Year)**

Health at a Glance 2015: OECD Indicators by OECD Publishing. Reproduced with permission of OECD Publishing via Copyright Clearance Center

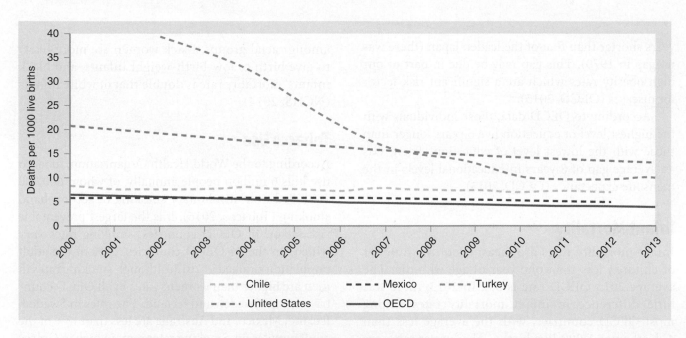

FIGURE 3-10 **Trends in Infant Mortality, Selected OECD Countries, 2000–13**

Health at a Glance 2015: OECD Indicators by OECD Publishing. Reproduced with permission of OECD Publishing via Copyright Clearance Center

Alcohol Use

Alcohol use is associated with several serious health diseases such as cirrhosis of the liver and strokes. It is a contributing factor to vehicular accidents, violence, and suicide, among other events. Alcohol causes more than 3.3 million deaths worldwide annually. Alcohol abuse causes reduced work productivity.

Alcohol consumption, as determined by annual sales, is 2.3 gallons per adult across OECD countries. Austria, Estonia, and the Czech Republic report 3-gallons-per-adult

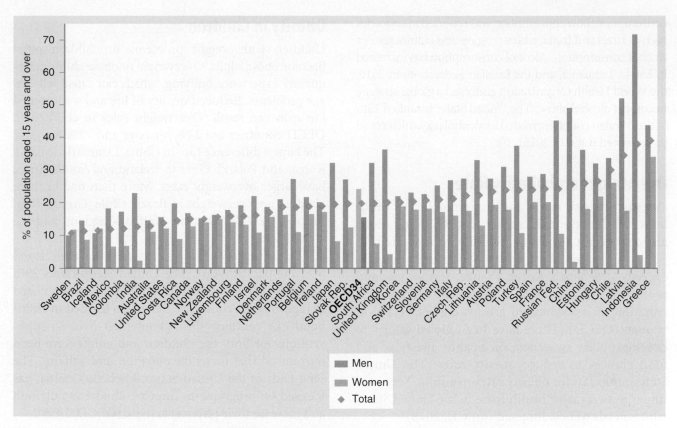

FIGURE 3-11   Daily Smoking in Adults, 2013 (or Nearest Year)

Health at a Glance 2015: OECD Indicators by OECD Publishing. Reproduced with permission of OECD Publishing via Copyright Clearance Center

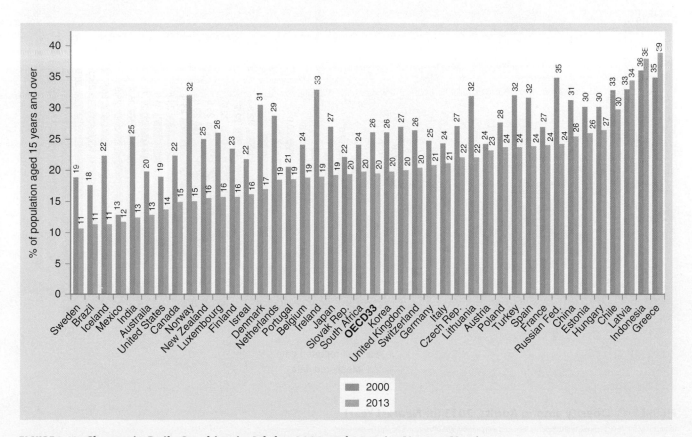

FIGURE 3-12   Change in Daily Smoking in Adults, 2000 and 2013 (or Nearest Year)

Health at a Glance 2015: OECD Indicators by OECD Publishing. Reproduced with permission of OECD Publishing via Copyright Clearance Center

consumption. Low consumption was reported in countries such as Israel and India, where religion and culture restrict alcohol consumption. Alcohol consumption has increased in Latvia, Lithuania, and the Russian Federation. In 2010, the World Health Organization endorsed a global strategy to combat alcohol abuse. The United States is ranked 13th of the 34 rated countries related to alcohol use which could be improved (OECD, 2015).

Overweight and Obesity Rates

Obesity is a risk factor for numerous health problems. OECD countries report that 53.8% of adults are overweight or obese. Obesity has affected all populations. In 22 of the 34 countries, the rate exceeds 50%. Japan, Korea, France, and Switzerland report much lower rates. Obesity tends to be more common in less educated groups and especially in women (OECD). There have been global efforts to develop public awareness on healthy lifestyles and food choices to reduce obesity rates. The United States ranks last for obesity rates in adults. This continues to be a major health issue in the United States which needs to be addressed (OECD, 2015).

Obesity in Children

Children with weight problems in children often become obese adults. Overweight or obese children frequently experience bullying, which can cause self-image problems. Reduced quality of life and a shortened life span can result. Overweight rates in children in OECD countries are 24% for boys and 22% for girls. The largest differences are in China, Denmark, Iceland, Korea, and Poland. Girls in Ireland and South Africa have larger overweight rates. More than one in three children are overweight in Brazil, Chile, Greece, Italy, Mexico, New Zealand, the United Kingdom, and the United States.

Unfortunately, child obesity rates have increased over the past 30 years. The United States ranks 29th in obesity rates in children. The rates have stabilized in high-income countries. Behaviors learned in childhood can continue throughout their lives so interventions for both the children and adults have been introduced that focus on nutrition and activity. The First Lady of the United States, Michelle Obama, has focused on programs to improve children's nutrition and increase their physical activity (OECD, 2015).

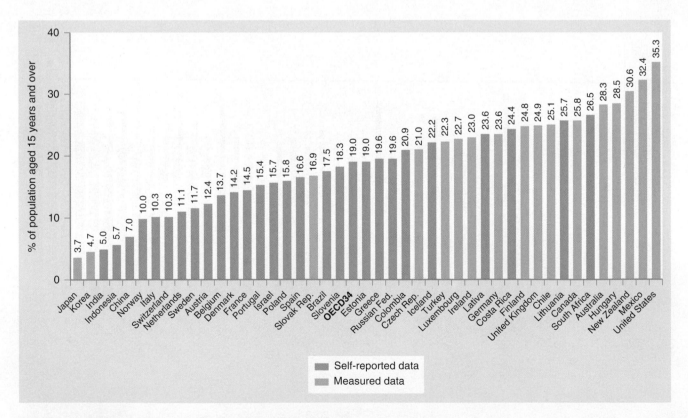

FIGURE 3-13 Obesity among Adults, 2013 (or Nearest Year)

Health at a Glance 2015: OECD Indicators by OECD Publishing. Reproduced with permission of OECD Publishing via Copyright Clearance Center

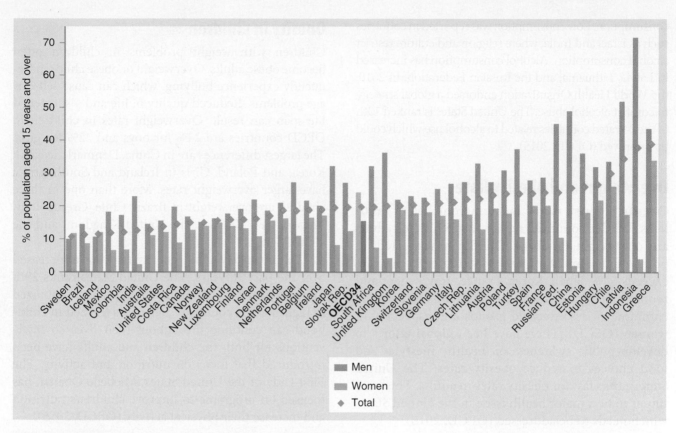

FIGURE 3-11 Daily Smoking in Adults, 2013 (or Nearest Year)

Health at a Glance 2015: OECD Indicators by OECD Publishing. Reproduced with permission of OECD Publishing via Copyright Clearance Center

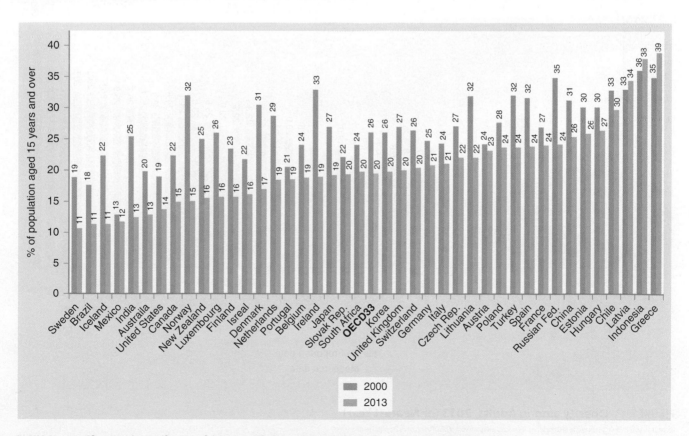

FIGURE 3-12 Change in Daily Smoking in Adults, 2000 and 2013 (or Nearest Year)

Health at a Glance 2015: OECD Indicators by OECD Publishing. Reproduced with permission of OECD Publishing via Copyright Clearance Center

consumption. Low consumption was reported in countries such as Israel and India, where religion and culture restrict alcohol consumption. Alcohol consumption has increased in Latvia, Lithuania, and the Russian Federation. In 2010, the World Health Organization endorsed a global strategy to combat alcohol abuse. The United States is ranked 13th of the 34 rated countries related to alcohol use which could be improved (OECD, 2015).

Overweight and Obesity Rates

Obesity is a risk factor for numerous health problems. OECD countries report that 53.8% of adults are overweight or obese. Obesity has affected all populations. In 22 of the 34 countries, the rate exceeds 50%. Japan, Korea, France, and Switzerland report much lower rates. Obesity tends to be more common in less educated groups and especially in women (OECD). There have been global efforts to develop public awareness on healthy lifestyles and food choices to reduce obesity rates. The United States ranks last for obesity rates in adults. This continues to be a major health issue in the United States which needs to be addressed (OECD, 2015).

Obesity in Children

Children with weight problems in children often become obese adults. Overweight or obese children frequently experience bullying, which can cause self-image problems. Reduced quality of life and a shortened life span can result. Overweight rates in children in OECD countries are 24% for boys and 22% for girls. The largest differences are in China, Denmark, Iceland, Korea, and Poland. Girls in Ireland and South Africa have larger overweight rates. More than one in three children are overweight in Brazil, Chile, Greece, Italy, Mexico, New Zealand, the United Kingdom, and the United States.

Unfortunately, child obesity rates have increased over the past 30 years. The United States ranks 29th in obesity rates in children. The rates have stabilized in high-income countries. Behaviors learned in childhood can continue throughout their lives so interventions for both the children and adults have been introduced that focus on nutrition and activity. The First Lady of the United States, Michelle Obama, has focused on programs to improve children's nutrition and increase their physical activity (OECD, 2015).

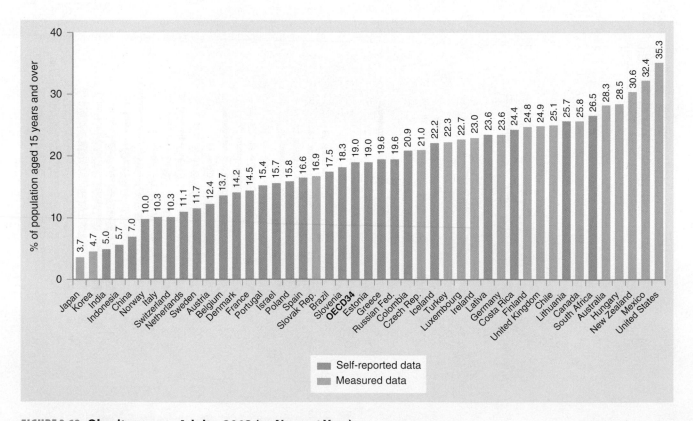

FIGURE 3-13 **Obesity among Adults, 2013 (or Nearest Year)**

Health at a Glance 2015: OECD Indicators by OECD Publishing. Reproduced with permission of OECD Publishing via Copyright Clearance Center

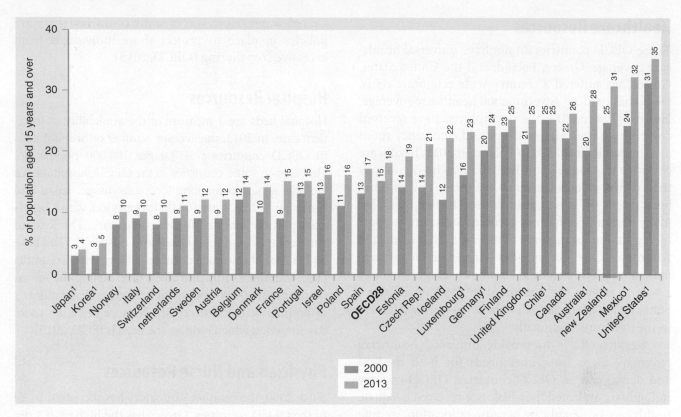

FIGURE 3-14 Increasing Obesity among Adults in OECD Countries, 2000 and 2013 (or Nearest Years)

Health at a Glance 2015: OECD Indicators by OECD Publishing. Reproduced with permission of OECD Publishing via Copyright Clearance Center

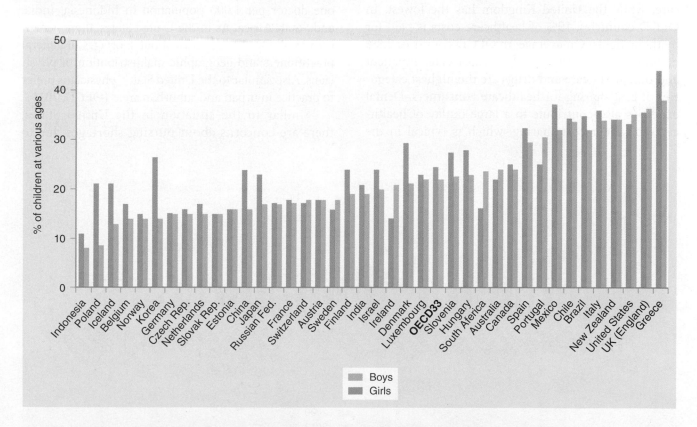

FIGURE 3-15 Measured Overweight (Including Obesity) among Children, 2013 (or Nearest Year)

Health at a Glance 2015: OECD Indicators by OECD Publishing. Reproduced with permission of OECD Publishing via Copyright Clearance Center

Healthcare Resources

Three OECD countries do not have universal healthcare coverage: Greece, Poland, and the United States. Greece has suffered a country-wide economic crisis, which has reduced governmental healthcare coverage. However, since 2014, the unemployed have received coverage for prescription drugs and emergency room care in public hospitals. In Poland in 2012, healthcare coverage was reduced for individuals who do not pay their contributions. Universal healthcare coverage has been discussed as an option for the United States for many decades but has not garnered sufficient support for legislation for this type of measure. That is why the Affordable Care Act includes a mandate for individuals to purchase health insurance coverage. This was a way to reduce the uninsured in the United States. Statistics have indicated that there has been a decrease in the uninsured nationally.

Despite efforts to provide universal healthcare coverage, there are unmet needs for both medical and dental care in OECD countries. OECD-country individuals indicated they have not received adequate health care or dental care because of location, waiting lists, and lower incomes, which prevented cost sharing. The United States has the highest rate of unmet care, while the United Kingdom has the lowest. In OECD countries, 19% of healthcare costs is paid for by the patients. On average, in OECD countries 2.8% of household spending is for health care. Inpatient and outpatient care and drugs are the highest categories of cost sharing for healthcare consumers. Dental expenses also contribute to a large outlay of healthcare-consumer cost sharing, which is typical in the United States. However, in some countries, there are policies in place to protect those individuals from excessive cost sharing (OECD, 2015).

Hospital Resources

Hospital beds are a measure of the availability of inpatient care. In 2013, the average number of hospital beds in OECD countries was 4.6 per 100,000 population. However, in some countries in the OECD, hospital beds are also allocated for long-term care usage. Japan and Korea have 11 beds per 100,000 population, with a significant portion allocated for long-term care. The Russian Federation (9), Germany (8.3), and Austria (7.7) all have higher than the average number of beds, with Columbia (1.5), Indonesia (1.0), and Chile (0.5) having the lowest numbers per 100,000 population. In general, the number of hospital beds has decreased because there are more day surgeries, which reduces the need (OECD, 2015).

Physician and Nurse Resources

Since 2000, the number of doctors has increased in all of the OECD countries. Greece has the highest, 6.3 per 1,000 population. Chile had the lowest number of doctors, less than 2.0 per 1,000 population. There is less than one doctor per 1,000 population in Indonesia, India, and South Africa. As in the United States, there is concern in all OECD countries about shortages of general practitioners and geographic maldistribution of physicians. Also similar to the United States, physicians prefer to practice in urban and suburban areas (OECD, 2015).

Similar to the situation in the United States, there are concerns about nursing shortages due to

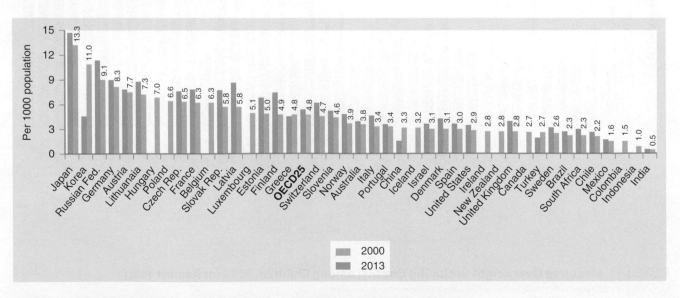

FIGURE 3-16 **Hospital Beds Per 1,000 Population, 2000 and 2013 (or Nearest Year)**

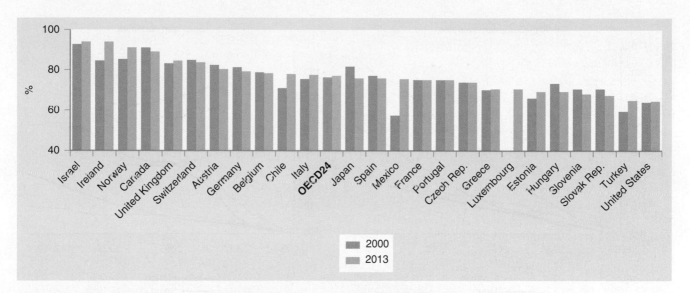

FIGURE 3-17 **Occupancy Rate of Curative (Acute) Care Beds, 2000 and 2013 (or Nearest Year)**

Health at a Glance 2015: OECD Indicators by OECD Publishing. Reproduced with permission of OECD Publishing via Copyright Clearance Center

increased life expectancy resulting in an increased need to access health care. Overall, the nurse rate has increased since 2000 in almost all OECD countries. There were an average of 3 nurses per 1 doctor in the OECD countries. In 2013, there were 9 nurses per 1,000 population in OECD countries. There are 14 nurses per 1,000 population in Switzerland, Norway, Finland, and Denmark. The OECD countries with the lowest proportions of nurses are

Turkey, Mexico, and Greece (1–4 nurses per 1,000 population).

In response to the nursing shortage, there has been more advanced training for nurses. The United States has a robust nurse-practitioner degree curriculum, with many states allowing nurse practitioners to prescribe drugs. This type of healthcare provider is an excellent alternative to a physician because it is a more cost-effective alternative for providing care.

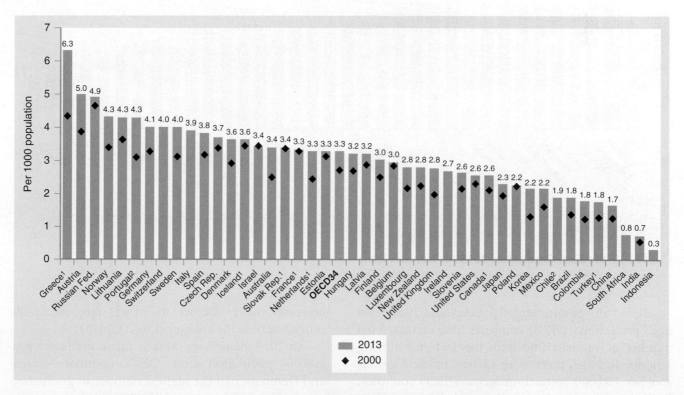

FIGURE 3-18 **Practicing Doctors per 1,000 Population, 2000 and 2013 (or Nearest Year)**

Health at a Glance 2015: OECD Indicators by OECD Publishing. Reproduced with permission of OECD Publishing via Copyright Clearance Center

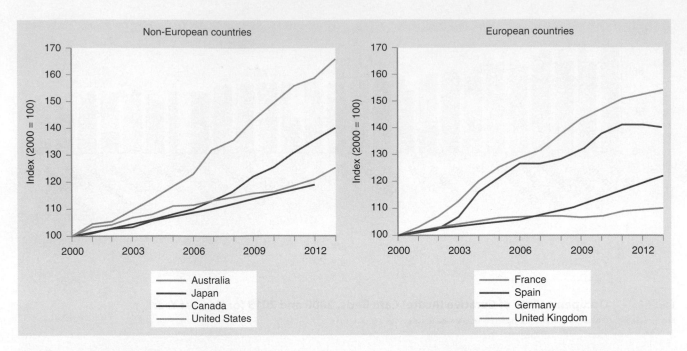

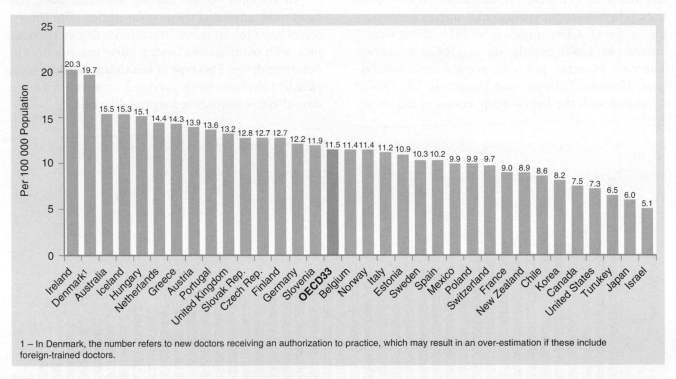

1 – In Denmark, the number refers to new doctors receiving an authorization to practice, which may result in an over-estimation if these include foreign-trained doctors.

FIGURE 3-20 **Medical Graduates, 2013 (or Nearest Year)**

Based on governmental policies and healthcare need projections, OECD countries have increased the number of students into both medical and nursing schools. In 2013, there were 12 new medical graduates per 100,000 population across OECD countries. Ireland had the highest number of medical graduates. Israel had the lowest number of medical graduates;

however, many doctors in Israel were medically trained outside the country (OECD, 2015).

In 2013, there were 50 new nurse graduates per 100,000 population across OECD countries. Korea and Denmark had the highest number of graduates, nearly 90 graduates per 100,000 population, with Mexico and the Czech Republic producing 15

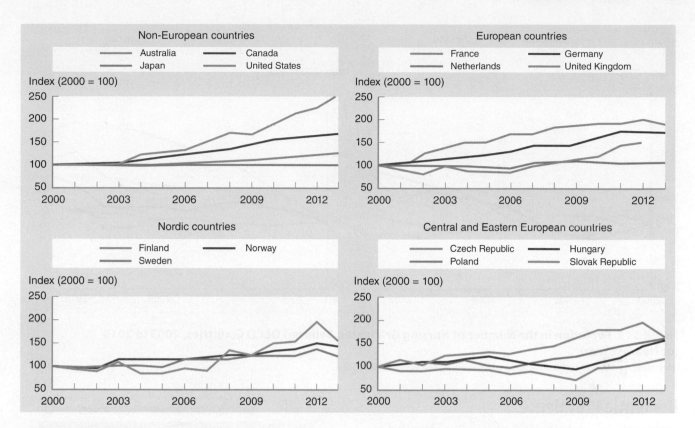

FIGURE 3-21 **Evolution in the Number of Medical Graduates, Selected OECD Countries, 2000 to 2013 (or Nearest Year)**

Health at a Glance 2015: OECD Indicators by OECD Publishing. Reproduced with permission of OECD Publishing via Copyright Clearance Center

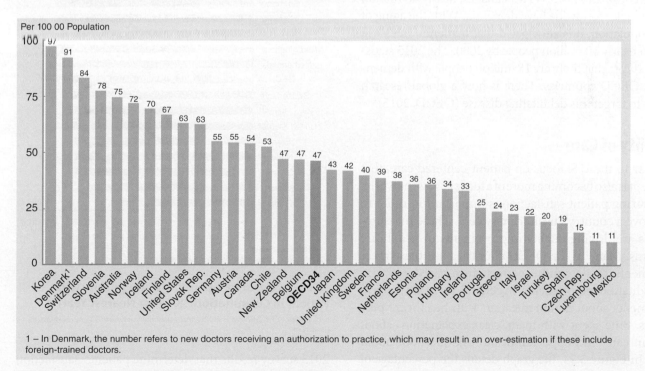

1 – In Denmark, the number refers to new doctors receiving an authorization to practice, which may result in an over-estimation if these include foreign-trained doctors.

FIGURE 3-22 **Nursing Graduates, 2013 (or Nearest Year)**

Health at a Glance 2015: OECD Indicators by OECD Publishing. Reproduced with permission of OECD Publishing via Copyright Clearance Center

graduates per 100,000 population. The U.S. nursing graduate rates have increased 70% from 2003 to 2013, to 20 per 100,000 population. With the passage of the Affordable Care Act, it is anticipated that there will continue to be an increased need for nurses (OECD, 2015).

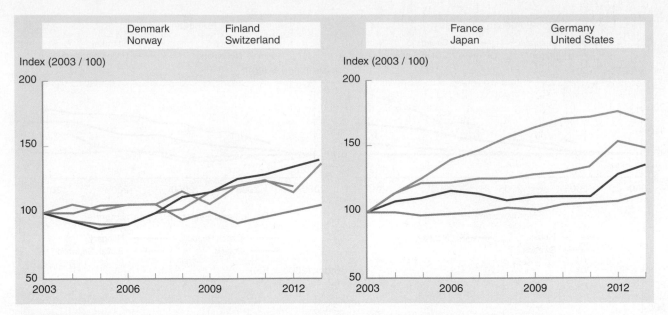

FIGURE 3-23 **Evolution in the Number of Nursing Graduates, Selected OECD Countries, 2003 to 2013 (or Nearest Year)**

Health at a Glance 2015: OECD Indicators by OECD Publishing. Reproduced with permission of OECD Publishing via Copyright Clearance Center

Dementia Prevalence

Dementia is a global term for brain disorders that can lead to brain disease that diminishes cognitive functions. Alzheimer's disease is the most common form of dementia. According to 2015 WHO statistics, nearly 48 million individuals worldwide have dementia. With the aging of the population, it is anticipated that dementia rates will rise to nearly 80 million people by 2030. The 2015 statistics indicate that there are 18 million people with dementia in OECD countries. There is now a global research effort to target this debilitating disease (OECD, 2015).

Quality of Care

Similar to the U.S. focus on patient-centered care, that concept is also becoming more of a focus across the world. Measuring patient satisfaction is important in order to improve a country's healthcare system. These measurements are driving quality improvements in healthcare systems. Many of the OECD countries use these measurements to determine performance-based pay and accreditation requirements. In general, there are positive comments about communication with healthcare providers, time spent with them, clear explanations about patient care, and opportunities to ask questions about care. In Figure 3.24, the graph details the percentage of patients who feel they had enough time with their doctors in consultation. The average for OECD countries is 85%. Belgium, the Czech Republic, and Luxembourg all had more than 90% of patients reporting adequate consultation time with their doctors. The United States had 80.9%, below the OECD average. Figure 3.25 details the

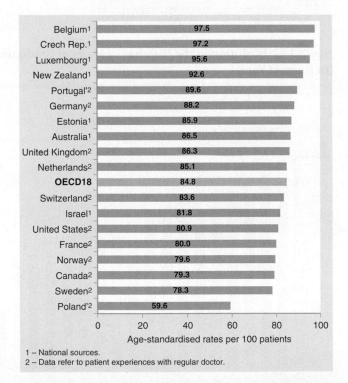

1 – National sources.
2 – Data refer to patient experiences with regular doctor.

FIGURE 3-24 **Doctor Spending Enough Time with Patient in Consultation, 2013 (or Nearest Year)**

Health at a Glance 2015: OECD Indicators by OECD Publishing. Reproduced with permission of OECD Publishing via Copyright Clearance Center

2013 survey results that determine patients' satisfaction with easy-to-understand explanation of their care from the doctor. The average OECD 2013 patient satisfaction level was 87.9%, with the United States reporting 86.3%. Figure 3.26 details patients' satisfaction in 2013 with the doctor giving them the opportunity to ask questions and raise concerns. The average patient satisfaction

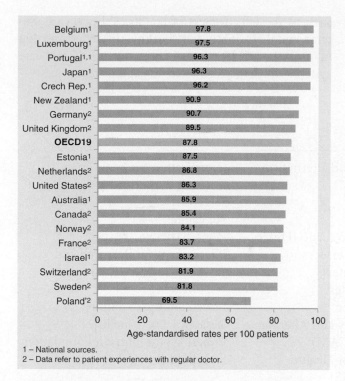

FIGURE 3-25 **Doctor Providing Easy-to-Understand Explanations, 2013 (or Nearest Year)**

Health at a Glance 2015: OECD Indicators by OECD Publishing. Reproduced with permission of OECD Publishing via Copyright Clearance Center

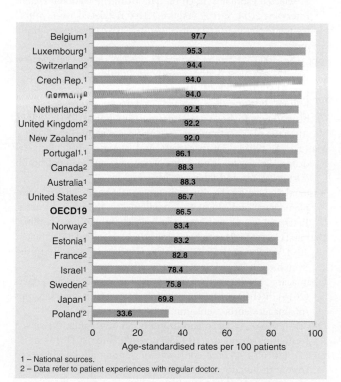

FIGURE 3-26 **Doctor Giving Opportunity to Ask Questions or Raise Concerns, 2013 (or Nearest Year)**

Health at a Glance 2015: OECD Indicators by OECD Publishing. Reproduced with permission of OECD Publishing via Copyright Clearance Center

response was 85%, with the U.S. response rate 86.7%, which is above the average. Figure 3.27 details the 2013 satisfaction rates with the doctors involving patients in

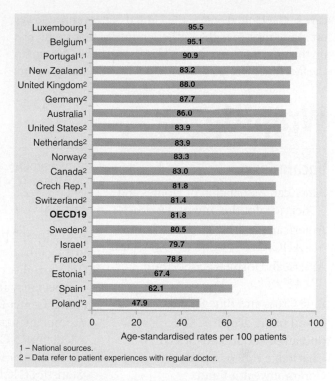

FIGURE 3-27 **Doctor Involving Patient in Decisions about Care and Treatment, 2013 (or Nearest Year)**

Health at a Glance 2015: OECD Indicators by OECD Publishing. Reproduced with permission of OECD Publishing via Copyright Clearance Center

decisions about their care. The 2013 average was 81.3%, with the United States reporting 83.9%, which is above the average (OECD, 2015).

▶ Conclusion

The U.S. healthcare system is a complicated system comprised of both public and private resources. Health care is available to those who have health insurance or who are entitled to health care through a public program. One can think of the healthcare system as several concentric circles that surround the most important stakeholders in the center circle: the healthcare consumers and providers. Immediately surrounding this relationship are health insurance companies and governmental programs, healthcare facilities, pharmaceutical companies, and laboratories, all of which provide services to consumers to ensure they receive quality health care, as well as support providers to ensure they provide quality health care. The next circle consists of peripheral stakeholders that do not have an immediate impact on the main relationship but are still important to the industry. These consist of the professional associations, the research organizations, and the medical and training facilities.

It is important to assess the system from an international perspective. Comparing different statistics from the OECD is valuable to assess the health of the United States. Despite the amount of money spent on health care in the United States, the United States ranked lower on many measures than other countries that spend less on their healthcare systems. These statistics may point to the fact that there is a combination of influencing factors such as the effectiveness of countries' healthcare systems, and their citizens have healthier lifestyles, and that many of the OECD countries have universal healthcare systems which increase access to healthcare services.

Wrap-Up

Vocabulary

American Association of Homes and Services for the Aging (AAHSA)

American Health Care Association (AHCA)

American Hospital Association (AHA)

Blue Cross and Blue Shield

Brand name drugs

Bureau of Labor Statistics (BLS)

Charitable care or bad debt

Commonwealth Fund

Complementary and alternative medicine (CAM)

Duty to treat

Generic drugs

Gross domestic product (GDP)

Home healthcare services

Infant mortality rates

Life expectancy rates

National Center for Complementary and Alternative Medicine (NCCAM)

National Center for Health Statistics (NCHS)

Organisation for Economic Cooperation and Development (OECD)

Per capita

Pew Charitable Trusts

Pharmaceutical Research and Manufacturers of America (PhRMA)

Professional associations

Residential care facilities

Robert Wood Johnson Foundation

Stakeholder

References

American Association of Homes and Services for the Aging. (2016). Retrieved from http://www.aahsa.org/about.aspx

American Diabetes Association. (2016). Diabetes basics. Retrieved from http://www.diabetes.org/diabetes-basics/

American Hospital Association. (2016). Trendwatch Chartbook 2015. http://www.aha.org/research/reports/tw/chartbook/2015/chart3-8.pdf

American Hospital Association (2016). Financial Fact Sheets. http://www.aha.org/content/15/uncompensatedcarefactsheet.pdf

American Health Care Association. (2016). Retrieved from http://www.ahcancal.org/about_ahca/who_we_are/Pages/default.aspx

American Hospital Association. (2016). Retrieved from http://www.aha.org

Bureau of Labor Statistics. (2016a). http://www.bls.gov/news.release/pdf/ecopro.pdf

Bureau of Labor Statistics. (2016b). Industries at a glance: Nursing and residential care facilities. Retrieved from http://www.bls.gov/iag/tgs/iag623.htm

Bureau of Labor Statistics. (2016c). Occupational outlook handbook: Healthcare occupations. Retrieved from http://www.bls.gov/ooh/healthcare/

Bureau of Labor Statistics. (2016d). Occupational outlook handbook: Home health and personal care aides. Retrieved from http://www.bls.gov/ooh/healthcare/home-health-and-personal-care-aides.htm#tab-2

Bureau of Labor Statistics. (2016e). Industries at a glance: Ambulatory health care services: NAICS 621. Retrieved from http://www.bls.gov/iag/tgs/iag621.htm

Bureau of Labor Statistics. (2016f). Occupational outlook handbook. Medical and clinical laboratory technologists and technicians. Retrieved from http://www.bls.gov/ooh/healthcare/medical-and-clinical-laboratory-technologists-and-technicians.htm

Centers for Disease Control and Prevention. (2016a). Early release of selected estimates based on data from the National Health Interview 2014 Survey (Figure 1.1b). Retrieved from http://www.cdc.gov/nchs/data/nhis/earlyrelease/earlyrelease201506.pdf

Jonas, S. (2003). *An introduction to the U.S. health care system* (pp. 17–45). New York, NY: Springer Publishing.

Herper, M. (2013). The Cost of Creating a New Drug Now $5 Billion, Pushing Big Pharma to Change. Retrieved from http://www.forbes.com/sites/matthewherper/2013/08/11/the-cost-of-inventing-a-new-drug-98-companies-ranked/

Mandal, A. (2014). Drug patents and generic pharmaceutical drugs. Retrieved from http://www.news-medical.net/health/Drug-Patents-and-Generics.aspx

National Center for Health Statistics. (2016). The use of complementary and alternative medicine in the United States. Retrieved from http://www.cdc.gov/nchs/nhis/nhis_nhsr.htm

National Center for Health Statistics. (2015). Health, United States, 2014, Adults aged 55–64. NHCS, Hyattsville, MD. Retrieved from http://www.cdc.gov /nchs/hus/index.htm

Obamacare enrollment figures and sign up numbers quick facts (2015). Retrieved from http://obamacarefacts.com/sign-ups/obamacare-enrollment-numbers/

OECD. (2016a). Tobacco consumption among adults. Retrieved from http://dx.doi.org/10.1787/health_glance-2011-16-en

OECD. (2016b). Alcohol consumption among adults. Retrieved from http://dx.doi.org/10.1787/health_glance-2011-17-3n

OECD. (2016). Health at a glance. Retrieved from http://www.oecd-ilibrary.org/social-issues-migration-health/health-at-a-glance_19991312

Occupational Safety and Health Administration. (2015). https://www.osha.gov/newsrelease/nat-20150625.html

Pharmaceutical Research and Manufacturers of America. (2016). Retrieved from http://www.phrma.org/about_phrma/

Tobacco. (2016). Retrieved from http://www.who.int/mediacentre/factsheets/fs339/en/

▶ **Notes**

▶ **Student Activity 3-1**

In Your Own Words

Based on this chapter, please provide a definition of the following vocabulary words in your own words. DO NOT RECITE the text definition.

Duty to treat:

_____

_____

Infant mortality rate:

_____

_____

Life expectancy rates:

_____

_____

_____

Charitable care or bad debt:

_____

_____

Complementary and alternative medicine:

_____

_____

Outpatient care centers:

_____

_____

Professional associations:

_____

_____

Residential care facilities:

_____

_____

▶ **Student Activity 3-2**

Real-Life Applications: Case Scenario One

You have decided to become a health education teacher for a high school. One of your first class lessons will be on explaining the complexity of the U.S. healthcare system to your students.

Activity

You want to be creative, so you have your students role play the stakeholders in the healthcare system. You also want them to understand how the United States compares to other countries. You develop a lesson plan that is outlined below. Your lesson plan outlines the major stakeholders in the system and how they interact with each other.

Responses

_____

_____

_____

_____

_____

_____

_____

_____

_____

_____

_____

_____

_____

_____

_____

_____

_____

Case Scenario Two

Your grandmother will be moving to a continuing-care retirement community and is unsure of how to evaluate such facilities. She asked you for assistance.

Activity

Visit the American Association of Homes and Services for the Aging (AAHSA) to find out what information is available for continuing-care communities. Give that information to your grandmother to help her make a decision.

Responses

_____

_____

_____

_____

_____

_____

_____

_____

_____

_____

_____

_____

_____

_____

_____

_____

_____

Case Scenario Three

You eventually would like to work for a pharmaceutical company. You decided to perform research on pharmaceutical companies such as Pfizer and GlaxoSmithKline. You actually did not realize that there are brand name drugs and generic drugs.

Activity

Perform an Internet search on the difference between generic and brand name drugs. Discuss the difference between the two products.

Responses

_____

_____

_____

_____

_____

_____

_____

_____

_____

_____

_____

_____

_____

_____

_____

_____

Case Scenario Four

Your aunt has had back problems for years and rather than have surgery, she decides to research alternative medicine. You had never heard of this type of medicine and was curious if it can help people.

Activity

You perform a research on the term and provide a summary of the types of treatments alternative medicine provides.

Responses

_____

_____

_____

_____

_____

_____

_____

_____

_____

_____

_____

_____

_____

_____

_____

_____

_____

▶ Student Activity 3-3

Internet Exercises

Write your answers in the space provided.

- Visit each of the websites listed here.
- Name the organization.
- Locate the organization's mission statement on the website.
- Provide a brief overview of the activities of the organization.
- How do these organizations participate in the U.S. healthcare system?

Websites

http://www.who.int

Organization Name:

_____

_____

Mission Statement:

_____

_____

_____

Overview of Activities:

_____

_____

_____

Importance of Organization to U.S. Health Care:

_____

_____

_____

http://www.commonwealthfund.org

Organization Name:

_____

_____

Mission Statement:

_____

_____

_____

Overview of Activities:

_____

_____

_____

Importance of Organization to U.S. Health Care:

_____

_____

_____

http://www.phrma.org

Organization Name:

_____

_____

Mission Statement:

_____

_____

_____

Overview of Activities:

_____

_____

_____

Importance of Organization to U.S. Health Care:

_____

_____

_____

http://www.oecd.org

Organization Name:

_____

_____

Mission Statement:

_____

_____

_____

Overview of Activities:

_____

_____

_____

Importance of Organization to U.S. Health Care:

_____

_____

_____

http://www.diabetes.org

Organization Name:

_____

_____

Mission Statement:

_____

_____

_____

Overview of Activities:

_____

_____

_____

Importance of Organization to U.S. Health Care:

_____

_____

_____

http://www.ahcancal.org

Organization Name:

_____

_____

Mission Statement:

_____

_____

_____

Overview of Activities:

_____

_____

_____

Importance of Organization to U.S. Health Care:

_____

_____

_____

▶ Student Activity 3-4

Discussion Questions

The following are suggested discussion questions for this chapter.

1. Which of the OECD statistics about the United States surprised you?

_____

_____

_____

2. Identify three stakeholders and their role in the healthcare industry.

    _____

    _____

    _____

    _____

    _____

    _____

3. Do you feel the United States should have a universal healthcare system? Defend your answer.

    _____

    _____

    _____

    _____

    _____

    _____

    _____

4. Select one of the OECD countries and discuss three of its statistics. You cannot pick the United States.

    _____

    _____

    _____

    _____

    _____

    _____

    _____

5. Select three statistics for the United States and comment on their ranking among the other countries.

    _____

    _____

    _____

    _____

    _____

_____

_____

_____

Student Activity 3-5
Current Events
Perform an Internet search and find a current events topic over the past three years that is related to this chapter. Provide a summary of the article and the link to the article and why the article relates to the chapter.

_____

_____

_____

_____

_____

_____

_____

_____

_____

_____

_____

_____

_____

_____

_____

_____

_____

_____

_____

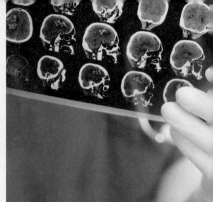

CHAPTER 4

Government's Role in U.S. Health Care

▶ Introduction

During the Depression and World War II the United States had no funds to start a universal healthcare program—an issue that had been discussed for years. As a result, a private-sector system was developed that did not provide healthcare services to all citizens. However, the government's role in providing healthcare coverage evolved to being a regulatory body to ensure that the elderly and poor were able to receive health care. The passage of the **Social Security Act of 1935** and the establishment of the Medicaid and Medicare programs in 1965 mandated the government's increased role in providing healthcare coverage. Also, the State Children's Health Insurance Program (SCHIP), now the Children's Health Insurance Program, established in 1997 and reauthorized by the Affordable Care Act (ACA) through 2019, continues to expand the government's role in children's health care. The laws require states, upon enactment, to maintain current income eligibility levels for CHIP through September 30, 2019 (CHIP, 2016). In addition to the reauthorization of the CHIP program, the ACA increased governmental interaction with the healthcare system by developing several of the governmental initiatives that focus on increasing the ability of individuals to make informed decisions about their health care.

In these instances, the government increased accessibility to health care as well as provided financing for health care to certain targeted populations. This chapter will focus on the different roles the federal, state, and local governments play in the U.S. healthcare system. This chapter will also highlight different governmental programs and regulations that focus on monitoring how health care is provided.

▶ History of the Role of Government in Health Care

Social regulation focuses on organizations' actions, such as those in the healthcare industry, that impact an individual's safety. Social regulations focus on protecting individuals as employees and consumers (Carroll & Buchholtz, 2015). These types of regulations are common in the U.S. healthcare system. The healthcare industry claims it is the most regulated industry in the world. It is important to mention that in addition to governmental regulations, there are nongovernmental regulations of U.S. health care by accrediting bodies such as the Joint Commission, which began over 80 years ago and accredits nearly 21,000 healthcare organizations and programs (The Joint Commission, 2016). However, regulatory oversight is mainly handled at the federal, state, and local governmental levels.

▶ U.S. Government Agencies

Regulatory healthcare power is shared among federal and state governments. State governments have a dominant role of regulating constituents in their jurisdiction. To ensure success in this regulatory process, state governments also developed local government levels to provide direct services to constituents and regulate their geographic region. Legislatures establish the legal framework for state and local governmental authority (Jonas, 2003).

Important Federal Government Agencies

Many federal agencies are responsible for a sector of healthcare. The **U.S. Department of Health and Human Services (HHS)** is the most important federal agency. It is a cabinet-level department of the executive branch of the federal government. The Secretary of the HHS provides advice to the President of the United States regarding health and human services policy (Pozgar, 2014). HHS collaborates with state and local governments because many HHS services are provided at those levels. There are 11 operating divisions: the **Centers for Disease Control and Prevention (CDC)**, the **Administration for Community Living (ACL)**, the **National Institutes of Health (NIH)**, the **Agency for Toxic Substances and Disease Registry (ATSDR)**, the **Indian Health Service (IHS)**, the **Health Resources and Services Administration (HRSA)**, the **Agency for Healthcare Research and Quality (AHRQ)**, the **Substance Abuse and Mental Health Services Administration (SAMHSA)**, the **U.S. Food and Drug Administration (FDA)**, the **Administration for Children and Families (ACF)**, and the **Centers for Medicare and Medicaid Services (CMS)**. Each of these agencies will be discussed individually (HHS, 2016).

Secretary Deputy Secretary Chief of Staff

The Executive Secretariat (ES)

Office of Health Reform (OHR)

Office of Intergovernmental and External Affairs (IEA)

Office of the Secretary

Office of the Assistant Secretary for Administration (ASA)

Office of the Assistant Secretary for Financial Resources (ASFR)

Office of the Assistant Secretary for Health (OASH)

Office of the Assistant Secretary for Legislation (ASL)

Office of the Assistant Secretary for Planning and Evaluation (ASPE)

Office of the Assistant Secretary for Preparedness and Response (ASPR)*

Office of the Assistant Secretary for Public Affairs (ASPA)

Office for Civil Rights (OCR)

Departmental Appeals Board (DAB)

Office of the General Counsel (OGC)

Office of Global Affairs (OGA)*

Office of Inspector General (OIG)

Office of Medicare Hearings and Appeals (OMHA)

Office of the National Coordinator for Health Information Technology (ONC)

Operating Divisions

Administration for Children and Families (ACF)

Administration for Community Living (ACL)

Agency for Healthcare Research and Quality (AHRQ)*

Agency for Toxic Substances and Disease Registry (ATSDR)*

Centers for Disease Control and Prevention (CDC)*

Centers for Medicare & Medicaid Services (CMS)

Food and Drug Administration (FDA)*

Health Resources and Services Administration (HRSA)*

Indian Health Service (IHS)*

National Institutes of Health (NIH)*

Substance Abuse and Mental Health Services Administration (SAMHSA)*

* Components of the Public Health Service

Administratively supported by the Office of the Assistant Secretary for Health

Centers for Disease Control and Prevention (CDC)

The CDC was established in 1946 and is headquartered in Atlanta, Georgia, with 10 additional U.S. locations. Its mission is saving and protecting the health of Americans. The CDC is available 24/7 to respond to any manmade or natural event. By connecting state and local health departments across the United States, the CDC can discover patterns of disease and respond when needed. The CDC has created four health goals, which focus on (1) healthy people in healthy places, (2) preparing people for emerging health threats, (3) positive international health, and (4) healthy people at all stages of their life. To achieve these goals, the CDC focuses on six areas: health impact, customer focus, public health research, leadership, globalization, and accountability. The CDC website provides information on disease, healthy living, emergency preparedness, injury prevention, environmental health, workplace safety, data and statistics, and global health. The CDC also provides specific information for travelers, infants and children, pregnancies, and state and tribal associations. It is the lead U.S. agency for disease outbreaks, such as Ebola and Zika (CDC, 2016).

Administration for Community Living (ACL)

All Americans—including people with disabilities and older adults—should be able to live at home with the supports they need, participating in communities that value their contributions. To help meet these needs, the HHS created a new organization, the ACL.

Established in 2012, the ACL brings together the efforts and achievements of the Administration on Aging, the Administration on Intellectual and Developmental Disabilities, and the HHS Office on Disability to serve as the federal agency responsible for increasing access to community supports, while focusing attention and resources on the unique needs of older Americans and people with disabilities across the lifespan.

The ACL mission is to maximize the independence, well-being, and health of older adults, people with disabilities across the lifespan, and their families and caregivers. Since its inception, it has developed elderly housing initiatives, new models of community care for the elderly and people with disabilities, a partnership with the Veterans' Administration to counsel veterans on their ongoing service needs, and a national network of increased transportation access for the elderly and people with disabilities (ACL, 2016).

Agency for Toxic Substances and Disease Registry (ATSDR)

The ATSDR, headquartered in Atlanta, Georgia, and administered organizationally with the CDC, was established in 1985 and is authorized by the Comprehensive Environmental Response, Compensation, and Liability Act of 1980 (CERCLA; more commonly known as the Superfund law). The ATSDR is responsible for finding and cleaning the most dangerous hazardous waste sites in the country. Specific functions include public health assessments of waste sites, health consultations concerning specific hazardous substances, health surveillance and registries, response to emergency releases of hazardous substances, applied research in support of public health assessments, information development and dissemination, and education and training concerning hazardous substances. The ATSDR's mission is to protect the public against harmful exposures and disease-related exposures to toxic substances. The ATSDR is the lead federal public health agency responsible for determining human health effects associated with toxic exposures, preventing continued exposures, and mitigating associated human health risks. ATSDR is administered organizationally with the CDC. The ATSDR has 10 regional offices within the Environmental Protection Agency (EPA) across the country (ATSDR, 2016).

National Institutes of Health (NIH)

Established in 1930 and headquartered in Bethesda, Maryland, the NIH is the primary federal agency for research toward preventing and curing disease worldwide. Its mission is the pursuit of knowledge about the nature and behavior of living systems and the application of that knowledge to extend healthy life and reduce the burdens of illness and disability. The NIH is comprised of 27 institutes and centers that focus on different diseases and conditions, including cancer, ophthalmology, heart, lung, and blood disorders, genes, aging, alcoholism and drug abuse, infectious diseases, chronic diseases, children's diseases, and mental health. Although the NIH has sponsored external research, it also has a large internal research program. Nearly 150 Nobel Prize winners have received NIH funding, which has led to the development of the MRI, how viruses can cause cancer, insights into cholesterol control, and other important advances in medicine (NIH, 2016).

Health Resources and Services Administration (HRSA)

Created in 1982 and headquartered in Rockville, Maryland, the HRSA is the primary federal agency for improving access to healthcare services for people in every state who are uninsured, isolated, or medically vulnerable. The five organizational goals are improving access to quality healthcare, strengthening the health care workforce, building healthy communities, improving health equity, and strengthening HRSA management and operations. The HRSA has six bureaus: primary health care, health professions, healthcare systems, maternal and child health, the HIV/AIDS bureau, and the Bureau of Clinician Recruitment and Service. The HRSA provides funding to grantees that provide health care to those vulnerable populations. It also oversees organ, bone marrow, and cord blood donation; supports programs against bioterrorism; and maintains databases that protect against healthcare malpractice and healthcare waste, fraud, and abuse. Tens of millions of Americans get affordable health care and other help through the HRSA's 100-plus programs and more than 3,000 grantees (HRSA, 2016).

Agency for Healthcare Research and Quality (AHRQ)

Created in 1989 and headquartered in Rockville, Maryland, the agency's mission is to improve the quality, safety, efficiency, and effectiveness of health care for all U.S. citizens. The AHRQ's cutting-edge research helps people make more informed decisions and improve the quality of healthcare services. AHRQ focuses on the following areas of research: healthcare costs and utilization, information technology, disaster preparedness, medication safety, healthcare consumerism, prevention of illness, and special-needs populations. The AHRQ has a National Partnership Network, which includes over 600 federal, state, and local health agencies, health professional groups, patient and caregiver advocacy groups, health systems, and businesses committed to improving the quality of health care through informed decision making. These organizations support the AHRQ's efforts to share evidence-based resources with patients and caregivers, health professionals, and others in their communities (AHRQ, 2016).

Indian Health Service (IHS)

Established in 1921 and headquartered in Rockville, Maryland, the mission of IHS is to raise the physical, mental, social, and spiritual health of American Indians and Alaska Natives to the highest level. Also part of its mission is to ensure that comprehensive, culturally acceptable personal and public health services are available and accessible to American Indian and Alaska Native people. It also is responsible for promoting American Indian and Alaska Native communities and cultures and for honoring and protecting the inherent sovereign rights of these people. The IHS provides a comprehensive health-service-delivery system for approximately 1.9 million American Indians and Alaska Natives who belong to 566 federally recognized tribes. Twelve area IHS sites provide services to constituents (IHS, 2016).

Substance Abuse and Mental Health Services Administration (SAMHSA)

Established in 1992, the SAMHSA is the main federal agency for improving access to quality substance abuse and mental health services in the United States by working with state, community, and private organizations. The Administrator of the Substance Abuse and Mental Health Services Administration co-chairs the HHS Behavioral Health Coordinating Council (BHCC), which is a coordinating body within the HHS established in 2010 by the HHS Secretary. The BHCC's chief goals are to share information and identify and facilitate collaborative, action-oriented approaches to address the HHS behavioral health agenda without duplication of effort across the HHS. The SAMHSA is the umbrella agency for mental health and substance abuse services, which includes the **Center for Mental Health Services (CMHS)**, the **Center for Substance Abuse Prevention (CSAP)**, and the **Center for Substance Abuse Treatment (CSAT)**. The **Center for Behavioral Health Statistics and Quality (CBHSQ)** is responsible for data collection, analysis, and dissemination of critical health data to assist policymakers, providers, and the public for use in making informed decisions regarding the prevention and treatment of mental and substance use disorders (SAMHSA, 2016).

U.S. Food and Drug Administration (FDA)

Established in 1906 as a result of the **Federal Food, Drug, and Cosmetic Act**, the FDA is responsible for ensuring that the following products are safe: food, human and veterinary products, biologic products, medical devices, cosmetics, and electronic products. The FDA is also responsible for ensuring that product information is accurate. The following is a summary of FDA responsibility for each category:

1. Food: The FDA ensures that food labeling contains accurate information. Also, the FDA regulates the safety of all food except poultry and meat and oversees bottled water, dietary supplements, infant formulas, and food additives.
2. Veterinary products: The FDA has oversight of the production of livestock feed, pet food, and veterinary drugs and devices.
3. Human drugs: The FDA has regulatory oversight of both prescription and over-the-counter (OTC) drug development and

labeling, which includes the manufacturing standards for these drug products.

4. Biologics: The FDA has oversight of vaccines, blood and blood products, cellular and gene therapy products, tissue and tissue products, and allergenics.

5. Medical devices: The FDA has authority for premarket approval for any new devices, as well as developing standards for their manufacturing and performance, and also must track reports of any malfunction of these devices. The FDA has oversight of dental devices.

6. Cosmetics: The FDA oversees both the safety and labeling of cosmetic products.

7. Electronic products: The FDA develops and regulate standards for microwaves, television receivers, and diagnostic equipment such as X-ray equipment, laser products, ultrasonic therapy equipment, and sunlamps. It also must accredit and inspect any mammography facilities.

8. Tobacco products: Cigarettes, cigarette tobacco, roll your own tobacco, and smokeless tobacco. The FDA regulates the manufacture, distribution and marketing of all tobacco products. Starting in August 2016, the FDA will begin to apply and enforce key provisions of the Family Smoking Prevention and Tobacco Control Act as it relates to the sale, marketing, and manufacturing of e-cigarettes.

The FDA is also responsible for advancing public health by speeding up innovations to make medicine and food more effective, safer, and more affordable. It is also responsible for ensuring that the public receives accurate information to be able to make informed decisions about using medicine and food products. The FDA also plays a significant role in the nation's counterterrorism capability. The FDA fulfills this responsibility by ensuring the security of the food supply and by fostering development of medical products to respond to deliberate and naturally emerging public health threats (USFDA, 2016).

Administration for Children and Families (ACF)

The ACF, which has 10 regional offices, is responsible for federal programs that promote the economic and social well-being of families, children, individuals, and communities. Their mission is to empower people to increase their own economic well-being, support

communities that have a positive impact on the quality of life of their residents, partner with other organizations to support Native American tribes, improve needed access to services, and work with special-needs populations. The ACF also has programs that target human trafficking and refugees (ACF, 2016).

Centers for Medicare and Medicaid Services (CMS)

The CMS was established when the Medicare and Medicaid programs were signed into law in 1965 by President Lyndon B. Johnson as a result of the Social Security Act. At that time, only half of those 65 years or older had health insurance. Medicaid was established for low-income children, the elderly, the blind, and the disabled and was linked with the Supplemental Security Income program (SSI). In 1972, Medicare was extended to cover people under the age of 65 with permanent disabilities. The CMS also has oversight of SCHIP, Title XXI of the Social Security Act, which is financed by both federal and state funding and is administered at the state level.

Headquartered in Baltimore, Maryland, the CMS has over 20 offices that oversee different aspects of programs. The primary responsibility of CMS is to provide policy, funding, and oversight to healthcare programs for elderly and poor individuals. For many years, the CMS was a geographically based structure with 10 field offices. In 2007, it was reorganized to a consortia structure based on the priorities of Medicare health plans and financial management, Medicare fee for service, Medicaid and children's health, surveys and certification, and quality assurance and improvement. The consortia are responsible for oversight of the 10 regional offices for each priority. In 2010, the Center for Program Integrity was developed as part of the CMS; it focuses on best practices for program implementation (CMS, 2016a). As part of the Affordable Care Act, the Innovation Center was established. Congress created the Innovation Center for the purpose of testing "innovative payment and service delivery models to reduce program expenditures while preserving or enhancing the quality of care" for those individuals who receive Medicare, Medicaid, or Children's Health Insurance Program (CHIP) benefits. The CMS also oversees the ACA Health Insurance Marketplace (CMS, 2016b).

Occupational Safety and Health Administration (OSHA)

Established on December 29, 1970, and part of the U.S. Department of Labor, the **Occupational Safety and Health Administration (OSHA)** was established to govern workplace environments to ensure that employees have a safe and healthy environment. The Act covers most private sector employees. OSHA requires states to develop their own job safety and health programs, which can be approved by OSHA. States can apply for approval for their plans and receive up to 50% funding for their programs. There are currently 22 states that have programs that protect both private and public sector employees (OSHA, 2016).

Under OSHA enforcement, the following legislation ensures that healthcare workers are protected. The **Hazard Communication Standard (HCS)** ensures that all hazardous chemicals are properly labeled and that companies are informed of these risks (Hazard Communication, 2016). The **Medical Waste Tracking Act** requires companies to have medical waste disposal procedures so that there is no risk to employees and the environment (Environmental Protection Agency, 2016). The **Occupational Exposure to Blood-borne Pathogen Standard** developed behavioral standards for employees who deal with blood products, such as wearing gloves and other equipment and disposal of blood collection materials (OSHA Quicktakes, 2016).

Surgeon General and U.S. Public Health Service

The **Surgeon General** is the U.S. chief health educator who provides information on how to improve the health of the U.S. population. The Surgeon General, who is appointed by the President of the United States, and the Office of the Surgeon General oversee the operations of the commissioned **U.S. Public Health Service Corps**, which provides support to the Surgeon General. The U.S. Public Health Service Commissioned Corps consists of 6,700 public health professionals who are stationed within federal agencies and programs. These commissioned employees include various professionals such as dentists, nurses, physicians, mental health specialists, environmental health specialists, veterinarians, and therapists. The Surgeon General serves a four-year term and reports to the Secretary of HHS. The Surgeon General focuses on certain health priorities for the United States and publishes reports on these issues. In 2010, the Affordable Care Act designated the Surgeon General as the chair of the National Prevention Council, which provides coordination and leadership among 20 executive departments with respect to prevention, wellness, and health promotion activities (Office of the Surgeon General, 2016).

Department of Homeland Security (DHS)

The **Department of Homeland Security (DHS)** was established in 2002 as a result of the 2001 terrorist attack on the United States. It consists of 22 different federal departments with over 240,000 employees and focuses on protecting the United States. The **Federal Emergency Management Agency (FEMA)**, which is responsible for managing catastrophic events, was integrated into the DHS in 2003. Together, they are responsible for coordinating efforts at all governmental levels to ensure emergency preparedness for any catastrophic events such as bioterrorism; chemical and radiation emergencies; mass casualties as a result of explosions, natural disasters, and severe weather; and disease outbreaks. They coordinate with the CDC to ensure there are plans in place to quickly resolve these events. In conjunction with FEMA, the DHS has also developed a **National Incident Management System (NIMS)**, which provides a systematic, proactive approach to all levels of government and private sector agencies to collaborate and ensure there is a seamless plan to manage any major incidents. It is the essential foundation to the **National Preparedness System (NPS)**, which outlines an organized process for an integrated preparedness system for any disaster (DHS, 2016).

Office of the Assistant Secretary for Preparedness and Response (ASPR)

The **Office of the Assistant Secretary for Preparedness and Response (ASPR)** was created under the Pandemic and All Hazards Preparedness Act in the wake of Hurricane Katrina to prevent, prepare, and respond to the adverse health effects of public health emergencies and disasters. ASPR focuses on preparedness planning and response; building federal emergency medical operational capabilities; countermeasures research, advance development, and procurement; and grants to strengthen the capabilities of hospitals and healthcare systems in public health emergencies and medical disasters. The office provides federal support, including medical professionals through the ASPR's **National Disaster Medical System**, to augment state and local capabilities during an emergency or disaster. The **Office of Emergency Management** provides support and coordination of federal, state, and local activities during times of emergency. The Secretary of HHS delegates to the ASPR the leadership role for all health and medical services support function in a health emergency or public health event (PHE, 2016).

State Health Departments' Role in Health Care

The U.S. Constitution gives state governments the primary role in providing health care for their citizens. Most states have several different agencies that are responsible for specific public health services. There is usually a lead state agency with approximately 20 agencies that target health issues like aging, living, and working environments, as well as alcoholism and substance abuse. Many state agencies are responsible for implementing certain federal acts, such as the Clean Water Act, the Clean Air Act, the Food, Drug, and Cosmetic Act, and the Safe Drinking Water Act (Turnock, 2007). **State health departments** monitor communities to identify health problems. Additionally, they diagnose and investigate health problems and provide education about health issues. They also develop policies to support community health. They must enforce laws and regulations to promote health and safety. Most state agencies are responsible for or share responsibility for federal programs related to maternal and infant health services and cancer prevention. They are responsible for providing population-based services for the CDC's health priorities, which include motor vehicle injuries, HIV, obesity, food safety, tobacco use, teen pregnancy, and nutrition. Vital statistics collected include deaths, births, marriages, and health and disease statuses of the population. These statistics are important to collect because they serve as a basis for funding. The **Council of State and Territorial Epidemiologists (CSTE)** decides which diseases should be considered reportable to the CDC, which then produces the **Morbidity and Mortality Weekly Report (MMWR)**. The MMWR is an estimate of the prevalence of disease throughout the country (Association of State and Territorial Health Officials, 2016).

State health departments also license health professionals such as physicians, dentists, chiropractors, nurses, pharmacists, optometrists, and veterinarians who practice within the state. Further, they inspect and license healthcare facilities such as hospitals and nursing homes. Most state agencies provide technical assistance to their local health departments in the following areas: (1) quality improvement, (2) data management, (3) public health law, (4) human resource management, and (5) policy development. It is important to emphasize that the state health department provides oversight to local health departments, which are directly responsible for providing public health activities for their community (Mays, 2008). State agencies are funded primarily by federal sources, state resources, and Medicaid and Medicare, with the remaining sources supplied by fines and fees, indirect federal funding, and other minor sources (Association of State and Territorial Health Officials Profile, 2016).

Local Health Departments' Role in Health Care

Local health departments are the governmental organizations that provide most of the direct services to the population. There are 2,800 local health departments across the United States. Although their organizational structures may differ, their basic role is to provide direct public health services to their designated areas. It is difficult to generalize as to the types of services offered by local health departments because they do vary according to geographic location, but most are involved in communicable disease control. The following are highlights of the types of direct services offered by local health departments:

- Over 90% of local health departments provide adult and children immunizations.
- Over 90% offer communicable/infectious disease surveillance.
- Over 80% offer tuberculosis screening and 75% offer tuberculosis treatment.
- Over 75% offer environmental surveillance.
- Approximately 70% offer population nutrition services.
- Nearly 75% provide school/day care center inspection.
- Nearly 85% provide activities to address health disparities.
- Approximately 75% provide food safety education (NACCHO, 2016).

Local health departments receive funding from their state government and the federal government, direct funding such as from the CDC, reimbursement for services from Medicaid and Medicare, private health insurance, and fees for services. Because of population size and coverage, local health department funding varies from state to state. Local sources are the greatest contributor to funding local health departments, followed by state allocations, Medicare and Medicaid, fees, and other federal funding (NACCHO, 2016). However, the ACA has strengthened the position of the local health departments by providing funding opportunities for educating the public health workforce and increasing the focus on preventive services that are traditionally performed by the local health departments (Historic Health Reform Legislation, 2013).

▶ Conclusion

The government plays an important role in the quality of the U.S. healthcare system. The federal government provides funding for state and local governmental programs. Federal healthcare regulations are implemented and enforced at the state and local levels. Funding is primarily distributed from the federal government to the state government, which then allocates funding to local health departments. Local health departments provide the majority of services for their constituents. More local health departments are working with local organizations such as schools and physicians to increase their ability to provide education and prevention services.

The DHS and FEMA now play an integral role in the management and oversight of catastrophic events, such as natural disasters, earthquakes, floods, pandemic diseases, and bioterrorism. The DHS and FEMA collaborate closely with the CDC to ensure that both the state and local health departments have a crisis management plan in place for these events. These attacks are often horrific and frightening with a tremendous loss of life, and as a result, the state and local health departments need to be more prepared to deal with catastrophic events. They are required to develop plans and be trained to deal effectively with many of these catastrophic issues. Finally, the Affordable Care Act has increased government involvement in the healthcare industry to promote access to a quality healthcare system.

Wrap-Up

Vocabulary

Administration for Children and Families (ACF)

Administration for Community Living (ACL)

Agency for Healthcare Research and Quality (AHRQ)

Agency for Toxic Substances and Disease Registry (ATSDR)

Center for Behavioral Health Statistics and Quality (CBHSQ)

Center for Mental Health Services (CMHS)

Center for Substance Abuse Prevention (CSAP)

Center for Substance Abuse Treatment (CSAT)

Centers for Disease Control and Prevention (CDC)

Centers for Medicare and Medicaid Services (CMS)

Council of State and Territorial Epidemiologists (CSTE)

Department of Homeland Security (DHS)

Emergency preparedness

Federal Emergency Management Agency (FEMA)

Federal Food, Drug, and Cosmetic Act (FDCA)

Hazard Communication Standard (HCS)

Health Resources and Services Administration (HRSA)

Indian Health Service (IHS)

Local health departments

Medical Waste Tracking Act

Morbidity and Mortality Weekly Report (MMWR)

National Disaster Medical System

National Incident Management System (NIMS)

National Institutes of Health (NIH)

National Preparedness System

Occupational Exposure to Blood-borne Pathogen Standard

Occupational Safety and Health Administration (OSHA)

Office of Emergency Management

Office of the Assistant Secretary for Preparedness and Response (ASPR)

Social regulation

Social Security Act of 1935

State health departments

Substance Abuse and Mental Health Services Administration (SAMHSA)

Surgeon General

U.S. Department of Health and Human Services (HHS)

U.S. Food and Drug Administration (FDA)

U.S. Public Health Service Corps

References

Administration for Children and Families (ACF). (2016). What we do. Retrieved from http://www.acf.hhs.gov/about/what-we-do

Administration for Community Living (ACL). (2016). Retrieved from http://www.acl.gov/About_ACL/Index.aspx

Agency for Healthcare Research and Quality (AHRQ). (2016). Retrieved from http://www.ahrq.gov/about/mission/glance/index.html

Agency for Toxic Substances and Disease Registry (ATSDR). (2016). Retrieved from http://www.atsdr.cdc.gov/about/index.html

ASPR. (2016). Office of the Assistant Secretary for preparedness and response. Retrieved from http://www.phe.gov/about/aspr/Pages/default.aspx

Association of State and Territorial Health Officials (ASTHO). (2016). Profile. Retrieved from http://www.astho.org/about/.org/about/

Carroll, A., & Buchholtz, A. (2015). *Business and society: Ethics and stakeholder management*. Mason, OH: Cengage.

Centers for Disease Control and Prevention (CDC). (2016). Retrieved from http://www.cdc.gov/about/

Centers for Medicare and Medicaid Services (CMS). (2016a). About CMS. Retrieved from http://www.cms.gov/About-CMS/About-CMS.html

Centers for Medicare and Medicaid Services (CMS). (2016b). Innovation Center. Retrieved from http://innovation.cms.gov/

Children's Health Insurance Program (CHIP). (2016). Retrieved from http://www.medicaid.gov/medicaid-chip-program-information/by-topics/childrens-health-insurance-program-chip/childrens-health-insurance-program-chip.html

Coalition for Health Services Research (CHSR). (2016). Retrieved from http://www.chsr.org/about.htm

Council of State and Territorial Epidemiologists (CSTE). (2016). Retrieved from http://www.cste.org/dnn/AboutCSTE/AboutCSTE/tabid/56/Default.aspx

Department of Homeland Security (DHS). (2016). Retrieved from http://www.dhs.gov/xabout/index.shtm

Environmental Protection Agency (EPA). (2016). Medical Waste Tracking Act of 1988. Retrieved from http://www.epa.gov/osw/nonhaz/industrial/medical/tracking.htm

Hazard Communication. (2016). Retrieved from http://www.osha.gov/dsg/hazcom/index.html

Health and Human Services (HHS). (2016). Retrieved from http://www.hhs.gov/about/

Health Resources and Services Administration (HRSA). (2016). Retrieved from http://www.hrsa.gov/about/index.html

Historic Health Reform Legislation. (2016). Retrieved from NAC-CHO LHU Profile, 2016.

Indian Health Service (IHS). (2016). Retrieved from http://www.ihs.gov/PublicInfo/PublicAffairs/Welcome_Info/IHSintro.asp

Jonas, S. (2003). *An introduction to the U.S. health care system* (pp. 17–45). New York, NY: Springer Publishing.

Mays, G. (2008). Organization of the public health delivery system. In L. Novick & C. Morrow (Eds.), *Public health administration: Principles for population-based management* (pp. 69–126). Sudbury, MA: Jones and Bartlett.

NACCHO. (2016). Local health department responsibilities. Retrieved from http://www.naccho.org/topics/infrastructure/profile/resources/index.cfm#anchor7

National Institutes of Health (NIH). (2016). Retrieved from http://www.nih.gov/about/mission.htm

Occupational Safety and Health Administration (OSHA). (2016). Retrieved from http://www.osha.gov/about.html

Office of the Surgeon General. (2016). Retrieved from http://www.surgeongeneral.gov/about/index.html

Pozgar, G. (2014). *Legal and ethical essentials of health care administration*. Sudbury, MA: Jones & Bartlett Learning.

Public health departments partner across regions to expand services. (2011). Retrieved from http://www.rwjf.org/en/culture-of-health/2011/11/public-health-departments-partner-across-regions-to-provide-expanded-services.html

Substance Abuse and Mental Health Services Administration (SAMHSA). (2016). Retrieved from http://www.oas.samhsa.gov

The Joint Commission. (2016). About The Joint Commission. Retrieved from http://www.jointcommission.org/about_us/about_the_joint_commission_main.aspx

Turnock, B. (2007). *Essentials of public health*. Sudbury, MA: Jones and Bartlett.

U.S. Food and Drug Administration (FDA). (2016). Retrieved from http://www.fda.gov/AboutFDA/WhatWeDo/WhatFDARegulates/default.htm

▶ **Notes**

▶ **Student Activity 4-1**

In Your Own Words

Based on this chapter, please provide a description of the following concepts in your own words. DO NOT RECITE the text description.

Hazard Communication Standard (HCS):

_____

_____

National Network on Aging:

_____

_____

U.S. Public Health Service Corps:

_____

_____

Morbidity and Mortality Weekly Report (MMWR):

_____

_____

National Incident Management System:

_____

_____

National Disaster Medical System:

_____

_____

Office of Emergency Management:

_____

_____

Public Health Accreditation Board:

_____

_____

Social Security Act of 1935

_____

_____

Office of the Assistant Secretary for Preparedness and Response (ASPR):

_____

_____

U.S. Surgeon General:

_____

_____

▶ Student Activity 4-2

Real-Life Applications: Case Scenario One

You are interested in the Food and Drug Administration and its most recent new role of oversight of e-cigarettes. Many of your friends use e-cigarettes and you are not sure if they are a healthy alternative to cigarettes.

Activity

Perform an Internet search of the FDA and its regulation of e-cigarettes and the health implications of e-cigarettes, and present your findings to the class.

Responses

_____

_____

_____

_____

_____

_____

_____

_____

_____

_____

_____

_____

_____

_____

_____

_____

_____

Case Scenario Two

You have been assigned as an intern at FEMA for the summer. You are not familiar with this governmental organization but want to be familiar with its mission and activities prior to your start date.

Activity

Perform an Internet search and prepare a report for the class on FEMA and its activities. Be specific about its role in the healthcare system.

Responses

_____

_____

_____

_____

_____

_____

_____

_____

_____

_____

_____

_____

_____

_____

_____

_____

_____

_____

_____

_____

Case Scenario Three

You are thinking about continuing your education but are not sure what area of health care is of interest to you. Your friend just obtained her master of public health degree. Before you decide what degree you want to obtain, you decide to perform additional research on what is the goal of public health.

Activity

Go to the Centers for Disease Control and Prevention website and review five recent activities regarding public health. Prepare a report for the class.

Responses

_____

_____

_____

_____

_____

_____

_____

_____

_____

_____

_____

_____

_____

_____

_____

_____

_____

Case Scenario Four

You have decided you would like to become a federal government worker in the healthcare industry but are unsure of which organization would be of interest to you.

Activity

Select three of the federal government organizations identified in this chapter and provide a summary of their activities.

Responses

_____

_____

_____

_____

_____

_____

_____

_____

_____

_____

_____

_____

_____

_____

_____

_____

_____

▶ **Student Activity 4-3**

Internet Exercises

Write your answers in the space provided.

- Visit each of the websites listed here.
- Name the organization.
- Locate the organization's mission statement on the website.
- Provide a brief overview of the activities of the organization.
- How do these organizations participate in the U.S. healthcare system?

Websites

http://www.atsdr.cdc.gov

Organization Name:

_____

_____

Mission Statement:

_____

_____

_____

Overview of Activities:

_____

_____

_____

Importance of Organization to U.S. Health Care:

_____

_____

_____

http://www.hrsa.gov

Organization Name:

_____

_____

Mission Statement:

_____

_____

_____

Overview of Activities:

_____

_____

_____

Importance of Organization to U.S. Health Care:

_____

_____

_____

http://www.fda.gov

Organization Name:

_____

_____

Mission Statement:

_____

_____

_____

Overview of Activities:

_____

_____

_____

Importance of Organization to U.S. Health Care:

_____

_____

_____

http://www.ihs.gov

Organization Name:

_____

_____

Mission Statement:

_____

_____

_____

Overview of Activities:

_____

_____

_____

Importance of Organization to U.S. Health Care:

_____

_____

_____

http://www.acl.gov

Organization Name:

_____

_____

Mission Statement:

_____

_____

_____

Overview of Activities:

_____

_____

_____

Importance of Organization to U.S. Health Care:

_____

_____

_____

http://www.acf.hhs.gov

Organization Name:

_____

_____

Mission Statement:

_____

_____

_____

Overview of Activities:

_____

_____

_____

Importance of Organization to U.S. Health Care:

_____

_____

_____

▶ Student Activity 4-4

Discussion Questions

The following are suggested discussion questions for this chapter.

1. Discuss the role of the FDA in the healthcare industry.

_____

_____

_____

2. Why was the Department of Homeland Security (DHS) established? Why was FEMA integrated into the DHS?

_____

_____

_____

_____

_____

_____

3. What is the difference between the role of the state health department and the local health department in providing health services?

_____

_____

_____

_____

_____

_____

4. Go to the ASTHO website. Based on your research, why is it important to state agencies?

_____

_____

_____

_____

_____

_____

_____

5. What is the purpose of the Public Health Accreditation Board? Perform an Internet search to see if your state and local health departments have received accreditation.

_____

_____

_____

_____

_____

_____

_____

_____

▶ **Student Activity 4-5**

Current Events

Perform an Internet search and find a current events topic over the past three years that is related to this chapter. Provide a summary of the article and the link to the article and why the article relates to the chapter.

_____

_____

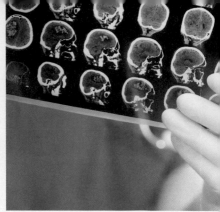

CHAPTER 5

Public Health's Role in Health Care

DID YOU KNOW THAT?

- In 1842, Edwin Chadwick reported that the poor had higher rates of disease—a fact that still exists today.
- Established in 1905, the civic organization Rotary International has played a huge role in eradicating polio through international vaccine programs.
- In 1916, the Johns Hopkins University, located in Baltimore, Maryland, established the first school of public health.
- In 1992, a national exercise program for Medicare patients, Silver Sneakers, was created to provide free access to organized exercise at national fitness chains.
- A newer form of surveillance is called biosurveillance, which monitors patterns of unusual disease that may be the result of human intervention.
- Public health marketing is an innovative approach to public health practice because it draws from the business discipline of marketing and adds science-based health strategies of promotion and prevention.

▶ Introduction

There are two important definitions of public health. In 1920, **public health** was defined by Charles Winslow as the science and art of preventing disease, prolonging life, and promoting physical health and efficiency through organized community efforts for the sanitation of the environment, control of community infections, and education of individuals regarding hygiene to ensure a standard of living for health maintenance (Winslow, 1920). Sixty years later, the **Institute of Medicine (IOM)**, in its 1988 *Future of Public Health* report, defined public health as an organized community effort to address public health by applying scientific and technical knowledge to promote health (IOM, 1988). Both definitions point to broad community efforts to promote health activities to protect the population's health status. The Affordable Care Act is also emphasizing the importance of prevention and wellness. The establishment of the Prevention and Public Health Fund has supported several community-based public health programs. To date, the Fund has invested in a broad range of evidence-based activities including community and clinical prevention initiatives; research, surveillance, and tracking; public health infrastructure; immunizations and screenings; tobacco prevention; and public health workforce and training. As of 2016, funding has been allocated to public health priorities including Alzheimer's disease prevention, chronic disease self-management, diabetes prevention, hospital promotion of breastfeeding, and lead poisoning prevention (HHS, 2016).

The development of public health is important to note as part of the basics of the U.S. healthcare system because its development was separate from the development of private medical practices. Public health specialists view health from a collectivist and preventative care viewpoint: to protect as many citizens as possible from health issues and to provide strategies to prevent health issues from occurring. The definitions cited in the previous paragraph emphasize this viewpoint. Public health concepts were in stark contrast to traditional medicine, which focused on the relationship between a provider and a patient. Private practitioners held an individualistic viewpoint—people more often would be paying for their services from their health insurance or from their own pockets. Physicians would be providing their patients guidance on how to cure their diseases, not preventing disease. This chapter will discuss the concept of health and healthcare delivery and the role of public health in delivering health care. The concepts of primary, secondary, and tertiary prevention and the role of public health in those delivery activities will be highlighted. Discussion will also focus on the origins of public health, the major role epidemiology plays in public health, the role of public health in disasters, core public health activities, the collaboration of public health and private medicine, and the importance of public health consumers.

▶ What Is Health?

The World Health Organization (WHO) defines **health** as the state of complete physical, mental, and social well-being and not merely the absence of disease or infirmity (WHO, 1942). The IOM defines health as a state of well-being and the capability to function in the face of changing circumstances. It is a positive concept emphasizing social and personal resources as well as physical capabilities (IOM, 1997). According to the Society for Academic Emergency Medicine (SAEM), health is a state of physical and mental well-being that facilitates the achievement of individual and societal goals (SAEM, 1992). All of these definitions focus on the impact an individual's health status has on his or her quality of life.

Health has several determinants or influences that impact the status of an individual's health. The individual lifestyle factors such as age, sex, and **constitutional factors** are direct determinants of a person's health. Within the immediate environment of an individual, there are social and community networks—external influences on health. In addition to the **social and community networks**, there are also the general **macroenvironmental conditions** of socioeconomic, cultural, and environmental conditions that impact health, such as education, work environment, living and working conditions, healthcare services, food production, unemployment, water and sanitation, and housing. These **determinants of health** depicted in **FIGURE 5-1** tie into the role of public health in the healthcare delivery system because public health focuses on the impact of these determinants on an individual's health. Public health provides health education and other preventive activities to consumers so they will understand the negative impact these determinants may have on their health status. These activities are often categorized as primary, secondary, and occasionally tertiary prevention (Determinants of Health, 2016).

Primary prevention activities focus on reducing disease development. Smoking cessation programs, immunization programs, educational programs for pregnancy, and employee safety education are all examples of primary prevention programs. **Secondary prevention** activities refer to early detection and

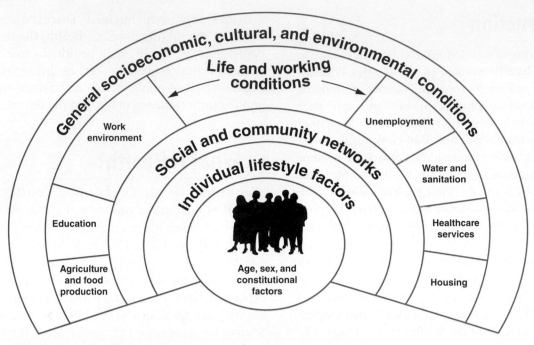

FIGURE 5-1 **Dahlgren and Whitehead Model of Health Determinants, 1991**

Dalhgren, G., & Whitehead, M (1991). Policies and Strategies to Promote Social Equity in Health. Stockholm, Sweden: Institute for Future Studies. Reprinted by permission.

treatment of diseases. The goal of secondary prevention is to stop the progression of disease. Blood pressure screenings, colonoscopies, and mammograms are examples of secondary prevention. **Tertiary prevention** activities focus on activities to rehabilitate and monitor individuals during disease progression.

Activities may also include patient behavior education to limit disease impact and reduce progression (What researchers mean, 2016). Although public health professionals may participate in each area of prevention activities, they focus primarily on primary and secondary prevention. See **TABLE 5-1**.

TABLE 5-1 Primary, Secondary, and Tertiary Prevention

	Primary	Secondary	Tertiary
Aim	Reduce disease development	Prevent disease progression by early detection and intervention	Disease management to reduce progress
Disease Phase	Specific risk factors associated with disease onset Factors associated with protection against disease	Early disease stage	Later disease stages
Target	Total population, selected groups, and healthy individuals	Early disease individuals with established high-risk factors	Patients
Examples	– Immunization programs – Education programs for pregnancy – Smoking cessation programs	– Blood pressure screenings – Mammograms – Colonoscopies	– Rehabilitation of stroke patients – Self-management programs for chronic individuals – Patient behavior education

▸ Origins of Public Health

During the 18th and 19th centuries, the concept of public health was born. Edwin Chadwick, Dr. John Snow, and Lemuel Shattuck demonstrated a relationship between the environment and disease that established the foundation of public health.

In 1842, **Edwin Chadwick** published the *Report on the Sanitary Condition of the Labouring Population of Great Britain*. His report highlighted the relationship between unsanitary conditions and disease (Rosen, 1958). As Chief Commissioner of the Poor Law Commission, Chadwick was responsible for relief to the poor in England and Wales. He became the champion of reform for working conditions. His report illustrated that the poor had higher rates of disease than the upper class, a fact that still exists today. His activities became the basis for U.S. public health activities (Rosen, 1958). He was also responsible for the implementation of the 1848 Public Health Act, which created England's first national board of health. Unfortunately, in 1854, the Parliament did not renew the Act, which consequently dissolved the board of health. Although dissolved, the concept of public health was born because this Act, using data, identified several public health issues that were assigned to national and local boards. Public health issues such as water, sewerage, environment, safety, and food were a focus of the act. By identifying these community issues, people began to focus on improving the community's health status (Ashton & Sram, 1998).

Dr. John Snow, a famed British anesthesiologist, is more famous for investigating the cholera epidemics in London in the 1800s. He made the connection between contaminated water and the spread of cholera. Dr. Snow surveyed local London residents and discovered that those who were ill had retrieved water from a specific neighborhood pump on Broad Street. When the pump handle was removed, the disease ceased. This famous Broad Street pump incident became a classic example of an epidemiologic investigation that studies the causes between disease and external sources (Ellis, 2008).

Lemuel Shattuck, who has been called the architect of the public health infrastructure, wrote the landmark report, *Report of the Sanitary Commission of Massachusetts*. It was ignored for many years but finally, in the 19th century, it became central to the development of state and local public health activities (Rosen, 1958).

As a result of their work, public health law was enacted and, by the 1900s, public health departments were focused on the environment and its relationship to disease outbreaks. Disease control and health education also became integral components of public health departments.

▸ What Is Public Health?

Overview of the Public Health System

According to the Centers for Disease Control and Prevention (CDC), public health systems are commonly defined as "all public, private, and voluntary entities that contribute to the delivery of essential public health services within a jurisdiction." **FIGURE 5-2** provides an overview of the components of public health, which include (CDC, 2016a):

- Public health agencies at state and local levels
- Healthcare providers
- Public safety agencies
- Human service and charity organizations
- Education and youth development organizations
- Recreation and arts-related organizations
- Economic and philanthropic organizations
- Environmental agencies and organizations

In 1945, in conjunction with Haven Emerson and C.E.A Winslow, the **American Public Health Association** (APHA) issued a set of guidelines for the basic functions of the local health department, including (Emerson, 1945):

- Vital statistics: data management of the essential facts on births, deaths, and reportable diseases
- Communicable disease control: management of tuberculosis, venereal disease, and malaria
- Sanitation: management of the environment, including milk, water, and dining
- Laboratory services
- Maternal and child health: management of school-aged children's health
- Health education of the general public

These functions remained the cornerstone of public health until the 1960s when the APHA, reacting to cultural and political changes, revised the definition of the core public health functions. The APHA issued the following guidelines for the core public health functions (APHA, 2016):

- Health surveillance, planning, and program development
- Health promotion of local health activities
- Development and enforcement of sanitation standards
- Health services provisions

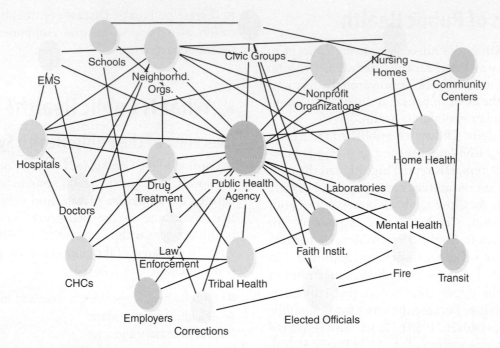

FIGURE 5-2 **Public Health Participants**

The IOM, as a result of an in-depth study of public health, stated that the three **core public health functions** of public health are (IOM, 1988):

- Assessment, which includes surveillance, identifying problems, data collection, and analysis
- Policy development, which includes developing policies to address public problems
- Assurance, which includes evaluating policies that meet program goals

These core public health functions became accepted by public health departments; however, there was some confusion about the terminology. In 1994, the Public Health Steering Committee, as part of the U.S. Public Health Service, issued a list of essential public health services that provided specific information on the implementation of the core public health functions and how they should be implemented (see **TABLE 5-2**).

▶ The Epidemiology Triangle

Epidemiology is the study of disease distribution and patterns among populations. Epidemiologists search for the relationship of those patterns of disease to the causes of the disease. They scientifically collect data to determine what has caused the spread of the disease. Epidemiology is the foundation for public health because its focus is to prevent disease from reoccurring. Epidemiologists identify three major risk factor

categories for disease. These three factors are called the **epidemiology triangle** (see **FIGURE 5-3**), which consists of the host, which is the population that has the disease; the agent or organism, which is causing the disease; and the environment, or where the disease is occurring (CDC, 2016b). Public health workers attempt to assess each factor's role in why a disease occurs. Based on this research, public health workers develop prevention strategies to alter the interaction between the host, the disease, and the environment so the disease occurrences will be less severe or will not occur again.

For example, a person (host) can be vaccinated against a disease to prevent the host from carrying the disease (agent). Procedures can be implemented such as sanitary regulations to protect the community condition (environment) from contamination.

▶ Epidemiologic Surveillance

An important component of epidemiology is **surveillance**, which is the monitoring of patterns of disease and investigating disease outbreaks to develop public health intervention strategies to combat disease. A new form of surveillance involves **biosurveillance**, which focuses on early detection of unusual disease patterns that may be due to human intervention. In 2012, as part of the National Security Strategy, a national strategy for biosurveillance was outlined that focused on an

TABLE 5-2 10 Essential Public Health Services Describing the Public Health Activities That All Communities Should Undertake

1. Monitor health status to identify and solve community health problems.

2. Diagnose and investigate health problems and health hazards in the community.

3. Inform, educate, and empower people about health issues.

4. Mobilize community partnerships and action to identify and solve health problems.

5. Develop policies and plans that support individual and community health efforts.

6. Enforce laws and regulations that protect health and ensure safety.

7. Link people to needed personal health services and ensure the provision of health care when otherwise unavailable.

8. Ensure competent public and personal healthcare workforce.

9. Evaluate effectiveness, accessibility, and quality of personal and population-based health services.

10. Research for new insights and innovative solutions to health problems.

Reproduced from Centers for Disease Control and Prevention. (2016). Core Functions of Public Health and How They Relate to the 10 Essential Services. Retrieved from http://www.cdc.gov/nceh/ehs/ephli/core_ess.htm

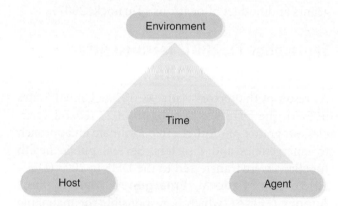

FIGURE 5-3 Epidemiological Triangle

Reproduced from Centers for Disease Control and Prevention. (2013). Understanding the Epidemiologic Triangle through Infectious Disease. Retrieved from http://www.cdc.gov/bam/epi-triangle.html

integrated decision-making strategy of activities at all levels. As the lead agency for public health activities, the CDC's role in supporting the strategy is to continue making the best use of electronic health data, managing unstructured health data, integrating biosurveillance data so health-related information can be shared rapidly, and strengthening global disease detection and cooperation with global health partners (CDC, 2016). Historically, surveillance activities have been passive and been initiated by public health workers through routine disease reports. However, public health has become more proactive by initiating contact with providers to assess any unusual disease pattern.

▶ Environmental Health

Since John Snow linked disease with environmental factors, the field of **environmental health** has been an integral component of public health. Environmental health workers often are responsible for investigating environmental hazards in the community and monitoring and enforcing environmental regulations. A subset of environmental health workers is occupational health workers, who focus on ensuring employees' working conditions are safe. Both state and local health departments have environmental health departments that are responsible for investigating and enforcing local regulations. The CDC has identified 10 essential environmental health services that relate to the core functions of public health assessment, policy development, and assurance (CDC, 2013c) (see **TABLE 5-3**).

▶ Emergency Preparedness

Federal Response

Public health preparedness is defined by the Department of Homeland Security (DHS) and the Federal Emergency Management Agency (FEMA) as "a continuous cycle of planning, organizing, training, equipping, exercising, evaluating, and taking

TABLE 5-3 Essential Health Services and Core Public Health Functions of Environmental Health

Assessment

Monitor environmental and health status to identify and solve community environmental health problems

Diagnose and investigate environmental health problems and health hazards in the community

Policy Development

Inform, educate, and empower people about environmental health issues

Mobilize community partnerships and actions to identify and solve environmental health problems

Develop policies and plans that support individual and community environmental health efforts

Assurance

Enforce laws and regulations that protect environmental health and ensure safety

Link people to needed environmental health services and ensure the provision of environmental health services when otherwise unavailable

Ensure a competent environmental health workforce

Evaluate effectiveness, accessibility, and quality of personal and population-based environmental health services

Research for new insights and innovative solutions to environmental health problems

Centers for Disease Control and Prevention. (2016). Core Functions of Public Health and How They Relate to the 10 Essential Services. Retrieved from http://www.cdc.gov/nceh/ehs/ephli/core_ess.htm

corrective action in an effort to ensure effective coordination during incident response." This cycle is one element of a broader National Preparedness System to prevent, respond to, and recover from natural disasters, acts of terrorism, and other disasters (DHS, 2016). These planning protocols are in place to manage a large-scale event: a natural disaster such as a hurricane, massive flooding, or chemical or oil spills, or a manmade disaster, such as the Boston Marathon bombing in 2013 or the terrorist attack of September 11, 2001. During a public health emergency, such as the California wildfires, Superstorm Sandy in New Jersey, and the tornados in Oklahoma, risk communication protocols are implemented to inform the public regarding the health issue and what should be done during a severe situation. Dissemination of information is handled through multimedia efforts such as radio, television, and print media. Depending on the level of disease threat, the federal government may intervene in a disease outbreak. If not, state and local public health departments are responsible for monitoring the disease threat. Unfortunately, severe public health crises can create secondary disease threats. These crises also can have an extreme psychological impact on the public. The public needs to be informed. Since the terrorist attacks in 2001, simulations of public health emergencies have been staged across vulnerable areas of the United States, including large urban areas such as New York City and Las Vegas, to plan

for these possible events. Public health funding for state activities such as these are largely from CDC grants and budget allocations (Turnock, 2007).

September 11, 2001, Terrorist Attack Impact on Public Health

As result of the terrorist attacks on the United States in 2001, the DHS was created from 22 federal agencies, programs, and offices to coordinate an approach to emergencies and disasters. Several public health functions were transferred to the DHS in 2003 (DHS, 2016). The **Federal Emergency Management Agency (FEMA)**, which is responsible for managing catastrophic events, was integrated into the DHS in 2003. Together, they are responsible for coordinating efforts at all governmental levels to ensure emergency preparedness for any catastrophic events such as bioterrorism; chemical and radiation emergencies; mass casualties as a result of explosions, natural disasters, and severe weather; and disease outbreaks. They coordinate with the CDC to ensure there are plans in place to quickly resolve these events.

Within the DHS, the Emergency Preparedness and Response Directorate coordinates emergency medical response in the event of a public health emergency. Some states have created their own homeland security offices that coordinate with the federal DHS. The **National Response Framework (NRF)**, created by the DHS, presents the guiding principles that enable all response partners to prepare for and provide a unified national response to disasters and emergencies. It establishes a comprehensive, national, all-hazards approach to domestic incident response. The NRF defines the principles, roles, and structures that organize how we respond as a nation. It also describes how communities, states, the federal government, the private sector, and nongovernmental partners collaborate to coordinate national response. Further, it describes "best practices" for managing incidents and builds on the **National Incident Management System (NIMS)**, which provides a framework for managing incidents. Information on the NRF, including documents, annexes, references, briefings, and trainings, can be accessed from the NRF Resource Center (FEMA, 2016).

▶ State and Local Response to Disasters

State and Local Health Department Planning in Emergency Preparedness

The state and local health departments play a major role in managing emergencies. The CDC has developed national standards for both state and local health departments to develop capabilities to deal with emergencies as part of their strategic plans. The following are the capabilities as outlined by the CDC (2016d):

- Capability 1: **Community preparedness**: The local health department has to assess its own and the community's capability to respond quickly to a threat. It is also important to assess the impact of the threat.
- Capability 2: **Community recovery**: The ability to collaborate with community partners (e.g., healthcare organizations, businesses, schools, and emergency management) to plan and advocate for the rebuilding of public health, medical, and mental–behavioral health systems to at least a level of functioning comparable to pre-incident levels, and improved levels when possible.
- Capability 3: **Emergency operations coordination**: The ability to direct and support an event or incident with public health or medical implications by establishing a standardized, scalable system of oversight, organization, and supervision consistent with jurisdictional standards and practices and with the National Incident Management System.

- Capability 4: **Emergency public information and warning system**: The ability to develop, coordinate, and disseminate information, alerts, warnings, and notifications to the public and incident management responders.
- Capability 5: **Fatality management**: The ability to coordinate with other organizations (e.g., law enforcement, healthcare, emergency management, and medical examiner or coroner) to ensure the proper recovery, handling, identification, transportation, tracking, storage, and disposal of human remains and personal effects; certify cause of death; and facilitate access to mental and behavioral health services for the family members, responders, and survivors of an incident.
- Capability 6: **Information sharing**: The ability to conduct multijurisdictional, multidisciplinary exchange of health-related information and situational awareness data among federal, state, local, territorial, and tribal levels of government and the private sector. This capability includes the routine sharing of information as well as issuing of public health alerts to federal, state, local, territorial, and tribal levels of government and the private sector in preparation for, and in response to, events or incidents of public health.
- Capability 7: **Mass care**: The ability to coordinate with partner agencies to address the public health, medical, and mental and behavioral health needs of those impacted by an incident at a congregate location. This capability includes the coordination of ongoing surveillance and assessment to ensure that health needs continue to be met as the incident evolves.
- Capability 8: **Medical countermeasure dispensing**: The ability to provide medical countermeasures (including vaccines, antiviral drugs, antibiotics, antitoxin, etc.) in support of treatment or prophylaxis (oral or vaccination) to the identified population in accordance with public health guidelines, recommendations, or both.
- Capability 9: **Medical materiel management and distribution**: The ability to acquire, maintain (e.g., cold-chain storage or other storage protocol), transport, distribute, and track medical materiel (e.g., pharmaceuticals, gloves, masks, and ventilators) during an incident and to recover and account for unused medical materiel, as necessary, after an incident.
- Capability 10: **Medical surge**: The ability to provide adequate medical evaluation and care during events that exceed the limits of the normal medical infrastructure of an affected community. It

encompasses the ability of the healthcare system to survive a hazard impact and maintain or rapidly recover operations that were compromised.

■ Capability 11: **Nonpharmaceutical interventions**: The ability to recommend to the applicable agency (if not public health) and implement, if applicable, strategies for disease, injury, and exposure control. Strategies include the following: isolation and quarantine of diseased individuals; restrictions on movement and travel advisories; and warnings of high-risk areas that may be hot zones for disease outbreaks.

■ Capability 12: **Public health laboratory testing**: The ability to conduct rapid and conventional detection, characterization, confirmatory testing, data reporting, investigative support, and laboratory networking to address actual or potential exposure to all hazards. Hazards include chemical, radiological, and biological agents in multiple matrices that may include clinical samples, food, and environmental samples (e.g., water, air, and soil). This capability supports routine surveillance, including pre-event or pre-incident and post-exposure activities.

■ Capability 13: **Public health surveillance and epidemiological investigation**: The ability to create, maintain, support, and strengthen routine surveillance and detection systems and epidemiological investigation processes, as well as to expand these systems and processes in response to incidents of public health significance.

■ Capability 14: **Responder safety and health**: The ability to protect public health agency staff responding to an incident and the ability to support the health and safety needs of hospital and medical facility personnel, if requested.

■ Capability 15: **Volunteer management**: The ability to coordinate the identification, recruitment, registration, credential verification, training, and engagement of volunteers to support the jurisdictional public health agency's response to incidents of public health significance.

Incident Command System and Public Health

The **Incident Command System (ICS)** is used by police, fire, and emergency management agencies. The ICS eliminates many communication problems, spans of control, organizational structures, and differences in terminology when multiple agencies respond to an emergency event. The ICS is a coordinator for an emergency event. It controls situations and makes decisions about how to manage emergencies. The ICS coordinates all responders to the event, which increases management effectiveness. Local public health agencies work with first responders such as fire and rescue, emergency medical service, law enforcement, physicians, and hospitals in managing health-related emergencies. Most local public health agencies provide epidemiology and surveillance, food safety, communicable disease control, and health inspections. Many state public health agencies provide laboratory services. Because public health is now considered an integral component to battling terrorism and, consequently, a matter of national security, federal funding has dramatically increased. The Emergency Management Institute, which is the training unit for FEMA, provides training both on ground and online (free of charge) individuals who are interested in emergency preparedness (FEMA, 2016).

▶ Bioterrorism

According to the CDC, **bioterrorism** is an attack on a population by deliberately releasing viruses, bacteria, or other germs or agents that will contribute to illness or death in people (CDC, 2016e). These can be spread throughout the environment through air or water or in food. These agents can be difficult to detect and may take a period of time to spread. The DHS, the American Red Cross (ARC), the American Medical Association (AMA), and the Environmental Protection Agency (EPA) have developed educational campaigns regarding the U.S. response to bioterrorism. Since the September 11, 2001, terrorist attacks on the United States, bioterrorism has become a reality.

More than 20 federal departments and agencies have roles in preparing for a bioterrorist attack. In 2002, the **Public Health Security and Bioterrorism Preparedness and Response Act** provided grants to hospitals and public health organizations to prepare for bioterrorism as a result of September 11, 2001. Funding supports increased public health infrastructures and programs and increased laboratory testing, and the development of programs to detect bioterrorist threats. The **U.S. Food and Drug Administration (FDA)** also has additional responsibilities in the detection of food as a threat to community health (USFDA, 2016). Bioterrorism preparedness involves federal, state, and local health departments as well as input from other organizations. When a disaster, such as a bioterrorist attack, occurs, responses from both the federal and the state level may take as much as 24 hours; therefore, it is vital that local health departments, because they are at the front line of public health interventions, have a plan in place for immediate intervention. In terms of emergency responders, local health departments are the frontline organizations to assess an emergency situation (Turnock, 2007).

▶ Public Health Functions and Administration

Accreditation of Public Health Departments

The 2003 IOM report discussed above recommends a national accreditation system for public health agencies because there is no national accrediting body to institute standards. In 2004, the CDC and the Robert Wood Johnson Foundation (RWJF) funded a study, the **Exploring Accreditation Project (EAP)**, to assess accreditation of public health agencies. Based on this information, in 2007, the **Public Health Accreditation Board (PHAB)** was formed as a nonprofit organization dedicated to improving and protecting the health of the public by advancing the quality and performance of tribal, state, local, and territorial public health departments. This accreditation ensures that the health departments deliver the core functions of public health and essential public health services. In 2011, public health department accreditation became mandatory. Based on population served, there is a fee for this accreditation. As of February 2016, there were 96 accredited health departments with 258 departments in the process of the accreditation program (PHAB, 2016).

National Association of Local Boards of Health

Established in 1992, as a membership organization, the **National Association of Local Boards of Health (NALBOH)** informs, guides, and is the national voice for boards of health. In today's public health system, the leadership role of boards of health makes them an essential link between public health services and a healthy community. NALBOH provides technical expertise in governance and leadership, board development, health priorities, and public health policy at the local level (About NALBOH, 2016).

Influence of the Institute of Medicine Reports on Public Health Functions

In 1988, the IOM published a report, *The Future of Public Health*, which indicated that although the health

of the American people has been improved through public health measures such as consumer food regulations, water safety standards, and control of epidemic diseases, the public has come to take public health measures for granted. The report indicated that there was an attrition of public health activities in protecting the community because of this attitude (IOM, 1988). The report established recommendations for reorganizing public health that emphasized population-based strategies rather than personal healthcare delivery. There was poor collaboration between public health and private medicine, no strong mission statement, weak leadership, and politicized decision making. Three core public health functions were identified: **assessment**, **policy development**, and **assurance**. Assessment was recommended because it focused on systematic continuous data collection of health issues, which would ensure that public health agencies were vigilant in protecting the public. Policy development was also mentioned but the recommendation was to ensure that any policies were based on valid data to avoid any political decision making. Policy development was recommended to include planning at all health levels, not just at the federal level. Federal agencies should support local health planning. Assurance focused on evaluating any processes that had been put in place to ensure that the programs were being implemented appropriately (IOM, 1988). These core functions will ensure that public health remains focused on the community, has programs in place that are effective, and has an evaluation process in place to determine whether programs work.

In 2002, the IOM published a second, more in-depth report, *The Future of the Public's Health in the 21st Century*, based on the 1988 report, which analyzed public health as a system. The 2002 report discussed several deficiencies first noted in their 1988 report. Deficiencies included:

- Fragmented governmental public health infrastructures;
- Passive community participation in public health activities;
- Lack of healthcare delivery coordination;
- Lack of participation of businesses in influencing health activities;
- Lack of coordination of media with the health arena; and
- Lack of academic institutions in community-based health activities.

Recommendations to rectify these deficiencies included:

- Development of a national commission to establish a framework for state public health law reform;

- Development of active partnerships between public health agencies and communities;
- Offering by insurance plans of preventive services as part of their plans;
- Collaboration between businesses and communities to develop health promotion programs;
- Expansion of public service announcements by media outlets to include health promotion marketing; and
- Increased funding for researchers who are interested in public health practice research (IOM, 2002).

The public health community continues to work on these deficiencies. Since the 2002 report, the IOM has published hundreds of reports including a global health perspective due to the recent Ebola outbreak and most recently the Zika virus (IOM, 2016).

▶ Healthy People Reports

The Healthy People series is a federal public health planning tool produced by the CDC that assesses the most significant health threats and sets objectives to challenge these threats (Novick & Morrow, 2008). The first major report, published in 1979, *Healthy People: The Surgeon General's Report on Health Promotion and Disease Prevention*, discussed five goals of public health: reduce mortality rates among children, adolescents, young adults, and adults and increase independence among older adults. Objectives were set for 1990 to accomplish these goals (HHS, 1979).

The **Healthy People 2000** report released in 1990, the *National Health Promotion and Disease Prevention Objectives*, was created to implement a new national prevention strategy with three major goals: increase life expectancy, reduce health disparities, and increase access to preventive services. Three categories (health promotion, health prevention, and preventive services) and surveillance activities were emphasized. *Healthy People 2000* provided a vision to reduce preventable disabilities and death. Year 2000 target objectives were set throughout the years to measure progress. An evaluation report in 2002 found that only 21% of the objectives were met, with an additional 41% indicating progress. Unfortunately, in the critical areas of mental health, there were significant reversals in any progress. There was also minor progress in the areas of chronic diseases and diabetes (CDC, 2013f).

The **Healthy People 2010** report, *Understanding and Improving Health*, based on the previous *Healthy People* reports and their progress, was released in 2000 (HHS, 2000). The report contained a health promotion and disease prevention focus to identify preventable threats to public health and to set goals to reduce the threats. There were two major goals: to increase the quality and years of healthy life and to eliminate health disparities. Nearly 1,000 objectives were developed with 28 focus areas. Focus areas ranged from access to care, food safety, education, and environmental health to tobacco and substance abuse. An important component of the *Healthy People 2010* report was the development of an infrastructure to ensure public health services are provided in a systematic approach. Infrastructure includes skilled labor, information technology, organizations, and research. A final review of the 2010 report indicated that of the 733 final objectives, 48% of those objectives demonstrated improvement toward their stated target, 23% met or exceeded their targets, and 24% moved away from their target objectives. These results indicate measured success (CDC, 2016g). Like *Healthy People 2000*, its major goals were to increase quality of life and life expectancy and to reduce health disparities. The goals for these reports are consistent with both Winslow's and the IOM's definitions of public health.

In 2010, **Healthy People 2020** was released. It contains 1,200 objectives that focus on 42 topic areas. According to the CDC, a smaller set of Healthy People 2020 objectives, called leading health indicators (LHIs), has been targeted to communicate high-priority health issues. The new interactive HealthyPeople.gov web site replaces the traditional print publication released for previous Healthy People initiatives. Objective information including objective number, objective text, baseline, target, and data source used can be found on the HealthyPeople.gov website (CDC, 2016h).

▶ Public Health Infrastructure

U.S. public health activities are delivered by many organizations, including government agencies at the federal, state, and local levels and nongovernment organizations including healthcare providers, community organizations, educational institutions, charitable organizations, philanthropic organizations, and businesses (Mays, 2008).

Government Contributions to Public Health

Federal

The federal government has the ability to formulate and implement a national policy agenda for public health (Lee, 1994). It also has the power to allocate funding to both governmental and nongovernmental organizations for public health programs at the state government level. If there is a major health threat in a community, direct federal activity may occur, such as investigating a disease outbreak or providing assistance during a major disaster. The majority of the federal government's activities focus on policy and regulatory development and funding allocation to public health programs. The major federal agency responsible for public health activities is the HHS and one of its agencies, the CDC, which is responsible for the following activities (Pointer, Williams, Isaacs, & Knickman, 2007):

- Data gathering and analysis, and surveillance and control
- Conducting and funding research
- Providing assistance to state and local government programs
- Formulating health policy
- Ensuring food and drug safety
- Ensuring access to health services for the poor and elderly
- Providing direct services to special populations

State

State public health agencies follow two basic models: a freestanding agency structure that reports directly to the state's governor or an organizational unit with a larger agency structure that includes other healthcare activities. The key feature of state agencies is their relationship with their local public health agencies, which are responsible for implementing state policy and regulations. Most states have public health activities distributed across many agencies that include environmental protection, human services, labor, insurance, transportation, housing, and agriculture (Mays, 2008).

Additional activities include (Pointer et al., 2007):

- Licensure of healthcare professionals
- Inspection and licensure of healthcare facilities
- Collection of vital statistics
- Epidemiologic studies
- Crisis management of disease outbreaks
- Disease registry
- Laboratory services
- Implementation and analysis of health policy
- Community health education

Local

Local government health departments are directly responsible for performing the majority of community public health services. The National Association of County and City Officials (NACCHO), which is the national advocacy organization for the 2800 local health departments nationwide, released the operational definition of a local health department, which is "what people in any community can reasonably expect from their local governmental public health presence. These activities include: adult and children immunizations, communicable disease surveillance, tuberculosis screening and treatment, environmental surveillance, population nutrition services, school/day care center inspections, health disparity activities, and food and safety education" (NACCHO, 2016c).

NACCHO has also developed a communications toolkit with fact sheets regarding public health departments. TABLE 5-4 is a fact sheet used to market the importance of public health departments to the community (NACCHO, 2016b).

Public Health Accreditation

In May 2007, the **Public Health Accreditation Board** was established to set standards for voluntary national accreditation for both state and local health departments. This accreditation ensures that the health departments deliver the core functions of public health and essential public health services. In 2011, public health department accreditation became mandatory. There is an accreditation fee, the amount of which is based on population served. As of February 2016, there were 96 accredited health departments with 258 departments in the process of the accreditation program (PHAB, 2016).

Medical Reserve Corps (MRC)

The Medical Reserve Corps was created in 2002 after the September 11, 2001, terrorist attacks. They operate under the umbrella of the DHHS but are housed primarily in local health departments nationwide. There are 1,000 MRCs, staffed by volunteer physicians, nurses, dentists, pharmacists, and other community workers who provide services during emergencies. They provided service during Superstorm Sandy, the domestic Ebola crisis, and the Boston Marathon bombing. The MRC network covers over 90% of the U.S. population (MRC, 2016).

Nongovernmental Public Health Activities

National Association of County and City Health Officials (NACCHO)

NACCHO is the advocacy organization for local health departments. Established in 1993 and located

TABLE 5-4 What Does the Local Public Health Department Do in Your Community?

Your local health department (LHD)—you may know it as your local "health department" or "public health department"—is a leader in improving the health and well-being of your community. This fact sheet describes the roles performed by LHDs in communities throughout the United States.

- Protects you from health threats, the everyday and the exceptional. Your LHD guards multiple fronts to defend you from any health threat, regardless of the source, and works tirelessly to prevent disease outbreaks. Your LHD makes sure the tap water you drink, the restaurant food you eat, and the air you breathe are all safe. It's ready to respond to any health emergency—be it bioterrorism, SARS, West Nile Virus, or an environmental hazard.

"Not content with merely a 'clipboard' role, checking for compliance with regulations, Marquette County (MI) food service health inspectors organize and conduct classes to advise restaurant managers how best to meet current food safety standards. These inspectors are resources as well as enforcers."

- Educates you and your neighbors about health issues. Your LHD gives you information that allows you to make healthy decisions every day, like exercising more, eating right, quitting smoking, or simply washing your hands to keep from spreading illness. They provide this information through public forums in your community, public service announcements in the media, programs in schools, health education in homes and clinics, and detailed websites. During a public health emergency, your LHD provides important alerts and warnings to protect your health.

"Effective health education can be fun and can promote creativity and self-esteem. Marquette County (MI)'s Health Education Division sponsors annual school-based tobacco control billboard contests. Kids' winning designs are displayed on highway billboards throughout the county."

- Provides healthy solutions for everyone. Your LHD offers the preventive care you need to avoid chronic disease and to help maintain your health. It provides flu shots for the elderly and helps mothers obtain prenatal care that gives their babies a healthy start. Your LHD also helps provide children with regular check-ups, immunizations, and good nutrition to help them grow and learn.

"Health professionals and seniors know that foot problems are a major source of disability. Every month, public health nurses hold foot care clinics at every senior center in Marquette County (MI). The nurses examine feet for problems, refer clients for assistance, and provide counseling on how to avoid disease complications and discomfort and 'be a friend to your feet.'"

- Advances community health. Your LHD plays a vital role in developing new policies and standards that address existing and emerging challenges to your community's health while enforcing a range of laws intended to keep you safe. Your LHD is constantly working—through research and rigorous staff training—to maintain its unique expertise and deliver up-to-date, cutting-edge health programs.

"Treatment for HIV/AIDS has evolved rapidly during the last several years. The staff of the Marquette County (MI) health department keeps up to date in preventing the spread of this awful epidemic through periodic, state-run training sessions."

Adapted with permission from the National Association for County and City Officials (NACCHO). http://www.naccho.org/advocacy/marketing/toolkit/upload/Fact_Sheet_1.doc

in Washington, DC, NACCHO provides support to nearly 3,000 local health department members, which include city, county, district, metro, and tribal agencies. NACCHO is staffed by nearly 100 physicians and public health experts and a 32-member board of directors that lobbies Congress for its public health agenda, promotes public health, and provides support for members (NACCHO, 2016a).

NACCHO has recently focused on providing guidance to local health departments on ways to market public health activities and their role in public health. As discussed earlier, in collaboration with the CDC, it provides support for **Mobilizing for Action through Planning and Partnerships (MAPP)**, a community-driven strategic planning process for improving community health. In collaboration with World Ways

Social Marketing, NACCHO has developed a logo with the tagline "Prevent, Promote, Protect," which can be used nationally by local health departments to help the public understand their role.

Community hospitals have been important to public health. The Hill-Burton Act of 1943, which financed hospital construction projects, required hospitals to provide charitable services and thus helped establish a tradition of charitable services among community hospitals. Hospitals may operate primary care clinics and sponsor health education programs and health screening fairs. The Joint Commission (TJC) requires hospitals to participate in community-health-assessment activities (TJC, 2013).

Ambulatory or outpatient care providers such as physician practices also contribute to community public health. Physicians may serve on local public health organizations or provide services to the uninsured for reduced fees. Hospitals, clinics, and nursing homes may also contribute to public health. Health insurers and managed care providers also make important public health contributions. All types of healthcare providers cooperate with state and local health departments by providing immunizations, offering patient education, screening for communicable diseases, and reporting disease information to health departments (Pointer et al., 2007). Health insurers and managed care providers have a large network of clients to encourage health promotion and health education activities. For example, a physical activity program for senior citizens, **Silver Sneakers**, was developed in 1992 and encouraged the elderly to participate in organized exercise at national fitness chains. Data is being collected to assess if those seniors visited their providers less because their health status increased. It is a free program to Medicare or Medicare supplement participants. In 2016, over 13,000 fitness facilities nationwide accepted the Silver Sneakers program (Healthways Silver Sneakers Fitness Program, 2016). The Affordable Care Act of 2010's focus is on primary and preventive care as well as increased access and improving the quality of healthcare services.

Nonprofit agencies such as the **American Cancer Society**, the **American Heart Association**, and the **American Lung Association** have active health promotion and health screening programs at the national, state, and local levels. The **United Way** is a civic organization that is active in identifying health risks and implementing community public health programs to target these risks. Established in 1905, the civic organization **Rotary International** is responsible for efforts to eradicate polio through vaccine programs throughout the world (Rotary International, 2016).

Philanthropic organizations such as the RWJF have provided funding for public health activities, including community education and intervention programs. The RWJF's goal is to improve the health of all Americans, and it has provided substantial funds for research activities to combat public health issues such as obesity and smoking (RWJF, 2016).

Council of State and Territorial Epidemiologists (CSTE)

Established in 1992 and headquartered in Atlanta, Georgia, the **Council of State and Territorial Epidemiologists (CSTE)** is a professional organization of over 1,000 public health epidemiologists who work in state and local health departments and provide technical assistance to the **Association of State and Territorial Health Officials (ASTHO)** and to the CDC for research and policy issues. They provide expertise in the areas of maternal child health, infectious diseases, environmental health, injury epidemiology, occupational health, and public health informatics (CSTE, 2016).

Association of State and Territorial Health Officials (ASTHO)

The ASTHO is a nonprofit organization that provides support for state and territorial health agencies. Members provide research, expertise, and guidance for health policy issues. The federal government looks to ASTHO for expertise in developing health policy. ASTHO members frequently testify in front of Congress regarding major health issues. They advocate for increased public health funding and campaign against any funding reductions. ASTHO provides training opportunities for state public health leaders. All states and U.S. territories and the District of Columbia belong to ASTHO (ASTHO, 2016).

Public health, nursing, and medical schools are also major contributors to public health activities. Faculty from these schools often provide technical assistance to local public health organizations and often partner with organizations to establish health programs. The schools may also provide specific educational programs that are tailored to community needs. Educational accreditation organizations are also encouraging educational programs to participate in community health activities. Harvard University's School of Public Health has established several centers to advance research in public health, such as health communication, injury control, AIDS, health promotion, and population and development studies (Harvard School of Public Health, 2013).

▶ Public Health Education and Health Promotion

Public health educational strategies are a crucial component to public health interventions. **Health education** focuses on changing health behavior through educational interventions such as multimedia education and classes. **Health promotion**, a broader intervention term in public health, encompasses not only educational objectives and activities but also organizational, environmental, and economic interventions to support activities conducive to healthy behavior (Pointer et al., 2007).

Public Health Education Campaign

Educational strategies inform the community about positive health behavior, targeting those at risk to change or maintain positive health behavior. Many public health campaigns are performed by the local public health department and in collaboration with community organizations. There are several steps to planning and developing a successful **public health educational campaign** (Minnesota Department of Health, 2013).

- The first step in implementing a public health education campaign is to perform a community assessment to determine at-risk populations. Developing an effective educational campaign to target high-risk populations requires community participation.
- The next step is collaborating with the community for input on health issues and prioritizing target health issues.
- The third step is performing surveillance activities for specific data related to mortality and morbidity rates.
- The fourth step is to develop a pilot study to assess the effectiveness of the proposed campaign.
- The fifth step is to revise the campaign based on the pilot study.
- The sixth step is to implement the chosen campaign for a period of time.
- The seventh step is to perform an evaluation of the impact of the campaign and revise, if needed.

Minnesota Department of Health, 2013.

Public Health Education Evaluation

Educational activities can be difficult to measure because of their abstract nature. It is important that specific outcome measures are developed prior to the campaign. Each measure should address the following parameters: (1) specific target group, (2) change in and type of behavior, (3) time frame for change, and (4) defined geographic area of change (Novick & Morrow, 2008).

Health Promotion Activities

Most health promotion campaigns have more community health objectives than health educational campaigns that focus on specific target populations. Health promotion focuses on a comprehensive coordinated approach to long-term health behavior changes by influencing the community through educational activities (Minnesota Department of Health, 2013). When the focus is at the community level, it is necessary to address **lifestyle behaviors** and to include cultural, economic, psychological, and environmental factors. Examples of health promotion include nutritional, genetic, or family counseling that would encompass health education activities. Health promotion may also include other community development activities such as occupational and environmental control and immunization programs (Turnock, 2007).

Public Health Marketing

According to the CDC, **health marketing** is an innovative approach to public health practice. Public health marketing draws from the business discipline of marketing theory and adds science-based health strategies of promotion and prevention. It involves creating, communicating, and delivering health information and interventions using customer-oriented and science-based strategies to protect and promote health in diverse populations (CDC, 2016i). Marketing research is used to deliver messages to educate the public on priority health issues.

Social media is electronic communication dedicated to community-based input, interaction, content-sharing, and collaboration. Websites and applications dedicated to forums, microblogging, social networking, social bookmarking, social curation, and wikis are among the different types of social media (Social Media, 2013). The most famous example is Facebook. Social media can be easily used as part of a health communications program.

Social media has also become a communication tool for patient engagement, employees, and providers. According to a September 2011 employee survey of IT professionals, administrators, and physicians, 75% use social media for professional purposes within their employment. The Mayo Clinic and the U.S. Department of Veterans Affairs are exploring ways to use social media for patient engagement, including education (Most Health IT Pros Use Social Media, 2011). Hospitals and academic medical centers are establishing more YouTube channels and Twitter accounts nationwide. Physicians use Twitter to communicate easily and quickly with other physicians. YouTube provides an opportunity for brief videos regarding certain healthcare education.

Because of the continued increase in social media use, the CDC Health Communicator's Social Media Toolkit (2011) contains recommendations for social media use in the healthcare industry:

1. Perform market research to determine key educational messages.
2. Review social media sites by user statistics and demographics.
3. Start a social media campaign by using low-risk tools such as podcasts and videos.
4. Base the educational messages in science.
5. Develop a system of easy viral sharing by patients so everyone can benefit from the message.
6. Social media users should listen to each other. If patients are voicing concerns or questions, they need to be answered.
7. Leverage social networks to expand the message. An average Facebook user has 130 friends with whom he or she can easily share a health message.

In addition to these recommendations, the federal government has established two websites for social media best practices and governance policies: http://govsocmed.pbworks.com/Web-2-0-Governance-Policies-and-Best-Practices http://socialmediagovernance.com/policies.php (CDC 2016j).

▶ Collaboration of Public Health and Private Medicine

Public health and private medicine have traditionally focused on different aspects of U.S. health. Public health focuses on primary prevention, specifically on the prevention of disease. Public health practitioners' approach is to develop strategies to promote community health. Private medicine has traditionally focused on tertiary care or providing a cure to individuals or patients. These approaches have traditionally been in conflict. In the 1920s, when public health clinics were treating the poor, private medicine felt threatened because these clinics were viewed as competitors (Reiser, 1996).

Prior to these activities, there were some collaborative activities in the early 1800s and early 1900s—many physicians were involved in public health. They realized the importance of public health in the role of infectious diseases. However, public health efforts were later resisted by physicians. They resented mandatory tuberculosis reporting, as well as immunization programs (Council on Scientific Affairs, 1990). When antibiotics were developed to combat diseases and the financial benefit of reimbursement of tertiary care by health insurance companies was realized, physicians' interest in public health dissipated (Lasker, 1997). They became more hostile because public health was viewed as a direct competitor.

Over the last decade, there has been an increase in the collaboration between public health and private medicine. In 1994, the AMA and the APHA established a long-term commitment that instituted the following initiatives to formalize a partnership: creation of joint research and local and national networks, development of a strategic plan, and development of a shared vision of health care. There has been an increase in collaborative efforts between the AMA and the CDC to develop healthcare programs to combat disease. The AMA is recognizing that obesity is a disease and should be treated as a disease rather than a behavior (AMA, 2016). With the increased prevalence of obesity, diabetes, and other chronic health conditions, this collaboration is crucial to develop strategies to reduce the rates of these diseases in the United States.

▶ Conclusion

Public health is challenged by its very success because consumers now take public health measures for granted. There are several successful vaccines that have targeted all childhood diseases, tobacco use has decreased significantly, accident prevention has increased, workplaces are safer because of the Occupational Safety and Health Administration (OSHA), the fluoridation of water is established, and there is a decrease in mortality from heart attacks (Novick & Morrow, 2008). NACCHO and ASTHO are important support organizations for both state and local governments by providing policy expertise, technical advice, and lobbying at the federal level for appropriate funding and regulations. When some major event occurs like a natural disaster, people immediately think that public health will automatically control these problems. The public may not realize how much effort, dedication, and research take place to protect the public. The Medical Reserve Corps provides needed support during difficult times.

As a healthcare consumer, it is important to recognize the role that public health plays in our health care. If you are sick, you go to your physician for medical advice, which may mean receiving a prescription. However, there are often times that you may not go see your physician because you do not have health insurance or you do not feel that sick or you would like to change one of your lifestyle behaviors. Public health surrounds consumers with educational opportunities to change a health condition or behavior. You can visit the CDC's website, which provides information about different diseases and health conditions. You can also visit your local health department. CDC has become very proactive in developing successful social media campaigns regarding public health issues. Traditional medicine has also become entrenched in social media as well. These tools are an effective way to communicate with a society that is so connected with social media applications on a daily basis.

The concept of public health has been more publicized in the 21st century because of the terrorist attacks of 2001, the anthrax attacks in post offices, the natural disasters of Hurricane Katrina and Superstorm Sandy, the Boston Marathon bombing, the Ebola and Zika virus epidemics, and flooding in the Midwest. Funding has increased for public health activities because of these events. The concept of bioterrorism is now a reality. Because public health is now considered an integral component to battling terrorism and consequently a matter of national security, federal funding dramatically increased. In addition to these major public health issues, the goal of the Affordable Care Act is to improve the accessibility and quality of the U.S. healthcare system. There are nearly 50 healthcare reform initiatives that are being implemented during 2010–2017 and beyond. Many of these initiatives focus on public health.

Wrap-Up

Vocabulary

American Cancer Society
American Heart Association
American Lung Association
American Public Health
  Association
Assessment
Association of State and
  Territorial Health Officials
  (ASTHO)
Assurance
Biosurveillance
Bioterrorism
Community preparedness
Community recovery
Constitutional factors
Core public health functions
Council of State and Territorial
  Epidemiologists (CSTE)
Determinants of health
Edwin Chadwick
Emergency operations
  coordination
Emergency public information
  and warning system
Environmental health
Epidemiology
Epidemiology triangle

Exploring Accreditation Project
  (EAP)
Fatality management
Federal Emergency Management
  Agency (FEMA)
Health
Health education
Health marketing
Health promotion
Healthy People 2000 report
Healthy People 2010 report
Healthy People 2020 report
Incident Command System
  (ICS)
Information sharing
Institute of Medicine (IOM)
John Snow
Lemuel Shattuck
Lifestyle behaviors
Macroenvironmental conditions
Mass care
Medical countermeasure
  dispensing
Medical materiel management
  and distribution
Medical Reserve Corps (MRC)
Medical surge

Mobilizing for Action through
  Planning and Partnership
  (MAPP)
National Association of County
  and City Health Officials
  (NACCHO)
National Association of Local
  Boards of Health (NALBOH)
National Incident Management
  System (NIMS)
National Response Framework
  (NRF)
Nonpharmaceutical interventions
Policy development
Primary prevention
Public health
Public Health Accreditation
  Board (PHAB)
Public health educational
  campaign
Public health laboratory testing
Public health preparedness
Public Health Security and
  Bioterrorism Preparedness
  and Response Act
Public health surveillance and
  epidemiological investigation

Responder safety and health
Rotary International
Secondary prevention
Silver Sneakers

Social media
Social and community networks
Surveillance
Tertiary prevention

U.S. Food and Drug
   Administration (FDA)
United Way
Volunteer management

References

About NALBOH. (2016). Retrieved from http://www.nalboh.org/About.htm

American Medical Association (AMA). (2016). Retrieved from http://www.ama-assn.org/ama/pub/advocacy/current-topics-advocacy.shtml

HHS, Prevention and Public Health Fund. (2016). Retrieved from http://www.hhs.gov/open/prevention/index.html

10 essential public health services. (2016). Retrieved from http://www.apha.org/about/news/pressreleases/2013/Historic+Affordable+Care+Act+offers+great+promise+for+protecting+nation's+health.htm

Ashton, J., & Sram, I. (1998). Millennium report to Sir Edwin Chadwick. *British Medical Journal*, 317, 592–596.

Association of State and Territorial Health Officials. (2016). Retrieved from http://www.astho.org/about/

Centers for Disease Control and Prevention (CDC). (2011). The health communicator's social media toolkit. Retrieved from http://www.cdc.gov/socialmedia/tools/guidelines/pdf/socialmediatoolkit_bm.pdf

CDC. (2016a). Core functions and capabilities of state public health laboratories. Retrieved from http://www.cdc.gov/mmwr/preview/mmwrhtml/rr5114a1.htm

CDC. (2016b). Understanding the epidemiologic triangle through infectious disease. Retrieved from http://www.bam.gov/teachers/activities/epi_1_triangle.pdf

CDC. (2016c). Environmental health services. Retrieved from http://www.cdc.gov/nceh/ehs/ephli/core_ess.htm

CDC. (2016d). Public health emergency response guide for state, local, and tribal public health directors. Retrieved from http://www.bt.cdc.gov/planning/responseguide.asp

CDC. (2016e). Bioterrorism. Retrieved from http://emergency.cdc.gov/bioterrorism/

CDC. (2016f). Healthy People 2000. Retrieved from http://www.cdc.gov/nchs/healthy_people/hp2000.htm

CDC. (2016g). Healthy People 2010. Retrieved from http://www.cdc.gov/nchs/data/hpdata2010/hp2010_final_review_overview.pdf

CDC. (2013h). Healthy People 2020. Retrieved from http://www.cdc.gov/nchs/healthy_people/hp2020.htm

CDC. (2016i). What is health marketing? Retrieved from http://www.cdc.gov/healthmarketing/whatishm.htm

Council of State and Territorial Epidemiologists. (2016). About CSTE. Retrieved from http://www.cste.org/?page=About_CSTE

Council on Scientific Affairs. (1990). The IOM report and public health. *Journal of American Medical Association*, 264, 4, 508–509.

Creation of the Department of Homeland Security. (2016). Retrieved from http://www.dhs.gov/creation-department-homeland-security

Determinants of health. (2016). Retrieved from http://healthypeople.gov/2020/implement/assess.aspx

Ellis, H. (2008). John Snow: Early anesthetist and pioneer of public health. *British Journal of Hospital Medicine*, 69, 2, 113.

Emerson, H. (1945). *Local health units for the nation* (p. viii). New York, NY: The Commonwealth Fund.

Federal Emergency Management Agency (FEMA). (2016). NRF Resource Center. Retrieved from http://www.fema.gov/nrf

Harvard School of Public Health. (2013). Research centers. Retrieved from www.hsph.harvard.edu/research/

Healthways Silver Sneakers Fitness Program. (2016). Retrieved from http://www.silversneakers.com

Institute of Medicine (IOM). (1988). *The future of public health*. Washington, DC: National Academies Press.

IOM. (1997). *Improving health in the community*. Washington, DC: National Academies Press.

IOM. (2002). *The future of the public's health in the 21st century*. Washington, DC: National Academies Press.

The Joint Commission (TJC). (2016). Hospital Accreditation. Retrieved from http://www.jointcommission.org/Accreditation Programs/Hospitals/

Lasker, R. (1997). *Medicine & public health: The power of collaboration*. New York, NY: Academy of Medicine.

Lee, B. (1994). *Health policy and the politics of health care: Nation's health* (4th ed.). Sudbury, MA: Jones and Bartlett.

Mays, G. (2008). Organization of the public health delivery system. In L. Novick & C. Morrow (Eds.), *Public health administration: Principles for population-based management* (pp. 69–126). Sudbury, MA: Jones and Bartlett.

Medical Reserve Corps (MRC). (2016). Retrieved from http://naccho.org/advocacy/funding-priorities

Minnesota Department of Health. (2016). Community health promotion. Retrieved from http://www.health.state.mn.us/divs/hpcd/chp/hpkit/index.htm

Most health IT pros use Social Media. (2011). Retrieved from http://www.informationweek.com/healthcare/mobile-wireless/most-health-it-pros-use-social-media/231601331

National Association of County and City Health Officials (NACCHO). (2016a). About NACCHO. Retrieved from http://www.naccho.org/about/.

NACCHO. (2016b). Mobilizing for action through planning and partnerships. Retrieved from http://naccho.org/topics/infrastructure/mapp/index.cfm?&render

NACCHO. (2016c). Operational Definition of a Functional Local Health Department. Retrieved from http://archived.naccho.org/advocacy/marketing/toolkit/upload/PubHCommunications Toolkit.doc.

National strategy for biosurveillance. (2016). Retrieved from http://www.cdc.gov/surveillancepractice/reports/nbs.html.

Novick, L., & Morrow, C. (2008). A framework for public health administration and practice. In L. Novick & C. Morrow (Eds.), *Public health administration: Principles for population-based management* (pp. 35–68). Sudbury, MA: Jones and Bartlett.

Plan and prepare for disasters, DHS (2016). Retrieved from http://www.dhs.gov/topic/plan-and-prepare-disasters

Pointer, D., Williams, S., Isaacs, S., & Knickman, J. (2007). *Introduction to U.S. health care*. Hoboken, NJ: Wiley Publishing.

Public Health Accreditation Board. (2016). Retrieved from http://www.phaboard.org/news-room/accreditation-activity/

Reiser, S. (1996). Medicine and public health. *Journal of American Medical Association*, 276, 17, 1429–1430.

Robert Wood Johnson Foundation (RWJF). (2016). Retrieved from http://www.rwjf.org/about/

Rosen, G. (1958). A history of public health. New York: MD Publications.

Rotary International. (2016). Retrieved from http://www.rotary.org

Social Media. (2016). Retrieved from http://whatis.techtarget.com/definition/social-media

Society for Academic Emergency Medicine (SAEM), Ethics Committee. (1992). An ethical foundation for health care: An emergency medicine perspective. *Annals of Emergency Medicine* 21 (11): 1381–1387.

Turnock, B. (2007). *Essentials of public health*. Sudbury, MA: Jones and Bartlett.

U.S. Department of Health and Human Services (HHS). (1979). Healthy people: The Surgeon General report on health promotion and disease prevention. Publication no. 79-55071. Washington, DC: Public Health Service.

U.S. Department of Health and Human Services (HHS). (2000). Healthy people 1979. Retrieved from http://www.healthypeople.gov/document/html/uih/uih_bw/uih_2.htm#determanats

U.S. Food and Drug Administration. (2016). Counterterrorism legislation. Retrieved from http://www.fda.gov/Emergency-Preparedness/Counterterrorism/BioterrorismAct/default.htm What researchers mean by primary, secondary and tertiary prevention (2016). Retrieved from http://www.iwh.on.ca/wrmb/primary-secondary-and-tertiary-prevention

World Health Organization (WHO). (1942). Retrieved from http://www.who.int/about/definition/en/print.html.

WHO. (2016). Health promotion. Retrieved from http://www.who.int/healthpromotion/en/

Winslow, C. (1920). The untitled fields of public health. *Science*, 51, 23.

▶ Notes

▶ **Student Activity 5-1**

In Your Own Words

Based on this chapter, please provide a description of the following concepts in your own words. DO NOT RECITE the text description.

Exploring Accreditation Project (EAP):

_____

_____

Determinants of health:

_____

_____

Mobilizing for Action through Planning and Partnership (MAPP):

_____

_____

Healthy People Reports:

_____

_____

Incident Command System (ICS):

_____

_____

Institute of Medicine (IOM):

_____

_____

Health promotion:

_____

_____

National Response Framework (NRF):

_____

_____

Public Health marketing:

_____

_____

▶ Student Activity 5-2

Real-Life Applications: Case Scenario One

Because of all of the media attention on terrorism, your grandparents, who are elderly, are very concerned about terrorist attacks on the United States. They hear the concept of "bioterrorism" and are worried they will be poisoned. They do not understand the role public health departments play in protecting the public from terrorism. As the director of the local health department, you explain that you have a disaster plan prepared in case there is a natural or manmade disaster in the community.

Activity

(1) Define bioterrorism and how it can impact a community; (2) describe the coordination of the federal, state, and local health departments in a catastrophic event such as bioterrorism; and (3) explain the role that the public health department has in protecting special groups such as the disabled and elderly.

Responses

_____

_____

_____

_____

_____

_____

_____

_____

_____

_____

_____

_____

_____

_____

_____

_____

_____

Case Scenario Two

You are a business marketing major. You want to provide your expertise to your friend who is a public health nurse. She feels the need to market health strategies on reducing cigarette smoking in teens.

Activity

Develop a social media campaign for your friend using three forms of social media.

Responses

_____

_____

_____

_____

_____

_____

_____

_____

_____

_____

_____

_____

_____

_____

_____

_____

_____

_____

_____

Case Scenario Three

You have been offered a position with the American Public Health Association. You were not sure if it was a for-profit or nonprofit organization and whether its mission is to make money or to help people. You want to be sure that this will be a good fit for you.

Activity

Visit the American Public Health Association website and review the mission statement and the level of activities. Develop a pros and cons list to determine if you should take the job.

Responses

_____

_____

_____

_____

_____

_____

_____

_____

_____

_____

_____

_____

_____

_____

_____

_____

_____

_____

Case Scenario Four

You are working in a restaurant and are concerned about some safety issues. You mentioned it to the manager but the manager was not concerned. You feel you need to look for answers in another direction.

Activity

Visit the Occupational Safety and Health Administration website to find out what you can do regarding the issues in your workplace.

Responses

_____

_____

_____

_____

_____

_____

_____

_____

_____

_____

_____

_____

_____

_____

_____

_____

_____

_____

▶ Student Activity 5-3

Internet Exercises

Write your answers in the space provided.

- Visit each of the websites listed here.
- Name the organization.
- Locate the organization's mission statement on the website.
- Provide a brief overview of the activities of the organization.
- How do these organizations participate in the U.S. healthcare system?

Websites

http://www.fema.gov/nrf

Organization Name:

_____

_____

Mission Statement:

_____

_____

_____

Overview of Activities:

_____

_____

_____

Importance of Organization to U.S. Health Care:

_____

_____

_____

http://www.saem.org

Organization Name:

_____

_____

Mission Statement:

_____

_____

_____

Overview of Activities:

_____

_____

_____

Importance of Organization to U.S. Health Care:

_____

_____

_____

http://www.apha.org

Organization Name:

_____

_____

Mission Statement:

_____

_____

_____

Overview of Activities:

_____

_____

_____

Importance of Organization to U.S. Health Care:

_____

_____

_____

http://www.hsph.harvard.edu/research

Organization Name:

_____

_____

Mission Statement:

_____

_____

Overview of Activities:

_____

_____

Importance of Organization to U.S. Health Care:

_____

_____

_____

http://www.silversneakers.com

Organization Name:

_____

_____

Mission Statement:

_____

_____

_____

Overview of Activities:

_____

_____

_____

Importance of Organization to U.S. Health Care:

_____

_____

_____

http://www.medicalreservecorps.gov

Organization Name:

_____

_____

Mission Statement:

_____

_____

_____

Overview of Activities:

_____

_____

_____

Importance of Organization to U.S. Health Care:

_____

_____

_____

▶ **Student Activity 5-4**

Discussion Questions

The following are suggested discussion questions for this chapter.

1.   Define public health marketing. Do you think it will help change people's unhealthy behaviors?

_____

_____

_____

2.   What is the difference between the roles of the state health department and the local health department in providing health services?

_____

_____

_____

_____

_____

3.   Go to the ASTHO website. Based on your research, why is it important to state health departments?

_____

_____

_____

_____

_____

4. What is the purpose of the Public Health Accreditation Board? Do you feel it has been successful in its goals?

_____

_____

_____

_____

_____

_____

_____

_____

5. Discuss three of the capabilities developed by the CDC as national standards for emergency preparedness.

_____

_____

_____

_____

_____

_____

_____

_____

_____

▶ Student Activity 5-5

Current Events

Perform an Internet search and find a current events topic over the past three years that is related to this chapter. Provide a summary of the article and the link to the article and why the article relates to the chapter.

_____

_____

_____

_____

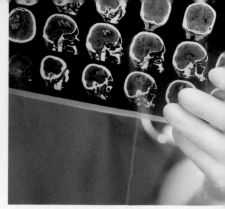

CHAPTER 6

Inpatient and Outpatient Services

LEARNING OBJECTIVES

The student will be able to:

- Identify and discuss three milestones of the history of the hospital.
- Define and discuss the different hospitals by their ownership classification.
- Describe the difference between hospitals by who they serve.
- Identify the different types of outpatient care settings.
- Analyze the utilization trends of both inpatient and outpatient services.
- Evaluate the difference between inpatient and outpatient services.

DID YOU KNOW THAT?

- Hospitals are the foundation of our healthcare system.
- Other terms related to "hospital" include hospitality, host, hotel, and hospice.
- Voluntary hospitals are called voluntary because their funding comes from the community voluntarily.
- According to the Urgent Care Association 2014 Benchmarking Survey, the number of urgent care centers has decreased from 9,000 in 2011 to 6,400 in 2013, with an average charge of less than $150 compared to the average emergency room visit cost of $1,354.
- Women seek healthcare services more frequently than men.
- Public hospitals are the oldest type of hospital and are government owned.
- Religious hospitals were developed as a way to perform spiritual work.

▶ Introduction

Inpatient services are services that involve an overnight stay of a patient. Historically, the U.S. healthcare industry was based on the provision of inpatient services provided by hospitals and outpatient services provided by physicians. As our healthcare system evolved, hospitals became the mainstay of the healthcare system, offering primarily inpatient with limited outpatient services. Over the past two centuries, hospitals have evolved from serving the poor and homeless to providing the latest medical technology to serve the seriously ill and injured (Shi & Singh, 2008). Although their original focus was inpatient services, as a result of cost containment and consumer preferences, more outpatient services are now being offered by hospitals. Hospitals have evolved into medical centers that provide the most advanced service. Hospitals can be classified by who owns them, length of stay, and type of services provided. Inpatient services typically focus on acute care, which includes secondary and tertiary care levels that most likely require inpatient care. Inpatient care is very expensive and, throughout the years, has been targeted for cost-containment measures. Hospitals have begun offering more outpatient services that do not require an overnight stay and are less financially taxing on the healthcare system. The percentage of the U.S. gross domestic product comprised of healthcare expenditures continues to increase, and consequently, more cost-containment measures have evolved. Outpatient services have become more prevalent because they are less expensive and they are preferred by consumers. This chapter will discuss the evolution of outpatient and inpatient healthcare services in the United States.

▶ History of Hospitals

The word hospital comes from the Latin word *hospes*, which means a visitor or host who receives a visitor. From this root word, the Latin *hospitalia* evolved, which means an apartment for strangers or guests. "Hospital" was a word in the Old French language. As it evolved in England in the 15th century, the meaning shifted to a home for the infirm, poor, or elderly. The modern definition of "an institution where sick or injured are given medical or surgical care" was developed in the 16th century. The name Hôtel-Dieu, "the hotel of God," was commonly given to hospitals in France during the Middle Ages (American Hospital Association, 2016).

Greek temples were, more than 5,000 years ago, the first type of hospital, with similar institutions in Egyptian, Hindu, and Roman cultures. Egyptian physicians were the first to use castor oil, opium, and peppermint as medications. Manhattan Island claimed the first U.S. hospital in 1663 for ill soldiers. They were the precursor of the **almshouses** or **poorhouses** that were developed in the 1820s to primarily serve the poor. The first almshouse was in Philadelphia; it was operated by the Quakers and open only to members of their faith. Eventually, in 1732, a public almshouse was established and eventually evolved into the Philadelphia General Hospital. The first incorporated hospital in America was the Pennsylvania Hospital, also in Philadelphia. Philadelphia is also credited with having the first quarantine station for immigrants (Pozgar, 2014).

In 1789, the Public Hospital of Baltimore was established for the indigent and, in 1889, it became Johns Hopkins Hospital, which exists today as one of the best hospitals in the world (Sultz & Young, 2006). In the 1850s, a hospital system was finally developed, but the conditions were deplorable because of the staff of unskilled providers.

Hospitals were owned primarily by the physicians who practiced in them (Relman, 2007), and therefore became more cohesive among providers because they had to rely on each other for referrals and access to hospitals, which gave them more professional power (Rosen, 1983).

In the early 20th century, with the establishment of standardized medical education, hospitals became accepted across socioeconomic classes and developed into the symbol of medicine. With the establishment of the American Medical Association (AMA), which protected the interests of providers, providers became more prestigious. In the 1920s, because of the development of medical technological advances, increases in the quality of medical training and specialization, and the economic development of the United States, the establishment of hospitals became the symbol of the institutionalization of health care and the acknowledgment of the medical profession as a powerful presence (Torrens, 1993). During the 1930s and 1940s, the ownership of hospitals changed from physician owned to church related and government operated (Starr, 1982). Religious orders viewed hospitals as an opportunity to perform their spiritual good works, so religion played a major role in the development of hospitals. Several religious orders established hospitals that still exist today.

In 1973, the first Patient Bill of Rights was introduced to represent the healthcare consumer in hospital care (AHA, 2016a). In 1972, the AHA had all hospitals display a "Patient Bill of Rights" in their institutions

(Sultz & Young, 2006). In 1974, the National Health Planning and Resources Development Act required states to have **certificate of need (CON)** laws to ensure the state approved any capital expenditures associated with hospital and medical facilities' construction and expansion. The Act was repealed in 1987, but as of January 2016, 36 states still have some type of CON mechanism (National Conference of State Legislatures, 2016). The concept of CON was important because it encouraged state planning to ensure their medical systems are based on need.

Hospitals are the foundation of our healthcare system. As our health insurance system evolved, the first type of insurance was hospital insurance. As society's health needs increased, expansion of different medical facilities increased. There was more of a focus on ambulatory or outpatient services because U.S. healthcare consumers preferred outpatient services and it was more cost effective. In 1980, the AHA estimated that 87% of hospitals offered outpatient surgery (Duke University Libraries, 2016). Although hospitals are still an integral part of our healthcare delivery system, the method of their delivery has changed. "Hospitalists," created in 1996, are providers that focus specifically on the care of patients when they are hospitalized (Nabili, 2013). This new type of provider recognized the need for providing quality hospital care. More hospitals have recognized the trend of outpatient services and have integrated those types of services into their delivery. In 2000, as a result of cuts required by the Balanced Budget Act of 1997, the federal government authorized an outpatient Medicare reimbursement system, which has supported hospital outpatient services efforts. There are over 5,600 hospitals in the United States. In 2013, hospitals employed almost 6 million employees and received over 600 million outpatient visits and 6.160 million visits to their emergency departments. More outpatient surgeries are now being performed outside the hospital center and in ambulatory surgery centers. There are nearly 5,600 hospitals in the United States, with almost the same number of ambulatory surgery centers (American Hospital Association, 2016a).

Hospital Types by Ownership

There are three major types of hospitals by ownership: (1) public, (2) voluntary or community, and (3) proprietary hospitals. **Public hospitals** are the oldest type of hospital and are owned by the federal, state, or local government. **Federal hospitals** generally do not serve the general public but operate for federal beneficiaries such as military personnel, veterans, and Native Americans. The U.S. Department of Veterans Affairs (VA) hospitals are the largest group of federal hospitals. They have high utilization rates by veterans. Taxes support part of their operations. In 2014, there were 211 federal hospitals. County and city hospitals are open to the general population and are supported by taxes. Many of these hospitals are located in urban areas to serve the poor and the elderly. Larger public hospitals may be affiliated with medical schools and are involved in training medical students and other healthcare professionals (Shi & Singh, 2008). Their services are primarily reimbursed by Medicare and Medicaid services and have high utilization rates. In 2014, there were 1,003 state and local hospitals (AHA, 2016b).

Voluntary hospitals are privately (not government) owned and nonprofit facilities. They are considered voluntary because their financial support is the result of community organizational efforts. Their focus is their community. Private, nonprofit hospitals are the largest group of hospitals. In 2014, there were over 3,000 nonprofit hospitals. **Proprietary hospitals** or investor-owned hospitals are for-profit institutions and are owned by corporations, individuals, or partnerships. Their primary goal is to generate a profit. They have the lowest utilization rates. In 2014, there were 1,053 proprietary hospitals (AHA, 2016b).

Hospital Types by Specialty

Hospitals may be classified by what type of services they provide and their target population. A general hospital provides many different types of services to meet the general needs of its population. Most hospitals are general hospitals. Specialty hospitals provide services for a specific disease or target population. Some examples are psychiatric, children's, women's, cardiac, cancer, rehabilitation, and orthopedic hospitals.

Other Hospital Classifications

Hospitals can be classified as single-unit or multiunit operations. Two or more hospitals may be owned by a central corporation. Multiunit hospitals are the result of the merging or acquiring of other hospitals that have financial problems. These chains can be operated as for-profit, nonprofit, or government owned. These hospitals often formed systems because it was more cost efficient. In 2014, over 3,000 hospitals, or 53% of all hospitals, are part of hospital systems. Hospitals can also be classified by length of stay. A short-stay or **acute care hospital** focuses on patients who stay an average of less than 30 days. Community hospitals are short term. A **long-term care hospital** focuses on patients who stay an average of more than 30 days. Rehabilitation and chronic disease hospitals are examples of long-term care hospitals. More than 90% of hospitals are acute or short-term (AHA, 2016b).

Hospitals can be classified by geographic location—rural or urban. Urban hospitals are located in a county with designated urban or city geographic areas. Rural hospitals are located in a county that has no urban areas. In 2014, there were 1,855 rural community hospitals. Urban hospitals tend to pay higher salaries and consequently offer more complex care because of the highly trained providers and staff. In 2014, there were 3,000 urban hospitals. Rural hospitals tend to see more poor and elderly patients and, consequently, have financial issues (AHA, 2016b). As a result of this issue, the **Medicare Rural Hospital Flexibility Program (MRHFP)** was created as part of the Balanced Budget Act of 1997. The MRHFP allows some rural hospitals to be classified as **critical access hospitals** if they have no more than 25 acute care beds, and are at least 35 miles away from another hospital, provide emergency care, and are eligible for grants to increase access to consumers. This classification enables them to receive additional Medicare reimbursement called cost plus. **Cost plus reimbursement** allows for capital costs, which enables these facilities to expand (Centers for Medicare & Medicaid Services [CMS], 2016).

Teaching hospitals are hospitals that have one or more graduate resident programs approved by the AMA. **Academic medical centers** are hospitals organized around a medical school. There are approximately 400 teaching hospitals that are members of the **Council of Teaching Hospitals and Health Systems** in the United States and Canada. These institutions offer substantial programs and are considered elite teaching and research institutions affiliated with large medical schools (Association of American Medical Colleges, 2016).

Safety-net hospitals are hospitals that provide more charitable care than other hospitals. They receive hospital disproportionate share payments from the Center for Medicare and Medicaid Services on the assumption they would be providing more uncompensated care to those populations. However, with the passage of the mandate of the voluntary expansion of Medicaid coverage in the Affordable Care Act, it was assumed there would be less uncompensated care.

As discussed previously, **church-related hospitals** are developed as a way to perform spiritual work. The first church-affiliated hospitals were established by Catholic nuns. These hospitals are community general hospitals. They could be affiliated with a medical school. **Osteopathic hospitals** focus on a holistic approach to care. They emphasize diet and environmental factors that influence health as well as the manipulation of the body. Their focus is preventive care. Historically, osteopathic hospitals were developed as a result of the antagonism between the different approaches to medicine—traditional or allopathic medicine versus holistic. Current trends indicate that practitioners of both branches of medicine now serve in each others' hospitals and respect the focus of each others' treatment (Shi & Singh, 2008).

▶ Hospital Governance

Hospitals are governed by a **chief executive officer** (CEO), a board of trustees or board of directors, and the chief of medical staff. The CEO or president is ultimately responsible for the day-to-day operations of the hospital and is a board of trustees' member. CEOs provide leadership to achieve their mission and vision. The **board of trustees** is legally responsible for hospital operations. It approves strategic plans and budgets and has authority for appointing, evaluating, and terminating the CEO. Boards often form different committees such as quality assurance, finance, and planning. In a recent AHA survey, CEOs indicated that in most hospitals, the two standing committees were **finance** and **quality**. Economic conditions and legal requirements have forced boards to become more goal oriented, so boards have developed very specific objectives that focus on quality and safety as well as finances. Hospital governance has evolved as hospital structures have changed. There are more hospitals that belong to a system of hospitals with one board that oversees the system making the individual hospital boards' subsidiary boards (Totten, 2012).

The **chief of medical staff** or **medical director** is in charge of the medical staff–physicians that provide clinical services to the hospital. The physicians may be in private practice and have admitting privileges to the hospital and are accountable to the board of trustees. The medical staff is divided according to specialty or department, such as obstetrics, cardiology, and radiology. There may be a **chief of service** that leads each of these specialties. The **operational staff** is a parallel line of staff with the medical staff. They are responsible for managing nonmedical staff and performing nonclinical, administrative, and service work (Longest & Darr, 2008; Pointer et al., 2007). It is in the best interest of the institution that the operational staff and the medical staff collaborate to ensure smooth management of the facility.

The medical staff also have committees, such as the following: a **credentials committee** that reviews and grants admitting privileges to physicians, a bylaws committee that reviews bylaw changes, a planning committee that oversees activities that relate to the mission and vision, a **medical records committee** that oversees patient records, a **utilization review committee** that ensures inpatient stays are clinically appropriate, an **infection control committee** that focuses on minimizing infections in the hospital, and a **quality improvement committee** that is responsible for quality improvement programs (Pozgar, 2014).

▶ Hospital Licensure, Certification, and Accreditation

State governments oversee the licensure of healthcare facilities, including hospitals. States set their own standards. It is important to note that all facilities must be licensed but do not have to be accredited. **State licensure** focuses on building codes, sanitation, equipment, and personnel. Hospitals must be licensed to operate with a certain number of beds.

Certification of hospitals enables them to obtain Medicare and Medicaid reimbursement. This type of certification is mandated by the U.S. Department of Health and Human Services (HHS). All hospitals that receive Medicare and Medicaid reimbursement must adhere to **conditions of participation** that emphasize patient health and safety. **Accreditation** is a private standard developed by accepted organizations as a way to meet certain standards. For example, accreditation of a hospital by The Joint Commission (TJC) means that hospitals have met Medicare and Medicaid standards and do not have to be certified. Medicare and Medicaid have also authorized the American Osteopathic Organization to jointly accredit their types of hospitals with TJC (TJC, 2016a). It is important to mention that TJC has had tremendous impact on how healthcare organizations are accredited. Since its formation in 1951, TJC has expanded its accreditation beyond hospitals. It accredits ambulatory care, assisted living, behavioral health care, and home care organizations; hospitals;

laboratory services; long-term care facilities; and office-based surgery centers. Accreditation of managed care organizations such as preferred providers and managed behavioral organizations ended in 2006 (The Joint Commission, 2016b).

International Organization for Standardization

Established in 1947 in Geneva, Switzerland, the **International Organization for Standardization (ISO)** is a worldwide organization that promotes standards from different countries. Although this is not an accrediting organization, those organizations that register with the ISO are promoted as having higher standards. ISO 9000 (quality management focus) and ISO 14000 (environmental management focus) are management standards that are applicable to any organization, including healthcare organizations, and many healthcare organizations are registered with the ISO. For example, the ISO has standards for healthcare informatics and medical devices (ISO, 2016).

▶ Patient Rights

The **Patient Self-Determination Act of 1990** requires hospitals and other facilities that participate in the Medicare and Medicaid programs to provide patients, upon admission, with information on their rights; it is also referred to as the Patient Bill of Rights. If you enter any hospital, you will see the Bill of Rights posted on its walls. This law requires that the hospital maintain confidentiality of patients' personal and medical information. Patients also have the right to be provided accurate and easy-to-understand information about their medical condition so they may give **informed consent** for any of their medical care.

The Affordable Care Act (ACA) created an additional Patient Bill of Rights that focuses on implementing consumer-oriented practices from insurance companies, which will help children and adults with preexisting conditions to obtain and keep insurance coverage, to end lifetime reimbursement limits on healthcare insurance reimbursements, and to increase the opportunities for consumers to choose their physicians (Fact Sheet, 2016).

▶ Current Status of Hospitals

Many hospitals have experienced financial problems. As a result of the increased competition of outpatient services (which are often more cost effective, efficient, and consumer friendly) and reduced reimbursement from Medicare and Medicaid, many hospitals have developed strategies to increase their financial stability. Due to pressure to develop cost-containment measures, hospitals are forming huge systems and building large physician workforces. In order to compete with the ACA's mandated state health insurance marketplaces where consumers can purchase health insurance, health insurance companies are developing relationships with hospitals, creating joint marketing plans, and sharing patient data (Matthews, 2011).

Over the years, outpatient services have become the major competitors of hospitals. Advanced technology has enabled more ambulatory surgeries and testing, which has resulted in the development of many specialty centers for radiology and imaging, chemotherapy treatment, kidney dialysis, and so on. These services were often performed in a hospital. What is even more interesting is that physicians or physician groups own some of the centers. They are receiving revenue that used to be hospital revenue. Hospitals have recognized that fact and have embraced outpatient services as part of their patient care. Hospitals have to continue to focus on revenue generation by operating more outpatient service opportunities; they own 25% of urgent care centers in the United States, 21% have ownership interest in ambulatory surgery centers, and 3% have sole ownership of outpatient centers (AHA, 2016a).

Quality Improvement Processes

Hospitals are employing different methods to improve quality and control costs. Their focus is the **Institute of Medicine's definition of quality in health care, which encompasses the following six dimensions.** Figure 6-1 represents the relationships of the patient and the quality dimensions of healthcare:

1. Safety: No medical errors that endanger the patient
2. Patient Centeredness: Patients informed about their care, producing a healthy outcome
3. Efficiency: Delivery of effective care in an economic manner
4. Effectiveness: Evidence-based medicine that produces a healthy outcome
5. Equity: Access to healthcare in order to produce a healthy outcome
6. Timeliness: Care is given in a timely manner to produce a healthy outcome (Six domains of healthcare quality, 2016).

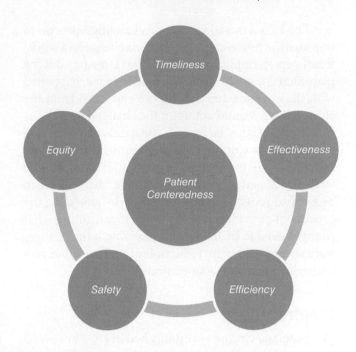

They also use the following models to assess quality health care:

- Lean Six Sigma: This approach, developed by Motorola, uses statistics to identify and eliminate defects in patient care. Healthcare facilities use this approach to focus on quality improvement processes and thereby improve patient health outcomes. This organizational effort is based on data-driven decision making. Lean six sigma drives customer satisfaction and bottom-line results by reducing variation in processes that could result in unsafe practices and waste that promotes inefficient use of resources, while promoting the use of work standardization, thereby creating a safer environment in the healthcare workplace as well as establishing a competitive advantage.
- **Plan Do Study Act (PDSA):** The Institute for Healthcare Improvement uses a four-step cycle to focus on improvement of workflow in the healthcare industry.

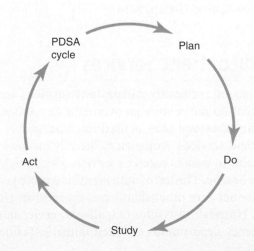

The PDSA model focuses on changing a process to improve the process. Providers **plan** change in a workflow (step 1), implement the change (**Do**-carry out the plan-Step 2), **study and summarize** what happened with the change (step 3), observe and learn from the change (Step 3), and **act** upon the change (Step 4).

Many of the large U.S. hospitals are working with the Joint Commission Center for Transforming Healthcare to implement processes that target safe and quality patient care. For example, the PDSA can be used to reduce medication errors by analyzing the process of providing medications, determining what changes need to be made, and assessing if the changes were successful by the reduction of medication errors (American Hospital Association, 2016b).

Leapfrog Group

The Leapfrog Group was established in 1998 by several large employers that purchase healthcare to find ways to assess the quality of health care services. The founders believed they could take "leaps" forward with their employees by rewarding hospitals that achieve quality and safety performance. In 2001, the Leapfrog Group initiated an annual hospital survey, endorsed by the National Quality Forum, to assess hospital safety performance standards to reduce preventable medical mistakes The surveys can be voluntarily completed by any U.S. hospital and are implemented annually. The survey data is for public consumption so consumers can find out which safety issues are occurring in their local hospitals. The 2015 survey includes data on computerized prescriber order entry, maternity care, and ICU physician staffing.

In June 2012, the Leapfrog Group initiated the Hospital Safety Score, a letter-grade rating of how well hospitals protect patients from accidents, infections, injuries, and errors. These data are collected from the Leapfrog Hospital Survey, the CMS, and the American Hospital Association to calculate a letter grade safety rating (Leapfrog Group, 2016).

▶ Outpatient Services

As discussed previously, **outpatient services** are services that do not require an overnight stay. Often, the term **ambulatory care** is used interchangeably with outpatient services. Ambulatory literally means a person is able to walk to receive a service, which might not always be true. The term "outpatient" is a more general term for services other than inpatient services (Jonas, 2003). Hospitals also offer outpatients service in their emergency departments and their outpatient clinics.

Physician Offices

The basic form of an outpatient service is a patient seeing his or her physician in the physician's office. Both general practitioners and specialists offer ambulatory care as either solitary practitioners or in group practice.

Traditionally, physicians established solo practices, but as the costs of running a practice increased, more physicians have established group practices (Pointer et al., 2007).

Hospital Emergency Services

Hospital emergency medical services are an integral part of the American healthcare system. Emergency departments provide care for patients with emergency healthcare needs. There were 160 million emergency department visits in 2013 (CDC, 2016a). Emergency department use is more likely among low-income people, people in fair or poor health, the elderly, infants and young children, and people with Medicaid coverage (CDC, 2016b). Hospitals traditionally provide inpatient services, though nearly all community hospitals provide emergency services that are considered outpatient services. Although emergency departments have the technology to treat emergency situations, many emergency rooms are used for nonemergency issues.

Hospital-Based Outpatient Clinics

Many outpatient clinics are found in teaching hospitals. They use outpatient clinics as an opportunity to teach and perform research. The clinics are categorized as surgical, medical, and other. Larger teaching hospitals may have 100 specialty and subspecialty clinics (Jonas, 2003). They may operate as part of the hospital or as a hospital-owned entity.

Urgent and Emergent Care Centers

Urgent and emergent care centers were first established in the 1970s, and are used for consumers who need medical care but whose situation is not life-threatening. This would take the place of the hospital emergency room visit. The medical issue usually occurs outside traditional physician office hours, so these centers see patients in the evenings and on weekends and holidays. Many of these centers are both walk-in and appointment facilities. They do not take the place of a patient's primary care provider. These centers are conveniently located and may be in strip malls or medical buildings so they are accessible for consumers. It is important to note that many managed care organizations will reimburse member visits because they are less expensive than an emergency room visit (Sultz & Young, 2006). The urgent care centers relieve the emergency departments from seeing patients who do not have life-threatening situations. It is anticipated that there will be an increase in urgent care centers because of this need.

According to the Urgent Care Association 2014 Benchmarking Survey, the number of urgent care centers has decreased from 9,000 in 2011 to 6,400 in 2013, with an average charge of less than $150 compared to the average ER visit cost of $1,354. Approximately 85% of the centers have a physician on site at all times, and 75% of the physicians are board certified in a primary specialty (Bannon, 2015).

Physicians (35.4%), private investors and insurers (30.5%), and hospitals (25.2%) are the top three owners of urgent care centers. Private equity firms invested nearly $4 billion in healthcare services in 2013, fueled predominantly by urgent care centers. This type of medical care has become the consumer preference because there is less wait time than for an emergency room visit (Dolan, 2013).

Ambulatory Surgery Centers

Ambulatory surgery centers (ASCs) are for surgeries that do not require an overnight stay. Physicians have taken the lead in developing ASCs. The first ASC was established in 1970. It provided an opportunity for physicians to have more control over their surgical practices as they grew frustrated by hospital policies, wait times for surgical rooms, and delays in new equipment. Advances in technology and newer anesthesia drugs to help patients recover more quickly from grogginess have enabled more surgeries to be performed on an outpatient basis. ASCs might focus on general surgical procedures that involve the abdomen, whereas specialized surgical centers focus on orthopedic surgery, plastic surgery, and gynecologic surgery. Some centers offer a combination of both general and specialized surgeries. Outpatient surgery is a major contributor to growth in ambulatory care. Approximately 8 million surgeries are performed in 4,000 ASCs annually. The most common procedure areas include ophthalmology; gastroenterology; orthopedic; ear, nose, and throat; gynecology; and plastic surgery. ASCs contribute to healthcare cost containment. Procedures at ASCs cost nearly 50% less than inpatient surgeries. Hospitals have ownership interest in 21% of ASCs and have sole ownership in 3% of ASCs. Patient surveys indicate over 90% customer satisfaction with their care and service (ASCA, 2016). **Health Centers** (HCs), which originated in the

1960s as part of the war on poverty, are organizations that provide culturally competent primary healthcare services to the uninsured or indigent population such as minorities, infants and children, patients with HIV, substance abusers, homeless persons, and migrant workers. They are supported by the Health Resources and Services Administration (HRSA) and operate on four fundamentals:

1. Located in high-service-need community;
2. Governed by a community board;
3. Provide comprehensive primary care; and
4. Must achieve performance objectives (HRSA, 2016b).

HCs often are located in urban and rural areas where there is a designated need. They enter a contract with the state or local health department to provide services to designated populations. They also provide links with social workers, Medicaid, and Health Insurance Program (HIP). As part of the ACA, funding increased for HCs. HCs may be organized as part of the local health department or other health service; they also operate at schools. In 2014, over 1,000 HCs received federal funding, providing care to over 22 million patients. HCs provide more preventive services to their designated populations, including healthcare education, mammograms, pap smears, and adult immunizations, than do other healthcare providers (DHHS, 2016c; Community Health Centers, 2016).

Home Health Agencies

Home health agencies and **visiting nurse agencies** provide medical services in a patient's home. The earliest form of home health care was developed by Lillian Wald, who created the Visiting Nurse Service of New York in 1893 to service the poor. In 1909, she persuaded the Metropolitan Life Insurance Company to include nursing home care in their policies (Lilian Wald, 2016). This care is often provided to elderly or disabled individuals or patients who are too weak to come to the hospital or physician's office or have just been released from the hospital. Contemporary home health services include both medical and social services, incorporating skilled nursing care and home health aide care, such as dispensing medications, assisting with activities of daily living, and meal planning. Physical, speech, and occupational therapy can also be provided at home. Medical equipment such as oxygen tanks and hospital beds may also be provided. Annually, approximately 4.7 million people receive home health services that are provided by approximately 12,000 agencies. These agencies can be private nonprofit, governmental, or private for-profit. Almost 80% of the agencies are for profit (Home health care, 2016). Although the home healthcare industry is very popular with patients, there have been continued problems with the quality of home health care being offered, as well as issues with fraudulent Medicare reimbursement for services not needed. Although most states offer licensing for home health agencies, it is important that home health agencies be Medicare certified because they are required to comply with CMS regulations. In 2011, approximately 3.4 million Medicare beneficiaries received home health services from almost 12,000 home health agencies. Access to home health care is generally adequate: 99% of beneficiaries live in a ZIP code where a Medicare home health agency operates, and 98% live in an area with two or more agencies. In 2011, Medicare implemented two major changes to strengthen program integrity for Medicare home health services. In April 2011, CMS implemented an ACA requirement for a face-to-face encounter with a physician or nurse practitioner when home health care is ordered. They can also receive accreditation from the Community Health Accreditation Program (CHAP) (Medpac, 2016).

Employee Assistance Programs

Employee assistance programs (EAPs) are a type of occupational health program, dating back to the 1940s, as an intervention for employee drug and alcohol abuse. The program has expanded to offer other services such as tobacco cessation programs, mental health counseling, and disease management and prevention health (Employee Assistance Programs, 2016).

▶ Other Health Services

Respite Care

Often, family and friends become the major caregivers of chronically ill patients. This continuous care can become stressful for those caregivers. These caregivers may still be working full time and have other family members that need their attention. As a result of this issue, **respite care** or **temporary care programs** were formally established in the 1970s to provide systematic relief to those caregivers who need a break. It also forestalls the ill patient from being placed in a facility. A variety of programs are considered respite programs, such as adult day care, furloughs to facilities for the patient, and in-home aides. Long-term care insurance may pay for a portion of respite care. Respite care is typically 14 to 21 days per year (DHHS, 2016).

Hospice

Hospice care provides care for patients who have a life-threatening illness and comfort for the patients' family members. It dates back to medieval times and focuses on a type of care, not a specific place of care; on palliative care, not curative treatment; and on the quality of life. Medicare, private health insurance, and Medicaid cover hospice care for qualified patients. Some hospice programs offer healthcare services on a sliding-fee-scale basis for patients with limited resources. The VA and private insurance plans will cover hospice services. A typical hospice care team includes the following:

- Doctors
- Nurses
- Home health aides
- Clergy or other spiritual counselors (e.g., minister, priest, rabbi)
- Social workers
- Volunteers
- Occupational, physical, and speech therapists

The family of the terminally ill patient is also involved in the care giving. Hospice services can be offered as both inpatient and outpatient services. Hospitals may have designated hospice units. Home health agencies may also offer a hospice program. Donations allow hospice care facilities to provide care at no cost to those who cannot afford it (WebMD, 2016).

Adult Day Services Centers

Adult day services centers are day programs that provide a medical model of care, with medical and therapeutic services; a social model, with meals, recreation, and some basic medical health; or a medical–social model, with social interaction and intensive medical-related activities, all depending on the needs of the patients. Adult day services centers were developed in the 1960s based on research that indicated that they were an opportunity to provide a break for informal caregivers as well as to prolong the patient's life at home. The average age of the adult day services center recipient is 72 years old, and two-thirds are women. There are 4,800 adult day services centers in the United States. They typically operate five days per week during normal business hours although some centers may offer weekend services (DHHS, 2016).

In 1979, the **National Adult Day Services Association (NADSA)** was formed to promote these types of community services. It has established national standard criteria for the operation of adult day services centers. Many adult day services centers are regulated by state licensing and may be certified by a particular community agency. They are often affiliated with larger formal healthcare or skilled nursing care facilities, medical centers, or senior organizations. More frequently, adult day services participants have higher levels of chronic conditions and disease, such as hypertension (46%), physical disability (42%), cardiovascular disease (34%), diabetes (31%), mental illness (25%), and developmental disability (20%). Approximately 50% of attendees have a form of dementia (NADSA, 2016).

Senior Centers

Established by the Older Americans Act of 1965, **senior centers** provide a broad array of services for the older population. Services provided include meal and nutrition programs, education, recreational programs, health and wellness programs, transportation services, volunteer opportunities, counseling, and other services.

According to 2015 statistics, there are 11,000 senior centers in the United States, serving approximately 1 million seniors every day; users spend 3 hours per day, 1 to 3 times per week, at the centers; 75% of users are women; and the average age of attendees is 75 years of age (National Council on Aging [NCOA], 2016). Funding is received from state and local governments, grants, and private donations.

Located in Washington, DC, NCOA is a not-for-profit advocacy agency for the senior population. As part of the NCOA, the **National Institute of Senior Centers (NISC)** is a network of senior center professionals who promote senior centers. It is the only national program dedicated to the welfare of senior centers. It sponsors a national voluntary accreditation program for senior centers (NCOA, 2016). With the estimated increase in life expectancy, senior centers will continue to expand and offer more services to seniors who have chronic disease that can be managed on an outpatient basis.

Women's Health Centers

Women have unique health needs that require specialized medical facilities. Recognizing this need, in 1991, the HHS established an **Office on Women's Health** (OWH). There are currently 10 regional offices that oversee women's health activities nationwide. Women's life expectancy is approximately 7 years longer than men's and will represent a larger portion of the elder population. The OWH mission is to promote women's and girls' health by gender-specific health activities (DHHS, 2016a).

Meals on Wheels of America

Established in 1954, the **Meals on Wheels Association of America (MOWAA)** is the oldest and largest national organization representing community-based senior nutrition programs; it has 5,000 member programs. These programs provide well over 1 million meals to seniors every day. Some programs serve meals at senior centers, some deliver meals directly to the homes of seniors whose mobility is limited, and many provide both services. Federal funding for Meals on Wheels is provided by the Senior Nutrition Program, authorized by the 1972 Older Americans Act. In October 2011, the U.S. Administration on Aging (AoA) entered into a cooperative agreement with MOWAA to establish a new National Resource Center on Nutrition and Aging (NRC). The primary role of the NRC is to cultivate innovative ideas related to nutrition and aging in the United States. As MOWAA members continued to receive increased demand for their services, they realized they needed to investigate more cost-effective ways to deliver meals to seniors. In 2015, they implemented a 15-week research study to determine which type of meal delivery methods were both cost effective and impactful on their seniors. The study results fully support the importance of the daily contact of the senior clients and the MOWAA workers (MOWAA, 2016).

Planned Parenthood Federation of America

Planned Parenthood Federation of America (PPFA) is a 90-year-old organization that provides family services to men, women, and teenagers regarding sexual health, family planning, and more, both online and at sites across the United States. Planned Parenthood provides sexual and reproductive health care, education, information, and outreach to nearly 5 million women, men, and adolescents worldwide in a single year.

Planned Parenthood accepts Medicaid but also offers services based on a sliding-fee scale. Planned Parenthood also works with partner organizations worldwide to improve the sexual health and well-being of individuals and families everywhere. Planned Parenthood has 59 independent local affiliates that operate more than 650 health centers throughout the United States. Planned Parenthood often is the only source of family planning for a large proportion of the women we serve (PPFA, 2016).

American Red Cross

Founded in 1881 and headquartered in Washington, DC, the **American Red Cross (ARC)** provides emergency response to victims of war and natural and manmade disasters around the world. It also offers services to the indigent and the military, analyzes and distributes blood products, provides education, and organizes international relief programs. Approximately 91 cents of every dollar spent is invested in humanitarian programs. There are over 700 local chapters with 35,000 employees supported by 500,000 volunteers in the United States. The ARC responds to approximately 70,000 U.S. disasters annually. It has a network of 13 million volunteers in 87 countries (ARC, 2016).

The PPFA's and the ARC's services are examples of the types of outpatient services offered in different communities across the United States. Organizations have recognized that outpatient services are preferred by healthcare consumers and are cost effective. Many physicians have established outpatient services as a way to satisfy consumer preference.

Doctors Without Borders

Established in 1971 by physicians and journalists in France, **Doctors Without Borders** is an international medical organization that provides quality medical care to individuals threatened by violence, catastrophe, lack of health care, natural disasters, epidemics, or wars in 60 countries. Eighty-eight cents of every dollar spent by the organization goes to direct program support. Staff are recruited from the communities where the crises are occurring as well as from the United States. The organization won the Nobel Peace Prize in 1999. A U.S. component of this organization was established in 1990 and recently raised $133 million in funding (Doctors Without Borders, 2016).

Remote Area Medical Volunteer Corps

Remote Area Medical (RAM) was founded in 1985 to develop a mobile, efficient workforce to provide free health care in areas of need worldwide. The first services delivered by the Remote Area Medical Volunteer Corps in the United States were in the Appalachian Mountains of the southeast, where 42% of the population is classified as rural, as compared to the national average of 20%. Volunteer physicians, nurses, and other healthcare professionals provide general medical, surgical, eye, dental, and veterinary care to thousands of individuals worldwide. However, 60% of their services are provided in the United States. RAM determines where the centers are most needed and set up a mobile healthcare unit for weekend services only.

RAM established a foundation in 1996 for the sole purpose of raising funds for RAM activities (RAM, 2016).

Telemedicine

According to the HRSA Office of Rural Health Policy, telemedicine or telehealth was developed about 40 years ago. This type of healthcare delivery uses technology for providing healthcare services and is an efficient method of providing outpatient care. Telemedicine is a new model for delivering health care—it moves information electronically to consumers quickly and efficiently without a patient physically seeing a healthcare provider. Telemedicine uses electronic information and telecommunication technologies to support long-distance clinical health care, patient and professional health-related education, public health, and health administration. Even in the reimbursement fee structure, there is usually no distinction made between services provided on site and those provided through telemedicine and often no separate coding required for billing of remote services.

According to the American Telemedicine Association, examples of the types of telemedicine provided include the following:

- **Primary care and specialist referral services** may involve a primary care or allied health professional providing a consultation with a patient or a specialist assisting the primary care physician in rendering a diagnosis. This may involve the use of live interactive video or the use of stored and forwarded transmission of diagnostic images, vital signs, or video clips along with patient data for later review.
- **Remote patient monitoring**, including home telehealth, uses devices to remotely collect and send data to a home health agency or a remote diagnostic testing facility (RDTF) for interpretation. Such applications might include a specific vital sign, such as blood glucose or heart ECG or a variety of indicators for homebound patients. Such services can be used to supplement the use of visiting nurses.
- **Consumer medical and health information** includes the use of the Internet and wireless devices for consumers to obtain specialized health information and online discussion groups to provide peer-to-peer support.
- **Medical education** provides continuing medical education credits for health professionals and special medical education seminars for targeted groups in remote locations.

Delivery mechanisms for telemedicine include the following:

- **Networked programs** link tertiary care hospitals and clinics with outlying clinics and community health centers in rural or suburban areas. The links may use dedicated high-speed lines or the Internet for telecommunication links between sites. ATA estimates the number of existing telemedicine networks in the United States at roughly 200 providing connectivity to over 3,000 sites.

- **Point-to-point connections** using private high-speed networks are used by hospitals and clinics that deliver services directly or outsource specialty services to independent medical service providers. Such outsourced services include radiology, stroke assessment, mental health, and intensive care services.

- **Monitoring center links** are used for cardiac, pulmonary, or fetal monitoring; home care; and related services that provide care to patients in the home. Often normal land-line or wireless connections are used to communicate directly between the patient and the center, although some systems use the Internet.

- **Web-based e-health patient service sites** provide direct consumer outreach and services over the Internet. Under telemedicine, these include those sites that provide direct patient care (What is telemedicine, 2016).

The Office for the Advancement of Telehealth (OAT), part of the HRSA's Office of Rural Health Policy, promotes the use of telehealth technologies for healthcare delivery, education, and health information services. The HRSA's mission is to ensure quality health care for underserved, vulnerable, and special-needs populations (HRSA, 2016a).

▶ Conclusion

Although hospitals admit 35 million individuals annually, the healthcare industry has recognized that outpatient services are a cost-effective method of providing quality health care and has therefore evolved into providing quality outpatient care. This type of service is the preferred method of receiving health care by many consumers. In 2015, there were over 900 million visits to doctor's offices, which is the traditional method of ambulatory care (CDC, 2016b). However, as medicine has evolved and more procedures, such as surgeries, can be performed on an outpatient basis, different types of outpatient care have evolved. As discussed previously, there are more outpatient surgical centers, imaging centers, urgent and emergent care centers, and other services that used to be offered on an inpatient basis. There will continue to be an increase in outpatient services being offered. Technology will increase the quality and efficiency of health care for consumers. Telemedicine will also become a more widely used model for health care because of continued advances in technology. The implementation of patient electronic health record systems nationwide will be the impetus for the development of more electronic healthcare services.

Wrap-Up

Vocabulary

Academic medical centers
Accreditation
Acute care hospital
Adult day services centers
Almshouses
Ambulatory care
Ambulatory surgery centers
American Red Cross (ARC)
Board of trustees
Certificate of need (CON)
Certification
Chief executive officer
Chief of medical staff
Chief of service

Church-related hospitals
Conditions of participation
Consumer medical and health information
Cost plus reimbursement
Council of Teaching Hospitals and Health Systems
Credentials committee
Critical access hospitals
Doctors Without Borders
Employee assistance programs
Federal hospitals
Finance committee
Health Center

Home health agencies
Hospice care
Hospital emergency medical services
Infection control committee
Informed consent
Inpatient services
International Organization for Standardization (ISO)
IOM quality dimensions
Long-term care hospital
Meals on Wheels Association of America (MOWAA)
Medical director

Medical education
Medical records committee
Medicare Rural Hospital
    Flexibility Program (MRHFP)
Monitoring center links
National Adult Day Services
    Association (NADSA)
National Institute of Senior
    Centers (NISC)
Networked programs
Office on Women's Health
Operational staff
Osteopathic hospitals
Outpatient services

Patient Self-Determination Act
    of 1990
PDSA cycle
Planned Parenthood Federation
    of America (PPFA)
Point-to-point connections
Poorhouses
Primary care and specialist
    referral services
Proprietary hospitals
Public hospitals
Quality committee
Quality improvement committee
Remote Area Medical (RAM)

Remote patient monitoring
Respite care
Senior centers
State licensure
Teaching hospitals
Telemedicine
Temporary care programs
Urgent and emergent care
    centers
Utilization review committee
Visiting nurse agencies
Voluntary hospitals
Web-based e-health patient
    service sites

References

AHA. (2016a). A patient bill of rights. Retrieved from http://www.patienttalk.info/AHA-Patient_Bill_of_Rights.htm

AHA. (2016b). 2016 Health and hospital trends. Retrieved from http://www.aha.org/aha/research-and-trends/health-and-hospital-trends/2013.html

Ambulatory Surgery Center Association (ASCA). (2013). Retrieved from http://www.ascassociation.org/faqs/faqaboutascs/#1

American Hospital Association. (2016a). Trends affecting hospitals and health systems. Retrieved from http://www.aha.org/research/reports/tw/chartbook/index.shtml

American Hospital Association (AHA). (2016). Center for hospital and health administration history. Retrieved from http://www.aha.org/research/rc/chhah/index.shtml

American Red Cross (ARC). (2016). Our history. Retrieved from http://www.redcross.org/about-us/history

ASCA. (2016b). A positive trend in health care. Retrieved from http://www.ascassociation.org/ASCA/Resources/ViewDocument/?DocumentKey=7d8441a1-82dd-47b9-b626-8563dc31930c.

Association of American Medical Colleges (AAMC). (2016). Council of Teaching Hospitals and Health Systems. Retrieved from https://www.aamc.org/members/coth/DHHS. (2016a).

Barnet, S. (2015). 20 things to know about urgent care/2015. Retrieved from http://www.beckershospitalreview.com/lists/20-things-to-know-about-urgent-care-2015.html?tmpl=component&print=1&layout=default&page=

Buchbinder, S., & Shanks, N. (2007). Introduction to health care management. Sudbury, MA: Jones and Bartlett.

CDC. (2016a). National hospital medical care ambulatory survey. Retrieved from http://www.cdc.gov/Nchs/ahcd.htm

Centers for Disease Control and Prevention (CDC). (2016b). Ambulatory care use and physician visits. Retrieved from http://www.cdc.gov/nchs/fastats/docvisit.htm

Centers for Medicare and Medicaid Services (CMS). Home Health Agency (HHA) Center. (2016). Retrieved from http://www.cms.hhs.gov/center/hha.asp

Community health centers and rural health clinics. (2016). Retrieved from http://www.aha.org/advocacy-issues/rural/CHCandRHC.shtml

Department of Health and Human Services (DHHS). (2016). Respite care. Retrieved from http://www.eldercare.gov/ELDERCARE.NET/Public/Resources/Factsheets/Respite_Care.aspx

DHHS. (2016b). Adult day care. Retrieved from http://www.eldercare.gov/ELDERCARE.NET/Public/Resources/Factsheets/Adult_Day_Care.aspx

DHHS. (2016c). Recovery act: Community health centers Retrieved from http://www.hhs.gov/recovery/hrsa/healthcentergrants.html

Doctors Without Borders. (2016). History & principles. Retrieved from http://www.doctorswithoutborders.org/aboutus/?ref=nav-footer

Dolan, P. (2016). Urgent care surge fueled by pressures on health system. Retrieved from http://www.amednews.com/article/20130415/business/130419964/2/

Duke University Libraries. (2016). Timeline of medicine. Retrieved from http://library.duke.edu/digitalcollections/mma/timeline.html

Fact Sheet: The Affordable Care Act's new patient Bill of Rights. (2016). Retrieved from http://www.healthreform.gov/newsroom/new_patients_bill_of_rights.html

Golia, N. (2016). Three insurers take the plunge into telehealth. Retrieved from DHHS. (2012a).

Health care law expands community health centers, services more patients. (July 1, 2012). Retrieved from http://www.hhs.gov/news/press/2012pres/06/20120620a.html

Health Resources and Services Administration. (2016a). Telehealth. Retrieved from http://www.hrsa.gov/ruralhealth/about/telehealth/

Health Resources and Services Administration. (2016b). What is a health center? Retrieved from http://bphc.hrsa.gov/about/

Home health care. (2016). Retrieved from http://www.cdc.gov/nchs/fastats/home-health-care.htm

Hospice care. (2016) Retrieved from http://www.eldercare.gov/ELDERCARE.NET/Public/Resources/Factsheets/Hospice_Care.aspx

International Organization for Standardization (ISO). (2016). Retrieved from http://www.iso.org

Jonas, S. (2003). *An introduction to the U.S. health care system.* New York, NY: Springer Publishing.

Leapfrog Group. (2016). Current Leapfrog initiatives. Retrieved from http://www.leapfroggroup.org/about_leapfrog/other_initiatives

Lillian Wald. (2016). Retrieved from http://www.vnsny.org/community/our-history/lillian-wald/

Longest, B., & Darr, K. (2008). *Managing health services organizations and system*. Baltimore, MD: Health Professions Press.

Mathews, A. W. (Dec. 12, 2011). The future of U.S. healthcare. Retrieved from http://online.wsj.com/article/SB10001424052970204319004577084553869990554.html

Meals on Wheels Association of America (MOWAA). (2016). Key initiatives, projects and grants. Retrieved from http://www.mowaa.org/page.aspx?pid=296

Medpac. (2016). Home health care services, Chapter 8. Retrieved from http://www.medpac.gov/chapters/Mar12_Ch08.pdf

Nabili, S. (2016). What is a hospitalist? Retrieved from http://www.medicinenet.com/script/main/art.asp?articlekey=93946

National Adult Day Services Association (NADSA). (2016). Adult day services: Overview and facts. Retrieved from http://www.nadsa.org/adsfacts/default.asp

National Conference of State Legislatures. (2016). Certificate of need: State health laws and programs. Retrieved from http://www.ncsl.org/default.aspx?tabid=14373

National Council on Aging. (2016). Retrieved from http://www.ncoa.org/content.cfm?sectionID=46

Office of Disability Employment Policy. (2016). Employee Assistance Programs for a new generation of employees. Retrieved from http://www.dol.gov/odep/documents/employeeassistance.pdf

Planned Parenthood Federation of America (PPFA). (2016). Retrieved from http://www.plannedparenthood.org/about-us/index.htm

Pointer, D., Williams, S., Isaacs, S., & Knickman, J. (2007). *Introduction to U.S. health care*. Hoboken, NJ: Wiley Publishing.

Pozgar, G. (2014). *Legal and ethical essentials of health care administration*. Sudbury, MA: JB Learning.

Relman, A. (2007). *A second opinion: Rescuing America's health care* (pp. 15–67). New York, NY: Public Affairs.

Remote Area Medical Volunteer Corps (RAM). (2016). Retrieved from http://www.ramusa.org/about/history.htm

Rosen, G. (1983). *The structure of American medical practice 1875–1941*. Philadelphia: University of Pennsylvania Press.

Shi, L., & Singh, D. (2008). *Delivering health care in America*. Sudbury, MA: Jones and Bartlett.

Six domains of healthcare quality. (2016). Retrieved from http://www.ahrq.gov/professionals/quality-patient-safety/talkingquality/create/sixdomains.html

Starr, P. (1982). *The social transformation of American medicine*. Cambridge, MA: Basic Books.

Substance Abuse and Mental Health Services Administration (SAMHSA). (2016). Retrieved from http://www.samhsa.gov

Sultz, H., & Young, K. (2006). *Health care USA: Understanding its organization and delivery* (5th ed.). Sudbury, MA: Jones and Bartlett.

The Joint Commission (TJC). (2016a). Accreditation and certification preparation. Retrieved from http://www.jointcommissioninternational.org/Quality-and-Safety-Risk-Areas/Accreditation-and-Certification/

The Joint Commission. (2016b). Ambulatory health care Retrieved from http://www.jointcommission.org/accreditation/ambulatory_healthcare.aspx

Torrens, P. R. (1993). Historical evolution and overview of health services in the United States. In S. J. Williams & P. R. Torrens (Eds.), *Introduction to health services* (4th ed.). Clifton Park, NY: Delmar Publishers.

Totten, M. (2012). Hospital governance in the US: An evolving landscape. Issue 1, Spring. Retrieved from http://www.greatboards.org/newsletter/2012/greatboards-newsletter-spring-2012.pdf

WebMD. (2016). Hospice care. Retrieved from http://www.webmd.com/balance/tc/hospice-care-topic-overviewPage=2

What is telemedicine? (2016). Retrieved from http://www.americantelemed.org/about-telemedicine/what-is-telemedicine#.VtDRdOZChSU

▶ **Notes**

▶ Student Activity 6-1

In Your Own Words

Based on this chapter, please provide an explanation of the following concepts in your own words. DO NOT RECITE the text.

Cost plus reimbursement:

_____

_____

Respite care:

_____

_____

Patient Self-Determination Act of 1990:

_____

_____

Public hospitals:

_____

_____

Voluntary hospitals:

_____

_____

Proprietary hospitals:

_____

_____

Certification:

_____

_____

Accreditation:

_____

_____

Ambulatory care:

_____

_____

▶ **Student Activity 6-2**

Real-Life Applications: Case Scenario One

You just received your Master of Health Administration degree and decided you would like to pursue a career in hospital management. You cannot decide what type of hospital you would like to apply to and decide to investigate the different types of hospitals that are available.

Activity

(1) Identify three different types of hospitals that are available for your employment; and (2) based on your research, select a hospital type and state why you chose this type of hospital.

Responses

_____

_____

_____

_____

_____

_____

_____

_____

_____

_____

_____

_____

_____

_____

_____

_____

_____

Case Scenario Two

One of your friends was just released from the hospital. She was pleased with her care but was not sure about her physician, who told her she was a "hospitalist." You had not heard of the term before either.

Activity

Perform an Internet search on the term "hospitalist." Define the term and find out if there are any current statistics on hospitalist use.

Responses

_____

_____

_____

_____

_____

_____

_____

_____

_____

_____

_____

_____

_____

_____

_____

_____

Case Scenario Three

Your mother is a volunteer at a hospice facility. She often comes home emotionally exhausted. You have never visited a hospice and asked if you could go with her next time. She agrees. Prior to your visit, you want to understand the concept of a hospice.

Activity

Perform an Internet search on the subject to understand the mission and goals of hospice programs. Write up your research and share it with your mother.

Responses

_____

_____

_____

_____

_____

_____

_____

_____

_____

_____

_____
_____
_____
_____
_____
_____
_____
_____

Case Scenario Four

As part of your internship, you will be assigned this semester to an adult day services center. You are only familiar with child day care centers so you decide to do some research before you start your internship.

Activity

Perform an Internet search on adult day services centers in your area and develop an information report to share with your classmates.

Responses

_____
_____
_____
_____
_____
_____
_____
_____
_____
_____

_____

_____

_____

_____

_____

_____

_____

▶ **Student activity 6-3**

Internet Exercises

Write your answers in the space provided.

■ Visit each of the websites listed here.
■ Name the organization.
■ Locate the organization's mission statement on the website.
■ Provide a brief overview of the activities of the organization.
■ How do these organizations participate in the U.S. healthcare system?

Websites

http://www.doctorswithoutborders.org

Organization Name:

_____

_____

Mission Statement:

_____

_____

_____

Overview of Activities:

_____

_____

Importance of Organization to U.S. Health Care:

_____

_____

_____

http://www.4woman.gov

Organization Name:

_____

_____

Mission Statement:

_____

_____

_____

Overview of Activities:

_____

_____

_____

Importance of Organization to U.S. Health Care:

_____

_____

_____

http://www.ramusa.org

Organization Name:

_____

_____

Mission Statement:

_____

_____

_____

Overview of Activities:

_____

_____

_____

Importance of Organization to U.S. Health Care:

_____

_____

_____

http://www.swiftmd.com

Organization Name:

_____

_____

Mission Statement:

_____

_____

_____

Overview of Activities:

_____

_____

_____

Importance of Organization to U.S. Health Care:

_____

_____

_____

http://www.ncoa.org

Organization Name:

_____

_____

Mission Statement:

_____

_____

_____

Overview of Activities:

_____

_____

_____

Importance of Organization to U.S. Health Care:

_____

_____

_____

http://www.ascassociation.org

Organization Name:

_____

_____

Mission Statement:

_____

_____

_____

Overview of Activities:

_____

_____

_____

Importance of Organization to U.S. Health Care:

_____

_____

_____

▶ **Student Activity 6-4**

Discussion Questions

The following are suggested discussion questions for this chapter.

1. Why do you think outpatient services are so popular with healthcare consumers? Discuss your experience with outpatient services.

_____

_____

_____

_____

2. What are urgent care centers? Have you or someone you know used these centers?

_____

_____

_____

_____

_____

3. Discuss at least two of the IOM quality dimensions.

_____

_____

_____

_____

_____

4. Visit the Doctors Without Borders website. Report back to the discussion board on one of the organization's recent activities.

_____

_____

_____

_____

_____

_____

_____

_____

_____

5. What is telemedicine? Give examples of telemedicine. Would you use telemedicine to receive care from your healthcare provider?

_____

_____

_____

_____

_____

_____

_____

_____

▶ **Student Activity 6-5**

Current Events

Perform an Internet search and find a current events topic over the past three years that is related to this chapter. Provide a summary of the article and the link to the article and why the article relates to the chapter.

The Navigate Companion Website for this text is a great source for additional information on the U.S. healthcare system. You can gain a new perspective on many of the topics presented in this chapter by visiting http://go.jblearning.com/Niles2e. You'll find additional student activities, further reading, and interactive study tools that explore:

- Discuss the history of hospitals
- Discuss the different types of outpatient services
- Discuss the importance of the IOM quality dimensions

_____

_____

_____

_____

_____

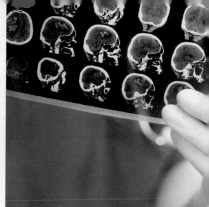

CHAPTER 7

U.S. Healthcare Workforce

LEARNING OBJECTIVES

The student will be able to:

- Describe five types of physicians and their roles in health care.
- Describe six types of nurse professionals and their roles in health care.
- Describe six types of other health professionals and their roles in health care.
- Discuss the issue of geographic maldistribution of physicians and its impact on access to care.
- Describe the difference between primary, secondary, tertiary, and quaternary care.
- Define allied health professionals and their role in the healthcare industry.

DID YOU KNOW THAT?

- The healthcare industry is one of the largest employers in the United States, with a workforce of 18 million workers.
- Approximately 65% of U.S. physicians are specialists, which includes surgeons, cardiologists, and psychiatrists.
- Quaternary care is an extension of tertiary care and is considered cutting-edge specialty medicine.
- Since the 1990s, physicians who specialize in the care of hospitalized patients are called "hospitalists."
- Women represent nearly 80% of the healthcare workforce.
- With the passage of the ACA, there will be shortage of physicians.

▶ Introduction

The healthcare industry is the fastest growing industry in the U.S. economy, employing a workforce of nearly 20 million healthcare workers. Considering the aging of the U.S. population and the impact of the Affordable Care Act, it is expected that the healthcare industry will continue to experience strong job growth. Job growth in many healthcare sectors is outpacing that in other industries (Centers for Disease Control and Prevention [CDC], 2016). When we think of healthcare providers, we automatically think of physicians and nurses. However, the healthcare industry is composed of many different health service professionals, including dentists, optometrists, psychologists, chiropractors, podiatrists, nonphysician practitioners (NPPs), administrators, and allied health professionals. It is important to identify allied health professionals because they provide a range of essential healthcare services that complement the services provided by physicians and nurses. This category of health professionals is an integral component of providing quality health.

Health care can occur in varied settings. Physicians have traditionally operated in their own practices but they also work in hospitals, mental health facilities, managed care organizations, and community health centers. They may also hold government positions or teach at a university. They could be employed by an insurance company. Health professionals, in general, may work at many different organizations, both for profit and nonprofit. Although the healthcare industry is one of the largest employers in the United States, there continue to be shortages of physicians in certain geographic areas of the country. Rural areas continue to suffer physician shortages, which limits consumer access to health care. There have been different incentive programs to encourage physicians to relocate to rural areas, but shortages still exist. In most states, only physicians, dentists, and a few other practitioners may serve patients directly without the authorization of another licensed independent health professional. Those categories authorized include chiropractic, optometry, psychotherapy, and podiatry. Some states authorize midwifery and physical therapy (Jonas, 2003). There also continues to be a shortage of registered nurses nationwide, with the most need identified in the south and the west. There is also a shortage of qualified nursing faculty to teach in nursing schools, which limits the number of students enrolled in registered nursing programs. The American Association of Colleges of Nursing (AACN) is discussing this issue with policy makers (AACN, 2016).

With the passage of the Affordable Care Act, it is anticipated there will continue to be a shortage of physicians. According to a 2015 AMAC study, there will be a shortage of physicians by 2025 in both primary and specialty care (Physician Supply, 2016). This chapter will provide a description of the different types of healthcare professionals and their role in providing care in the U.S. system.

▸ Primary, Secondary, and Tertiary Care

Three important concepts of care need to be emphasized: primary, secondary, and tertiary care. **Primary care** is the essential component of the U.S. healthcare

system because it is the point of entry into the system—where the patient makes first contact with the system. Primary care focuses on continuous and routine care of an individual. It may be delivered by a physician, nurse practitioner, midwife, or physician's assistant. Categories of primary care practitioners usually include family practitioners, pediatricians, internal medicine providers, obstetricians and gynecologists, psychiatrists, and emergency medicine physicians (Jonas, 2003). The focus of a primary care provider is to ensure patient access to the system by coordinating the delivery of healthcare services. Primary care is often referred to as essential health care and could include health education, counseling, and other preventive services. **Secondary care** focuses on short-term interventions that may require a specialist's intervention. Examples of secondary care include hospitalizations, routine surgery, specialty consultation, and rehabilitation. **Tertiary care** is a complex level of medical care, typically done by surgeons—physicians who perform operations to treat disease, physical problems, and injuries. This type of care is usually based on a referral from a primary care provider. Examples of tertiary care providers are orthopedic surgeons who operate on broken bones, oncology surgeons who remove cancerous tumors, and cardiac surgeons who operate on the heart. A new term, **quaternary care**, is an extension of tertiary care and refers to highly specialized, cutting-edge tertiary care. This is performed in research facilities and highly specialized facilities. An example of this type of care is proton beam therapy, which is a cutting-edge technology used to treat prostate cancer (Torrey, 2011).

▸ Physician Education

Physicians play a major role in providing healthcare services. They have been trained to diagnose and treat patient illnesses. Depending on their training, physicians have participated in primary, secondary, and tertiary care. All states require a license to practice medicine. Physicians must receive their medical education from an accredited school that awards either a **Doctor of Medicine (MD)** or a **Doctor of Osteopathic Medicine (DO)**. Many students prepare for medical school by majoring in a premedical undergraduate program, which often consists of science and mathematics. Undergraduate students are also required to take the MCAT—the Medical College Admission Test.

In order to provide direct patient care, physicians must take a licensing examination in the desired state of practice once they complete a residency. State licensing requirements may vary. This residency or training may take 3–8 years. The residency is important because it allows physicians to learn about a certain specialty of interest while providing them with on-the-job training. The length of the residency program can be as short as 3 years for a family practice and as long as 10 years for different surgery specialties. Most states require physicians to participate in continuing medical education (CME) activities to maintain state licensure.

The major difference between an MD and a DO is their approach to treatment. DOs tend to stress preventive treatments and use a **holistic approach** to treating a patient, which means they focus not only on the disease but also on the entire person. Most DOs are generalists. MDs use an **allopathic approach**, which means MDs actively intervene in attacking and eradicating disease and focus their efforts on the disease (BLS, 2016a).

Wages for physicians and surgeons are among the highest of all occupations. According to the Medical Group Management Association's Physician Compensation and Production Survey, median total compensation for physicians varies with their type of practice. In 2014, physicians practicing primary care received total median annual compensation of $241,273 and physicians practicing in medical specialties received total median annual compensation of $411,852. Job prospects should be good for physicians who are willing to practice in rural and low-income areas, because these areas tend to have difficulty attracting physicians. Job prospects also should be good for physicians in specialties dealing with health issues that largely affect aging baby boomers. For example, physicians specializing in cardiology and radiology will be needed because the risks for heart disease and cancer increase as people age. The growing and aging population is expected to drive overall growth in the demand for physician services as consumers continue to seek high levels of care that uses the latest technologies, diagnostic tests, and therapies (BLS, 2016b).

▶ Generalists and Specialists

Generalists can be primary care physicians, family care practitioners, general internal medicine physicians, or general pediatricians. Their focus is preventive services such as immunizations and health examinations. They treat less severe medical problems and often serve as a gatekeeper for a patient, which means they coordinate patient care if the patient needs to see a specialist for more complex medical problems. **Specialists** are required to be certified in their area of specialization. This may require additional years of training, as discussed in the previous paragraph, and require a **board certifying or credentialing examination**. The most common specialties are dermatology, cardiology, pediatrics, pathology, psychiatry, obstetrics, anesthesiology, specialized internal medicine, gynecology, ophthalmology, radiology, and surgery (Shi & Singh, 2008). The board certification is often associated with the quality of the healthcare provider's services because board certification requires more training. The **National Practitioner Data Bank (NPDB)** is an electronic information repository created by Congress. It contains information on medical malpractice payments and certain adverse actions related to health care practitioners, entities, providers, and suppliers. Federal law specifies the types of actions reported to the NPDB, who must submit the reports, and who can obtain copies of the reports. Organizations authorized to access these reports use them to make licensing, credentialing, privileging, or employment decisions. Individuals and organizations that are subjects of these reports have access to their own information. The reports are confidential and not available to the public (NPDB, 2016).

The www.healthgrades.com website was developed as a consumer tool to review other consumer ratings of physicians, dentists, and hospitals in the consumer's geographic areas. Consumers can find a provider by health condition or medical procedure. There is also a rating tool for hospitals (Healthgrades, 2016).

▶ Differences Between Primary and Specialty Care

Primary care is the initial contact between the healthcare provider and the patient. If needed, **specialty care** will be a result of a primary care evaluation. The primary care physician will ultimately coordinate the health care of the patient if additional specialty care is required. If a patient has a chronic condition, the primary care provider will coordinate the overall care of the individual (Torrey, 2011). In a managed care environment, which focuses on cost containment, the primary care physician becomes the gatekeeper of the patient's care by referring a patient to a specialist for additional care. Primary care students spend most of their focus in ambulatory settings learning about different diseases, whereas specialty care students spend time in an inpatient setting focusing on special patient conditions.

Patterns of Physician Supply

The concept of **geographic maldistribution** has occurred because physicians prefer to practice in urban and suburban areas where there is a higher probability of increased income. Recruiting physicians to rural areas is difficult because of the working conditions, reduced income, and reduced access to technology, which is more available in urban and suburban areas. Another issue in physician supply is the increasing proportion of specialists to generalists, which is called **specialty maldistribution**. The supply of specialists has increased more than 100% over the last 20 years, while the supply of generalists has increased only 18%. The Affordable Care Act mandate of expanding health insurance coverage will add an additional 34 million consumers to the healthcare system. President Obama called for an increase in primary care physicians, nurse practitioners, and physician assistants to manage this huge increase (Petterson et al., 2012).

▶ Types of Healthcare Providers

Hospitalists

A **hospitalist** is a physician who provides care to hospitalized patients. This new type of physician, which evolved in the 1990s, is usually a general practitioner and is becoming more popular—because they spend so much time in the hospital setting, they can provide more efficient care. They replace a patient's primary care physician while the patient is hospitalized. A hospitalist monitors the patient from admittance to discharge, acting as a primary care provider for inpatient medicine. However, they normally do not have a relationship with the patient prior to admittance. They coordinate the care within the hospital among the specialty physicians and other healthcare practitioners. Hospitalists comprise 9% of the primary care workforce and 4% of the overall physician workforce, which is approximately 30,000 in the United States (Association of American Medical Colleges [AAMC], 2016).

Nonphysician Practitioners

It is important to mention the general term **nonphysician practitioner (NPP)**, which includes nonphysician clinicians (NPCs) and mid-level practitioners (MLPs). The specific professionals of this category will be discussed in depth in this chapter, but it is important to mention their importance generally in providing health care. They are sometimes called **physician extenders** because they often are used as a substitute for physicians. They are not involved in total care of a patient so they collaborate closely with physicians. Categories of NPPs include physician assistants (PAs), nurse practitioners (NPs), and certified nurse practitioners (CNPs). NPPs have been favorably received by patients because they tend to spend more time with patients (Shi & Singh, 2008).

Physician Assistants

Physician assistants (PAs), a category of NPPs, provide a range of diagnostic and therapeutic services to patients. They take medical histories, conduct patient examinations, analyze tests, make diagnoses, and perform basic medical procedures. They are able to prescribe medicines in all but three states. They must be associated with and supervised by a physician but the supervision does not need to be direct. In many areas where there is a shortage of physicians, PAs act as primary care providers. They collaborate with physicians by telephone and onsite visits. Students take classes and participate in clinical settings. They are required to pass a national certification exam and may take additional education in surgery, pediatrics, emergency medicine, primary care, and occupational medicine. Their average salary is $95,520 (BLS, 2016c).

Nurses

Nurses constitute the largest group of healthcare professionals and provide the majority of care to patients. They are the patient's advocate. There are several different types of nurses that provide patient care and several different levels of nursing care based on education and training.

Although nursing supply and demand is cyclical, during recent years there has been a continued nursing shortage, particularly of registered nurses (Casselman, 2013).

Licensed Practical Nurses and Licensed Vocational Nurses

There are approximately 700,000 **licensed practical nurses (LPNs)** (called **licensed vocational nurses (LVNs)** in California and Texas) in the United States. They are the largest group of nurses and provide basic nursing care. Education is offered by community colleges or technical schools. Training takes approximately 12–14 months and includes both education and supervised clinical practice. LPNs have a high school diploma and take a licensing exam. The 2014 median salary is approximately $42,490.

Their job responsibilities include patient observation, taking vital signs, keeping records, assisting patients with personal hygiene, and feeding and dressing patients, which are considered **activities of daily living (ADLs)**. In some states, LPNs administer some medications. They work primarily in hospitals, home health agencies, and nursing homes.

Many LPNs work full time and earn their Bachelor of Science in Nursing (BSN) degree to increase their career choices (BLS, 2016d).

Registered Nurses

A **registered nurse** (RN) is a trained nurse who has been licensed by a state board after passing the national nursing examination. RNs can be registered in more than one state. Employment of RNs is projected to grow 16% from 2014 to 2024, much faster than the average for all occupations. Growth will occur for a number of reasons, including an increased emphasis on preventive care; growing rates of chronic conditions, such as diabetes and obesity; and demand for healthcare services from the baby-boomer population, as they live longer and have more active lives.

There are different levels of registered nursing based on education.

- **Associate Degree in Nursing (ADN)**: Two-year program offered by community colleges.
  There are three-year diploma programs offered by hospitals. There is no degree offered but under-graduate credit may be earned. They are very expensive and are being offered less often.
- **Bachelor of Science in Nursing (BSN)**: The most rigorous of the nursing programs. Programs offered by colleges and universities normally take 4–5 years. Students perform both classroom activity and clinical practice activity. Their job responsibilities include recording symptoms of any disease, implementing care plans, assisting physicians in examinations and the treatment of patients, administering medications and performing medical procedures, supervising other personnel such as LPNs, and educating patients and families about follow-up care. The majority of RNs work in hospitals. Depending on the level of education, the average 2014 annual income was $66,640.
- **Advanced practice registered nurses (APN)** or mid-level practitioners are nurses who have

experience and education beyond the requirements of an RN. They operate between the RN and MD, which is why they are called **mid-level practitioners**. They normally obtain a Master of Science in Nursing (MSN) with a specialty in the field of practice. There are four areas of specialization: clinical nurse specialists (CNSs), certified registered nurse anesthetists (CRNAs), nurse practitioners (NPs), and certified nurse–midwives (CNMs). The 2014 median salary was $102,670. Depending on the state, many of these certifications allow for a nurse to provide direct care including writing prescriptions. (BLS, 2016e).

Nurse Anesthetists, Nurse Practitioners, and Certified Nurse–Midwives

Nurse anesthetists (CRNAs) provide anesthesia and related care before, during, and after surgical, therapeutic, diagnostic, and obstetrical procedures. They also provide pain management and some emergency services. Before a procedure begins, nurse anesthetists discuss with a patient any medications the patient is taking as well as any allergies or illnesses the patient may have, so that anesthesia can be safely administered. Nurse anesthetists then give a patient general anesthesia to put the patient to sleep so they feel no pain during surgery or administer a regional or local anesthesia to numb an area of the body. They remain with the patient throughout a procedure to monitor vital signs and adjust the anesthesia as necessary. Their 2014 median salary was $153,780.

As stated earlier, NPPs are an integral component of providing quality health care in the United States. **Nurse practitioners (NPs)** are the largest categories of advanced practice nurses (APNs). The first group of NPs was trained in 1965 at the University of Colorado. In 1974, the American Nursing Association developed the Council of Primary Care Nurse Practitioners, which helped substantiate the role of NPs in patient care. Over the last two decades, several specialty NP boards have been established, such as pediatrics and reproductive health for certification of NPs. On January 1, 2013, the American Academy of Nurse Practitioners (founded in 1985) and the American College of Nurse Practitioners (founded in 1995) merged to form the American Association of Nurse Practitioners (AANP), the largest full-service national professional membership organization for NPs.

NPs are required to obtain an RN and a master's degree or doctoral degree. They may receive a certificate program and complete direct-patient-care clinical training. NPs emphasize health education and promotion as well as disease treatment—referred to as care and cure. NPs spend more time with patients and, as a result, patient surveys indicate satisfaction with NPs' care. NPs may specialize in pediatric, family, geriatric, or psychiatric care. Most states allow NPs to prescribe medications. They practice in ambulatory, acute, and long-term settings. Their 2014 median salary was $95,350 (AANP, 2016). They are a very cost-effective alternative to a physician. They have played a role in the expanded health services prescribed by the Affordable Care Act.

Certified nurse–midwives (CNMs) are RNs who have graduated from a nurse–midwifery education program that has been accredited by the American College of Nurse–Midwives' Division of Accreditation. Nurse–midwives have been practicing in the United States for nearly 90 years. They must pass the national certification exam to receive the designation of CNM. Nurse–midwives are primary care providers for women who are pregnant. They must be recertified every 8 years. Recent salaries are reported at $96,970. **Certified midwives (CMs)** are individuals who do not have a nursing degree but have a related health background. They must take the midwifery education program, which is accredited by the same organization. They must also pass the same national certification exam to be given the designation of CM. The recent reported salary is $70,000 (American College of Nurse–Midwives, 2016).

Certified Nursing Assistants or Nursing Aides

Certified nursing assistants (CNAs) are unlicensed patient attendants who work under the supervision of physicians and nurses. They answer call bells from patients who need their service; assist patients with personal hygiene and ordering meals; change bedding; and assist patients with their ADLs. Most CNAs are employed by nursing care facilities. There are approximately 1.5 million CNAs in the healthcare industry. They are required to receive 75 hours of training and are required to pass a competency examination. Their average pay is extremely low and they are often overlooked for pay and advancement, creating a high turnover in their field despite the fact that they provide much needed services to the patient. Their 2014 reported median salary was $25,100 (BLS, 2016).

▶ Other Independent Healthcare Professionals

Dentists

Dentists prevent, diagnose, and treat tooth, gum, and mouth diseases. They are required to complete four years of education from an accredited dental school after receiving a bachelor's degree. They are awarded a Doctor of Dental Surgery (DDS) or Doctor of Dental Medicine (DDM). Some states may require a specialty license. The first two years of dental school are focused on dental sciences. The last two years are spent in a clinical environment. Dentists may take an additional two to four years of postgraduate education in orthodontics (teeth straightening), oral surgery, public health dentistry, etc. In 2014, there were over 150,000 dentists in the United States—over 90% were in private practice and were primarily general practitioners. Job growth is projected to be approximately 18% between 2014 and 2024. The 2014 median salary was $154,650. There is no industry priority to target this population (BLS, 2016f).

Dentists are often helped by **dental assistants**. Dental assistants work directly with dentists in the preparation and treatment of patients. Some states require assistants to graduate from an accredited program and pass a state exam. Some states have no formal educational requirements. Dental assistants who do not have formal education may learn their duties through on-the-job training. They do not have to be licensed but there are certification programs available. The 2010 median pay was $35,390. Job growth is projected at 31% from 2010 to 2020 (BLS, 2016g).

Dental hygienists clean teeth, examine patients for oral diseases, and provide other preventive dental care. They educate patients on ways to improve and maintain oral health. Dental hygienists typically need an associate's degree in dental hygiene. Every state requires dental hygienists to be licensed, but licensing requirements vary by state. Employment is expected to grow by 19% between 2014 and 2024, much faster than the average for all occupations. Ongoing research linking oral health and general health will continue to spur the demand for preventive dental services provided by dental hygienists. The 2014 median pay was $71,520 (BLS, 2016h).

Pharmacists

Pharmacists are responsible for dispensing medication that has been prescribed by physicians. They also advise both patients and healthcare providers on potential side effects of medications. All Doctor of Pharmacy programs require applicants to have taken postsecondary courses such as chemistry, biology, and anatomy. Applicants need at least two to three years of undergraduate study; for some programs, applicants must have a bachelor's degree. For most programs, applicants also must take the Pharmacy College Admissions Test (PCAT). All states license pharmacists. After they finish the PharmD, prospective pharmacists must pass two exams to get a license. One exam is in pharmacy skills and knowledge and the other is in pharmacy law. In May 2014, the median annual wage of pharmacists was $120,950. Employment of pharmacists is expected to increase by 3% from 2014 to 2024, which is slower than average (BLS, 2016i).

Chiropractors

Chiropractors have a holistic approach to treating their patients, which means they focus on the entire body with emphasis on the spine. They believe the body can heal itself with no medication or surgery. Chiropractors treat patients with health issues involving the musculoskeletal system, which is made up of bones, muscles, ligaments, and tendons. They manipulate the body with their hands or with a machine. Becoming a chiropractor requires earning a Doctor of Chiropractic (DC) degree and getting a state license. Doctor of Chiropractic programs take four years to complete and require three years of previous undergraduate college education for admission. Although specific requirements vary by state, all jurisdictions require the completion of an accredited Doctor of Chiropractic program to be licensed in the state. In May 2014, the median annual wage of chiropractors was $66,720. Employment of chiropractors is expected to increase by 17% from 2014 to 2024 (BLS, 2016j).

Optometrists

Optometrists, also known as Doctors of Optometry or ODs, are the main providers of vision care. They examine people's eyes to diagnose vision problems. Optometrists may prescribe eyeglasses or contact lenses. Optometrists also test for glaucoma and other eye diseases, diagnose conditions caused by systemic diseases, such as diabetes and high blood pressure, and refer patients to other health practitioners. Optometrists often provide preoperative and postoperative care to cataract patients, as well as to patients who have had laser vision correction or other eye surgery.

Optometrists need a Doctor of Optometry (OD) degree. In 2015, there were 23 accredited Doctor of Optometry programs in the United States, one of which was in Puerto Rico. All states require optometrists to be licensed. All prospective optometrists must have an OD from an accredited optometry school and must complete all sections of the National Boards in Optometry to be licensed in a state. Some states require an additional exam. Employment of optometrists is expected to grow by 27% from 2014 to 2024. In 2014, the median annual wage of optometrists was $101,410 (BLS, 2016k).

Psychologists

Psychologists study the human mind and human behavior. Some psychologists work independently, doing research or working only with patients. Others work as part of a healthcare team, collaborating with physicians, social workers, and others to treat illness and promote overall wellness. Most clinical, counseling, and research psychologists need a doctoral degree. Psychologists can complete a Ph.D. in psychology or a Doctor of Psychology (Psy.D.) degree. A Ph.D. in psychology is a research degree that culminates in a comprehensive exam and a dissertation based on original research. In clinical, counseling, school, or health service settings, students usually complete a one-year internship as part of the doctoral program. The Psy.D. is a clinical degree and is often based on practical work and examinations rather than a dissertation. In most states, practicing psychology or using the title of "psychologist" requires licensure or certification. The American Board of Professional Psychology awards specialty certification in 13 areas of psychology, such as clinical health, couples and families, psychoanalysis, or rehabilitation. Although board certification is not required for most psychologists, it can demonstrate professional expertise in a specialty area. Some hospitals and clinics do require certification. In those cases, candidates must have a doctoral degree in psychology, state license or certification, and any additional criteria of the specialty field. In May 2014, the median annual wage of psychologists was $70,700. Overall employment of psychologists is expected to grow 22% from 2014 to 2024 (BLS, 2016l).

Podiatrists

Podiatrists provide medical and surgical care for people suffering from foot, ankle, and lower-leg problems. They diagnose illnesses, treat injuries, and perform surgery. Podiatrists must have a Doctor of Podiatric Medicine (DPM) degree, which is a four-year degree after earning a bachelor's degree. Admission to DPM programs usually also requires taking the Medical College Admission Test (MCAT). In 2014, there were nine colleges of podiatric medicine in the United States. The 2014 median annual wage of podiatrists was $120,700. Employment of podiatrists is expected to increase by 14% from 2014 to 2024 (BLS, 2016m).

▶ Allied Health Professionals

In the early 20th century, healthcare providers consisted of physicians, nurses, pharmacists, and optometrists. As the healthcare industry evolved with increased use of technology and sophisticated interventions, increased time demands were placed on these healthcare providers. As a result, a broader spectrum of healthcare professionals with skills that complemented these primary healthcare providers evolved. These **allied health professionals** assist physicians and nurses in providing care to their patients. The impact of technology has increased the number of different specialties available. They can be divided into four main categories: laboratory technologists and technicians, therapeutic science practitioners, behavioral scientists, and support services (The Association of Schools of Allied Health Professionals [ASAHP], 2016).

Laboratory or clinical laboratory technologists and technicians have a major role in diagnosing disease, assessing the impact of interventions, and applying highly technical procedures. Examples of this category include radiologic technology and nuclear medicine technology. Therapeutic science practitioners focus on the rehabilitation of patients with diseases and injuries. Examples of this category include physical therapists, radiation therapists, respiratory therapists, dieticians, and dental hygienists.

Behavioral scientists such as social workers and rehabilitation counselors provide social, psychological, and community and patient educational activities (Sultz & Young, 2006). This chapter cannot list all allied health professionals, but a list of those allied health careers that have accredited education programs will be discussed.

The **Commission on Accreditation of Allied Health Education Programs (CAAHEP)** accredits 2,000 U.S. programs that offer 28 allied health specialties. This section will provide a brief summary of the different allied healthcare jobs that contribute to providing quality health care. This information was obtained from the CAAHEP website and the Bureau of Labor Statistics (CAAHEP, 2016a).

Anesthesiologist Assistant

Under the direction of an anesthesiologist and as a team member of the anesthesia care component of surgical procedures, this specialty physician assistant assists with implementing an anesthesia care plan. Activities include performing presurgical and surgical tasks and possibly also assisting in administrative and educational activities. The **anesthesiologist assistant (AA)** primarily is employed by medical centers. In 2014, median annual salaries ranged from $110,000 to $120,000 for 40 hours work per week. Acceptance into an AA educational program requires an undergraduate premedical education, which consists of sciences such as biology, chemistry, physics, and mathematics. The AA program length of duration is 24–27 months (CAAHEP, 2016b).

Cardiovascular Technologist

At the request of a physician, a **cardiovascular technologist** performs diagnostic examinations for cardiovascular issues. Basically, they assist physicians in treating cardiac (heart) and peripheral vascular (blood vessel) problems. They may also review and record clinical data, perform procedures, and obtain data for physician review. They may provide services in any medical setting but are primarily in hospitals. They also operate and maintain testing equipment and may explain test procedures. These allied health professionals generally work a 5-day, 40-hour week that may include weekends. In 2014, their wages averaged $55,210. A high school diploma or qualifications in a clinically related allied position is required to enter an education program, which may last from one to four years depending on the background of the student (CAAHEP, 2016c).

Cytotechnologist

Cytology is the study of the structure and function of cells. **Cytotechnologists**, a category of clinical laboratory technologists, are specialists who collaborate with pathologists to evaluate cellular material. This material is used by pathologists to diagnose cancer and other diseases. Cytotechnologists prepare slides of body cells and examine these cells microscopically for abnormalities that may signal the beginning of a cancerous growth. Most cytotechnologists work in hospitals. In 2014, cytotechnologists' median annual salary was $66,000. In order to enter into their educational program, applicants should have a background in the biological sciences. Applicants must have an undergraduate degree in order to qualify for national certification (CAAHEP, 2016d).

Diagnostic Medical Sonographer

Under the supervision of a physician, this specialist provides patient services using medical ultrasound, which photographs internal structures. **Sonography** uses sound waves to generate images of the body for the assessment and diagnosis of various medical conditions. Sonography commonly is associated with obstetrics and the use of ultrasound imaging during pregnancy. This specialist gathers data to assist with disease management in a variety of medical facilities including hospitals, clinics, and private practices. They may assist with patient education. In addition to working directly with patients, **diagnostic medical sonographers** keep patient records. They also may prepare work schedules, evaluate equipment purchases, or manage a sonography or imaging department. Diagnostic medical sonographers may specialize in obstetric and gynecologic sonography (the female reproductive system), abdominal sonography (the liver, kidneys, gallbladder, spleen, and pancreas), neurosonography (the brain), breast sonography, vascular sonography, or cardiac sonography.

Sonographers work approximately 40 hours per week but may have weekend and evening hours. In 2014, the median annual salary was $62,000, with job growth projected to be 24% between 2014 and 2024. Colleges and universities offer formal training in both two- and four-year programs, culminating in an associate or a bachelor's degree. Applicants to a one-year educational program must have relevant clinical experience. There are two-year programs, which are the most prevalent, that will accept high school graduates with an education in basic sciences (CAAHEP, 2016e).

Emergency Medical Technicians and Paramedics

People who are ill, have had an accident, or have been wounded often depend on the competent care of **emergency medical technicians (EMTs)** and **paramedics**. EMTs and paramedics work with patients who require immediate medical attention. EMTs and paramedics provide this vital service as they care for and transport the sick or injured to a medical facility for appropriate medical care.

In general, EMTs and EMT–paramedics (EMT-Ps) provide emergency medical assistance because of an accident or illness that has occurred outside the medical setting. EMTs and paramedics work under guidelines approved by the physician medical director of a healthcare organization to assess and manage medical emergencies. They are trained to provide lifesaving measures. EMTs provide basic life support, and EMT–Ps provide advanced life support measures. They may be employed by an ambulance company, fire department, public emergency medical services company, or hospital or a combination thereof. They may be paid or be volunteers from the community. Both EMTs and EMT–Ps must be proficient in cardiopulmonary resuscitation (CPR). They learn the basics of different types of medical emergencies. EMT–Ps perform more sophisticated procedures. They also receive extensive training in patient assessment. The work is not only physically demanding but also can be stressful, sometimes involving life-or-death situations. In 2014, the median annual salary was approximately $31,700.

Firefighters may also be trained as EMTs. EMT training is offered at community colleges, technical schools, hospitals, and academies. EMTs require 40 hours of training, whereas EMT–Ps require 200–400 hours of training. Applicants for the programs are expected to have a high school diploma or the equivalent. The National Registry of Emergency Medical Technicians (NREMT) certifies emergency medical service providers at five levels: First Responder, EMT-Basic, EMT-Intermediate (which has two levels called 1985 and 1999), and Paramedic. All 50 states require certification for each of the EMT levels. Job growth is projected to be 24% between 2014 and 2024 (CAAHEP, 2016f).

Exercise Physiologists

Exercise physiologists assess, design, and manage individual exercise programs for both healthy and unhealthy individuals. Clinical exercise physiologists work with a physician when applying programs for patients that have demonstrated a therapeutic benefit for the patient. In 2014, their median salary, depending on geographic area and experience, was $46,270. These allied health professionals may work with fitness trainers, exercise science professionals, or physicians in cardiac rehabilitation in hospital settings. Applicants for two-year programs should have an undergraduate degree in exercise science. Job growth projections between 2014 and 2024 is 11%, which is higher than average (CAAHEP, 2016g).

Medical Assistant

Supervised by physicians, **medical assistants** must have the ability to multitask. Over 60% of medical assistants work in medical offices and clinics. They perform both administrative and clinical duties. Medical assistants are employed by physicians more than any other allied health assistant. In 2014, their median salary was $29,960. Their educational program consists of an associate degree, a certificate, or a diploma program. Job growth is estimated to be 23% between 2014 and 2024 (CAAHEP, 2016h).

Medical Illustrator

Medical illustrators are trained artists who visually portray scientific information to teach both professionals and the public about medical issues. They may work digitally or traditionally to create images of human anatomy and surgical procedures as well as three-dimensional models and animations. Medical illustrators may be self-employed or work for pharmaceutical companies, advertising agencies, or medical schools. In 2014, the median salary was $62,000. Applicants must have an undergraduate degree with a focus on art and premedical education. The program is two years and results in a master's degree (CAAHEP, 2016i).

Orthotist and Prosthetist

These specialists address neuromuscular and skeletal issues and develop a plan and a device to rectify any issues. The **orthotist** develops devices called "othoses" that focus on the limbs and spines of individuals to increase function. The **prosthetist** designs "prostheses" or devices for patients who have limb amputations to replace the limb function. Most of these allied health professionals work in hospitals, clinics, colleges, and medical schools. In 2014, the median salary was $64,400, with an estimated job growth between 2014 and 2024 of 23%, which is higher than average. The required education may be achieved through a four-year program or a certificate program that varies in length from six months to two years. Applicants for four-year programs should have a high school diploma. Applicants for certificate programs must have a four-year degree (CAAHEP, 2016j).

Perfusionist

A **perfusionist** operates equipment to support or replace a patient's circulatory or respiratory function. Perfusion involves advanced-life-support techniques. Perfusionists may be responsible for administering blood byproducts or anesthetic products during a surgical procedure. They may be employed by hospitals, surgeons, or group practices. The 2014 median salary was $109,773. The prerequisites for educational programs vary depending on the length of the program, which can range from one to four years, depending on the individual's experience (CAAHEP, 2016k).

Personal Fitness Trainer

Personal fitness trainers are familiar with different forms of exercise. They have a variety of clients who they serve one-on-one or in group activities. They may work with exercise science professionals or physiologists in corporate, clinical, or commercial fitness centers, country clubs, or wellness centers. In 2014, their median pay was $39,740. The educational programs consist of a one-year certificate or a two-year associate degree program. Applicants must have a high school diploma or equivalent for program entry (CAAHEP, 2016l).

Polysomnographic Technologist

Polysomnographic technologists perform sleep tests and work with physicians to provide diagnoses of sleep disorders. They monitor brain waves, eye movements, and other physiological activity during sleep, analyze this information, and provide it to the patient's physician. They work in sleep disorder centers that may be affiliated with a hospital or operate independently. In 2014, the median salary was $52,000. Applicants for the education programs should have a high school diploma or equivalent. The educational program can be a two-year associate degree or a one-year certificate program (CAAHEP, 2013m).

Recreational Therapist

Recreational therapists provide individualized and group recreational therapy for individuals experiencing limitations in life activities as a result of a disabling condition, illness or disease, aging, or developmental factors. Recreational therapists use a variety of educational, behavioral, recreational, and activity-oriented strategies with clients to enhance functional performance and improve positive lifestyle behaviors designed to increase independence, effective community participation, and well-being.

Recreational therapists work in clinical settings, such as hospitals, psychiatric or skilled nursing facilities, substance abuse programs, and rehabilitation centers. Recreational therapists treat and rehabilitate individuals with specific medical, social, and behavioral problems, usually in cooperation with physicians; nurses; psychologists; social workers; and speech, physical, and occupational therapists.

A bachelor's degree with a major in recreational therapy or therapeutic recreation, or a major in recreation with a specialization in recreational therapy or therapeutic recreation, is required for national certification. Specific requirements can be obtained from the National Council for Therapeutic Recreation

Certification. Job growth is expected to be 12% between 2014 and 2024 due to the aging of the U.S. population. Median pay in 2014 for certified therapists was $44,000 (CAAHEP, 2014n).

Transfusion Medicine Specialists or Specialists in Blood Banking Technology

Transfusion medicine specialists or specialists in blood banking (SBB) technology provide routine and specialized tests for blood donor centers, transfusion centers, laboratories, and research centers. In 2014, the median salary was $55,000. Applicants for the educational programs must be certified in medical technology and have an undergraduate degree from an accredited educational institution. If they are not certified, they must have a degree from an accredited institution with a major in a biological or physical science and have appropriate work experience. This allied health program ranges from one to two years (CAAHEP, 2016o).

Surgical Assistant

A **surgical assistant** is a specialized physician's assistant. Surgical assistants' main goal is to ensure the surgeon has a safe and sterile environment in which to perform. They determine the appropriate equipment for the procedure, select radiographs for a surgeon's reference, assist in moving the patient, confirm procedures with the surgeon, and assist with the procedure as directed by the surgeon. The educational programs range from 10 to 22 months long. In 2014, median annual pay was $75,000. Applicants must have a bachelor of science or higher degree or an associate degree in an allied health field with three years of recent experience, current CPR–basic life support certification, acceptable health and immunization records, and computer literacy (CAAHEP, 2016p).

Surgeon Technologist

Surgeon technologists are key team members of medical practitioners providing surgery. They are responsible for preparing the operating room by equipping the room with the appropriate sterile supplies and verifying the equipment is working properly. Prior to surgery, they also interact with the patient to ensure he or she is comfortable, monitor the patient's vital signs, and review the patient's charts. During surgery, they are responsible for ensuring all surgery team members maintain a sterile environment and providing instruments to the surgeons. After surgery, they prepare the room for the next patient. They

may also provide follow-up care in the postoperative room. They work in hospitals or outpatient settings, and they may be self-employed. In 2014, the median annual salary was $43,350. Applicants for the educational programs must have a high school diploma or equivalent. The programs range from 12 to 24 months long (CAAHEP, 2016q).

▶ Non-CAAHEP Allied Health Professionals

The following job descriptions are important allied health professionals but are not a CAAHEP program.

Pharmacy Technicians

Pharmacy technicians typically do the following:

- Take from customers or health professionals the information needed to fill a prescription;
- Count tablets and measure amounts of other medication for prescriptions;
- Compound or mix medications, such as preparing ointments;
- Package and label prescriptions;
- Accept payment for prescriptions and process insurance claims; and
- Do routine pharmacy tasks, such as answering phone calls from customers.

Many pharmacy technicians learn how to perform their duties through on-the-job training. Others attend postsecondary education programs in pharmacy technology at vocational schools or community colleges, which award certificates. These programs typically last one year or less and cover a variety of subjects, such as arithmetic used in pharmacies, recordkeeping, ways of dispensing medications, and pharmacy law and ethics. Technicians also learn the names, actions, uses, and doses of medications. Many training programs include internships, in which students get hands-on experience in a pharmacy. The median annual salary of pharmacy technicians was $29,810 in 2014, and employment is expected to grow by 9% between 2014 and 2024 (BLS, 2016n).

Psychiatric Technicians and Aides

Psychiatric technicians and aides care for people who have mental illness or developmental disabilities. The two occupations are related, but technicians typically provide therapeutic care, and aides help patients in their daily activities. Psychiatric technicians typically enter the occupation with a postsecondary certificate. Programs in psychiatric or mental health technology are commonly offered by community colleges and technical schools. Psychiatric technician programs include courses in biology, psychology, and counseling. The programs also may include supervised work experience or cooperative programs, in which students gain academic credit for structured work experience. The median annual salary of psychiatric technicians was $28,470 in 2014. Employment of psychiatric technicians is expected to increase 5% from 2014 to 2024 (BLS, 2016o).

Respiratory Therapist

There are two levels of **respiratory therapists**: certified respiratory therapist and registered respiratory therapist. The entry-level respiratory therapist performs basic respiratory care procedures under the supervision of a physician or an advanced-level therapist. Entry-level therapists review patient data, including tests and previous medical history; implement and monitor any respiratory therapy under the supervision of a physician; and may be involved in the home care of a patient. Entry-level therapists are employed in hospitals, nursing care facilities, clinics, sleep labs, and home care organizations. In 2014, the median pay was $56,730.

Applicants are required to have a high school degree or equivalent. The educational program consists of a two-year program leading to an associate's degree. An advanced-level respiratory therapist participates in clinical decision making such as diagnosing lung and breathing disorders, recommending treatment methods, providing patient education, and developing and recommending care plans in collaboration with a physician. Becoming an advanced-level therapist can be achieved through increased education such as a bachelor's or master's degree (BLS, 2016p).

Health Services Administrators

It is important to discuss the importance of **health services administrators** and their role in health care. They can be found at all levels of a healthcare organization. They may be managing hospitals, clinics, nursing homes, community health centers, and other types of healthcare facilities. Top-level administrators are responsible for strategic planning and the overall success of the organization and for its financial, clinical, and operational outcomes. Mid-level administrators also play a leadership role in departments and are responsible for managing their area of responsibility. They may manage departments or individual programs. Administrators at all levels work with top

administrators to achieve organizational goals. As healthcare costs continue to increase, it is important that health services administrators focus on efficiency and effectiveness at all levels of management. The 2014 median annual pay was $92,000 (BLS, 2016q).

Health services administration is taught at both the undergraduate and master's levels. The most common undergraduate degree is a degree in healthcare administration, although most generalist management positions require a master's degree. Undergraduate degrees may be acceptable for entry-level management positions. Approximately 40% of hospitals employ health services administrators.

The most common master's degrees are the Master of Health Services Administration (MHA), the Master of Business Administration (MBA) with a healthcare emphasis, and the Master of Public Health (MPH). The MHA or MBA degree provides a more business-oriented education that health administrators need for managing healthcare organizations. However, having an MPH degree also provides insight into the importance of public health as an integral component of our healthcare system (BLS, 2016q).

Home Health and Personal Care Aides

Home health and personal care aides help people who are disabled, chronically ill, or cognitively impaired, as well as older adults who need assistance. They assist with activities such as bathing and dressing, and they provide services such as light housekeeping. In some states, home health aides may be able to give medication to a client or check the client's vital signs under the direction of a nurse or other healthcare practitioner. Home health and personal care aides work most often in a client's home or small group homes. There is no formal education required; however, if they work in a certified home health agency or hospice facility, they must receive formal training. The 2014 median pay was $21,380. The projected growth of this occupation between 2014 and 2024 is nearly 40%, due to the increased popularity of home health care (BLS, 2016r).

▶ Conclusion

Healthcare personnel comprise one of the largest labor forces in the United States. This chapter provided an overview of the different types of employees in the healthcare industry. Some of them require many years of education; however, some of these positions can be attained upon completion of 1–2 year programs. The healthcare industry will continue to progress as U.S. trends in demographics, disease, and public health pattern change, and cost and efficiency issues, insurance issues, technological influences, and economic factors continue to evolve. More occupations and professions will develop as a result of these trends. The major trend that will impact the healthcare industry is the aging of the U.S. population. The BLS predicts that half of the next decades' fastest growing job categories will be in the healthcare industry. The Affordable Care Act will continue to have an impact on the positive growth for this industry.

Wrap-Up

Vocabulary

Activities of daily living (ADLs)
Advanced practice nurse (APN)
Allied health professionals
Allopathic approach
Anesthesiologist assistant (AA)
Associate degree in nursing (ADN)
Bachelor of Science in Nursing (BSN)
Board certifying or credentialing examination
Cardiovascular technologist
Certified midwives (CMs)
Certified nurse–midwives (CNMs)
Certified nursing assistants (CNAs)
Chiropractors
Commission on Accreditation of Allied Health Education Programs (CAAHEP)
Cytotechnologists
Dental assistants
Dental hygienists
Dentists
Diagnostic medical sonographer

Doctor of Medicine (MD)
Doctor of Osteopathic Medicine (DO)
Emergency medical technician (EMT)
Emergency medical technician-paramedic (EMT-P)
Exercise physiologists
Generalists
Geographic maldistribution
Health services administrators
Holistic approach
Home health and personal care aides
Hospitalists
Licensed practical nurses
Licensed vocational nurses
Medical assistants
Medical illustrators
Mid-level practitioners
National Practitioner Data Bank
Nonphysician practitioner
Nurse anesthetists (CRNAs)
Nurse practitioner (NP)
Optometrists
Orthotist

Perfusionists
Personal fitness trainer
Pharmacists
Pharmacy technician
Physician assistant (PA)
Physician Compare website
Physician extender
Podiatrists
Polysomnographic technologist
Primary care
Prosthetist
Psychiatric technicians and aides
Psychologists
Quaternary care
Recreational therapists
Registered nurse
Respiratory therapist
Secondary care
Sonography
Specialists
Specialty care
Specialty maldistribution
Surgeon technologist
Surgical assistant
Tertiary care
Transfusion medicine specialist

References

Allsup, Inc. (2016). Making the most of Social Security and Medicare benefits. Retrieved from https://www.allsup.com/personal-finance/financial-planning/financial-planning-for-family-caregivers/make-the-most-of-social-security-and-medicare

American Public Health Association (APHA). (2016). Workmen's compensation reform. Retrieved from http://www.apha.org/NR/rdonlyres/B240302E-94EF-4456-966F-6AEF329C289E/0/WorkersCompDraftNov102009.pdf

Bach, P. (2008). Cost sharing for health care: Whose skin? Which game? *New England Journal of Medicine*, 358, 4, 411–413.

Bihari, M. (2010). Understanding the Medicare Part D donut hole. Retrieved from http://healthinsurance.about.com/od/medicare/a/understanding_part_d.htm?p=1

Blue Cross Blue Shield (BCBS). (2016). Retrieved from http://www.bcbs.com/about-the-association/

Buchbinder, S., & Shanks, N. (2007). *Introduction to health care management*. Sudbury, MA: Jones and Bartlett.

Centers for Medicare and Medicaid Services (CMS). (2016a). Medicare program—general information. Retrieved from http://www.cms.gov/Medicare/Medicare-General-Information/MedicareGenInfo/index.html

CMS. (2016a). National health expenditures 2014 highlights. Retrieved from http://www.cms.gov/Research-Statistics-Data-and-Systems/Statistics-Trends-and-Reports/NationalHealthExpendData/Downloads/highlights.pdf

CMS. (2016b). National health expenditures projections 2014–2024. Retrieved from http://www.cms.gov/Research-Statistics-Data-and-Systems/Statistics-Trends-and-Reports/NationalHealthExpendData/Downloads/Proj2012.pdf

CMS. (2016c). How Medicare Advantage plans work? Retrieved from http://www.medicare.gov/sign-up-change-plans/medicare-health-plans/medicare-advantage-plans/how-medicare-advantage-plans-work.html

CMS. (2016d). Drug coverage (Part D). Retrieved from http://www.medicare.gov/part-d/

CMS. (2016e). Medicaid information by topic. Retrieved from http://www.medicaid.gov/Medicaid-CHIP-Program-Information/By-Topics/By-Topic.html

CMS. (2016f). Center for Medicare and Medicaid Innovation. Retrieved from http://innovation.cms.gov

CMS. (2016g). Innovation models. Retrieved from http://innovation.cms.gov/initiatives/index.html#views=models

CMS. (2016h). Community First Choice. Retrieved from http://www.medicaid.gov/Medicaid-CHIP-Program-Information/By-Topics/Long-Term-Services-and-Support/Home-and-Community-Based-Services/Community-First-Choice-1915-k.html

CMS. (2016i). Details for title: On eve of Medicare anniversary, over 6.6 million seniors save over $7 billion on drugs (July 29, 2013). Retrieved from http://cms.gov/Newsroom/MediaReleaseDatabase/Press-Releases/2013-Press-Releases-Items/2013-07-29.html

CMS. (2016j). Self-insured plan. Retrieved from https://www.healthcare.gov/glossary/self-insured-plan/

CMS. (2016k). National health expenditure data. Retrieved from http://www.cms.gov/Research-Statistics-Data-and-Systems/Statistics-Trends-and-Reports/NationalHealthExpendData/index.html?redirect=/nationalhealthexpenddata

CMS. (2016l). Medicare ACOs continue to improve quality of care, generate shared savings. Retrieved from https://www.cms.gov/Newsroom/MediaReleaseDatabase/Press-releases/2015-Press-releases-items/2015-08-25.html

Costs of care (2016). Retrieved from http://longtermcare.gov/costs-how-to-pay/costs-of-care/

Department of Health and Human Services (DHHS). (2016a). Long-term care insurance. Retrieved from http://www.longtermcare.gov/LTC/Main_Site/Paying_LTC/Private_Programs/LTC_Insurance/index.aspx

Department of Labor (DOL). (2016). Office of Worker's Compensation Programs. Retrieved from http://www.dol.gov/esa/owcp/dfec/regs/compliance/wc.htm

DHHS. (2016). Long term care: Where you live matters. Retrieved from http://longtermcare.gov/where-you-live-matters/

Emanuel, E. (2008). *Health care, guaranteed*. New York, NY: Public Affairs.

Enthoven, A. & Fuchs, V. (2006). Employment-based health insurance: Past, present and future. *Health Affairs, 25*, 6, 1538–1547.

Feldstein, P. (2005). *Health care economics*. Clifton Park, NY: Thomson/Delmar Learning.

Griffin, D., Black, N., Bronstein, S. & Devine, C. (2015). Veterans still facing major medical delays at VA hospitals. Retrieved from http://www.cnn.com/2015/10/20/politics/veterans-delays-va-hospitals/

Judson, K., & Harrison, C. (2006). *Law & ethics for medical careers*. New York, NY: McGraw-Hill.

Kaiser Family Foundation. (May 2012). Focus on health reform: Massachusetts health care reform: Six years later. Retrieved from http://kaiserfamilyfoundation.files.wordpress.com/2013/01/8311.pdf

Health care spending (2016). Retrieved from http://www.healthsystemtracker.org/interactive/health-spending-explorer/?display=U.S.%2520%2524%2520Billions&service=Hospitals%252CPhysicians%2520%2526%2520Clinics%252CPrescription%2520Drug&rangeType=single&years=2012&source=Total%2520National%2520Health%2520Expenditures&tab=2

Indian Health Services (IHS). (2016). Retrieved from http://www.ihs.gov/index.cfm?module=About

Kliff, S. (2012). Study: Fewer employers are offering health insurance. Retrieved from http://www.washingtonpost.com/blogs/wonkblog/post/study-fewer-employers-are-offering-health-insurance/2012/04/24/gIQAfGH6eT_print.html

Longest Jr., B., & Darr, K. (2008). *Managing health services organizations and systems*. Baltimore, MD: Health Professions Press.

McLean, R. (2003). *Financial management in health care organizations* (pp. 12–19). Clifton Park, NY: Thomson/Delmar Learning.

edicare.gov. (2016). What's Medicare supplement (Medigap) insurance? Retrieved from http://www.medicare.gov/supplement-other-insurance/medigap/whats-medigap.html

Miller, S. (2012). 6.3% health premium increases projected for 2013. Retrieved from http://www.shrm.org/hrdisciplines/benefits/articles/pages/health-premiums-2013.aspx

National Health Expenditures (2016). Retrieved from https://www.cms.gov/research-statistics-data-and-systems/statistics-trends-and-reports/nationalhealthexpenddata/downloads/highlights.pdf

National PACE Association. (2016). About NPA. Retrieved from http://www.npaonline.org/website/article.asp?id=5

Niles, N. (2011). *Basics of U.S. healthcare reform*. Sudbury, MA: Jones and Bartlett.

Noe, R., Hollenbeck, J., Gerhart B., & Wright, P. (2009). *Fundamentals of human resource management* (3rd ed., 29–30). New York, NY: McGraw-Hill/Irwin.

Nolo. (2016). Workers' compensation benefits FAQ. Retrieved from http://www.nolo.com/legal-encyclopedia/your-right-to-workers-comp-benefits-faq-29093.html

Pointer, D., Williams, S., Isaacs, S., & Knickman, J. (2007). *Introduction to U.S. health care*. Hoboken, NJ: Wiley Publishing.

Shi, L., & Singh, D. (2008). *Delivering health care in America* (4th ed.). Sudbury, MA: Jones and Bartlett.

Starr, P. (1982). *The social transformation of American medicine*. Cambridge, MA: Basic Books.

Sultz, H., & Young, K. (2006). *Health care USA: Understanding its organization and delivery* (5th ed.). Sudbury, MA: Jones and Bartlett.

Thomasson, M. (2016). Health insurance in the United States. Retrieved from http://eh.net/encyclopedia/article/thomasson.insurance.health.us

TRICARE. (2016). Retrieved from http://tricare.mil/tma/About TMA.aspx

Wilensky, G. (2006). Consumer driven health plans: Early evidence and potential impact on hospitals. *Health Affairs, 25*, 1, 174–186.

▶ **Notes**

▶ **Student Activity 7-1**

In Your Own Words

Based on this chapter, please provide an explanation of the following concepts in your own words. DO NOT RECITE the text.

Doctor of Medicine:

_____

_____

Doctor of Osteopathic Medicine:

_____

_____

Allopathic approach:

_____

_____

Psychologist:

_____

_____

Respiratory therapist:

_____

_____

Medical illustrator:

_____

_____

Emergency medical technician:

_____

_____

Transfusion medicine specialist:

_____

_____

Certified midwives:

_____

_____

Board certifying or credentialing examination:

_____

_____

▶ **Student Activity 7-2**

Real-Life Applications: Case Scenario One

You have heard that the healthcare industry is a growing industry for employment. You are unsure of the types of careers available to you.

Activity

You have chosen to explore the area of nursing and have provided the information here regarding nursing opportunities. For each of these opportunities, you will provide (1) educational requirements, (2) job responsibilities, and (3) average wages.

Nursing Options

Licensed practical nurse:

_____

_____

_____

_____

_____

Registered nurse:

_____

_____

_____

_____

_____

Case Scenario Two

Your friend has decided to research the area of allied health professionals as an opportunity for a career in health care and has provided the information here regarding two opportunities in this area. He will provide (1) educational requirements, (2) job responsibilities, and (3) average wages.

Activity

Your friend has decided to visit the CAAHEP website to research two accredited allied health professional jobs that are of interest to him and has added his research below.

Allied Health Professionals

Surgical assistant:

_____

_____

_____

_____

_____

Transfusion medical specialist:

_____

_____

_____

_____

_____

Case Scenario Three

You just moved to a rural community from an urban community and you want to establish relationships with physicians at your new home. You were surprised to find out how few choices you have. You decide to investigate why this is occurring.

Activity

Look on the Internet to find out information on geographic maldistribution. Write a report for your family and friends regarding this major issue.

Responses

_____

_____

_____

_____

_____

_____

_____

_____

_____

_____

_____

_____

_____

_____

_____

_____

Case Scenario Four

You have just been introduced to the different types of health care typically provided by physicians and other healthcare providers.

Activity

You ask your older sister, who is in medical school, to explain the differences and provide examples of primary, secondary, tertiary, and quaternary care.

Responses

_____

_____

_____

_____

_____

_____

_____

_____

_____

_____

_____

_____

_____

_____

_____

_____

_____

▶ **Student Activity 7-3**

Internet Exercises

Write your answers in the space provided.

- ■ Visit each of the websites here.
- ■ Name the organization.
- ■ Locate the organization's mission statement on the website.

- Provide a brief overview of the activities of the organization.
- How do these organizations participate in the U.S. healthcare system?

Websites

http://www.aanp.org

Organization Name:

_____

_____

Mission Statement:

_____

_____

_____

Overview of Activities:

_____

_____

_____

Importance of Organization to U.S. Health Care:

_____

_____

_____

http://www.asahp.org

Organization Name:

_____

_____

Mission Statement:

_____

_____

_____

Overview of Activities:

_____
_____
_____

Importance of Organization to U.S. Health Care:

_____
_____
_____

http://www.caahep.org

Organization Name:

_____
_____

Mission Statement:

_____
_____
_____

Overview of Activities:

_____
_____
_____

Importance of Organization to U.S. Health Care:

_____
_____
_____

http://www.aamc.org

Organization Name:

_____
_____

Mission Statement:

_____

_____

Overview of Activities:

_____

_____

_____

Importance of Organization to U.S. Health Care:

_____

_____

_____

http://bhpr.hrsa.gov

Organization Name:

_____

_____

Mission Statement:

_____

_____

_____

Overview of Activities:

_____

_____

_____

Importance of Organization to U.S. Health Care:

_____

_____

_____

http://www.aapa.org

Organization Name:

_____

_____

Mission Statement:

_____

_____

_____

Overview of Activities:

_____

_____

_____

Importance of Organization to U.S. Health Care:

_____

_____

_____

▶ Student Activity 7-4

Discussion Questions

The following are suggested discussion questions for this chapter.

1. Which of the allied health professional jobs would you like to choose as a career and why?

_____

_____

_____

_____

2. What is a physician extender? Would you as a patient use a physician extender? Defend your decision.

_____

_____

_____

_____

_____

_____

3. What is geographic maldistribution? Do you believe it is a problem?

_____

_____

_____

_____

_____

_____

_____

4. What is specialty maldistribution?

_____

_____

_____

_____

_____

_____

_____

5. Discuss the different nurse career options. Which one would you choose and why?

_____

_____

_____

_____

_____

_____

_____

_____

▶ **Student Activity 7-5**

Current Events

Perform an Internet search and find a current events topic over the past three years that is related to this chapter. Provide a summary of the article and the link to the article and why the article relates to the chapter.

_____

_____

_____

_____

_____

_____

_____

_____

_____

_____

_____

_____

_____

_____

_____

_____

_____

_____

_____

_____

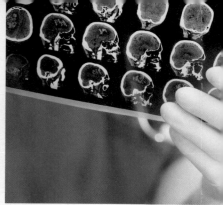

CHAPTER 8

Healthcare Financing

▶ Introduction

The percentage of the U.S. gross domestic product (GDP) devoted to healthcare expenditures has increased over the past several decades. In 2014, the United States spent $2.6 trillion on health care or 17.5% of GDP, which is the highest percentage of GDP spent on health care for any country in the world. The Centers for Medicare and Medicaid Services (CMS) predicts annual healthcare costs will be $4.64 trillion by 2024, which represents nearly 20% of the U.S. GDP (CMS, 2016a). The increase in healthcare spending can be attributed to three causes: (1) When prices increase in an economy overall, the cost of medical care will increase and, even when prices are adjusted for inflation, medical prices have increased. (2) As life expectancy increases in the United States, more individuals will require more medical care for chronic diseases, which means there will be more healthcare expenses. (3) As healthcare technology and research provide for more sophisticated and more expensive procedures, there will be an increase in healthcare expenses (Pointer, Williams, Isaacs, & Knickman, 2007). Three areas account for over 60% of national healthcare expenditures: hospital care, physician and clinical services, and prescription drugs (Health spending explorer, 2016). Unlike countries that have universal healthcare systems, payment of healthcare services in the United States is derived from (1) **out-of-pocket payments** or **cost sharing** from patients who pay entirely or partially for services rendered; (2) health insurance plans, such as indemnity plans or managed care organizations; (3) public or governmental funding such as Medicare, Medicaid, and other governmental programs; and (4) health savings accounts (HSAs) (Buchbinder & Shanks, 2007; Shi & Singh, 2008; Sultz & Young, 2006). Much of the burden of healthcare expenditures has been borne by private sources—employers and their health insurance programs. Individuals may continue to pay their health insurance premiums through the Consolidated Omnibus Budget Reconciliation Act (COBRA) once they are unemployed, but most individuals cannot afford to pay the expensive premiums. As a result of the passage of the Affordable Care Act (ACA) of 2010, the government has played a proactive role in developing a healthcare system that is more consumer oriented. The Act is requiring more employers to offer health insurance benefits and requiring individuals to purchase healthcare insurance if they can afford it from the health insurance marketplaces. The Act also requires health insurance plans to provide more information about their plans to their members so they can make informed decisions about their healthcare.

To understand the complexity of the U.S. healthcare system, this chapter will provide a breakdown of U.S. healthcare spending by source of funds, and the major private and public sources of funding for these expenditures. It is important to reemphasize that there are three parties involved in providing health care: the provider, the patient, and the fiscal intermediary such as a health insurance company or the government. Therefore, also included in the chapter is a description of how healthcare providers are reimbursed for their services and how reimbursement rates were developed for both private and public funds.

▶ Healthcare Spending by Service Type

This data is a summary from the CMS website of the different healthcare spending categories.

Overview

Hospital and Clinical Services

Spending for hospital care increased over 4% in 2014, compared to 3.5% growth in 2013. The growth in spending was due to an increase in the use of services. Hospital services experienced growth from Medicaid, private health insurance, and Medicare patients. Affordable Care Act coverage also contributed to increased hospital spending by Medicaid and private health insurers.

Private health insurance and Medicare spending on clinical services grew in 2014 because there was an increase in clinical service use by consumers as well as an increase in prices. Spending on specialty care such as chiropractic services, podiatry, and optometry increased nearly 5%, compared to a growth rate of 4.6% in 2010. Dental services increased 3% in 2014, which was a slight increase of 1.3% from 2013. Out-of-pocket spending for dental services, which accounts for 40% of dental spending, increased 0.2% in 2014, compared to a growth rate of 1% in 2013.

Home Health Care

Home health-care agency use increased 4.8% in 2014, up from 3.3% in 2013. The increase in 2014 spending was the result of the increase from Medicare and Medicaid spending for home health care, which accounts for 77% of overall home healthcare spending.

Nursing Care and Continuing Care Retirement Community Spending

Nursing care and continuing care retirement community spending increased 3.6% in 2014 compared to 2.4% in 2013. This increase can be attributed to Medicare and Medicaid spending.

Prescription Drugs

Prescription drug spending grew over 12% in 2014, a stark increase from a growth rate of 0.4% in 2010. The difference in the growth rates was due to price increases for brand-name prescription drugs, although consumers are continuing to purchase more generic drugs. Prices also increased for generic drugs (CMS, 2016a).

▶ Healthcare Spending by Sources of Funds

Medicare spending grew nearly 6% in 2014, an increase from the 2013 growth rate of 3%. The spending increase was the result of the overall growth in prices of drugs and services. Medicaid spending increased 11% in 2014, an increase from the 2013 growth rate of 6%. The increase in spending was due to new enrollees as a result of the Affordable Care Act. Private health insurance spending increased over 4% in 2014, which was higher than the 2013 growth rate of 1.6%. The difference in spending rates is most likely due to the number of enrollees in the health insurance marketplace. Out-of-pocket spending grew 1.3% in 2014, which was lower than the 2013 growth rate of 2.1%. The decrease in spending could be attributed to the decrease in the number of uninsured individuals nationwide (National Health Expenditures, 2014).

▶ Health Insurance as a Payer for Healthcare Services

Like life insurance or homeowner's insurance, **health insurance** was developed to provide protection should a covered individual experience an event that required health care. In 1847, a Boston insurance company offered sickness insurance to consumers. During the 19th century, large employers such as coal mining and railroad companies offered medical services to their employees by providing company doctors. Fees were taken from their pay to cover the service. In 1913, union-provided health insurance was administered by the International Ladies Garment Workers, which negotiated health insurance was negotiated as part of employment contracts. During this period, there were several proposals for a national health insurance program, but the efforts failed. The American Medical Association (AMA) was worried that any national health insurance would impact the financial security of providers. The AMA persuaded the federal government to support private insurance efforts. Employer-based health insurance grew rapidly post–World War II for three decades, with some stability for one decade and then an eventual decline in coverage since the late 1980s (Enthoven & Fuchs, 2006). However, it is still the major method of providing health care in the United States.

In 1929, a group hospital-insurance plan was offered to teachers in Texas. The teachers contracted for 21 days of hospital care for a $6.00 premium. This was the basic concept from which prepaid healthcare plans evolved. This also became the foundation of the nonprofit Blue Cross Blue Shield (BCBS) plans. To placate the AMA, BCBS initially offered only hospital insurance in order to avoid infringement of physicians' incomes (BCBS, 2013; Thomasson, 2013).

In 1935, the Social Security Act was enacted, creating Social Security, which was considered "old age" insurance. During this period, there was continued discussion of a national health insurance program. But with the impact of the Depression and World War II, there was no funding for such a program. The government's view was that Social Security was sufficient to protect consumers. These events were a catalyst for the development of a health insurance program that included private participation. Although a universal health coverage program was proposed during President Clinton's administration in the 1990s, it was never passed. In 2006, Massachusetts passed a bill requiring health coverage for all citizens. State data from 2010 indicates that Massachusetts had the lowest uninsured-resident rates in the country because of this initiative, although the state's healthcare premiums were also among the highest nationwide (Kaiser Family Foundation, 2012; Thomasson, 2013). In the 1960s, President Johnson signed into law Medicare and Medicaid, which protect elderly, disabled, and indigent individuals. President Nixon signed into law the Health Maintenance Act of 1973, which focused on effective cost measures for health delivery and was the basis for the current health maintenance organizations (HMOs). Also, in the 1980s, diagnosis-related groups (DRGs) and prospective payment guidelines were established to provide directions for treatment. These DRGs were attached to appropriate insurance reimbursement categories for treatment. Also, in the 1980s and 1990s, several consumer laws were passed. COBRA was passed to provide health insurance protection if an individual changes jobs. In 1993, the Family and Medical Leave Act (FMLA) was passed to protect an employee in the event of a family illness. Employees can receive up to 12 weeks of unpaid leave, and their health insurance is covered during this period. Also, in 1996, the Health Insurance Portability and Accountability Act (HIPAA) was passed, which mandated stricter confidentiality rules regarding the health information of individuals. The Affordable Care Act of 2010 eliminated lifetime and unreasonable annual caps or limits on healthcare reimbursement with annual limitations, provided assistance for the uninsured with preexisting conditions, prohibited denial of insurance coverage for preexisting conditions for children, created a temporary national high-risk pool for health insurance for individuals with preexisting conditions who have no insurance, and extended coverage for dependents up to age 26 (Niles, 2011).

▶ Types of Health Insurance

Health insurance, particularly employer-provided health insurance, is the primary source of payment of healthcare services in the United States. Unfortunately, employer-provided health insurance has become very expensive for businesses, resulting in the increase in cost sharing by employees (Emanuel, 2008). There are four types of private insurance: group insurance, individual private health insurance, self-insurance, and managed care plans. **Group insurance** anticipates that a large group of individuals will purchase insurance through their employer, and the risk is spread among those paying individuals. If an individual is self-employed, such as a small-business owner or a farmer, he or she may purchase **individual private health insurance**. Unlike group insurance, the risk is determined by the individual's health. Premiums, deductibles, and copayments are much higher for this type of insurance. Established in the 1970s, **self-funded or self-insurance** programs are health insurance programs that are implemented and controlled by the company itself. **Managed care plans** are a type of health program that combines administrative costs and service costs for cost control.

Health insurance is a financing mechanism intended to protect insureds from using their personal funds when expensive care is required. Having insurance also decreases the likelihood of delays in seeking treatment that may result in increased healthcare costs (Sultz & Young, 2006). Approximately 84% of the population is covered by some form of health insurance. All insurance plans fall into three categories: **voluntary health insurance (VHI)**, social insurance, and public welfare insurance. VHI is a type of private health insurance that is provided by nonprofit and for-profit health plans such as BCBS. **Social insurance** is provided by the government at all levels: federal, state, and local. An example of this type of insurance is Medicare. **Public welfare insurance** is based on financial need. The primary example of public welfare insurance is **Medicaid**.

All insurance plans define a contract among the beneficiaries, the purchasers (the employers and government), the health plan organizations, and the providers who deliver the services (Pointer et al., 2007). There are also self-insurance programs that are administered by employers, who bear the financial risk of providing their own health insurance to their employees. The funds to operate the program are derived from employee premiums. Reimbursement of health services is taken from this pool of funds rather than from another health insurance company.

There are two forms of payment, fee for service and prepayment, which provide the basis for all health insurance coverage. **Fee for service**, developed by BCBS, is based on the concept of a person purchasing coverage for certain benefits, using the health insurance coverage for these designated benefits, and paying the provider for the services provided. The provider may be paid by the insurance coverage or out of pocket by the patient. In a **prepayment** concept, the individual pays a fixed, predetermined amount for the services rendered. Managed care organizations follow a prepayment model (Sultz & Young, 2006).

▶ Cost Sharing of Health Services

Most insurance policies require a contribution from the covered individual in the form of a copayment, deductible, or coinsurance. This concept is called cost sharing. Used in both fee-for-service and prepaid plans, **copayments** are costs that patients must pay at the time they receive the services. It is a designated dollar amount. For, **coinsurance**, a type of copayment that is part of a fee-for-service policy, the patient pays a percentage of the cost of the services. A typical coinsurance portion is 20% paid by the individual, with the remaining 80% paid by the health insurance plan. **Deductibles** are payments that are required prior to the insurance paying for services rendered in a fee-for-service plan. Deductible amounts vary among individual and family health insurance plans and cover one calendar year. For example, an individual may have a $250 deductible per calendar year, which means they must pay the $250 before their health insurance covers the services. The growth in health insurance premiums is an excellent barometer to measure changes in private health insurance costs. Since 2007, health insurance premiums have increased approximately 6% annually. The rise in premium costs has increased the percentage of health insurance cost sharing borne by consumers (Miller, 2012). The main issue with the increase in cost sharing is its impact on individuals utilizing healthcare services. A study published in the *New England Journal of Medicine* concluded that adding an additional cost-sharing measure, such as a copayment of $10, reduced the number of women who received mammographies. These results concur with those of similar studies that examined cost sharing for health-screening services (Bach, 2008). Recognizing this trend, the ACA mandated that several types of preventive screenings will no longer require cost sharing.

Types of Health Insurance Policies

Comprehensive health insurance policies provide benefits that include outpatient and inpatient services, surgery, laboratory testing, medical equipment purchases, therapies, and other services such as mental health, rehabilitation, and prescription drugs. Most comprehensive policies have some exclusion attached to their policies. The opposite of comprehensive health insurance policies are basic or **major medical policies**, which reimburse hospital services such as surgeries and any expenses related to any hospitalization. There are limits on hospital stays. **Catastrophic health insurance** policies cover unusual illnesses with a high deductible and have lifetime reimbursement caps. There are also specific health insurance policies such as **disease-specific policies** for cancer and **medigap** or **Medicare supplement** or **medsup policies** that provide supplemental insurance coverage for Medicare patients (Shi & Singh, 2008).

▶ Types of Health Insurance Plans

There are two basic types of insurance plans: **indemnity plans**, which are fee-for-service plans, and managed care plans, which include health maintenance organizations, preferred provider organizations (PPOs), and point-of-service (POS) plans. Indemnity plans or fee-for-service plans are contracts between a beneficiary and a health plan but there is no contract between the health plan and providers. The beneficiary pays a premium to the health plan. When the beneficiary receives a healthcare service, the plan will reimburse the beneficiary based on an established fee for a particular service regardless of the provider's fees. The beneficiary will then reimburse the provider directly (Sultz & Young, 2006). The managed care plan is a special type of health plan that focuses on cost containment of health services. The first type of managed care organization was the HMO, which evolved in the 1970s. As managed care organizations evolved, different types of managed care organizations developed.

Managed care plans combine health services and health insurance functions to reduce administrative costs. For example, employers contract with a health plan for services on behalf of their employees. The employer is required to pay a set amount per enrolled employee on a monthly basis. The contracted health plan has a contract with certain providers to whom it pays a fixed rate per member on a monthly basis for certain services. Enrolled employees may cost share with a copayment. There is no deductible. The enrolled employees have restrictions on their choice of providers or incur larger copayments if they choose a provider out of the network.

A recent trend in health insurance plans is **consumer-driven health plans (CDHPs)** that are tax-plans with high deductible coverage. The most common CDHPs are **health reimbursement arrangements (HRAs)** and HSAs. HRAs, or **personal care accounts**, began in 2001 as a result of an Internal Revenue Service (IRS) regulation. An HRA is funded by the employer but owned by the employees and remains with the company if the employee leaves. This has been an issue because it has no portability (Wilensky, 2006).

A **health savings account (HSA)**, which was authorized by the **Medicare Prescription Drug, Improvement, and Modernization Act of 2003**, pairs high-deductible plans with fully portable employee-owned tax-advantaged accounts. This plan encourages consumers to become more cost conscious when using the healthcare system because they are using their own funds for healthcare services. The HSA, unlike the HRA, is a portable account, which means it can be transferred to another employer when the employee changes jobs. HSAs encourage consumers to understand healthcare service pricing because these accounts are paired with a high deductible. America's Health Insurance Plans (AHIP), an industry trade association, estimates that 4% of firms that offered benefits also offered an HSA or HRA (Wilensky, 2006).

Other types of CDHPs include **flexible spending accounts (FSAs)** and **medical savings accounts (MSAs)**. FSAs provide employees with the option of setting aside pretax income to pay for out-of-pocket medical expenses. Employees must submit claims for these expenses and are reimbursed from their spending accounts. The drawback is that the amount set aside must be spent within one year. Any unspent dollars cannot be rolled over so it is very important to be specific about the projected medical expenses. Mandated as part of HIPAA, MSAs allow workers employed in firms with 50 or fewer employees, and who have high-deductible health insurance plans, to set aside pretax dollars to be used for healthcare premiums and nonreimbursed healthcare expenses (Buchbinder & Shanks, 2007).

As discussed previously, self-funded or self-insurance programs are health insurance programs that are implemented and controlled by the company itself. They retain all of the risk in providing health insurance to their employees by paying any claims from their employees. Both the employee and the employer pay into the fund. The employer maintains a trust that is overseen by federal regulation. All claims are paid from the trust. The company will purchase reinsurance from another insurance company to protect itself from any catastrophic losses. The **reinsurance** sets a **stop-loss measure** that limits the amount the company will pay for claims (CMS, 2016i).

Long-Term Care Insurance

As life expectancy continues to increase in the United States, more people will require more healthcare services for chronic conditions. Unfortunately, Medicare and traditional health insurance policies do not pay for long-term care. Approximately 70% of people over age 65 will require long-term care at some point in their lives. Medicaid will pay for long-term care if you qualify for their program. The Department of Veterans Affairs may pay for long-term care for service-related disabilities and other eligible veterans' conditions. **Long-term care insurance** was developed to cover services such as assistance with **activities of daily living** (personal hygiene, feeding, and dressing oneself) as well as care in an institutional setting. The cost of long-term care insurance can vary based on the type and amount of services selected as well as the age at time of purchase and healthcare status. An average monthly cost for a semi-private room in a nursing facility is $6,235 or $4,000 for an assisted living facility (Costs of care, 2016).

An individual already receiving long-term care or in ill health might not qualify for long-term care insurance. Most long-term care insurance policies are comprehensive, which means they will cover expenses for home health care, hospice, respite care, assisted living and nursing homes, Alzheimer's disease special care, and adult day services centers. Long-term care policy costs vary greatly based on age and type of policy. The **National Clearinghouse for Long-Term Care Information** has provided the following information for purchasing long-term care insurance:

- The policyholder can select a daily benefit amount and how much is paid on a daily basis, depending on the healthcare setting. The type of healthcare setting can also be identified, such as home health care or skilled nursing facility.
- The policyholder can select a lifetime amount the policy will provide, which can range from $100,000 to $300,000. More expensive policies will allow unlimited coverage with no dollar limit, which is unusual. Premiums are typically $3,000 per year. Most policies will provide two to five years of long-term care coverage.
- The policyholder can also select an inflation option, which adjusts the coverage amount as the policyholder ages.
- Some policies may pay for long-term care provided to the policyholder by family members or friends. The policy may also provide reimbursement for equipment or transportation.

More employees are now offering long-term care insurance as an option to their employees. Employers do not contribute to the premium cost but may negotiate a better group rate. Long-term care insurance is becoming more popular because individuals are recognizing that Medicare will not pay for long-term care unless it is a medical necessity. Medicaid will pay for long-term care, but only for those individuals who qualify for the program (DHHS, 2016b).

Long-Term Care Financial Crisis

As the population lives longer, more people will need long-term care services; however, the majority of Americans do not plan for long-term care. Governmental programs account for 63% of long-term care funding, with Medicaid providing for 40% of that amount and Medicare 23% of that amount. Nationally, the median annual cost of a private room in a nursing home is over $90,000. Although Medicaid was originally developed for lower-income individuals, more middle-income needy individuals will be tapping into Medicaid because they do not have the funds to pay for their long-term care.

The federal government has been examining different alternatives to purchase long-term care insurance. For example, consumers who have been concerned about losing money on their premiums if they never use long-term care insurance can purchase a premium return rider on the policy, although doing so is expensive. A more grassroots opportunity for the elderly are community networks that the elderly can join so they can access long-term care support services.

Village Movement

In 2001, in Boston, Massachusetts, a group formed a nonprofit, Beacon Hill Village, which formed a network to provide services to older homeowners that allowed them to remain in their homes longer and maintain their independence. The network typically acts as a liaison to connect homeowners to needed workers. This membership organization's annual dues are approximately $600 and there is a network of contractors and volunteers who offer services that would typically be offered in a retirement community. There are nearly 200 villages around the country and more in development (Calmus, 2013).

▶ Public Financing of Healthcare Services

Since 1965, public financing has played a large role in providing healthcare services to elderly, disabled, and indigent individuals. Medicare and Medicaid are the two largest government-sponsored health insurance programs in the United States. Medicaid is a welfare program that is administered at the state government level. Medicare, Title XVIII of the Social Security Act, provides medical care for (1) individuals who are 65 years old or older, (2) disabled individuals who are entitled to Social Security benefits, and (3) people who have end-stage renal disease (Shi & Singh, 2008). Medicare is an **entitlement program** because people, after paying into the program for years from their wages, are entitled to receive benefits. It is important to emphasize that Medicare and Medicaid have provided increased access to healthcare services. The number of uninsured individuals in the United States would be much higher if these programs did not exist (Enthoven & Fuchs, 2006).

Medicare

The CMS has oversight of Medicare. In 2016, there are currently 57 million Medicare enrollees. This number will continue to increase as life expectancy increases. Medicare is the healthcare industry's largest payer. It was originally designed as a two-part structure: Part A for hospital insurance and Part B for supplemental or voluntary medical insurance. Recently, two additional parts were added: Part C/Medicare Advantage and Part D, which is a prescription-drug-plan benefit. The following summary information is from the medicare .gov website.

Medicare Part A: Hospital Insurance

Medicare Part A is primarily financed from payroll taxes and is considered hospital insurance. Employer and employees contribute to the Social Security

(Medicare) fund. Employees contribute 1.45% of wages, which is matched by employers. Self-employed individuals pay 2.9% of earnings. You pay no premium if you or your spouse paid Medicare taxes for at least 10 years. If an individual did not pay Medicare payroll taxes, your monthly 2016 premium is $411. In general, Part A covers hospital care, skilled nursing facility care, nursing home care (as long as custodial care is not the only care you need), hospice, and home health services (CMS, 2016a).

Medicare Part B: Original Medicare–Voluntary Medical Insurance

Medicare Part B is a supplemental health plan to cover physician services. It is financed 24% from enrollee premiums and 76% from federal treasury funds. Part B covers two types of services: medically necessary services—services or supplies that are needed to diagnose or treat your medical condition and that meet accepted standards of medical practice; and preventive services—health care to prevent illness (like the flu) or detect it at an early stage, when treatment is most likely to work best. The ACA has mandated there is no cost sharing for many preventive services. Part B covers things like clinical research, ambulance services, durable medical equipment (DME), mental health treatment, inpatient care, outpatient care, partial hospitalization, getting a second opinion before surgery, and limited outpatient prescription drugs. Part B is made available when enrollees sign up for Part A. Enrollees typically pay $104.90 per month (CMS, 2016a).

Medicare Part C: Medicare Advantage

Medicare Part C is also referred to as Medicare Advantage, and it can be considered a managed care model. It covers all services in Parts A and B. This program was designed to move Medicare patients into more cost-effective health insurance programs such as HMOs or PPOs. Medicare pays a fixed amount for your care every month to the companies offering Medicare Advantage Plans. These companies must follow rules set by Medicare. However, each Medicare Advantage Plan can charge different out-of-pocket costs and have different rules for how you get services. Some of these plans do offer vision, prescription, and dental plans (CMS, 2016b).

Medicare Part D: Prescription Drug Benefit

The Medicare Prescription Drug Improvement and Modernization Act of 2003 (MMA), which authorized

Medicare Part D, produced the largest additions and changes to Medicare. Tax revenues of the federal government support the majority of the program costs. Its purpose was to provide seniors with relief from high prescription costs. Like Part B, it is a voluntary program because enrollees pay a premium for coverage. Medicare Part C has Part D benefits rolled into their program. Private health insurance companies contract with Medicare to provide services. Effective January 1, 2006, this program developed a prescription drug program for enrollees. The following is a summary of Part D benefits (CMS 2016c):

- Affordable prescription drug plans were made available for Medicare Advantage plan enrollees and traditional Medicare health plans.
- For seniors who are considered indigent, the MMA established a low-income subsidy for the costs of Part D.

There was an issue with the Medicare Part D coverage gap, more commonly known as the "**donut hole**," for Medicare Part D beneficiaries that the Affordable Care Act should remedy.

There was an issue with the Medicare Part D coverage gap, more commonly known as the donut hole for Medicare Part D. The coverage gap or donut hole starts after the beneficiary and the drug plan together have spent a designated amount for the covered drugs. The donut hole changes every year. For example, in 2016, once the beneficiary enters the coverage gap ($3,310), the individual must pay 45% of the plan's cost for covered brand drugs and 58% of the plan's covered generic drugs. The beneficiary pays these percentages until he or she has reached the end of the coverage gap ($4,850 in 2016) and then a copayment for each covered drug is paid until the end of the year. Not all beneficiaries will reach the coverage gap because their drug costs are not that high. This increase in beneficiary out-of-pocket payments was very expensive for those enrolled and often resulted in individuals not obtaining necessary medication because of cost. Since the passage of the ACA, 6.6 million Medicare enrollees who were impacted by the donut hole have saved over $7 billion on prescription drugs, which averages $1,061 per beneficiary. In addition to the $250 rebate check, those impacted received discounts and increased coverage. They will continue to receive these benefits until the coverage gap is closed in 2020 (Centers for Medicare & Medicaid Services, 2016h).

Medigap or Medicare Supplement Plan or Medsup

Medicare covers less than half of total healthcare costs for enrollees, which leaves them with substantial out-of-pocket expenses. To cover these expenses, Medicare enrollees can receive additional coverage from (1) Medicaid if the Medicare enrollee is eligible, (2) enrollment in Medicare Advantage, which can provide supplemental coverage, (3) employer-sponsored retiree insurance, or (4) supplemental insurance policies from private insurance companies, which are called medigap or medsup policies. Medsup plans cover copays, deductibles, and coinsurance, which can be very expensive. Medicare has created 10 medsup plans that vary by state. Depending on the selected plan, the premiums will vary. Medicare Part C (Medicare Advantage) enrollees are not eligible for medsup plans (Medicare.gov, 2016).

Medicaid

Medicaid, Title XIX of the Social Security Act, provides health insurance to the indigent. It is a welfare program that is administered at the state government level. Medicaid and the CHIP program provide coverage to one in five people in the United States. Individuals who meet the requirements of both Medicare and Medicaid can be dually enrolled. Medicaid spending varies based on the status of the U.S. economy. It is not a federally mandated program; however, all states have Medicaid. Managed care enrollment has controlled Medicaid spending. Eligible people include (1) families with children receiving support under the Temporary Assistance for Needy Families (TANF) program, (2) people receiving Supplemental Security Income (SSI), (3) children and pregnant women with income at or below 133% of the federal poverty level, and (4) children whose parents have income too high for Medicaid but too low for private insurance (CMS, 2016d).

The ACA has requested that states expand their Medicaid programs to provide more coverage to individuals. As of 2016, 28 states have expanded their Medicaid program. The ACA created **Community First Choice** as an optional Medicaid benefit, which focuses on community health services to Medicaid enrollees with disabilities. This will enable consumers to receive care at home or at community health centers rather than going to a hospital or other facility. This option became available on October 1, 2011, and provides a 6% increase in federal matching payments to states for expenditures related to this option (CMS, 2016g). These mandates will enable lower-income consumers and children to have access to health care at an affordable cost.

All states administer their own program so eligibility varies by state. State programs must match federal funding and must provide the following:

inpatient and outpatient hospital services, physician care, nursing facility services, home health services, prenatal care, family planning services, health services for children under age 21, midwife services, and pediatric and family nurse practitioner services. State programs are responsible for at least 40% of the costs for provider services and must equally share the administrative costs of the Medicaid programs (CMS, 2016d). States have the right to determine the eligibility criteria for Medicaid enrollment, optional services to provide, methods and rates for provider payments, and utilization limits for services. As of 2016, five states have opted for this benefit (Pointer et al., 2007).

Children's Health Insurance Program

Authorized by the Balanced Budget Act of 1997, and codified as Title XXI of the Social Security Act, the State Children's Health Insurance Program (SCHIP), now the **Children's Health Insurance Program (CHIP)**, was initiated in response to the number of children who are uninsured in the United States. The CHIP gave states $40 billion over a decade to provide health care for these children. This program offers additional funds to states to expand Medicaid benefits to children younger than 19 years of age who otherwise may not qualify because their family income exceeds Medicaid levels.

The ACA of 2010 maintains the CHIP eligibility standards in place as of enactment through 2019. The law extended CHIP funding until October 1, 2015, when the already enhanced CHIP federal matching rate increased by 23%, bringing the average federal matching rate for CHIP to 93%. The ACA also provided an additional $40 million in federal funding to continue efforts to promote enrollment in Medicaid and CHIP (DHHS, 2016a).

Program of All-Inclusive Care for the Elderly

Also authorized by the Balanced Budget Act of 1997, the **Program of All-Inclusive Care for the Elderly (PACE)** is a comprehensive healthcare delivery system funded by Medicare and Medicaid. Oversight is provided by the CMS, and is modeled from a San Francisco, California, senior healthcare center, On Lok Senior Health Services. The PACE model focuses on providing community-based care and services to people who otherwise need nursing home levels of care. The philosophy is that seniors with chronic care needs are better served in the

community when possible. PACE organizations provide care and services in the home, the community, and the PACE center. They have contracts with many specialists and other providers in the community to make sure that patients get the care they need. Many PACE participants get most of their care from staff employed by the PACE organization in the PACE center. PACE centers must meet state and federal safety requirements.

Implemented at the state level, PACE can be offered as a Medicaid option. Participants must be Medicare eligible or 55 years or older with a disability, live in a PACE area, and be certified for nursing home care. An interdisciplinary team assesses the needs of the patient and develops a long-term plan. The PACE model provides services of Medicaid and Medicare but in an integrated manner. The National Pace Association Primary Care Committee has developed care models and prevention guidelines specifically for PACE patients who have diabetes, chronic heart failure, kidney disease, or pulmonary disease. PACE providers are reimbursed from Medicare and Medicaid payments. As of 2016, there were 117 PACE programs operational in 32 states. The CMS has issued guidelines for PACE programs to market their services (National PACE Association, 2016).

Worker's Compensation

The employer is financially liable for employees who become injured or ill as a result of working conditions. **Worker's compensation** is a state-administered program. Employees may receive cash for lost wages, payment for medical treatment, survivor's death benefits, and indemnification for loss of skills. Although worker's compensation is not a traditional health insurance program, it does provide medical benefits. The main difference between employer health insurance programs and worker's compensation is that the employer must cover the full cost of the benefits (DOL, 2016).

The worker's compensation program protects both the employer and the employee if there is a job-related injury and illness. Worker's compensation is a state program so benefits vary by state. Employees are eligible for this program for the following issues: (1) medical care, (2) death, (3) disability, and (4) rehabilitation services. Most employees receive approximately 66.66% of their earnings, which are tax-free. Workers compensation programs are funded by the employer, which either contracts with a commercial insurer or self-insures. Depending on the industry and the risk of injury, rates can vary from 1% of the payroll to 100% of the payroll. Like unemployment insurance, rates can also vary based on the **experience rating** of the company, meaning how often they have used the workmen's compensation program for employees who have been injured on the job. If the experience rating is high, their rates will be high (Noe et al., 2009).

These laws fall under **no-fault liability** or no-fault insurance, developed to avoid costly legal fees because there is no process to assess blame. The employee does not have to demonstrate that the employer was in the wrong, and the employer is protected from lawsuits unless it can be demonstrated that it was grossly negligent in the working conditions (Nolo, 2013). Unfortunately, there are disparities of how worker's compensation programs are implemented in each state. States often differ on the scope of permanent disability benefits and mental health coverage resulting from work. Experts estimate that 1 of 20 occupational disease victims receives workers' compensation benefits and 1 of 100 for occupational cancer. The American Public Health Association recommends that a national database be established on worker injuries, illnesses, toxic exposures, and diseases (APHA, 2016). As of this writing, worker's compensation is not reformed.

Other Prospective Reimbursement Methods

Tricare

The U.S. Department of Defense operates the Military Health Services System (MHHS), which provides medical services to active duty and retired members of the armed services. As the active duty numbers increased, a special medical care program called **TRICARE** was developed to respond to the growing needs of retired members. As a major component of the Military Health System, TRICARE combines the healthcare resources of the uniformed services with networks of civilian healthcare professionals, institutions, pharmacies, and suppliers to provide access to high-quality healthcare services while maintaining the capability to support military operations. TRICARE is regionally managed, structured after managed care, and coordinates the efforts of the Navy, Army, and Air Force. It has an HMO-type operation, a PPO-type organization, and a traditional fee-for-service program. There are 11 TRICARE regions in the United States, with other TRICARE operations in Europe, Latin America, and the Pacific. TRICARE provides benefits to

9.4 million beneficiaries worldwide. In 2015, the TRICARE system covered 1.450 million admissions, 49.345 million outpatient visits, 119,000 births, and 128.2 million prescriptions filled (TRICARE, 2016).

Veteran's Health Administration

In April 2014, CNN reported that 40 veterans had died while waiting for care provided by the Veteran's Health Administration in their Phoenix, Arizona site. This report was verified by governmental audits. Additional investigations indicated that 120,000 veterans had never received care, and there were huge waiting lists for veterans to receive care. In August 2014, President Obama signed legislation regarding funding for a complete overhaul of the VA system. There has been a continued focus on improving the VA to ensure veterans have timely medical treatment (Griffn, Black, Bronstein, & Devine, 2015).

Indian Health Service

The Indian Health Service (IHS) is the principal federal healthcare provider and health advocate for Indian people, and its goal is to raise their health status to the highest possible level. The IHS provides a comprehensive health service delivery system for American Indians and Alaska Natives who are members of 566 federally recognized tribes across the United States. The IHS is staffed by approximately 15,000 employees made up of a mixture of civil servants, federal employees, and U.S. Public Health Services (USPHS) commissioned officers (IHS, 2016).

▶ Reimbursement Methods of Private Health Insurance Plans

As healthcare costs have escalated, the government has developed various mechanisms aimed at standardizing reimbursement for healthcare services. In response, insurance companies developed standards for **usual, customary, and reasonable (UCR) services** based on community and state surveys of provider charges. If there was a difference in the reimbursement rates, the provider asked the patient to pay the difference. The problem with fee-for-service reimbursement methods is that it may have become a tool for some physicians to increase the number of services provided to the patient as a way to increase their income (Shi & Singh, 2008).

Insurance companies, managed care organizations, and the government are referred to as **third-party payers**. The other parties are the patient and the healthcare provider. The payment function in health care determines how much is reimbursed for the services. Fee for service, which was discussed previously, is the preferred method of reimbursement by providers. Historically, providers set the rate for their services that the government and health insurance companies paid without question. This type of **retrospective reimbursement** determines the amount of reimbursement after the delivery of services and provides little financial risk to providers. This method contributed to the increase in healthcare costs (Feldstein, 2005).

The most common type of reimbursement is a **service benefit plan**. This type of **prospective reimbursement** method was developed and used primarily by managed care organizations. The employer has a contract with a benefit plan and pays a premium for each of its employees. Employees usually also pay a portion of the premium to the health plan. The health plan contracts with certain providers and facilities to provide services to their beneficiaries at a specified rate and makes payments directly to the providers for their services (McLean, 2003).

Beneficiaries–employees and their families may have a cost-sharing arrangement with their employer for these services, such as deductibles and coinsurance payments, that supply payment to providers upon the receipt of a service. HMOs are examples of service benefit plans. In a managed care organization, the organization reimburses the provider at a **capitated rate**, which means they receive a set rate for serving enrolled patients regardless of how much care the provider gives. This type of capitation is also used by Medicaid and Medicare for their managed care programs (Pointer et al., 2007).

Per diem rates or per patient per day rates is a defined dollar amount per day for care provided. This is the most common form of reimbursement to hospitals. **Cost-plus reimbursement**, a type of retrospective reimbursement, was the traditional method used by Medicare and Medicaid to establish per diem rates for inpatient services. Under this method, reimbursement rates for institutions are based on the total costs incurred in operating the institution that are used to calculate the per diem or per patient day rate. The method is called cost-plus because, in addition to the operating costs, the reimbursement rate allows a portion of the capital costs to determine the rate (Buchbinder & Shanks, 2007; Shi & Singh, 2008; Sultz & Young, 2006).

▶ Governmental Reimbursement Methods for Healthcare Services

The federal government has sought to control healthcare expenditures through programs such as **diagnosis-related groups (DRGs)**, **ambulatory patient groups (APGs)**, **ambulatory payment categories (APCs)**, **home health resource groups (HHRGs)**, **resource utilization groups (RUGs)**, and **resource-based relative value scales (RBRVSs)**. States also used regulatory efforts such as a **certificate of need (CON)** to control expenditures by requiring an assessment to certify that a hospital is needed for a designated area. Also, Medicaid growth costs have been limited by hospital preadmission screening, limiting hospital stays, reducing per diem rates, increasing copayments, and decreasing service coverage. Reducing Medicaid reimbursements creates issues of **cost shifting**. Healthcare organizations must find other ways to be reimbursed or they will not be profitable so they cost shift by raising the prices to privately insured patients to offset the small reimbursement charges of Medicaid and Medicare (Feldstein, 2005).

Hospital Reimbursement

In 1982, Congress passed the **Tax Equity and Fiscal Responsibility Act (TEFRA)** and the **Social Security Amendments of 1983** to manage Medicare cost controls. There was a mandate to hospitals for a **prospective payment system** (PPS) to establish reimbursement rates for certain conditions. The CMS reimburses hospitals per admission and per diagnosis, which is based on a DRG—a prospective payment system for hospitals established through the Social Security Amendments of 1983. Each DRG group represents similar diagnoses of diseases that are expected to have similar use of hospital services. The amount of reimbursement is set per discharge of a patient. Hospitals that can provide services at lower costs may keep the difference in the reimbursement rates (Longest & Darr, 2008).

Medicare Hospital Readmission Reduction Program

Effective 2013, the Hospital Readmission Reduction Program (HRRP), established by the Affordable Care Act, penalizes most acute care hospitals with higher Medicare readmission rates within a 30-day period than the national average. Specialty hospitals such as children's, cancer, psychiatric, and rehabilitative are exempt. The penalty for excessive readmissions is 1% of their claims in 2013, 2% in 2014, and 3% in 2015 and beyond.

CMS has been posting individual hospital readmission rates on its *Hospital Compare* website, in addition to other measures of quality and patient satisfaction, since 2009. Designed for use by Medicare consumers as well as researchers, this website also provides comparisons of each hospital's Medicare readmission performance to the national average by indicating whether the hospital is "better/worse/no different" than the U.S. National rate (Boccuti & Casillas, 2015).

Most U.S. hospitals will get less money from Medicare in fiscal 2016 because too many patients return within 30 days of discharge. Only 799 out of more than 3,400 hospitals subject to the Hospital Readmissions Reduction Program performed well enough on the CMS' 30-day readmission program to face no penalty. Thirty-eight hospitals will be subject to the maximum 3% reduction (Rice, 2015).

This program is an attempt for hospitals to focus on recurring medical issues such as medication errors, surgery errors and hospital based infections. Hospitals across the country are focusing on quality improvement programs to improve patient health outcomes.

Resource-Based Relative Value Scale (RBRVS)

Under the Omnibus Budget Reconciliation Act of 1989, Medicare developed a new initiative, the RBRVS, to reimburse physicians according to a relative value assigned to a service. This is the most common physician-fee schedule. This reimbursement is divided into three components: physician work, practice expenses, and malpractice insurance. Medicare pays a flat fee for physician visits based on the Healthcare Common Procedure Coding System, which is used to code professional services. The RBRVS, implemented in 1992, has become a standard Medicare Part B reimbursement method. It is also widely used by Medicaid, worker's compensation payers, and private payers. This system increased reimbursement for family and general practice by approximately 15%. Also, physicians who had not signed a Medicare participation agreement (which requires accepting Medicare reimbursement as the full payment for services) were prevented from **balance billing**, so the physician is not able to bill the patient the difference between Medicare payments and the physician

charges. The statute limited the amount the physician could balance bill the patient (Longest & Darr, 2008).

Ambulatory Patient Groups (APGs) and Ambulatory Payment Categories (APCs)

Ambulatory patient groups (APGs) were developed in the 1980s and are a system of codes that explain the number and types of services used in an ambulatory visit. Similar to the DRG classification, patients per APG had similar clinical classifications, resource use, and costs. Implemented in August 2000, ambulatory payment categories (APCs) were adapted from the APGs. The APCs divide all outpatient services into 300 procedural groups or classifications based on similar clinical content such as surgery, medical, and ancillary services. Each APC is assigned a payment weight based on the median cost of services within the APC. The rates are also adjusted for wage differential by location. This type of rate is a bundled rate established by Medicare (CMS, 2016).

Resource Utilization Groups (RUG)

This type of prospective payment system for skilled nursing facilities, used by Medicare, provides for a per diem based on the clinical severity of patients. A classification system called resource utilization groups (RUG), a type of DRG, was designed to differentiate patients based on how much they use the resources of the facility. As the patient's condition changes, the rate of reimbursement changes. A per diem rate was established using these classifications (Longest & Darr, 2008; Shi & Singh, 2008).

Home Health Resource Groups (HHRG)

Implemented in October 2000, the home health resource group (HHRG), which is a prospective payment used by Medicare, pays a fixed predetermined rate for each 60-day episode of care, regardless of the services. All services are bundled under a home health agency.

The HHRG uses 80 distinct groups to classify patients' conditions (Longest & Darr, 2008).

The **Center for Medicare and Medicaid Innovation**'s goal is to support the development and testing of innovative healthcare payment and service delivery models. They have seven different categories of quality improvement projects for payment and care models, including accountable care organizations, value-based purchasing, and coordinated and prevention care.

Traditionally, Medicare makes separate payments to providers for each of the individual services they furnish to beneficiaries for a single illness or course of treatment. This approach can result in fragmented care with minimal coordination across providers and healthcare settings. Payment rewards the quantity of services offered by providers rather than the quality of care furnished. Research has shown that bundled payments can align incentives for providers—hospitals, post-acute care providers, physicians, and other practitioners—allowing them to work closely together across all specialties and settings. The following are different types of research projects that explore different payment initiatives (CMS, 2016e).

The CMS Demonstration Models

The **Bundled Payments Initiative** is composed of four broadly defined models of care, which link payments that multiple service beneficiaries receive during an episode of care. Model 1 includes an episode of care focused on the acute care inpatient

hospitalization. Awardees agree to provide a standard discount to Medicare from the usual Part A hospital inpatient payments.

Models 2 and 3 involve a **retrospective bundled payment** arrangement in which actual expenditures are reconciled against a target price for an episode of care. Model 4 involves a prospective bundled payment arrangement, in which a lump-sum payment is made to a provider for the entire episode of care. Over the course of the three-year initiative, the CMS will work with participating organizations to assess whether the models being tested result in improved patient care and lower costs to Medicare (see **TABLE 8-1**).

Accountable Care Organizations

According to the CMS website, **accountable care organizations (ACOs)** are groups of providers and hospitals who volunteer to give coordinated care to Medicare patients. The goal of ACOs is to ensure that patients, especially ones with chronic conditions, receive timely care while avoiding duplication

TABLE 8-1 Bundled Payments Models Initiative

Model 1: Retrospective Acute Care Hospital Stay Only

Under Model 1, the episode of care is defined as the inpatient stay in the acute care hospital. Medicare will pay the hospital a discounted amount based on the payment rates established under the Inpatient Prospective Payment System used in the original Medicare program. Medicare will continue to pay physicians separately for their services under the Medicare Physician Fee Schedule. Under certain circumstances, hospitals and physicians will be permitted to share gains arising from the providers' care-redesign efforts. Participation will begin as early as April 2013 and no later than January 2014 and will include most Medicare fee-for-service discharges for the participating hospitals.

Model 2: Retrospective Acute Care Hospital Stay plus Post-Acute Care

In Model 2, the episode of care will include the inpatient stay in the acute care hospital and all related services during the episode. The episode will end either 30, 60, or 90 days after hospital discharge. Participants can select up to 48 different clinical condition episodes.

Model 3: Retrospective Post-Acute Care Only

For Model 3, the episode of care will be triggered by an acute care hospital stay and will begin at initiation of post-acute care services with a participating skilled nursing facility, inpatient rehabilitation facility, long-term care hospital, or home health agency. The post-acute care services included in the episode must begin within 30 days of discharge from the inpatient stay and will end either a minimum of 30, 60, or 90 days after the initiation of the episode. Participants can select up to 48 different clinical condition episodes.

Model 4: Acute Care Hospital Stay Only

Under Model 4, the CMS will make a single, prospectively determined bundled payment to the hospital that would encompass all services furnished during the inpatient stay by the hospital, physicians, and other practitioners. Physicians and other practitioners will submit "no-pay" claims to Medicare and will be paid by the hospital out of the bundled payment. Related readmissions for 30 days after hospital discharge will be included in the bundled payment amount. Participants can select up to 48 different clinical condition episodes.

Modified from the Centers for Medicare and Medicaid Services. (2016). Bundled Payments for Care Improvement (BPCI) initiative: General information. Retrieved from http://innovation.cms.gov/initiatives/bundled-payments/

of services and preventing medical errors. Medicare has developed three major programs for providers to become ACOs:

- **Medicare Shared Savings Program**—a program that helps Medicare fee-for-service program providers becomes an ACO.
- **Advance Payment ACO Model**—a supplementary incentive program for smaller practices and physician-based and rural providers in the Shared Savings Program. They receive monthly payments to use for coordinated care.
- **Pioneer ACO Model**—a program designed for early adopters of coordinated care. Any monetary savings are shared with Medicare (CMS, 2016f).

In 2014, 20 Pioneer and 333 Shared Savings Program ACOs generated more than $411 million in savings, which includes all ACOs savings and losses. These results show that ACOs with more experience in the program tend to perform better over time. Since passage of the Affordable Care Act, more than 420 Medicare ACOs have been established, serving more than 7.8 million Americans with Original Medicare as of January 1, 2015 (CMS, 2016).

▶ Healthcare Financial Management

Although for-profit and nonprofit healthcare organizations have different missions, both types of organizations have financial objectives to achieve. The most common are (1) generating a reasonable net income to continue effective operations, (2) setting prices for services, (3) contracting management of third-party payers such as Medicare and Medicaid and health service providers, (4) analyzing information for cost control, (5) adhering to governmental regulations such as reimbursement methods, and (6) minimizing financial risk (Buchbinder & Shanks, 2007). To ensure these objectives are met, many healthcare organizational structures include the following positions to supervise the financial management function. The **chief financial officer (CFO)** supervises the **comptroller**, who is charged with accounting and reporting functions. The CFO may also supervise the **treasurer**, who is responsible for cash management, banking relations, accounts payable, etc. An **internal auditor**, who reports to the CFO, ensures that accounting procedures are performed in accordance with appropriate regulations (McLean, 2003). All of these positions ensure that the organization is focusing on its mission to provide quality healthcare services. If there is no strong financial management system in place, the organization will fail.

▶ Funds Disbursement

After services are delivered, the agency has to verify and pay the claims received from the providers. Disbursement of funds, which is often called **claims processing**, is carried out in accordance with the administrative procedures of the program. Most insurance companies and managed care organizations have a claims department to process payments. Self-funded insurance programs often hire a third-party administrator to process claims. Medicare and Medicaid contract with commercial insurance companies to process claims for them (Pointer et al., 2007).

▶ Conclusion

As healthcare expenditures continue to increase, the major focus of the healthcare industry is cost control in both the public and private sectors. For years, healthcare costs were unchecked. The concept of retrospective reimbursement methods for healthcare services, which mean that a provider submitted a bill to a health insurance company that automatically reimbursed the provider, had no incentive to control costs in health care. This type of reimbursement method contributed to expensive health care for both the healthcare insurance companies and the individual who was paying out of pocket for their services. The establishment of a prospective reimbursement system for Medicare—developed based on care criteria for certain conditions regardless of provider costs—was an incentive system for providers to manage how they were providing services. The DRGs, RUGs, and RBRVSs are examples of this type of reimbursement method. The focus now is efficiency and quality.

Also, the implementation of managed care organizations has focused on cost control. Although healthcare spending decreased in the 1990s, healthcare costs have continued to increase since. The implementation of CDHPs has assisted individuals with controlling healthcare costs by providing opportunities to save money for health care while obtaining a tax advantage. The Center for Medicare and Medicaid Innovation's new demonstration projects may provide data that supports new effective payment models that tie quality care with reimbursement. The Medicare Hospital Readmission Program is also an attempt to focus the hospitals on quality improvement in their healthcare.

Wrap-Up

Vocabulary

Accountable care organizations (ACOs)

Activities of daily living

Advance Payment ACO Model

Ambulatory patient groups (APGs)

Ambulatory payment categories (APCs)

Balance billing

Bundled Payments Initiative

Capitated rate

Catastrophic health insurance

Center for Medicare and Medicaid Innovation

Certificate of need (CON)

Chief financial officer (CFO)

Children's Health Insurance Program (CHIP)

Claims processing

Coinsurance

Community First Choice

Comprehensive health insurance policies

Comptroller

Consumer-driven health plans

Copayments

Cost-plus reimbursement

Cost sharing

Cost shifting

Deductibles

Diagnosis-related group (DRG)

Disease-specific policies

Donut hole

Entitlement program

Experience rating

Fee for service

Flexible spending accounts (FSAs)

Group insurance

Health insurance

Health reimbursement arrangements (HRAs)

Health savings accounts (HSAs)

Home health resource group (HHRG)

Indemnity plans

Individual private health insurance

Internal auditor

Long-term care insurance

Major medical policies

Managed care plans

Medicaid

Medical saving accounts (MSAs)

Medicare Hospital Readmission Program

Medicare Part A

Medicare Part B

Medicare Part C

Medicare Part D

Medicare Prescription Drug Improvement and Modernization Act of 2003

Medicare Shared Savings program

Medigap or Medicare supplemental or medsup policies

National Clearinghouse for Long-Term Care Information

No-fault liability

Out-of-pocket payments

Personal care accounts

Per diem rates

Pioneer ACO Model

Prepayment

Program of All-Inclusive Care for the Elderly (PACE)

Prospective reimbursement

Prospective payment system

Public welfare insurance

Reinsurance

Resource-based relative value scales (RBRVSs)

Resource utilization group (RUG)

Retrospective bundled payments

Retrospective reimbursement

Self-funded or self-insurance

Service benefit plan

Social insurance

Social Security Amendments of 1983

Stop-loss measure

Tax Equity and Fiscal Responsibility Act (TEFRA)

Third-party payer

Treasurer

TRICARE

Usual, customary, and reasonable (UCR) services

Voluntary health insurance (VHI)

Workers' compensation

References

Allsup, Inc. (2016). Making the most of Social Security and Medicare benefits. Retrieved from https://www.allsup .com/personal-finance/financial-planning/financial-plan ning-for-family-caregivers/make-the-most-of-social-security -and-medicare

American Public Health Association (APHA). (2016). Workmen's compensation reform. Retrieved from http://www.apha.org /NR/rdonlyres/B240302E-94EF-4456-966F-6AEF329C289E/0 /WorkersCompDraftNov102009.pdf

Bach, P. (2008). Cost sharing for health care: Whose skin? Which game? *New England Journal of Medicine*, 358, 4, 411–413.

Bihari, M. (2010). Understanding the Medicare Part D donut hole. Retrieved from http://healthinsurance.about.com/od /medicare/a/understanding_part_d.htm?p=1

Blue Cross Blue Shield (BCBS). (2016). Retrieved from http ://www.bcbs.com/about-the-association/

Buchbinder, S., & Shanks, N. (2007). *Introduction to health care management*. Sudbury, MA: Jones and Bartlett.

Boccuti C. & Casillas, G., (2015). Aiming for fewer u-turns: The Medicare Hospital Readmission program. Retrieved from http://kff.org/medicare/issue-brief/aiming-for-fewer-hospital -u-turns-the-medicare-hospital-readmission-reduction-program/

Calmus, D. (2013). The long term care financing crisis. Center for Policy Innovation, Retrieved from http://www.heritage.org /research/reports/2013/02/the-long-term-care-financing-crisis

Centers for Medicare and Medicaid Services (CMS). (2016a). Medicare program—general information. Retrieved from http://www.cms.gov/Medicare/Medicare-General-Information/MedicareGenInfo/index.html

CMS. (2016a). National health expenditures 2014 highlights. Retrieved from http://www.cms.gov/Research-Statistics-Data-and-Systems/Statistics-Trends-and-Reports/NationalHealthExpendData/Downloads/highlights.pdf

CMS. (2016b). National health expenditures projections 2014–2024. Retrieved from http://www.cms.gov/Research-Statistics-Data-and-Systems/Statistics-Trends-and-Reports/NationalHealthExpendData/Downloads/Proj2012.pdf

CMS. (2016c). How Medicare Advantage plans work? Retrieved from http://www.medicare.gov/sign-up-change-plans/medicare-health-plans/medicare-advantage-plans/how-medicare-advantage-plans-work.html

CMS. (2016d). Drug coverage (Part D). Retrieved from http://www.medicare.gov/part-d/

CMS. (2016e). Medicaid information by topic. Retrieved from http://www.medicaid.gov/Medicaid-CHIP-Program-Information/By-Topics/By-Topic.html

CMS. (2016f). Center for Medicare and Medicaid Innovation. Retrieved from http://innovation.cms.gov

CMS. (2016g). Innovation models. Retrieved from http://innovation.cms.gov/initiatives/index.html#views=models

CMS. (2016h). Community First Choice. Retrieved from http://www.medicaid.gov/Medicaid-CHIP-Program-Information/By-Topics/Long-Term-Services-and-Support/Home-and-Community-Based-Services/Community-First-Choice-1915-k.html

CMS. (2016i). Details for title: On eve of Medicare anniversary, over 6.6 million seniors save over $7 billion on drugs (July 29, 2013). Retrieved from http://cms.gov/Newsroom/MediaReleaseDatabase/Press-Releases/2013-Press-Releases-Items/2013-07-29.html

CMS. (2016j). Self-insured plan. Retrieved from https://www.healthcare.gov/glossary/self insured plan/

CMS. (2016k). National health expenditure data. Retrieved from http://www.cms.gov/Research-Statistics-Data-and-Systems/Statistics-Trends-and-Reports/NationalHealthExpendData/index.html?redirect=/nationalhealthexpenddata

CMS. (2016l). Medicare ACOs continue to improve quality of care, generate shared savings. Retrieved from https://www.cms.gov/Newsroom/MediaReleaseDatabase/Press-releases/2015-Press-releases-items/2015-08-25.html

Costs of care. (2016). Retrieved from http://longtermcare.gov/costs-how-to-pay/costs-of-care/

Department of Health and Human Services (DHHS). (2016a). Long-term care insurance. Retrieved from http://www.longtermcare.gov/LTC/Main_Site/Paying_LTC/Private_Programs/LTC_Insurance/index.aspx

Department of Labor (DOL). (2016). Office of Worker's Compensation Programs. Retrieved from http://www.dol.gov/esa/owcp/dfec/regs/compliance/wc.htm

DHHS. (2016). Long term care: Where you live matters. Retrieved from http://longtermcare.gov/where-you-live-matters/

Emanuel, E. (2008). *Health care, guaranteed*. New York, NY: Public Affairs.

Enthoven, A. & Fuchs, V. (2006). Employment-based health insurance: Past, present and future. *Health Affairs*, 25, 6, 1538–1547.

Feldstein, P. (2005). *Health care economics*. Clifton Park, NY: Thomson/Delmar Learning.

Griffin, D., Black, N., Bronstein, S. & Devine, C. (2015). Veterans still facing major medical delays at VA hospitals. Retrieved from http://www.cnn.com/2015/10/20/politics/veterans-delays-va-hospitals/

Judson, K., & Harrison, C. (2006). *Law & ethics for medical careers*. New York, NY: McGraw-Hill.

Kaiser Family Foundation. (May 2012). Focus on health reform: Massachusetts health care reform: Six years later. Retrieved from http://kaiserfamilyfoundation.files.wordpress.com/2013/01/8311.pdf

Health care spending (2016). Retrieved from http://www.healthsystemtracker.org/interactive/health-spending-explorer/?display=U.S.%2520%2524%2520Billions&service=Hospitals%252CPhysicians%2520%2526%2520Clinics%252CPrescription%2520Drug&rangeType=single&years=2012&source=Total%2520National%2520Health%-2520Expenditures&tab=2

Indian Health Services (IHS). (2016). Retrieved from http://www.ihs.gov/index.cfm?module=About

Kliff, S. (2012). Study: Fewer employers are offering health insurance. Retrieved from http://www.washingtonpost.com/blogs/wonkblog/post/study-fewer-employers-are-offering-health-insurance/2012/04/24/gIQAfGH6eT_print.html

Longest Jr., B., & Darr, K. (2008). *Managing health services organizations and systems*. Baltimore, MD: Health Professions Press.

McLean, R. (2003). *Financial management in health care organizations* (pp. 12–19). Clifton Park, NY: Thomson/Delmar Learning..

Medicare.gov. (2016). What's Medicare supplement (Medigap) insurance? Retrieved from http://www.medicare.gov/supplement-other-insurance/medigap/whats-medigap.html

Miller, S. (2012). 6.3% health premium increases projected for 2013. Retrieved from http://www.shrm.org/hrdisciplines/benefits/articles/pages/health-premiums-2013.aspx

National Health Expenditures (2016). Retrieved from https://www.cms.gov/research-statistics-data-and-systems/statistics-trends-and-reports/nationalhealthexpenddata/downloads/highlights.pdf

National PACE Association. (2016). About NPA. Retrieved from http://www.npaonline.org/website/article.asp?id=5

Niles, N. (2011). *Basics of U.S. healthcare reform*. Sudbury, MA: Jones and Bartlett.

Noe, R., Hollenbeck, J., Gerhart B., & Wright, P. (2009). *Fundamentals of human resource management* (3rd ed., 29–30). New York, NY: McGraw-Hill/Irwin.

Nolo. (2016). Workers' compensation benefits FAQ. Retrieved from http://www.nolo.com/legal-encyclopedia/your-right-to-workers-comp-benefits-faq-29093.html

Pointer, D., Williams, S., Isaacs, S., & Knickman, J. (2007). *Introduction to U.S. health care*. Hoboken, NJ: Wiley Publishing.

Rice, S., (2015). Most hospitals face 30 day readmission penalty in 2016. Retrieved from http://www.modernhealthcare.com/article/20150803/NEWS/150809981

Shi, L., & Singh, D. (2008). *Delivering health care in America* (4th ed.). Sudbury, MA: Jones and Bartlett.

Starr, P. (1982). *The social transformation of American medicine*. Cambridge, MA: Basic Books.

Sultz, H., & Young, K. (2006). *Health care USA: Understanding its organization and delivery* (5th ed.). Sudbury, MA: Jones and Bartlett.

Thomasson, M. (2016). Health insurance in the United States. Retrieved from http://eh.net/encyclopedia/article/thomasson.insurance.health.us

TRICARE. (2016). Retrieved from http://tricare.mil/tma/About TMA.aspx

Wilensky, G. (2006). Consumer driven health plans: Early evidence and potential impact on hospitals. *Health Affairs*, 25, 1, 174–186.

▶ Notes

▶ Student Activity 8-1

Based on this chapter, please provide an explanation of the following concepts in your own words. DO NOT RECITE the text.

Reinsurance:

_____

_____

Flexible spending accounts (FSAs):

_____

_____

Prospective reimbursement:

_____

_____

Diagnosis-related group (DRG):

_____

_____

Resource utilization group (RUG):

_____

_____

Coinsurance:

_____

_____

Consumer-driven health plans:

_____

_____

Cost sharing:

_____

_____

Entitlement program:

_____

_____

_____

▶ Student Activity 8-2

Real-Life Applications: Case Scenario One

Your grandmother just turned 65 and is very confused about Medicare. She doesn't understand why there are four parts to this health insurance program. She has asked you to help her with enrolling in Medicare.

Activity

(1) List the different parts of Medicare, and (2) explain what each part is and why it may be important to your grandmother.

Responses

_____

_____

_____

_____

_____

_____

_____

_____

_____

_____

_____

_____

_____

_____

_____

_____

_____

_____

Case Scenario Two

Your health insurance is paid for by your family. You continually hear your parents complain about cost sharing in their health insurance costs. You are not familiar with the term.

Activity

Perform research to identify cost sharing in the U.S. healthcare system. Define cost sharing and how the cost is shared with the employer and employees like your parents. Develop a report and share it with your parents.

Responses

_____

_____

_____

_____

_____

_____

_____

_____

_____

_____

_____

_____

_____

_____

_____

_____

_____

_____

Case Scenario Three

As life expectancy continues to increase in the United States, you are encouraging your older siblings to start planning ahead. You indicate to them they should think about long-term care insurance. They said they have never heard of it.

Activity

You decide to perform research on long-term care insurance and how it is used. You prepare a report for your siblings.

Responses

_____

_____

_____

_____

_____

_____

_____

_____

_____

_____

_____

_____

_____

_____

_____

_____

_____

_____

_____

_____

Case Scenario Four

One of your friends recently left the military. He is happy that he has medical benefits under TRICARE. You are not familiar with this program.

Activity

You decide to research TRICARE and what type of benefits it provides to military members. Write your results and present to the class.

Responses

_____

_____

_____

_____

_____

_____

_____

_____

_____

_____

_____

_____

_____

_____

_____

_____

▶ **Student Activity 8-3**

Internet Exercises

Write your answers in the space provided.

- Visit each of the websites listed here.
- Name the organization.
- Locate the organization's mission statement on the website.
- Provide a brief overview of the activities of the organization.
- How do these organizations participate in the U.S. healthcare system?

Websites

http://www.tricare.mil

Organization Name:

_____

_____

Mission Statement:

_____

_____

_____

Overview of Activities:

_____

_____

Importance of Organization to U.S. Health Care:

_____

_____

_____

http://www.npaonline.org

Organization Name:

_____

_____

Mission Statement:

_____

_____

_____

Overview of Activities:

_____

_____

_____

Importance of Organization to U.S. Health Care:

_____

_____

_____

http://www.familiesusa.org

Organization Name:

_____

_____

Mission Statement:

_____

_____

_____

Overview of Activities:

_____

_____

_____

Importance of Organization to U.S. Health Care:

_____

_____

_____

http://www.innovations.ahrq.gov

Organization Name:

_____

_____

Mission Statement:

_____

_____

_____

Overview of Activities:

_____

_____

_____

Importance of Organization to U.S. Health Care:

_____

_____

_____

http://www.schip-info.org

Organization Name:

_____

_____

Mission Statement:

_____

_____

_____

Overview of Activities:

_____

_____

_____

Importance of Organization to U.S. Health Care:

_____

_____

_____

http://www.ebms.com

Organization Name:

_____

_____

Mission Statement:

_____

_____

Overview of Activities:

_____

_____

_____

Importance of Organization to U.S. Health Care:

_____

_____

_____

▶ **Student Activity 8-4**

Discussion Questions

The following are suggested discussion questions for this chapter.

1. What is long-term care insurance? Do you think this is a useful tool? Would you buy it?

_____

_____

_____

_____

2. Discuss the three types of Medicare accountable care organizations. Do you think these are a great way to provide care? Defend your answer.

_____

_____

_____

_____

_____

_____

3. What is the donut hole? How would you fix this?

_____

_____

_____

_____

_____

_____

4. Visit the www.cms.gov website and go to the innovation center. Discuss one of the innovation methods you found on the website and its potential contribution to health care.

_____

_____

_____

_____

_____
_____
_____
_____
_____

5. Review the PACE website. What do you think of this association?

_____
_____
_____
_____
_____
_____
_____
_____

▶ Student Activity 8-5

Current Events

Perform an Internet search and find a current events topic over the past three years that is related to this chapter. Provide a summary of the article and the link to the article and why the article relates to the chapter.

_____
_____
_____
_____
_____
_____
_____
_____

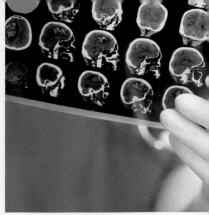

CHAPTER 9

Managed Care Impact on Healthcare Delivery

▶ Introduction

Managed care is a healthcare delivery system organized to manage cost, utilization, and quality. Managed care refers to the cost management of healthcare services by controlling who the consumer sees and how much the service costs. **Managed care organizations (MCOs)** were introduced 40 years ago, but became more entrenched in the healthcare system when the Health Maintenance Organization Act of 1973 was signed into law by President Nixon (Medicaid, 2016). Healthcare costs were spiraling out of control during that period. Encouraging the increase in the development of HMOs, the first widely used managed care model, would help to control the healthcare costs. MCOs' integration of the financial industry with the medical service industry resulted in controlling the reimbursement rate of services, which allowed MCOs more control over the health insurance portion of health care (Sultz & Young, 2006). Physicians were initially resistant to managed care models because they were threatened by loss of income. As the number of managed care models increased, physicians realized they had to accept this new form of healthcare delivery and, if they participated in a managed care organization, it was guaranteed income. Managed care health plans have become a standard option for consumers. Medicare Part C, which is commonly called Medicare Advantage, offers managed care options to their enrollees. Medicaid managed care provides for the delivery of Medicaid health benefits and additional services through contracted arrangements between state Medicaid agencies and MCOs that accept a set payment per member per month (capitation) for these services. Many employers offer managed care plans to their employees. This chapter will discuss the evolution of managed care and why it developed, the different types of managed care, the MCO assessment measures used for cost control, issues regarding managed care, and how managed care has impacted the delivery of healthcare services.

▶ History of Managed Care

The delivery of health care traditionally evolved around the individual relationship between the provider and the patient–consumer. The payment was either provided by a health insurance company or paid out of pocket by the consumer. This **fee-for-service (FFS)** system or **indemnity plan** increased the cost of health care because there were no controls on how much to charge for the provider's service. As

healthcare costs continued to spiral out of control throughout the decades, more experiments with contract practice and prepaid service occurred randomly across the U.S. healthcare system (Shi & Singh, 2008).

According to the Tufts Managed Care Institute, from 1850 to 1900, railroad, mining, and lumber companies provided their employees with healthcare services. The companies contracted with a physician to provide services to their employees at a rate per worker (which is a capitation rate because it limits the amount the provider will be paid per service). These companies had to contract with a physician because of the remoteness of work locations.

A managed care pioneer, Dr. Michael Shadid, started a farmer cooperative health plan in 1929 in Oklahoma. He enrolled several hundred families, who paid a set fee and received care from Dr. Shadid. Also, in 1929, the Los Angeles Department of Health contracted with physicians to provide healthcare services to 2,000 workers and families. In 1933, Dr. Sidney Garfield contracted with 5,000 construction workers to prepay for their healthcare. In 1938, he contracted with Henry Kaiser to provide medical care to his workers for a dam project.

When group health insurance programs were formed in the 1940s, corporations' power to manage healthcare coverage decreased and health insurance companies' power increased. The health insurance companies and providers had no incentives to control the costs of services. The concept of contractual practices and capitation were not adopted nationwide, which pleased the American Medical Association (AMA) because providers could increase their income with a traditional FFS practice. As a result of this system, healthcare costs continued to increase dramatically (Tufts Managed Care Institute, 2016).

The concept of managed care has been evolving seriously since the early 1930s. The Committee on the Costs of Medicare Care recommended in 1932 that health care should be reorganized into a type of prepaid formula to control costs of services (Committee on the Costs of Medical Care, 1932). The FFS system was recognized even then as inefficient because there was no patient care coordination between the primary care provider and other providers. There was also no focus on minimizing cost of services.

In the early 1930s and 1940s, several health plans adopted the concept of prepaid practice plans: the Group Health Association of Washington, the Group Health Cooperative of Puget Sound, the Health Insurance Plan of Greater New York, the Group Health Plan of Minneapolis, and the Kaiser Permanente Medical Care program, which became the model for

HMOs. According to the Kaiser Permanente website, the Kaiser Permanente Plan was developed in 1933 as a result of providing care to construction, shipyard, and steel workers for Kaiser Industries, which they owned during this period. Dr. Sidney Garfield, a surgeon, recognized the potential to provide care to the thousands of workers involved in extensive projects, so he built a hospital and set up a practice to care for these workers. Unfortunately, he often did not receive pay for his services because the insurance companies were not timely in their reimbursement and some workers were uninsured. Harold Hatch, an insurance agent, developed the prepaid concept of medical care. Dr. Garfield would receive insurance remuneration up front per day for each worker. This system worked extremely well and was used for several different industrial projects until 1945, when many of these large projects were completed. Kaiser Permanente opened this type of managed care system to the public in 1945. Enrollment increased to 300,000 members as a result of union membership. Kaiser Permanente, located in Oakland, California, has continued this type of concept successfully. It is the largest nonprofit health plan today, with 9.1 million members and nearly $51 billion in operating revenue (Kaiser Permanente, 2016).

Legislative Influence on Managed Care Development

In 1973, President Nixon signed into law the HMO Act. This Act authorized $375 million in funding (loans and grants) for HMO expansion of existing facilities, thus rewarding HMOs for focusing on cost control. The Act also required that any business that had 25 or more employees offer an HMO option if available. According to a 2004 report on managed care by the AMA's Council on Medical Services, over the next 30 years, several legislative acts were passed that impacted how managed care developed (Hoven, 2004).

Amendments in 1976 and 1978 to the HMO Act of 1973 relaxed requirements for HMOs and restricted funding for HMO assistance programs for 2 years. In 1988, the HMO Act was amended to allow employees to contribute less to HMO plans than to traditional FFS plans. In 1982, the Tax Equity and Fiscal Responsibility Act reduced federal funding for health care, including HMOs. The Balanced Budget Act of 1997 established Medicare+Choice (M+C; Part C) which developed different structures for managed care plans. In 2003, the Medicare Prescription Drug, Improvement, and Modernization Act of 2003 replaced M+C with Medicare Advantage (Hoven, 2004).

Over the past three decades, MCOs' strategies have increased their exposure. More companies have become interested in controlling healthcare costs and routinely offer managed care plans to their employees.

Managed Care Characteristics

Regardless of the type of MCO, all MCOs have five common characteristics (Knight, 1998):

- They all establish relationships with organizations and providers to offer a designated set of services to their members.
- They all establish criteria for their members to utilize the MCO.
- They all establish measures to estimate cost control.
- They all provide incentives to encourage health service resources.
- They all provide and encourage utilization of programs to improve the health status of their enrollees.

The MCO provides comprehensive services that include primary, secondary, and tertiary care. Depending on the type of MCO, physicians may work exclusively for the MCO or may be under contract with the MCO. MCOs will also contract with hospitals and outpatient clinics to ensure they provide comprehensive services.

Different Types of Managed Care Models

There are six organizational structures of MCOs.

1. **Health maintenance organizations (HMOs):** HMOs are the oldest type of managed care. Members must see their primary care provider first in order to see a specialist. There are four types of HMOs: staff model, group model, network model, and the independent practice association (Bihari, 2010).

   - The **staff model** hires providers to work at a physical location. The **group model** negotiates with a group of physicians exclusively to perform services. This was the first type of HMO model introduced by Kaiser Permanente.
   - The **network model** is similar to the group model, but providers may see other patients who are not members of the HMO. There is a negotiated rate for service for members to see providers who belong to the network.
   - The **independent practice associations (IPAs)** contract with a group of physicians who are in private practice to

see MCO members at a prepaid rate per visit. The physicians may sign contracts with many HMOs. The physicians may also see non-HMO patients. This type of HMO was a result of the HMO Act of 1973.

2. **Preferred provider organizations (PPOs):** These providers agree to a relative value-based fee schedule or a discounted fee to see members. They do not have a gatekeeper like the HMO so a member does not need a referral to see a specialist. The PPO does not have a copay but does have a deductible. This plan was developed by providers and hospitals to ensure that nonmembers could still be served while providing a discount to MCOs for their members. A member may see a provider not in the network but they may pay more out of pocket for their services. The bill could be as much as 50% of the total bill. They are currently the most popular type of plan (American Heart Association, 2013).

3. **Exclusive provider organizations (EPOs):** These are similar to PPOs but they restrict members to a list of preferred or exclusive providers.

4. **Physician hospital organizations (PHOs):** These organizations include physician hospitals, surgical centers, and other medical providers that contract with a managed care plan to provide health services (Judson & Harrison, 2006).

5. **Point-of-service (POS) plans:** The POS plans are a blend of the other MCOs—a type of HMO–PPO hybrid. They encourage but do not require that plan members use a primary care provider who will become the gatekeeper of services. Members will receive lower fees if they use a gatekeeper model. They may also see an out-of-network provider at any time but will be charged a higher rate. This type of plan was developed as a result of complaints about the inability of members to choose their provider (American Heart Association, 2016).

6. **Provider-sponsored organizations (PSOs):** These organizations are owned or controlled by healthcare providers. This is an emerging term that describes provider organizations that are formed to directly contract with purchasers to deliver healthcare services. PSOs are formed by

organizations such as IPAs. However, unlike IPAs, they assume insurance risk for their beneficiaries (Bihari, 2010).

▶ The Managed Care Organization Payment Plan

Depending on the type of MCO structure, the financing structure with providers may differ as well.

There are three major types of provider remuneration: capitation, discounted fees, and salaries. With a **capitation policy** or per member per month policy, the provider is paid a fixed monthly amount per member, often called a **per member per month (PMPM) payment**. This member fee is given to the provider regardless of how often the members use the service and the types of services used. The provider is responsible for providing all services deemed necessary.

Discounted fees are a type of FFS but are discounted based on a fee schedule. The provider supplies the service and then can bill the MCO based on the fee schedule developed by the MCO. Each service can be billed separately. The provider anticipates a large referral pool from the MCO so they will accept the discounted rates.

Salaries are the third method of payment. In this instance, the provider is actually an employer of the MCO. Some type of bonus is distributed annually among the providers based on how often services have been used by members. So although they receive a salary, they will be rewarded by additional performance measures (The Geometry Center, 2016).

▶ Cost-Control Measures of Managed Care Organizations

Restriction on Provider Choice

Members of an MCO often have restrictions on their choice for a provider. As the types of MCOs have evolved over the years, the restrictions have lessened, but there is a financial penalty such as a higher copayment or higher deductible for choosing a provider outside the network.

Gatekeeper

In some MCOs, the primary care provider is the **gatekeeper** of all of the care for the patient member. Any secondary or tertiary care would be coordinated by the gatekeeper or primary care provider. The primary care provider is responsible for the case management of a member patient. If additional medical services are needed, the primary care provider must refer the member patient for additional services. Some members do not like having a gatekeeper and would prefer to make these decisions themselves. As a result of this model, some MCOs require a preauthorization of services by the MCO. Many MCOs have clinical guidelines to determine service approval (Buchbinder & Shanks, 2007).

Services Review

Utilization review evaluates the appropriateness of the types of services provided. According to Shi and Singh (2008), there are three types of utilization reviews: prospective, concurrent, and retrospective. **Prospective utilization review** is implemented before the service is actually performed by having the procedure authorized by the MCO, having the primary care provider decide to refer the member for the service, or assessing the service based on the clinical guidelines. **Concurrent utilization reviews** are decisions that are made during the actual course of service, such as length of inpatient stay and additional surgery. **Retrospective utilization review** is an evaluation of services once the services have been provided. This may occur to assess treatment patterns of certain diseases. This type of review may include a financial review to assure accuracy of billing. **Practice profiling**, an offshoot of retrospective utilization review, examines specific provider patterns of practice. This is a type of employee performance review because the focus is to determine which provider also fits in with the organizational culture of the MCO (Spector, 2004).

▸ Medicare and Medicaid Managed Care

Medicare Managed Care or Medicare Part C

As stated previously, the M+C program was created as a result of the Balanced Budget Act of 1997. Implemented in 2000, the purpose of M+C was to encourage Medicare enrollees to use managed care services. Medicare offered risk plans and cost plans for their enrollees. **Risk plans** pay a premium per member that is based on the member's county of residence. Members could use both in-network and out-of-network providers. The risk plans cover all Medicare services and vision and prescription care. **Medicare cost plans** are a type of HMO and have

similar rules to Medicare Advantage plans. The CMS reimburses the MCOs on a preset monthly basis per enrollee based on a forecasted budget. The reimbursement rate is based on the reasonable cost of providing services. Cost plans allow members to pursue care outside the network. If that occurs, the services are covered under the original Medicare (CMS, 2016a).

In 2003, the Medicare Prescription Drug, Improvement, and Modernization Act (MMA) renamed the program **Medicare Advantage** (MA) and allowed PPOs as an option. It also allowed enrollees to participate in private fee-for-service (PFFS) plans as part of the MA. The CMS evaluated the administration of the MA program and, based on that evaluation, developed strategies to encourage more MCO participation. Despite these improvements, managed care enrollment initially dropped nearly 2 million in 2004. With changes in MA, 2006 enrollment surpassed the M+C enrollment. As a result of the MMA, the newly revamped MA program has been a financial boost to MCOs. Enrollment in MA continued to increase each year. In addition, in 2016, more Medicare Advantage plans will offer supplemental benefits for enrollees, such as dental, vision, and hearing benefits. Between 2010, when the Affordable Care Act was enacted, and 2016, premiums were expected to decrease by nearly 10 percent and enrollment was projected to increase by more than 50 percent to approximately 17.4 million enrollees, which represents about 32 percent of the Medicare population (CMS, 2016). At the same time, beneficiaries are receiving higher quality care.

Medicaid Managed Care

According to the Medicaid website, states have traditionally provided people with Medicaid benefits using a fee-for-service system; however, in the past 15 years, states have more frequently implemented a managed care delivery system for Medicaid benefits. More states are requiring people to enroll in a managed care program. Increasing numbers of states are using **Managed Long Term Services and Supports (MLTSS)**, a CMS Medicaid program, as a strategy for expanding home- and community-based services to ensure quality and increase efficiency. When states implement an MLTSS program, they can use any one of the following types of entities:

- **MCOs**—Like HMOs, these companies agree to provide most Medicaid benefits to people in exchange for a monthly payment from the state.

- **Limited benefit plans**—These companies may look like HMOs but only provide one or two Medicaid benefits (like mental health or dental services).
- **Primary care case managers**—These individual providers (or groups of providers) agree to act as an individual's primary care provider and receive a small monthly payment for helping to coordinate referrals and other medical services (CMS, 2016c).

Managed care plans use the gatekeeper model, HMOs, and prepaid health plans. **Carve outs** are services that Medicaid is not obligated to pay for under an MCO contract. Carve outs have occurred because the MCO cannot provide the service or it is too expensive. Unfortunately, mental health services and substance abuse treatment services are often categorized as carve-out services (CMS, 2016b).

According to the Medicaid Managed Care website, those states that have a Medicaid managed care program must have a written CMS-approved strategy for improving their programs and perform an external quality review to ensure they are providing quality care. To assist in these efforts, the CMS has updated the State Quality Strategy Toolkit available at: http://www.medicaid.gov/Medicaid-CHIP-Program-Information/By-Topics/Quality-of-Care/Downloads/Quality-Strategy-Toolkit-for-States.pdf. The External Quality Review analyzes the program on quality, timeliness, and access to the healthcare services that a MCO, prepaid inpatient health plan, or their contractors furnish to Medicaid beneficiaries. The CMS has created a new External Quality Review (EQR) Toolkit to assist states and external quality review organizations in completing the annual EQR technical report. This toolkit is available at http://www.medicaid.gov/Medicaid-CHIP-Program-Information/By-Topics/Quality-of-Care/Quality-of-Care-External-Quality-Review.html. This type of quality assurance activity is in concert with the goals of the Affordable Care Act to improve the quality of the U.S. healthcare system.

▶ Assessment of Managed Care Models

National Committee on Quality Assurance

From a healthcare consumer perspective, when an organization's top priority is cost control, there may be concerns about losing a level of quality. As managed care was integrated into Medicaid and Medicare, the government also became more involved in the evaluation of managed care providers. Also, as competition increased in the managed care arena, there was fear that more services would be reduced to maintain lower premiums (Sultz & Young, 2006). As a result of these issues, the **National Committee on Quality Assurance (NCQA)** was established to maintain the quality of care in health plans.

The NCQA was established in 1990 to monitor health plans and improve healthcare quality. Its focus is to measure, analyze, and improve healthcare programs. The NCQA accredits MCOs and, although a voluntary review process, the process includes surveys completed by managed care experts and physicians. They evaluate access and service and quality of the MCO's providers, primary prevention activities, and case management for the chronically ill. An organization can be accredited at three levels: excellent, commendable, or accredited. This accreditation, although voluntary, has alleviated concerns about the MCOs' focus on cost control. The NCQA has developed a report card of accredited health plans that consumers can access on the NCQA's website. In the past, the NCQA had developed different criteria for the different types of MCOs. The NCQA developed standards and guidelines for all MCOs, regardless of their organizational structure. Since 2006, the NCQA has developed standards specifically for Medicaid Managed Care accreditation. There are currently 41 states that recognize the NCQA accreditation for both their Medicaid Managed care and commercial managed care programs. Additionally, the NCQA has a physician directory that recognizes quality practices. As the MCO industry has become very competitive, it is to the benefit of an MCO to become accredited. The Affordable Care Act has many quality assurance initiatives connected with the NCQA (NCQA, 2016a).

Health Plan Employer Data and Information Set

The **Health Plan Employer Data and Information Set (HEDIS)** was established by the NCQA in 1989. It is used by over 90% of all health plans to measure service and quality of care. The reported data is available to MCOs and physicians. Because so many health plans submit data to this HEDIS database and because the measures are so specifically defined, one can create comparisons of health plan performance. Health plans also use HEDIS results to assess performance and calculate physician and healthcare plan rankings. These results can be very helpful to the healthcare consumer (HEDIS, 2016b).

HEDIS also measures health issues such as medication use patterns, breast cancer rates, rates of chronic diseases such as diabetes, childhood health issues, high blood pressure issues, heart disease, and mental health disease, and health plans' treatment of these major health issues. Healthcare plans and providers use this database for performance assessment, and consumers may access this information through the State of the Health Care Quality Report, which analyzes the healthcare system. The Committee on Performance Measurement has members that represent consumers, providers, health plans, employers, and other stakeholders, who decide what type of data should be collected by HEDIS and what types of measures should be used (HEDIS, 2016b). There are four standards that are the focus of an NCQA review: quality management, utilization standards, members' rights and responsibilities, and services (NCQA, 2016b).

▶ Managed Care Accreditation

Although the Joint Commission and the NCQA can accredit different types of MCOs, since 1983, the **Accreditation Association for Ambulatory Health Care (AAAHC)** has been reviewing and accrediting managed care organizations. In 2012, its standards were revised to focus on managed care principles, including members' rights, care coordination, enrollee records accuracy, credentialing of provider networks, quality improvement, and health education. The AAAHC has received **Medicare Deemed Status** from the CMS, which means that the AAAHC can survey Medicare Advantage HMO and PPO plans. In 2014, it launched an accreditation program for surgical specialty and critical access hospitals and hospitals with less than 200 beds. Also in 2014, nine state governments recognized the AAAHC accreditation plan for healthcare plans. The AAAHC is the largest accreditor of health plans in Florida (AAAHC, 2016).

▶ Issues with Managed Care Operations

Several years ago, survey results indicated that physicians who contract with several MCOs were concerned with providing quality care to their patients because the MCOs' focuses are on cost. However, managed care options have become an integral component of the healthcare system, so assurance of quality and cost measures have been implemented to assist with managed care quality of care while maintaining cost effective care. The AMA has developed a **National Managed Care Contract (NMCC)**, which is designed to comply with the managed care laws of all 50 states and the District of Columbia, as well as with federal requirements.

The comprehensive information it provides covers the business relationship between physicians and MCOs. Using the NMCC, physicians can better understand, evaluate, and negotiate managed care contracts.

Physicians are also concerned with physician network rentals or **silent PPOs**, which are unauthorized third parties outside the contract between the MCO and the physician that gain access to the MCO discount rates. Examples of these network rentals are automobile insurers or workmen's compensations insurers. They obtain the physician's rates from a database. The main insurer who has the contract with the physician does not provide the information to the physician, and the third parties continue to benefit from the discounted rates. This scheme takes money from the physicians because they are obtaining discounts fraudulently. Physicians have pursued legal action against MCOs due to issues with reimbursement such as the abuse of these discounted rates by unauthorized users. The AMA has an educational service for physicians to determine if a silent PPO is being implemented (Advocacy Resource Center, 2016).

The concept of **medical loss ratio** or the minimum amount of dollars a healthcare plan spends on providing care rather than administration has been targeted by the Affordable Care Act. Under the Affordable Care Act, insurance companies must spend 80–85% of member premium revenues on medical care and healthcare quality improvement. If they do not meet that minimum percentage, the insurance companies must provide a rebate to their customers. The Kaiser Foundation estimates that the medical loss ratio in 2014 for the individual market—including coverage purchased since January 1, 2014, under new ACA rules as well as plans bought prior to then under pre-ACA insurance rules—will range from 81% to 87% (Levitt, Claxon, & Cox, 2015).

▶ Challenges to Managed Care

Below are some issues confronting managed care organizations.

1. Moving to a value-based reimbursement: This type of model is being implemented by Medicare. It is a cultural change in a managed care system that can be difficult because such systems' original focus was cost containment. It will be necessary to work closely with providers regarding this type of payment model.

2. Data-driven decision making: The trend is decision making based on current information to provide the best decisions and

healthy outcomes for patients. The challenge is to have data accessible so providers can make decisions using appropriate data. Performance dashboards are an excellent tool to be able to obtain data from different sources in an organization and create reports that can be beneficial.

3. Increasing drug costs: The continued increase in prescription drug prices is a challenge to managed care organizations. As cost sharing continues to grow for consumers, some might be unable to pay for their drugs. Pundits indicate that focusing more on generic drugs may be a possibility. Using a pharmacy benefit management system may also be cost effective.

4. Healthcare consumer advocacy: Consumers have more information available to them to make an informed decision about their health insurance plans, which means the choice between one plan over another may come down to each plan's customer service. Healthcare organizations now are marketing their plans to consumers because consumers now have a choice.

5. Increasing healthcare systems: To become more cost effective, systems are merging and developing larger healthcare systems that may be difficult to compete against because of the options they can provide to healthcare consumers. Independent healthcare systems may have to assess their plans and their offerings to compete with the larger systems (Westgate, 2015).

▶ Conclusion

The managed care model for healthcare delivery was developed for the primary purpose of containing healthcare costs. By administering both the healthcare services and the reimbursement of these services, and therefore eliminating a third-party health insurer, the industry felt that this model would be very cost-effective. Both the consumer–patient and the physician's concerns were the same—providing quality care while focusing predominantly on cost. Consumers were also worried about losing freedom to choose their primary care provider. Physicians were concerned about loss of income.

As managed care evolved, managed care models developed that allowed more choice for both the consumer and the physician. Eventually, there were models such as PPOs and POS plans that allowed consumers to more freely choose their providers. There is a financial disincentive to use a provider outside the network of the MCO. From a provider perspective, providers are also able to see non-MCO patients, which increases their income. The provider also receives a financial disincentive because any MCO patient was given health care at a discounted rate.

There also have been issues with how MCOs have reimbursed physicians. The issue with silent PPOs has financially hurt physicians. Physicians have also had problems with timely reimbursement from MCOs. There were issues with fraudulent reimbursement rates of out-of-network services, which resulted in members paying exorbitant out-of-pocket expenses. However, the American Medical Association has developed tools to assist physicians with managed care contracting and reimbursement processes. The Affordable Care Act mandate that insurance companies must spend 80–85% of their premium revenues on quality care or be penalized with fines, give rebates to their members, or both will be an incentive for MCOs to provide quality and affordable care. As healthcare organizations continue to focus on providing quality care and cost reduction, having a database such as HEDIS can provide important information to both healthcare providers and consumers.

Wrap-Up

Vocabulary

Accreditation Association for Ambulatory Health Care
Capitation plan
Carve outs
Concurrent utilization reviews

Discounted fees
Exclusive provider organizations (EPOs)
Fee-for-service (FFS)
Gatekeeper

Group model
Health maintenance organization (HMO)
Health Plan Employer Data and Information Set (HEDIS)

Indemnity plan
Independent practice associations
  (IPAs)
Limited benefit plans
Managed Care Long Term
  Services and Support
  (MLTSS)
Managed care organizations
  (MCOs)
Medical loss ratio
Medicare Advantage
Medicare cost plans

Medicare Deemed Status
National Committee on Quality
  Assurance (NCQA)
National Managed Care Contract
  (NMCC)
Network model
Per member per month (PMPM)
  payment
Physician hospital organizations
  (PHOs)
Point-of-service (POS) plans
Practice profiling

Preferred provider organizations
  (PPOs)
Primary care case managers
Prospective utilization review
Provider sponsored organizations
  (PSOs)
Retrospective utilization review
Risk plans
Salaries
Silent PPOs
Staff model
Utilization review

References

Accreditation Association for Ambulatory Health Care (AAAHC). (2016). About AAAHC. Retrieved from http://www.aaahc.org/about/

Advocacy Resource Center. (2016). Retrieved from http://www.ama-assn.org/resources/doc/arc/x-ama/reg-rental-network-ppos-issue-brief.pdf

American Heart Association. (2016). Managed health care plans. Retrieved from http://www.americanheart.org/presenter.jhtml?identifier=4663

Buchbinder, S., & Shanks, N. (2007). *Introduction to health care management*. Sudbury, MA: Jones and Bartlett.

Centers for Medicare & Medicaid Services (CMS). (2016a). Other Medicare managed plans. Retrieved from http://www.medicare.gov/sign-up-change-plans/medicare-health-plans/other-health-plans/other-medicare-health-plans.html

CMS. (2016b). Managed care. Retrieved from http://www.medicaid.gov/Medicaid-CHIP-Program-Information/By-Topics/Delivery-Systems/Managed-Care/Managed-Care.html

CMS. (2016c). Medicaid Managed Long Term Services and Support. Retrieved from http://www.medicaid.gov/Medicaid-CHIP-Program-Information/By-Topics/Delivery-Systems/Medicaid-Managed-Long-Term-Services-and-Supports-MLTSS.html

Committee on the Costs of Medical Care. (1932). *Medical care for the American people: The final report*. Chicago, IL: University of Chicago Press.

Healthcare Effectiveness Data and Information Set (HEDIS). (2016a). HEDIS and performance management. Retrieved from http://www.ncqa.org/HEDISQualityMeasurement.aspx

HEDIS. (2016b). HEDIS and quality compass. Retrieved from http://www.ncqa.org/HEDISQualityMeasurement/WhatisHEDIS.aspx

Hoven, A. (2004). Impact of the health maintenance act of 1973. *Report of the Council on Medical Services*, CMS Report 4-A-04.

Judson, K., & Harrison, C. (2006). *Law & ethics for medical careers*. New York, NY: McGraw-Hill.

Kaiser Permanente. (2013). Our history. Retrieved from http://xnet.kp.org/newscenter/aboutkp/historyofkp.html

Knight, W. (1998). *Managed care: What it is and how it works*. Gaithersburg, MD: Aspen Publishers.

Lambrew, J. (2013). Good news: Americans saved billions thanks to the Affordable Care Act. Retrieved from http://www.potusnews.net/category/Jeanne-Lambrew.aspx

Levitt, L., Claxton, G., & Cox, C. (2015). How have insurers fared under the Affordable Care Act? Retrieved from http://kff.org/private-insurance/perspective/how-have-insurers-fared-under-the-affordable-care-act/

Mann, C. (2012). CMCS informational bulletin: November 19th. Retrieved from http://www.medicaid.gov/Federal-Policy-Guidance/downloads/CIB-11-19-12.pdf

Medicaid managed care. (2016). Retrieved from https://www.medicaid.gov/medicaid-chip-program-information/by-topics/delivery-systems/managed-care/managed-care-site.html

Moeller, P. (2012). Lower Medicare Advantage premiums attract seniors. Retrieved from http://money.usnews.com/money/blogs/the-best-life/2012/02/07/lower-medicare-advantage-premiums-attract-seniors_print.html

National Committee for Quality Assurance (NCQA). (2013a). About the NCQA. Retrieved from http://www.ncqa.org/AboutNCQA.aspx

NCQA. (2016b). NCQA accreditation for health insurance exchanges and alignment with ACA. Retrieved from http://www.ncqa.org/Programs/Accreditation/HealthPlanHP/Accreditation/AlignmentwithACA.aspx

Shi, L., & Singh, D. (2008). *An Introduction to Healthcare in America: A systems approach*. Sudbury, MA: Jones and Bartlett.

Spector, R. (2004). Utilization Review and Managed Health Care Liability. *Southern Medical Journal*, 97 (3): 284–286.

Sultz, H., & Young, K. (2006). *Health care USA: Understanding its organization and delivery* (5th ed.). Sudbury, MA: Jones and Bartlett.

The Geometry Center. (2016). How do health care plans pay for physicians? Retrieved from http://www.geom.uiuc.edu/usenate/payreport/how.html

Tufts Managed Care Institute. (2016). A brief history of managed care. Retrieved from http://www.thci.org/downloads/BriefHist.pdf

Westgate, A. (2015). Top 5 industry challenges of 2016. Retrieved from http://managedhealthcareexecutive.modernmedicine.com/managed-healthcare-executive/news/top-5-industry-challenges-2016

▶ Notes

▶ Student Activity 9-1

In Your Own Words

Based on this chapter, please provide an explanation of the following concepts in your own words. DO NOT RECITE the text.

Managed care:

_____

_____

Health maintenance organizations:

_____

_____

Preferred provider organizations:

_____

_____

Medicare Deemed Status:

_____

_____

Point-of-service plans:

_____

_____

Indemnity plan:

_____

_____

Carve outs:

_____

_____

Fee-for-service plans:

_____

_____

Medical loss ratio:

_____

_____

Silent PPOs:

_____

_____

▶ **Student Activity 9-2**

Real-Life Applications: Case Study

A friend, who had been a dependent on her parents' insurance, recently graduated from college and was offered a full-time healthcare management position. When she started to complete her human resource (HR) application, the HR manager asked her what type of healthcare plan she chose. Her new employer offered several different healthcare plans: fee-for-service, HMO, PPO, and POS plans. She was very confused and asked you to explain the managed care plans to her.

Activity

(1) Describe the characteristics of these healthcare plans, and (2) identify the differences between the HMO and PPO plans.

Responses

_____

_____

_____

_____

_____

_____

_____

_____

_____

_____

_____

_____

_____

_____

_____

_____

_____

_____

Case Scenario Two

You had heard that the premiums for your health insurance plan may decrease as a result of the Affordable Care Act's requirement that insurance companies spend a certain amount of their premium revenue on their plans. You were interested to find out if this was true.

Activity

Perform an Internet search on medical loss ratios. Describe the concept and why it could decrease the cost sharing of your health insurance coverage.

Responses

_____

_____

_____

_____

_____

_____

_____

_____

_____

_____

_____

_____

_____

_____

_____

_____

_____

_____

Case Scenario Three

For years, your parents had a traditional fee-for-service health insurance. They are now required to switch to a managed care product. They are very upset because they love their physicians. However, their physicians did tell them they had contracted with certain MCOs to provide services. Your parents were still confused.

Activity

Explain the managed care principle and which program would enable them to still use their practitioners.

Responses

_____

_____

_____

_____

_____

_____

_____

_____

_____

_____

_____

_____

_____

_____

_____

_____

Case Scenario Four

As a healthcare consumer who recently switched to a managed care health plan, you were very worried about the quality of the care provided to you. You were wondering if there were any reviews of these types of programs to determine the quality of healthcare services offered.

Activity

Discuss the different types of reviews used to assess managed care organizations.

Responses

_____

_____

_____

_____

_____

_____

_____

_____

_____

_____

_____

▶ **Student Activity 9-3**

Internet Exercises

Write your answers in the space provided.

- ◼ Visit each of the websites listed here.
- ◼ Name the organization.
- ◼ Locate the organization's mission statement or values statement on the website.
- ◼ Provide a brief overview of the activities of the organization.
- ◼ How do these organizations participate in the U.S. healthcare system?

Websites

http://www.ncqa.org

Organization Name:

_____

_____

Mission Statement:

_____

_____

_____

Overview of Activities:

_____

_____

_____

Importance of Organization to U.S. Health Care:

_____

_____

_____

http://www.aaahc.org

Mission Statement:

_____

_____

_____

Overview of Activities:

_____

_____

_____

Importance of Organization to U.S. Health Care:

_____

_____

_____

http://www.americanheart.org

Organization Name:

_____

_____

Mission Statement:

_____

_____

_____

Overview of Activities:

_____

_____

_____

Importance of Organization to U.S. Health Care:

_____

_____

_____

http://managedhealthcareexecutive.modernmedicine.com

Organization Name:

_____

_____

Mission Statement:

_____

_____

_____

Overview of Activities:

_____

_____

_____

Importance of Organization to U.S. Health Care:

_____

_____

_____

http://www.managedcare.com

Organization Name:

_____

_____

Mission Statement:

_____

_____

_____

Overview of Activities:

_____

_____

_____

Importance of Organization to U.S. Health Care:

_____

_____

_____

http://www.amednews.com

Organization Name:

_____

_____

Mission Statement:

_____

_____

_____

Overview of Activities:

_____

_____

_____

Importance of Organization to U.S. Health Care:

_____

_____

_____

▶ **Student Activity 9-4**

Discussion Questions

The following are suggested discussion questions for this chapter.

1. Why was managed care developed? Do you think managed care is a good way to provide healthcare services? Why or why not?

_____

_____

_____

_____

2. What is the difference between an HMO and a PPO? Which one do you prefer? Search the Internet to find one HMO and one PPO.

_____

_____

_____

_____

_____

3. What is a medical loss ratio? How does it impact healthcare consumers?

_____

_____

_____

4. Discuss the importance of the National Committee on Quality Assurance on U.S. health care.

5. Select one of the new initiatives that NCQA will be administering. Which one do you think is the most valuable for healthcare services? Defend your answer.

▸ Student Activity 9-5

Current Events

Perform an Internet search and find a current events topic over the past three years that is related to this chapter. Provide a summary of the article and the link to the article and why the article relates to the chapter.

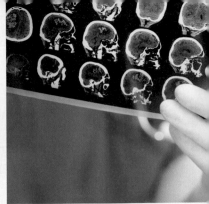

CHAPTER 10

Information Technology Impact on Health Care

LEARNING OBJECTIVES

The student will be able to:

- Define and discuss health information technology, health information systems, and health or medical informatics.
- Evaluate the importance of the Office of the National Coordinator for Health Information Technology to health care.
- Discuss the pros and cons of electronic health records.
- Discuss the importance of Dr. Octo Barnett to healthcare technology.
- Evaluate the impact of information technology on healthcare stakeholders.
- Discuss the Million Hearts initiative and its importance to health.

DID YOU KNOW THAT?

- Both President Bush and President Obama supported the initiative for electronic health records.
- E-prescribing is a form of a clinical decision support system.
- The average cost to install an EHR software system in a physician's office is $55,000.
- There is a new product called Electronic Aspirin, which is an implant on the side of the head normally affected by a headache.
- The Food and Drug Administration (FDA) has approved a medical robot that can make rounds, checking on patients in different rooms.
- The Microsoft HealthVault, Microsoft's version of an electronic patient record, now has a feature that allows a patient to preregister for hospital procedures and admissions.

▶ Introduction

The general term **informatics** refers to the science of computer application to data in different industries. **Health** or **medical informatics** is the science of computer application that supports clinical and research data in different areas of health care. It is a methodology of how the healthcare industry thinks about patients and how their treatments are defined and evolved. For example, **imaging informatics** applies computer technology to organs and tissue (Coiera, 2003; Open Clinical, 2016). **Health information systems** are systems that store, transmit, collect, and retrieve this data (Anderson, Rice, & Kominski, 2007). The goal of **health information technology (HIT)** is to manage the health data that can be used by patients–consumers, insurance companies, healthcare providers, healthcare administrators, and any stakeholder that has an interest in health care (Goldstein & Blumenthal, 2008).

HIT impacts every aspect of the healthcare industry. All of the stakeholders in the healthcare industry use HIT. **Information technology (IT)** has had a tremendous impact on the healthcare industry because it allows faster documentation of every transaction. When an industry focuses on saving lives, it is important that every activity has a written document that describes the activity. Computerization of documentation has increased the management efficiency and accuracy of healthcare data. The main focus of HIT is the national implementation of an electronic patient record. Both President Bush and President Obama have supported this initiative.

This is the foundation of many IT systems because it will enable different systems to share patient information, which will increase the quality and efficiency of health care. This chapter will discuss the history of IT, different applications of IT health care, and the status of electronic health records and barriers for its national implementation.

▶ History of Information Technology in the Healthcare Industry

Computers' first widespread use was in the 1960s as a result of the implementation of Medicaid and Medicare. Healthcare providers were inundated with forms to complete for both programs. In order to receive reimbursement from both programs, services needed to be tracked and forms needed to be completed and submitted to these programs. Therefore, computers were used to assist with the financial management of these programs (Buchbinder & Shanks, 2007). As a result of computer integration, more healthcare providers recognized the efficiency of computers to manage programs. Hospitals particularly recognized the efficiency of electronic billing. During the 1960s, hospitals developed their own computer systems that housed their financial information. The hospitals were responsible for the maintenance of these systems. These systems, which were large mainframe systems, required a large staff to maintain their operations. All of the hospitals' data was stored on these mainframe computers. Computer programs were developed by the hospitals to extract data reports. These mainframe computers were very expensive. They were eventually replaced in the 1970s with minicomputers, which were more efficient, more cost effective, and easier to maintain. These minicomputers were connected to a main computer that stored all of the data. They were also used to enter information. Eventually, specific computer systems were developed for laboratories and clinics. It is important to mention Dr. G. Octo Barnett, who is a Professor of Medicine at Harvard Medical School and the former senior scientific director at the Laboratory of Computer Science at Massachusetts General Hospital (Appleby, 2008). He developed the first computer program for healthcare applications, called MUMPS, in 1964, which became the basis of very sophisticated programs used today.

During the 1980s and 1990s, the development and widespread use of personal computers (PCs) revolutionized information systems and technology. PCs were not reliant on a main computer for analyses. They were able to generate more sophisticated reports. PCs were often linked as a network to share information among different departments in hospitals. The development of the PC also enabled more computerization of physician practices. In the 2000s, the application of IT has increased in the healthcare industry with cutting-edge new applications such as Electronic Aspirin and the national implementation of electronic health information.

The establishment of a **chief information officer (CIO)** in healthcare organizations emphasized how important information systems and technology had become to healthcare organizations. The U.S. healthcare system has been the world leader for developing cutting-edge technology in health care. It has impacted how diagnostic procedures are performed, how data is collected and disseminated, how medicine is delivered, how providers treat their patients, and how surgeries are performed. There are several healthcare stakeholders that are impacted by technology. Consumers, providers, employers, researchers, all governmental levels, nonprofit and for-profit health-care organizations, and insurance payers have all been impacted by technology (eJobDescription, 2016). Technological advances have been blamed, in part, for the continued rise of healthcare expenditures, but the results of technological advances cannot be disputed.

▶ Electronic Health Records

History

The Institute of Medicine (IOM) has published a series of reports over the past several years that focus on improving the quality of health care in the United States. In 2001, it published the report *Crossing the Quality Chasm: A New Health System for the 21st Century*, which stresses the importance of improving IT infrastructure. The IOM emphasized the importance of an electronic health record (EHR), an electronic record of patients' medical history. The report also discussed the importance of patient safety by establishing data standards for collecting patient information (IOM, 2001).

In 1991 and 1997, the IOM issued reports that focused on the impact of computer-based patients' records as important technology for improving health care (Vreeman, Taggard, Rhine, & Wornell, 2006). There are two concepts in electronic patient records that are used interchangeably but are different—the **electronic medical record (EMR/EHR)** and the **electronic health record (EHR)**. The **National Alliance for Health Information Technology (NAHIT)** defines the EMR as the electronic record of health-related information on an individual that is accumulated from one health system and is utilized by the health organization that is providing patient care while the EHR accumulates more patient medical information from many health organizations that have been involved in the patient care. Simply, the EMR is an EHR that can be integrated with other systems (MNT, 2016b). The IOM has been urging the healthcare industry to adopt the electronic patient record but initially costs were too high and the health community did not embrace the recommendation. This discussion will focus on the EHR.

As software costs have declined, more healthcare providers have adopted the use of the EHR system. The EHR system can be used in hospitals, healthcare providers' offices, and other types of healthcare facilities. It enables healthcare organizations to monitor patient safety and care. In 2003, the U.S. Department of Health and Human Services (DHHS) began to promote the use of HIT, including the use of the EHR. The IOM was asked to identify essential elements for the establishment of an EHR. The IOM broadly defined an EHR to include (IOM, 2016):

- The collection of longitudinal data on a person's health;
- Immediate electronic access to this information; and
- Establishment of a system that provides decision support to ensure the quality, safety, and efficiency of patient care.

According to the DHHS, the Health Information Technology for Economic and Clinical Health (HITECH) Act, which was enacted as part of the 2009 American Recovery and Reinvestment Act, was designed to stimulate the adoption of health information technology in the United States. The Office of the National Coordinator (ONC) for Health Information Technology is responsible for implementing the incentives and penalties program. The ONC has developed "meaningful use" guidelines for physicians and others that will help them receive incentive payments and avoid penalties in the future (DHHS, 2016).

Incentives to Use Electronic Health Records: Meaningful Use

In accordance with the HITECH Act, the Centers for Medicaid and Medicare Services (CMS) established incentives to encourage "**meaningful use**" of EHRs to increase patient care quality and safety. Meaningful use, as defined by the CMS, has established core measures that healthcare providers must meet to determine the EHR system is being adequately used. Stage 1, defined in 2010, focused on patient data and medical history. Stage 2, effective in 2014, increased the physician use of computerized physician order entry and clinical decision support to improve patient health outcomes.

Beginning in 2016, penalties will be issued to providers that fail to meet the program's requirements in the preceding year. Stage 3 objectives are focused on improving the interoperability of EHR systems in different practices. Prior to moving to Stage 3, the CMS established a "Modified Stage 2" (2015–2017), which combined the requirements of stage 1 and 2 for physicians. This modification was to reduce reporting requirements and assist with the transition to stage 3. Both healthcare professionals and hospitals are eligible for the program. They can participate in the Medicare, Medicare Advantage, or Medicaid program but cannot receive incentives for all of the programs. They must choose which program for which to receive the incentives.

Eligible healthcare professionals could participate for up to five continuous years and receive up to $44,000 for those years. Providers must demonstrate meaningful use on an annual basis. The last year for provider enrollment was 2014; however, to receive maximum participation, providers must have enrolled by 2012. Effective 2015, providers who did not demonstrate meaningful use were subjected to a fine up to 5% of their incentive amount. Medicaid professionals can also be involved in the meaningful use of the EHR system. Nearly all states are administering the program. The federal government will pay 90% of the state's cost for implementing this type of electronic system. Medicaid incentives are higher than the Medicare program—up to $63,750 over six years.

Specified criteria for meaningful use for hospitals was established to review their EHR systems. As of October 2015, more than 479,000 healthcare providers received payment for participating in the Medicare and Medicaid EHR incentive programs. For Stage 3, the CMS will focus on advanced use of certified EHR technology to support health information exchange and interoperability, advanced quality measurement, and maximizing clinical effectiveness and efficiencies (CMS, 2016d).

Benefits of Electronic Health Records

Several studies have been performed to assess the impact of the EHR on healthcare delivery. Administrators of several healthcare delivery systems reported many benefits to the implementation of an EHR. Many administrators cited the capability of more comprehensive reporting that integrated both clinical and administrative data. It also provided an opportunity to analyze and review patient outcomes because of the standardization of the clinical assessments. Also noted was the development of electronic automated reports that improved the discharge of a patient. The reports also provided an opportunity for the administrator to assess the workload of a department. The EHR also improved operational efficiency. The EHR had excellent capabilities to process and store data. Administrators further reported that the computerized documentation took 30% less time than the previous handwritten notes (Shields et al., 2007).

Several studies indicated there was an improvement in interdepartmental communication. The EHR provided aggregate data in the patient records to other departments, and the information about the patient was legible. The actual design and implementation of an EHR system contributed to the development of a more interdisciplinary approach to patient care (Ventres & Shah, 2007; Whitman & David, 2007). The implementation of an EHR system led to improved data accuracy because it reduced the need to replicate data. The EHR system also provided a platform for routine

data quality assessments, which was important to maintain the accuracy of the EHR data. The EHR system provides an opportunity for future research. The data captured in the database could be used to analyze outcomes and develop baseline data for future research.

▶ Barriers to Electronic Health Record Implementation

From the perspective of a user such as a physician's office, a major issue with EHR implementation is the cost of implementing the system. Software purchases, hardware, network upgrades, training, and computer personnel must be considered in the purchase of the system. The average cost of installation for a practice is $55,000 (Daigrepont & McGrath, 2011).

According to Valerius (2007), migrating from a hard-copy system to an electronic system requires several components, including a physician order communication or results retrieval, electronic document control management, point-of-care charting, electronic physician order entry and prescribing, clinical decision support system, provider patient portals, personal health records, and population health. When an organization implements an electronic system, there are changes in the workflow because much of the process was previously manual. Training is required for both healthcare professionals and staff to fully utilize the system.

When purchasing a system for patient electronic records, sometimes there were equipment or software inadequacies that created a much slower system for processing data. If the system failed, it created frustration for healthcare professionals and administrators. Both of these problems emphasized the need for adequate training for both the providers and staff. Much of the initial training required overtime for the staff. Most of the training lasted approximately four months. Continued training was also required for maintenance of the system (Valerius, 2007).

The critical success factors medical practices need to consider for successful HIT implementation include the following (Daigrepont & McGrath, 2011):

- Uniform adoption of technology by all participants;
- Reliable HIT infrastructure;
- A system that is appropriate for the practice;
- A plan that details the milestones of the implementation of the system; and
- Ongoing training of all employees to ensure optimal use of the EHR.

A focus of EHR implementation is the development of standards for the type of data collected so it can be exchanged between two systems. However, the American Academy of Pediatrics (AAP) has indicated that EHRs lack specific functions for pediatric patients such as child abuse reporting and newborn screening. The AAP has developed additional standards that EHR vendors could integrate into their products (Robeznieks, 2013).

In October 2008, Microsoft announced its **Health-Vault** website (HealthVault, 2016) that enables patients to develop **electronic patient records** free of charge. These electronic health records are the patient component of the electronic health record. It is up to the individual as to how much medical information the person wants to store online with this website. The website also has links to several health websites that can assist with exercise programs, heart issues, drug reactions, software that allows users to share their medical information with their providers, and so on. In November 2008, the Cleveland Clinic agreed to pilot data exchanges between HealthVault and the Cleveland Clinic's personal health record system. The clinic enrolled 250 patients in the areas of diabetes, hypertension, and heart disease to test the system. The patients tested their health status at home using blood pressure monitors, weight scales, heart rate monitors, and glucometers. The patients tested themselves, and the reports were uploaded to the clinic using HealthVault. They were also able to access health education material on HealthVault regarding their diseases. This is the first pilot study in the country to assess this tool. The 2010 results of the pilot study indicated that there was a 26–71% increase in time intervals between doctor appointments. Heart patients made more appointments with their physicians as well (iMedicalApps, 2013). In 2010, Microsoft released a new version of HealthVault, Healthvault Community Connect, which allows patients to preregister for hospital procedures and admissions via the hospital's web portal. Patients can create a HealthVault personal e-health record account. When patients are discharged from the hospital, copies of their hospital care are uploaded to the patient's HealthVault account for the patient's accessibility. Microsoft HealthVault can now communicate with many healthcare websites, mobile applications, and personal health devices, which enable patients to more quickly upload their health data (HealthVault, 2016).

Computerized information systems that are seen in finance, manufacturing, and retail have not achieved the same penetration in health care. EHRs have captured the attention of politicians, insurance companies, and practitioners as a way to improve patient safety because patient information will be more complete and standardized, which will enhance the decision-making process of practitioners (Murer, 2007). Major barriers

to EHR implementation have been discussed, including training and financial impacts on organizations as the system becomes integrated with daily operations. However, there are legal issues associated with the implementation of an EHR.

There may be medical malpractice concerns when a physician initially adopts an EHR due to errors when transferring patient data from a paper system to an electronic system. Another legal issue is the electronic definition of a legal patient record. A traditional patient record is a folder containing a paper trail of patient visits, prescriptions, and tests. During a trial, what constitutes an electronic patient record? A report is generated by the EHR software that does not look like the actual screen data of the patient. As with patients' paper files, there are certainly issues with medical errors related to entering the patient information into the system. For example, a family physician using an EHR system nearly prescribed the incorrect medication because of an incorrect click of the mouse. Lastly, the other issue is the protection of the data. Depending on who has access to the patient data in the healthcare facility, there may be breaches of confidentiality (Gamble, 2012).

▶ Clinical Decision Support Systems

Artificial Intelligence (AI) is a field of computerized methods and technologies created to imitate human decision making. A technique of AI is **expert systems** (ESs), which were developed to imitate experts' knowledge in decision making (Coiera, 2003). **Electronic clinical decision support systems** (CDSSs) are designed to integrate medical information, patient information, and a decision-making tool to generate information to assist with cases. They are a type of knowledge-base system. The key functions of a CDSS are (1) administrative, (2) case management, (3) cost control, and (4) decision support. Administrative protocols consist of clinical coding and documentation for procedure approval and patient referrals if necessary. Case management control focuses on the management of patients to ensure they are receiving timely interventions. Cost control is a focus because the system monitors orders for tests and medication, which reduces unnecessary interventions (Perreault & Metzger, 1999).

Specifically, ESs can be used to alert and remind healthcare providers of a patient's condition change or to have a laboratory test or an intervention performed. An ES can also assist with a diagnosis using the system's database. The system can expose any weaknesses in a treatment plan or check for drug interactions and allergies. A system can also interpret imaging tests routinely to flag any abnormalities. It is important to note that the more complex duties of a system require the integration of an EHR system so the system can interface with the patient data (Coiera, 2003).

Research over the past several years has indicated that CDSSs have many potential benefits, which can be classified into three categories: (1) improved patient safety, (2) improved quality of care, and (3) improved efficiency in healthcare delivery. Although the barriers to implementation were identified previously, the benefits for many institutions have outweighed those barriers so they have found ways to utilize these CDSSs. More CDSSs are being developed to provide information for various types of diseases (Open Clinical, 2016).

Computerized Physician Order Entry

Computerized physician order entry (CPOE) systems are CDSSs that enable a patient's provider to enter a prescription order or order for a lab or diagnostic test in a computer system, which typically is now part of an electronic health record system. The order entry has four components: (1) information is entered from a handheld device, laptop, or desktop computer; (2) the provider orders a test, prescription, or procedure; (3) the device is connected to a decision support system that alerts providers to any problems with their orders; and (4) the system can be integrated into the overall computer system of the organization. The CPOE first appeared in 1971 when NASA Space Center and Lockheed Corporation developed a system for a hospital in California. It improves quality assurance in patient care, thus reducing medical errors (Ash, Gorman, Seshardri, & Hersch, 2004).

E-prescribing, a form of CPOE, consists of medication history, benefits information, and processing new and existing prescriptions. With an e-prescribing system, the user–clinician signs into a system with a password to verify identify. The user–clinician provides a patient identification code so the user–clinician can review the patient's medication list, prescribe a new drug and designate which pharmacy will fill the prescription (HRSA, 2016).

Over 90% of pharmacies can accept electronic prescriptions (Surescripts, 2016). Errors can occur in medication ordering and administration because of similar sounding names, similar dosages, and similar labeling. E-prescribing can be performed on a desk computer, a laptop, or a handheld device, which will record physicians' prescription orders and thereby eliminate the need for an individual to read a handwritten prescription. CPOE also has a decision support

system that includes possible drug interactions and dosage information that help physicians make the best decisions possible for patients.

Section 132 of the Medicare Improvements for Patients and Providers Act of 2008 (MIPPA) authorized incentives to encourage physicians to e-prescribe. In January 2009, Medicare and some private healthcare plans began paying a bonus to physicians who e-prescribe to their Medicare patients. Since 2012, Medicare has also penalized physicians who do not e-prescribe by reducing their reimbursement rates by 1%, 1.5% for 2013, and 2% for 2014 and all subsequent years (CMS, 2016b). IT companies are providing free software to physicians to encourage them to electronically prescribe. This system can be used alone but it is best used with the EHR system because it integrates the information from the patient's EHR into its decision making.

▶ Pharmacy Benefit Managers

Technology-based tools provide exceptional value to the prescription benefits of a health insurance program. E-prescribing will become more commonplace with the mandates of Medicare. In order to manage this technology effectively and efficiently, a **pharmacy benefit manager** (PBM) uses technology-based tools to assess and evaluate the management of the prescription component so it can be customized to address the needs of the organization. PBMs are companies that administer drug benefits for employers and health insurance carriers. They contract with managed care organizations, self-insured employers, Medicaid and Medicare managed care plans, federal health insurance programs, and local-government organizations. They provide an opportunity for employers to offer reduced prices for their employees. In 2016, approximately 266 million patients with drug coverage received benefits through a PBM. There are 30 PBM companies, with three major PBM companies covering 78% of the market. The PBM integrates medical and pharmacy data of the population to determine which interventions are the most cost effective and clinically appropriate. They operate within healthcare systems such as Kaiser or retail operations such as CVS (Balto, 2015).

▶ Drug–Drug Interactions

Drug–drug interactions (DDIs) are used by software programs to alert pharmacists and clinicians about potential drug interactions. These alerts can be notifying the provider that two drugs may interact or there may be management strategies provided regarding the DDIs. DDI software programs can be very beneficial to providers but must be updated continually to ensure there is current information provided regarding drug interactions (Murphy et al., 2009).

▶ Telehealth

Telehealth is the broad term that encompasses the use of IT to deliver education, research, and clinical care. An important activity of telehealth is the use of email between providers and their patients. **E-health** refers to the use of the Internet by both consumers and healthcare professionals to access education, research, and products and services. There are several websites such as WebMD and Healthline that provide consumers with general healthcare information. Sometimes telemedicine is best understood in terms of the services provided and the mechanisms used to provide those services.

Telemedicine refers to the use of IT to enable healthcare providers to communicate with rural healthcare providers regarding patient care or to communicate directly with patients regarding treatment. The ultimate goal of telemedicine is to improve the patient's health status. The basic form of telemedicine is a telephone consultation. There are growing IT applications for telemedicine, including smart phones, video conferencing, and email (American Telemedicine Association, 2016). Telemedicine is most frequently used in pathology and radiology because images can be transmitted to a distant location where a specialist will read the results. Telemedicine is becoming more common because it increases healthcare access in remote locations such as rural areas. It is also a cost-effective mode of treatment. Telemedicine includes:

1. Synchronous electronic consulting between primary care providers and specialists;
2. Remote patient monitoring, which includes sending patient data to a remote location electronically;
3. Provision of electronic health consumer information; and
4. Provision of medical education to healthcare professionals.

The information can be sent electronically via networks and websites (American Telemedicine Association, 2016).

▶ Avera Ecare

Beginning in 1993, Avera offered eConsult services to rural, frontier, and critical-access hospitals that were part of the Avera Health system. Avera eConsult completes more than 900 virtual visits each month with patients in 100-plus clinics and hospitals. Since eConsult services launched in 1993, they have provided support to approximately 35 medical specialties. Ten years later, eCARE expanded to provide eICU care, the first 24-hour, on-demand service that allows staff at partner facilities to connect virtually via a video and audio call for immediate assistance from board-certified providers. In addition, Avera eCARE delivers 24/7 access to medical specialists for underserved populations and communities.

Since Avera ePharmacy services began in 2008, they have provided remote pharmacy coverage for just over 700,000 patients, including 170,000 in 2015. For the 60-plus facilities currently in their network, they reviewed 630,000 medication orders in 2015 for any adverse drug events.

In 2009, Avera eCare established eEmergency, which provides rural providers with immediate electronic access to emergency-certified physicians and nurses to help them with diagnosis of patients with critical conditions. It is an example of tele-emergency services. Rural clinicians and administrators agreed that eEmergency services have demonstrated significant impact on the quality of clinical services provided in rural areas.

Avera eCare recently established eCorrectionalHealth which provides medical consults to South Dakota prisons. In 2015, they completed 500 video consults and 150 service-related calls and eLongTermCare, which serves 30 long-term care facilities. In all of these instances, this type of electronic medical serve does provide cost savings to medical facilities because it requires no onsite visits (Avera eCare, 2016).

▶ Million Hearts

Million Hearts is a national initiative to prevent one million heart attacks by 2017. The focus is to educate providers and patients on the "ABCS" through the use of HIT:

> Aspirin therapy as needed
> Blood Pressure Control
> Cholesterol Management
> Smoking Cessation.

Million Heart EHR optimization guides assist providers with optimizing their EHR systems with the ABCS. They help providers with improving their EHR data to maximize the Million Harts clinical data measures. The government is requesting EHR vendors to work to develop guides for their systems to customize it for Million Hearts ABCS data (Million Hearts, 2016).

▶ Chief Information Officer

As more healthcare services are delivered electronically, many healthcare organizations have designated a chief information officer (CIO) to manage the organization's information systems. Some organizations may also refer to this position as a **chief technology officer (CTO)** or they may have both. Normally, the CIO is a vice president of the organization and the CTO reports to that position. The CIO also integrates HIT into the organization's strategic plan. The CIO must have knowledge of current information technologies as they apply to the healthcare industry and how new technology can apply to the organization. The CIO is also responsible for motivating employees whenever there is any technological change (Oz, 2006). C. Martin Harris, the CIO of the Cleveland Clinic, feels that the challenge of the CIO (who, he believes, is a change agent) is to move from the implementing of the EHR to continuing to provide quality care to the patient by developing an integrated system model regardless of the organization's size or location. As more health care is being delivered by technology, it will be the responsibility of the CIO to develop a model that is patient oriented rather than operations oriented (Harris, 2008).

▶ Council for Affordable Quality Health Care

The Council for Affordable Quality Health Care (CAQH), a nonprofit organization, consists of alliances of health plans and trade associations that discuss efficiency initiatives to streamline healthcare administration by working with healthcare plans, providers, the government, and consumers. One initiative is creation of a **Committee on Operating Rules for Information Exchange (CORE)**, which borrows from the banking industry's standards for one of the largest electronic payment systems in the world. Based on stakeholder input, CORE has set up standards and operating rules for streamlining processes between providers and healthcare plans. This system allows for real-time access to patient information pre- and post-care. Established by the DHHS, the Health Information Technology Standards Panel (HITSP) utilized the CORE platform in its first set of data standards. HITSP is working toward the national integration of both public and private healthcare data standards for sharing among all organizations. As part of the required data standards mandated by the Affordable Care Act, CORE is being used for data exchange of EHRs to ensure compliance with the Health Insurance Portability and Accountability Act (HIPAA) and other standards. To date, 200 CORE certifications have been obtained (CAQH, 2016).

▶ Other Applications

Enterprise Data Warehouse

Enterprise data warehouses (EDWs) are developed to provide information that helps organizations in strategic decision making. Data warehousing requires an integration of many computer systems across an organization. Business EDWs collect numeric data to assess trends. Retail, banking, and manufacturing use EDWs because these industries usually have repetitive actions that can be easily categorized. For example, banks have savings accounts, CDs, Roth IRAs, money markets, and so on. It is very easy to analyze that type of data. Healthcare transactions can occur in the hospital, in community health centers, and in physicians' offices, and each transaction is unique. Other patient healthcare data may not be numeric (Inmon, 2007). There is written information, such as a physician's prognosis, that needs to be integrated into a system. Therefore, a healthcare EDW must be developed that acknowledges these differences. One of the first healthcare systems to utilize an EDW was the Veterans Health Administration (VHA) (VHA, 2016).

The Centers for Medicaid and Medicare Services Enterprise Data Warehouse

In 2006, the CMS, as a pilot study, developed the largest EDW in history to gather hospital, prescription, and physician data to analyze the claims data for Medicare and Medicaid, based on the belief that integration of the data would enable the CMS to analyze the number of claims submitted by providers. Use of the EDW also assisted in identifying any potential fraud and abuse. The CMS determined the EDW was successful but was concerned that it was a claims-oriented warehouse. Therefore, part of the CMS's EDW strategy is the Integrated Data Repository (IDR), which integrates data from CMS and its partners in a consistent, secure, multi-view environment that includes providers, patients, claims, drug information, and other data as needed (CMS, 2016a).

Radio Frequency Identification

Radio frequency identification (RFID) chips transmit data to receivers. Each of these chips is uniquely identified by a signal indicating where it is located. RFID has been used in the business industry for inventory management by placing a chip on each of the pieces of inventory. Walmart was one of the first retailers to use RFID technology to manage its massive inventory. Recently, RFID technology is being used in many aspects of healthcare industry operations. RFID can be used for the following (GAO RFID, 2016):

- Tracking pharmaceuticals as they are shipped from the manufacturer to the customer;
- Tracking pharmaceutical inventory in a healthcare facility;
- Tracking wait time in emergency rooms;
- Tracking the use of what is being used in surgeries;
- Tracking costly medical equipment to ensure easy access;
- Identifying providers in hospitals to ensure efficiency in care;
- Identifying laboratory specimens to reduce medical errors;
- Tracking patients, including infants, while they are hospitalized;
- Tracking hazardous materials that pose a public health threat; and
- Tracking hand washing to ensure employee compliance.

The following are specific examples of how RFID technology is used in the healthcare industry:

- Wake Forest Baptist Medical Center (North Carolina) sewed RFID tags into the seams of x-ray protection vests in an effort to reduce the time it takes to locate the vests for governmental inspections.
- Texas Health Harris Methodist Hospital is using RFID tags deployed to patients and staff to trace people who come into contact with patients with a contagious, potentially dangerous infection such as tuberculosis.
- Sanraku Hospital, a 270-bed hospital in Tokyo, used a handheld reader with RFID tags in patient wristbands to match drugs with prescription information in electronic medical records (Balm, 2013).

▶ Applied Health Information Technology

The PhreesiaPad

Chaim Indig and Evan Roberts spent one year examining the healthcare market. As young entrepreneurs, they believed that the healthcare industry was the best entry for them to start a business. They realized that patient check in at doctors' offices was a problem. Backed by venture capital firms and with advice from medical professionals, they developed PhreesiaPad, a wireless digital device with a touch-screen keyboard that allows patients to enter their demographic information and the reason they are visiting the doctor. This point-of-service technology eliminates the need for patients to replicate their information each time they visit the doctor. The software automatically verifies patients' insurance information. If they have a copay or balance, they can pay with a credit or debit card. When the patient is finished, a report is automatically generated for the doctor to review before seeing the patient. This increases office efficiency, shortens visit rates, and reduces error rates. This information can also be uploaded to an EHR (Phreesia, 2016).

According to a study conducted by the Medical Group Management Association (MGMA), approximately 30% of patients leave their clinician's office without making any payment, and it takes practices an average of 3.3 billing statements before a patient's outstanding balance is paid in full. Phreesia is a tool that can rectify these financial issues (Leatherbury, 2012).

PatientPoint (Formerly Healthy Advice Network)

PatientPoint provides education to patients electronically while they are in the waiting room or an exam room. Health education information is customized with brand advertising messages displayed on digital flat screens in physicians' waiting rooms. There are 25-minute loops of brand materials that focus on prevention and management of disease. PatientPoint has programs in over 31,000 locations. PatientPoint serves more than 70,000 healthcare providers and 750 hospitals nationwide, impacting 113 million patients and creating more than 586 million patient and caregiver exposures each year (PatientPoint, 2016).

MelaFind Optical Scanner

The **MelaFind optical scanner** is not for definitive diagnosis but rather to provide additional information a doctor can use in determining whether to order a biopsy. The goal is to reduce the number of patients left with unnecessary biopsy scars, with the added benefit of eliminating the cost of unnecessary procedures. The MelaFind technology (MELA Sciences, Irvington, NY) uses missile navigation technologies originally paid for by the U.S. Department of Defense to optically scan the surface of a suspicious lesion at 10 electromagnetic wavelengths (Gidalovtiz, 2014).

55555

Electronic Aspirin

A technology under clinical investigation at Autonomic Technologies, Inc. (Redwood City, CA) is a patient-powered tool for blocking pain-causing signals at the first sign of a headache. The system involves the permanent implant of a small nerve-stimulating device in the upper gum on the side of the head normally affected by the headache. When a patient senses the onset of a headache, he or she places a handheld remote controller on the cheek nearest the implant. The resulting signals block the pain-causing neurotransmitters (Intellitechaz, 2015).

Robotic Checkups

Medical robots can make rounds, checking on patients in different rooms and managing their individual charts and vital signs without direct human intervention. The RP-VITA Remote Presence Robot produced jointly by iRobot Corp. and InTouch Health is the first such autonomous navigation remote-presence robot to receive FDA clearance for hospital use. The device is a mobile cart with a two-way video screen and medical monitoring equipment, programmed to maneuver through healthcare facilities. This is an innovative method of telemedicine (iRobot, 2016).

Sapien Heart Valve

The **Sapien heart valve** is a life-saving alternative to open-heart surgery for patients who need a new valve but for whom surgery is considered high risk. Manufactured by Edwards Life Sciences (Irvine, CA), the Sapien has been available in Europe but was approved for use by the FDA in 2011, and is finding its first use in U.S. heart centers—where it is limited only to the most at-risk patients. The Sapien valve is inserted by catheter from a small incision near the rib cage. The valve material is made of bovine tissue attached to a stainless-steel stent, which is expanded by inflating a small balloon in the valve space. A simpler procedure with much shorter hospitalizations could have a positive impact on healthcare costs (Edwards Lifesciences Corporation, 2016).

Acuson P10

Siemens has introduced a pocket-sized ultrasound, **Acuson P10**, which can be used for traditional applications of diagnostic and screening tests. It is designed for quick and easy use in emergency medicine, cardiology, ICU, and OB/GYN situations. In each of these situations, the device provides a quick view of anatomy and tissue. It can be used in outpatient areas, intensive care units, and rescue helicopters to provide instant information to make a diagnosis. The results can be viewed on the screen but can also be uploaded to a computer. This technology eliminates the need for the provider to send the patient to an imaging center (MNT, 2016a).

Piccolo Xpress Chemistry Analyzer

The size of a shoebox, Piccolo xpress is a compact, portable chemistry analyzer that delivers blood test results quickly. The provider places blood and the like on a small disc and slides the disc into the Piccolo xpress. The provider requests tests to be performed using the device's touch-screen display. The device can print a hard-copy report in approximately 12 minutes, or the information can be transferred to an EHR. This technology expedites the provider's ability to diagnose a patient (Piccolo xpress, 2016).

▶ The Importance of Health Information Technology

In a recent study focused on the implementation and management of IT in the hospital setting, Szydlowski and Smith (2009) interviewed six hospital CIOs (or their equivalents) and nurse managers to assess why they used HIT. The CIOs indicated they used HIT to streamline administrative processes in the organization. They all recognized the substantial cost to invest in HIT but understood that the investment was long term and that it would ultimately be very cost efficient. The nurse managers focused on the ability to reduce medical errors as a result of HIT. They also indicated that having electronic patient data ultimately contributed to more efficient and effective clinical decision making. The barriers to successful implementation identified by both the CIOs and the nurse managers were inadequate training on HIT and the amount of time needed to become familiar with HIT. The concerns the CIOs indicate are also applicable to other healthcare settings such as physician offices and outpatient facilities.

From a consumer perspective, health information technology can mean safer care. Electronic health records can provide a more complete picture of a person's health status. E-prescribing may reduce medical errors because pharmacists will not have to interpret poor physician writing. Sharing medical information with other providers electronically may reduce the number of tests a consumer could receive. In case of a disaster in which paper records could be destroyed, having an electronic copy of consumer medical records could save a life (Why is health information, 2016).

Technology can produce innovative ways to improve patient care, and for all of the providers that is the main goal.

▶ Conclusion

The healthcare industry has lagged behind other industries utilizing IT as a form of communicating important data. Despite that fact, there have been specific applications developed for HIT such as e-prescribing, telemedicine, ehealth, and specific applied technologies such as the PatientPoint, MelaFind optical scanner, the Phreesia Pad, Sapien heart valve, robotic checkups, Electronic Aspirin, Accuson P10, and the Piccolo xpress, which were discussed in this chapter. Healthcare organizations have recognized the importance of IT and have hired CIOs and CTOs to manage their data. However, healthcare consumers need to embrace an electronic patient record, which is the basis for the Microsoft Health Vault. This will enable patients to be treated effectively and efficiently nationally. The patient health record can be integrated into the electronic health records that are being utilized nationwide. Having the ability to access a patient's health information could assist in reducing medical errors. As a consumer, utilizing a tool like HealthVault could provide an opportunity to consolidate all medical information electronically so, if there are any medical problems, the information will be readily available. The major IT issue in healthcare is the need to establish the interoperability of EHR systems nationwide. This communication between systems will enable patients to be treated more quickly because there will be immediate access to their most current medical information. Although the federal government has indicated this communication between systems is necessary to ensure the full success of electronic health records system, progress continues to be slow.

Wrap-Up

Vocabulary

Acuson P10
Artificial intelligence
Avera eCare
Chief information officer (CIO)
Chief technology officer (CTO)
Committee on Operating Rules for Information Exchange (CORE)
Computerized physician order entry
Drug–drug interactions
E-health
Electronic aspirin
Electronic clinical decision support systems
Electronic health record (EHR)

Electronic medical record (EMR/EHR)
Electronic patient record
Enterprise data warehouse
E-prescribing
Expert system
Health information systems (HIS)
Health information technology (HIT)
HealthVault
Healthy Advice Network
Imaging informatics
Informatics
Information technology (IT)

Meaningful use
Medical informatics
Melafind optical scanner
Million Hearts
National Alliance for Health Information Technology (NAHIT)
PatientPoint
Pharmacy benefit manager
Piccolo xpress Chemistry Analyzer
Radio frequency identification
Robotic checkups
Sapien heart valve
Telehealth
Telemedicine

References

American Telemedicine Association. (2016). What is telemedicine? Retrieved from http://www.americantelemed.org/learn

American Telemedicine Association. (2016). Telemedicine case studies. Retrieved from http://www.americantelemed.org/learn/telemedicine-case-studies/case-study-full-page/avera-ecare-supports-675-rural-clinicians-in-the-delivery-of-highest-quality-care

Anderson, R., Rice, T., & Kominksi, G. (2007). *Changing the U.S. health care system*. San Francisco, CA: Jossey-Bass.

Appleby, C. (2008). IT visionary: G. Octo Barnett, MD. *Most Wired Magazine*. Retrieved from http://www.hhnmostwired.com/hhnmostwiredapp/jsp/articledisplay.jsp?dcrpath=HHNM

Ash, J., Gorman, P., Seshadri, V., & Hersh, W. (2004). Computerized physician order entry in U.S. hospitals: Results of a 2002 survey. *Journal of the American Medical Informatics Association, 11*(2), 95–99.

Avera eCare. (2016). Retrieved from http://www.averaecare.org/ecare/who-we-are/about-avera-ecare/

Balm, S. (2013). 5 ways the healthcare industry is implementing RFID technology. Retrieved from http://medcitynews

.com/2013/12/5-ways-hospitals-implementing-rfid-tags-emerging-trend-healthcare/

Balto, D. (2015). The state of competition in the PBM and pharmacy marketplaces. Retrieved from https://judiciary.house.gov/Balto-testimony

Buchbinder, S., & Shanks, N. (2007). *Introduction to health care management*. Sudbury, MA: Jones and Bartlett.

CAQH. (2016). What are operating rules? Retrieved from http://www.caqh.org/CORE_rules.php

Centers for Medicare and Medicaid Services (CMS). (2016a). CMS Integrated Data Repository (IDR). Retrieved from http://www.cms.gov/Research-Statistics-Data-and-Systems/Computer-Data-and-Systems/IDR

CMS. (2016b). Electronic prescribing (eRx) incentive program. Retrieved from http://www.cms.gov/Medicare/Quality-Initiatives-Patient-Assessment-Instruments/ERxIncentive/index.html?redirect=/erxincentive

CMS. (2016c). Meaningful use. Retrieved from http://www.cms.gov/Regulations-and-Guidance/Legislation/EHRIncentivePrograms/Meaningful_Use.html

CMS. (2016d). Medicare and Medicaid EHR incentive program basics. Retrieved from http://www.cms.gov/Regulations-and-Guidance/Legislation/EHRIncentivePrograms/Basics.html

Coiera, E. (2003). *The guide to health informatics* (2nd ed.). London: Hodder Arnold.

Daigrepont, J., & McGrath, J. (2011). EHR critical success factors. In *Complete guide and toolkit to successful EHR adoption* (pp. 13–21). Chicago, IL: HIMSS.

Department of Health and Human Services (DHHS). (2016). Health information technology. Retrieved from http://www.hhs.gov/healthit/onc/background

eJobDescription. (2016). Chief information officer job description. Retrieved from http://www.ejobdescription.com/CIO_Job_Description.html

Edwards Lifesciences Corporation. (2016). Edwards Sapien transcatheter heart valve. Retrieved from http://www.edwards.com/products/transcathetervalve/Pages/THVcategory.aspx

Federal Trade Commission. (2016). FTC and DOJ issue report on competition and health care. Retrieved from http://www.ftc.gov/opa/2004/07/healthcarerpt.shtm

Gamble, M. (2012). 5 legal issues surrounding electronic medical records. Retrieved from http://www.beckershospitalreview.com/legal-regulatory-issues/5-legal-issues-surrounding-electronic-medical-records.html

GAO RFID. (2016). RFID for healthcare industry. Retrieved from http://healthcare.gaorfid.com

Goldstein, M., & Blumenthal, D. (2008). Building an information technology infrastructure. *Journal of Law, Medicine & Ethics*, 709–715.

Gidalevitz, Y. (2014). Reduce the number of melanoma skin cancer biopsies with MelaFind in your #MEDTECH-TOOLBOX. Retrieved from https://www.fortis.edu/blog/healthcare/reduce-the-number-of-melanoma-skin-cancer-biopsies-with-melafind-in-your-medtechtoolbox/id/3062

Harris, C. (2008). C. Martin Harris, CIO, Cleveland Clinic. *Health Management Technology*, 29(7), 10.

HealthVault. (20166). Overview. Retrieved from https://www.healthvault.com/us/en/overview

iMedicalApps. (2016). Cleveland Clinic pilots Microsoft HealthVault. Retrieved from http://www.imedicalapps.com/2010/03/microsoft-healthvault-community-connect-cleveland-clini/

Inmon, B. (2007). Data warehousing in a health care environment. *The Data Newsletter*. Retrieved from http://tdan.com/print/4584

Institute of Medicine (IOM). (2001). Crossing the quality chasm: A new health system for the 21st century. Retrieved from http://www.iom.edu/Reports/2001/Crossing-the-Quality-Chasm-A-New-Health-System-for-the-21st-Century.aspx

Intellitechaz (20156). Three innovations in medical practice. Retrieved from http://www.intellitechaz.com/blog/category/electronic-aspirin/

iRobot. (2016). InTouch Health and iRobot announce first customers to install RP-VITA, the new face of -telemedicine. Retrieved from http://www.irobot.com/us/Company/Press_Center/Press_Releases/Press_Release.aspx?n=050613

Leatherbury, L. (2012). Phreesia increases productivity, improves collections for medical practices. *South Florida Hospital News*. Retrieved from http://southfloridahospitalnews.com/page/Phreesia_Increases_Productivity_Improves_Collections_for_Medical_Practices/7158/1/

Leung, L. (2008). Internet embeddedness: Links with online health information seeking, expectancy value/quality of health information websites, and Internet usage patterns. *Cyber Psychology & Behavior*, 11(5), 565–569.

Million Hearts. (2016). Retrieved from https://www.healthit.gov/providers-professionals/million-hearts

MNT. (2016a). ACUSON P10 crosses healthcare boundaries: Handheld pocket ultrasound carries out essential obstetric scanning in Tanzania. Retrieved from http://www.medicalnewstoday.com/articles/114511.php

MNT. (2016b). The National Alliance for Health Information Technology explores next set of strategic initiatives. Retrieved from http://www.medicalnewstoday.com/articles/101878.php

Murer, C. (2007). EHRS: Issues preventing widespread adoption. *Rehab Management*, 20, 38–39.

Murphy, J., Malone, D., Olson, B., Grizzle, A., Armstrong, E., & Skrepnek, G. (2009). Development of computerized alerts with management strategies for 25 serious drug-drug interactions. *American Journal of Health-System Pharmacists*, 66, 38–44.

Open Clinical. (2016). Health informatics. Retrieved from http://www.openclinical.org/healthinformatics.html

Oz, E. (2006). *Management information systems*. Mason, OH: Thomson Southwestern.

PatientPoint. (2013). About us. Retrieved from http://www.patientpoint.com/aboutus/formerly-healthy-advice.aspx

Perreault, L., & Metzger, J. (1999). A pragmatic framework for understanding clinical decision support. *Journal of Health Care Information Management*, 13, 2, 5–21.

Phreesia. (2016). Phreesia news. Retrieved from http://www.phreesia.com/news.asp

Piccolo xpress. (2016). Overview. Retrieved from http://www.piccoloxpress.com/products/piccolo/overview

Robeznieks, A. (2013). Pediatricians offer model for kids' EHRs. Retrieved from http://www.modernphysician.com/article/20130404/MODERNPHYSICIAN/304049975

Shields, A., Shin, P., Leu, M., Levy, D., Betancourt, R., Hawkins, D., & Proser, M. (2007). Adoption of health information technology in community health centers: Results of a national survey. *Health Affairs*, 26(3), 1373–1383.

Singer, J. (2013). EHRs are a tool not a solution: The NYC primary care information project. Retrieved from http://healthaffairs.org/blog/2013/03/13/ehrs-are-a-tool-not-a-solution-the-nyc-primary-care-information-project

Surescripts. (2012). National Progress Report on EPrescribing and Safe-Rx Rankings. Retrieved from http://www.surescripts.com/about-e-prescribing/progress-reports/national-progress-reports#downloads

Szydlowski, S., & Smith, C. (2009). Perspectives from nurse leaders and chief information officers on health information technology implementation. *Hospital Topics: Research and Perspectives on Healthcare*, *87*(1), 3–9.

Valerius, J. (2007). The electronic health record: What every information manager should know. *The Information Management Journal*, *4*(1), 56–59.

Ventres, W., & Shah, A. (2007). How do EHRs affect the physician patient relationship? *American Family Physician*, *75*(9), 1385–1390.

Vreeman, D., Taggard, S., Rhine, M., & Worrell, T.W. (2006). Evidence for electronic health record systems in physical therapy. *Physical Therapy*, *86*, 3, 434–446.

Walker, J.M. (2013). Using the EHR to transform healthcare. Retrieved from http://www.ehcca.com/presentations/hitsymposium/walker_2a.pdf

What is telemedicine (2016). Retrieved from http://www.americantelemed.org/about-telemedicine/what-is-telemedicine#.VtOYA-ZChSU

Whitman, J.C., & David, S. (2007). Effectively integrating your EMR/EHR initiative. *The Physician Executive*, *33*(5), 56–59.

Why is health information technology important to me? (2016). Retrieved from http://www.ak-ehealth.org/for-patients/why-is-health-information-technology-important-to-me/

▶ **Notes**

▶ **Student Activity 10-1**

In Your Own Words

Based on this chapter, please provide an explanation of the following concepts in your own words. DO NOT RECITE the text.

Health information technology:

_____

_____

Expert systems:

_____

_____

Electronic health records:

_____

_____

Legacy systems:

_____

_____

Enterprise data warehouse:

_____

_____

Radio frequency identification:

_____

_____

PatientPoint:

_____

_____

Computerized physician order entry (CPOE) systems:

_____

_____

Phreesia Pad:

_____

_____

▶ # Student Activity 10-2

Complete the following case scenarios based on the information provided in the chapter. Your answer must be IN YOUR OWN WORDS.

Real-Life Applications: Case Scenario One

As the office manager of a cardiologist, you heard there was a program called Million Hearts that could benefit her patients.

Activity

You decide to research the Million Hearts project to present to your boss.

Responses

_____

_____

_____

_____

_____

_____

_____

_____

_____

_____

_____

_____

_____

_____

_____

_____

_____

Case Scenario Two

As a new physician, one of your goals is to increase access to health care in the rural areas of your state. You have heard that telemedicine may be an opportunity for you.

Activity

You perform research on the advantages and disadvantages of telemedicine for your practice.

Responses

_____

_____

_____

_____

_____

_____

_____

_____

_____

_____

_____

_____

_____

_____

_____

_____

_____

Case Scenario Three

You were just promoted to CIO of your hospital. One of your goals is to improve the efficiencies of hospital operation. You heard that RFID is a viable option to pursue.

Activity

Perform research on RFID technology and its application to the healthcare industry. Select three types of RFID applications that will work for your hospital and develop a report for your CEO.

Responses

_____

_____

_____

_____

_____

_____

_____

_____

_____

_____

_____

_____

_____

_____

_____

_____

_____

_____

Case Scenario Four

Your friend lives in a rural area that has no nearby healthcare system. They are starting a telemedicine program near her. She is very worried about this new concept.

Activity

Perform research and find healthcare organizations that use telemedicine. Discuss your findings with your friend.

Responses

_____

_____

_____

_____

_____

_____

_____

_____

_____

_____

_____

_____

_____

_____

_____

_____

_____

_____

_____

▶ **Student Activity 10-3**

Internet Exercises

Write your answers in the space provided.

- ■ Visit each of the websites listed here.
- ■ Name the organization.
- ■ Locate the organization's mission statement on the website.
- ■ Provide a brief overview of the activities of the organization.
- ■ How do these organizations participate in the U.S. healthcare system?

Websites

http://www.millionhearts.hhs.gov

Organization Name:

_____

_____

Mission Statement:

_____

_____

Overview of Activities:

_____

_____

_____

Importance of Organization to U.S. Health Care:

_____

_____

_____

http://www.patientpoint.com

Organization Name:

_____

_____

Mission Statement:

_____

_____

_____

Overview of Activities:

_____

_____

_____

Importance of Organization to U.S. Health Care:

_____

_____

_____

http://www.healthdatamanagement.com

Organization Name:

_____

_____

Mission Statement:

_____

_____

_____

Overview of Activities:

_____

_____

_____

Importance of Organization to U.S. Health Care:

_____

_____

_____

http://www.nationalehealth.org

Organization Name:

_____

_____

Mission Statement:

_____

_____

_____

Overview of Activities:

_____

_____

_____

Importance of Organization to U.S. Health Care:

_____

_____

http://www.phreesia.com

Organization Name:

_____

_____

Mission Statement:

_____

_____

_____

Overview of Activities:

_____

_____

_____

Importance of Organization to U.S. Health Care:

_____

_____

_____

http://www.healthvault.com

Organization Name:

_____

_____

Mission Statement:

_____

_____

Overview of Activities:

_____

_____

_____

Importance of Organization to U.S. Health Care:

_____

_____

_____

_____

▶ Student Activity 10-4

Discussion Questions

The following are suggested discussion questions for this chapter.

1. What is radio frequency identification? Using the textbook and the Internet, discuss three ways this technology applies to health care.

_____

_____

_____

_____

_____

_____

2. What is PatientPoint? Do you think this is an effective way to educate patients? Defend your answer.

_____

_____

_____

_____

_____

_____

3. What is Electronic Aspirin? What are the advantages and disadvantages of this new product. Would you use this product? Defend your answer.

_____

_____

_____

_____

_____

_____

_____

_____

_____

_____

_____

4. What are two advantages and two disadvantages of EHR? What is meaningful use? What are the barriers to implementing an EHR system?

_____

_____

_____

_____

_____

_____

_____

_____

5. Discuss the concept of telemedicine and explain whether you believe it is beneficial to health care.

_____

_____

_____

_____

_____

_____

_____

▶ **Student Activity 10-5**

Current Events

Perform an Internet search and find a current events topic over the past three years that is related to this chapter. Provide a summary of the article and the link to the article and why the article relates to the chapter.

_____

_____

_____

_____

_____

_____

_____

_____

_____

_____

_____

_____

_____

_____

_____

_____

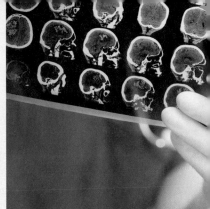

CHAPTER 11

Healthcare Law

DID YOU KNOW THAT?

- The Ethics in Patient Referral Act of 1989 was passed because providers were referring patients to medical services in which they or family members had a financial interest.
- *Qui tam*, a concept used in antitrust law, is Latin for *he who sues*. A *qui tam* provision enables individuals to sue providers for fraudulent activity against the federal government, recovering a portion of the funds returned to the government.
- In response to the Affordable Care Act antifraud initiatives, over 15,000 Medicare providers were expelled from the system for fraudulent activity.
- According to civil law, a surgeon's performance of surgery without consent could be considered assault and battery.
- The most important relationship in the healthcare system is the relationship between the patient—the healthcare consumer—and their provider, which could be a physician or an organization such as a clinic or hospital where the physician has a relationship.
- Defensive medicine occurs when clinicians order more tests and provide more services than necessary to protect themselves from malpractice lawsuits.

▶ Introduction

To be an effective healthcare manager, it is important to understand basic legal and ethical principles that influence the work environment, including the legal relationship between the organization and the consumer—the healthcare provider and the patient. The basic concepts of law, both civil and criminal healthcare law, tort reform, employment-related legislation, safety in the workplace, and the legal relationship between the provider and the patient will be discussed in this chapter.

▶ Basic Concepts of Healthcare Law

The healthcare industry is one of the most heavily regulated industries in the United States. Those who provide, receive, pay for, and regulate healthcare services are affected by the law (Miller, 2006). **Law** is a body of rules for the conduct of individuals and organizations. Law is created so there is a minimal standard of action required by individuals and organizations. **Public law** enforces relationships between entities and the government, and **private law** deals with issues among individual. Public law is created by federal, state, and local governments. As the judicial system interprets previous legal decisions regarding a case, judges are creating **common law** (Pozgar, 2014). The minimal standard for action is federal law, although state law may be more stringent. Legislative bodies such as the U.S. Congress create laws that are called **statutes**. Both common law and statutes are then interpreted by administrative agencies by developing **rules and regulations**.

There are civil and criminal laws that affect the healthcare industry. **Civil law**, an example of private law, focuses on wrongful acts against individuals and organizations based on contractual violations. **Torts**, derived from the French word for *wrong*, is a category of wrongful acts, in civil law, which may not have a preexisting contract. To prove a civil infraction, you do not need as much evidence as in a criminal case. **Criminal law**, an example of public law, is concerned with actions that are illegal based on court decisions. In order to convict someone of a criminal activity, guilt must be proved beyond a reasonable doubt. The most common types of criminal law infractions in the healthcare field are Medicare and Medicaid fraud (Miller 2006).

As stated earlier, torts are wrongdoings inflicted on individuals or organizations regardless of whether a contract is in place. There are several different types of violations that can apply to health care. There are two basic healthcare torts: (1) negligence, which involves the unintentional omission of an act that would contribute to the positive health of a patient; and (2) intentional torts, such as assault and **battery** or invasion of privacy (Pozgar, 2014).

An example of **negligence** would be if a provider does not give appropriate care or withholds care and injury to the patient results. In the healthcare industry, an **intentional tort** such as assault and battery would be a surgeon performing surgery on a patient without his or her consent (Bal, 2009). Invasion of privacy would be the release of patients' health records. Privacy issues relating to patient information is a major issue in the healthcare industry. These activities are categorized under the term *medical malpractice*.

According to the *American Heritage Dictionary* (2000), **medical malpractice** is the "improper or negligent treatment of a patient by a provider which results in injury, damage or loss" (p. 1060). According to the Institute of Medicine's (IOM) landmark report *To Err Is Human*, medical malpractice has resulted in approximately 80,000–100,000 deaths per year. Unfortunately, recent research indicates that this data is low. Preventable medical errors are the third leading cause of death in the United States, and the estimates are over 400,000 even though there have been many patient safety standards implemented to lower this amount (McCann, 2014). Disputes over improper care of a patient have hurt both providers and patients. Patients have sued physicians because they feel their provider has not provided them the proper level of care compared to the standard of care in the industry.

To prove negligence, four legal elements must be proved: (1) a professional duty owed to the patient as determined by the standard of care, (2) breach of such duty, (3) injury caused by the breach, and (4) proven causation between the action and the injury. There are four types of damages considered: (1) economic damages are a fixed price based on a loss of an object; (2) **noneconomic damages** are not a fixed amount and include pain and suffering from the negligence; (3) compensatory damages include both economic and noneconomic damages; and (4) punitive damages, which are uncommon, are intended to punish the defendant (Pozgar, 2014).

▶ Tort Reform

As a result of the number of medical malpractice claims in the United States, malpractice insurance premiums have increased. This has resulted in the concept of **defensive medicine**, which means that providers often order more tests and provide more services than necessary to protect themselves from malpractice lawsuits. Surveys of physicians over the years reveal over 70% of physicians admit to defensive medicine practices because they are afraid of litigation (Sekhar & Vyas, 2013). Historically, there have been malpractice insurance crises during the 1970s, 1980s, and, most recently, the beginning of this century (Danzon, 1995). The issues in the 1970s led to joint underwriting measures that required insurance companies to offer medical malpractice if the physician purchased other insurance. In some states, compensation funds were established to offset large award settlements. The number of malpractice suits lessened but the dollar amounts of awards were still huge. During the mid-1980s, the premiums were rising again—nearly 75%. It was determined that any initiatives established in the 1970s were not effective (Rosenbach & Stone, 1990). A third malpractice insurance crisis occurred in the 2000s. Issues with obtaining medical malpractice insurance in several states have increased, forcing physicians to join underwriting associations, which can charge exorbitant premiums.

As a result of the recent malpractice insurance crisis, more states have adopted statutory caps on the monetary damages that a plaintiff can recover in malpractice claims. State officials felt that a cap on monetary damages would have the most impact on malpractice insurance premiums because the less an insurance company has paid out in insurance claims, the less the insurance company would have to raise insurance rates. Over half of the states have established caps on awards. For example, Florida, Kansas, Maryland, Massachusetts, Michigan, North Carolina, and Texas have established noneconomic damages caps for different medical cases. An example of a noneconomic damage policy is that of Texas, which has implemented the following:

- A per-claimant **$250,000** cap on noneconomic damages in medical malpractice cases against a physician or health care provider;
- For a single healthcare institution, a per-claimant **$250,000** cap on noneconomic damages; and
- For multiple healthcare institutions, an overall cap of **$500,000** per claimant for noneconomic damages, and no single institution can be on the hook for more than **$250,000** in noneconomic damages, per claimant.

As stated earlier, noneconomic damages include compensation for things like pain and suffering and emotional distress. Noneconomic damages are said to be more "subjective," which is why many states have focused on caps for this type of damage (NOLO, 2016).

Many legal factors have contributed to the increase in claims. Voluntary hospitals are no longer exempt from malpractice suits. The fact that employers now have to take responsibility for their employees' wrongdoing has also increased claims. The concept of informed consent for the patient has expanded and therefore increased claims. The acceptable **standard of care**, which used to be strictly based on a locality rule, has now become a state or national standard, which has also resulted in increased claims (Pozgar, 2014). Statutes specifying the acceptable standard of care in a malpractice suit in a local setting were replaced by a national or state standard. This increased the ability to locate expert witnesses who would testify at a trial regarding the standard of care given to the plaintiff.

Some physicians are leaving private practice because they can no longer afford the premiums—they are now in administrative positions at all levels of government, are academicians, or are teaching at medical schools. The malpractice insurance issues have forced many states to review their malpractice guidelines. Some states' **tort reform**, which has imposed limits on the amount awarded, continues to cause controversy. However, recent federal studies have indicated that imposing caps on awards may be an effective method to reduce malpractice costs and to discourage frivolous lawsuits. In addition, the U.S. Supreme Court ruled that any awards must be included in an individual's taxed income (Miller, 2006).

The Legal Relationship between the Provider and Consumer

The most important relationship in the healthcare system is the relationship between the patient—the healthcare consumer—and his or her provider, which could be a physician or an organization such as a clinic or hospital where the physician has a relationship. This relationship can be considered a contract: an agreement, either oral or written, between two or more parties that designates legally enforceable activities (Pozgar, 2016). A physician can establish a contractual relationship with a patient in three ways: (1) establishing a **contractual relationship to care for a designated population**, (2) establishing an **express contract** with a patient under mutual agreement, or (3) establishing a relationship under an **implied contract** (Laws, 2016).

In order for a contract to exist, there must be four components: (1) agreement between two parties, (2) both parties must be competent to consent to the agreement, (3) the agreement must be of value, and (4) the agreement must be legally enforceable. If any of these components are missing, the parties are not bound by the agreement to comply with the terms (Buchbinder & Shanks, 2007). This chapter will discuss several types of contracts as they pertain to health care.

A contract to care for a designated population is indicative of a health maintenance organization (HMO) or managed care contract. A physician is contractually required to care for those member patients of a managed care organization. They may sign contracts to provide care for hospitals, schools, or long-term care facilities that have designated populations (Miller, 2006).

An express contract is a simple contract—merely a mutual agreement of care between the physician and patient. The physician may define the limitations of the contract, including the parameters of care. The physician may decide to practice only in a certain geographic area or, if a specialist, to provide services only in that area of specialty. An implied contract can be implied from a physician's actions. If a physician gives advice regarding medical treatment, there is an implied contract (Laws, 2016). The relationship between a patient and hospital, a **contractual right to admission**, can be considered a contract if a hospital has contracted to treat certain members of an organization, like a managed care organization; if so, the hospital is required to treat those members. A second example of this type of contractual right to admission is if governmental hospitals, such as county hospitals, are required to provide care for patients regardless of ability to pay (Miller, 2006).

How Does a Relationship with a Provider End?

According to the American Medical Association (AMA), once a patient and physician relationship has started, the physician is legally and ethically obligated to continue the relationship until the patient no longer requires the physician's care. There may be practical reason for a relationship to end, such as geographic relocation or change of healthcare insurance. If a patient becomes noncompliant and abusive, the physician has the right to end a relationship. However, to protect the physician from being accused of "**patient abandonment**," the physician must take steps to properly end the relationship. If a patient withdraws from the relationship with the provider, then the physician no longer has a duty to provide follow up. Also, if medical care is no longer needed, the relationship naturally is completed. If a patient is transferred to another provider, the provider then establishes a relationship with the new patient. However, a physician could withdraw from a relationship by giving sufficient notice or providing the patient with a referral. However, if a physician withdraws from a relationship

without sufficient reason, the provider may be liable for breach of contract or patient abandonment. The AMA (2016) provides the following five steps for a physician to terminate a relationship:

1. Giving the patient written notice, preferably certified mail;
2. Providing the patient with a specific reason for termination;
3. Continuing to provide care for a reasonable period of time so the patient can find other care;
4. Providing assistance to the patient to find other care; and
5. Offering to transfer all medical records with patient permission.

▶ Healthcare-Related Legislation

Healthcare Consumer Laws

Other legislative acts will be discussed thoroughly throughout the text; however, these acts directly impact how health care is provided to consumers.

Hill-Burton Act

The **Hill-Burton Act** of 1946, also known as the Hospital Survey and Construction Act, was passed because the federal government recognized the lack of hospitals in the United States during the 1940s. Federal grants were provided to states for hospital construction to ensure there were 4.5 beds per 1,000 people (Shi & Singh, 2008). This act had a huge influence on creating more hospitals nationally. If a hospital received federal funds because of the Hill-Burton Act, it agreed to a community service requirement, so any person residing in the area of the hospital cannot be denied treatment in the portion of the hospital financed by the Hill-Burton Act. (There are exceptions, for lack of needed services, unavailability of the services needed, or the patient's ability to pay.) The program stopped providing funds in 1997, but approximately 150 healthcare facilities nationwide are still obligated to provide free or reduced-cost care. Since 1980, more than $6 billion in uncompensated services have been provided to eligible patients through Hill-Burton. Hospitals that are under the Hill-Burton Act are required to post notices about the program in their admitting area. These notices must be easy to read and in languages appropriate to the community (HRSA, 2016).

Emergency Medical Treatment and Active Labor Act

The **Emergency Medical Treatment and Active Labor Act (EMTALA)** of 1986, enforced by the Centers for Medicare and Medicaid Services (CMS) and the Office of Inspector General (OIG), requires Medicare participants to receive emergency care from a hospital or medical entity that provides dedicated emergency services. This was passed as part of the Consolidated Omnibus Budget Reconciliation Act of 1985 (COBRA). This requirement is a type of fiduciary duty that means the healthcare provider or organization is obligated to provide care to someone who has placed his or her trust in them (CMS, 2016). This law is also called the "antidumping" statute because, prior to the enactment of this law, many hospitals dumped Medicare patients. Penalties for violating EMTALA include the following:

1. A hospital can be fined between $25,000 and $50,000 per violation.
2. Hospitals can be excluded from the Medicare program.
3. Physicians can be fined up to $50,000 per violation.
4. Physicians can be excluded from Medicare and Medicaid.

The original act was amended in 2000 and 2006 to strengthen the law. The CMS issued guidelines that further explained the act. This legislation protects consumers to ensure they receive appropriate emergency care when they present themselves to regulated hospitals and medical organizations (CMS, 2016).

Children's Health Insurance Program

The **Children's Health Insurance Program (CHIP)** was enacted under the Balanced Budget Act of 1997, is Title XXI of the Social Security Act, and is jointly financed by federal and state funding and administered by the states and the CMS. The purpose of this program is to provide coverage for low-income children (younger than age 19) whose family income exceeds the income-level requirements of Medicaid. As an incentive for states to expand their coverage programs for children, Congress created an "enhanced" federal matching rate for CHIP that is generally about 15 percentage points higher than the Medicaid rate— averaging 71% nationally. For example, if a state has a 50% match rate for Medicaid, they may have a 65% match rate for CHIP (Financing, 2016). Children who are eligible for Medicaid or covered by private health insurance cannot participate in CHIP (National Health Law Program, 2016). Approximately 8 million children who are uninsured and ineligible for public assistance have been positively impacted by this program. Children who are eligible for state health benefit plans are not eligible for CHIP. Studies have indicated that this program has improved access to health insurance for children (Kaiser Family Foundation, 2016).

Benefits Improvement and Protection Act

The **Benefits Improvement and Protection Act of 2000 (BIPA)**, formally called the Medicare, Medicaid, and CHIP Benefits Improvement and Protection Act, modifies Medicare payment rates for many services. It also adds coverage for preventive and therapeutic services. It increases federal funding to state programs. From a healthcare consumer perspective, it protects Medicare beneficiaries by granting them the ability to appeal providers' terminations of services (BIPA, 2016). It requires providers to issue a written notice to the patient that coverage has been terminated, giving an end date for the termination. The patient has the right to appeal the decision.

The **HIPAA National Standards** of 2002 or Privacy Rule is intended to further protect patient's personal medical records and other personal health information maintained by healthcare providers, hospitals, insurance companies, and health plans. It gives patients new rights to access of their records, restricts the amount of patient information released, and establishes new restrictions on researchers' access (U.S. Department of Health & Human Services, 2016a).

Antitrust Laws

The purpose of **antitrust law** is to protect the consumer by ensuring there is a market driven by competition so the consumer has a choice for health care. In a sense, antitrust laws protect competition so the consumer has a choice. Antitrust laws apply to most healthcare organizations. There are both federal and state antitrust laws. There are four main antitrust federal laws that will be discussed in this chapter: the Sherman Antitrust Act, the Clayton Act, the Federal Trade Commission Act, and the Robinson-Patman Act (the amendment to the Clayton Act). These acts are important to know because they were developed to ultimately protect the healthcare consumer and those who provide healthcare services.

The **Sherman Act of 1890** focuses on eliminating **monopolies**, which are healthcare organizations that control a market so that the consumer has no choice in health care. It also targets **price fixing** among competitors; price fixing prevents consumers from paying a fair price because competitors establish a certain price (by either increasing or lowering prices) among themselves to stabilize the market. Healthcare facilities may also have an agreement on **market division**. This illegal action occurs when one or more health organizations decide which type of services will be offered at each organization. **Tying** refers to healthcare providers that will only sell a product to a consumer who will also buy a second product from them. **Boycotts** are also illegal according to this act. When healthcare providers have an agreement to not deal with anyone outside their group, that is considered interfering with the consumers' rights to choose. **Price information exchange** of services between providers can also be illegal (Miller, 2006). Healthcare providers are protected under the act if it has been determined that hospitals have exclusive contracts with certain providers, which excludes other providers from use of the hospital. This could be a violation of the act. Violations of the act are considered federal crimes.

The **Clayton Act of 1914** was passed to supplement the Sherman Act, as amended by the Robinson-Patman Act, which issues further restrictions on mergers and acquisitions. With the increasing development of hospital chains, this act has focused on hospitals. There are no criminal penalties for violations of this act, unlike the Sherman Act. Any organization considering a merger or acquisition above a certain size must notify both the Antitrust Division of the U.S. Department of Justice (DOJ) and the Federal Trade Commission (FTC). The act also prohibits other business practices that, under certain circumstances, may harm competition. The act also allows individuals to sue for three times their actual damages plus legal costs.

The **Hart-Scott-Rodino Antitrust Improvement Act of 1976**, an amendment to the Clayton Act, ensures those hospitals and other entities that entered mergers, acquisitions, and joint ventures must notify the DOJ and the FTC before any final decisions are made. This is a requirement for any hospitals with greater than $100 million in assets acquiring a hospital with more than $10 million in assets (Buchbinder & Shanks, 2007). The DOJ and the FTC will make the final decision on these proposals. This ensures there will not be any type of monopoly within a certain geographic area.

There are two federal agencies that enforce antitrust violations: the **Federal Trade Commission** (FTC) and the **Department of Justice** (DOJ). The FTC, established in 1914 by the **Federal Trade Commission Act**, is one of the oldest federal agencies and is charged with the oversight of commercial acts and practices. Two major activities of the FTC are to maintain free and fair competition in the economy and to protect consumers from misleading practices.

The FTC may issue "cease and desist orders" to companies to ensure they stop their practices until a court decides what the company may do (Carroll & Buchholtz, 2015). The DOJ, headed by the U.S. Attorney General, was established in 1870 to handle U.S. legal issues, including the enforcement of federal laws. The DOJ and the FTC collaborate on antitrust law enforcement (FTC, 2016).

Informed Consent

The concept of **informed consent** is based on the patient's right to make an informed decision regarding medical treatment. It is a legal requirement in all 50 states. It is more than a patient signing an informed consent form—it is the communication between the provider and patient regarding a specific medical treatment. The provider is responsible for discussing the following information with the patient: the diagnosis, if it has been established; the nature of a proposed treatment or operation, including the risks and benefits, any alternatives, and the risks and benefits of the alternatives; and the risks and benefits of not agreeing to the procedure or treatment (AMA, 2016). If a patient did not provide informed consent for a procedure or treatment, it is considered a case of negligence. It is the duty of the physician to provide sufficient information to the patient to enable the patient to evaluate the proposed treatment before giving consent. If the patient does not understand the information, the consent is not considered an informed consent.

A medical emergency may eliminate the need for an informed consent. If a patient cannot clinically give consent to a lifesaving medical treatment, **statutory consent** may be considered, which presumes a reasonable person would give consent to the lifesaving procedure. Consent may be implied in nonemergency situations. If a patient volunteers for a procedure, implying consent, without an oral or written verification, the patient might be considered to have given an informed consent (Pozgar, 2016).

Informed consent is a basic patient right. It is important that the physician provides information that the patient clearly understands so the patient can evaluate the risks and benefits of the intervention.

▶ Patient Bill of Rights

The **Patient Self-Determination Act of 1990** requires hospitals, nursing homes, home health providers, hospices, and managed care organizations that provide services to Medicare- and Medicaid-eligible patients to supply information on patient rights to patients upon admission. It applies to almost every type of healthcare facility. The facility must provide adult patients with written information, under state law, about making healthcare decisions. Based on the concept of informed consent, in 1972 the Board of Trustees of the American Hospital Association developed a Patient Bill of Rights. The **Patient Bill of Rights** states that the patient has the right to all information from this provider regarding any testing, diagnoses, and treatments. This information must be provided to the patient in terms that the patient will be able to understand (Rosner, 2004). Eligible health organizations will have the Patient Bill of Rights displayed.

▶ Healthcare Fraud

The most common criminal violation in the healthcare industry is healthcare fraud, which typically involves illegal acts for financial gain. Fraud can be perpetrated by a variety of healthcare stakeholders: multistate organized-crime rings that improperly bill Medicare for $40 million dollars of home health care, a single physician who brings in an extra $20,000 per year by regularly "up-coding" office procedures (upgrading simple procedures to a more complicated procedure to increase billing), or healthcare systems that systematically defraud Medicare of hundreds of millions of dollars (Mahar, 2016). Increases in healthcare costs that have impacted public health insurance programs, such as Medicare and Medicaid, have emphasized the need to combat fraud and abuse of the healthcare system. Healthcare fraud costs the healthcare system and its stakeholders $80 billion annually. The FBI is responsible for investigating healthcare fraud. The Department of Justice and Human Services Medicare Fraud Strike Force is designed to combat fraud (OIG, 2016). The centerpiece for fraud recovery is the False Claims Act.

The **False Claims Act**, also known as the Lincoln law, enacted in 1863, was originally passed to protect the federal government against defense contractors during the Civil War. The False Claims Act has been amended several times throughout the years, and, in the 1990s, was amended with a focus on healthcare fraud, most notably Medicare and Medicaid fraud. The False Claims Act of 1995 imposes criminal penalties on anyone who tries to present fictitious claims for payment to the federal government. It is one of the most powerful governmental tools to combat health care fraud. This act also provides financial incentives for whistleblowers—allowing employees to blow the whistle about contractor fraud against the federal government. Private plaintiffs fulfill this role pursuant to

the *qui tam* provisions of the act. The Deficit Reduction Act of 2005 encouraged states to crack down on healthcare fraud by giving the states additional incentives under their own fraud law. The *qui tam* provisions allow whistle blowers to receive between 15% and 25% of proceeds in the case. As a result of the financial incentive program, the federal government has received billions in returned funds (Carroll & Buchholtz, 2015).

The Fraud Enforcement and Recovery Act of 2009 (FERA) and the Affordable Care Act (ACA) of 2010 further strengthened the False Claims Act. The FERA expanded potential liability for false claims by applying the FCA to a broader range of transactions, reducing the proof required to establish illegal activities, and expanding the pool of potential whistleblowers that may bring retaliation claims. The Affordable Care Act provided an additional $350 million over 10 years to help fund new initiatives to effectively fight fraud. It also called for more stringent Federal Sentencing Guidelines for healthcare fraud (Mahar, 2016).

Medicare Fraud Strike Force

Established in 2007, this task force uses both federal and local law enforcement agencies to combat healthcare fraud. As of September 2015, the task force had indicted nearly 2,000 people and recouped $1.8 billion. In September 2015, it caught 200 people who defrauded Medicare and Medicaid by more than $700 million. In 2016, the task force has recouped over $200 million from nine different fraud schemes (OIG, 2016).

Ethics in Patient Referral Act of 1989

The Stark laws (named after Representative Pete Stark who authored the legislation), also known as the **Physician Self-Referral Laws** or the **Ethics in Patient Referral Act of 1989**, prohibit physicians, including dentists and chiropractors, from referring Medicare and Medicaid patients to other providers for **designated health services** in which they have a financial interest. These laws directly prohibit many referrals that may increase a provider's or family members' financial interest. Designated health services include clinical laboratory services, outpatient prescription drug services, physical and occupational therapy, and imaging services such as magnetic resonance imaging (MRI), and the like. The statute became effective on January 1, 1995, but the regulations interpreting the statute were not released until January 4, 2001 (Gosfield, 2003). Additional Stark amendments expanded the types of services for which a physician cannot refer Medicare and Medicaid patients if the physician or a family member

Patients' Bill of Rights

As a patient in the hospital in New York State you have the right, consistent with law, to:

1) Understand and use these rights. If for any reason you do not understand or you need help, the hospital MUST provide assistance, including an interpreter.

2) Receive treatment without discrimination as to race, color, religion, sex, national origin, disability, sexual orientation or source of payment.

3) Receive considerate and respectful care in a clean and safe environment free of unnecessary restraints.

4) Receive emergency care if you need it.

5) Be informed of the name and position of the doctor who will be in charge of your care in the hospital.

6) Know the names, positions and functions of any hospital staff involved in your care and refuse their treatment, examination or observation.

7) A no smoking room.

8) Receive complete information about your diagnosis, treatment and prognosis.

9) Receive all the information that you need to give informed consent for any proposed procedure or treatment. This information shall include the possible risks and benefits of the procedure or treatment.

10) Receive all the information you need to give informed consent for an order not to resuscitate. You also have the right to designate an individual to give this consent for you if you are too ill to do so. If you would like additional information, please ask for a copy of the pamphlet "Do Not Resuscitate Orders-A Guide for Patients and Families."

11) Refuse treatment and be told what effect this may have on your health.

12) Refuse to take part in research. In deciding whether or not to participate, you have the right to a full explanation.

13) Privacy while in the hospital and confidentiality of all information and records regarding your care.

14) Participate in all decisions about your treatment and discharge from the hospital. The hospital must provide you with a written discharge plan and written description of how you can appeal your discharge.

15) Review your medical record without charge. Obtain a copy of your medical record for which the hospital can charge a reasonable fee. You cannot be denied a copy solely because you cannot afford to pay.

16) Receive an itemized bill and explanation of all charges.

17) Complain without fear of reprisals about the care and services you are receiving an to have the hospital respond to you and if you request it, a written response. If you are not satisfied with the hospital's response, you can complain to the New York State Health Department. The hospital must provide you with the Health Department telephone number.

18) Authorize those family members and other adults who will be given priority to visit consistent with your ability to receive visitors.

19) Make known your wishes in regard to anatomical gifts. You may document your wishes in your health care proxy or on a donor card, available from the hospital.

Public Health Law (PHL) 2803 (1) (g) Patients' Rights, 10NYCRR, 405.7.405.7 (a) (1), 405.7 (a) (2)
11003 Dev.9/97 Rev. 5/01

FIGURE 11-1 Patient Bill of Rights

has a financial interest in the service. These regulations protect consumers by ensuring they will receive objective referrals for health services.

Fraud in the healthcare industry is easy to commit for several reasons. The governmental system assumes providers are trustworthy, it is easy to obtain a government-issued provider number for Medicare and Medicaid, and perpetrators might think it is easy to escape notice when committing fraud. Also, the penalties historically were low. As a result of these factors, there were Medicare providers who would sell access to their program ID number. The ACA antifraud initiatives should help to reduce these fraudulent activities (Mahar, 2016).

▶ # Employment-Related Legislation

As part of healthcare law, it is important to be familiar with the impact on employees of employment-related healthcare legislation. Employment-related legislation is enacted to ensure protection of employers' and employees' rights in the workplace. The following section outlines major employment-related legislation that influences the healthcare industry.

Title VII of the Civil Rights Act of 1964

This landmark act prohibits discrimination based on race, sex, color, religion, and national origin. Discrimination means treating people differently. This legislation is the key legal piece to equal opportunity employment. Two components to this legislation, which will be discussed later, are disparate treatment and disparate impact. It applies to employers with 15 or more employees. This act is enforced by the U.S. Equal Employment Opportunity Commission (EEOC).

The **Civil Rights Act of 1964, Title VII**, created a concept of protected classes to protect these groups from employment discrimination in compensation and conditions or privileges of employment. The protected classes include sex, age, national origin, race, and religion. A current major issue within the purview of discrimination legislation is sexual harassment. According to the EEOC, **sexual harassment** is defined as unwelcome sexual conduct that has a negative impact on the employee. There are two major categories of sexual harassment: (1) quid pro quo sexual harassment, which occurs when sexual activities occur in return for an employment benefit; and (2) hostile work environment, which occurs when the behavior of coworkers is sexual in nature and creates an uncomfortable work atmosphere. The creation of a hostile work environment is the more common type of sexual harassment. Several court decisions indicate that repeated suggestive joke telling and lewd photos on display can be legally considered to be a hostile work environment. In the healthcare industry, nurses sometimes experience sexual harassment from colleagues, physicians, and patients. There might also be discrimination against LGBTQ individuals.

Examples of LGBTQ-Related Sex Discrimination Claims

Some examples of LGBTQ-related claims that the EEOC views as unlawful sex discrimination include:

- Failing to hire an applicant because she is a transgender woman.
- Firing an employee because he is planning or has made a gender transition.
- Denying an employee equal access to a common restroom corresponding to the employee's gender identity.
- Harassing an employee because of a gender transition, such as by intentionally and persistently failing to use the name and gender pronoun that correspond to the gender identity with which the employee identifies, and which the employee has communicated to management and employees.
- Denying an employee a promotion because he is gay or straight.
- Discriminating in terms, conditions, or privileges of employment, such as providing a lower salary to an employee because of sexual orientation, or denying spousal health insurance benefits to a female employee because her legal spouse is a woman, while providing spousal health insurance to a male employee whose legal spouse is a woman.
- Harassing an employee because of his or her sexual orientation, for example, by derogatory terms, sexually oriented comments, or disparaging remarks for associating with a person of the same or opposite sex.
- Discriminating against or harassing an employee because of his or her sexual orientation or gender identity, in combination with another unlawful reason, for example, on the basis of transgender status and race, or sexual orientation and disability (What you should know about the EEOC, 2016).

Civil Rights Act of 1991

Title VII only allowed damages for back pay. This act enables individuals to receive both **punitive damages**, which are damages that punish the defendant, and **compensatory damages** for financial or psychological harm. This act applies to employers with 15 or more employees. The upper limit to damages is based on the size of the company: $50,000 for employers with 15 to 100 employees; $100,000 for companies with 101 to 200 employees; $200,000 for employers with 201 to 500 employers; and $300,000 for employers with more than 500 employees. This act is enforced by the EEOC.

The 1991 law extended the possibility of individuals collecting damages related to sex, religious, or disability-related discrimination. Some organizations had developed a policy of adjusting scores on employment tests so a certain percentage of a protected class would be hired. This amendment to Title VII specifically prohibits quotas, which are diversity goals to increase the number of protected class members in a work force (Gomez-Mejia, Balkin & Cardy, 2012).

Age Discrimination in Employment Act (ADEA) of 1967

This act protects employees and job applicants 40 years old and older from discrimination as it applies to hiring, firing, promotion, layoffs, training, assignments, and benefits. Older employees file lawsuits for age discrimination in job termination. It applies to employers with 20 or more employees and is enforced by the EEOC.

During difficult economic times, older employees might have a greater tendency to file complaints with the EEOC because of their termination. Many older workers tend to have higher salaries and businesses may lay them off illegally. In November 2010, Hawaii Professional Homecare Services was sued by the EEOC because the owner fired a 54-year-old employee, referring to her as a "bag of old bones" and claiming that because she sounded old over the phone, the owner did not want her representing the company (U.S. EEOC, 2010).

Older Workers Benefit Protection Act of 1990

This act amended the ADEA. Its goal is to ensure that older workers' employee benefits are protected and that organizations provide the same benefits to both younger and older workers. The act also gives employees time to decide if they would accept early retirement options and allows employees to change their mind if they have signed a waiver of their right to sue. The act is enforced by the EEOC.

Rehabilitation Act of 1973

This law applies to organizations that receive financial assistance from federal organizations, including the U.S. Department of Health and Human Services, and forbids discriminating against individuals with disabilities in terms of employee benefits and job opportunities. These organizations and employers include many hospitals, nursing homes, mental health centers, and human services programs. Employers with 50 or more employees and federal contracts of $50,000 or more must submit written affirmative action plans. The PPACA amends this act by requiring all healthcare manufacturers to redesign medical equipment so healthcare providers can accommodate individuals with disabilities. Healthcare provider locations must also be accessible to those with disabilities. This act is enforced by the Office of Federal Contract Compliance Programs (OFCCP).

Equal Pay Act of 1963

This act, which amended the Fair Labor Standards Act and is enforced by the U.S. Department of Labor, mandates that all employers award pay fairly to men and women if it is determined their jobs have equal responsibilities and require the same skills. It can be difficult to assess whether two employees are performing exactly the same job. One employee may have additional duties, which would affect pay. The current trend in business is pay for performance, so some employees may earn more if they perform better. However, research consistently states that women earn less than men. An individual who alleges pay discrimination may file a lawsuit without informing the EEOC.

Executive Orders 11246 (1965), 11375 (1967), and 11478 (1969)

The President of the United States, for federal agency directions, writes executive orders, some of which focus on discrimination issues, and require affirmative action based on these factors. These orders affect both federal contractors and employers with 50 or more employees.

An **affirmative action plan** is a strategy that encourages employers to increase the diversity of their workforce by hiring individuals based on race, sex, and age. These potential employees must be qualified for the job. Although an affirmative action plan encourages hiring protected-class candidates, an employer cannot set quotas for this process. They can develop strategies to encourage applications from diverse candidates.

An employer who develops an affirmative action plan must perform an analysis of the demographics of the current workforce compared to the eligible pool of qualified applicants. The employer must also calculate the percentage of those protected classes in the qualified applicants. The percentages are compared to determine if there was an underrepresentation of diverse employees in the organization. If it is determined the current workforce is not diverse, then an employer develops a timetable to hire diverse employees that also includes a recruitment plan.

Pregnancy Discrimination Act of 1978

The Pregnancy Discrimination Act of 1978 was an amendment to Title VII of the Civil Rights Act of 1964. This act protects female employees who are discriminated against based on pregnancy-related conditions, which constitutes illegal sex discrimination. A pregnant woman must be treated like anyone with a medical condition. For example, an organization must allow sick leave for pregnant women with morning sickness if the organization also allows sick leave for other nausea-causing illnesses (Gomez-Mejia, Balking, & Cardy, 2012). This act applies to employers with at least 15 employees and is enforced by EEOC.

Americans with Disabilities Act of 1990 (ADA)

The ADA focuses on individuals in the workplace who are considered disabled. There are three sections: Section I contains employment limitations, while Section II and Section III target local government organizations, hotels, restaurants, and grocery stores. This act applies to employers who have 15 employees or more and is enforced by the EEOC. According to the law, a disabled person is someone who has a physical or mental impairment that limits the ability to hear, see, speak, or walk. The act was passed to ensure that those individuals who have a disability but can perform primary job functions are not discriminated against. According to the act, disabilities included learning, mental, epilepsy, cancer, arthritis, mental retardation, AIDS, asthma, and traumatic brain injury. A nursing home cannot refuse to admit a person with AIDS who requires a nursing service if the facility has that type of service available (DOL, 2016). Individuals with alcohol and other drug abuse are not covered under the ADA. Individuals who are morbidly obese can be considered disabled if the obesity was related to a physical cause.

Title I of the ADA states that employment discrimination is prohibited against individuals with disabilities who can perform essential functions of a job with or without reasonable accommodation. *Essential functions* are job duties that must be performed to be a satisfactory employee. *Reasonable accommodation* is an employer's reasonable action to accommodate a disabled individual, such as providing special computer equipment or furniture to accommodate a physical limitation. The reasonable accommodation should not cause undue financial hardship to the employer.

Individuals with disabilities have mental or physical limitations in areas such as walking, speaking, breathing, sitting, seeing, and hearing. Individuals with **intellectual disabilities** have an IQ less than 70–75 and problems with social skills, and the disability must have begun before the person turned 18 years of age. Intellectual disabilities must significantly limit major life activities such as walking, seeing, hearing, thinking, speaking, learning, concentrating, and working. The ADA amendments of 2008 expanded living activities to include bodily functions such as bladder, circulatory, neurological, and digestive functions.

Role of Equal Employment Opportunity Commission (EEOC)

The EEOC, created by Title VII of the Civil Rights Act of 1964, is responsible for processing complaints, issuing regulations, and collecting information from employers.

Processing Complaints

An individual who thinks he or she is being discriminated against can file a complaint with the EEOC, which notifies the employer. The employer is responsible for safeguarding any written information regarding the complaint. The EEOC then investigates the complaint to determine if the employer did violate any laws. If a violation is found, the EEOC uses conciliation or negotiation to attempt to resolve the issue without going to court. If conciliation is not successful, litigation or going to trial is the next step. Most employers prefer to avoid litigation because it is costly and might damage their reputation. Most cases are resolved by conciliation.

Issuing Regulations

The EEOC is responsible for developing regulations for any EEOC law and its amendments. It has written regulations for the ADA, the ADEA, and the Equal Pay Act. It also issues guidelines on other issues, such as sexual harassment and affirmative action.

Information and Education

The EEOC acquires information from employers regarding their practices. Employers with 100 or more employees must file an EEO-1 report that reflects the number of women and minorities who hold positions. This report is used to assess any potential discrimination trends. The EEOC also provides employers with written and electronic media education on discrimination. It sends this information to human resources departments, which disseminate the information with training classes.

These pieces of legislation focus on equal employment opportunity in the workplace. These laws ensure that protected classes, as outlined in the Civil Rights Act of 1964, are provided opportunities for equal employment without bias or discrimination. In addition to this landmark legislation, the ADEA, the Older Workers Benefit Protection Act, and the ADA establish standards for treating individuals who are older than 40 years and those individuals who have a disability are also treated fairly in their terms of employment. Both the ADEA and the ADA were further strengthened by passage of the Lilly Ledbetter Fair Pay Act regarding pay discrimination. In addition, the Pregnancy Discrimination Act and the Equal Pay Act target discrimination against women. Despite the amount of antidiscrimination legislation, discrimination continues to exist in the work environment.

Occupational Safety and Health Act of 1970

This act is also important to the healthcare industry because of the high incidence of employee injury. In healthcare jobs, there is a higher risk of exposure to workplace hazards such as airborne and blood-borne infectious diseases, physical injuries from lifting patients, and needle stick injuries. This law was passed to ensure that employers have a **general duty** to provide a safe and healthy work environment for their employees, which is very important for the healthcare industry because of potential exposure to bacteria, viruses, and contaminated fluids.

Employers are also required to inform employees of potential hazardous conditions and Occupational Safety and Health Administration (OSHA) standards. Posters and other materials are displayed for employees' education. OSHA is responsible for enforcing these provisions. The National Institute for Occupational Safety and Health (NIOSH) was also established as part of this act to provide research to support the standards. OSHA enforces the **Hazard Communication Standard** that requires companies to label hazardous materials. Information is contained on **Material Safety Data Sheets (MSDSs)**, which are provided to employees via the Internet or on site. OSHA has also issued a standard for exposure to human immunodeficiency virus (HIV), hepatitis B virus (HBV), and other blood-borne pathogens. This standard is crucial to the healthcare industry because of increased risk of exposure by nurses and laboratory workers.

OSHA has also developed standards for **personal protective equipment (PPE)**, required when employees might be exposed to hazardous materials or working conditions. Companies must also maintain records of employee accidents. OSHA provides workers with the rights to receive training, keep a copy of their medical records, and request OSHA inspections of their workplace (Occupational Safety & Health Administration, U.S. Department of Labor, 2016a).

OSHA has also developed standards for **ergonomics**, which is the study of working conditions that affect the physical condition of employees. Studies indicate that repetitive motion can create employee injuries. A common disorder is **carpal tunnel syndrome**, a wrist injury that often occurs from repetitive hand motions in jobs such as grocery cashiers and computer users. Employers can provide ergonomic-friendly equipment and guidelines for ergonomic actions to eliminate these types of injuries. Ergonomic equipment and actions are important to the healthcare industry because many workers often lift patients to and from beds, operating tables, and wheelchairs (Occupational Safety & Health Administration, U.S. Department of Labor, 2016b).

Immigration Reform and Control Act (1988)

The **Immigration Reform and Control Act of 1988** (IRCA) requires employers with one or more employees to verify that all job applicants are U.S. citizens or authorized to work in the United States. Most employees are only aware of this legislation because of the I-9 form all new employees must complete. There are three categories, A, B, and C, on the form. Category A establishes identity and eligibility to work, such as a passport, a Permanent Resident Card, or a Permanent Alien Registration Receipt Card. Category B establishes the individual's identity. Acceptable proof of identity includes a driver's license and different types of identification cards with photographs. Category C focuses on eligibility of an employee to work. Documentation includes a Social Security card or a birth certificate. If an employee cannot provide this information, he or she must provide documentation in both Category B and Category C. This prohibits any company from hiring illegal aliens and penalizes employers who hire illegal aliens. However, immigrants with special skill sets or those who can satisfy a labor shortage in the United States, such as nurses, will be permitted to work in the United States. This act is enforced by the U.S. Department of Labor.

▶ Other Employment-Related Legislation

Consumer Credit Protection Act (Title III) of 1968

This act prohibits employers from terminating an employee if the individual's earnings are subject to garnishment due to debt issues. This act also limits the weekly garnishment amount from employees' pay and is enforced by the Federal Deposit Insurance Corporation (FDIC).

Drug Free Workplace Act of 1988

This act requires any employers that receive federal grants or have a federal contract of $25,000 or greater to certify that they operate a drug-free workplace. They must provide education to their employees about drug abuse. Many employers now offer drug testing. The act is enforced by the U.S. Department of Labor.

Worker Adjustment and Retraining Notification Act of 1989

Employers with 100 employees or more must give their employees 60 days' notice of layoffs and business closings. This act is enforced by the U.S. Department of Labor.

Employee Retirement Income Security Act of 1974 (ERISA)

ERISA regulates pension and benefit plans for employees, including medical and disability benefits. It protects employees because it forbids employers from firing an employee to prevent the employee from receiving health benefits. Employees may change the benefits provided under their plans, but employers cannot force an employee to leave so that the employer does not have to pay the employee's medical coverage.

Consolidated Omnibus Budget Reconciliation Act of 1986 (COBRA)

COBRA, an amendment to ERISA, was passed to protect employees who lost or changed employers so they could keep their health insurance if they paid 102% of the full premium (Anderson, Rice, & Kominski 2007). The act was passed because, at the time, people were afraid to change jobs, resulting in the concept of **job lock** (Emanuel, 2008). With the establishment of the Healthcare Insurance Marketplace, individuals may find more affordable health insurance plan options rather than using the COBRA option.

Health Insurance Portability and Accountability Act of 1996 (HIPAA)

HIPAA was passed to promote patient information and confidentiality in a secure environment. The *Standards for Privacy of Individually Identifiable Health Information* (the **Privacy Rule**) established the first set of national standards for the protection of certain health information. The major goal of the Privacy Rule is to ensure that individuals' health information is properly protected while allowing the flow of health information needed to provide and promote high-quality health care for patients and to protect the public's health and well-being. There are two exceptions to the Privacy Rule: if the patient requests the disclosure of their information or there is an investigation. This act is enforced by the Department of Health and Human Services' Office for Civil Rights and the U.S. Department of Justice.

It is vitally important that patient information is protected in accordance with HIPAA. With the increased use of technology in healthcare, patient information may be more at risk.

Releasing patient information is more complex because of the introduction of information technology to the healthcare industry. For example, patient information may be faxed, as long as only necessary information is transmitted and safeguards are implemented. Physicians may also communicate via email as long as safeguards are implemented.

Health Information Technology for Economic and Clinical Health Act of 2009

Effective September 23, 2009, this act amends HIPAA by requiring stricter notification protocols for breach of any patient information. The notification must occur within 60 days of the breach, and the media must also be informed of the breach. These new rules apply to any associates of the health organizations. In addition to the Privacy Rule, the **Security Rule** was implemented; it applies to e-PHI or electronic patient information. The Security Rule was developed because of the increased use of electronic patient records. These new rules also apply to any associates of the health plans. It also increased HIPAA's civil and criminal penalties for violating consumers' privacy regarding health information. Civil penalties were increased to $1.5 million per calendar year, which was a huge increase in the original penalty cap of $25,000. The criminal penalties of up to $50,000–$250,000 and 10 years' incarceration remained the same.

Releasing patient information is more complex because of the introduction of information technology to the healthcare industry. For example, patient information may be faxed as long as only necessary information is transmitted and safeguards are implemented. Physicians may also communicate via email as long as safeguards are implemented.

Employee wellness programs, which can include promotion of exercise, health risk appraisals, disease management, and healthcare coaching, have become a popular employee benefit. However, there have been legal issues surrounding the implementation of wellness programs in the workplace because they discriminate based on the health conditions of employees. HIPAA states that wellness programs that are part of a group health plan must be designed to promote health and cannot be a subterfuge that discriminates against an employee based on a health condition. Many wellness programs also offer incentives for wellness program performance. The incentive program must be designed so that all employees may participate in the incentive program regardless of health conditions, which means the incentive–rewards program must be flexible to adapt to employees who want to participate but may be restricted based on a health condition (DOL, 2016).

Family and Medical Leave Act of 1993 (FMLA)

The FMLA requires employers with 50 or more employees within a 75-mile radius who work more than 25 hours per week and who have been employed more than 1 year to provide up to 12 weeks of unpaid leave, during any 12-month period, to provide care for a family member or the employee himself or herself. This benefit can also include post childbirth or adoption. Employers must provide healthcare benefits, although they are not required to provide wages during the leave. Individuals who are among the organization's highest paid 10% of all employees are not covered by the act. The employer is also supposed to provide the same job or a comparable position upon the employee's return. The U.S. Department of Labor announced a final rule in 2015 to amend the term "spouse" to include legal-same-sex-marriage spouses (DOL, 2016).

Mental Health Parity Act of 1996

This act requires the equality or parity of lifetime and annual limits of health insurance reimbursements for mental health care. Unfortunately, the act did not require employers to offer mental health coverage, it did not impose limits on deductibles or coinsurance payments, and it did not cover substance abuse. This federal legislation spurred several states to implement their own parity legislation (Anderson, Rice, & Kominski, 2007). The Wellstone Act or the **Mental Health Parity and Addiction Equity Act of 2008** amends the Mental Health Parity Act of 1996 to include substance abuse treatment plans as part of group health plans.

Genetic Information Nondiscrimination Act of 2008

This act prohibits U.S. insurance companies and employers from discriminating based on information derived from genetic tests. Genetic information includes information about an individual's genetic tests and the genetic tests of an individual's family members, as well as information about the manifestation of a disease or disorder in an individual's family members (i.e., family medical history). Family medical history is included in the definition of genetic information because it is often used to determine whether someone has an increased risk of getting a disease, disorder, or condition in the future. Genetic information also includes an individual's request for, or receipt of, genetic services, or the participation in clinical research that includes genetic services by the individual or a family member of the individual, and the genetic information of a fetus carried by an individual or by a pregnant woman who is a family member of the individual and the genetic information of any embryo legally held by the individual or family member using an assisted reproductive method. Specifically, it forbids insurance companies from discriminating through reduced coverage or price increases. It also prohibits employers from making adverse employment decisions based on a person's genetic factors (EEOC, 2016a)

Lilly Ledbetter Fair Pay Act of 2009 (FPA)

This act, an amendment to Title VII of the Civil Rights Act of 1964, also applies to claims under the Age Discrimination Act of 1967 and the ADA, provides protection against unlawful employment practices related to compensation discrimination. This act was named after Lilly Ledbetter, an employee of Goodyear Tire and Rubber Company who found out near her retirement that her male colleagues were paid more than she was and then brought suit. The U.S. Supreme Court ruled that she should have filed a suit within 180 days of the date that Goodyear paid her less than her peers. This act allows the statute of limitations to restart every 180 days from the time the worker receives a paycheck (EEOC, 2016b).

To avoid litigation, Sedhom (2009) suggests the implementation of a program coordinated by senior management and human resources to help protect employers from being accused of unfair employment practices. The following summarizes the steps of the program:

1. Establish compensation criteria.
2. Develop pay audits and document these audits for several years.
3. Document retention processes related to pay.
4. Train managers on providing objective performance evaluations.
5. Develop and implement a rigorous statistical analysis of pay distributions.

Patient Protection and Affordable Care Act or Affordable Care Act of 2010 (ACA)

This act has had a major impact on the U.S. healthcare system; therefore, a separate chapter has been devoted to the act and its mandates. A brief summary of the ACA is included in this chapter because it is considered landmark legislation and should be mentioned.

The **Patient Protection and Affordable Care Act (PPACA)** or, as it is commonly called, the **Affordable Care Act (ACA)**, and its amendment, the **Healthcare and Education Affordability Reconciliation Act of 2010**, was signed into law on March 23, 2010, by President Barack Obama. The goal of the act is to improve the accessibility and quality of the U.S. healthcare system. There are nearly 50 healthcare reform initiatives that are being implemented during 2010–2017 and beyond. The passage of this complex landmark legislation has been very controversial and continues to be contentious today.

There were national public protests and a huge division among the political parties regarding the components of the legislation. People, in general, agreed that the healthcare system needed some type of reform, but it was difficult to develop common recommendations that had majority support. Criticism, in part, focused on the increased role of government in implementing and monitoring the healthcare system. Proponents of healthcare reform reminded people that Medicare is a federal government entitlement program because when individuals reach 65 years of age, they can receive their health insurance from this program. Millions of individuals are enrolled in Medicare. Medicaid is a state-established public welfare program that provides health care benefits to millions of income-eligible individuals, including children.

On October 1, 2013, the federal government was shut down because some elected officials did not want the Affordable Care Act to proceed further. These politicians refused to approve a bill that would continue financial operations of the U.S. government. They attempted to include provisions defunding portions of the Affordable Care Act as part of the federal government funding bill. Governmental functions resumed on October 17, 2013, after the Continuing Appropriations Act of 2014 was enacted by Congress. Poll results indicated that public approval ratings of Congress declined significantly during the shutdown (Newport, 2013).

One ACA provision that has been generally supported is raising to age 26 the cut-off for health insurance coverage of dependents, even if the child is not living with his or her parents, is not declared a dependent on the parents' tax return, or is no longer a student. This would not apply to individuals who have employer-based coverage (DOL, 2013). Another positive mandate, also implemented in July 2010, was the establishment of a web portal, www.healthcare.gov, to increase consumers' awareness about their eligibility for specific healthcare insurance.

In addition to the two reforms discussed in the previous paragraphs, the following are selected major reforms that were also implemented in 2010:

- Elimination of lifetime and annual caps on healthcare reimbursement;
- Granting assistance for the uninsured with preexisting conditions; and
- Creation of a temporary reinsurance program for early retirees.

In the past, health insurance companies would establish an annual or lifetime cap on reimbursement for the use of healthcare insurance. These would be eliminated. Unlike the past, health insurance companies would also be prohibited from dropping individuals and children with certain conditions or not providing insurance to those individuals with preexisting conditions. The government would provide assistance to securing health insurance for these high-risk individuals.

The following are selected major reforms that have been implemented:

- Insurance companies are prohibited from setting insurance rates based on health status, medical condition, genetic information, or other related factors.

- A Health Insurance Marketplace Exchange, which is a marketplace where consumers can obtain information and buy health insurance, has been established. If the state opts not to establish a marketplace, individuals can use the federal marketplace website to obtain insurance.
- Most individuals must maintain minimum essential healthcare coverage or pay a fine.

In the past, there were issues with health insurance companies denying coverage based on health status or other conditions. Premiums now will be based on family type, geography, tobacco use, and age. In addition, states can establish Health Insurance Marketplace Exchanges to assist consumers with obtaining health insurance. If the state chooses not to establish a state-run operation, residents of the state will use the federal government website. Information is provided to consumers in a standardized format so they can compare the plans. Plans and cost will vary based on level of coverage. There are exceptions based on certain circumstances. By 2014, most consumers were responsible for obtaining health insurance or paying a penalty, which will increase each year they do not obtain health insurance coverage (Niles, 2010). According to an analysis by the Kaiser Family Foundation, as of the end of the third open enrollment under the ACA (2016), 12.7 million people had signed up for coverage in the health insurance marketplaces, up from 11.7 million in 2015 and 8.0 million in 2014. Recent data indicates that there will be attrition due to people paying their premiums, having their coverage terminated due to inconsistencies on their applications, or receiving health insurance through an employer. Actual enrollment may be closer to 10 million, which meets the HHS target (Levitt, Claxton, Demico, & Cos, 2016).

▶ Conclusion

To be an effective healthcare manager, it is important to understand basic legal principles that influence the work environment, including the legal relationship between the organization and the consumer—the healthcare provider and the patient and the employer and the employee. As both a healthcare manager and healthcare consumer, it is imperative that you are familiar with the different federal and state laws that impact the healthcare organization. It is also important that you understand the differences between civil and criminal law and the penalties that may be imposed for breaking those laws. Federal and state laws have been enacted and policies have been implemented to protect both the healthcare provider and the healthcare consumer. New laws have been passed and older laws have been amended to reflect needed changes regarding health care, to continue to protect participants from both a patient and an employee or employer perspective.

Wrap-Up

Vocabulary

Affirmative action plan
Age Discrimination in Employment Act of 1967
Americans with Disabilities Act of 1990
Antitrust law
Battery
Benefits Improvement and Protection Act of 2000 (BIPA)
Boycotts
Carpal tunnel syndrome
Children's Health Insurance Program (CHIP)
Civil law
Civil Rights Act of 1964, Title VII
Civil Rights Act of 1991
Clayton Act of 1914
Common law

Compensatory damages
Consolidated Omnibus Budget Reconciliation Act of 1986 (COBRA)
Consumer Credit Protection Act (Title III) of 1968
Contractual relationship to care for a designated population
Contractual right to admission
Criminal law
Defensive medicine
Department of Justice
Designated health services
Drug Free Workplace Act of 1988
Emergency Medical Treatment and Active Labor Act (EMTALA)
Employee Retirement Income Security Act of 1974 (ERISA)

Employee wellness programs
Equal Pay Act of 1963
Ergonomics
Ethics in Patient Referral Act of 1989
Executive Orders 11246 (1965), 11375 (1967), and 11478 (1969)
Express contract
False Claims Act
Family Medical Leave Act of 1993
Federal Trade Commission
Federal Trade Commission Act
General duty
Genetic Information Nondiscrimination Act of 2008
Hart-Scott-Rodino Antitrust Improvement Act of 1976
Hazard Communication Standard

Healthcare and Education
  Affordability Reconciliation Act
  of 2010
Health Information Technology for
  Economic and Clinical Health
  Act of 2009
Health Insurance Portability and
  Accountability Act of 1996
  (HIPAA)
Hill-Burton Act
HIPAA National Standards
Immigration Reform and Control
  Act of 1988
Implied contract
Informed consent
Intellectual disabilities
Intentional torts
Job lock
Law
Lilly Ledbetter Fair Pay Act of 2009
Material Safety Data Sheets (MSDSs)

Market division
Medical malpractice
Mental Health Parity Act of 1996
Mental Health Parity and
  Addiction Equity Act of 2008
Monopolies
Negligence
Noneconomic damages
Occupational Safety and Health
  Act of 1970
Older Workers Benefit Protection
  Act of 1990
Patient abandonment
Patient Bill of Rights
Patient Protection and Affordability
  Care Act or Affordable Care Act
  of 2010
Patient Self-Determination Act of
  1990
Personal protective equipment (PPE)
Physician Self-Referral Laws

Pregnancy Discrimination Act of
  1978
Price fixing
Price information exchange
Privacy rule
Punitive damages
Qui tam
Rehabilitation Act of 1973
Rules and regulations
Security Rule
Sexual harassment
Sherman Act of 1890
Standard of care
Statutes
Statutory consent
Tort
Tort reform
Tying
Worker Adjustment and
  Retraining Notification Act
  of 1989

References

American Heritage Dictionary. (2000). *Medical malpractice.* Boston: Houghton Mifflin.

American Medical Association (AMA). (2016). Ending the patient-physician relationship. Retrieved from http://www.ama-assn.org//ama/pub/physician-resources/legal-topics/patient-physician-relationship-topics/ending-patient-physician-relationship.page#

Anderson, R., Rice, T., & Kominksi, G. (2007). *Changing the U.S. health care system.* San Francisco, CA: Jossey-Bass.

Bal, B. (2009). An introduction to medical malpractice in the United States. *Clinical Orthopedics and Related Research,* 467(2), 339–347.

BIPA. (2016). Retrieved from https://www.ruralcenter.org/tasc/resources/medicare-medicaid-and-schip-benefits-improvement-and-protection-act-2000-bipa

Buchbinder, S., & Shanks, N. (2007). *Introduction to health care management.* Sudbury, MA: Jones and Bartlett.

Budnick, N. (2013). John Kitzhaber recommends reform for Oregon medical malpractice laws. Retrieved from http://www.oregonlive.com/health/index.ssf/2012/07/john_kitzhaber_rolls_out_his_r.html

Carroll, A., & Buchholtz, A. (2015). *Business society: Ethics and stakeholder management* (9th ed.). Mason, OH: Thomson/Southwestern.

Centers for Medicare and Medicaid Services (CMS). (2016). Emergency Medical Treatment & Labor Act (EMTALA). Retrieved from http://www.cms.hhs.gov/EMTALA

Clayton Act, 15 U.S.C. §§ 12–27. (1914). Retrieved from http://www.law.cornell.edu/uscode/text/15/12

Congressional Budget Office. (2001). H.R. 5661, Medicare, Medicaid, and SCHIP Benefits Improvement and Protection Act of 2000 (Incorporated in H.R. 4577, the Consolidated Appropriations Act): Cost estimate. Retrieved from http://www.cbo.gov/publication/13285

DefensiveMedicine. (2016). What is defensive medicine? Retrieved from http://defensivemedicine.org

Danzon, P. (1995). *Medical malpractice: Theory, evidence, and public policy.* Cambridge, MA: Harvard University Press.

Degnan, J.M., & Scoggin, S.A. (2007, July). Medical defense and health law. *IADC Committee Newsletter, 9.*

Draschler, D. (2010). Notes on: Year one of the Lilly Ledbetter Fair Pay Act. *Labor Law Journal,* 102–106.

EEOC. (2016a). Retrieved from http://www.eeoc.gov/laws/types/genetic.cfm

EEOC. (2016b). Retrieved from http://www.eeoc.gov/eeoc/publications/brochure-equal_pay_and_ledbetter_act.cfm

Emanuel, E. (2008). *Health care guaranteed.* New York, NY: Public Affairs.

Federal Trade Commission (FTC). (2016). About the FTC. Retrieved from http://www.ftc.gov/ftc/about.shtm

Financing. (2016). Retrieved from https://www.medicaid.gov/chip/financing/financing.html

Gomez-Mejia, L., Balkin, D., & Cardy, R. (2012). *Managing human resources.* Upper Saddle River, NJ: Pearson: 100–125.

Gosfield, A.G. (2003). The stark truth about the STARK law: Part I. *Family Practice Management,* 10(10), 27–33. Retrieved from http://www.aafp.org/fpm/2003/1100/p27.html

Hickman, J., Gilligan, M., & Patton, G. (2008). FMLA and benefit obligations: New rights under an old mandate. *Benefits Law Journal,* 21(3), 5–16.

Kaiser Family Foundation. (2016). Number of children ever enrolled in the Children's Health Insurance Program (CHIP). Retrieved from http://kff.org/other/state-indicator/annual-chip-enrollment

Kesselheim, A., & Studdert, D. (2008). Whistleblower-initiated enforcement actions against health care fraud and abuse in the United States, 1996–2005. *Annals of Internal Medicine,* 149(5), 342–349.

LaMance, K. (2012). State limits on medical malpractice awards. Retrieved from http://www.legalmatch.com/law-library/article/state-limits-on-medical-malpractice-awards

Laws. (2013). Express and implied contracts from a physician. (2013). Retrieved from http://malpractice.laws.com /professional-patient-relationship/express-implied-contracts -from-a-physician

Levitt, L, Claxton, L., Damico, G., & Cox, C. (2016). Assessing ACA marketplace enrollment. Retrieved from http://kff .org/private-insurance/issue-brief/assessing-aca-market place-enrollment/?utm_campaign=KFF-2016-March-Assessing -ACA-Enrollment&utm_source=hs_email&utm_medium =email&utm_content=26937070&_hsenc=p2ANqtz-96gs GlUVGkTGyZoOE7KdOa9wSOhSwJ1YEvYskNAw5_mm —UJo393VFNIRbnIYzmOT7B4hZZ8LFklcecv8d-yz5yx v5kQ&_hsmi=26937070

Mahar, M., (2016). Taking on the "epidemic" of health care fraud. Retrieved from http://www.theihcc.com/en/communities /policy_legislation/taking-on-the-epidemic-of-health-care -fraud_gs3lc2x7.html

McCann, E. (2014). Deaths by medical mistakes hit records. Retrieved from http://www.healthcareitnews.com/news/deaths -by-medical-mistakes-hit-records

Memmott, S., & Makwana, K. (2007). Beware the whistleblower within—Recent False Claims Act settlements remind industry that almost anyone can be a whistleblower. *Journal of Health Care Compliance*, 9, 47–65.

Miller, R. (2006). *Problems in health care law* (9th ed.). Sudbury, MA: Jones and Bartlett.

Moran, A. (2008). Wellness programs: What's permitted? *Employer Relations Law Journal, 342*(2), 111–116.

Moseley, G. (2015). *Managing legal compliance in the health care industry*. Sudbury, MA: JB Learning.

National Human Genome Research Institute. (2016). Retrieved November 10, 2009 from http://www.genome.gov/About/.

Newport, F. (2013). Congress' job approval falls to 11% amid gov't shutdown: Americans' approval of their own representative averages 44%. Retrieved from http://www.gallup.com/poll/165281 /congress-job-approval-falls-amid-gov-shutdown.aspx

Niles, N. (2010). *Basics of the U.S. health care system*. Sudbury, MA: Jones and Bartlett: 247–259.

Noe, R., Hollenbeck, J., Gerhart, B., & Wright, P. (2011). *Fundamentals of human resource management* (4th ed.). Boston, MA: McGraw Hill-Irwin.

Occupational Safety & Health Administration, U.S. Department of Labor. (2016a). Ergonomics. Retrieved from http://www.osha .gov/SLTC/ergonomics

Occupational Safety & Health Administration, U.S. Department of Labor. (2016b). Workers. Retrieved from http://www.osha .gov/workers.html

Office of Technology Assessment. (1993). *Impact of legal reforms on medical malpractice cost, (OTA-BP-H-19)*. Washington, DC: US Government Printing Office.

OIG, (2016). Retrieved from http://oig.hhs.gov/fraud/strike-force/

Pho, K. (2012). Patient centered medical malpractice reform in New Hampshire. Retrieved from http://www.kevinmd.com /blog/2012/04/patient-centered-medical-malpractice -reform-hampshire.html

Ringholz, J. (2005). An outline of the basic requirements of EMTALA, as it relates to compliance. *Journal of Health Care Compliance*, 35–36.

Rosenbach, M., & Stone, A. (1990). Malpractice insurance costs and physician practice—1981–1986. *Health Affairs, 9*, 176–185.

Rosner, F. (2004). Informing the patient about a fatal disease: From paternalism to autonomy—the Jewish view. *Cancer Investigation, 22*(6), 949–953.

Sekhar, M. & Vyas, N. (2013). Defensive medicine: A bane to healthcare. *Ann Med Health Sci Res.* 2013 Apr–Jun 3(2): 295–296.

Sedhom, S. (2009). Reacting to the Lilly Ledbetter Fair Pay Act: What every employer needs to know. *Employee Relations Law Journal, 35*(3), 3–8.

Shi, L., & Singh, D. (2008). *Essentials of the U.S. health care delivery system*. Sudbury, MA: Jones and Bartlett.

Sultz, H., & Young, K. (2006). *Health care USA: Understanding its organization and delivery* (5th ed.). Sudbury, MA: Jones and Bartlett.

USLegal. (2016). Noneconomic damages law and legal definition. Retrieved from http://definitions.uslegal.com/n /non-economic-damages

U.S. Department of Health & Human Services. (2016a). Health information privacy. Retrieved from http://www.hhs.gov/ocr /privacy/hipaa/administrative

U.S. Department of Health & Human Services. (2016b). Medical treatment in Hill Burton funded healthcare facilities. Retrieved from http://www.hhs.gov/ocr/civilrights/understanding/Medical %20Treatment%20at%20Hill%20Burton%20Funded%20 Medical%20Facilities/

U.S. Department of Labor. (2016). Young adults and the Affordable Care Act: Protecting young adults and eliminating burdens on families and businesses. Retrieved from http://www .dol.gov/ebsa/newsroom/fsdependentcoverage.html

U.S. Department of Labor (DOL). (2016). Nondiscrimination and wellness programs in health coverage in the group market: Rules and regulations. Retrieved from http://www.dol.gov /ebsa/Regs/fedreg/final/2006009557.htm

U.S. Equal Employment Opportunity Commission (EEOC). (2010). EEOC sues Hawaii healthcare professionals for age discrimination. Retrieved from http://www.eeoc.gov/eeoc /newsroom/release/9-28-10.cfm

What you should know about the EEOC and the LGBTQ worker. (2016). Retrieved from https://www.eeoc.gov/eeoc/newsroom /wysk/enforcement_protections_lgbtq_workers.cfm

▶ **Notes**

▶ **Student Activity 11-1**

In Your Own Words

Based on this chapter, please provide an explanation of the following concepts in your own words as they apply to healthcare law. DO NOT RECITE the text.

Criminal law:

_____

_____

Civil law:

_____

_____

Battery:

_____

_____

Defensive medicine:

_____

_____

Torts:

_____

_____

Affirmative action plan:

_____

_____

Qui tam:

_____

_____

Standard of care:

_____

_____

Job lock:

_____

_____

Privacy rule:

_____

_____

▸ Student Activity 11-2

Complete the following case scenarios based on the information provided in the chapter. Your answer must be **IN YOUR OWN WORDS.**

Real-Life Applications: Case Scenario One

As a new healthcare administrator, you are in charge of orientation for four new employees regarding employment law. One of the employees is a woman, one has a disability, one is African American, and one is a Muslim. You feel it is important to emphasize laws that were passed to protect employees from discrimination.

Activity

Select the laws you feel are the most important to the new employees. Provide a brief description of each law and their impact on the new employees.

Responses

_____

_____

_____

_____

_____

_____

_____

_____

_____

_____

_____

_____

_____

_____

_____

_____

_____

Case Scenario Two

Your physician has informed you that she can no longer be your primary care provider. Her office manager called to tell you there would be a letter sent to you confirming that change. You are confused because you did not request this change.

Activity

Perform research on how a physician is required to end a relationship and develop a letter to your physician stating your findings.

Responses

_____

_____

_____

_____

_____

_____

_____

_____

_____

_____

_____

_____

_____

_____

_____

_____

_____

_____

_____

Case Scenario Three

Your cousin is involved in a lawsuit. He is the claimant of the case. You were very surprised and you asked him to give you a summary of the problem. He mentioned the words "noneconomic damages," "standard of care," and "medical malpractice." You were not sure what these words meant so you decided to do some research on them.

Activity

Research these three terms and provide specific "real-world" examples of the application of these terms.

Responses

_____

_____

_____

_____

_____

_____

_____

_____

_____

_____

_____

_____

_____

_____

_____

_____

Case Scenario Four

You just joined a company and one of the benefits was an employee wellness program. You were not sure what type of program it was and whether you would use the program.

Activity

Perform research on different types of employee wellness programs and discuss the relationship between employee wellness programs and the HIPAA law.

Responses

_____

_____

_____

_____

_____

_____

_____

_____

_____

_____

_____

_____

_____

_____

_____

_____

_____

_____

▶ Student Activity 11-3

Internet Exercises

Write your answers in the space provided.

- ▪ Visit each of the websites listed here.
- ▪ Name the organization.
- ▪ Locate the organization's mission statement on the website.
- ▪ Provide a brief overview of the activities of the organization.
- ▪ How do these organizations participate in the U.S. healthcare system?

Websites

http//:www.justice.gov

Organization Name:

_____

_____

Mission Statement:

_____

_____

_____

Overview of Activities:

_____

_____

_____

Importance of Organization to U.S. Health Care:

_____

_____

_____

http://www.americanbar.org

Organization Name:

_____

_____

Mission Statement:

_____

_____

_____

Overview of Activities:

_____

_____

_____

Importance of Organization to U.S. Health Care:

_____

_____

_____

http://www.healthlaw.org

Organization Name:

_____

_____

Mission Statement:

_____

_____

_____

Overview of Activities:

_____

_____

_____

Importance of Organization to U.S. Health Care:

_____

_____

_____

http://www.eeoc.gov

Organization Name:

_____

_____

Mission Statement:

_____

_____

_____

Overview of Activities:

_____

_____

_____

Importance of Organization to U.S. Health Care:

_____

_____

_____

http://www.medicalmalpractice.com

Organization Name:

_____

_____

Mission Statement:

_____

_____

_____

Overview of Activities:

_____

_____

_____

Importance of Organization to U.S. Health Care:

_____

_____

_____

http://www.hg.org/health-law.html

Organization Name:

_____

_____

Mission Statement:

_____

_____

_____

Overview of Activities:

_____

_____

_____

Importance of Organization to U.S. Health Care:

_____

_____

_____

▶ Student Activity 11-4

Discussion Questions

The following are suggested discussion questions for this chapter.

1. Discuss the concepts of negligence and intentional torts and give examples of these in the healthcare industry.

_____

_____

_____

_____

_____

_____

2. What is tort reform? Do you believe tort reform is necessary?

_____

_____

_____

_____

_____

_____

3. Discuss three employment-related pieces of legislation that you feel are very important and why.

_____

_____

_____

_____

_____

_____

_____

4. What is an affirmative action plan? Research on the Internet and discuss with your classmates the issues regarding this type of plan.

_____

_____

_____

_____

_____

_____

_____

_____

_____

5. What is defensive medicine? Do you think physicians really do this? Research on the Internet and locate current information on this topic to share with your classmates.

_____

_____

_____

_____

_____

_____

_____

_____

▶ **Student Activity 11-5**

Current Events

Perform an Internet search and find a current events topic over the past three years that is related to this chapter. Provide a summary of the article and the link to the article and why the article relates to the chapter.

_____

_____

_____

_____

_____

_____

_____

_____

_____

_____

_____

_____

_____

_____

_____

_____

_____

_____

_____

_____

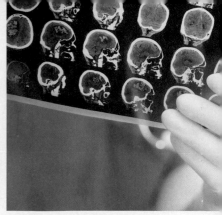

CHAPTER 12

Healthcare Ethics

DID YOU KNOW THAT?

- The concept of *bioethics* evolved as a result of the Nazis' human experimentation in the World War II prisoner camps.
- Eighteen people die daily waiting for an organ transplant.
- Xenotransplantation, which is transferring organs from one species to another, was first performed in 1984 when Baby Fae, a 5-pound infant, received the heart of a baboon.
- Euthanasia is from the Greek language, meaning *good death*.
- As the cost of U.S. medical procedures has increased, medical tourism is becoming popular as more citizens travel overseas to have medical procedures performed because the procedures are less expensive overseas.
- Workplace bullying is common in the healthcare industry.

▶ Introduction

Legal standards are the minimal standard of action established for individuals in a society. Ethical standards are considered one level above a legal action because individuals make a choice based on what is the "right thing to do," not what is required by law. There are many interpretations of the concept of ethics. Ethics has been interpreted as the moral foundation for standards of conduct (Taylor, 1975). The concept of **ethical standards** applies to actions that are hoped for and expected by individuals. Actions may be considered legal but not ethical. There are many definitions of ethics but, basically, **ethics** is concerned with what are right and wrong choices as perceived by society and individuals.

The concept of ethics is tightly woven throughout the healthcare industry. It has been dated back to Hippocrates, the father of medicine, in the 4th century BC, and evolved into the Hippocratic Oath, which is the foundation for the ethical guidelines for patient treatment by physicians. In 1847, the American Medical Association (AMA) published a *Code of Medical Ethics* that provided guidelines for the physician–provider relationship, emphasizing the duty to treat a patient (AMA, 2016a). To this day, physicians' actions have followed codes of ethics that demand the "**duty to treat**" (Wynia, 2007).

Applying the concept of ethics to the healthcare industry has created two areas of ethics: medical ethics and bioethics. **Medical ethics** focuses on the decisions healthcare providers make concerning medical treatment of patients. Euthanasia or physician-assisted suicide would be an example of a medical ethics topic. **Advance directives** are orders that patients give to providers to ensure that, if they are terminally ill and incompetent to make a decision, certain measures will not be taken to prolong that patient's life. If advance directives are not provided, the ethical decision of when to withdraw treatment may be placed on the family and provider. These issues are legally defined, although there are ethical ramifications surrounding these decisions.

This chapter will focus primarily on **bioethics**. This field of study is concerned with the ethical implications of certain biologic and medical procedures and technologies, such as cloning; **alternative reproductive methods**, such as in vitro fertilization; organ transplants; genetic engineering; and care of the terminally ill (Adelaide Center for Bioethics and Culture, 2016). Additionally, the rapid advances in medicine in these areas raised questions about the influence of technology on the field of medicine (Coleman, Bouesseau, & Reis, 2008).

It is important to understand the impact of ethics in different aspects of providing health care. Ethical dilemmas in health care are situations that test a provider's belief and what the provider should do professionally. Ethical dilemmas are often a conflict between personal and professional ethics. A **healthcare ethical dilemma** is a problem, situation, or opportunity that requires an individual, such as a healthcare provider, or an organization, such as a managed care practice, to choose an action that could be unethical. A decision-making model is presented that can help resolve ethical dilemmas in the healthcare field (Niles, 2013). This chapter will discuss ethical theories, codes of healthcare conduct, informed consent, confidentiality, special populations, research ethics, ethics in public health, end-of-life decisions, genetic testing and profiling, and biomedical ethics, which focus on technology use and health care.

▶ Healthcare Stakeholder Management Model

A **stakeholder** is an individual or group that has an interest in an organization or activity. This term should not be confused with a "shareholder," who actually has a financial interest in an organization because he or she owns part of the organization. The concept of **stakeholder management** focuses on the relationship between organizations and all of their constituents, including shareholders, and how management recognizes the different expectations of each group. For example, a customer stakeholder would have a large interest in an organization where he or she purchases a product or a service. For some organizations, the government is an important stakeholder because the government regulates the organization's activities. Managing the interests of all of the stakeholders is a challenge for management, particularly in the healthcare industry. The pressure that stakeholders may impose on a manager can impact the manager's ethical decision-making process (Carroll & Buchholtz, 2015).

The basic stakeholder relationship in the healthcare industry is the relationship between the physician–clinician and the patient. However, Oddo (2001) has proposed that there are several other stakeholders that play a role in their relationship. Patients will have relationships that impact their interaction with the physician. The physician also has relationships with other stakeholders who have expectations of the physician. For example, the patient will have family and friends and the health insurance company or the government that is paying for the health procedure. The family and friends have expectations that the physician will cure their friend or family member. They have an emotional relationship. The health insurance company's relationship with the patient is professional. The company will reimburse standardized treatment procedures.

The physician's stakeholder relationships are more complex. Physicians may be a part of a managed care facility or have admitting privileges at a hospital so they have the relationship with that entity and the entity might have expectations of how they will treat patients. Physicians are also impacted by health insurance companies, which want them to treat patients according to standardized diagnostic procedures. Drug companies have an interest in the physician because they want the provider to use their products. All of these stakeholders have expectations based on the simple relationship between the patient and the provider. When these stakeholders place undue pressure on this relationship, the decision-making process of the provider may not always place the patient first, although, as stated previously, the provider is ethically bound to treat the patient.

Basic Concepts of Ethics in the Healthcare Workplace

Ethical standards are considered above legal standards because individuals make a choice based on what is the "right thing to do," not what is required by law. There are many interpretations of the concept of ethics. Ethics has been interpreted as the moral foundation for standards of conduct (Taylor, 1975). The concept of *ethical standards* applies to actions that are hoped for and expected by individuals. There are many definitions of ethics but, basically, ethics is concerned with what are right and wrong choices as perceived by society and its individuals. Ethical dilemmas are often a conflict between personal and professional ethics. A *healthcare ethical dilemma* is a problem, situation, or opportunity that requires an individual, such as a healthcare provider, to choose an action between two obligations (Niles, 2011). The dilemma occurs when the ethical reasoning of the decision maker may conflict with the ethical reasoning of the patient and the institution. Dilemmas are often resolved because of the guidelines provided by codes of medical ethics of medical associations or healthcare institutions, ongoing training, and implementing ethical decision-making models.

Healthcare Codes of Ethics

As a result of many public ethical crises that have occurred, particularly in the business world, many organizations have developed written **codes of ethics**, which are guidelines for industry participants' actions.

Codes of ethics provide a standard for operation so that all participants understand that if they do not adhere to this code, there may be negative consequences. The healthcare industry is no different.

Physicians have been guided by many healthcare codes of ethics. The statement of ethics discussed previously in this chapter is a type of code of ethics; the AMA created a code of ethics for physicians in 1847. This code was revised and adopted in 2001. Each category of healthcare professional has a code of conduct. In 1985, the **American Nurses Association (ANA)** established a code for nurses, which was revised in 1995 and most recently in 2015 (ANA, 2016). Healthcare executives have a code of ethics that was established in 1941 that discusses the relationship with their stakeholders. The **American College of Healthcare Executives (ACHE)** represents 30,000 executives internationally who participate in the healthcare system (ACHE, 2016). They also offer ethical policy statements on relevant issues such as creating an ethical culture for employees. In addition, they offer an ethics self-assessment tool that enables employees to target potential areas of ethical weakness. Many hospitals have established a code of ethics, which may help providers when they are dealing with medical situations such as organ donations.

Interestingly, the **Advanced Medical Technology Association** (AdvaMed), an industry association that represents medical products, has also developed a code of ethics that addresses interactions with healthcare professionals who are potential customers of their products. Their ethical issues are similar to the pharmaceutical industry because they want physicians to use their medical devices and encourage the use by providing physicians with incentives such as gifts or paying for healthcare providers' travel or medical conferences (Advanced Medical Technology Association, 2016).

How to Develop a Code of Ethics

A code of ethics must be written clearly, because employees at all organizational levels will utilize it. If a certain employee category needs a specific code of ethics, then a written code should be specifically developed for that category. The code must be current in laws and regulations. Driscoll and Hoffman (2000) recommend the following outline for developing a code of ethics:

1. Memorable Title
2. Leadership Letter
3. Table of Contents
4. Introduction
5. Core Values of the Organization

6. Code Provisions
7. Information and Resources

The code of ethics must be a user-friendly resource for the organization. It should be updated to include current laws and regulations. The language should be specific as to what the organization should expect from its employees and training should be provided on the code of ethics so employees understand the organization's expectations.

▶ Workplace Bullying

In 1992, Andrea Adams, a BBC journalist, coined the term **workplace bullying**, describing an ongoing harassing workplace behavior between employees, which results in negative health outcomes for the targeted employees (Adams, 1992). Workplace bullying is receiving increased attention worldwide as a negative organizational issue. It is considered a serious and chronic workplace stressor that can lead to diminished work productivity and work quality (Hoel, Faragher, & Cooper, 2004). This negative behavior is considered bullying if it is repeated over an extended period of time. It can occur between colleagues, supervisors, or supervisees, although the bully is often the supervisor. Definitions also include negative verbal or nonverbal behavior such as snide comments, verbal or physical threats, or items being thrown. Employees have also reported less aggressive behavior, such as demeaning comments about work or continual gossip. The literature has reported an increased incident of bullying reported in healthcare organizations (Ayoko, Callan, & Hartel, 2003; Vartia, 2001; Djurkovic, McCormack, & Casimir, 2008).

Workplace Bullying in Healthcare

The Center for American Nurses, the American Association of Critical-Care Nurses, the International Council of Nurses, and the National Student Nurses Association have all issued statements regarding the need for healthcare organizations to eliminate bullying in the healthcare workplace. Often, verbal abuse also occurs toward nurses by physicians or patients and their families. **Lateral violence** also occurs, defined as "nurse to nurse" aggression and demonstrated by both verbal and nonverbal behavior (American Nurses Association, 2016). In a 2014 Kaplan Survey of 2,000 nursing graduates, 48% indicated they were concerned about being bullied or working in hostile work environment and 38% knew nurses who were bullied or worked in a hostile work environment (Kaplan, 2014).

Legal Implications of Workplace Bullying

There is no federal legislation in the United States that forbids workplace bullying. Since 2003, 30 states have introduced anti-workplace-bullying bills (WBI, 2016). However, there are two federal laws that can be applied in workplace bullying: the Occupational Safety and Health (OSHA) Act of 1970 and Title VII of the Civil Rights Act of 1964. The OSHA Act of 1970 states that employers must provide a safe and healthful working environment or their employees. Under Title VII of the Civil Rights Act, if an employee in a protected class (e.g., gender, religion, ethnicity) is bullied by another employee, the action might be illegal based on the concept of a hostile work environment.

Recommendations to Eliminate Workplace Bullying

To date, there is no federal legislation that specifically addresses workplace bullying. In order to reduce the prevalence of workplace bullying, it is important that employers implement policies to eliminate this behavior. The following are recommendations for organizations, including in health care (LaVan & Martin, 2007):

1. Adopt a policy of zero tolerance for workplace bullying and develop measures to discipline bullies in the workplace.
2. Create an organizational culture that focuses on a positive work environment enabling all individuals to pursue their careers.
3. Reward behaviors that encourage teamwork and collaboration among employees and their supervisors.
4. Develop an educational program for all employees on what constitutes workplace bullying.

Workplace bullying continues to be a pervasive organizational problem worldwide. In the United States, the Workplace Bullying Institute has developed a Healthy Workplace Bill that precisely defines workplace bullying and extends protection to employees against this type of behavior. There is no specific federal legislation against anti-bullying so bullying will continue to be legal, unfortunately. It is important that workplace bullying educational programs and organizational policies be implemented to ensure that employees will be protected against this type of negative behavior. The results can be devastating from both an organizational and individual level.

In 2008, **The Joint Commission** developed a standard for workplace bullying called "intimidating and disruptive behaviors in the workplace." They issued the following statement:

> *Intimidating and disruptive behaviors can foster medical errors, contribute to poor patient satisfaction and to preventable adverse outcomes, increase the cost of care, and cause qualified clinicians, administrators, and managers to seek new positions in more professional environments. Safety and quality of patient care is dependent on teamwork, communication, and a collaborative work environment. To assure quality and to promote a culture of safety, health care organizations must address the problem of behaviors that threaten the performance of the health care team. (The Joint Commission, 2008, p. 1)*

Two leadership standards are now part of The Joint Commission's accreditation provisions: The first requires an institution to have "a code of conduct that defines acceptable and disruptive and inappropriate behaviors." The second requires an institution "to create and implement a process for managing disruptive and inappropriate behaviors" (Yamada, 2004).

The Joint Commission standard focused on the impact of these types of behavior on patient care quality. The Joint Commission requires healthcare institutions to create a code of conduct that defines appropriate behavior and has a system in place to manage inappropriate behavior such as workplace bullying. In addition to the stance of The Joint Commission, the Center for Professional Health at the Vanderbilt University Medical Center has developed a program for treating and remediating disruptive behaviors by physicians (Minding the Workplace, 2016).

In July 2015, the ANA updated its code of ethics to include this statement:

> *All registered nurses and employers in all settings, including practice, academia, and research must collaborate to create a culture of respect, free of incivility, bullying, and workplace violence. Best practice strategies based on evidence must be implemented to prevent and mitigate incivility, bullying, and workplace violence; to promote the health, safety, and wellness of registered nurses; and to ensure optimal outcomes across the health care continuum. (ANA, 2016)*

This code of ethics can be applied to any stakeholder in the health care industry.

▶ Ethics and the Doctor–Patient Relationship

The Physician Code of Ethics has been in existence as long as the American Medical Association (1947). It is a living document and in its most recent update (2001), the following statements discuss the relationship between the patient and physician:

> *A patient-physician relationship exists when a physician serves a patient's medical needs, generally by mutual consent between physician and patient (or surrogate). In some instances the agreement is implied, such as in emergency care or when physicians provide services at the request of the treating physician. In rare instances, treatment without consent may be provided under court order.*

> *The relationship between patient and physician is based on trust and gives rise to physicians' ethical obligations to place patients' welfare above their own self-interest and above obligations to other groups, and to advocate for their patients' welfare. Within the patient-physician relationship, a physician is ethically required to use sound medical judgment, holding the best interests of the patient as paramount (AMA, 2016)*

In 2004, the **American College of Physicians and Harvard Pilgrim Health Care Ethics Program** developed a statement of ethics for managed care. The following is a summary of the statements (Povar et al., 2004):

- Clinicians, healthcare plans, insurance companies, and patients should be honest in their relationships with each other.
- These parties should recognize the importance of the clinician and patient relationship and its ethical obligations.
- Clinicians should maintain accurate patient records.
- All parties should contribute to developing healthcare policies.
- The clinician's primary duty is the care of the patient.
- Clinicians have the responsibility to practice effective and efficient medicine.
- Clinicians should recognize that all individuals, regardless of their position, should have health care.
- Healthcare plans and their insurers should openly explain their policies regarding reimbursement of types of health care.
- Patients have a responsibility to understand their health insurance.

- Health plans should not ask clinicians to compromise their ethical standards of care.
- Clinicians should enter agreements with healthcare plans that support ethical standards.
- Confidentiality of patient information should be protected.
- Clinicians should disclose conflicts of interest to their patients.
- Information provided to patients should be clearly understood by the patient.

This statement was developed as a result of the continued economic and policy changes in the healthcare industry. It provided guidelines to healthcare practitioners, healthcare organizations, and the healthcare insurance industry about ethical actions in the changing healthcare environment.

▶ Physician–Patient Relationship Model

It is important to further discuss the relationship between the practitioner and the patient. There are several different models that can be applied to this relationship. Veatch (1972) identified four models that apply to the doctor–patient relationship: engineering model, priestly model, contractual model, and collegial model.

The **engineering model** focuses on patients and their power to make decisions about their health care. The provider gives the patient all of the necessary information to make a decision. The provider empowers the patient with knowledge to make a decision. The **priestly model** assumes the doctor will make the best decisions for the patient's health. The patient assumes a very passive role, giving the provider great power in the decision-making process. This is a very traditional relationship that often would occur between physicians and elderly individuals who were taught to revere the medical world. The **contractual model**, based on a legal foundation, assumes there is an agreement between the two parties, assuming mutual goals. It is a relationship between the two parties with equal power. The patient understands the legal ramifications of the relationship. The **collegial model** assumes trust between the patient and doctor and that decision making is an equal effort (Veatch, 1972). These models are dependent on what type of relationship a patient expects with his or her practitioner. In any case, in each model, ethics plays a role in the relationship. Although the provider may play different roles in each of these models, the underlying foundation is the assumption that the doctor's actions are ethical, representing the best interest of the patient.

According to Beauchamp and Childress (2001) and Gillon (1994), the role of ethics in the healthcare industry is based on five basic values that all healthcare providers should observe:

- **Respect for autonomy:** Decision making may be different and healthcare providers must respect their patients' decisions even if they differ from their own.
- **Beneficence:** The healthcare provider should focus on the patient's best interests when making a decision.
- **Nonmalfeasance:** The healthcare provider will cause no harm when taking action.
- **Justice:** Healthcare providers will make fair decisions.
- **Dignity:** Patients should be treated with respect and dignity.

Each of these principles will be discussed in depth because these concepts are important to understanding the role of ethics in the healthcare industry. **Autonomy**, which is defined as self-rule, is an important concept to health care because it is applied to **informed consent**, which requires a provider to obtain the permission of a patient who has been provided adequate information to make a decision regarding intervention. Informed consent is a legal requirement for medical intervention. As part of the autonomy concept, it is also important that providers respect the decision of their patient even if the patient's decisions do not agree with the provider's recommendation. For example, a friend who has been diagnosed with a very advanced stage of cancer was told by her provider that she could enroll her in an experimental program that would give her 2–3 months to live. The intervention is very potent with severe side effects. My friend decided to try a homeopathic medicine to attack her disease. Her doctor was not in agreement with her choice but she respected her patient's decision. She told her that if she needed pain medication, she could come see her and she would help her. This situation is an excellent example of autonomy in medicine.

Beneficence in the healthcare industry means that the best interest of the patient should always be the first priority of the healthcare provider and healthcare organizations. **Nonmalfeasance** further states that healthcare providers must not take any actions to harm the patient. As discussed in the paragraph on autonomy, this concept appears to be very easy to understand; however, there may be disagreement between the provider and the patient as to what is best for the patient. For example, Jehovah's Witnesses, a religious sect, do not believe in blood transfusions and will not give consent during an operation for a transfusion to occur, despite the procedure's ability to possibly save a life (Miller, 2006). The provider has been trained to believe in beneficence and malfeasance. However, from the provider's point of view, if he or she respects the wishes of the patient and family in such a situation, the provider will be potentially harming the patient.

Justice or fairness in the healthcare industry emphasizes that patients should be treated equally and that health care should be accessible to all. Justice should be applied to the way healthcare services are distributed, which means that healthcare services are available to all individuals. Unfortunately, in the United States, the healthcare system does not provide accessibility to all citizens. Access to health care is often determined by the ability to pay either out of pocket or by an employer- or government-sponsored program. In countries with universal healthcare coverage, justice in the healthcare industry is more prevalent. Despite the passage of the Affordable Care Act, there are still millions of uninsured individuals in the United States: Can one say that justice has not prevailed in the healthcare industry (Centers for Disease Control and Prevention, 2016)?

▶ Pharmaceutical Marketing to Physicians

There have been many cases regarding how drug companies market their products to physicians. Over the past two decades, this relationship has received more scrutiny because of its appearance of unethical behavior. The drug companies provide free samples and information to physicians because the companies want providers to prescribe or recommend their products. Although providers deny that these "perks" influence their decisions in choosing drugs, federal legislation— the **Physician Payment Sunshine Act**—was passed in 2010 as part of the Affordable Care Act (effective August 2013) and requires manufacturers of drugs, medical devices, and other healthcare products with relationships with Medicare and Medicaid providers and CHIP programs to submit annual reports regarding payments and items of value. They must also report ownership interests held by physicians and their families (AMA, 2016b). In 2002, the **Pharmaceutical Research and Manufacturers of America (PhRMA)** implemented a new code of conduct governing physician–industry relationships, which it updated in 2009 (PhRMA, 2016). The code discourages gifts to physicians and other monetary rewards, emphasizing the relationship should focus on enhancing the quality of treatment of the patient. It emphasizes ethical marketing to physicians. These types of codes of conduct

provide guidelines for the relationship between the provider and the companies, thereby providing more accountability for the use of certain prescriptions by providers. This type of relationship can test the ethical relationship between the provider and patient.

▶ Decision Model for Healthcare Dilemmas

Healthcare dilemmas require guidelines to process a solution to the dilemma. Codes of ethics and HR training can assist with a solution. Employee training can include a decision-making model that will assist the individual to process the steps in resolving the situation. The PLUS ethical decision-making model consists of the following (Ethics Resource Center, 2016):

1. Identification of the dilemma;
2. Identification of the conflicting ethics of each party;
3. Identification of alternatives to a solution;
4. Identification of the impact of each alternative; and
5. Selection of the solution.

Application of the Decision-Making Model

Healthcare Dilemma (discussed earlier): An oncologist has a patient with an advanced stage of melanoma (skin cancer). Prognosis: 3–6 months to live. The oncologist has developed an experimental treatment program that has severe side effects but may give the patient an additional six months. The patient prefers alternative remedies, such as homeopathic solutions (natural remedies).

Step 1: *Define the problem.* This is the most important part of the process. This step should define the problem and the ultimate outcome of the decision-making process.
Application: The problem is the differing views of treatment by the physician and the patient. The physician does not believe in homeopathic remedies. The ultimate outcome of the decision-making process is to prolong the life of the patient, if possible.

Step 2: *Identify the alternative(s) to the problem.* List the possible alternatives to the desired outcome. Attempt to identify at least three as a minimum, but five are preferred.

Alternative 1: Patient accepts experimental treatment program.

Alternative 2: Patient rejects experimental treatment program.

Alternative 3: Physician researches homeopathic remedies for patient.

Alternative 4: Physician refuses to research homeopathic remedies for patient.

Alternative 5: Patient seeks other medical advice from different physician.

Alternative 6: Physician refers patient to physician who is an expert in homeopathic medicine.

Step 3: *Evaluate the identified alternatives*. Discuss the positive and negative impact of each alternative.

Alternative 1: Patient accepts experimental treatment program.

Positive: Patient's cancer is eradicated or is in remission.

Negative: Treatment has no impact on cancer. Patient dies.

Alternative 2: Patient rejects experimental treatment program.

Positive: Cancer goes into remission.

Negative: Patient dies shortly.

Alternative 3: Physician researches homeopathic remedies for patient.

Positive: Physician finds a homeopathic remedy that can be used in conjunction with experimental program. Patient accepts treatment. Cancer is eradicated or goes into remission.

Negative: Physician finds no homeopathic solution that can be used in conjunction with experimental program. Patient refuses treatment. Patient dies shortly.

Alternative 4: Physician refuses to research homeopathic remedies for patient.

Positive: Patient believes in physician and agrees to try experimental program. Program is successful.

Negative: Patient cuts ties with physician. Receives no treatment and dies shortly.

Alternative 5: Patient seeks other medical advice from different physician.

Positive: Patient finds a physician who agrees with homeopathic remedies. Patient accepts homeopathic remedies and cancer is eradicated or goes into remission.

Negative: Patient does not find a physician who would help her and dies quickly, trying to find someone.

Alternative 6: Physician refers patient to physician who is expert in homeopathic medicine.

Positive: Patient is treated with a homeopathic solution that prolongs her life.

Negative: Patient is treated with a homeopathic solution that does not prolong her life.

Step 4: *Make the decision*. In the healthcare industry, the decision must include the patient's best interest and his or her values, which can be conflicting at times. However, patients have the right to make an informed decision about their health. In this instance, alternative 6 is chosen, because the patient believes in homeopathic medicine. The physician, who does not believe in natural remedies, respected the patient's beliefs, which differed from hers, but she still wanted to help the patient. The physician wanted to be involved in the patient care by supporting the beliefs of her patient.

Step 5: *Implement the decision*. Once the decision is made, the physician actually finds a physician to help her patient. The primary physician said she would provide any assistance with pain medication if needed.

Step 6: *Evaluate the decision*. The patient accepted the referral of the new physician and entered a homeopathic treatment program. The patient lived three more years with a high quality of life.

This decision-making model is an excellent method of resolving many types of healthcare dilemmas. This model can be utilized in employee training on ethical issues in the healthcare workplace.

▶ Ethics and Public Health

In contrast to the bioethicist view of the relationship between physician and patient, ethical analysis has expanded to public health. There are several ethics issues in public health that focus on the design and implementation of measures to monitor and improve the community's health (Coleman et al., 2008). Issues in public health include inaccessibility to health care for certain populations, response to bioterrorism, research in developing countries, health promotion and its infringement on an individual's lifestyle choices, and public health's response to emergencies. The concept of **paternalism** and public health is the concern that individual freedom will be restricted for the sake of public health activities because the government infringes on individual choices for the sake of protecting the community (Ascension Health, 2016).

The **Nuffield Council on Bioethics**, based in Great Britain, has proposed a stewardship model that outlines the principles public health policy makers should utilize globally. This model addresses the issues of paternalism in public health. The **stewardship model** states that public health officials should achieve the stated health outcomes for the population while minimizing restrictions on people's freedom of choice.

The focus of public health is to reduce the population's health risks from other people's actions such as drunk driving, smoking in public places, environmental conditions, inaccessibility to health care, and unsafe working environments. While promoting a healthy lifestyle, according to the Nuffield Council on Bioethics, it is also important that public health programs do not force people into programs without their consent or introduce interventions that may invade people's privacy. The Council also introduced the concept of an intervention ladder, which establishes a ranking of the type of public health intervention introduced, which may minimize people's choices. The higher the intervention is on the ladder, the more justification is required for the action (Nuffield Council on Bioethics, 2016).

Childress, Faden, and Gaare (2002) specify five justifications for public health interventions that infringe on individual choices. The criteria are (1) effectiveness, (2) need, (3) proportionality, (4) minimal infringement, and (5) public education. **Effectiveness** is essential to demonstrate that the public health efforts were successful and, therefore, it was necessary to limit individual freedom of choice. The need for a public health intervention must be demonstrated to limit individual freedom. If the **proportionality** of the public health intervention outweighs freedom of choice, then the intervention must be warranted. If the public health intervention satisfies effectiveness, need, and proportionality, the least restrictive intervention or **minimal infringement** on individual freedoms should be considered first. Lastly, public health workers must provide **public education** to explain their interventions and why the infringement on individual choices is warranted. For example, bioterrorism is now a viable threat. If it has been determined that a public health threat exists as a result of some biological weapons, then mandatory blood tests, possible quarantines, and other measures that would infringe on individual freedom of choice must be implemented (Buchanan, 2008).

Another public health ethical issue is the duty of practitioners to treat individuals during a public health crisis. If there is a natural disaster, what is the duty to treat? During Hurricane Katrina, several healthcare professionals volunteered to stay behind in a local hospital. Unfortunately, several patients in the hospital died and the providers were accused of murdering their patients. As a result of this incident, many professionals are now wary of volunteering during a crisis even though state good Samaritan laws may provide protection from civil liability for volunteers during a crisis. From providers' perspective, they commit to an ethical reaction but might be rewarded with a criminal liability. Physicians practicing in free clinics are protected

by federal law. Federal lawmakers should pass legislation that protects these healthcare professionals during public health emergencies (Wynia, 2007).

▶ Ethics and Research

Conducting research involving human subjects requires the assessment of the risks and benefits to the human subjects, which must be explained clearly to them before the consent to participate in the research is given. The principles of ethical research are outlined in **Institutional Review Boards (IRBs)**. An IRB is a group that has been formally designated to review and monitor biomedical research involving human subjects. An IRB has the authority to approve, require modifications in (to secure approval), or disapprove research. This group review serves an important role in the protection of the rights and welfare of human research subjects (Food and Drug Administration [FDA], 2016). Any organization that performs research should develop an IRB. The ethical component of an IRB is to protect the participants of the study. The IRBs require the researchers to maximize the benefits and minimize the risks to participants and explain these assessments clearly. It is important that the IRB does not approve a study that imposes significant risks on the subjects.

Assuming the study clears the IRB's assessment of risks and benefits, it is important the subjects understand the study and its impact on them. Informed consent, as it relates to treatment, is one of the basic ethical protections for human subject research. It is designed to protect human subjects and increase autonomy. Informed consent protects human subjects because it allows the individual to consider personal issues before participating in medical research. Informed consent increases autonomy because it provides individuals with the opportunity to make a choice to exercise control over their lives (Mehlman & Berg, 2008). Research informed consent requires the disclosure of appropriate information to assist the individual in project participation. Both the U.S. Department of Health and Human Services (HHS) and the FDA have outlined the common rule elements of informed consent.

Common rule elements include a written statement that includes the purpose and duration of the study; the procedures and, if they are experimental, any foreseen risks and potential benefits; and any alternative procedures that may benefit the subject (FDA, 2013; Korenman, 2009). Additional requirements are needed for children, pregnant women, people with disabilities, mentally disabled people, prisoners, and so on. It is clear that the IRB must provide guidelines for parents whose children participate in research and for subjects with mental disabilities, who could be unduly influenced (Mehlman & Berg, 2008).

▶ Bioethical Issues

Designer or Donor Babies

Alternative reproductive methods are methods of conception that parents use to have children. An example is in vitro fertilization, which means that the embryo is fertilized in a clinic using the sperm from the father. **Preimplantation genetic diagnosis (PGD)** can be used to test embryos for tissue compatibility with their siblings prior to being transplanted into the mother. If one of the siblings becomes ill, the "designer baby" can save the existing sibling's life by providing bone marrow transplants. If it has been determined that the embryo is not compatible, it could be destroyed. This procedure is considered very controversial because many people consider the embryo to be early human life. Also, are the physicians and parents "playing God" by determining whether the embryo should be saved? Does this type of control dehumanize **procreation** or creation of life? Another issue is the impact on the child, who will eventually be aware that he or she was created to save a sibling (Dayal & Zarek, 2008).

Cloning

All human beings possess **stem cells**, which are "starter" cells for the development of body tissue that has yet to be formed into specialized tissues for certain parts of the body (Sullivan, 2006). The term **cloning** applies to any procedure that creates a genetic replica of a cell or organism. There are two major types of cloning: **reproductive cloning**, which creates cloned babies; and **therapeutic** or **research cloning**, which uses the same process but the focus is replicating sources for stem cells to replace damaged tissues. The most famous reproductive clone was Dolly, the sheep that was cloned in 1996 from an adult cell (Baylis, 2002). Several countries have banned cloning for reproductive purposes but have been more lenient in therapeutic cloning. There are several ethical issues regarding cloning. Researchers worldwide have attempted human cloning with no success. Some feel that cloning humans is unnatural and playing God rather than allowing procreating to progress naturally. Some people, however, have cloned their pets, which has created an uproar. People are highly focused on the reproductive cloning issues rather than the potential research success of cloning that could result in effective treatment of many diseases. However,

therapeutic cloning also is considered unethical because it is destroying embryos to obtain healthy stem cells for research.

Research has focused on stem cells that could replace damaged body tissues from spinal injuries or cure ailments such as Parkinson's disease. These stem cells could be derived from surplus human embryos that are stored at in vitro fertilization clinics and were not used for fertility procedures. The ethical issue, similar to the designer baby issues, is that, in order to use the stem cells, researchers would be destroying human embryos; many people consider embryos to be human life. The issue in both cases also is what should happen to the excess embryos that are stored in clinics. Studies have indicated there may be an estimated 400,000 embryos stored in U.S. clinics that may eventually be destroyed (The Coalition of Americans for Research Ethics, 2016). Could these embryos be used to develop therapies and cures for disease?

Genetic Testing

Genetic testing is carried out on populations based on age, gender, or other risk factors to determine if they are at risk for a serious genetic disease or if they have a carrier gene that they may pass on to their children. Genetic tests may be analyzed from bodily tissue, including blood, mouth-lining cells, saliva, hair, skin, tumors, or fluid surrounding the fetus during pregnancy (National Human Genome Research Institute [NHGRI], 2016). The specimen is analyzed by a laboratory. There are several different types of tests:

- **Diagnostic testing** is used to identify the disease when a person is exhibiting symptoms.
- **Predictive and asymptomatic testing** (no symptoms) is used to identify any gene changes that may increase the likelihood of a person developing a disease.
- **Carrier testing** is used to identify individuals who carry a gene that is linked to a disease. The individual may exhibit no symptoms but may pass the gene to offspring, who may develop the disease or carry the gene themselves.
- **Prenatal testing** is offered to identify fetuses with potential diseases or conditions.
- Newborn screening is performed during the first 1–2 days of life to determine if the child has a disease that could impact its development.
- **Pharmacogenomic testing** is performed to assess how medicines react to an individual's genetic makeup.
- **Research genetic testing** focuses on how genes impact disease development.

The **Human Genome Project**, a long-term government-funded project completed in 2003, identified all of the 20,000–25,000 genes found in human DNA. Researchers catalogued these genes, which has made it easier to quickly determine the genes an individual possesses. As a result of genetics research, several genes have been identified as markers of predictors of disease in families such as breast cancer, colon cancer, cystic fibrosis, and Down syndrome in fetuses (Oak Ridge National Laboratory [ORNL], 2016).

Although information gained from genetic testing is important to individuals and their families, there are several ethical issues regarding genetic testing. If employers were aware of this information, would they use it to discriminate against employees? Would parents decide against having a child because of a result of a genetic test? How accurate are the genetic tests? There are no regulations regarding genetic tests so individuals and families may make decisions based on faulty laboratory tests. It is important that genetic testing is provided in conjunction with genetic counseling to ensure that individuals understand the results. Recently, private companies have developed home kits for genetic testing. This type of information without discussion with a genetic counselor or physician may have repercussions because an individual may make decisions based on lack of comprehension.

Euthanasia: Treating the Terminally Ill

End-of-life issues can be an ethical challenge. Healthcare providers may find this difficult to understand because they have been trained to save lives. **Euthanasia** is the term most often associated with end-of-life issues. Euthanasia, a Greek word that means *good death*, may seem unethical because you are allowing an individual to die. Letting a patient die may be morally justifiable if it has been determined that any medical intervention is completely futile. There are two major types of euthanasia: voluntary and nonvoluntary. **Voluntary euthanasia** is assisting a patient with ending his or her life at the patient's request. **Nonvoluntary euthanasia** means ending the life of an incompetent patient usually at the request of a family member. The two most famous nonvoluntary euthanasia cases involved Karen Quinlan and Terri Schiavo. In 1975, the New Jersey Supreme Court granted Ms. Quinlan's father the right to remove his daughter's respirator, which resulted in her death 10 years later. She had remained in a coma or persistent vegetative state for 10 years. Because she was not able to make the decision herself, the judge granted the father the right to limit any medical interventions to continue

her life. Terri Schiavo suffered a heart attack in 1990 and remained in a coma on a feeding tube until 2005, when the Florida Supreme Court allowed her husband to remove her feeding tube despite her parent's protests (University of Miami Ethics Programs, 2016).

There is confusion regarding the difference between euthanasia and physician-assisted suicide. **Physician-assisted suicide** refers to the physician providing the means for death, most often with a prescription for a drug. The patient, not the physician, will ultimately administer the lethal medication. Euthanasia generally means that the physician would act directly, for instance by giving a lethal injection, to end the patient's life.

Although euthanasia is illegal in all states, physician-assisted suicide is legal in Oregon (1994), Washington (2008), Vermont (2013), and California (2017), so it is important to examine end-of-life issues because many of us will face them ourselves or with a loved one. The **Oregon Death with Dignity Act** (DWDA) was passed in 1994 and became effective in 1997. Since the state started tracking data in 1998, 1,545 individuals have received prescriptions under the act's authority, and 991 of them have ingested the medication and died as a result. Between 1998 and 2013, written prescriptions increased annually at 12%. During 2014 and 2015, the average annual rate doubled to 24%. During 2015, the death rate was 38.6 DWDA deaths per 10,000 total deaths (DWDA, 2016). The Washington mandate, effective 2009, was modeled after the Oregon law. In both states, the patient needs to be deemed terminal by two physicians. If physicians have doubts about a patient's mental state, a mental health professional will be consulted. The patient must make an oral request and a witnessed written request and another request 15 days later. The physicians must inform the patient about hospice and palliative care options (O'Reilly, 2009). Between 2009 and 2014, 725 patients received written prescriptions, and 712 used the prescription. The number of participants increased from 65 in 2009 to 176 in 2014. The number of patients who ingested the medication was 64 in 2009, 86 in 2010, 121 in 2013, and 171 in 2014. A survey of terminal patients showed they requested the prescriptions because they felt they were becoming a burden on their families, losing their independence, and losing the ability to enjoy life (Washington State Department of Health, 2016).

This legislation is controversial and has generated much commentary throughout the country and worldwide. Healthcare providers who support euthanasia believe that (1) it is an opportunity to relieve the pain a patient is experiencing at the end of his or her life; (2) it is an example of autonomy in life by allowing a person to choose when he or she is dying; and (3) it allows an opportunity to be released from a life that no longer has quality. Healthcare providers who believe that euthanasia is unethical feel that (1) it devalues the concept of life, (2) it may merely be an opportunity to contain medical costs for both the families and health insurance companies and, most importantly, (3) a provider should not be directly involved in killing a patient (Sullivan, 2005). The opponents of euthanasia also feel that a physician cannot, with medical certainty, tell patients that they will die within six months. The patient's emotional state and response to medication may alter that prognosis.

Dr. Jack Kevorkian and Dr. Phillip Nitschke

It is important to mention two physicians who have strongly supported euthanasia throughout the years. U.S. physician Dr. Jack Kevorkian, or Dr. Death as he was called, had provided assisted-suicide services to at least 45 ill patients. In 1989, he developed a suicide machine that allowed patients to administer a lethal injection of medication to themselves. In 1997, the U.S. Supreme Court ruled that individuals who want to kill themselves, but are physically unable to do so, have no constitutional right to end their lives. Dr. Kevorkian was sentenced to 10–25 years in prison that same year. He was paroled in 2007 because he was in failing health and died in 2011 (Notable Names Database, 2013).

Australian physician Dr. Phillip Nitschke travels internationally presenting "how to commit suicide" clinics. Several years ago, he created a concoction from household ingredients that he calls the "Peaceful Pill." He believes that if there is a right to life, there is also a right to die and that individuals should have the right to choose to end life. He does not restrict this right to just the terminally ill. He also believes that the depressed, the elderly, and the grieving should have the right to end their lives (Exit International, 2016).

Transplantation

Transplantation is the general procedure of implanting a functional organ from one person to another. This procedure can include blood transfusions or complicated procedures such as heart and lung transplants and bone marrow transplants. Organ transplants are becoming a more common approach to the treatment of diseased organs, making organ donations important to saving lives. Many patients have a significant chance for long-term survival because of impressive gains in the field (Burrows, 2004; Woloschak, 2003). There are two major ethical and legal issues associated with

organ transplants between humans: (1) the decision-making process for who receives the organ; and (2) financial remuneration from selling organs, which has resulted in a black market for buying organs. It is important to note that since 1984, as a result of the passage of the National Organ Transplant Act, it is illegal in the United States to buy and sell organs, which has resulted in a black market for organs. By 1990, many countries and the World Health Organization had issued similar bans. The Ethics Committee of the Transplantation Society issued a policy statement further supporting the ban on illegally buying and selling organs (Friedman & Friedman, 2006).

Who Should Receive the Organ?

According to the **American Transplant Foundation**, more than 121,000 people in the United States are currently on the waiting list for a lifesaving organ transplant and more than 6,500 die annually waiting for a transplant (American Transplant Foundation, 2016). In the United States, there is an organ waiting list managed by the **United Network for Organ Sharing**. Under the current UNOS, patients awaiting a transplant are assigned a priority based on medical need. For patients waiting for a heart transplant, those on life support or in intensive care have highest priority. Kidneys are allocated based on a point system maintained by the UNOS. Liver transplants also include guidelines on alcohol abuse, which often destroys livers. UNOS guidelines require six months of sobriety prior to a transplant. Should the alcoholic receive a liver transplant at all? Some organ transplant centers will not provide any liver transplants to any alcoholics (UNOS, 2016).

The UNOS has developed several types of calculators for each type of organ donation to determine survival rates. What is of interest is the types of calculators utilized when determining organ donations for pediatric patients. In 2010, the UNOS Ethics committee updated their transplantation policy. Justifications for organ priority is based on four areas: lifespan account, fair innings account, maximum principle, and the concept of utility. The lifespan account assesses lifespan and quality of life. The fair innings account assumes that every individual deserves to live a full life and the allocation of society's resources should try to maximize each individual's opportunity to reach a full life. The maximum principle states that when allocating a scarce resource such as an organ, inequalities will exist. Therefore, those who are the most disadvantaged should benefit the most. Finally, the concept of utility focuses on the greatest percentage of survival when receiving an organ (HHS, 2016).

Consent for Organ Donations

As stated in the previous paragraph, organ donations may also occur when a person dies. Depending on the state of residence, individuals may enroll in a program that gives permission for organ harvesting when they die, alleviating the pressure on families of having to make that decision to harvest the organs. However, some states require permission from the family, which places pressure on them. Some families feel it is unethical to donate their family member's body for science because of religious or personal philosophical reasons.

There has been a continued increase in donors over the decades. In 2015, there were 15,000 donors with 31,000 patients receiving an organ transplant. Despite these numbers, there continue to be long waiting lists for organs, and every day people die while waiting for a transplant (Organ Procurement and Transplantation Network, 2016).

In other parts of the world, countries use **presumed consent**, which means that if a parent does not actively oppose the transplantation, the procedure automatically occurs. In the United States, the consent must be actively received from the family first. As a result of presumed consent, those countries receive significantly more donations (Burrows, 2004). Is it an ethical policy to assume the family will consent to organ donations? Oftentimes, a family is frozen with grief and cannot make a coherent decision; however, more people do receive organ donations.

Organ Transplants from Family Member

Often, organ transplants may occur between two family members because it has been determined that the compatibility is very high, which would result in less risk for an organ to be rejected. An ethical issue with this situation is the pressure a family member feels from other family members to agree to give one of their organs to another member. Most parents would gladly donate organs to their sick offspring. What about siblings who don't like each other? Should they feel compelled to give an organ? Are they being pressured by other family members to go into surgery? The donors are also at risk. Any time surgery is performed there is a risk to the individual. Should physicians provide a "medical excuse" to the potential family donor as a way to rationalize their decision not to give their organ to a family member? The family member should not be coerced or forced to have the surgery.

Financial Payoff for Organ Donations

Living-donor organ transplantation is the only field in medicine in which two individuals are ultimately involved—the person donating the organ and the person receiving the organ. Because of the success of organ transplantation, more treatments are focusing on this alternative. As stated previously, the statistics indicate that the need for organ donations is far outstripping the number of donors. In the United States, 18 states offer a tax incentive to donate organs or marrow. These states are Arkansas, Georgia, Idaho, Iowa, Louisiana, Maryland, Massachusetts, Minnesota, Mississippi, New Mexico, New York, North Dakota, Ohio, Oklahoma, South Carolina, Utah, Virginia, and Wisconsin. Louisiana residents who donate are allowed to take a tax credit of as much as $10,000 on their state income taxes for travel, lodging, and lost wages related to the donation process (American Transplant Foundation, 2016).

Also, as a result of the increasing need for organs, a **black market**, which is an illegal form of commerce, has developed for the buying and selling of organs. The World Health Organization indicates that there are 10,000 illegal organ purchases worldwide on an annual basis, which is considered a conservative estimate. In China, 11,000 organs are harvested from political prisoners each year without anesthetic. There are massive illegal kidney transplants due to the rise of diabetes worldwide (Tomlinson, 2015). From a supply and demand perspective, when there is a scarcity of supply, the demand and the price for the demand will continue to escalate.

As a result of the inequity of healthcare costs between the United States and other countries, the concept of **medical tourism** or "medical value travel" has evolved. U.S. organ transplants can cost $100,000, but are considerably less expensive overseas. IndUShealth and Global Health Administrators, Inc. have collaborated with insurance companies to arrange for U.S. residents to obtain medical treatment in India. United Group Programs offers living and deceased organ donor transplants from foreign countries such as Thailand (Bramstedt & Xu, 2007). Medical tourism has become so popular that the first medical tourism association was formed. The Medical Tourism Association, also referred to as the Medical Travel Association (MTA), is the first membership-based international nonprofit trade association for the medical tourism and global healthcare industry, comprised of international hospitals, healthcare providers, medical travel facilitators, insurance companies, and other affiliated companies and members with the common goal of promoting quality health care worldwide (Medical Tourism Association, 2016). Although these programs are cost effective, concerns about follow-up care or complications may determine the effectiveness of these medical value plans. Are these programs ethical? Are insurance companies focusing on cost rather than safety of the patient? Is the patient fully aware of the risk of these types of options?

Xenotransplantation

Another type of transplantation is **xenotransplantation**, which is the transfer of organs from one species to another. This has evolved as a result of the shortage of human organs available for donation. The first xenotransplantation was the transfer of a baboon heart into a five-pound infant in 1984. Baby Fae survived three weeks before the baboon heart was rejected (Ascension Health, 2016). Since that time, several other xenotransplants have occurred using pig livers and hearts. Pigs are the preferred choice for xenotransplantation. There have been few successful xenotransplants because of the high risk of rejection.

Although xenotransplantation is promising, the ethical objection from some observers is that we are killing animals for these procedures, which are considered experimental. Is there a difference between killing animals for food and killing them for organ transplants? Although we may be ultimately saving lives, for some individuals, xenotransplantation is not ethical. Another issue is the transmission of animal disease to humans. If xenotransplantation is to be successful, it is important that the animals be screened for any diseases humans may contract, such as rabies and viruses. The Food and Drug Administration is responsible for regulating xenotransplantation activities.

▶ Conclusion

Several ethical issues involving the healthcare industry and its stakeholders are discussed in this chapter. There are two components of ethics in health care: medical ethics, which focus on the treatment of the patient; and bioethics, which focus on technology and how it is utilized in health care. The most important stakeholder in health care is the patient. The most important relationship with this stakeholder is his or her healthcare provider. Their relationship is impacted by the other stakeholders in the industry, including the government, which regulates healthcare provider activities; the insurance companies who interact with both provider and patient; and healthcare facilities, such as hospitals or managed care facilities, with which the physician has a relationship. All of these stakeholders can influence how a healthcare provider interacts with the patient because they have an interest in the outcome. For that reason, many organizations that

represent these stakeholders have developed codes of ethics so individuals are provided guidance for ethical behavior. Codes of ethics for the physicians and other healthcare providers, nurses, pharmaceutical companies, and medical equipment companies emphasize how these stakeholders should interact with both the healthcare providers and patients. These codes of conduct also apply to the relationship between employees in a healthcare facility. The issue of workplace bullying has been a continued problem for many years. The Joint Commission issued a statement and guidelines for workplace behavior in the healthcare industry. The Joint Commission indicated that this type of behavior can be destructive, resulting in medical errors.

Another major area of ethics is the treatment of patients who are dying. Euthanasia, including physician-assisted suicide, illegal in all states but Oregon, Washington, and most recently, Vermont, has been a controversial patient issue for years. Some people support euthanasia because they feel it is the individual's right to choose when they want to end their life and they should have assistance from a physician, if needed. Opponents feel it is unethical because it is the responsibility of a physician to save a life, or not to take a life. This issue is tied into advance directives, which a patient gives to the provider requesting that certain treatments be administered or not. If the patient is incompetent, advance directives provide guidance on how the provider should treat the patient at the end of his or her life.

Another area of ethical discussion is organ transplantation. There are not enough organ donors in the United States, thereby creating a long waiting list. With limited supply, the ethical dilemma of organ transplants is how to determine who should receive an organ. For example, the famous New York Yankee baseball player, Mickey Mantle, a long-time alcoholic, received a liver transplant, which he needed as a result of his alcoholism. There was a public outcry because people felt that he received the liver because he was famous. Although the doctors explained that was not the case, people were upset because they felt that his addiction caused the liver failure. Why should he receive a new liver after he damaged his first one? As a result of designer or donor babies, children must be included in the transplant discussion. Should parents have another child specifically to save the ill child's life? Children designated as donor babies may have emotional issues because they will eventually be aware that they were created specifically for their sibling's transplant needs.

When Dolly the sheep was cloned in 1995, she created an international furor. There are diametrically opposed views on cloning. Opponents feel that cloning takes the natural procreation process and turns it into a scientific experiment. Supporters feel that the scientific community has provided an opportunity to recreate a specimen, at will, with the desired genes.

And, finally, it is necessary to address the ethical foundation of our healthcare system. With millions of uninsured citizens in the United States, is it unethical that there is no universal healthcare system? The United States is one of very few industrialized nations that has no universal healthcare coverage. Other nations have

stated that health care is a right, not a privilege. Is it unethical for the United States to have a system that does not provide for all citizens? The recent legal battles over the implementation of the individual mandate to purchase health insurance indicates the various beliefs of access to healthcare insurance to most citizens. This text cannot provide answers to ethical situations because ethics are viewed differently by each individual. This chapter can only provide questions for readers so they can assess their ethical viewpoint as it relates to the healthcare industry.

Wrap-Up

Vocabulary

Advance directives
Advanced Medical Technology Association
Alternative reproductive methods
American College of Healthcare Executives (ACHE)
American College of Physicians and Harvard Pilgrim Health Care Ethics Program
American Nurses Association
American Transplant Foundation
Autonomy
Beneficence
Bioethics
Black market
Carrier testing
Cloning
Codes of ethics
Collegial model
Common rule
Contractual model
Diagnostic testing
Dignity
Duty to treat
Effectiveness

Engineering model
Ethical standards
Ethics
Euthanasia
Genetic testing
Healthcare ethical dilemma
Human Genome Project
Informed consent
Institutional Review Boards (IRBs)
Justice
Lateral violence
Medical ethics
Medical tourism
Minimal infringement
Nonmalfeasance
Nonvoluntary euthanasia
Nuffield Council on Bioethics
Oregon Death with Dignity Act
Paternalism
Preimplantation genetic diagnosis (PGD)
Pharmaceutical Research and Manufacturers of America
Pharmacogenomic testing
Physician-assisted suicide

Physician Payment Sunshine Act
Predictive and asymptomatic testing
Prenatal testing
Presumed consent
Priestly model
Procreation
Proportionality
Public education
Reproductive cloning
Research cloning
Research genetic testing
Respect for autonomy
Stakeholder
Stakeholder management
Stem cells
Stewardship model
The Joint Commission
Therapeutic cloning
Transplantation
United Network for Organ Sharing (UNOS)
Voluntary euthanasia
Workplace bullying
Xenotransplantation

References

Adams, A. (1992). *Bullying at work*. London: Virago Press: 1–20.
Adelaide Center for Bioethics and Culture. (2016). Healthcare, Retrieved from http://www.bioethics.org.au/Resources/Resource%20Topics/Healthcare.html
Advanced Medical Technology Association (AMTA). (2016). Code of ethics. Retrieved from http://advamed.org/issues/code-of-ethics
American College of Healthcare Executives (ACHE). (2016). About ACHE. Retrieved from http://www.ache.org/aboutache.cfm

American Medical Association (AMA). (2016a). Medical Code of Ethics. Retrieved from http://www.ama-assn.org/ama/pub/physician-resources/medical-ethics/code-medical-ethics/opinion10015.page
American Medical Association (AMA). (2016b). Toolkit for physician financial transparency reports (Sunshine Act). Retrieved from https://www.ama-assn.org/ama/pub/advocacy/topics/sunshine-act-and-physician-financial-transparency-reports.page
American Nurses Association (ANA). (2016a). Lateral violence and bullying in nursing. Retrieved from http://nursingworld

.org/Mobile/Nursing-Factsheets/lateral-violence-and
-bullying-in-nursing.html

ANA. (2016b). Ethics. Retrieved from http://www.nursingworld
.org/MainMenuCategories/EthicsStandards.aspx

ANA. (2016b). Incivility, bullying and workplace violence. Retrieved
from http://www.nursingworld.org/MainMenuCategories
/WorkplaceSafety/Healthy-Nurse/bullyingworkplaceviolence
/Incivility-Bullying-and-Workplace-Violence.html

American Transplant Foundation. (2016). Facts and myths.
Retrieved from http://www.americantransplantfoundation
.org/about-transplant/facts-and-myths/

Ascension Health. (2016). Cases. Retrieved from http://www
.ascensionhealth.org/ethics/public/cases/case4.asp

Ayoko, O., Callan, V., & Hartel, C. (2003). Workplace conflict, bullying and counterproductive behaviors. *International Journal
of Organizational Analysis*, 11, 283–301.

Baylis, F. (2002). Human cloning: Three mistakes and an alternative. *Journal of Medicine and Philosophy*, 27(3), 319–337.

Beauchamp, T., & Childress, J. (2001). *Principles of biomedical ethics* (5th ed.). Oxford: Oxford University Press.

Berman, R. (2005). Lethal legislation. *Robert Kennedy School
Review*, 6, 13–18.

Bilefsky, D. (2013, April 29). Five convicted in Kosovo organ trafficking. New York Times. Retrieved from http://www.nytimes.
com/2013/04/30/world/europe/in-kosovo-5-are-convicted
-in-organ-trafficking.html?_r=0

Bramstedt, K., & Xu, J. (2007). Checklist: Passport, plane ticket, organ
transplant. *American Journal of Transplantation*, 7, 1698–1701.

Buchanan, D. (2008). Autonomy, paternalism and justice: Ethical
priorities in public health. *American Journal of Public Health*,
98, 15–21.

Burkett, L. (2007). Medical tourism. Concerns, benefits, and the
American legal perspective. *The Journal of Legal Medicine*, 28,
223–245.

Burrows, L. (2004). Selling organs for transplantation. *The Mount
Sinai Journal of Medicine*, 71(4), 251–254.

Campbell, E. (2007). Doctors and drug companies—Scrutinizing
influential relationships. *New England Journal of Medicine*,
357, 18, 1796–1796.

Carroll, A., & Buchholtz, A. (2015). Business society: Ethics and
stakeholder management (9th ed.). Mason, OH: Thomson/
Southwestern.

Centers for Disease Control and Prevention (CDC). (2016).
Health insurance coverage. Retrieved from http://www.cdc
.gov/nchs/fastats/hinsure.htm

Childress, J., Faden, R., & Gaare, R. (2002). Public health ethics:
Mapping the terrain. *Journal of Law, Medicine & Ethics*, 30,
170–178.

The Coalition of Americans for Research Ethics. (2016). Do no
harm. Retrieved from http://www.stemcellresearch.org

Coleman, C., Bouesseau, M., & Reis, A. (2008). The contribution of
ethics to public health. *Bulletin of the World Health Organization*,
86(8), 578–589.

Davis, R. (2008). More elderly patients are having transplantation surgery. Retrieved from http://www.usatoday.com/news
/health/2008-02-04-transplant_N.htm

Dayal, M., & Zarek, S. (2008). Preimplantation genetic diagnosis. Retrieved from http://emedicine.medscape.com/article
/273415-overview

Death with Dignity Act, 1994, Oregon. (2016). Retrieved from
https://public.health.oregon.gov/ProviderPartnerResources
/EvaluationResearch/DeathwithDignityAct/Documents
/requirements.pdf

Death with Dignity Act, 2009, Washington. (2016). Retrieved from
http://www.doh.wa.gov/portals/1/Documents/Pubs/422-109
-DeathWithDignityAct2014.pdf

Djurkovic, N., McCormack, D., & Casimir, G. (2008). Workplace
bullying and intention to leave: The modernizing effect of perceived organizational support. *Human Resource Management
Journal*, 18(4), 405–420.

Ethics Resource Center. (2016). The PLUS decision making
model. Retrieved from http://www.ethics.org/resource/plus
-decision-making-model

Exit International. (2016). Voluntary euthanasia and assisted suicide information by Exit International. Retrieved from http
://www.exitinternational.net

Food and Drug Administration (FDA). (2016). Information sheet
guidance for institutional review boards, clinical investigators,
and sponsors. Retrieved from http://www.fda.gov/oc/ohrt
/irbs/facts.html#IRBOrg

Friedman, E., & Friedman, A. (2006). Payment for donor kidneys:
Pros and cons. *International Society of Nephrology*, January,
960–962.

Gillon, R. (1994). Principles of medical ethics. *British Medical
Journal*, 309, 184.

Giuliano, K. (1997). Organ transplants: Tackling the tough ethical
questions. *Nursing*, 27, 34–40.

Hoel, H., Faragher, B., & Cooper, C. (2004). Bullying is detri-
mental to health but all bullying behaviors are not necessarily
equally damaging. *British Journal of Guidance & Counseling*,
32(3), 367–387.

Kaplan Survey. (2014). Retrieved from http://www.workplacebul
lying.org/kaplan/

Keashly, L. (2001). Interpersonal and systemic aspects of emotional abuse at work: The target's perspective. *Violence and
Victims*, 16, 233–268.

Korenman, S.G. (2009). Teaching the responsible conduct of
research in humans. Retrieved from http://ori.hhs.gov/education
/products/ucla/chapter2/page04b.htm

LaVan, H., & Martin, W. (2007). Bullying in the U.S. workplace:
Normative and process-oriented ethical approaches. *Journal of
Business Ethics*, 83, 147–165.

Medical Tourism Association (MTA). (2016). About the MTA.
Retrieved from http://www.medicaltourismassociation.com
/en/about-the-MTA.html

Mehlman, M., & Berg, J. (2008). Human subjects' protections in
biomedical enhancement research: Assessing risk and benefit
and obtaining informed consent. Journal of Law, *Medicine &
Ethics*, 36(3), 546–559.

Miller, R. (2006). *Problems in health care law* (9th ed.). Sudbury,
MA: Jones and Bartlett.

Minding the Workplace. (2009). Workplace bullying in healthcare I: The Joint Commission standards. Retrieved from http
://newworkplace.wordpress.com/2009/12/15/workplace-bullying
-in-healthcare-i-the-joint-commission-standards/

Morgan, S., Harrison, T., Long, S., Afifi, W., Stephenson, M., &
Reichert, T. (2005). Family discussions about organ donations:
How the media influences opinions about organ donations.
Clinical Transplant, 19, 674–682.

National Human Genome Research Institute. (2016). Regulation of genetic tests. Retrieved from http://www.genome
.gov/10002335

Niles, N. (2011). *Basics of the U.S. health care system*. Sudbury,
MA: Jones and Bartlett.

Niles, N. (2013). *Basic concepts of health care human resource management*. Sudbury, MA: Jones and Bartlett: 50.

Notable Names Database. (2016). Jack Kevorkian. Retrieved from http://www.nndb.com/people/272/000023203/

Nuffield Council on Bioethics Report. (2016). Public health: Ethical issues guide to the report. Retrieved from http://www.nuffieldbioethics.org/fileLibrary/pdf/Public_Health_-_short_guide.pdf

Oak Ridge National Laboratory (ORNL). (2016). Human Genome Project information. Retrieved from http://www.ornl.gov/sci/techresources/Human_Genome/home.shtml

Oddo, A. (2001). Health care ethics: A patient-centered decision model. *Journal of Business Ethics*, 29, 126.

O'Reilly, K.B. (2009). Five people die under new Washington physician-assisted suicide law. Retrieved from http://www.amednews.com/article/20090706/profession/307069977/7

Organ Procurement and Transplantation Network, Health Resources and Services Administration, U.S. Department of Health & Human Services. (2016). Donors recovered in U.S. by donor type. Retrieved from http://optn.transplant.hrsa.gov/latestData/viewDataReports.asp

Peng, T. (2008). Opening the books. Retrieved from http://www.newsweek.com/id/160894?from=rss?nav=slate

Pharmaceutical Research and Manufacturers of America (PhRMA). (2016). About PhRMA. Retrieved from http://www.phrma.org/about

Povar, C., Blumen, H., Daniel, J., Daub, S., Evans, L., Holm, R., Campbell, A. (2004). Ethics in practice: Managed care and the changing health care environment. *American College of Physicians*, 4(2), 131–136.

Scheper-Hughes, N. (2003). Keeping an eye on the global traffic in human organs. *Lancet*, 361, 1645–1648.

Sullivan, D. (2005). Euthanasia versus letting die: Christian decision-making in terminal patients. Ethics and Medicine, 21(2), 109–118.

Sullivan, D. (2006). Stem cells 101—An audio/MP3 version. Retrieved from http://www.bioethics.com/?page_id=533

Sultz, H., & Young, K. (2006). *Health care USA: Understanding its organization and delivery* (5th ed.). Sudbury, MA: Jones and Bartlett.

University of Miami Ethics Programs. (2016). Schiavo timeline, part 1. Retrieved from http://www.miami.edu/index.php/ethics/projects/schiavo/schiavo_timeline/

Taylor, P. (1975). *Principles of ethics: An introduction to ethics* (2nd ed.). Encino, CA: Dickinson.

The Joint Commission. (July 9, 2008). Behaviors that undermine a culture of safety. Sentinel Event Alert, 40. Retrieved from http://www.jointcommission.org/assets/1/18/SEA_40.PDF

United Network for Organ Sharing (UNOS). (2016). FAQ. Retrieved from https://www.unos.org/transplantation/faqs/

Tomlinson, S. (2015). Inside the illegal hospitals performing thousands of black market organ transplants every year for $200,000 a time. Retrieved from http://www.dailymail.co.uk/news/article-3031784/Inside-illegal-hospitals-performing-thousands-black-market-organ-transplants-year-200-000-time.html

Vartia, M. (2001). Consequences of workplace bullying with respect to the well-being of its targets and the observers or bullying. *Scandinavian Journal of Work Environment and Health*, 27, 63–59.

Veatch, R. (1972). Medical ethics: Professional or universal. *Harvard Theological Review*, 65, 531–559.

Washington State Department of Health. (2016). Washington State Department of Health 2012 Death with Dignity Act Report: Executive summary. Retrieved from http://www.doh.wa.gov/portals/1/Documents/Pubs/422-109-DeathWithDignityAct2012.pdf

Wazana, A. (2000). Physicians and the pharmaceutical industry: Is a gift ever just a gift? *Journal of American Medical Association*, 283, 373–380.

Woloschak, G. (2003). Transplantation: Biomedical and ethical concerns raised by the cloning stem cell debate. Zygon, 8, 599–704.

Workplace Bullying Institute (2016). Healthy Workplace Bill. Retrieved from http://healthyworkplacebill.org/

Wynia, M. (2007). Ethics and public health emergencies: Encouraging responsibility. *The American Journal of Bioethics*, 7, 1–4.

Xue, J., Ma, J., & Louis, T. (2001). Forecast of the number of patients with end-stage renal disease in the United States to the year 2010. *Journal of American Sociological Nephrology*, 12, 2753–2758.

Yamada, D. C. (2004). Crafting a legislative response to workplace bullying. Employee Rights and Employment Policy Journal, 8, 475. Retrieved from http://ssrn.com/abstract=1303725

▶ Notes

▶ **Student Activity 12-1**

In Your Own Words

Based on this chapter, please provide an explanation of the following concepts in your own words. DO NOT RECITE the text.

Paternalism:

_____

_____

Medical tourism:

_____

_____

Therapeutic cloning:

_____

_____

Stem cell:

_____

_____

Transplantation:

_____

_____

Xenotransplantation:

_____

_____

Presumed consent:

_____

_____

Autonomy:

_____

_____

Stewardship model:

_____

_____

Institutional Review Boards:

_____

_____

▶ ## Student Activity 12-2

Real-Life Applications: Case Scenario One

A friend from high school, pregnant with her third child, moved into your neighborhood. She told you that her eldest child was very ill and required a bone marrow transplant. There were no matching donors on the national list. She and her husband decided to have a baby who could be used to save her other child. She asked what you thought of her actions. Before making any statements that could hurt your friend, you decide to do some research on the topic.

Activity

(1) Explain this type of procedure and what the procedure entails, (2) identify any ethical issues associated with this type of procedure, and (3) provide an opinion on this procedure—would you do it or not and why?

Responses

_____

_____

_____

_____

_____

_____

_____

_____

_____

_____

_____

_____

_____

_____

_____

_____

Case Scenario Two

You need a back operation but cannot afford your cost share of the operation. You have heard that other countries may offer less expensive medical procedures. You decide to investigate this option.

Activity

Perform an Internet search and use textbook information on medical tourism. Locate two countries that offer lower-cost surgeries. Write a report and submit to the class.

Responses

_____

_____

_____

_____

_____

_____

_____

_____

_____

_____

_____

_____

_____

_____

_____

_____

_____

Case Scenario Three

One of your best friends is on the waiting list for a new liver. According to current research, there is a huge waiting list for organ donations. Several states have offered tax incentives to encourage organ donation. You are unsure of how to encourage her to be optimistic.

Activity

You decide to do research on tax incentives in the different states and other options to encourage organ donation.

Responses

_____

_____

_____

_____

_____

_____

_____

_____

_____

_____

_____

_____

_____

_____

_____

_____

_____

Case Scenario Four

You and your friend were discussing euthanasia and whether it is an ethical procedure. Your friend does not believe in it but you feel it is an option depending on the circumstance. You think of your great grandmother who is terminally ill but is in pain and is on life support.

Activity

Using the textbook and the Internet, research both the pros and cons of euthanasia.

Responses

_____

_____

_____

_____

_____

_____

_____

_____

_____

_____

_____

_____

_____

_____

_____

_____

_____

_____

▶ **Student Activity 12-3**

Internet Exercises

Write your answers in the space provided.

- Visit each of the websites listed here.
- Name the organization.
- Locate the organization's mission statement on the website.
- Provide a brief overview of the activities of the organization.
- How do these organizations participate in the U.S. healthcare system?

Websites

http://www.nursingworld.org

Organization Name:

_____

_____

Mission Statement:

_____

_____

_____

Overview of Activities:

_____

_____

_____

Importance of Organization to U.S. Health Care:

_____

_____

_____

http://www.thehastingscenter.org

Organization Name:

_____

_____

Mission Statement:

_____

_____

_____

Overview of Activities:

_____

_____

_____

Importance of Organization to U.S. Health Care:

_____

_____

_____

http://www.phrma.org

Organization Name:

_____

_____

Mission Statement:

_____

_____

_____

Overview of Activities:

_____

_____

_____

Importance of Organization to U.S. Health Care:

_____

_____

_____

http://www.procon.org

Organization Name:

_____

_____

Mission Statement:

_____

_____

_____

Overview of Activities:

_____

_____

_____

Importance of Organization to U.S. Health Care:

_____

_____

_____

http://www.ornl.gov

Organization Name:

_____

_____

Mission Statement:

_____

_____

_____

Overview of Activities:

_____

_____

_____

Importance of Organization to U.S. Health Care:

_____

_____

_____

http://stemcells.nih.gov

Organization Name:

_____

_____

Mission Statement:

_____

_____

_____

Overview of Activities:

_____

_____

_____

Importance of Organization to U.S. Health Care:

_____

_____

_____

▶ **Student Activity 12-4**

Discussion Questions

The following are suggested discussion questions for this chapter.

1. If you were going to develop a code of ethics for this class, what behavior components should be included?

_____

_____

_____

_____

_____

_____

_____

2. Do you believe in cloning? Do you think humans should be cloned? Defend your answer.

_____

_____

_____

_____

_____

_____

_____

3. What is your definition of ethics? What do you think are some unethical situations in the healthcare industry?

    _____

    _____

    _____

    _____

    _____

    _____

    _____

4. What is workplace bullying? Have you witnessed this behavior in the workplace? Do you consider this behavior unethical? Defend your answer.

    _____

    _____

    _____

    _____

    _____

    _____

    _____

5. What is voluntary euthanasia? Do you believe there should be national legislation to make it legal in all states? Defend your answer.

    _____

    _____

    _____

    _____

    _____

    _____

    _____

▶ **Student Activity 12-5**

Current Events

Perform an Internet search and find a current events topic over the past three years that is related to this chapter. Provide a summary of the article and the link to the article and why the article relates to the chapter.

_____

_____

_____

_____

_____

_____

_____

_____

_____

_____

_____

_____

_____

_____

_____

_____

_____

_____

_____

_____

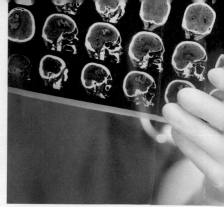

CHAPTER 13

Mental Health Issues

▸ Introduction

According to the World Health Organization, mental wellness or mental health is an integral and essential component of health. It is a state of well-being in which an individual can cope with normal stressors, can work productively, and is able to make a contribution to his or her community. Mental health behavioral disorders can be caused by biological, psychological, and personality factors. By 2020, behavioral health disorders will surpass all physiological diseases as a major cause of disability worldwide (World Health Organization, 2016). Mental disorders are the leading cause of disability in the United States. Mental illnesses can impact individuals of any age, race, religion, or income. According to the Substance Abuse and Mental Health Services Administration's 2014 National Survey, an estimated 43.6 million (18.1%) Americans age 18 or older experienced some form of mental illness. In 2014, 20.2 million adults (8.4%) had a substance use disorder. Anxiety disorders are the most common type of mental disorders, followed by depressive disorders. Different mental disorders are more likely to begin and occur at different stages in life and are thus more prevalent in certain age groups. Lifetime anxiety disorders generally have the earliest age of first onset, most commonly around age 6 (SAMHSA, 2016). Although mental health is a disease that requires medical care, its characteristics set it apart from traditional medical care. U.S. Surgeon General David Satcher released a landmark report in 1999 on mental health and illness, *Mental Health: A Report of the Surgeon General*. The Surgeon General's report on mental health defines **mental disorders** as conditions that alter thinking processes, moods, or behavior and result in dysfunction or stress. The condition can be psychological or biological in nature. The most common conditions include **phobias**, which are excessive fear of objects or activities; substance abuse; and affective disorders, which are emotional states such as depression. Severe mental illness includes schizophrenia, major depression, and psychosis. Obsessive-compulsive disorders (OCD), intellectual disabilities, Alzheimer's disease, and dementia are also considered mentally disabling conditions. According to the report, mental health ranks second to heart disease as a limitation on health and productivity (U.S. Public Health Service, 1999). People who have mental disorders often exhibit feelings of anxiety or may have hallucinations or feelings of sadness or fear that can limit normal functioning in their daily life. Because the causes or etiologies of mental health disorders are less defined and less understood compared to traditional medical problems, interventions are less developed than in other areas of medicine (Anderson, Rice, & Kominski, 2007). This chapter will discuss the following topics: the history of the U.S. mental healthcare system, a background of healthcare professionals, mental healthcare law, insurance coverage for mental health, barriers to mental health care, the populations at risk for mental disorders, the types of mental health disorders as classified by the American Psychiatric Association's **Diagnostic and Statistical Manual of Mental Disorders (DSM)**, liability issues associated with mental health care, an analysis of the mental healthcare system, and guidelines and recommendations to improve U.S. mental health care.

▸ History of U.S. Mental Health Care

Over the past three centuries, the mental health system has consisted of a patchwork of services that has become very fragmented (Regier et al., 1993). Initially, mentally ill individuals were relegated to care by their families. State governments built **insane asylums**, later known as hospitals. In the mid-18th century, the state of Pennsylvania opened a hospital in Philadelphia where the mentally ill were housed in the basement. During this period, Virginia was the first state to build an asylum in its capital city, Williamsburg. If the mentally ill were not cared for by their families or sent to an asylum, they were found in jails or almshouse. It was not until the 19th century that the mentally ill were treated with sensitivity. This **moral treatment** approach was used earlier in Europe with success. Mental health patients in hospitals were treated while participating in work and educational activities. The first mental health reformers in the United States were Dorothea Dix and Horace Mann, who crusaded for this moral movement by convincing the public that some mentally ill patients can be treated in a controlled environment outside the confines of an asylum. Asylums should be focused on housing mentally ill individuals with chronic, untreatable conditions. During this period, more states built more asylums, which became overcrowded. It is important to note that the local governments were responsible for funding the care of asylum residents, which resulted in deteriorating conditions and exposure of the patients to inhumane treatment. Between 1894 and World War I, state care acts were passed that mandated state funding for treatment. Asylums were renamed mental hospitals. Psychiatric units were also opened in general hospitals to promote mental health as part of general health care (Regier et al., 1993).

After World War I, many war veterans returned home with mental disorders, or what is now known as PTSD (posttraumatic stress disorder), because of their war experiences. It was not until the 1930s that medications for mental health treatment became available. However, other controversial treatments were used, such as **electrotherapy**. Brain surgery or lobotomies became a method to treat the mentally ill. World War II further focused the government on mental health issues and the **National Institute of Mental Health** (NIMH) was created. Governmental funding was awarded for mental health training and research. The U.S. Department of Veterans Affairs (VA) established psychiatric hospitals and clinics. During this period, most health care focused on inpatient services. The VA also developed mental health disorder categories in order to better treat war veterans. By the mid-1950s, over 500,000 mental health patients were being treated in government mental health hospitals. In 1952, the **American Psychiatric Association** published the first *DSM*, which was coordinated with the World Health Organization's (WHO) International Classification of Disease (American Psychiatric Association, 2016a) to encourage acceptance of mental health disorders.

Finally, the first psychoactive medication was developed that allowed outpatient treatment of mentally disabled patients. In 1955, the **U.S. Commission on Mental Health** was established. It investigated the quality of mental hospitals and allocated funding for outpatient facilities. As more **psychotropic medications** were developed, Congress provided more funding allocations for community-based services. Medicaid, Medicare, Supplemental Security Income (SSI), Social Security, and disability insurance became accessible for mental health care (Grob, 1983, 1994; Sultz & Young, 2006).

During the 1960s and 1970s, community mental health centers were developed and supported by the federal government. Most of the funding focused on the less severe mentally ill who could live normally with outpatient services. In the late 1970s, President Carter appointed a Presidential Committee on Mental Health, which had limited success; however, Medicaid payments for outpatient mental health services were increased. By 1990, most mental health services were offered as outpatient services. Research in the 1990s indicated that the reason people did not seek assistance for mental health disorders was shame and embarrassment. The Mental Health Parity Act was passed in 1996 to ensure adequate coverage for mental health illnesses and that annual lifetime reimbursement limits on mental health services were similar to other medical benefits.

In 2002, President George W. Bush established the **New Freedom Commission on Mental Health**, which was charged with implementing an analytical study on the U.S. mental health service system and developing recommendations to improve the public mental health system that could be implemented at the federal, state, and local levels. This was the first study performed since 1978 when President Jimmy Carter's Mental Health Commission's report was published. In 2003, the New Freedom Commission issued a final report that contained nearly 20 recommendations that focused primarily on mental illness recovery, including a comprehensive approach to mental health care, such as the screening of mental illness for children and other high-risk populations (APA, 2003).

The **Mental Health Parity and Addiction Equity Act of 2008** further supported mental health care by requiring insurance plans to offer mental health benefits and cost sharing similar to those of traditional medical benefits. Over the past 15 years, increased funding has increased the quality of mental health services. As with the 1996 act, there were loopholes that reduced the effectiveness of the 2008 act. The Obama administration recognized the importance of funding mental health initiatives, including teacher training programs for mental health awareness (Mohney, 2013). The Obama administration also issued the final rule on guidance to implement the regulations regarding the 2008 act. The final rule requires transparency of health plans on how they interpret medical coverage for mental health problems. The final rule should strengthen the impact of the 2008 act. The final rule applies to health insurance plans which became effective on July 1, 2014 (Moran, 2013).

▶ Background of Mental Health Services

Mental Health Professionals

Mental health problems impact not only the individual but family members and friends as well. As a result of the vast impact of mental health disabilities, behavioral services are provided by psychiatrists, psychologists, social workers, nurses, counselors, and therapists (Shi & Singh, 2008). Social workers receive training in counseling, normally a master's degree, and can provide support for an individual with a mental health disability. Family and vocational counselors and recreational therapists may also be involved in the treatment plan. Because mental illness often is complex and impacts many different aspects of life, often it is useful to have a variety of mental health professionals available for support and treatment. Most of these mental health professionals provide outpatient or ambulatory care for the mentally ill. Inpatient care may be offered in the psychiatric units of a hospital, mental hospitals, or substance abuse facilities (Pointer, Williams, Isaacs, & Knickman, 2007).

Psychiatrists are specialty physicians who can prescribe medication and admit patients to hospitals. **Psychologists**, who also participate in the treatment of mental health, cannot prescribe drugs but provide different types of therapy. Social workers focus on mental health counseling. Nurses may also specialize in psychiatric care. There may be additional counselors and therapists who participate in the treatment of the mentally disabled.

However, there are liability issues that mental health professionals may face. A recent study (Woody, 2008) indicated that there were seven reasons mental health professionals are at high risk for liability and complaints:

- When mental health professionals provide services to both children and their families they are at risk for more complaints from their patients regarding care. Families may be wary when a mental health professional provides services to their children.
- Because of increased governmental regulation of the licensing of practitioners, professionals no longer have a say in establishing standards for care.
- The litigious U.S. society has included the mental health profession in their complaints.
- Patients have become more distrustful of their providers and are not always willing to adhere to treatment guidelines. If they are not cured, they blame the provider.
- Managed care has imposed restrictions on the number of sessions, resulting in increased liability of providers.
- Because of the high cost of health care, more patients are abandoning their healthcare treatment, which has reduced revenues. As a result, practitioners have developed cost-cutting practices that may result in more errors.
- Mental health practitioners are ignoring their professional liability issues and do not hire professionals to resolve their problems. As a result, many practitioners are ill prepared to defend their actions and are found liable.

Mental Health Commitment Law

Commitment laws are laws that enable family members, law enforcement, or healthcare professionals to commit a person to a facility or a treatment program. **Voluntary commitment** occurs when people commit themselves willingly to receive care. If a person voluntarily commits for treatment, that person can leave of his or her own free will. **Involuntary commitment** occurs when people are forced to receive treatment or are committed to a facility against their wishes. A hearing must be held to prove the person is dangerous to himself or herself or others or is suffering from a mental disorder. If they are committed, they are not free to leave (Pointer et al., 2007). An involuntary commitment may occur as an outpatient mental health treatment plan. This type of involuntary commitment is normally a court-ordered program for mental health services.

Managed Care Behavioral Organizations

Mental health services are provided by distinct components of the healthcare system. There are specialty healthcare providers, as explained previously, such as psychiatrists and psychologists. However, the primary care provider (e.g., family physicians, internists) is often the initial contact for the mentally ill and may often serve as the treatment provider. An important component of mental health care is the social service sector, such as social service workers and counselors, who provide assistance to both the individual and the family. Finally, there is a growing sector of nonprofit groups and organizations for the mentally ill that provide education and support, including the **National Alliance on Mental Illness (NAMI)** and **Mental Health America**. These components are known as the **de facto mental health service system** (**FIGURE 13-1**) (U.S. Public Health Service, 1999).

Private insurance coverage for mental health conditions and substance abuse or behavioral care is less generous than the coverage for traditional medical care. Many small companies do not offer mental health coverage. Employers routinely impose higher employee copayments and may limit outpatient visit reimbursement. The **Mental Health Parity Act of 1996**, enacted in 1998, provided the mental health field with more equity for health insurance coverage to ensure mental health services were being reimbursed at the same level as traditional medical care. The Mental Health Parity and Addiction Equity Act of 2008 requires group health insurance plans (those with more than 50 insured employees) that offer coverage for mental illness and substance use disorders to provide those benefits in a no more restrictive way than all other medical and surgical procedures covered by the plan. It does not require

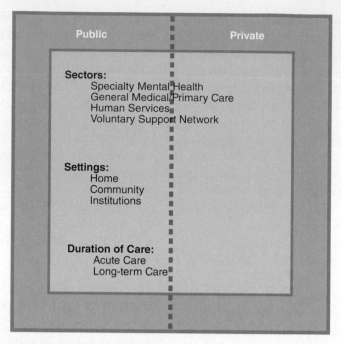

FIGURE 13-1 **The De Facto Mental Health Service System.**

U.S. Public Health Service. (1999). Mental health: A report of the Surgeon General. Retrieved from http://mentalhealth.samhsa.gov/features/surgeongeneralreport/chapter2/sec7.asp

group health plans to provide mental health and substance use disorder benefits, but when plans do provide these benefits, mental health and substance use disorder benefits must be provided at levels that are no lower and with treatment limitations that are no more restrictive than would be the case for the other medical and surgical benefits offered by the plan (SAMHSA, 2016b). Many mental health advocates were dismayed by the weakness of this legislation, so in November 2013, a final rule was issued for the 2008 act that includes the following consumer protections:

- "Ensuring that parity applies to intermediate levels of care received in residential treatment or intensive outpatient settings;
- Clarifying the scope of the transparency required by health plans, including the disclosure rights of plan participants, to ensure compliance with the law;
- Clarifying that parity applies to all plan standards, including geographic limits, facility-type limits, and network adequacy; and
- Eliminating the provision that allowed insurance companies to make an exception to parity requirements for certain benefits on the basis of 'clinically appropriate standards of care,' which clinical experts advised was not necessary and which is confusing and open to potential abuse" (MHPAEA, 2016).

Medicare and Medicaid are a large source of mental health funding, particularly for individuals with serious mental disabilities who often cannot work. Medicaid is the single largest payer for state-financed mental health care (Shi & Singh, 2008). Medicare does impose a 50% copayment rate for outpatient services other than initial diagnoses and drug management. The normal copayment rate is 20% for traditional medical care (Anderson, Rice, & Kominski, 2007). However, as a result of cost concerns over mental health care, managed care organizations contracted with external vendors that focused on mental health care. These external vendors became known as **managed behavioral healthcare organizations**.

There is still a stigma attached to being mentally disabled. Individuals may be embarrassed to admit they might have a mental health problem and ignore it, or they might not understand what is happening to them. Families can be embarrassed by having a relative who is mentally disabled. A patient's primary care provider may also be uncomfortable dealing with a patient that may have a mental health disorder.

Who Are the Mentally Ill?

The Diagnostic and Statistical Manual of Mental Disorders (DSM) is a guide published by the American Psychiatric Association that explains the signs and symptoms that mark more than 300 types of mental health conditions. Traditionally, mental health providers use the *DSM* to diagnose everything from anorexia to voyeurism and, if necessary, determine appropriate treatment. Health insurance companies also use the *DSM* to determine coverage and benefits and to reimburse mental health providers (Mayo Clinic, 2016). The *DSM* has been in publication since 1952 and periodically publishes an updated manual. The most recent update was in 2013.

However, the NIMH, the world's largest funding agency of mental health research, has refused to endorse the 2013 *DSM* (*DSM-5*) and will no longer fund mental health research based on the *DSM* mental health categories. The NIMH states that the *DSM* has not categorized mental health disorders based on objective science but more from inconsistent information gathered from clusters of symptoms that are then categorized as a mental health disorder. The NIMH is developing a new classification system of mental health disorders based on science and genetics. There have been petitions requesting an external review of the *DSM-5* (American Psychiatric Association, 2016b).

▶ Family and Caregivers

As with any chronic condition, family members and caregivers are often impacted by caring for afflicted individuals. Caregivers often do not think of themselves as needing any attention because their focus is on the afflicted family member. It is important to take some personal time out of the "caregiver mode" to take care of and reflect on the emotional needs of the caregiver. The following is some advice for caregivers on taking care of themselves:

1. Support groups: Caregivers may feel guilty if they resent their role as a caregiver. Do not judge your thoughts as bad, which will increase your stress; instead, recognize that other people may have the same feelings. Going to support groups to discuss your feelings provides an opportunity to deal with these issues.

2. Do not ignore personal relationships: Caregivers may unintentionally lose contact with friends. Set up times, even if only once per month, to see friends for a short period of time. These personal times provide an opportunity to step away from the caregiver mode.

It is very difficult to take care of someone else if the caregiver does not take care of himself or herself first. For additional information, please contact 1-800-950-NAMI (6264) or info@nami.org.

Here are additional resources about mental health illness support (SAMI, 2016).

Anxiety and Depression Association of America (ADAA): provides information on prevention, treatment, and symptoms of anxiety, depression, and related conditions.

Children and Adults with Attention-Deficit/Hyperactivity Disorder (CHADD): provides information and referrals on ADHD, including local support groups.

Depression and Bipolar Support Alliance (DBSA): provides information on bipolar disorder and depression and offers in-person and online support groups and forums.

International OCD Foundation: provides information on OCD and treatment referrals.

Schizophrenia and Related Disorders Alliance of America (SARDAA): maintains the Schizophrenia Anonymous programs, which are self-help groups and are now available as toll-free teleconferences.

Sidran Institute: helps people understand, manage, and treat trauma and dissociation and maintains a helpline for information and referrals.

TARA (Treatment and Research Advancements for Borderline Personality Disorder): offers a referral center for information, support, education, and treatment options for borderline personality disorder.

See more at: http://www.nami.org/Find-Support/NAMI-HelpLine/Top-25-HelpLine-Resources#sthash.LZlIFKub.dpuf

▶ Special Populations

Children and Adolescents

According to the NIMH, just over 20% (or 1 in 5) children, either currently or at some point during their life, have had a seriously debilitating mental disorder. Children might be diagnosed with one or more of the following: attention deficit hyperactivity disorder (ADHD), posttraumatic stress disorder, panic disorder, bipolar disorder, autism, depressive disorder, borderline personality disorder, eating disorder, social phobia, and schizophrenia. In some instances, these disorders can follow them throughout their lives. It is particularly difficult to assess teenagers' mental disorders because of characteristics of that stage in life. Many teens are worried about peer pressure, family issues, schoolwork and activities, and post-high school planning. It is important that there is open communication with both children and teens, with either their parents, counselors, or friends, to ensure that if there is a mental disorder, it will be addressed. Suicide is a major concern among children and adolescents; it is the fifth leading cause of death among ages 5–14 years (Agency for Healthcare Research and Quality, 2002; NIMH, 2016a).

Treatment for Children and Adolescents

According to the **American Psychological Association** (APA), it is important that parents recognize problems in their children so that they can be treated appropriately. The most common mental disorders are depression, ADHD, and conduct disorders. Although there is limited research on mental disorders in children, it is estimated that 1 in 10 children may suffer from persistent feelings of sadness, which can lead to depression. In some instances, children may not be able to verbalize their emotions, so it is important to notice any behavioral changes such as poor school performance, loss of interest in hobbies, angry outbursts, anxiety, alcohol or drug abuse, and irrational behavior. Treatment for children can consist of therapy or a combination of therapy and medication (SAMHSA, 2016a).

Elderly and Mental Health

As the U.S. population ages and life expectancies continue to increase, mental health disorders will become more prevalent in the elderly. As we age, we will experience loss of family members and friends, which is a major trigger of depression and possibly suicide. Unfortunately, many elderly people are not treated for mental illness, for several reasons. Often the elderly are being treated for other traditional illnesses, so the focus is treating those illnesses. Also, as we age, society assumes that we lose our memory and some of our faculties as part of the normal aging process, which is not an inevitable fact, so primary care providers and family members do not attribute these symptoms to dementia or Alzheimer's disease, both mental disorders. It is also more difficult to see a specialist because of lack of transportation. The elderly are focused on seeing their primary care provider for their main ailments, so both the patient and the provider may ignore the symptoms. Also, the primary care provider may not be comfortable addressing mental health issues. If the primary care provider does refer the elderly patient to a psychologist, the psychologist might not have optimal training; a recent APA survey indicated

that fewer than 30% of psychologists have had graduate coursework in **geropsychology**, which deals with mental health issues in the elderly, and that 70% would be interested in attending programs in geropsychology. The APA has provided geropsychology guidelines for older adults (American Psychological Association, 2016). Finally, the family of an elderly person may not want to acknowledge the problems because they may be afraid of hurting the person's feelings. Alzheimer's disease and other dementias are difficult for a family member to acknowledge, knowing the end result of these diseases. It is important that the primary care provider, the family, and the patient work together to assess the elderly patient's mental status.

Common Types of Mental Disorders in the Elderly

Depression may strike more than 10% of the elderly population. It can imitate dementia because its victims withdraw, cannot focus, and appear confused at times. **Dementias**, which have symptoms of memory loss and confusion, are often considered a part of growing old—but they are not an inevitable part of the aging process. Only 15% of the elderly population suffers from dementia. Of that percentage, over 60% suffer from Alzheimer's disease, for which there is no cure as of this writing. Approximately 40% of dementias are caused by conditions such as high blood pressure or a stroke or other diseases such as Parkinson's disease and Huntington's disease, which are disorders that, in their advanced stages, can cause dementia (American Psychiatric Association, 2016).

Alzheimer's disease causes the death of brain cells that control memory. The longer the person has Alzheimer's disease, the greater the memory loss as more cells die. One million people 65 years or older have severe Alzheimer's disease with approximately 2 million in the moderate stages of the disease (American Psychiatric Association, 2016).

Pseudo dementias (also known as false dementias) may develop as a result of medications, drug interactions, poor diet, or heart and gland diseases. These dementias may occur accidentally because of these conditions. Many elderly have multiple prescriptions so it is important to note any potential interactions that could result in dementia. Also, if the elderly person has poor nutritional habits, dementia could result. It is important that family members or providers monitor the dietary habits of the elderly patient. Fortunately, because of the causes, most of these pseudo dementias are reversible if treated (American Psychiatric Association, 2016).

Mental Health and Culture, Race, and Ethnicity

Mental health disorders occur across race and culture; however, according to the NIMH, diverse communities are often underserved. The following is mental health information related to the LGBTQ community, African Americans, the Latino community, Asian Americans, and American Indians Alaskan Natives.

LGBTQ

The lesbian, gay, bisexual, transgender, and questioning populations are almost three times more likely to experience depression or an anxiety disorder. For **LGBTQ** people age 10–24 years old, suicide is one of the leading causes of death. An estimated 20–30% of LGBTQ individuals report substance abuse problems compared to 9% of the population generally.

The fear of coming out or being discriminated against for sexual orientation can lead to mental health disorders. Thoughts of suicide and substance abuse can be issues with this community. Some LGBTQ individuals also hide their orientation from the mental health system because of fear of being ridiculed. The term "**minority stress**" stems from the social stigma, prejudice, denial of civil rights, victimization, and family rejection that can occur. With any population that experiences mental health distress, it is important that people feel comfortable reaching out for assistance.

The following is a list of resources to locate LGBTQ specific providers:

- Use the Gay and Lesbian Medical Association's Provider Directory to look through a list of inclusive medical providers.
- Check out the Healthcare Equality Index to find the LGBTQ-inclusive policies of organization leaders in healthcare.
- Review resources on the rights and experiences of LGBTQ people in mental health care, including the Center for American Progress and the National Transgender Discrimination Survey (NAMI, 2016).

African Americans

Some African Americans are hesitant to access mental health care due to prior misdiagnoses, inadequate treatment, and cultural misunderstandings. There is a small, although increasing, percentage of psychologists, psychiatrists, and social workers who are African American. Many African Americans rely on religious and social communities for social support, so rather than visit a specialist, they may rely on spiritual guidance. Unfortunately, there is a higher percentage of African Americans in the foster home system, homeless population, and prison. Those environments have a higher level of mental health disorders than other environments.

Latino Community

Approximately 16% of Hispanic adults live with a mental health condition. The Latino population has been identified as a high-risk group for depression, anxiety, and substance abuse. Like the African American population, Latinos may seek treatment from the clergy rather than specialists. There is a small percentage of Latinos who are mental health professionals, so the comfort level might be lower between patient and provider. This is also tied to language barriers. Like African Americans, Latinos are overrepresented in the prison and juvenile justice system (NAMI, n.d.).

NAMI has established an educational program, "Sharing Hope," for both the African American and Latino communities with the goal of increasing mental health awareness in their communities and the resources available to them.

Asian Americans

Approximately 14% of Asian adults live with a mental health condition. The Asian American population is composed of 50 cultures with different languages and religious traditions. Asian Americans have the highest life expectancy of any ethnic group in the United States. Mental health disorders are lower among Asians than whites. Overall, Asian Americans are much less likely to report mental health disorders to friends or medical professionals, sometimes because they feel mental illness is shameful and consider it a personal weakness. The suicide rates of elderly and young Asian American women are higher than those of women of other ethnicities. They will seek help for mental health disorders from alternative medicine providers; however, if they delay treatment, for example because of embarrassment, their problems might become more severe. As with the Hispanic population, there may be language barriers between Asian American patients and mental healthcare providers (APA, 2016).

American Indians and Alaskan Natives

Over 28% of American Indian or Alaskan Native adults live with a mental health condition. Recent statistics indicate that American Indian and Alaskan Native youths use alcohol by 14 years old. They use marijuana and prescription drugs at twice the rate of the national average. Many of these youths believe their parents are permissive with this type of behavior, which encourages them. However, the federal Indian Health Service (IHS) has established a public health marketing campaign targeted to youths to resist drug and alcohol use. The IHS currently funds 11 centers nationwide that address mental health and substance abuse disorders by providing holistic health care, which is accepted by this culture.

The IHS also uses **telebehavioral health**, which is a method of service delivery that broadens the availability to, quality of, and access to care across all behavioral health program areas. Using video conferencing technology, telebehavioral health services allow "real time" visits with a behavioral health specialist in another location who can assist in the evaluation, diagnosis, management, and treatment of health problems (IHS, 2016).

It is important to recognize the differences in cultural beliefs and adapt the system to recognize these value systems. Language barriers may also be a reason why minority cultures do not access the system. Hiring mental health counselors and providers who are from the same culture would be a first step in encouraging more culturally diverse individuals to use the system.

Women and Mental Health

Depression affects women significantly more than men—women who are depressed experience episodes nearly twice as often as men who are depressed. They tend to experience it earlier, longer, and more severely. Women may experience depression as a result of biologic and social reasons. **Premenstrual dysphoric disorder**, a severe disorder in which depression and anxiety co-occur with menstruation, impacts between 3% and 5% of women. Women may also feel depressed as a result of infertility, miscarriage, and menopause. Married women suffer depression more than married men. The more children a woman has, the more likely it is she will suffer from depression. Women who have been victims of sexual abuse or domestic violence may also suffer from depression.

By the year 2030, 20% of the population will be 65 years or older. Per decade above 65 years of age, the proportion of women increases because their life expectancy is higher than that of men. Older women comprise the large majority of nursing home residents. Unfortunately, women in nursing homes often do not receive mental health care. Throughout their lives, women have been traditional caregivers. Women

may provide family members with up to 13 hours of care per day for more than 20 years for both physical and emotional illnesses (Bradley, 2003). As a result of this role, many elderly women experience more depression and anxiety. Unfortunately, research indicates that healthcare providers do not provide appropriate mental health care to a large majority of older females (Qualls, Segal, Norman, Niederehe, & Gallagher-Thomson, 2002).

Homeless People and Mental Health

An estimated 26% of homeless adults staying in shelters live with serious mental illness and an estimated 46% live with severe mental illness or substance use disorders.

The health status of homeless individuals is overall poor because of lack of housing. They are exposed to more disease and do not have adequate access to health care, so their health status deteriorates over time. Mental health and substance abuse problems are common in the homeless population. As a result of lack of stability, it is difficult to provide adequate mental health care and general health care to homeless individuals (National Alliance to End Homelessness, 2016).

▶ Mental Health Issues and Disasters, Trauma, and Loss

Disasters can impact communities and their residents. Natural disasters can be natural, such as hurricanes, earthquakes, floods, and tornadoes, or manmade events, such as the September 11, 2001, terrorist attacks or the wars in Iraq and Afghanistan. Many losses occur after these events, such as the loss of family and loved ones, pets, neighbors, colleagues, and the community infrastructure such as schools, churches, and homes. These disasters may be short or long term. These events may impact individuals emotionally, by causing fear and anxiety because of the uncertainty in their lives. According to the **International Society for Traumatic Stress Studies (ISTSS)**, individuals may experience feelings of shock, disbelief, grief, anger, guilt, helplessness, and emotional numbness. They may have difficulty with cognitive thinking and may experience physical reactions such as fatigue and illness (ISTSS, 2001). They may also have difficulty interacting with others. As with any mental health condition, it is important to reach out for assistance before the condition controls an individual's life.

Mental Health Impact of Terrorist Attacks and Natural Disasters

September 11, 2001

Terrorist attacks are different than natural disasters such as hurricanes, earthquakes, avalanches, or tornados because these attacks are deliberately aimed at harming large numbers of people. An evaluation of the federal emergency mental health program indicated that over 1 million New Yorkers received one or more face-to-face counseling or public education services as a result of the September 11 terrorist attacks (Neria et al., 2007). Interestingly, the emotional impact of the terrorist attacks was felt nationwide. The federal emergency preparedness model of the **Federal Emergency Management Agency** (FEMA) and the **Substance Abuse and Mental Health Services Administration (SAMHSA)** is helpful to victims with short-term mental health issues as a result of different types of disasters (Felton, 2004). The **American Psychological Association Task Force on Promoting Resilience in Response to Terrorism** has produced fact sheets that are intended to provide information to psychologists assisting those target populations impacted by terrorist events (APA, 2016). However, those inflicted with long-term mental health issues as a result of these types of events are often not treated. The assumption is that the traditional healthcare system will treat individuals with long-term mental illnesses. However, as discussed previously, individuals who have long-term mental health issues feel stigmatized about seeking mental health services. Those individuals who have experienced traumatic events often feel uncomfortable because they feel that they should have recovered from the events without help.

Hurricane Katrina

Hurricane Katrina devastated nearly 90,000 square miles that were declared a natural disaster area. At least 1 million individuals, including 370,000 school-aged children, were displaced. Many were evacuated to the 46 unaffected states (Cook, 2006). Parents were very anxious because their homes were destroyed and they had to start new lives elsewhere, which was not their choice. The Centers for Disease Control and Prevention (CDC) surveyed Hurricane Katrina survivors in October 2005 and found that 50% needed mental health services and 33% needed an intervention, with only 2% actually receiving assistance (Weisler, Barbee, & Townsend, 2006). Mental health providers reported grief, anxiety, and fear. This experience was magnified for survivors who had a previous history of trauma

and who suffered from mental health disorders. Long-term mental health care is needed for the survivors of Hurricane Katrina. It is critical that mental health issues be included in the health care of those impacted by events such as terrorist incidents and natural disasters. Mental health issues do not only impact the survivors but also the providers of care to those survivors.

▶ Mental Health and Veterans

With nearly 155 hospitals serving nearly 8 million war veterans and current servicemen, the VA operates the largest healthcare system and is the largest single employer of psychologists in the country. In 1989, the **National Center for Posttraumatic Stress Disorder** was created within the VA to address the needs of military-related **posttraumatic stress disorder** (PTSD) (National Center for PTSD, 2016). Of the 1.7 million veterans returning from Afghanistan and Iraq, 20% suffer from posttraumatic stress disorder or major depression. Mental health issues are the leading cause of hospitalizations for active-duty military members. According to recent research, military suicides can be the result of many untreated mental illnesses (American Psychiatric Association, 2016). Many veterans seek help outside the VA healthcare system. Their main reason for not seeking help is fear of being stigmatized for seeking these types of service. This fear of stigmatization is similar in the general population. There are new military healthcare models to ensure that mental health services are being offered confidentially to allay these fears. The Department of Defense follows privacy guidelines established by the Health Insurance Portability and Accountability Act (HIPAA) and the Privacy Rule.

Embedded Behavioral Health (EBH)

The **Embedded Behavioral Health Model** focuses on early intervention and treatment to promote soldier readiness (before, during, and after deployment). The EBH develops multidisciplinary teams to improve access to behavioral care by setting up work areas and working with unit leaders to ensure availability of these resources. The EBH serves as entry into behavioral health care. The EBH is currently working with the Army (EBH, 2016).

▶ Managed Behavioral Health Care

Managed behavioral healthcare organizations (MBHOs), also known as behavioral healthcare carve outs, are specialized managed care organizations that focus on mental health services. According to the National Committee for Quality Assurance (NCQA), an MBHO can be part of a health plan, an independent organization, or be supported by healthcare providers.

MBHOs dominate private mental health coverage. Research has indicated that MBHOs have reduced mental health treatment costs (Zuvekas, Rupp, & Norquist, 2008). The NCQA's **Managed Behavioral Healthcare Organization Accreditation Program** provides consumers, employers, and others with information about the quality of the nation's managed behavioral healthcare organizations. NCQA accreditation includes a rigorous review against standards for improving behavioral healthcare access and services and the process of credentialing practitioners. Currently, there are 300 MBHOs that serve 120 million U.S. citizens. The NCQA program is designed to:

- Develop accountability measures for quality of care;
- Provide employers and consumers with MBHO information;
- Develop quality improvement MBHO programs; and
- Encourage coordination of behavioral care with medical care treatment (NCQA, 2013).

National Institute for Mental Health Strategic Plan

As the lead federal government agency on mental health, the NIMH developed a long-term strategic plan for mental health care in the United States. The plan, revised in 2013, identified four core areas of focus:

Strategic Objective 1: Promote Discovery in the Brain and Behavioral Sciences to Fuel Research on the Causes of Mental Disorders

We will support basic, translational, and clinical research to gain a more complete understanding of the genetic, neurobiological, behavioral, environmental, and experiential factors that contribute to mental disorders.

Strategic Objective 2: Chart Mental Illness Trajectories to Determine When, Where, and How to Intervene

We will chart the course of mental disorders over the lifespan in order to understand ideal times and methods for intervention to preempt or treat mental disorders and hasten recovery.

Strategic Objective 3: Develop New and Better Interventions That Incorporate the Diverse Needs and Circumstances of People with Mental Illnesses

We will improve existing approaches and devise new ones for the prevention, treatment, and cure of mental illness, allowing those who may suffer from these disorders to live full and productive lives.

Strategic Objective 4: Strengthen the Public Health Impact of NIMH-Supported Research

Through research, evaluation, and collaboration, we will further develop the dissemination capacity of the Institute to help close the gap between the development of new, research-tested interventions and their widespread use by those most in need (NIMH, 2013b).

The Virginia Tech Massacre: A Case Study of the Mental Health System

On April 16, 2007, a senior Virginia Tech student, Seung Hui Cho—who had been diagnosed with and treated for severe anxiety disorders in middle school until his junior year of high school, had been accused of stalking two female students at Virginia Tech, had been declared mentally ill by a Virginia special justice, and was asked to seek counseling by at least one Virginia Tech professor—killed 32 people, students, and professors. It was the worst school massacre in U.S. history.

Virginia Governor Tim Kaine gave the Virginia Tech Review Panel the task of reviewing Cho's mental health history. According to the panel's findings, even as a young boy, Cho was extremely shy and often refused to speak. He was uncomfortable in his school surroundings and was often bullied. As a result of testing, he did receive counseling throughout middle and high school until he was 18 years of age. He had responded well to the counseling but did not want to continue the counseling, so his parents allowed him to stop. When he decided to go to Virginia Tech, the school did not know of his mental health issues because of personal privacy rules. The **Family Educational Rights and Privacy Act of 1974 (FERPA)** and the **Americans with Disabilities Act** (ADA) generally allow for special-education records to be transferred to a higher education facility. However, the law prohibits a college or university from making an inquiry pre-admission about an applicant's disability status. After a student's admission, the higher education facility may make inquiries on a confidential basis. Cho could have made his disability known to the university but chose not to. Unfortunately, Virginia law allowed Cho to purchase a handgun without detection by the National Instant Criminal Background Check System (NCIS) (Virginia Tech Review Panel, 2007). This tragedy led to the first major federal gun control measure in more than a decade, which strengthened the NCIS, eliminating the legal loophole that allowed Cho to purchase a handgun (Cochran, 2008).

▶ Alternative Approaches to Mental Health Care

Alternative approaches to mental health care emphasize the relationships between the body, mind, and spirituality (SAMHSA, 2009). Established in 1992, the National Center for Complementary and Alternative Medicine at the National Institutes of Health evaluates different types of alternative therapies and treatments and whether to integrate them into traditional medicine culture. Different types of treatment, including techniques outlined in a fact sheet from the National Mental Health Information Center, are discussed below:

- **Self-help organizations:** Many mentally ill individuals often seek comfort in self-help organizations. They find solace with others who have experienced similar conditions. Many of them are nonprofit and are free of charge. Some also provide education and support to caregivers of mentally ill individuals. Often, these organizations are anonymous because of the stigma attached to mental disorders.
- **Nutrition:** Some research has demonstrated that certain types of diets may assist with certain mental disorders. Eliminating wheat and milk products may alleviate the severity of symptoms of children with autism.
- **Pastoral counseling:** Mental health counselors have recognized that incorporating spiritual guidance with traditional medical care may alleviate mental disorder symptoms.
- **Animal-assisted therapies:** Animals are often used to increase socialization skills and encourage communication among the mentally ill. Integrating animals into individuals' lives may alleviate some symptoms of mental illness.
- **Art therapy:** Art activities such as drawing, painting, and sculpting may help people express their emotions and may help treat disorders such as depression. There are certificates in art therapy for this purpose.
- **Dance therapy:** Moving one's body to music may help individuals recovering from physical abuse because the movement may help develop a sense of ease with their bodies.
- **Music therapy:** Research supports that music elevates a person's emotional moods. It has been used to treat depression, stress, and grief.

Culturally Based Healing Arts

Oriental and Native American medicine include the beliefs that wellness is a state of balance between the physical, spiritual, and emotional needs of an individual and that illness results from an imbalance (Center for Mental Health Services, 2009). Their remedies focus on natural medicine, nutrition, exercise, and prayers to regain the balance.

Acupuncture is the Chinese practice of the insertion of needles in specific points of the body to balance the system. Acupuncture has been used to treat stress and anxiety, depression, ADHD in children, and physical ailments. Acupuncture is often used in conjunction with chiropractic medicine.

Ayurveda medicine incorporates diet, meditation, herbal medicine, and nutrition to treat depression and to release stress.

Yoga is an Indian system that uses breathing techniques, stretching, and meditation to balance the body. Yoga is offered at many athletic clubs and gyms and has become a popular mainstream form of exercise. It has been used for depression and anxiety.

Native American practices include ceremonial dances and baptismal rituals as part of Indian health. These dances and rituals are used to treat depression, stress, and substance abuse.

Relaxation and Stress Reduction Techniques

Biofeedback is a technique that focuses on learning to control heart rate and body temperature. This technique may be used in conjunction with medication to treat depression and schizophrenia. Biofeedback may be used to control issues with stress and hyperventilation.

Visualization is when a patient creates a mental image of wellness and recovery. This may be used by traditional healthcare providers to treat substance abuse, panic disorders, and stress.

Massage therapy manipulates the body and its muscles and is used to release tension. It has been used to treat depression and stress.

Technology-Based Applications

Technology-aided development of electronic tools that can be used from home and increase access to isolated geographic areas can increase health care access for mentally ill individuals.

Telemedicine is when providers and patients are connected using the internet for communication for consultation. For example, mentally ill individuals living in rural areas have an opportunity to have access to providers.

Telephone counseling is an important part of mental health care. As stated previously, because of the stigma attached to receiving mental health services, some individuals prefer to talk to a counselor on the telephone because they do not have to face anyone and do not have to tell anyone where they are going if they have an appointment in an office. Counselors receive training for telephone counseling. Like telemedicine, telephone counseling provides an opportunity for outreach for individuals who live in isolated locations.

The Internet, including email services (**electronic communication**), has provided an opportunity to increase individuals' exposure to knowledge regarding their condition. Consumer groups and medical websites can be accessed anonymously.

Radio psychiatry has been used in the United States for over 30 years. Radio psychologists and psychiatrists provide advice, information, and referrals to consumers. Both the APA and the American Psychiatric Association have issued guidelines for radio show programs that focus on mental health.

Americans with Disabilities Act of 1990 and Mental Health

A mental impairment is defined by the Americans with Disabilities Act of 1990 (ADA) as "any mental or psychological disorder, such as mental retardation, organic brain syndrome, emotional or mental illness, and specific learning disabilities." The ADA requires an employer to make reasonable accommodations to those employees who are disabled.

The definition of disability in the ADA includes individuals with mental illness who:

1. Have a physical or mental impairment that substantially limits one or more major life activities of an individual;
2. Have a record of such an impairment; or
3. Are regarded as having such an impairment.

Examples of reasonable accommodations for people with severe mental illnesses are:

- Providing self-paced workloads and flexible hours;
- Modifying job responsibilities;
- Allowing leave (paid or unpaid) during periods of hospitalization or incapacity;
- Assigning a supportive and understanding supervisor;
- Modifying work hours to allow people to attend appointments with their psychiatrist;
- Providing easy access to supervision and supports in the workplace; and
- Providing frequent guidance and feedback about job performance (Mental health, 2016).

Conclusion

Mental health issues impact millions of U.S. residents. Mental health disabilities limit the life expectancy of individuals by many years. Historically, treatment of mental health disorders has been underfunded because of the attitude of the traditional healthcare system, confusion by health insurance companies, and mentally ill individuals' fear that they will be discriminated against because of their conditions. In 1999, Surgeon General David Satcher's report on mental health brought awareness to the issues with the U.S. mental healthcare system. The Mental Health Parity Act of 1996 was an attempt to establish a fair system of treatment between mental health disorders and traditional healthcare conditions by mandating that annual and lifetime limits be equal for mental health care and traditional health care. President Bush's Freedom Commission on Mental Health focused on an analysis of the mental health system and recommendations to improve mental health care.

The Mental Health Parity and Addiction Equity Act (2008) and its 2013 final rules further support mental health care by requiring insurance plans to offer benefits and cost-sharing provisions for mental health treatment that are similar to those for traditional medical care. Over the past 15 years, increased funding has improved the quality of mental health services. The Obama administration has recognized the importance of funding mental health initiatives, including teacher training programs for mental health awareness (Mohney, 2013).

Despite the progress in mental health care, there continues to be issue with the U.S. mental health care system. Recent tragedies such as the shootings at Sandy Hook Elementary School, the Aurora, Colorado movie theater, and the Navy Yard were committed by mentally ill individuals. Several questions must be answered in order to understand how mental health care can be administered to individuals who need it the most. Was there adequate access to mental health care for these individuals? Were these individuals properly diagnosed? Did their families recognize their problems? Did they refuse care? The U.S. mental healthcare system continues to be analyzed to ensure that these types of tragedies cease.

Wrap-Up

Vocabulary

Acupuncture
Alternative approaches to mental health care
Alzheimer's disease
American Psychiatric Association
American Psychological Association
Americans with Disabilities Act
Animal-assisted therapies
Art therapy
Ayurveda
Biofeedback
Dance therapy
De facto mental health service system
Dementia
Diagnostic and Statistical Manual of Mental Disorders (DSM)
Electronic communication
Electrotherapy
Embedded Behavioral Health model
Family Educational Rights and Privacy Act of 1974 (FERPA)
Federal Emergency Management Agency

Geropsychology
Hurricane Katrina
Insane asylums
International Society for Traumatic Stress Studies (ISTSS)
Involuntary commitment
LGBTQ
Managed Behavioral Healthcare Organization Accreditation Program
Managed behavioral healthcare organizations
Massage therapy
Mental disorders
Mental Health America
Mental Health Parity Act of 1996
Mental Health Parity and Addiction Equity Act of 2008
Minority stress
Moral treatment
Music therapy
National Alliance on Mental Alliance (NAMI)
National Center for Posttraumatic Stress Disorder
National Institute of Mental Health

Native American practice
New Freedom Commission on Mental Health
Nutrition
Pastoral counseling
Phobias
Posttraumatic stress disorder
Premenstrual dysphoric disorder
Pseudo dementias
Psychiatrists
Psychologists
Psychotropic medications
Radio psychiatry
Self-help organizations
Substance Abuse and Mental Health Services Administration (SAMHSA)
Task Force on Promoting Resilience in Response to Terrorism
Telebehavioral health
Telemedicine
Telephone counseling
U.S. Commission on Mental Health
Visualization
Voluntary commitment
Yoga

References

Agency for Healthcare Research and Quality (AHRQ). (2002). Specialized training helps ER nurses better manage children at risk for suicide. Retrieved from http://archive.ahrq.gov/research/feb02/0202RA8.htm

American Psychiatric Association. (2016a). DSM: History of the manual. Retrieved from http://www.psychiatry.org/practice/dsm/dsm-history-of-the-manual

American Psychiatric Association. (2016b). Recent updates to proposed revisions for *DSM-5*. Retrieved from http://www.dsm5.org/Pages/RecentUpdates.aspx

American Psychiatric Association. (2016). Seniors. Retrieved from http://www.psychiatry.org/mental-health/people/seniors

American Psychiatric Association. (2016). Military. http://www.psychiatry.org/mental-health/people/military

American Psychological Association (APA). (July, 2003). Office of Public Affairs. American Psychological Association applauds final report of President's New Freedom Commission on Mental Health. American Psychological Association Press Release. Retrieved from http://www.apa.org/releases/mentalhealth_rpt.html

American Psychological Association (APA). (2006). Asian-American mental health. Retrieved from http://www.apa.org/monitor/feb06/health.aspx

American Psychological Association (APA). (2016a). Retrieved from http://www.apa.org/helpcenter/terror-exposure.aspx

American Psychological Association (APA). (2016). Guidelines for Psychological Practice with Older Adults. Retrieved from http://www.apa.org/practice/guidelines/older-adults.aspx

Anderson, R., Rice, T., & Kominski, G. (2007). *Changing the U.S. Healthcare System* (439–479). San Francisco, CA: Jossey-Bass.

Bradley, P. (2003). Family caregiver assessment: Essential for effective home health care. *Journal of Gerontological Nursing*, 29, 29–36.

Center for Mental Health Services. (2016). Alternative approaches to mental health care. Retrieved from http://mentalhealth.samhsa.gov/publications/allpubs/ken98-0044/default.asp

Cochran, J. (January 12, 2008). New gun control law is killer's legacy. Retrieved from http://abcnews.go.com/Politics/story?id=4126152

Cook, G. (2006). Schooling Katrina's kids. *American School Board Journal*, 193, 18–26.

Everett, A., Mahler, J., Biblin, J., Ganguli, R., & Mauer, B. (2008). Improving the health of mental health consumers. *International Journal of Mental Health*, 37(2), 8–48.

EBH. (2016). Retrieved from http://armymedicine.mil/Pages/EBH.aspx

Felton, C. (2004). Lessons learned since September 11 2001 concerning the mental health impact of terrorism, appropriate response strategies and future preparedness. *Psychiatry*, 67(2), 147–153.

Grob, G. (1983). *Mental illness and American society: 1875–1940*. Princeton, NJ: Princeton University Press.

Grob, G. (1994). *The mad among us: A history of the care of America's mentally ill*. New York: Free Press.

Indian Health Service (IHS). (2016). Behavioral health. Retrieved from http://www.ihs.gov/communityhealth/behavioralhealth

International Society for Traumatic Stress Studies (ISTSS). (2001). Mass disasters, trauma, and loss. Retrieved from http://www.istss.org/AM/Template.cfm?Section=PublicEducationPamphlets&Template=/CM/ContentDisplay.cfm&ContentID=1464

Kessler, R.C., Chiu, W.T., Colpe, L., Demler, O., Merikangas, K.R., Walters, E.E., & Wang, P.S. (2006). The prevalence and correlates of serious mental illness (SMI) in the National Comorbidity Survey Replication (NCSR). In Manderscheid, R.W., & Berry, J.T. (Eds.). *Mental health, United States, 2004* (DHHS Publication No. SMA-06-4195). Rockville, MD: Substance Abuse and Mental Health Services Administration.

NAMI. (2016). LGBTQ. Retrieved from http://www.nami.org/Find-Support/LGBTQ

Luongo, T. (2008). The Mental Health Parity and Addiction Equity Act of 2008: Equal footing for those suffering from mental health and addition disorders. Retrieved from http://www.hrtutor.com/en/news_rss/articles/2008/1202MentalHealthParityandAddictionEquityActof2008.aspx

Mayo Clinic. (2016). Mental health: What's normal and what is not. Retrieved from http://www.mayoclinic.com/health/mental-health/MH00042

McFarling, L., D'Angelo, M., Drain, M., Gibbs, D., & Olmstead, K. (2011). Stigma as a barrier to substance abuse and mental health treatment. *Military Psychology*, 23, 1–5.

Mental health. (2016). Retrieved from http://www.womenshealth.gov/mental-health/your-rights/americans-disability-act.html

MHPAEA. (2016). Retrieved from https://www.cms.gov/CCIIO/Programs-and-Initiatives/Other-Insurance-Protections/mhpaea_factsheet.html

National Alliance on Mental Illness (NAMI). (n.d.). Latino community mental health fact sheet. Retrieved from http://www.nami.org/Content/NavigationMenu/Find_Support/Multicultural_Support/Annual_Minority_Mental_Healthcare_Symposia/Latino_MH06.pdf

National Alliance to End Homelessness. (2016). Snapshot of homelessness. Retrieved from http://www.endhomelessness.org/pages/snapshot_of_homelessness

National Center for Posttraumatic Stress Disorder. (2013). About us. Retrieved from http://www.ptsd.va.gov/about/mission/history_of_the_national_center_for_ptsd.asp

National Committee for Quality Assurance (NCQA). (2013). Accreditation programs. Retrieved from http://www.ncqa.org/Programs/Accreditation.aspx

National Institute of Mental Health (NIMH). (2013a). Child and adolescent mental health. Retrieved from http://www.nimh.nih.gov/health/topics/childandadolescentmentalhealth/index.shtml

National Institute of Mental Health (NIMH). (2013b). The National Institute of Mental Health strategic plan. Retrieved from http://www.nimh.nih.gov/about/strategic-planning-reports/index.shtml

Neria, Y., Gross, R., Litz, B., Maguen, S., Insel, B., Seirmarco, G., … Marshall, R.D. (2007). Prevalence and psychological correlates of complicated grief among bereaved adults 2.5–3.5 years after September 11 attacks. *Journal of Traumatic Stress*, 20(3), 251–262.

Pointer, D., Williams, S., Isaacs, S., & Knickman, J. (2007). *Introduction to U.S. health care*. Hoboken, NJ: Wiley Publishing.

Qualls, S., Segal, D., Norman, D., Niederehe, G., & Gallagher-Thomson, D. (2002). Psychologists in practice with older adults: Current patterns, sources of training, and need for continuing education. *Professional Psychology: Research and Practice*, 33, 435–442.

Regier, D., Narrow, W., Rae, D., Manderscheid, R., Locke, B., & Goodwin, F. (1993). The de facto US mental and addictive disorders service system. Epidemiologic catchment area prospective 1-year prevalence rates of disorders and services. *Archives of General Psychiatry*, 50, 85–94.

Shi, L., & Singh, D. (2008). *Essentials of the U.S. health care delivery system*. Sudbury, MA: Jones and Bartlett.

Smith, H. (2007). Psychological service needs of older women. *Psychological Services*, 4, 277–286.

Substance Abuse and Mental Health Services Administration (SAMHSA). (2009). Alternative approaches to mental health care. Retrieved from http://mentalhealth.samhsa.gov/publications/allpubs/ken980044/default.asp

Substance Abuse and Mental Health Services Administration (SAMHSA). (2011). Leading change: A plan for SAMHSA's roles and actions: 2011–2014. Retrieved from http://store.samhsa.gov/shin/content//SMA11-4629/02-ExecutiveSummary.pdf

Substance Abuse and Mental Health Services Administration (SAMHSA). (2013a). Children and Adolescents with Mental, Emotional and Behavioral Disorders. Retrieved from http://mentalhealth.samhsa.gov/publications/allpubs/CA0006/default.asp

Substance Abuse and Mental Health Services Administration (SAMHSA). (2013b). The Mental Health Parity and Addiction Equity Act of 2008. Retrieved from http://www.samhsa.gov/healthreform/parity

Sultz, H., & Young, K. (2006). *Health care USA: Understanding its organization and delivery* (5th ed.). Sudbury, MA: Jones and Bartlett.

U.S. Public Health Service. (1999). Mental health: A report of the Surgeon General. Retrieved from http://mentalhealth.samhsa.gov/features/surgeongeneralreport/chapter2/sec7.asp

Virginia Tech Review Panel. (2007). Mass shootings at Virginia Tech: Report of the Review Panel presented to Governor Kaine, Commonwealth of Virginia. Retrieved from http://www.governor.virginia.gov/TempContent/techPanelReport.cfm

Weisler, R., Barbee, J., & Townsend, M. (2006). Mental health and recovery in the Gulf Coast after Hurricanes Katrina and Rita. *Journal of the American Medical Association*, 296, 585–588.

World Health Organization (WHO). (September, 2010). Mental health: Strengthening our response. Retrieved from http://www.who.int/mediacentre/factsheets/fs220/en/index.html

Woody, R. (2008). Obtaining legal counsel for child and family mental health practice. *The American Journal of Family Therapy*, 36, 323–331.

Zuvekas, S., Rupp, A., & Norquist, G. (2008). The impacts of mental health parity and managed care in one large employer group: A reexamination. *Health Affairs*, 24, 1668–1671.

▶ **Notes**

▶ **Student Activity 13-1**

In Your Own Words

Based on this chapter, please provide a definition of the following vocabulary words in your own words. DO NOT RECITE the text definition.

Posttraumatic stress disorder:

_____

_____

Mental disorders:

_____

_____

Moral treatment:

_____

_____

Involuntary commitment:

_____

_____

Telebehavioral health:

_____

_____

Embedded Behavioral Health model:

_____

_____

Visualization:

_____

_____

Psychiatrists:

_____

_____

New Freedom Commission on Mental Health:

_____

_____

Family Educational Rights and Privacy Act:

_____

_____

Ayurveda:

_____

_____

▶ Student Activity 13-2

Complete the following case scenarios based on the information provided in the chapter. Your answer must be IN YOUR OWN WORDS.

Real-Life Applications: Case Scenario One

You have been concerned about your grandmother recently. Yesterday, she left the stove on when she went to the grocery store. Your grandfather has been chronically ill for years and she is his main caregiver. She regularly visits her primary care provider, who has told her that it is nothing more than old age. You decide to research mental health issues among the elderly and have found very interesting statistics, particularly for women.

Activity

(1) Provide three statistics about mental health issues in women population; and (2) strategies on how to deal with womens' mental health issues.

Responses

_____

_____

_____

_____

_____

_____

_____

_____

_____

_____

_____

_____

_____

_____

_____

_____

_____

_____

Case Scenario Two

You are thinking about going to school to become a mental health professional. However, you have heard that mental health professionals face liability issues and complaints—but you are unsure why.

Activity

Perform research using this text and the Internet to find five reasons why mental health professionals are at high risk for complaints.

Responses

_____

_____

_____

_____

_____

_____

_____

_____

_____

_____

_____

_____

_____

_____

_____

_____

_____

Case Scenario Three

The American Psychiatric Association has developed a guide for diagnosing mental health disorders. This guide has been used for years by many mental health professionals. Recently, the American Psychological Association has been criticized heavily regarding the guide.

Activity

You are curious as to why this guide has been challenged for its quality. You perform research to determine what the issue is with this landmark publication.

Responses

_____

_____

_____

_____

_____

_____

_____

_____

_____

_____

_____

_____

_____

_____

_____

_____

_____

_____

Case Scenario Four

You are concerned about your grandmother who recently lost her spouse, your grandfather. You think she is depressed. You want to take her to her primary care provider for a checkup.

Activity

Prior to taking her to her doctor, you want to familiarize yourself with mental health issues in the elderly. You do some research to find out what mental health issues are common in the elderly population.

Responses

_____

_____

_____

_____

_____

_____

_____

_____

_____

_____

_____

_____

_____

_____

_____

_____

_____

_____

▶ Student Activity 13-3

Internet Exercises

Write your answers in the space provided.

- ■ Visit each of the websites listed here.
- ■ Name the organization.
- ■ Locate the organization's mission statement on the website.

- Provide a brief overview of the activities of the organization.
- How do these organizations participate in the U.S. healthcare system?

Websites
http://www.apa.org

Organization Name:

_____

_____

Mission Statement:

_____

_____

_____

Overview of Activities:

_____

_____

_____

Importance of Organization to U.S. Health Care:

_____

_____

_____

http://www.samhsa.gov

Organization Name:

_____

_____

Mission Statement:

_____

_____

Overview of Activities:

_____

_____

_____

Importance of Organization to U.S. Health Care:

_____

_____

_____

http://www.istss.org

Organization Name:

_____

_____

Mission Statement:

_____

_____

_____

Overview of Activities:

_____

_____

_____

Importance of Organization to U.S. Health Care:

_____

_____

_____

http://www.psych.org

Organization Name:

_____

_____

Mission Statement:

_____

_____

_____

Overview of Activities:

_____

_____

_____

Importance of Organization to U.S. Health Care:

_____

_____

_____

http://www.nimh.nih.gov

Organization Name:

_____

_____

Mission Statement:

_____

_____

_____

Overview of Activities:

_____

_____

_____

Importance of Organization to U.S. Health Care:

_____

_____

_____

http://www.nami.org

Organization Name:

_____

_____

Mission Statement:

_____

_____

_____

Overview of Activities:

_____

_____

_____

Importance of Organization to U.S. Health Care:

_____

_____

_____

▶ Student Activity 13-4

Discussion Questions

The following are suggested discussion questions for this chapter.

1. What is the *DSM*? Why is it important to mental health care?

_____

_____

_____

_____

_____

_____

_____

2.   Do you believe that mental health care is important to veterans and military?

_____

_____

_____

_____

_____

_____

_____

3.   What are some issues regarding the treatment of African American patients who experience mental health issues?

_____

_____

_____

_____

_____

_____

_____

_____

4.   Do you believe in holistic healing? Support your answer.

_____

_____

_____

_____

_____

_____

_____

_____

5. Do you think the Indian Health Service is important? Discuss its activities.

_____

_____

_____

_____

_____

_____

_____

_____

_____

▶ Student Activity 13-5

Current Events

Perform an Internet search and find a current events topic over the past three years that is related to this chapter. Provide a summary of the article and the link to the article and why the article relates to the chapter.

The Navigate Companion Website for this text is a great source for additional information on the U.S. health-care system. You can gain a new perspective on many of the topics presented in this chapter by visiting http://go.jblearning.com/Niles3e. You'll find additional student activities, further reading, and interactive study tools that explore:

- Strategies on how to deal with mental health issues as a caregiver;
- Dealing with mental health issues in minority populations;
- How insurance plans cover mental health services;
- And much more.

_____

_____

_____

_____

_____

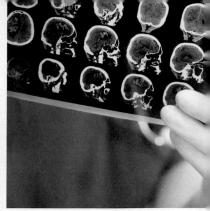

CHAPTER 14

Analysis of the U.S. Healthcare System

▶ Introduction

The U.S. healthcare system has long been recognized for providing state-of-the-art health care. It has also been recognized as the most expensive healthcare system in the world and the price tag is expected to increase. Despite offering two large public programs—Medicare and Medicaid for elderly, indigent, or disabled individuals—current statistics indicate that millions of individuals are uninsured, although the Affordable Care Act's individual mandate to purchase health insurance coverage has reduced those numbers

This chapter will compare the U.S. healthcare system and the healthcare systems of other countries and discuss whether universal healthcare coverage should be implemented in the United States. This chapter will also discuss trends that may positively impact the U.S. healthcare system, including the increased use of technology in prescribing medicine and providing health care, complementary and alternative medicine use, new nursing home models, accountable care organizations, and the universal-healthcare-coverage programs in Massachusetts and San Francisco, California. The Affordable Care Act (ACA) will also be discussed because of its major impact on the U.S. healthcare system.

▶ Highlights of the U.S. Healthcare System

The U.S. healthcare system is a complicated system that is composed of both public and private resources. Health care is available to those individuals who have health insurance or are entitled to health care through a public program or who can afford to pay out of pocket for their care.

The one commonality with the world's healthcare systems is that they all have consumers or users of their systems. Systems were developed to provide a service to their citizens. The U.S. healthcare system, unlike other systems in the world, does not provide healthcare access to all of its citizens. Healthcare expenditures comprise approximately 17.6% of the gross domestic product (GDP). Healthcare costs are very expensive and most citizens would be unable to afford it if they had to pay for it themselves. Individuals rely on health insurance to pay a large portion of their healthcare costs. Health insurance is predominantly offered by employers. According to the 2014 CDC National Health Survey, at the time of the survey there were 36 million uninsured individuals under the age of 65 in the United States, which was a decrease of 13 million from the CDC's 2011 survey. These new numbers

are the result of the Affordable Care Act mandate that required individuals to purchase health insurance. However, the number of underinsured individuals remains high, at 30 million. **Underinsured** individuals are people who have insurance but have high deductibles and out-of-pocket expenses compared to their income. People with health insurance through their jobs are increasingly underinsured, particularly employees who work for small firms. While people buying coverage on their own are still more likely to be underinsured than those with employer coverage (37% vs. 20%), the share of people with employer insurance who are underinsured has increased since over the last 15 years. In 2014, 14 million people had deductibles of at least 5% of their income (Thirty one million underinsured in 2014, 2015).

▶ Affordable Care Act Impact

The Patient Protection and Affordable Care Act of 2010 or Affordable Care Act and its amendments have focused on primary care as the foundation for the U.S. healthcare system (Goodson, 2010). The legislation has focused on several areas to improve the U.S. healthcare system including: quality, affordable, and efficient healthcare; public health and primary prevention of disease; healthcare workforce increases; community health; and increasing revenue provisions to pay for the reform. However, once the bill was signed, several states filed lawsuits. Several of these lawsuits argued that the Act violates the U.S. Constitution because of the mandate of individual healthcare insurance coverage and also infringes on states' rights because of the expansion of Medicaid (Arts, 2010). The 2012 U.S. Supreme Court decision that supported the constitutionality of the individual mandates should decrease the number of lawsuits. In October 2013, there were major problems with the operations of the federal government website (www.healthcare.gov) that houses the Health Insurance Marketplace. On October 1, the first day of the individual health insurance coverage mandate, consumers were unable to enroll in health insurance plans. State-run health insurance marketplaces also experienced the same types of technological issues, creating frustration as well. This major computer issue led to a firestorm of criticism. Despite these lawsuits and operational problems, this legislation has clearly provided opportunities to increase consumer empowerment in the healthcare system by providing temporary insurance to individuals with preexisting conditions until they can purchase their own insurance, eliminating lifetime and annual caps on health insurance payouts, improving the healthcare workforce, and providing databases so consumers can check the quality of their healthcare. The Affordable Care Act enables healthcare consumers to select a health insurance plan based on the amount of cost sharing the consumer wants. There are three types of plans: gold, silver, and bronze. Gold plans have the lowest cost sharing but are the most expensive. Silver plans have moderate cost sharing and are not as expensive as the gold plan, and the bronze plans have high cost sharing but the premiums are the lowest. This type of structure enables the consumer to select a plan that fits his or her budget. The ACA's focus is to increase the role of public health and primary care in the U.S. healthcare system while increasing accessibility to the system by providing affordable healthcare opportunities. Approximately 8 million people enrolled in the Marketplaces during 2014 open enrollment (October 2013 to April 2014), with 11.7 million estimated to have enrolled in the Marketplaces during 2015 open enrollment (November 2014 to February 2015). This includes 4.5 million people who reenrolled from 2014. As of June 30, 2015, 9.9 million people were still enrolled and had paid for a Marketplace plan, which is consistent with the U.S. Department of Health and Human Services' (HHS) original projection of 9.1 million (Obamacare enrollment, 2015).

▶ Government's Role

The government plays an important role in the quality of the U.S. healthcare system. **Social regulation** focuses on actions of organizations, such as those in the healthcare industry, that impact an individual's safety. Social regulations focus on protecting individuals as employees and consumers (Carroll & Buchholtz, 2015). These types of regulations are common in the U.S. healthcare system and are enforced by governmental agencies. The federal government provides funding for state and local governmental programs and sets policy for many aspects of the U.S. healthcare system. The federal government is also responsible for the implementation of Medicare, the entitlement program for the elderly. Federal healthcare regulations are implemented and enforced at the state and local levels. Funding is primarily distributed from the federal government to state governments, which then allocate funding to local health departments. Local health departments provide the majority of services for their constituents and are collaborating with local organizations such as schools and physicians to increase their ability to provide education and prevention services.

Many federal agencies are responsible for sectors of health care. The HHS is the most important federal agency. It is a cabinet-level department of the executive branch of the federal government. The Secretary of the HHS provides advice to the President of the United States regarding health and human services policy (Pozgar, 2014). HHS collaborates with state and local governments because many HHS services are provided at those levels. There are 11 operating divisions: the Centers for Disease Control and Prevention (CDC), the Administration for Community Living (ACL), the National Institutes of Health (NIH), the Agency for Toxic Substances and Disease Registry (ATSDR), the Indian Health Service (IHS), the Health Resources and Services Administration (HRSA), the Agency for Healthcare Research and Quality (AHRQ), the Substance Abuse and Mental Health Services Administration (SAMHSA), the U.S. Food and Drug Administration (FDA), the Administration for Children and Families (ACF), and the Centers for Medicare and Medicaid Services (CMS). Each of these governmental agencies has a specific mission that focuses on certain aspects of the U.S. healthcare system.

▶ Public Health

The development of public health is important to note as part of the basics of the U.S. healthcare system because its development was separate from the development of private medical practices. Public health specialists view health from a collectivist and preventative care viewpoint: to protect as many citizens as possible from health problems and to provide strategies to prevent health problems from occurring. Public health is challenged by its very success because consumers now take public health measures for granted. There are several successful vaccines that have targeted all childhood diseases, tobacco use has decreased significantly, accident prevention has increased, there are safer workplaces because of the Occupational Safety and Health Administration (OSHA), the fluoridation of water has been established, and there has been a decrease in mortality from heart attacks (Novick & Morrow, 2008). The National Association of County and City Health Officials (NACCHO) and the Association of State and Territorial Health Officials (ASTHO) are important support organizations for both state and local governments by providing policy expertise, technical advice, and lobbying at the federal level for appropriate funding and regulations. When some major event occurs like a natural or man-made disaster, people immediately think that public health will automatically control these problems. The public may not realize how much effort, dedication, and research takes place to protect the public. President Obama has recognized the importance of public health by supporting passage of the Affordable Care

Act, which focuses on increasing access to and quality of the U.S. healthcare system. The ACA also focuses on primary prevention activities, which are the foundation of public health.

It is important for healthcare consumers to recognize the role that public health plays in our health care. If you are sick, you go to your physician for medical advice, which may mean providing you with a prescription. However, sometimes you may not go see your physician because you do not have health insurance or you do not feel very sick or you would like to change one of your lifestyle behaviors. Public health surrounds consumers with educational opportunities to change a health condition or behavior. You can visit the Centers for Disease Control and Prevention website (www.cdc.gov) for information about different diseases and health conditions. You can also visit your local health department.

▶ Hospital and Outpatient Services

Many hospitals have experienced financial problems. As a result of the increased competition of outpatient services (which are often more cost effective, efficient, and consumer friendly) and reduced reimbursement from Medicare and Medicaid, many hospitals have developed strategies to increase their financial stability. Due to pressure to develop cost-containment measures, hospitals are forming huge hospital systems and building large physician workforces. In order to compete with the Affordable Care Act's mandated state healthcare exchanges where consumers can purchase health insurance, health insurance companies are developing relationships with hospitals and creating joint marketing plans and sharing patient data (Mathews, 2011).

Over the years, outpatient services have become the major competitors of hospitals. Advanced technology has enabled more ambulatory surgeries and testing, which has resulted in the development of many specialty centers for radiology and imaging, chemotherapy treatment, and kidney dialysis. Previously, these services were often performed in hospitals. What is even more interesting is that physicians or physician groups own some of the centers. They are receiving revenue that used to be hospital revenue. Hospitals have recognized that fact and have embraced outpatient services as part of their patient care. However, many hospitals, particularly in rural areas, have closed. Over 60 rural hospitals have closed since 2010 and over 670 rural hospitals in 42 states are vulnerable

to closure. Budget cuts and lower reimbursement rates from Medicare and Medicaid have impacted hospital revenues (Ellison, 2016).

Healthcare Personnel

The healthcare industry is the fastest growing industry in the U.S. economy, employing a workforce of nearly 20 million. Considering the aging of the U.S. population and the impact of the Affordable Care Act, it is expected that the healthcare industry will continue to experience strong job growth (Centers for Disease Control and Prevention, 2016). When we think of healthcare providers, we automatically think of physicians and nurses. However, the healthcare industry is comprised of many different health services professionals. The healthcare industry includes dentists, optometrists, psychologists, chiropractors, podiatrists, non-physician practitioners (NPPs), administrators, and allied health professionals. A new type of healthcare professional is the care coordinator, the fastest growing occupation, which integrates nursing, social work, and disability counseling for the elderly with chronic conditions who need additional assistance. It is important to identify allied health professionals because they provide a range of essential healthcare services that complement the services provided by physicians and nurses. This category of health professionals is an integral component of providing quality health.

Health care can occur in varied settings. Physicians have traditionally operated in their own practices but they also work in hospitals, mental health facilities, managed care organizations, and community health centers. They may also hold governmental positions or teach at a university. They could be employed by an insurance company. Health professionals, in general, may work at many different organizations, both for profit and nonprofit. Although the healthcare industry is one of the largest employers in the United States, there continue to be shortages of physicians in certain geographic areas of the country. Rural areas continue to suffer physician shortages, which limits consumer access to health care. There have been different incentive programs to encourage physicians to relocate to rural areas, but shortages still exist. In most states, only physicians, dentists, and a few other practitioners may serve patients directly without the authorization of another licensed independent health professional. Those categories authorized include chiropractic, optometry, psychotherapy, and podiatry. Some states authorize midwifery and physical therapy (Jonas, 2003). There also continues to be a shortage of registered nurses nationwide. The American Association of Colleges of Nursing (AACN) is publicizing this issue with policy makers (AACN, 2013).

Healthcare Expenditures

The percentage of the U.S. gross domestic product (GDP) devoted to healthcare expenditures has increased over the past several decades. The Centers for Medicare and Medicaid Services (CMS) predicts annual healthcare costs will be $4.64 trillion by 2020, which represents nearly 20% of the U.S. gross domestic product (CMS, 2016). The increase in healthcare spending can be attributed to three causes: (1) When prices increase in an economy overall, the cost of medical care will increase and, even when prices are adjusted for inflation, medical prices have increased; (2) as life expectancy increases in the United States, more individuals will require more medical care for chronic diseases, which means there will be more healthcare expenses; and (3) as healthcare technology and research provide for more sophisticated and more expensive procedures, there will be an increase in healthcare expenses (Pointer, Williams, Isaacs, & Knickman, 2007).

As healthcare expenditures continue to increase, the major focus of the healthcare industry is cost control, in both the public and private sectors. For years, healthcare costs were unchecked. The concept of retrospective reimbursement methods (when a provider submitted a bill for healthcare services to a health insurance company and was automatically reimbursed) gave healthcare insurers no incentive to control costs in health care. This type of reimbursement method contributed to expensive health care for both the healthcare insurance companies and the individual who was paying out of pocket for services. As a result, the establishment of a prospective reimbursement system for Medicare (reimbursement is based on care criteria for certain conditions, regardless of providers' costs) became an incentive for providers to manage how they were providing services. The Center for Medicare and Medicaid Innovation provided grants to healthcare organizations to explore different payment models based on performance.

The managed care model for healthcare delivery was developed for the primary purpose of containing healthcare costs. By administering both the healthcare services and the reimbursement of these services, and therefore eliminating a third-party health insurer, the industry felt that this model would be very cost effective. The consumer's (or patient's) and the physician's concerns were the same—worry about providing quality care while focusing predominantly on cost. The consumer was also worried about loss of freedom

to choose a primary care provider. The physician was worried about loss of income.

As managed care evolved, managed care organizations (MCOs) were developed, which allowed more choice for both the consumer and the physician. Eventually, there were models such as preferred provider organizations (PPOs) and point-of-service (POS) plans that allowed consumers to more freely choose their provider; however, there was a financial disincentive to use a provider outside the network of the MCO. Providers were also able to see non-MCO patients, which increased their income, but they also received a financial deterrent because any MCO patient was given health care at a discounted rate.

▶ Information Technology

The healthcare industry has lagged behind utilizing information technology (IT) as a form of communicating important data across healthcare systems nationally. Despite that fact, there have been specific applications developed for health IT, such as e-prescribing, telemedicine, and e-health, and specific applied technology, such as the PatientPoint, the MelaFind optical scanner, the Phreesia Pad, the Sapien heart valve, robotic checkups, Electronic Aspirin, Accuson P10, and the Piccolo xpress, which were discussed elsewhere in this text. Healthcare organizations have recognized the importance of IT and have hired chief information officers (CIOs) and chief technology officers (CTOs) to manage their data. However, healthcare consumers need to embrace use of electronic patient records. This will enable patients to be treated effectively and efficiently nationally. The patient health record can be integrated into the electronic health records that are being utilized nationwide. Having the ability to access a patient's health information could assist in reducing medical errors. Consumers' utilization of a tool like HealthVault could provide an opportunity to consolidate all medical information electronically, so if there are any medical problems, the information will be readily available.

▶ Healthcare Law

To be an effective healthcare manager, it is important to understand basic legal principles that influence the work environment, including the legal relationship between the organization and the consumer—the healthcare provider and the patient. As both a healthcare manager and healthcare consumer, it is imperative that you are familiar with the different federal and state laws that impact the healthcare organization. It is also important that as consumers and as employees of the healthcare industry, you understand the differences between civil and criminal law and the penalties that may be imposed for breaking those laws. Both federal and state laws have been enacted and policy has been implemented to protect both the healthcare provider and the healthcare consumer. New laws have been passed and older laws have been amended to reflect needed changes regarding health care to continue to protect participants, from both a patient and an employee–employer perspective.

U.S. citizens continue to experience some of the poorest health outcomes in the industrialized world. It is the responsibility of the government and policymakers, clinicians, and researchers to become involved in the progress of developing a systematic healthcare transformation in order to improve the health outcomes in this country. The goal of the *Healthy People* reports is to improve the quality of life and to eliminate health disparities among different segments of the population. These goals must be supported by lawmakers to ensure that at least a minimum standard is established and that health justice is achieved (Department of Health and Human Services [HHS], 2000). The Affordable Care Act and its mandates have attempted to rectify these problems.

▶ Healthcare Ethics

Legal standards are the minimal standard of action established for individuals in a society. Ethical standards are considered one level above a legal action because individuals make a choice based on what is the "right thing to do," not what is required by law. There are many interpretations of the concept of ethics. Ethics has been interpreted as the moral foundation for standards of conduct (Taylor, 1975). The concept of ethical standards applies to actions that are hoped for and expected by individuals. Actions may be considered legal but not ethical. There are many definitions of ethics but, essentially, ethics is concerned with what are right and wrong choices as perceived by society and individuals.

There are also several ethical issues involving the healthcare industry and its stakeholders. There are two components of ethics in health care: medical ethics, which focus on the treatment of the patient; and bioethics, which focus on technology and how it is utilized in health care. The most important stakeholder in health care is the patient. The most important relationship is this stakeholder's relationship with his or her healthcare provider. Their relationship is impacted

by the other stakeholders in the industry, including the government, which regulates healthcare provider activities; the insurance companies, which interact with both provider and patient; and healthcare facilities, such as hospitals or managed care facilities, where the physician has a relationship. All of these stakeholders can influence how a healthcare provider interacts with the patient because they have an interest in the outcome. For that reason, many organizations that represent these stakeholders have developed codes of ethics so individuals are provided guidance for ethical behavior. Codes of ethics for the physicians and other healthcare providers, nurses, pharmaceutical companies, and medical equipment companies were discussed previously and emphasize how these stakeholders should interact with both the healthcare providers and patients. These codes of conduct also apply to the relationship between employees in a healthcare facility. The issue of workplace bullying has been a continuous problem for many years. The Joint Commission issued a statement and guidelines for workplace behavior in the healthcare industry. The Joint Commission indicated that this type of behavior can be destructive, resulting in medical errors.

A major area of bioethics is the treatment of patients who are dying. Euthanasia, including physician-assisted suicide, which is illegal in all states but Oregon, Washington, and most recently, Vermont, has been a controversial patient issue for years. Supporters of euthanasia think it is the individual's right to choose when to end his or her life and individuals should have assistance from a physician, if needed. Opponents feel it is unethical because it is the responsibility of a physician to save a life, or not to take a life.

Another area of ethical discussion is organ transplantation. There are not enough organ donors in the United States, thereby creating a long waiting list. With limited supply, the ethical dilemma of organ transplants is how to determine who should receive an organ. The United States has a strict policy on organ donations; however, in other parts of the world black markets have developed to sell organs because of the continued demand. The World Health Organization indicates that there are 10,000 illegal organ purchases worldwide on an annual basis, which is considered a conservative estimate. In China, 11,000 organs are harvested from political prisoners each year without anesthetic. There are massive numbers of illegal kidney transplants due to the rise of diabetes worldwide.

When Dolly the sheep was cloned in 1995, an international furor ensued. There are diametrically opposed views on cloning. Opponents feel that cloning takes the natural procreation process and turns it into a scientific experiment. Supporters feel that the scientific community has provided an opportunity to recreate a specimen, at will, with the desired genes. Scientists in some countries have suggested they have cloned human beings.

Discrimination based on genetic testing has become illegal in the workplace. Although this information gained from genetic testing is important to individuals and their families, there are several ethical issues regarding genetic testing. Employers have discriminated against employees because of this information. These situations have generated many discussions from a bioethical perspective.

▶ Mental Health

Mental health issues impact millions of U.S. residents. Mental health disabilities reduce the life expectancy of individuals by several years. Treatment of mental health disorders has been traditionally underfunded because of the attitude of the traditional healthcare system, confusion by health insurance companies, and mentally ill individuals' fear of discrimination. In 1999, Surgeon General David Satcher's report on mental health brought awareness to the issues with the U.S. mental healthcare system. The Mental Health Parity Act of 1996 was an attempt to establish a fair system of treatment between mental health disorders and traditional healthcare conditions by mandating that mental health care annual and lifetime limits be equal to limits for traditional health care. President George W. Bush's Freedom Commission on Mental Health focused on an analysis of the mental health system and recommendations to improve mental health care.

The Mental Health Parity and Addiction Equity Act (2008) and its 2013 final rules further supported mental health care by requiring insurance plans to offer benefits for mental health care similar to traditional medical care benefits and similar cost sharing. However, mental health experts and legislators believed the Act was weak overall and recently passed a final rule that would strengthen the Act, increasing parity between mental health care insurance coverage and traditional health care insurance coverage. The Obama administration has recognized the importance of funding mental health initiatives, including teacher training programs for mental health awareness (Mohney, 2013).

▶ Trends in Health Care

Complementary and alternative medicine (CAM) is a group of diverse medical care practices that are not considered part of traditional medicine. "Complementary"

generally refers to using a nonmainstream approach together with conventional medicine. "Alternative" refers to using a nonmainstream approach in place of conventional medicine. **Integrative medicine** means a combination of alternative and complementary medicine with a mainstream approach.

Examples of CAM include acupuncture, chiropractic manipulation, diet therapies, meditation, natural products (e.g., flaxseed and fish oil), yoga, and massage. In 2012, approximately 40% of adults used CAM. CAM use is more predominant in females and those individuals with higher education and income. The National Center for Health's recent statistics indicate that back pain was the most common reason people used CAM (National Center for Complementary and Alternative Medicine, 2016). U.S. consumers spend an average of $34 billion on CAM. It is anticipated that more CAM therapies, particularly alternative medicine therapies, will be used by those individuals that are uninsured and underinsured.

Nursing Home Trends

In 2001, the Robert Wood Johnson Foundation funded a pilot project developed by Dr. Bill Thomas, the **Green House Project**, which is a unique type of nursing home that focuses on creating a residence that not only provides services but also is a home, not an institution where residents merely receive care. It alters the size of the facility, the physical environment, and delivery of services (Fine, 2009).

The home is managed by a team of workers who share the care of the residents, including cooking and housekeeping. Staff members who provide day-to-day care are certified nursing assistants (CNAs). All mandated professional personnel, such as physicians, nurses, social workers, and dieticians, form visiting clinical support teams that assess the **elders** and supervise their care (Kane, Lum, Cutler, Degenholtz, & Yu, 2007).

The residents can eat their meals when they choose. The word "patient" is not used; all residents are called "elders." The Green House is designed for 6–10 elders. Each resident has a private room and a private bathroom. The elders' rooms have lots of sunlight and are located near the kitchen and dining areas. There are patios and gardens for elders and staff to enjoy. Although these new types of nursing homes look like a residential home and resemble other hoes in their neighborhood, they adhere to all long-term housing requirements (Fine, 2009).

Residents can also have their own pets, which are not allowed in traditional nursing homes. According to a recent study performed by researchers at the University of Minnesota, the residents of the Green House are able to perform their activities of daily living longer and are less depressed than residents of traditional nursing homes and are able to be self-sufficient longer than residents of traditional nursing homes. The staff also enjoy working at the Green House, resulting in less turnover (Kane et al., 2007).

The first Green House was constructed in Tupelo, Mississippi. There are now over 100 homes in nearly 20 states. Another 130 homes are under development in 10 additional states. Dr. Thomas has partnered with the Robert Wood Johnson Foundation (RWJF) and NCB Capital Impact, a nonprofit organization that provides financial assistance to underserved communities. NCB Capital Impact has a loan program that provides financial assistance of up to $125,000 to support engineering, architectural, and other expenses for selected Green House sites. The borrower must contribute 25% of the loan amount (NCB Capital Impact, 2016).

Since 2002, the RWJF has awarded $12 million, primarily to NCB Capital Impact, to develop, test, and evaluate the Green House model. In 2011, the RWJF decided to expand its support, with the goal of helping the Green House model achieve greater reach and impact. With NCB Capital Impact, the RWJF announced a 10-year, $10 million low-interest credit line to finance the building of Green House homes. Specifically, this investment reduces the cost of financing Green House projects to serve low-income elders. RWJF support is helping to spread the Green House model across the United States. Today, hundreds of Green House homes are open or under development in many states. Research indicates that Green House operations are comparable in cost to those of traditional nursing homes (Robert Wood Johnson Foundation, 2016).

Value-Based Purchasing

Pay-for-performance (P4P) and **value-based purchasing (VBP)** are terms that describe healthcare payment systems that reward healthcare providers, including hospitals, physicians, and other providers, for their efficiency, which is defined as providing higher quality care for less cost. From a healthcare consumer's perspective, these stakeholders should hold healthcare providers accountable for both the cost and high quality of their care. Because historically, most health care in the United States has been provided by employers, in VBP, employers should select healthcare plans based on demonstrated performance of quality and cost-effective health care (Agency for Healthcare Research and Quality [AHRQ], 2016). For the past decade, the CMS has been collaborating with the National Quality Forum, The Joint Commission, the National Committee for Quality Assurance, the AHRQ, and the American Medical Association to implement initiatives to assess P4P systems nationwide.

The Affordable Care Act of 2010 established the **Hospital Value-Based Purchasing Program (HVBPP)**. It is a CMS initiative that rewards acute-care hospitals with incentive payments for the quality of care they provide to people with Medicare, not just the quantity of procedures performed. Hospitals are rewarded based on how closely they follow best clinical practices and how well they enhance patients' experiences of care. When hospitals follow proven best practices, patients receive higher quality care and see better outcomes. Hospital value-based purchasing is just one initiative the CMS is undertaking to improve the quality of care Medicare beneficiaries receive.

Beginning January 1, 2016, the CMS implemented a Home Health Value Based Purchasing Program (HHVBP) model among all home health agencies (HHAs) in nine states representing each geographic area in the nation. All Medicare-certified HHAs that provide services in Massachusetts, Maryland, North Carolina, Florida, Washington, Arizona, Iowa, Nebraska, and Tennessee will compete on value in the HHVBP model, where payment is tied to quality performance (CMS, 2016).

Accountable Care Organizations

According to the CMS website, Medicare **Accountable Care Organizations** (ACOs) are comprised of groups of doctors, hospitals, and other healthcare providers and suppliers who come together voluntarily to provide coordinated, high-quality care at lower costs to their Original Medicare patients. ACOs are patient-centered organizations in which the patient and providers are true partners in care decisions. Medicare beneficiaries will have better control over their health care, and providers will have better information about their patients' medical history and better relationships with patients' other providers. Provider participation in ACOs is purely voluntary, and participating patients will see no change in their Original Medicare benefits and will keep their freedom to see any Medicare provider. When an ACO succeeds in both delivering high-quality care and spending healthcare dollars more wisely, it will share in the savings it achieves for the Medicare program.

Medicare has developed several major programs for providers to become ACOs:

- **Medicare Shared Savings Program**—a program that helps Medicare fee-for-service program providers become an ACO. Over 400 providers are enrolled in the Medicare Shared Savings Program.

■ **Pioneer ACO Model**—a program designed for early adopters of coordinated care. Any monetary savings are shared with Medicare. This program has been less successful.

There were 32 ACOs enrolled in the Pioneer ACO model, but enrollment has dropped to 19 providers. According to recent results, nearly one-half of the ACOs improved patient quality of healthcare services, patient satisfaction, and saved money. However, the ACOs owed Medicare $4 million because they spent more on their patients than the traditional Medicare fee-for-service rates (Bleach, 2013).

● **Next Generation ACO Model**—Building on experience from the Pioneer ACO Model and the Medicare Shared Savings Program (Shared Savings Program), the Next Generation ACO Model offers a new opportunity in accountable care—one that sets predictable financial targets, enables providers and beneficiaries greater opportunities to coordinate care, and aims to attain the highest quality standards of care. There are 21 ACOS participating in this program.

■ **Advance Payment ACO Model**—a supplementary incentive program for smaller practices: physician-based and rural providers in the Shared Savings Program. They receive monthly payments to use for coordinated care. Currently 35 practices participate in the program.

● **Comprehensive ESRD Care Model**—The Comprehensive ESRD Care Model is designed to identify, test, and evaluate new ways to improve care for Medicare beneficiaries with end-stage renal disease (ESRD). Through the Comprehensive ESRD Care Model, the CMS will partner with healthcare providers and suppliers to test the effectiveness of a new payment and service delivery model in providing beneficiaries with patient-centered, high-quality care. There are 13 ESRD participants.

For example, California's **Integrated Healthcare Association's** (IHA) P4P program, started in 2003, has operated as the largest nongovernmental program nationally. The program targets 225 medical groups representing 35,000 physicians that contracted with the 10 largest health maintenance organizations (HMOs) and P4Ps in the state, which have 9 million enrollees. The program has four key components: a common set of measures and benchmarks, health plan incentive payments to physician organizations, public reporting of physician organization results, and public recognition awards. The IHA scored physician care based on the healthcare effectiveness data, information measures, and paid performance-based payments. These report cards are available to patients so they can review the performance of the health plans. The results are posted on the California Office of the Patient Advocate website (State of California, 2016). The concept of P4P is a valid concept for health care. Its goals of quality and access are similar to the goals of the Affordable Care Act. There are nearly 200 P4Ps worldwide that indicate improvements in clinical quality performances, although fewer improvements in patient satisfaction. These programs also encourage physicians to adopt clinical decision-support systems (Integrated Healthcare Association, 2016).

Electronic Prescribing

E-prescribing developed as a result of the Medicare Prescription Drug, Improvement and Modernization Act. Part D, which authorized a drug prescription program for enrollees, also supported a voluntary electronic prescription program for providers. With an e-prescribing system, the user–clinician signs into a system with a password to verify identify. The user–clinician provides a patient identification code so he or she can review the patient's medication list, prescribe a new drug, and designate which pharmacy will fill the prescription (HRSA, 2016).

E-prescribing not only is more efficient, but it also enhances patient safety. More than 7,000 medication-related deaths occur each year as a result of incompatible-drug interactions and drug allergies. These deaths are because of illegible handwritten prescriptions and because the healthcare provider is unaware of patient allergies. E-prescriptions are immediately notified about patient-specific drug allergies and potential drug interactions (Brunetti & Jay, 2009). According to the 2012 National Progress Report on E-Prescribing and Safe-RX Rankings, 93% of internists, 85% of cardiovascular specialists, and 84% of family practice providers have adopted e-prescribing. Nearly 70% of physicians' offices prescribe and nearly 90% of prescribers also use an electronic health record. Over 90% of pharmacies can accept electronic prescriptions (Surescripts, 2012).

Section 132 of the **Medicare Improvements for Patients and Providers Act of 2008 (MIPPA)** authorized incentives to encourage physicians to e-prescribe. In January 2009, Medicare and some private healthcare plans began paying a bonus to physicians who e-prescribe to their Medicare patients. Medicare will also penalize physicians who do not e-prescribe, by reducing reimbursement to them; in 2012, the reimbursement rate was reduced by 1%, in 2013, by 1.5%, and in 2014 and all later years, by 2%

(Electronic Prescribing Incentive Program, 2016). IT companies are providing free software to physicians to encourage them to electronically prescribe.

Telemedicine

Telemedicine refers to the use of information technology to enable healthcare providers to communicate with rural care providers regarding patient care or to communicate directly with patients regarding treatment. The basic form of telemedicine is a telephone consultation. Telemedicine is most frequently used in pathology and radiology because images can be transmitted to a distant location where a specialist will read the results. Telemedicine is becoming more common because it increases healthcare access in remote locations such as rural areas. It also is a cost-effective mode of treatment. It is also possible that employers and health plans recognize the potential to improve access to medical care while reducing medical costs (Gingrich, Boxer, & Brooks, 2008). In 2009, Avera eCare established eEmergency, which provides immediate electronic access of emergency certified physicians and nurses to rural providers to help them with diagnosis of patients with critical conditions. It is an example of tele-emergency services. Rural clinicians and administrators agreed that eEmergency services have demonstrated significant impact on the quality of clinical services provided in rural areas.

This type of consumer-centric approach is becoming more popular.

Radio Frequency Identification

Radio frequency identification (RFID) chips transmit data to receivers. Each of these chips is uniquely identified by a signal indicating where it is located. Businesses have used RFID for inventory management by placing a chip on each of the items of inventory. Walmart was one of the first retailers to use RFID technology to manage its massive inventory. Recently, RFID technology is being used in many aspects of the operations of the healthcare industry. RFID can be used for the following:

- Tracking pharmaceuticals as they are shipped from the manufacturer to the customer;
- Tracking pharmaceutical inventory in a healthcare facility;
- Tracking wait time in emergency rooms;
- Tracking the use of what is being used in surgeries;
- Tracking costly medical equipment to ensure easy access;
- Identifying providers in hospitals to ensure efficiency in care;

- Identifying laboratory specimens to reduce medical errors;
- Tracking patients, including infants, while they are hospitalized;
- Tracking hazardous materials that pose a public health threat; and
- Tracking hand washing to ensure employee compliance (RFID Solutions, 2016).

Robotic Surgery

Robots were first introduced as a surgical tool in 1987. **Robotic surgery** is a type of minimally invasive surgery (MIS) that it is less invasive than traditional surgery—there are smaller incisions, which reduce the risk of infection, shorten hospital stays, and reduce recuperation times. Surgeons manipulate robotic arms to perform surgeries normally performed by human hands. Surgeons have to be trained in robotic surgery and use a machine that will reduce the possibility of errors caused by tremors in their hands.

As robotic surgery became more popular, the National Aeronautic and Space Administration (NASA) developed the concept of **telesurgery** or **medical robotics and computer assisted surgery (MRCAS)**, which combines virtual reality, robots, and medicine. The U.S. Army also became involved in robotic surgery because they were interested in bringing surgery to the soldiers who were fighting and needed surgery immediately. They hoped robotic surgery would reduce war mortality rates. It is important to note that there are also other tools that can be used for MIS. Studies have indicated that some procedures, such as appendectomies, show very little difference in results whether performed by the traditional method or the robotic method. However, robotic surgeries performed on the prostate have shown significant positive outcomes (Guidarelli, 2006; Loisance, 2007).

The robotic system that has dominated the current market is the **da Vinci Surgical System**, which was developed by Intuitive Surgical of Sunnyvale, California. It is used in areas of cardiac, urologic, gynecologic, and general surgery. The initial investment for a da Vinci system is $2 million, with an annual upkeep of $100,000 (Intuitive Surgical, Inc., 2013). Despite the initial cost, experts feel that the actual procedure is cost effective because recuperation time is far less for the patients. The continued issue with telesurgery is patient injuries as a result of the use of robotic equipment. There have been continued issues with the DaVinci tool. The FDA, which regulates medical devices, received 3,700 reports in 2013 of injuries, deaths, and malfunctions from robotic surgery. Industry experts believe these adverse events are being underreported. (Langreth, 2013). In June 2014, there were 3,100 systems worldwide with 570,000 procedures performed (Lee, 2015). As with any technological advances, the costs should decrease and the tool will become more advanced and more efficient, but the safety issues must be addressed.

Drugstore Clinics

Rite Aid, Walgreen's, and CVS Health (CVS), three national chain pharmacies, have established **drugstore clinics**. CVS, the leader in this innovative type of health care, now has 1,100 **Minute Clinics** nationwide. CVS has decided to expand treatment options to include conditions typically handled by a physician. The goal is not to replace primary care providers but to increase access to health care. CVS is taking its role in retail health clinics very seriously. In September 2014, CVS stopped selling tobacco products at stores nationwide on grounds it was the ethical thing to do for customers. Walgreens, which has nearly 400 **Take Care Clinics** nationwide, will follow the CVS policy of stopping tobacco sales. Many of the patients who use drugstore clinics do not have a primary care provider (Modern Healthcare, 2013). According to the **Convenient Care Association** (CCA), since the walk-in clinics opened in 2000, retail clinics are now a common feature, with 10.5 million visits occurring annually at more than 1,800 retail clinics. Like urgent care clinics, retail clinics are open late and on weekends, and customers do not need an appointment. This type of access may encourage more individuals to seek health care (Bachrach, Frolich, Garcimnde, & Nevitt, 2015).

Care Managers and Patient Navigators

Care managers, or care coordinators, are individuals who provide a combination of nursing, social services, and disability assistance primarily to individuals who are eligible for both Medicare and Medicaid (dual eligibles), suffer from chronic conditions, and often cannot handle managing their own chronic conditions. The goal of a care coordinator is to prevent the patient's placement into a nursing home. Dual eligible patients utilize 35% of Medicare and Medicaid spending so this type of assistance with patient life issues may reduce governmental spending. According to the CMS, eight states have signed agreements with the CMS to develop care-coordination plans (Dickson, 2013).

Care coordination is the fastest growing occupation in the healthcare industry and care coordinators are primarily registered nurses who have received additional training in coordinated care, collaboration, and communication.

The Villages Health System

The Villages is one of the largest over-55 golf cart communities in the United States. The community developed a partnership with the University of South Florida to create a **patient-centered**, community-based and primary-care-driven healthcare system. A primary care network is being developed in which all residents have access to a **medical home** or care center that will be located within 10 minutes' access by golf cart. There are currently 6 care center facilities with 5–9 physicians in each care center that will serve as gatekeepers for patients' care. Although many patients are Medicare eligible, the physicians will be salaried and focused not on the quantity of patients they receive for their Medicare reimbursement but on the development of relationships with their patients. Each facility will serve a designated geographic area of patients. When specialty care is needed, the physicians will help patient with the referral. They will have extended hours and emergency operations. They will implement the electronic health record system to enable patient data sharing among the centers. They will also have on staff health coaches, who will work with patients on developing a healthy lifestyle as part of their health learning center. Patient surveys indicate they are very positive about this structure and have expressed interest in developing specialty care centers. It has also been ranked nationally as an excellent primary care provider system. However, in a stunning development, the Villages Health system announced the structure has left them with major debt so effective January 1, 2017, they will no longer be accepting any forms of health insurance except Medicare Advantage, the managed care of Medicare. This type of insurance provides more revenue for the system. This decision has left thousands of original Medicare members out of the system and will need to find new medical care. (The Villages Health, 2016).

▶ International Healthcare Systems

For years, there has been a movement toward healthcare reform in the United States; many people believe that because the United States is so powerful and wealthy, compared to the rest of the world, it should not have nearly 50 million uninsured citizens. However, universal healthcare coverage may not be the answer. It, too, has problems.

There is continued controversy over the expense of the U.S. healthcare system. If we spend so much of our gross domestic product on health care, why are there geographic disparities on who receives it? This may result in lower health indicators in the United States, such as life expectancy and infant mortality rates, compared to the rest of the world. Although the United States can provide state-of-the-art health care, the Institute of Medicine report estimates that 44,000–90,000 annual deaths are a result of medical errors (Kohn, Corrigan, & Donaldson, 1999). As with any large system, there are system errors that were just outlined. The United States is not the only country with a healthcare system that has problems.

▶ **Universal Healthcare Concepts**

Countries with national healthcare programs provide universal access to health care to all citizens. They have a **single-payer system**, which means the government pays for the healthcare services. There are three models for structuring a universal or national healthcare system: national health insurance, national health system, and socialized health insurance system. **National health insurance**, as in Canada, is funded by the government through general taxes, although the delivery of care is by private providers. In a **national health system**, as in Great Britain, taxes support the system but the government also manages the infrastructure for healthcare delivery. In a **socialized health insurance system**, as in Germany, the government mandates financial contributions by both employers and employees, with private providers delivering health care. Sickness funds, which are nonprofit insurance companies, collect the contributions and pay the healthcare providers (Shi & Singh, 2008). The U.S. healthcare system is employer–employee based and government funded. The U.S. system provides 100% coverage of people 65 years of age or older with the Medicare program, and 82% coverage for people younger than 65 years of age through employer-based insurance, Medicaid, Indian Health Services, Veterans' Administration (TRICARE), and the federal government employee program.

Infant mortality rates and life expectancy rates are common healthcare indicator comparisons among countries. Based on Organization for Economic Cooperation and Development data, Japan, Switzerland, and Sweden, which had the best infant mortality and life expectancy rates, were selected for discussion. These analyses will demonstrate that although these countries offer a type of universal healthcare coverage, they also have problems. The following country

information was primarily obtained from the 2015 Commonwealth Fund International Profiles of Health Care Systems.

Japan

Japan's social security system is divided into four components: social insurance, social welfare, public assistance, and public health. Participation in the universal public health insurance system (PHIS) is mandatory for every Japanese citizen. The system is regulated by the Japanese government. The PHIS has 3,400 insurers. Japan's health expenditures represent 10% of GDP. As part of the Japanese health insurance system, the insured pays a premium to the health insurance companies, and in case of a care visit, pays a 30% coinsurance rate to the healthcare institutions. The majority of medical facilities are privately owned. Medical fees are controlled by the government. There are more than 4,000 community comprehensive support centers to coordinate services for chronic diseases. Electronic health records are being used in designated areas as pilot projects. There is research to determine what is the best way to provide and maintain patient information to the providers and to the patients themselves. The Social Security and Tax Number System (SSTNS), a system of unique identifiers, was started in 2016 and is designed to be used as an identifier to medical services for citizens. Under the 2015 Health Care Reform Act, local governments will be responsible for administering community-based plans and to set and collect insurance premiums. Large hospitals will also be required to promote care coordination with community providers.

With a rapidly aging population with increasing chronic diseases, it is estimated that spending will rise by 3% annually. Income from health insurance premiums covers only 56% of social security expenses. The Japanese government is reforming the social security system to be more cost effective, with community-based care delivery and less hospital care. It is anticipated that Japan will triple government spending on health care in the next 20 years (Oi, 2015).

France

France's healthcare system has many characteristics of a socialized health insurance program similar to Germany and Japan. The system consists of statutory health insurance (SHI), funded by payroll taxes (64%), a national income tax (16%), alcohol and tobacco taxes, the drug industry and voluntary health insurance companies (12%), governmental subsidies (2%), and moneys from Social Security (6%). There is universal coverage, for approximately 99% of French citizens. The state has become increasingly involved in controlling health expenditures, which represent 11% of GDP. Cost sharing comes from coinsurance and copayments. A high-level electronic-health-record system is currently being implemented nationwide. Over 550,000 patients have an EHR, and an estimated 600 hospitals and 6,000 health care providers use the EHR. The SHI has faced tremendous deficits over the past several years, but the deficit has decreased dramatically as a result of country-wide initiatives. The initiatives include a reduction in the number of hospitals, the removal of 600 drugs from public reimbursement, an increase in generic-drug prescribing, and the increased use of over-the-counter drugs. France also has focused on cost containment through central purchasing.

Unlike in the United States, the French government makes it very difficult for insurance companies to deny any coverage because of preexisting conditions. Citizens who are very ill receive increased care and coverage, which is unlike the U.S. system, in which individuals may go financially bankrupt because of their cost sharing during a chronic disease.

All physicians in France participate in the nation's public health insurance (like Medicaid). The average American physician earns more than five times the average U.S. wage, while the average French physician makes only about two times the average French wage. However, in France, medical schools, although extremely competitive to enter, are tuition free. Therefore, French physicians enter their careers with minimal debt. Unlike U.S. physicians who pay high malpractice premiums, they pay much lower malpractice insurance premiums because lawsuits against physicians are much less common in France. French physicians have fewer administrative expenses because the government has created a standardized, efficient system for physician billing and patient reimbursement using electronic funds. It is interesting to note that the French government allows physicians to charge more than the government's reimbursement schedule, although physicians employed by hospitals are not allowed to set their own fees. Most physicians do not overcharge because of the intense competition in their field (Dutton, 2007).

Consumers have had no restrictions on physician selection; they may visit several physicians before they find the one they prefer. This type of **medical nomadism** drives up healthcare costs. In response to this issue, in 2005, the government established a **coordinated care pathway**, which is similar to the U.S. managed care system (Tanner, 2008). Individuals are encouraged to choose a preferred doctor and follow the doctor's pathway for their care. At this point, this is a choice, not a mandate; however, individuals' cost sharing does increase if they refuse to purchase generic drugs and do not use the coordinated care pathway system.

Switzerland

Switzerland's healthcare system is considered one of the best in the world, like that of the United States. It is unique because all residents are required to purchase health insurance, so, in a sense, it is a country with universal healthcare coverage. Approximately 99.5% of Swiss have health insurance paid for by mandatory statutory health insurance premiums (SHI). Health spending is 12% of GDP. Switzerland is tied with France as third most expensive of the OECD countries. Individuals buy insurance directly from private insurance providers. The Swiss system is similar to the "managed competition" healthcare plan proposed by Bill and Hillary Clinton in the early 1990s (Shafrin, 2008). Swiss law requires all citizens to purchase a health insurance package. Insurers cannot reject an applicant based on his or her health status. Healthier consumers pay higher premiums to subsidize the costs for the less healthy. Nonsmokers pay lower premiums than smokers. Insurers compete on price. Consumers, however, can adjust their premium up or down by choosing a larger or smaller annual deductible or by joining a managed care plan. Switzerland ranks second only to the United States in the ability of patients to choose their provider.

Unlike in the other countries discussed in this chapter, few Swiss employers provide insurance or contribute to insurance, so individuals bear the full cost of insurance plans. The government subsidizes the indigent. The Swiss healthcare insurance industry is private but regulated by the government. Swiss citizens pay more for health insurance than do citizens of other European countries. The government controls prescription drug prices, of which consumers pay 10% (Rovner, 2008). Like the United States and Japan, Switzerland has focused on health technology A national e-health service called eHealth Suisse is coordinated by the government. All providers must collect and store patient information electronically, and any health-related websites where the information is collected must be quality certified. Every citizen has an SHI subscription card, which has an encoded personal identification number that allows medical information to be coded on the card if the insurer agrees. As of this writing, the implementation of this type of technology is inconsistent across the country.

▶ Local Government Healthcare Reform

Massachusetts Universal Healthcare Program

In April 2006, the state of Massachusetts passed legislation to implement a type of universal healthcare coverage for its residents. The legislation mandated that all adult residents obtain health insurance coverage by July 1, 2007. At the time, 90% of residents had health care; the mandate would result in 98% of residents having health insurance. The law mandated that nearly every resident of Massachusetts obtain a minimum level of insurance coverage, provided free healthcare insurance for residents earning less than 150% of the federal poverty level (FPL), and mandated that employers with more than 10 "full-time" employees provide healthcare insurance. The law was amended significantly in 2008, 2010, and finally in 2014 to make it consistent with the federal Affordable Care Act. As with the Affordable Care Act, Massachusetts residents who did not purchase health insurance had to pay a fine. The purchase of health insurance was based on whether they could afford it or not. For those residents who did not register, a financial penalty of up to 50% of the health insurance plan cost would be assessed. By July 1, 2007, employers with 11 or more employees were required to provide health insurance coverage or pay a fair-share contribution of $295 annually per employee. Employers were also required to offer a Section 125 cafeteria plan that permits employees to purchase health care using pretax funds. A specially designed health coverage option was available for residents 19–36 years of age (Brown, 2013).

As part of the healthcare reform, Massachusetts established a clearinghouse system, the **Commonwealth Health Insurance Connector**, which facilitated the buying, selling, and administration of affordable, quality, private insurance coverage for small businesses and individuals. A major component of this reform was the provision of government-funded subsidies to low-income individuals to assist with the purchase of health insurance. Plans offered through the Commonwealth Care have no deductibles and are offered by Medicaid managed care organizations (Commonwealth Health Insurance Connector, 2016).

Any resident could purchase coverage through the clearinghouse and nonresidents could purchase insurance if their employer designated the nonresident as part of their group plan. Insurance purchased through this clearinghouse could be transferred within the state, during periods of unemployment, part-time employment, or self-employment (Haisimaier & Owcharenko, 2006). As a result of this program, an estimated 250,000 individuals have health insurance coverage. However, a major problem resulting from this new program is a shortage of primary care physicians. Many formerly uninsured people require the services of a primary care physician. There are now huge waiting lists to obtain appointments for an initial visit. This problem is reflective of the geographic maldistribution of primary care physicians in the United States—there are more specialists than there are primary care physicians. Massachusetts has passed incentive legislation, such as loan forgiveness for physician medical training, to encourage primary physicians to practice in the state. The incentives have increased the number of primary care physicians in the state. Massachusetts has the lowest uninsured rate in the nation at 4.9%. When the Affordable Care Act was implemented, the rate dropped to 3%. Hospitals are seeing fewer uninsured patients, and visits to emergency rooms for primary health care are down by approximately 33%. A benefit of this program is a healthier population (Dorsey, J., 2015).

Healthy San Francisco Program

In February 2006, then-San Francisco Mayor Gavin Newsom created a Universal Healthcare Council to develop a plan to provide access to health care for San Francisco's uninsured adults. This collaborative effort, comprised of representatives from the healthcare, business, labor, philanthropy, and research communities, met for four months. The council reviewed demographic and actuarial data, and heard from community advocates and employers to identify and quantify the needs of the uninsured. As a result of these meetings, in April 2007, the city's **Healthy San Francisco (HSF) Program** was established and made comprehensive health care available to the 73,000 uninsured San Francisco residents between 18 and 65 years of age. The San Francisco Department of Public Health (DPH) is responsible for the overall planning, development, implementation, and ongoing administration of Healthy San Francisco. Those eligible are required to obtain care at the San Francisco Medical Home Network, which consists of public health clinics, community clinics, and private providers.

Employers with 100 employees or more are also required to spend $1.76 per work hour per employee on health benefits. Employers with 20–99 employees are required to spend $1.17 per hour. It is not an insurance program, but a restructuring of the county's program for the uninsured (Department of Public Health, San Francisco, 2013). This type of managed care program provides inpatient and outpatient care, prescription coverage, lab services, and treatments for mental health and substance abuse. Any resident is eligible to apply for the program regardless of income status, preexisting conditions, or immigration status. Those eligible must choose a primary care provider home among the 14 clinics, and they are provided with an identification card and a handbook explaining the services. Small fees are charged based on income. Patient satisfaction surveys indicate the enrollees are very pleased with the HSF and would encourage others who are eligible to take advantage of the program (Kaiser Family Foundation, 2016). However, when the Affordable Care Act mandate became effective in 2014, enrollment dropped to 32,000 participants from a high of 65,000 in 2013. This reflects the transition from the HSF to Affordable Care Act programs.

Both the Massachusetts and the San Francisco programs focus on the uninsured in their geographic areas and attempt to provide affordable and quality medical care to all individuals, regardless of income. Both programs have benefitted from the ACA mandates.

▶ Lessons to Be Learned from Other Healthcare Systems

Japan, France, and Switzerland have different types of universal health insurance programs, but their systems all have flaws. Although Japan ranks at or near the top in the OECD country rankings for infant mortality rates and life expectancy, its healthcare system has problems. As in the United States, employer insurance provides a large percentage of the health care. As in the United States, the elderly use the healthcare system more than any other demographic and, as a result, Japan's healthcare spending is expected to triple over the next several years. In the United States, Medicare spending continues to be an issue; however, the Affordable Care Act has developed financing models for Medicare providers that may rectify this major problem.

France, which has been applauded for a quality healthcare system, also has financial problems. Similar to the United States, employers pay a portion of an employee's health insurance premium. However, unlike in the United States, employers are mandated to pay a percentage of the employee's salary to a national health insurance program, not to a private health insurance plan. In France, taxes on tobacco, alcohol, and pharmaceutical company revenues are used for health care. Similar to the United States, private health insurance companies participate in the healthcare industry because 90% of citizens purchase supplemental insurance. However, unlike in the United States, the sicker a French resident becomes, the more coverage he or she receives from the government. There is a mandate in the ACA that prohibits health insurance companies from denying coverage based on catastrophic illness. That mandate is a positive step in improving health care for those who are seriously ill. There are 30 chronic conditions for which the French government will pay coverage, such as cancer and diabetes. In the United States, some citizens become bankrupt if they have chronic conditions because they cannot pay for the out-of-pocket expenses. France's healthcare providers all participate in public health insurance, which is similar to Medicare and Medicaid. Unlike in the United States, physicians voluntarily enroll in the program. The French providers earn much less than U.S. providers but medical school tuition is free.

As with the U.S. system, France has developed strategies to deal with huge budget deficits for health care. Like the United States, France has developed a managed care–type program that encourages citizens to select a provider who will become the gatekeeper for their care or pay a higher amount out of pocket. Managed care contained costs in the United States during the 1990s and has become commonplace in the U.S. healthcare system.

Switzerland has an expensive healthcare system. The program is similar to the new healthcare system in Massachusetts because both require all of residents to purchase healthcare insurance. As in Japan, Swiss insurers cannot reject any applicant based on their health status. They also cannot make any profit on the basic insurance package but can make a profit on the supplemental insurance packages that most citizens buy. The government supports the indigent like the United States does with its Medicaid program.

The Affordable Care Act has targeted insurance companies by requiring them to spend at least 80% of premium revenues on providing quality care. The Affordable Care Act has also imposed a flat annual fee on the pharmaceutical companies, makers of medical devices, and health insurance providers, based on market share. There is also a 10% tax on indoor-tanning-bed facilities. Those moneys will be used to support the public portion of the U.S. healthcare system.

▶ Conclusion

The U.S. healthcare system continues to evolve. Technology will continue to have a huge impact on health care. Consumers have more information to make healthcare decisions because of information technology. Healthcare providers have more opportunities to utilize technology such as robotic surgery, e-prescribing, and clinical decision support systems that will assist them with diagnoses. The Green House Project is an exciting initiative that may transform how long-term care will be implemented. As our population becomes grayer, more citizens will want to live as independently as possible for a longer period of time, and the Green House Project is an excellent template for achieving this goal. All of these initiatives are exciting for the healthcare consumer. The implementation of an EHR, which will enable providers to share information about a patient's health history, will provide the consumer with the opportunity to obtain more cost-effective and efficient health care. The Veterans Administration hospitals use the EHR system. Duke University Health System also uses an EHR system in North Carolina (Ritzenthaler, 2009). There are hospitals, physician practices, and other healthcare organizations that utilize EHR systems across the country. Even though implementing the system nationally will be extremely expensive—costs have been estimated in the billions—it will eventually be a cost-saving measure for the United States. The Affordable Care Act has provided many incentives to improve the quality of and access to the U.S. healthcare system. The Center for Medicaid and Medicare Innovation has over 40 demonstration projects that focus on different types of financing models that are based on the performance of healthcare providers.

The discussion concerning different countries' healthcare systems indicate that all countries have problems with their healthcare systems. Establishing a universal healthcare system in the United States may not be the answer. There are aspects of each of these programs that could be integrated into the U.S. system. There are a surprising number of similarities. The major differences are in the area of the control the government places on pharmaceutical prices and health insurers. Some governments limit drug manufacturers' and insurers' profitability in order to increase healthcare access to their citizens. The main difference between these three countries and the United States is in the willingness of individuals to pay more so all citizens can receive health care. That collectivistic attitude does not prevail in the United States and would be difficult to institute. However, the mandates for both business and individuals to purchase health insurance coverage through the establishment of state health insurance marketplaces should improve the overall health of the United States.

Wrap-Up

Vocabulary

Accountable Care Organizations
Advance Payment ACO Model
Care manager
Commonwealth Health Insurance
   Connector
Comprehensive ESRD Care Model
Convenient Care Association
Coordinated care pathway
da Vinci Surgical System
Drugstore clinics
Elders
Electronic prescribing
   (e-prescribing)
Green House Project
Healthy San Francisco Program

Hospital Value-Based Purchasing
   Program
Integrated Healthcare Association
Integrative medicine
Medical homes
Medical nomadism
Medical robotics and computer
   assisted surgery (MRCAS)
Medicare Improvements for
   Patients and Providers Act of
   2008 (MIPPA)
Medicare Shared Savings Program
Minute Clinics
National health insurance
National health system

Next Generation ACO Model
Patient-centered
Pay-for-performance (P4P)
Pioneer ACO Model
Radio frequency identification
Robotic surgery
Single-payer system
Social regulation
Socialized health insurance
   system
Take Care Clinic
Telemedicine
Telesurgery
Underinsured
Value-based purchasing (VBP)

References

Affordable health care for America. (2010). Retrieved from http://www.speaker.gov/newsroom/legislation?id=0361

Agency for Healthcare Research and Quality (AHRQ). (2013). Theory and reality of value-based purchasing: Lessons from the pioneers. Retrieved from http://www.ahrq.gov/qual/meyerrpt.htm

Ambulatory Surgery Center Association (ASCA). (2013). Retrieved from http://ascassociation.org/faqs/faqaboutascs/#1

American Association of Colleges of Nursing (AACN). (2013). Nursing shortage. Retrieved from http://www.aacn.nche.edu/media-relations/fact-sheets/nursing-shortage

Arts, K. (2010). Legal challenges to health reform: An alliance for health reform toolkit. Retrieved from http://www.allhealth.org/publications/Uninsured/Legal_Challenges_to_New_Health_Reform_Law_97.pdf

Bachrach, D., Frohlich, J., Garcimonde, A., & Nevitt, K. (2015). The value proposition of value clinics. Retrieved from http://www.ccaclinics.org/research-a-resources/research

Bleasch, G. (2013). All Pioneer ACOs improved quality; only third lowered costs. Retrieved from http://www.modernhealthcare.com/article/20130716/NEWS/307169958/all-pioneer-acos-improved-quality-only-third-lowered-costs

Brown, K. (2008). Mass health care reform reveals doctor shortages. Retrieved from http://www.npr.org/templates/story/story.php?storyId=97620520

Brunetti, L., & Jay, R. (2009). Using technology for more effective pharmacy benefit management. *Benefits & Compensation Digest, 46*, 16–21.

Centers for Disease Control and Prevention (CDC). (2013). Workplace safety and health topics: Healthcare workers. Retrieved from http://www.cdc.gov/niosh/topics/healthcare

Centers for Medicare & Medicaid Services (CMS). (2013). Medicare program—General information. Retrieved from http://www.cms.gov/Medicare/Medicare General-Information/MedicareGenInfo/index.html

Centers for Medicare & Medicaid Services (CMS). (2016). Home Health Value Based Purchasing Model. Retrieved from https://innovation.cms.gov/initiatives/Home-Health-Value-Based-Purchasing-Model/faq.html

Commonwealth Health Insurance Connector Authority. (2013). Retrieved from http://www.mahealthconnector.org

Department of Health and Human Services (DHHS). (2000). Healthy People 2010. Retrieved from http://www.healthypeople.gov/Publications

Department of Public Health, San Francisco. (2013). Key facts and reports. Retrieved from http://healthysanfrancisco.org/about-healthy-san-francisco/key-facts-report

Dickson, V. (2013). Partners in health. Retrieved from http://www.modernhealthcare.com/article/20131221/MAGAZINE/312219933/?cslet=UnhOY2lLZjhMZkNkK2lneHNiZlNOSTRldWUzaXMyZlBNYnJCalE9PQ%3D%3D

Dorsey, J. (2015). Massachusetts health insurance. Retrieved from https://www.healthinsurance.org/massachusetts/

Dutton, P.V. (2007). France's model healthcare system. Retrieved from http://www.boston.com/news/globe/editorial_opinion/oped/articles/2007/08/11/frances_model_healthcare_system

Ellison, A. (2016). 673 rural hospitals vulnerable to closure: 5 things to know. Retrieved from http://www.beckershospitalreview.com/finance/673-rural-hospitals-vulnerable-to-closure-5-things-to-know.html

Fine, S. (May 31, 2009). Where to live as we age. *Parade Magazine,* 8–9.

Friedman, M., Schueth, A., & Bell, D. (2009). Interoperable electronic prescribing in the U.S.: A progress report. *Health Affairs, 28*(2), 393–403.

Gingrich, N., Boxer, R., & Brooks, B. (2008). Telephone medical consults answer the call for accessible, affordable and convenient health care. Retrieved from http://www.healthtransformation.net/galleries/defaultfile/teladoc.pdf

Goodson, J. (2010). Patient Protection and Affordable Care Act: Promise and peril for primary care. Retrieved from http://www.annals.org/content/early/2010/04/15/0003-4819-152-11-201006010-00249.full

Guidarelli, M. (2006). Robotic surgery. The Next Generation: An Introduction to Medicine, 2. Retrieved from http://www.nextgenmd.org/vol2–5/robotic_surgery.html

Haisimaier, E., & Owcharenko, N. (2006). The Massachusetts approach: A new way to restructure state health insurance markets and public programs. *Health Affairs, 25*(6), 1580–1590.

Hirschkorn, P. (June 25, 2012). Massachusetts' health care plan: 6 years later. Retrieved from http://www.cbsnews.com/2102-18563_162-57459563.html

Integrated Healthcare Association. (2016). Pay for performance overview. Retrieved from http://www.iha.org/performance_measurement.html

HRSA (2016). How does e-prescribing work? Retrieved from http://www.hrsa.gov/healthit/toolbox/HealthITAdoptiontoolbox/ElectronicPrescribing/epreswork.html

Intuitive Surgical, Inc. (2009). da Vinci surgery. Retrieved from http://www.davincisurgery.com

Japanese Nursing Association. (2013). Nursing in Japan. Retrieved from http://www.nurse.or.jp/jna/english/nursing/medical.html

Kaiser Family Foundation. (August, 2009). Survey of Healthy San Francisco Participants. Retrieved from http://www.healthysanfranciso.org/files/PDF/HSF_Satisfaction_Survey_Kaiser.pdf

Kane, R., Lum, T., Cutler, L., Degenholtz, H., & Yu, T. (2007). Resident outcomes in small house nursing homes: A longitudinal evaluation of the Initial Green House program. *Journal of Geriatrics Society, 55*(6), 832–839.

Katz, M. (2008). Golden Gate to health care for all? San Francisco's new universal access program. *New England Journal of Medicine, 258*(4), 327–329.

Kohn, L.T., Corrigan, J.M., & Donaldson, M.S. (1999). *To err is human: Building a safer health system.* Washington, DC: National Academy Press.

Langreth, R. (2013). Unreported robot surgery injuries open problems for FDA. Retrieved from http://www.bloomberg.com/news/2013-12-30/unreported-robot-surgery-injuries-open-questions-for-fda.htmlt

Lee, J. (2015). Intuitive surgical sees revenue, sales of da Vinci robot fall in 2014. Retrieved from http://www.modernhealthcare.com/article/20150113/NEWS/301139973

Loisance, A. (2007). Robotic surgery and telesurgery: Basic principles and description of a novel concept. *Journal de Chirugie, 3*(3), 211–214.

Mathews, A. W. (December 12, 2012). The future of U.S. health care. Retrieved from http://online.wsj.com/article/SB10001424052970204319004577084553869990554.html

Michael J. Bass Group. (2013). Patent valuation report update. Retrieved from http://michaelbass.com/PDF/Patent_Valuation.pdf

Modern Healthcare. (April 4, 2013). Walgreen clinics expand care into chronic illness. Retrieved from http://www.modernhealthcare.com/article/20130404/INFO/304049978

Mohney, G. (April 10, 2013). Obama budget includes $235 million for mental health care. Retrieved from http://abcnews.go.com/Health

/obama-budget-includes-235-million-mental-health-initiatives/story?id=18922699

National Center for Complementary and Alternative Medicine (NCCAM). (2013). About NCCAM. Retrieved from http://nccam.nih.gov/about

NCB Capital Impact. (2013). Retrieved from http://www.ncbcapitalimpact.org/default.aspx?id=146&terms=Green+House

Novick, L., & Morrow, C. (2008). A framework for public health administration and practice. In L. Novick & C. Morrow (Eds.), *Public health administration: Principles for population-based management* (pp. 35–68). Sudbury, MA: Jones and Bartlett.

Oi, M (2015). Who will look after Japan's elderly? Retrieved from http://www.bbc.com/news/world-asia-31901943

Organisation for Economic Cooperation and Development (OECD). (2012a). Retrieved from http://stats.oecd.org/Index.aspx?DataSetCode=CSP2009

Organisation for Economic Cooperation and Development (OECD). (2012b). France healthcare statistics. Retrieved from http://www.oecd.org/france

Pointer, D., Williams, S., Isaacs, S., & Knickman, J. (2007). *Introduction to U.S. health care*. Hoboken, NJ: Wiley Publishing.

State of California, Office of the Patient Advocate. (2013). PPO quality ratings summary. Retrieved from http://reportcard.opa.ca.gov/rc2013/pporating.aspx

Ritzenthaler, B.A. (2009). Healthcare and President Obama's address: Electronic health records are a key element to healthcare reform. Retrieved from http://generalmedicine.suite101.com/article.crm/healthcare_and_president_obamas_address

Robert Wood Johnson Foundation. (2013). Green House Research Collaborative. Retrieved from http://www.rwjf.org/en/research-publications/research-features/green-house-research-collaborative.html

Rovner, J. (2008). In Switzerland, a health care model for America? Retrieved from http://www.npr.org/templates/story/story.php?storyId=92106731

Shafrin, J. (2008). Health care around the world: Switzerland. Retrieved from http://healthcareeconomist.com/2008/04/23/healthcarearoundtheworldswitzerland/

Shi, L., & Singh, D. (2008). *Delivering health care in America*. Sudbury, MA: Jones and Bartlett.

Surescripts. (2012). National Progress Report on EPrescribing and Safe-RX Rankings. Retrieved from http://www.surescripts.com/about-e-prescribing/progress-reports/national-progress-reports#downloads

Tanner, M. (2008). The grass is not always greener—A look at national health care systems around the world. Cato Institute. *Policy analysis*, 613, 1–48.

Taylor, P. (1975). *Principles of ethics: An introduction to ethics* (2nd ed.). Encino, CA: Dickinson.

The Villages Health. (2013). About us. Retrieved from http://www.thevillageshealth.com/aboutus.php

Thirty one million underinsured in 2014. (2015). Retrieved from http://www.commonwealthfund.org/publications/press-releases/2015/may/underinsurance-brief-release

Torsoli, A. (January 3, 2013). France's health-care system is going broke. Retrieved from http://www.businessweek.com/articles/2013-01-03/frances-health-care-system-is-going-broke

Witsil, F. (March 28, 2013). Drugstore clinics: A rapidly growing option for sick people. Retrieved from http://www.freep.com/article/20130328/BUSINESS06/303280154/Drugstore-clinics-A-rapidly-growing-option-for-sick-people

Zigmond, J. (2013). CMS names ACOs leaving Pioneer program. Retrieved from http://www.modernhealthcare.com/article/20130716/NEWS/307169945/cms-names-acos-leaving-pioneer-program

▶ **Notes**

▶ **Student Activity 14-1**

In Your Own Words

Based on this chapter, please provide a description of the following concepts in your own words. DO NOT RECITE the text description.

Commonwealth Health Insurance Connector:

_____

_____

Coordinated care pathway:

_____

_____

Green House Project:

_____

_____

Healthy San Francisco Program:

_____

_____

Medical nomadism:

_____

_____

National health insurance:

_____

_____

National health system:

_____

_____

Pay-for-performance (P4P):

_____

_____

Single-payer system:

_____

_____

Robotic surgery:

_____

_____

▶ Student Activity 14-2

Complete the following case scenarios based on the information provided in the chapter. Your answer must be IN YOUR OWN WORDS.

Real-Life Applications: Case Scenario One

You need to do a research paper for your international healthcare class. Select one of the countries discussed in the chapter and assess two strengths of one of these systems.

Activity

Apply these two strengths to the U.S. healthcare system. Write a two-page report on how you would integrate these characteristics into U.S. health care.

Responses

_____

_____

_____

_____

_____

_____

_____

_____

_____

_____

_____

_____

_____

_____

_____

_____

_____

_____

Case Scenario Two

You have a friend that you believe is suffering from some mental health issues. You are concerned about him but do not know what to do.

Activity

Do an Internet search and review the different legislative acts that pertain to mental health. Research mental health statistics in the United States. Write a report that discusses these acts and the data you found regarding mental health in the United States.

Responses

_____

_____

_____

_____

_____

_____

_____

_____

_____

_____

_____

_____

_____

_____

_____

_____

_____

Case Scenario Three

Your family believes in a holistic approach to medicine. Family members have bad backs and they refuse to take prescription drugs. They believe that complementary and alternative medicine (CAM) is the best approach. You are not sure.

Activity

Research the field of CAM. Identify three ways that CAM is used to treat a medical problem.

Responses

_____

_____

_____

_____

_____

_____

_____

_____

_____

_____

_____

_____

_____

_____

_____

_____

_____

Case Scenario Four

Your parents have asked you to assist in placing your grandparents into a skilled nursing facility. They are very concerned about the care they will receive. You have heard of a new model of nursing home that may be appropriate for your grandparents.

Activity

Write up a report on the Green House Project and explain the differences between a traditional skilled nursing facility and the Green House Project.

Responses

_____

_____

_____

_____

_____

_____

_____

_____

_____

_____

_____

_____

_____

_____

_____

_____

_____

▶ **Student Activity 14-3**

Internet Exercises

Write your answers in the space provided.

- Visit each of the websites listed here.
- Name the organization.
- Locate the mission statement or statement of purpose on the website.
- Provide a brief overview of the activities of the organization.
- How do these organizations participate in the U.S. healthcare system?

Websites

http://www.healthline.com

Organization Name:

_____

_____

Mission Statement:

_____

_____

_____

Overview of Activities:

_____

_____

_____

Importance of Organization to U.S. Health Care:

_____

_____

_____

http://www.drugstorenews.com

Organization Name:

_____

_____

Mission Statement:

_____

_____

_____

Overview of Activities:

_____

_____

_____

Importance of Organization to U.S. Health Care:

_____

_____

_____

http://www.mahealthconnector.org

Organization Name:

_____

_____

Mission Statement:

_____

_____

_____

Overview of Activities:

_____

_____

_____

Importance of Organization to U.S. Health Care:

_____

_____

_____

http://www.ncbcapitalimpact.org

Organization Name:

_____

_____

Mission Statement:

_____

_____

_____

Overview of Activities:

_____

_____

_____

Importance of Organization to U.S. Health Care:

_____

_____

_____

http://www.nam.edu
National Academy of Medicine

Organization Name:

_____

_____

Mission Statement:

_____

_____

_____

Overview of Activities:

_____

_____

_____

Importance of Organization to U.S. Health Care:

_____

_____

_____

http://www.kff.org

Organization Name:

_____

_____

Mission Statement:

_____

_____

_____

Overview of Activities:

_____

_____

_____

Importance of Organization to U.S. Health Care:

_____

_____

_____

▶ **Student Activity 14-4**

Discussion Questions

The following are suggested discussion questions for this chapter.

1. What are accountable care organizations? What value can they provide to the healthcare industry?

_____

_____

_____

_____

_____

_____

2. Research a code of ethics of a healthcare organization and report back to the discussion board about your analysis of the code.

_____

_____

_____

_____

_____

_____

_____

3. What is e-prescribing? Do you think it will help reduce the number of mistakes that have occurred from handwritten prescriptions?

_____

_____

_____

_____

_____

_____

_____

4. What is telemedicine? Would you feel comfortable receiving medical care electronically?

_____

_____

_____

_____

_____

_____

_____

5. What is RFID? Provide three examples of RFID use in the healthcare industry.

_____

_____

_____

_____

_____

_____

_____

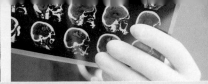

Glossary

A

Academic medical centers These are hospitals organized around a medical school that offer substantial programs and are considered elite teaching and research institutions affiliated with large medical schools.

Accountable Care Organizations Patient-centered organizations comprised of groups of doctors, hospitals, and other healthcare providers and suppliers who come together voluntarily to provide coordinated, high-quality care at lower costs.

Accreditation It is a private standard developed by accepted organizations as a way to meet certain standards.

Activities of daily living (ADLs) These are job responsibilities of licensed practical nurses that include patient observation, taking vital signs, keeping records, assisting patients with personal hygiene, and feeding and dressing patients.

Acupuncture A Chinese practice of insertion of needles in specific points of the body to balance the system.

Acuson P10 It is a pocket-sized portable ultrasound machine designed for quick and easy use in emergency medicine, cardiology, ICU, and OB/GYN situations for traditional applications of diagnostic and screening tests.

Acute care hospital A hospital with specialty-care for patients who stay an average of less than 30 days for short-term treatment.

Adult day services centers These are day programs that provide a medical model of care, with medical and therapeutic services; a social model, with meals, recreation, and some basic medical health; or a medical – social model, with social interaction and intensive medical-related activities, all depending on the needs of the patients.

Advance directives Orders that patients give to providers to ensure that, if they are terminally ill and incompetent to make a decision, certain measures will not be taken to prolong that patient's life.

Advance Payment ACO Model A supplementary incentive program for smaller practices and physician-based and rural providers in the shared savings program.

Advanced practice nurse (APN) A healthcare professional possessing a degree required for a licensure who may work independently depending on the state licensure requirements or in collaboration with physicians.

Affirmative action plan A strategy that encourages employers to increase the diversity of their workforce by hiring individuals based on race, sex, and age.

Affordable Care Act (ACA) An act intended to increase health insurance quality and affordability, lower the uninsured rate by expanding insurance coverage, and reduce the costs of healthcare.

Age Discrimination in Employment Act of 1967 An act that protects employees and job applicants 40 years old and older from discrimination as it applies to hiring, firing, promotion, layoffs, training, assignments, and benefits.

Allied health professionals A segment of the workforce that delivers services involving the identification, evaluation, and prevention of diseases and disorders; dietary and nutrition services; and rehabilitation and health systems management.

Allopathic approach An approach that actively intervenes in attacking and eradicating disease and focuses its efforts on the disease.

Almshouses Also known as poorhouses, they were established to serve the indigent by providing shelter while treating illness.

Alternative approaches to mental health care Therapies and treatments that emphasize the relationships between the body, mind, and spirituality.

Alternative reproductive methods A collection of methods for conceiving children through medical technology.

Alzheimer's disease A progressive mental deterioration that can occur in middle or old age, due to generalized degeneration of the brain.

Ambulatory care It literally means a person is able to walk to receive a healthcare service, which might not always be true; the term "ambulatory care" is used interchangeably with outpatient services.

Ambulatory patient groups (APGs) These groups were developed in the 1980s and are a system of codes that explain the number and types of services used in an ambulatory visit.

Ambulatory payment categories (APCs) These were adapted from the APGs, which divide all outpatient services into 300 procedural groups or classifications based on similar clinical content such as surgery, medical, and ancillary services and each APC is assigned a payment weight based on the median cost of services within the APC.

Ambulatory surgery centers A center for surgeries that does not require an overnight stay.

Americans with Disabilities Act of 1990 An act that focuses on individuals in the workplace who are considered disabled. This act applies to employers who have 15 employees or more and is enforced by the EEOC.

Anesthesiologist assistant (AA) A healthcare specialty physician assistant who assists with implementing an anesthesia care plan under the direction of an anesthesiologist and as a team member of the anesthesia care component of surgical procedures.

Animal-assisted therapies A type of treatment where animals are often used to increase socialization skills and encourage communication among the mentally ill.

Antitrust law A law to protect the consumer by ensuring there is a market driven by competition so the consumer has a choice for health care.

Art therapy A type of treatment where art activities such as drawing, painting, and sculpting may help people express their emotions and may help treat disorders such as depression.

Artificial intelligence A field of computerized methods and technologies created to imitate human decision making.

Assessment A regular and systematic investigation which includes surveillance, identifying problems, data collection, and analysis of the health problem to determine possible risks and hazards within the community.

Associate degree in nursing (ADN) A tertiary education nursing degree offered as a two-year program by community colleges and a three-year diploma program offered by hospitals.

Assurance A process of evaluating policies that meet program goals for provision of services to the public either directly or through regulation of other entities.

Autonomy Is defined as self-rule, is an important concept to health care because it is applied to informed consent, which requires a provider to obtain the permission of a patient who has been provided adequate information to make a decision regarding intervention.

Avera eCare It is part of the Avera Health system, which offered eConsult services to rural, frontier, and critical-access hospitals and delivers 24/7 access to medical specialists for underserved populations and communities.

Ayurveda A system that incorporates in its medicine diet, meditation, herbal medicine, and nutrition to treat depression and to release stress.

B

Bachelor of Science in Nursing (BSN) The most rigorous of the nursing programs offered by colleges and universities, it normally takes 4–5 years, where students perform both classroom activity and clinical practice activity.

Balance billing It is a bill raised for the difference between the amount the physician charges the patient and the amount that the patient's insurance company pays.

Battery A surgeon performing surgery on a patient without his or her consent.

Beneficence The basic value that the healthcare provider should focus on the patient's best interests when making a decision.

Benefits Improvement and Protection Act of 2000 (BIPA) An act formally called the Medicare, Medicaid, and CHIP Benefits Improvement and Protection Act, which modifies Medicare payment rates for many services.

Bioethics The study of the typically controversial ethical issues emerging from new situations and possibilities brought about by advances in biology and medicine.

Biofeedback A technique that focuses on learning to control heart rate and body temperature. This technique may be used in conjunction with medication to treat depression and schizophrenia.

Biosurveillance A new form of surveillance that focuses on early detection of unusual disease patterns that may be due to human intervention.

Bioterrorism An attack on a population by deliberately releasing viruses, bacteria, or other germs or agents that will contribute to illness or death in people.

Black market Underground economy, or shadow economy, is a market characterized by some form of noncompliant behavior with an institutional set of rules.

Board certifying or credentialing examination A certification required for specialists to be certified in their area of specialization, which requires additional years of training and is often associated with the quality of the healthcare provider's services.

Board of trustees It is legally responsible for hospital operations, approves strategic plans and budgets, and has authority for appointing, evaluating, and terminating the CEO.

Boycotts It means an expression of protest, a means of coercion or abstaining from using, buying, or dealing with and so on.

Brand name drugs A name given by the pharmaceutical company that makes a drug to stand out in the marketplace, though the product will have a generic name which is the drug's scientific name displayed somewhere on the product in small print.

Bundled Payments Initiative It is composed of four broadly defined models of care, which link payments that multiple service beneficiaries receive during an episode of care.

C

Cafeteria plan A type of employer-sponsored benefit plan that allows employees to select the type of benefits appropriate for their lifestyle.

Capitated rate The set rate received by the healthcare provider for serving enrolled patients regardless of how much care the provider gives. This type of capitation is also used by Medicaid and Medicare for their managed care programs.

Capitation plan A policy also known as per member per month policy in which the provider is paid a fixed monthly amount per member payment. This member fee is given to the provider regardless of how often the members use the service and the types of services used. The provider is responsible for providing all services deemed necessary.

Cardiovascular technologist A healthcare provider who performs diagnostic examinations for cardiovascular issues, basically assisting physicians in treating cardiac (heart) and peripheral vascular (blood vessel) problems.

Care manager A healthcare professional who provides a combination of nursing, social services, and disability assistance primarily to individuals who are eligible for both Medicare and Medicaid, suffer from chronic conditions, and often cannot handle managing their own chronic conditions.

Carpal tunnel syndrome A medical condition due to compression of the median nerve as it travels through the wrist at the carpal tunnel. It is a wrist injury that often occurs from repetitive hand motions in jobs such as grocery cashiers and computer users.

Carrier testing Test used to identify individuals who carry a gene that is linked to a disease.

Carve outs These are services for which Medicaid is not obligated to pay for under an MCO contract. Carve outs have occurred because the MCO cannot provide the service or it is too expensive.

Catastrophic health insurance An insurance policy that covers unusual illnesses with a high deductible and have lifetime reimbursement caps.

Center for Medicare and Medicaid Innovation A program that supports the development and testing of innovative healthcare payment and service delivery models.

Certificate of need (CON) An act to ensure that the state approved any capital expenditures associated with hospital and medical facility construction and expansion.

Certification A process through which an organization recognizes that accreditation eligibility requirements have been met.

Certified midwives (CMs) Healthcare professionals who do not have a nursing degree but undergo midwifery education program, which is accredited by the same organization. They must also pass the same national certification exam to be given the designation of CM.

Certified nurse–midwives (CNMs) Healthcare professionals who have graduated from a nurse–midwifery education program that has been accredited by the American College of Nurse–Midwives' Division of Accreditation.

Certified nursing assistants (CNAs) Healthcare professionals who work under supervision, assisting patients with eating, bathing, and dressing; taking some vital signs; making beds; noticing any changes in the physical or emotional state of a patient; and notifying a nursing supervisor.

Charitable care or bad debt It means either the healthcare providers do not expect payment after the person's inability to pay has been determined or the efforts to secure the payment have failed.

Chief executive officer A highest-ranking executive of a hospital who provides leadership to achieve their mission and vision and who is ultimately responsible for the day-to-day operations of the hospital and is a board-of-trustees member.

Chief financial officer (CFO) A highest-ranking executive who provides leadership and is responsible for complete accounting and the financial management system.

Chief information officer (CIO) An executive-level position in a company or other entity who manages the organization's information systems and has knowledge of current information technologies as they apply to the healthcare industry and how new technology can apply to the organization.

Chief of medical staff An in-charge of the medical staff–physicians that provides clinical services to the hospital.

Chief of service A person who is responsible for leading the specialty or department in a hospital.

Chief technology officer (CTO) An executive-level position in a company or other entity whose occupation is focused on scientific and technological issues within an organization.

Children's Health Insurance Program (CHIP) A program enacted under the Balanced Budget Act of 1997, is Title XXI of the Social Security Act, and is jointly financed by federal and state funding and administered by the states and the CMS to provide coverage for low-income children (younger than age 19) whose family income exceeds the income-level requirements of Medicaid.

Chiropractors Healthcare professionals who have a holistic approach to treating their patients, which means they focus on the entire body, with emphasis on the spine, believing that the body can heal itself with no medication or surgery.

Church-related hospitals These are community general hospitals developed as a way to perform spiritual work.

Civil law A private law that focuses on wrongful acts against individuals and organizations based on contractual violations.

Civil Rights Act of 1964, Title VII An act that prohibits discrimination based on race, sex, color, religion, and national origin and it is the key legal piece to equal opportunity employment. It created a concept of protected classes to protect these groups from employment discrimination in compensation and conditions or privileges of employment.

Civil Rights Act of 1991 An act that enables individuals to receive both punitive damages, which are damages that punish the defendant, and compensatory damages for financial or psychological harm.

Claims processing It is verification of claims received from the providers and disbursement of funds for the services that are delivered is often called as claims processing.

CLASS Independence Benefit Plan A self-funded long-term care insurance program for individuals with limited financial assistance.

Clayton Act of 1914 An act passed to supplement the Sherman Act, as amended by the Robinson-Patman Act, which issues further restrictions on mergers and acquisitions.

Cloning Any procedure that creates a genetic replica of a cell or organism.

Codes of ethics Guidelines for industry participants which provide a standard for operation so that all participants understand that if they do not adhere to this code, there may be negative consequences.

Coinsurance A type of copayment that is part of a fee-for-service policy. The patient pays a percentage of the cost of the services. A typical coinsurance portion is 20% paid by the individual, with the remaining 80% paid by the health insurance plan.

Collegial model A doctor–patient relationship that assumes trust between the patient and doctor and that decision making is an equal effort.

Commission on Accreditation of Allied Health Education Programs (CAAHEP) An agency of accreditation which accredits 2,000 U.S. programs that offer 28 allied health specialties.

Committee on Operating Rules for Information Exchange (CORE) It has set up standards and operating rules for streamlining processes between providers and healthcare plans. This system allows for real-time access to patient information pre- and post-care.

Common law A law established by the judicial system rather than by statutes enacted by legislatures that interprets previous legal decisions regarding a case when giving decisions in individual cases that have precedential effect on future cases.

Common rule Elements including a written statement that includes the purpose and duration of the study; the procedures and, if they are experimental, any foreseen risks and potential benefits; and any alternative procedures that may benefit the subject.

Commonwealth Fund A private foundation that aims to promote a high-performing healthcare system that achieves better access, improved quality, and greater efficiency, particularly for society's most vulnerable, including low-income people, the uninsured, minority Americans, young children, and elderly adults.

Commonwealth Health Insurance Connector A clearinghouse system which facilitates the buying, selling, and administration of affordable, quality, private insurance coverage for small businesses and individuals.

Community First Choice An optional Medicaid benefit, which focuses on community health services to Medicaid enrollees with disabilities.

Community preparedness Is the community's capability to prepare for, withstand, and recover from both the short- and long-term public health incidents.

Community recovery The ability to collaborate with community partners (e.g., healthcare organizations, businesses, schools, and emergency management) to plan and advocate for the rebuilding of public health, medical, and mental–behavioral health systems to at least a level of functioning comparable to pre-incident levels, and improved levels when possible.

Compensatory damages A sum of money awarded in a civil action by a court to indemnify a person for the particular loss, detriment, or injury suffered as a result of the unlawful conduct of another.

Complementary and alternative medicine (CAM) A group of diverse medical care practices that are not considered part of traditional medicine.

Comprehensive ESRD Care Model A model designed to identify, test, and evaluate new ways to improve care for Medicare beneficiaries with end-stage renal disease (ESRD).

Comprehensive health insurance policies A policy that provides benefits that include outpatient and inpatient services, surgery, laboratory testing, medical equipment purchases, therapies, and other services such as mental health, rehabilitation, and prescription drugs.

Comptroller An employee who is charged with accounting and reporting functions.

Computerized physician order entry It enables a patient's provider to enter a prescription order or order for a lab or diagnostic test in a computer system, which typically is now part of an electronic health record system.

Concurrent utilization reviews The decision that is made during the actual course of service, such as the length of inpatient stay and additional surgery.

Conditions of participation A proposed rule issued by Centers for Medicare and Medicaid Services (CMS) designed to protect patient health and safety and ensure quality of care.

Consolidated Omnibus Budget Reconciliation Act (COBRA) A law passed by the U.S. Congress in 1985 that required most employers with group health insurance plans to continue to offer temporary group health insurance for their employees in special circumstances for a period of up to 18 to 36 months depending on the situation.

Constitutional factors The factors like genetic, biological etc., that are highly significant for health which are seen as beyond the reach and influence of public health improvement strategies, policies, and practices.

Consumer Credit Protection Act (Title III) of 1968 An act that prohibits employers from terminating an employee if the individual's earnings are subject to garnishment due to debt issues. This act also limits the weekly garnishment amount from employees' pay and is enforced by the Federal Deposit Insurance Corporation (FDIC).

Consumer medical and health information It includes the use of the Internet and wireless devices for consumers to obtain specialized health information and online discussion groups to provide peer-to-peer support.

Consumer Operated and Oriented Plans (CO-OPs) A program that was included in the Patient Protection and Affordable Care Act in an effort to increase the competitiveness of state health insurance markets and improve choice in the individual and small group markets.

Consumer-driven health plans These are tax-plans with high deductible coverage that allow members to use health savings accounts (HSAs), Health Reimbursement Accounts (HRAs), or similar medical payment products to pay routine healthcare expenses directly.

Contractual model A doctor–patient relationship that is based on a legal foundation. It assumes there is an agreement between the two parties, assuming mutual goals.

Contractual relationship to care for a designated population A contract to care for a designated population is indicative of a health maintenance organization (HMO) or managed care contract. A physician is contractually required to care for those member patients of a managed care organization. They may sign contracts to provide care for hospitals, schools, or long-term care facilities that have designated populations.

Contractual right to admission A relationship between a patient and hospital, a contractual right to admission can be considered a contract if a hospital has contracted to treat certain members of an organization, like a managed care organization.

Coordinated care pathway A system established by the government, similar to the U.S. managed care system, where individuals are encouraged to choose a preferred doctor and follow the doctor's pathway for their care. Individuals are given a choice and not a mandate to follow.

Copayments A fixed fee or cost that individuals must pay prior to receiving specific medical services or treatments covered by their health insurance plan.

Core public health functions They are health surveillance, planning, and program development; health promotion of local health activities; development and enforcement of sanitation standards; and health services provisions.

Cost plus reimbursement A reimbursement given to rural hospitals as per the classification of MRHFP, which makes these hospitals eligible for grants to increase access to consumers.

Cost sharing A cost that individuals must pay prior to receiving specific medical services or treatments covered by their health insurance plan.

Cost shifting It occurs when a healthcare provider charges a patient with health insurance more than what it charges an uninsured patient for the same procedure or service, which means that those with insurance pay for the financial loss that the provider incurs by providing service to those who are not insured.

Cost-plus reimbursement A reimbursement given to rural hospitals as per the classification of MRHFP, which makes these hospitals eligible for grants to increase access to consumers.

Credentials committee A committee that reviews and grants admitting privileges to physicians.

Criminal law A system of law concerned with actions that are illegal based on court decisions. In order to convict someone of a criminal activity, guilt must be proved beyond a reasonable doubt. The most common types of criminal law infractions in the healthcare field are Medicare and Medicaid fraud.

Critical access hospitals Hospitals that are classified as having no more than 25 acute care beds, and are at least 35 miles away from another hospital, providing emergency care, and are eligible for grants to increase access to consumers.

Cures Acceleration Network A grants center established to encourage research in the cure and treatment of diseases.

Cytotechnologists A category of clinical laboratory technologists; they are specialists who collaborate with pathologists to evaluate cellular material.

D

da Vinci Surgical System A robotic system that has dominated the current market. It is used in areas of cardiac, urologic, gynecologic, and general surgery.

Dance therapy A type of treatment involving moving one's body to music to help individuals recovering from physical abuse because the movement may help develop a sense of ease with their bodies.

De facto mental health service system A growing sector of nonprofit groups and organizations for the mentally ill that provide education and support.

Deductibles These are payments that are required prior to the insurance paying for services rendered in a fee-for service plan.

Defensive medicine Results when providers order more tests and provide more services than necessary to protect themselves from malpractice lawsuits.

Dementia A wide range of symptoms associated with a decline in memory or other thinking skills severe enough to reduce a person's ability to perform everyday activities.

Dental assistants An aide who works directly with dentists in the preparation and treatment of patients.

Dental hygienists A healthcare professional who cleans teeth, examines patients for oral diseases, provides other preventive dental care, and educates patients on ways to improve and maintain oral health.

Dentist A healthcare professional who is required to complete four years of education from an accredited dental school after receiving a bachelor's degree, and prevent, diagnose, and treat tooth, gum, and mouth diseases.

Designated health services Services that include clinical laboratory services, outpatient prescription drug services, physical and occupational therapy, and imaging services such as magnetic resonance imaging (MRI), and the like.

Determinants of health The social and community networks and macroenvironmental conditions that influence the status of an individual's health.

Diagnosis-related group (DRG) It is a statistical system of classifying that divides possible diagnoses into more than 20 major body systems and subdivides them into almost 500 groups for the purpose of Medicare reimbursement.

Diagnostic and Statistical Manual of Mental Disorders (DSM) It is a guide published by the American Psychiatric Association that explains the signs and symptoms that mark more than 300 types of mental health conditions.

Diagnostic medical sonographer A healthcare professional who works under the supervision of a physician, this specialist provides patient services using medical ultrasound, which photographs internal structures.

Diagnostic testing Test used to identify the disease when a person is exhibiting symptoms.

Dignity The quality or state of being worthy.

Discounted fees A type of fee-for-service reimbursement but that is discounted based on a fee schedule. The provider supplies the service and then can bill the MCO based on the fee schedule developed by the MCO. Each service can be billed separately. The provider anticipates a large referral pool from the MCO so the provider will accept the discounted rates.

Disease-specific policies A policy that gives a lump-sum cash payment if the policyholder is diagnosed with any of the specific diseases predetermined in the policy document.

Doctor of Medicine (MD) A medical education from an accredited school that is required to apply for a license to practice medicine as physician to diagnose and treat patient illnesses.

Doctor of Osteopathic Medicine (DO) A medical education from an accredited school that is required to apply for a license to practice medicine as physician to diagnose and treat patient illnesses.

Doctors Without Borders An international medical organization that provides quality medical care to individuals threatened by violence, catastrophe, lack of health care, natural disasters, epidemics, or wars in 60 countries.

Donut hole A coverage gap in Medicare Part D that starts after the beneficiary and the drug plan together have spent a designated amount for the covered drugs.

Drug Free Workplace Act of 1988 This act requires any employers that receive federal grants or have a federal contract of $25,000 or greater to certify that they operate a drug-free workplace.

Drug–drug interactions When one drug affects the activity of another when both are administered together, it is called drug–drug interaction (DDI). DDI software programs alert pharmacists and clinicians about potential drug interactions.

Drugstore clinics Clinics that are run by nurse practitioners or physician assistants who provide routine care.

Duty to treat A code of medical ethics that provided guidelines for the physician–provider relationship, emphasizing the duty to treat a patient.

E

Edwin Chadwick Sir Edwin Chadwick was an English social reformer who worked to reform the Poor Laws and to improve sanitary conditions and public health.

Effectiveness One of the five justifications essential to demonstrate that the public health efforts were successful and, therefore, it was necessary to limit individual freedom of choice.

E-health Refers to the use of the Internet by both consumers and healthcare professionals to access education, research, and products and services.

Elder Justice Act An act passed as part of the Affordable Care Act, which targets to prevent and eliminate abuse, neglect, and exploitation of the elderly.

Elders The residents of a Green House.

Electronic aspirin A technology under clinical investigation at Autonomic Technologies, Inc. A patient-powered tool for blocking pain-causing signals at the first sign of a headache.

Electronic clinical decision support systems Systems that are designed to integrate medical information, patient information, and a decision-making tool to generate information to assist with cases.

Electronic communication A method of communication which refers to the transfer of writing, signals, data, sounds, images, signs, or intelligence sent via an electronic device using Internet, including email services.

Electronic health record (EHR) An electronic record of patients' medical history that can be used in hospitals, healthcare providers' offices, and other types of healthcare facilities. It enables healthcare organizations to monitor patient safety and care.

Electronic medical record (EMR/EHR) An electronic record of health-related information on an individual that is accumulated from one health system and is utilized by the health organization that is providing patient care. EMR is an EHR that can be integrated with other systems.

Electronic patient record The patient component of the electronic health record, which is an electronic record of patients' medical history.

Electronic prescribing (e-prescribing) A technology framework that allows physicians and other medical practitioners to write and send prescriptions to a participating pharmacy electronically instead of using handwritten or faxed notes or calling in prescriptions.

Electrotherapy Treatment that uses electric signals to interfere with the transmission of neural pain signals into the brain. It effectively slows down or distracts the message from the nerve to the brain. It is chiefly used in the treatment of various forms of paralysis.

Embedded Behavioral Health model A model that focuses on early intervention and treatment to promote soldier readiness (before, during, and after deployment).

Emergency medical technician (EMT) A healthcare professional who works with patients who require immediate medical attention, providing basic life support as they care for and transport the sick or injured to a medical facility for appropriate medical care.

Emergency medical technician-paramedic (EMT-P) A healthcare professional who works with patients who require immediate medical attention, providing advanced life support as they care for and transport the sick or injured to a medical facility for appropriate medical care.

Emergency Medical Treatment and Active Labor Act (EMTALA) An act that requires Medicare participants to receive emergency care from a hospital or medical entity that provides dedicated emergency services.

Emergency operations coordination It is the ability to direct and support an event or incident with public health or medical implications by establishing a standardized, scalable system of oversight, organization, and supervision consistent with jurisdictional standards and practices and with the National Incident Management System.

Emergency preparedness A process of ensuring that an organization has prepared for the first and immediate response for any catastrophic events such as bioterrorism; chemical and radiation emergencies; mass casualties as a result of explosions, natural disasters, and severe weather; and disease outbreaks.

Emergency public information and warning system It is the ability to develop, coordinate, and disseminate information, alerts, warnings, and notifications to the public and incident management responders.

Employee assistance programs An occupational health program, dating back to the 1940s, as an intervention for employee drug and alcohol abuse.

Employee Retirement Income Security Act of 1974 (ERISA) An act that regulates pension and benefit plans for employees, including medical and disability benefits.

Employee wellness programs Programs that include promotion of exercise, health risk appraisals, disease management, and healthcare coaching, which have become a popular employee benefit.

Employer health insurance A health insurance policy provided by an employer for the employees of a company.

Engineering model A doctor–patient relationship that focuses on patients and their power to make decisions about their health care.

Enterprise data warehouse It helps organizations in strategic decision making by integrating many computer systems across an organization.

Entitlement program The term refers to Medicare, as it is considered an entitlement program because people, after paying into the program for years from their wages, are entitled to receive benefits.

Environmental health It is the integral component of public health that focuses on the interrelationships between people and their environment, promotes human health and well-being, and fosters healthy and safe communities.

Epidemics The occurrence of cases of a disease spreading rapidly in excess of what would normally be expected in a defined community, geographical area, or season.

Epidemiology It is the study of disease distribution and patterns among populations and is the foundation for public health because its focus is to prevent disease from reoccurring.

Epidemiology triangle It consists of three major risk factor categories for disease, which consists of the host, which is the population that has the disease; the agent or organism, which is causing the disease; and the environment, or where the disease is occurring.

E-prescribing A form of computerized physician order entry, it consists of medication history, benefits information, and processing new and existing prescriptions. The user–clinician can review the patient's medication list, prescribe a new drug and designate which pharmacy will fill the prescription.

Equal Pay Act of 1963 An act that mandates that all employers award pay fairly to men and women if it is determined their jobs have equal responsibilities and require the same skills.

Ergonomics The study of working conditions that affect the physical condition of employees.

Essential Health Benefits (EHBs) A set of 10 specific healthcare benefits which health insurance plans must cover under the Affordable Care Act. Specific services may vary by state.

Ethical standards Basic concepts of ethics in the healthcare workplace that are considered above legal standards because individuals make a choice based on what is the "right thing to do," not what is required by law.

Ethics A system of moral principles that apply values and judgments to the practice of medicine.

Ethics in Patient Referral Act of 1989 An act that prohibits physicians, including dentists and chiropractors, from referring Medicare and Medicaid patients to other providers for designated health services in which they have a financial interest. These laws directly prohibit many referrals that may increase a provider's or family members' financial interest.

Euthanasia An act where a third party, usually a physician, terminates the life of an individual involving, but not limited to, a diagnosis of living in a situation that the individual considers to be worse than death or existing in a coma or in a persistent vegetative state.

Exclusive provider organizations (EPOs) An organization similar to preferred provider organizations but that restricts members to a list of preferred or exclusive providers.

Executive Orders 11246 (1965), 11375 (1967), and 11478 (1969) Orders written by the President of the United States, for federal agency directions that focus on discrimination issues, and require affirmative action based on these factors. These orders affect both federal contractors and employers with 50 or more employees.

Exercise physiologists Healthcare professionals who assess, design, and manage individual exercise programs for both healthy and unhealthy individuals.

Experience rating A method of rating in which the premium of workers' compensation is adjusted up or down based upon how often the workers got injured on the job. If the experience rating is high, the premium rates will be high.

Expert system A technique of artificial intelligence that was developed to imitate experts' knowledge in decision making.

Exploring Accreditation Project (EAP) The project was funded by the CDC and the Robert Wood Johnson Foundation (RWJF) to assess accreditation of public health agencies to ensure that the health departments deliver the core functions of public health and essential public health services.

Express contract A type of relationship a physician can establish with a patient to provide healthcare, which is a simple contract—merely a mutual agreement of care between the physician and patient.

F

False Claims Act An act also known as the Lincoln law, enacted in 1863, was originally passed to protect the federal government against defense contractors during the Civil War. The False Claims Act has been amended several times throughout the years, and, in the 1990s, was amended with a focus on healthcare fraud, most notably Medicare and Medicaid fraud.

Family Educational Rights and Privacy Act of 1974 (FERPA) A federal law that protects the privacy of student education records. The law applies to all schools that receive funds under an applicable program of the U.S. Department of Education.

Family Medical Leave Act (FMLA) An act that allowed employees up to 12 weeks of unpaid leave because of family illness.

Family Medical Leave Act of 1993 An act of the United States federal law requiring covered employers to provide employees job-protected and unpaid leave for qualified medical and family reasons.

Fatality management It is the ability to coordinate with other organizations to ensure the proper recovery, handling, identification, transportation, tracking, storage, and disposal of human remains and personal effects; certify cause of death; and facilitate access to mental and behavioral health services for the family members, responders, and survivors of an incident.

Federal Food, Drug, and Cosmetic Act (FDCA) It is a set of laws passed by Congress in 1938 giving authority to the U.S. Food and Drug Administration (FDA) to oversee the safety of food, drugs, and cosmetics.

Federal hospitals Hospitals that do not serve the general public but operate for federal beneficiaries such as military personnel, veterans, and Native Americans.

Federal Trade Commission It is one of the oldest federal agencies and is charged with the oversight of commercial acts and practices. Two major activities of the FTC are to maintain free and fair competition in the economy and to protect consumers from misleading practices.

Federal Trade Commission Act An act that outlaws unfair methods of competition and outlaws unfair acts or practices that affect commerce to protect the healthcare consumer and those who provide healthcare services.

Fee-for-service (FFS) A method in which healthcare providers are paid for each service performed.

Finance committee A committee that provides financial oversight for the organization.

Flexible spending accounts (FSAs) These accounts provide employees with the option of setting aside pretax income to pay for out-of-pocket medical expenses. Employees must submit claims for these expenses and are reimbursed from their spending accounts.

Flexner Report A report that evaluated medical schools in Canada and the United States and was responsible for forcing medical schools to develop curriculums and admission testing.

G

Gatekeeper A healthcare provider who is responsible for the administration of the patient's treatment and who coordinates and authorizes all medical services, laboratory studies, specialty referrals, and hospitalizations.

General duty Each employer shall furnish to each of his employees employment and a place of employment which are free from recognized hazards that are causing or are likely to cause death or serious physical harm to his employees.

Generalists Healthcare professionals who can be primary care physicians, family care practitioners, general internal medicine physicians, or general pediatricians, whose focus is preventive services such as immunizations and health examinations.

Generic drugs A drug that is equivalent to a brand name drug, only it has no patent protection and is sold at discounted prices.

Genetic Information Nondiscrimination Act of 2008 An act that prohibits U.S. insurance companies and employers from discriminating based on genetic test results.

Genetic testing Testing carried out on populations based on age, gender, or other risk factors to determine if they are at risk for a serious genetic disease or if they have a carrier gene that they may pass on to their children.

Geographic maldistribution An issue that occurs because physicians prefer to practice in urban and suburban areas where there is a higher probability of increased income.

Geropsychology A branch of psychology that seeks to address the concerns of older adults.

Graying of the population The increase in the proportion of older people in the population.

Green House Project An initiative aimed to provide long-term care for citizens becoming grayer and wanting to live as independently as possible for a long period of time.

Gross domestic product (GDP) The total value of all goods and services produced within a nation's geographic borders over a specified period of time.

Group insurance An insurance that covers a defined group of people which anticipates that a large group of individuals will purchase insurance through their employer, and the risk is spread among those paying individuals.

Group model A type of health maintenance organization that contracts and negotiates with a group of physicians exclusively to perform services.

H

Hart-Scott-Rodino Antitrust Improvement Act of 1976 An amendment to the Clayton Act, it ensures those hospitals and other entities that entered mergers, acquisitions, and joint ventures must notify the DOJ and the FTC before any final decisions are made.

Hazard Communication Standard (HCS) It ensures that all hazardous chemicals and toxic substances are properly labeled and requires employers to disclose these substances in workplaces and that companies are informed of the risks.

Health A state of complete physical, mental, and social well-being of a person.

Health Center Centers that originated in the1960s as part of the war on poverty, they are organizations that provide culturally competent primary healthcare services to the uninsured or indigent population such as minorities, infants and children, patients with HIV, substance abusers, homeless persons, and migrant workers.

Health education It focuses on changing health behavior through educational interventions such as multimedia education and classes.

Health information systems (HIS) Systems that store, transmit, collect, and retrieve health information data.

Health information technology (HIT) Technology used to manage the health data that can be used by patients–consumers, insurance companies, healthcare providers, healthcare administrators, and any stakeholder that has an interest in health care.

Health Information Technology for Economic and Clinical Health Act of 2009 This act amends Health Insurance Portability and Accountability Act of 1996 by requiring stricter notification protocols for breach of any patient information.

Health insurance A type of insurance coverage that pays for medical and surgical expenses incurred by the insured.

Health Insurance Marketplace A place run by the federal or state government where consumers can obtain information and buy health insurance coverage.

Health Insurance Portability and Accountability Act of 1996 (HIPAA) An act passed to promote patient information and confidentiality in a secure environment.

Health maintenance organization (HMO) An older type of managed healthcare system that takes both the financial risks associated with providing comprehensive medical services and the responsibility for healthcare delivery in a particular geographic area to its members, usually in return for a fixed, prepaid fee.

Health marketing An innovative approach to public health practice that does science-based health strategies of promotion and prevention involving creating, communicating, and delivering health information and interventions using customer-oriented and science-based strategies to protect and promote health in diverse populations.

Health Plan Employer Data and Information Set (HEDIS) Database established by the NCQA in 1989 and used by over 90% of all health plans to measure service and quality of care. The reported data is available to MCOs and physicians.

Health promotion A broader intervention term in public health, encompasses not only educational objectives and activities but also organizational, environmental, and economic interventions to support activities conducive to healthy behavior.

Health reimbursement arrangements (HRAs) Insurance which is funded by the employer but owned by the employees and remains with the company if the employee leaves. This has been an issue because it has no portability.

Health savings accounts (HSAs) A tax-advantaged medical savings account available to taxpayers who are enrolled in a high-deductible health plan (HDHP), which is fully portable.

Health services administrators A segment of the healthcare workforce found at all levels of a healthcare organization managing hospitals, clinics, nursing homes, community health centers, and other types of healthcare facilities.

HealthVault A website developed by Microsoft that enables patients to develop electronic patient records free of charge and it is up to the individual as to how much medical information the person wants to store online with this website.

Healthcare and Education Affordability Reconciliation Act of 2010 An act signed into law on March 23, 2010, by President Barack Obama to improve the accessibility and quality of the U.S. healthcare system.

Healthcare ethical dilemma A problem, situation, or opportunity that requires an individual, such as a healthcare provider, to choose an action between two obligations.

Healthy Advice Network Now known as PatientPoint, it provides education to patients electronically while they are in the waiting room or an exam room.

Healthy People 2000 report A report released in 1990, titled the National Health Promotion and Disease Prevention Objectives, was created to implement a new national prevention strategy with three major goals: increase life expectancy, reduce health disparities, and increase access to preventive services.

Healthy People 2010 report A report, Understanding and Improving Health, was released in 2000 which contained a health promotion and disease prevention focus to identify preventable threats to public health; major goals were to increase quality of life and life expectancy and to reduce health disparities.

Healthy People 2020 report A report released in 2010, it contains 1,200 objectives that focus on 42 topic areas. A smaller set of Healthy People 2020 objectives, called leading health indicators (LHIs), has been targeted to communicate high-priority health issues.

Healthy People reports (2000, 2010, 2020) The series of reports is a federal public health planning tool produced by the CDC that assesses the most significant health threats and sets objectives to challenge these threats.

Healthy San Francisco Program Healthy San Francisco is a program designed to make health care services available and affordable to uninsured San Francisco residents. It is operated by the San Francisco Department of Public Health (DPH).

Hill-Burton Act An act, also known as the Hospital Survey and Construction Act, passed because the federal government recognized the lack of hospitals in the United States during the 1940s. Federal grants were provided to states for hospital construction to ensure there were 4.5 beds per 1,000 people.

HIPAA National Standards Standards that ensure that individuals' health information is properly protected while allowing the flow of health information needed to provide and promote high-quality health care for patients and to protect the public's health and well-being.

Holistic approach An approach that focuses not only on the disease but also on the entire person.

Home health agencies An agency that provides medical services in a patient's home; often provided to elderly or disabled individuals or patients who are too weak to come to the hospital or physician's office or have just been released from the hospital.

Home health and personal care aides A segment of healthcare professionals who help people who are disabled, chronically ill, or cognitively impaired, as well as older adults who need assistance including in activities such as bathing and dressing.

Home health resource group (HHRG) It is a prospective payment used by Medicare, which pays a fixed predetermined rate for each 60-day episode of care, regardless of the services.

Home healthcare services Medical care in the home, provided primarily to elderly, chronically ill, or mentally impaired individuals.

Hospice care A holistic and philosophical approach to end-of-life care to make the individual as comfortable as possible during his or her final days, with an emphasis on pain control, symptom management, natural death, and quality of life to comfort the individual's physical body, while also supporting the family members as needed.

Hospital emergency medical services An integral part of the American healthcare system that provides care for patients with emergency healthcare needs.

Hospital Value-Based Purchasing Program A CMS initiative that rewards acutecare hospitals with incentive payments for the quality of care they provide to people with Medicare, not just the quantity of procedures performed.

Hospitalists A group of healthcare providers who engage exclusively in the care of patients when they are hospitalized.

Human Genome Project A long-term government-funded project completed in 2003, identified all of the 20,000–25,000 genes found in human DNA.

Hurricane Katrina A storm that was the costliest natural disaster, as well as one of the five deadliest hurricanes, in the history of the United States.

I

Imaging informatics Also known as radiology informatics or medical imaging informatics that aims to improve the efficiency, accuracy, usability and reliability of medical imaging services within health care.

Immigration Reform and Control Act of 1988 An act that requires employers with one or more employees to verify that all job applicants are U.S. citizens or authorized to work in the United States.

Implied contract A type of relationship a physician can establish with a patient to provide healthcare which can be implied from a physician's actions. If a physician gives advice regarding medical treatment, there is an implied contract.

Incident Command System (ICS) It is a coordinator for an emergency event and it controls situations and makes decisions about how to manage emergencies.

Indemnity plans In this mode, the payment was either provided by a health insurance company or paid out of pocket by the consumer. This increased the cost of health care because there were no controls on how much to charge for the provider's service.

Independence at home program A program that provides Medicare beneficiaries with at-home primary care and allocates any cost savings of this type of care to healthcare professionals who reduce hospital admissions and improve health outcomes.

Independent Payment Advisory Board A fifteen-member independent payment advisory board will present to Congress proposals for cost savings and quality performance measures.

Independent practice associations (IPAs) A type of healthcare provider organization composed of a group of independent practicing physicians who maintain their own offices and band together for the purpose of contracting their services to a health maintenance organization.

Indian Health Care Improvement Act (IHCIA) A permanent legal authority for the provision of health care to American Indians and Alaska Natives.

Individual private health insurance A health insurance policy in which the risk is determined by the individual's health. Premiums, deductibles, and copayments are much higher for this type of insurance.

Infant mortality rates The second widely used measurement of population health status that measures the chances of dying during the first year of life among those born alive in a particular year.

Infection control committee A committee that focuses on minimizing infections in the hospital.

Informatics A science of computer application to data in different industries.

Information technology (IT) Forms of technology used to create, store, exchange, and use information in its various forms.

Informed consent A legal written document that an individual signs to agree to a specific surgical or medical procedure or other course of treatment. The procedure is protected under federal and state medical consent laws.

Inpatient services Healthcare services that involve an overnight stay of a patient.

Insane asylums A hospital where the mentally ill were housed to be treated with sensitivity.

Institutional Review Boards (IRBs) A group that has been formally designated to review and monitor biomedical research involving human subjects.

Integrated Healthcare Association A statewide multi-stakeholder leadership group that promotes quality improvement, accountability, and affordability of health care in California.

Integrative medicine A combination of alternative and complementary medicine with a mainstream approach.

Intellectual disabilities A disability characterized by significant limitations in both intellectual functioning and in adaptive behavior, which covers many everyday social and practical skills.

Intentional torts It is a category of wrongful acts, in civil law, such as assault and battery or invasion of privacy.

Internal auditor An employee who ensures that accounting procedures are performed in accordance with appropriate regulations by conducting audits.

Involuntary commitment It is when people are forced to receive treatment or are committed to a facility against their wishes.

IOM quality dimensions A framework for quality assessment put forth by the Institute of Medicine (IOM), which includes six aims for the healthcare system, which are safe, effective, patient-centered, timely, efficient, and equitable.

Iron Triangle of Health Care A concept that focuses on the balance of three factors of a healthcare system: quality, cost, and accessibility to healthcare.

J

Job lock The inability of an employee to freely leave a job because doing so will result in the loss of employee benefits.

John Snow A famed British anesthesiologist, he is more famous for investigating the cholera epidemics in London in the 1800s.

Joint Commission A private, nonprofit organization that continues to improve the safety and quality of U.S. health care. It assesses performance improvement and provides accreditation to healthcare organizations.

Justice In the healthcare industry it emphasizes that patients should be treated equally and that health care should be accessible to all.

L

Lateral violence Defined as "nurse to nurse" aggression and demonstrated by both verbal and nonverbal behavior.

Law It is a body of rules for the conduct of individuals and organizations. Law is created so there is a minimal standard of action required by individuals and organizations.

Lemuel Shattuck He is known as the architect of public health infrastructure. He wrote the landmark report, Report of the Sanitary Commission of Massachusetts, which became central to the development of state and local public health activities.

LGBTQ The term refers to lesbian, gay, bisexual, transgender, and questioning populations.

Licensed practical nurses A healthcare professional who works primarily in hospitals, home health agencies, and nursing homes with job responsibilities that include patient observation, taking vital signs, keeping records, assisting patients with personal hygiene, and feeding and dressing patients.

Licensed vocational nurses Refer **Licensed practical nurses**.

Life expectancy rates The measurement of mortality rates from each age group in a population in a particular year that gives the summary of average number of years of life remaining for those of a particular age. It implies the number of years of expected life at birth.

Life qualifying event A change in situation—like getting married, having a baby, or losing health coverage—that can make a person eligible for a Special Enrollment Period, allowing them to enroll in health insurance outside the yearly Open Enrollment Period.

Lifestyle behaviors It refers to the interests, opinions, attitudes, way of life, values, or world view of an individual, group, or a culture.

Lilly Ledbetter Fair Pay Act of 2009 An amendment to Title VII of the Civil Rights Act of 1964 that provides protection against unlawful employment practices related to compensation discrimination.

Limited benefit plans A plan that offers one to two Medicaid benefits to the beneficiary as compared to the other major health plans.

Local health departments These are governmental organizations that provide most of the direct public health services to the population in their designated areas.

Long-term care hospital A hospital with specialty-care for patients with serious medical problems that require special and intense treatment for an extended period of time, usually more than 30 days.

Long-term care insurance A product designed to cover long-term services and supports, including personal and custodial care in a variety of settings such as your home, a community organization, or other facility and the policy reimburses policyholders a daily amount (up to a pre-selected limit) for services.

M

Macroeconomic conditions Factors such as changes in employment levels, gross national product (GNP), and prices that influence the state of economy.

Macroenvironmental conditions These are determinants of health which consist of socioeconomic, cultural, and environmental conditions that impact health, such as education, work environment, living and working conditions, healthcare services, food production, unemployment, water and sanitation, and housing.

Major medical policies A type of health insurance that covers the expenses associated with serious illness or hospitalization where there usually is a set amount, or deductible, for which the patient is responsible to pay.

Managed Behavioral Healthcare Organization Accreditation Program A program that provides consumers, employers, and others with information about the quality of the nation's managed behavioral healthcare organizations.

Managed behavioral healthcare organizations External vendors contracted with managed care organizations that focus on mental health services.

Managed Care Long Term Services and Support (MLTSS) Refers to the delivery of long-term services and supports through capitated Medicaid managed care programs.

Managed care organizations (MCOs) A healthcare delivery system organized to manage cost, utilization, and quality. Managed care refers to the cost management of healthcare services by controlling who the consumer sees and how much the service costs.

Managed care plans A type of health program that combines administrative costs and service costs for cost control.

Market division An illegal action as per the Sherman Act of 1890 which occurs when one or more health organizations decide which type of services will be offered at each organization.

Mass care It is the ability to coordinate with partner agencies to address the public health, medical, and mental and behavioral health needs D194 of those impacted by an incident at a congregate location.

Massage therapy A technique that manipulates the body and its muscles to release tension, and treat depression and stress.

Material Safety Data Sheets (MSDSs) A document that contains information on the potential hazards (health, fire, reactivity, and environmental) and how to work safely with the chemical product.

Meaningful use Core measures that healthcare providers must meet to determine the EHR system is being adequately used.

Medicaid A social protection program rather than a social insurance program where eligibility is determined largely by income. It is the largest source of funding for medical and health-related services for U.S. citizens living in poverty.

Medical assistants An aide employed by physicians more than any other allied health assistant who performs both administrative and clinical duties under the supervision of the physicians.

Medical countermeasure dispensing It is the ability to provide medical countermeasures in support of treatment or prophylaxis to the identified population in accordance with public health guidelines, recommendations, or both.

Medical director Refer **Chief of medical staff**.

Medical education It provides continuing medical education credits for health professionals and special medical education seminars for targeted groups in remote locations

Medical ethics Ethics in health care which focuses on the treatment of the patient.

Medical homes A team-based healthcare delivery model led by a healthcare provider that is intended to provide comprehensive and continuous medical care to patients with the goal of obtaining maximized health outcomes.

Medical illustrators A trained artist who visually portrays scientific information to teach both professionals and the public about medical issues, working digitally or traditionally to create images of human anatomy and surgical procedures as well as three-dimensional models and animations.

Medical informatics The science of computer application that supports clinical and research data in different areas of health care.

Medical loss ratio It is the percentage of insurance premium dollars spent on health care claims. Under the Affordable Care Act, insurance companies must spend 80–85% of member premium revenues on medical care and healthcare quality improvement. If they do not meet that minimum percentage, the insurance companies must provide a rebate to their customers.

Medical malpractice Improper or negligent treatment of a patient by a provider which results in injury, damage, or loss.

Medical materiel management and distribution It is the ability to acquire, maintain, transport, distribute, and track medical material during an incident and to recover and account for unused medical materiel, as necessary, after an incident.

Medical nomadism Consumers have had no restrictions on physician selection; they may visit several physicians before they find the one they prefer.

Medical records committee A committee that oversees patient records.

Medical Reserve Corps (MRC) It was created in 2002 after the September 11, 2001, terrorist attacks. They operate under the umbrella of the DHHS but are housed primarily in local health departments nationwide.

Medical robotics and computer assisted surgery (MRCAS) The concept of telesurgery which combines virtual reality, robots, and medicine, developed by the National Aeronautic and Space Administration (NASA).

Medical saving accounts (MSAs) A tax-advantaged account available to taxpayers who are enrolled in a high-deductible health plan (HDHP) and which is fully portable.

Medical surge It is the ability to provide adequate medical evaluation and care during events that exceed the limits of the normal medical infrastructure of an affected community. It encompasses the ability of the healthcare system to survive a hazard impact and maintain or rapidly recover operations that were compromised.

Medical tourism Travel of people to a place other than where they normally reside for the purpose of obtaining medical treatment in that country.

Medical Waste Tracking Act An act that requires companies to have medical waste disposal procedures so that there is no risk to employees and to the environment.

Medicare A health insurance program for people age 65 or older, people under age 65 with certain disabilities, and people of all ages with end-stage renal disease.

Medicare Advantage It is also referred to as Medicare Part C, considered as managed care model and it covers all services in Parts A and B. Each Medicare Advantage Plan can charge different out-of-pocket costs and have different rules for how you get services.

Medicare cost plans A type of Medicare health plan available in certain areas of the country having similar rules to Medicare Advantage plans. Cost plans allow members to pursue care outside the network.

Medicare Deemed Status A provider or supplier earns this when they have been accredited by a national accreditation program (approved by the Centers for Medicare & Medicaid Services) that they demonstrate compliance with certain conditions.

Medicare Hospital Readmission Program A program established by the Affordable Care Act, it penalizes most acute care hospitals with higher Medicare readmission rates within a 30-day period than the national average.

Specialty hospitals such as children's, cancer, psychiatric, and rehabilitative are exempt.

Medicare Improvements for Patients and Providers Act of 2008 (MIPPA) An act that authorized incentives to encourage physicians to e-prescribe.

Medicare Part A It is primarily financed from payroll taxes and is considered hospital insurance which in general covers hospital care, skilled nursing facility care, nursing home care (as long as custodial care is not the only care you need), hospice, and home health services.

Medicare Part B It is a supplemental health plan to cover physician services, as well as medically necessary services and preventive services.

Medicare Part C It is also referred to as Medicare Advantage, and it can be considered a managed care model and it covers all services in Parts A and B.

Medicare Part D It produced the largest additions and changes to Medicare where tax revenues of the federal government support the majority of the program costs and its purpose was to provide seniors with relief from high prescription costs.

Medicare Prescription Drug, Improvement, and Modernization Act A federal law of the United States, enacted in 2003, which created Medicare Part D, a prescription drug plan that provides different prescription programs to the elderly, based on their prescription needs.

Medicare Rural Hospital Flexibility Program (MRHFP) It is a program created as part of the Balanced Budget Act of 1997, which allows a small hospital to reconfigure its operations and be licensed as a critical access hospital (CAH), which enables the hospital to be reimbursed for services provided to Medicare patients for its reasonable cost of providing service.

Medicare Shared Savings program A program that helps Medicare fee-for-service program providers to become an accountable care organization.

Medigap or Medicare supplemental or medsup policies A policy, sold by private companies, can help pay some of the health care costs that Original Medicare doesn't cover, like copayments, coinsurance, and deductibles.

Melafind optical scanner A technology that uses missile navigation technologies originally paid for by the U.S. Department of Defense to optically scan the surface of a suspicious lesion at 10 electromagnetic wavelengths.

Mental disorders A syndrome characterized by clinically significant disturbance in an individual's cognition, emotion regulation, or behavior that reflects a dysfunction in the psychological, biological, or developmental processes underlying mental functioning.

Mental Health America A nonprofit group for the mentally ill that provides education and support.

Mental Health Parity Act (MHPA) An act that ensures adequate coverage for mental health illnesses and also ensures that annual lifetime reimbursement limits on mental health services were similar to other medical benefits.

Mental Health Parity Act of 1996 An act that provided the mental health field with more equity for health insurance coverage to ensure mental health services were being reimbursed at the same level as traditional medical care.

Mental Health Parity and Addiction Equity Act of 2008 An act that amends the Mental Health Parity Act of 1996 to include substance abuse treatment plans as part of group health plans.

Mid-level practitioners A segment of healthcare professionals who have experience and education beyond the requirements of a registered nurse and operate between the RN and MD.

Million Hearts A national initiative to prevent one million heart attacks by 2017.

Minimal infringement The least restrictive intervention that infringes on individual choices.

Minority stress It stems from the social stigma, prejudice, denial of civil rights, victimization, and family rejection that LGBTQ people face.

Minute Clinics Walk-in medical clinics staffed by nurse practitioners and physician assistants who specialize in family health care and are trained to diagnose, treat, and write prescriptions for common family illnesses.

Mobilizing for Action through Planning and Partnership (MAPP) A community-driven strategic planning process for improving community health that helps communities apply strategic thinking to prioritize public health issues and identify resources to address them.

Monitoring center links A center used for cardiac, pulmonary, or fetal monitoring; home care; and related services that provide care to patients in the home.

Monopolies These are healthcare organizations that control a market so that the consumer has no choice in health care.

Moral treatment An approach used earlier in Europe to treat mental health patients in hospitals while participating in work and educational activities.

Morbidity and Mortality Weekly Report (MMWR) It is a weekly report published by the Centers for Disease Control and Prevention (CDC) containing data on specific diseases as reported by state and territorial health departments and reports on infectious and chronic diseases, environmental hazards, natural or human-generated disasters, occupational diseases and injuries, and intentional and unintentional injuries.

Music therapy A type of treatment used to treat depression, stress, and grief based on research findings that music elevates a person's emotional moods.

N

National Clearinghouse for Long-Term Care Information A website developed by the US Department of Health and Human Services to provide information and resources to help a consumer plan for future long-term care (LTC) needs.

National Committee on Quality Assurance (NCQA) Established in 1990 to monitor health plans and improve healthcare quality, its focus is to measure, analyze, and improve healthcare programs.

National Defense Authorization Act An act to permit families of military service members to take a leave of absence if the spouse, parent, or child was called to active military service.

National Disaster Medical System It is a federally coordinated system that augments the Nation's medical response capability for assisting State and local authorities in dealing with the medical impacts of major peacetime disasters and to provide support to the military and the Department of Veterans Affairs medical systems in caring for casualties evacuated back to the U.S. from overseas armed conventional conflicts.

National Health Care Workforce Commission An advisory committee developed to review workforce needs and make recommendations to the federal government to ensure that national policies are in alignment with consumer needs.

National health insurance An insurance program funded by the government through general taxes, although the delivery of care is by private providers. It is a legally enforced scheme of health insurance that insures a national population against the costs of health care.

National health system A publicly funded national healthcare system in the United Kingdom that provides free or low-cost healthcare to all legal residents of the U.K. The medications are subsidized as well and prescriptions may be free when situations warrant.

National Incident Management System (NIMS) A systematic, proactive approach to guide departments and agencies at all levels of government, nongovernmental organizations, and the private sector to work together seamlessly and manage incidents involving all threats and hazards in order to reduce loss of life, property, and harm to the environment.

National Managed Care Contract (NMCC) A contract designed to comply with the managed care laws of all 50 states and the District of Columbia, as well as with federal requirements.

National Mental Health Act (NMHA) An act to amend the Public Health Service Act to provide for research relating to psychiatric disorders and to aid in the development of more effective methods of prevention, diagnosis, and treatment of such disorders, and for other purposes.

National Practitioner Data Bank It is an electronic information repository created by Congress, contains information on medical malpractice payments and certain adverse actions related to healthcare practitioners, entities, providers, and suppliers.

National Preparedness System An integrated preparedness system for risks that include events such as natural disasters, disease pandemics, chemical spills, and other manmade hazards, terrorist attacks, and cyber attacks.

National Prevention, Health Promotion, and Public Health Council A council established to develop a comprehensive national prevention and public health strategy.

National Response Framework (NRF) Created by the DHS, it presents the guiding principles that enable all response partners to prepare for and provide a unified national response to disasters and emergencies.

Native American practices Practices that include ceremonial dances and baptismal rituals as part of Indian health. These dances and rituals are used to treat depression, stress, and substance abuse.

Negligence A situation where a provider does not give appropriate care or withholds care, and injury to the patient results. Also, if a patient did not provide informed consent for a procedure or treatment, it is considered a case of negligence.

Network model An HMO model that contracts with multiple physician groups to provide services to HMO members; may involve large single and multispecialty groups. The physician groups may provide services to both HMO and non-HMO plan participants.

Networked programs Programs that link tertiary care hospitals and clinics with outlying clinics and community health centers in rural or suburban areas.

New Freedom Commission on Mental Health A commission charged with implementing an analytical study on the U.S. mental health service system and developing recommendations to improve the public mental health system that could be implemented at the federal, state, and local levels.

Newborns' and Mothers' Health Protection Act (NMHPA) An act that prevents health insurance companies from discharging a mother and child too early from the hospital.

Next Generation ACO Model A program that offers a new opportunity in accountable care—one that sets predictable financial targets, enables providers and beneficiaries greater opportunities to coordinate care, and aims to attain the highest quality standards of care.

No-fault liability Also known as no fault insurance, it is insurance that pays for healthcare services resulting from injury to an individual or damage to property in an accident, regardless of who is at fault for causing the accident.

Noneconomic damages It includes compensation for things like pain and suffering and emotional distress.

Nonmalfeasance The concept that healthcare providers must not take any actions to harm the patient.

Nonpharmaceutical interventions The ability to recommend to the applicable agency (if not public health) and implement, if applicable, strategies for disease, injury, and exposure control which include isolation and quarantine of diseased individuals; restrictions on movement and travel advisories; and warnings of high-risk areas that may be hot zones for disease outbreaks.

Nonphysician practitioner A professional sometimes called physician extender because they often are used as a substitute for physicians. They are not involved in the total care of a patient, so they collaborate closely with physicians.

Nonvoluntary euthanasia It is an act of ending the life of an incompetent patient usually at the request of a family member.

Nurse anesthetists (CRNAs) A healthcare professional who provides anesthesia and related care before, during, and after surgical, therapeutic, diagnostic, and obstetrical procedures and also provides pain management and some emergency services.

Nurse practitioner (NP) A healthcare professional who is trained and has clinical competence to provide services that are essential in the promotion, maintenance, and restoration of health and well-being of patients.

Nursing Home Compare website A website that allows consumers to compare information regarding quality of care and staffing information about nursing homes.

Nutrition A science that interprets the interaction of nutrients and other substances in food in relation to maintenance, growth, reproduction, health, and disease of an organism.

O

Occupational Exposure to Blood-borne Pathogen Standard It applies to all employers who have an employee(s) with occupational exposure to deal with blood products to follow behavioral standards such as wearing gloves and other equipment and disposal of blood collection materials.

Occupational Safety and Health Act of 1970 A federal law enacted in 1970, setting forth workplace rules and regulations to promote safety of workers to ensure that employers have a general duty to provide a safe and healthy work environment for their employees, which is very important for the healthcare industry because of potential exposure to bacteria, viruses, and contaminated fluids.

Older Workers Benefit Protection Act of 1990 An act to amend the Age Discrimination in Employment Act of 1967 to clarify the protections given to older individuals in regard to employee benefit plans, and for other purposes.

Operational staff A parallel line of staff with the medical staff responsible for managing nonmedical staff and performing nonclinical, administrative, and service work.

Optometrists A group of healthcare professionals known as Doctors of Optometry or ODs, they are the main providers of vision care by examining people's eyes to diagnose vision problems.

Oregon Death with Dignity Act An act that allows termination of life by an individual where a physician provides with a prescription for medications that the individual may use to end his or her life.

Orthotist A specialist who develops devices called "othoses" that focus on the limbs and spines of individuals to increase function.

Osteopathic hospitals Hospitals that focus on a holistic approach to care, with emphasis on diet and environmental factors that influence health as well as the manipulation of the body.

Out-of-pocket payments or expenses The amount of money that individuals must pay for health services or equipment that is not covered by the health insurance policies.

Outpatient services Health care for individuals needing services that do not require an overnight stay under clinical supervision or long-term care.

P

Pastoral counseling A type of counseling provided by spiritual people like ministers, rabbis, priests, and imams.

Paternalism It is the concern that individual freedom will be restricted for the sake of public health activities because the government infringes on individual choices for the sake of protecting the community.

Patient abandonment Is a form of medical malpractice that occurs when a physician terminates the doctor–patient relationship without reasonable notice or a reasonable excuse, and fails to provide the patient with an opportunity to find a qualified replacement care provider.

Patient Bill of Rights A law or a non-binding declaration that guarantees patients to get information, fair treatment, and autonomy over medical decisions, among other rights.

Patient Protection and Affordability Care Act or Affordable Care Act of 2010 An act that has major impact on the U.S. healthcare was signed into law on March 23, 2010, by President Barack Obama. The goal of the act is to improve the accessibility and quality of the U.S. healthcare system.

Patient Protection and Affordable Care Act (PPACA) An act enacted to increase the quality and affordability of health insurance, lower the uninsured rate by expanding public and private insurance coverage, and reduce the costs of healthcare for individuals and the government. It introduced mechanisms like mandates, subsidies, and insurance exchanges.

Patient Protection and Affordable Care Act of 2010 (PPACA, or ACA) An act enacted to increase the quality and affordability of health insurance, lower the uninsured rate by expanding public and private insurance coverage, and reduce the costs of healthcare for individuals and the government. It introduced mechanisms like mandates, subsidies, and insurance exchanges.

Patient Self-Determination Act of 1990 An act that requires hospitals and other facilities that participate in the Medicare and Medicaid programs to provide patients, upon admission, with information on their rights.

Patient-centered healthcare system It refers to providing care that is respectful of, and responsive to, individual patient preferences, needs and values, and ensuring that patient values guide all clinical decisions.

Patient-Centered Outcomes Research Institute A nonprofit private organization responsible for providing assistance to physicians, patients, and policymakers in improving health outcomes and perform research that targets quality and efficiency of care.

PatientPoint Formerly known as Healthy Advice Network, it provides education to patients electronically while they are in the waiting room or an exam room.

Pay-for-performance (P4P) A type of healthcare payment system that rewards healthcare providers for their efficiency in providing higher quality care at lesser cost.

PDSA cycle It is a four-step cycle that comprises plan, do, study, and act that focuses on improvement of workflow in the healthcare industry.

Per capita A phrase that is used widely in relation to economic data or population description which means for "each person" or "per person."

Per diem rates Also known as per patient per day rates, it is a defined dollar amount per day for care provided, which is the most common form of reimbursement to hospitals.

Per member per month (PMPM) payment A policy also known as capitation plan in which the provider is paid a fixed monthly amount per member payment. This member fee is given to the provider regardless of how often the members use the service and the types of services used. The provider is responsible for providing all services deemed necessary.

Perfusionists A healthcare professional who operates equipment to support or replace a patient's circulatory or respiratory function, including advanced-life-support techniques.

Personal care accounts The account is funded by the employer but owned by the employees and remains with the company if the employee leaves. This has been an issue because it has no portability.

Personal fitness trainer A professional familiar with different forms of exercise serving clients in one-on-one or in group activities and may closely work with exercise science professionals or physiologists in corporate, clinical, or commercial fitness centers, country clubs, or wellness centers.

Personal protective equipment (PPE) A standard developed by OSHA which required specialized clothing or equipment to employees who might be exposed to hazardous materials or working conditions.

Pesthouses A shelter or hospital used to quarantine people who had contagious diseases such as cholera.

Pew Charitable Trusts An independent nonprofit organization. Its stated mission is to serve the public interest by "improving public policy, informing the public, and stimulating civic life."

Pharmacists A segment of the healthcare workforce who are responsible for dispensing medication that has been prescribed by physicians and also advise both patients and healthcare providers on potential side effects of medications.

Pharmacogenomic testing It is a test performed to assess how medicines react to an individual's genetic makeup.

Pharmacy benefit manager A company that administers drug benefits for employers and health insurance carriers. It uses technology-based tools to assess and evaluate the management of the prescription component so it can be customized to address the needs of the organization.

Pharmacy technician A healthcare professional who performs all pharmacy-related functions, usually working under the direct supervision of a licensed pharmacist.

Phobias Excessive, illogical fear of objects or activities.

Physician assistant (PA) A segment of the healthcare workforce in the category of NPPs, who provide a range of diagnostic and therapeutic services to patients, take medical histories, conduct patient examinations, analyze tests, make diagnoses, and perform basic medical procedures.

Physician Compare website A website that helps to find and choose physicians and other healthcare professionals enrolled in Medicare so that patients can make informed choices about health care, as required by the Affordable Care Act (ACA) of 2010.

Physician extender A professional also called as nonphysician practitioner and often used as a substitute for physicians. They are not involved in the total care of a patient and so they collaborate closely with physicians.

Physician hospital organizations (PHOs) Organizations that include physician hospitals, surgical centers, and other medical providers that contract with a managed care plan that helps providers attain market share, improve bargaining power, and reduce administrative costs.

Physician Payment Sunshine Act An act passed in 2010 as part of the Affordable Care Act and requires manufacturers of drugs, medical devices, and other healthcare products with relationships with Medicare and Medicaid providers and CHIP programs to submit annual reports regarding payments and items of value.

Physician Self-Referral Laws Laws that prohibit physicians, including dentists and chiropractors, from referring Medicare and Medicaid patients to other providers for designated health services in which they have a financial interest.

Physician-assisted suicide It refers to the physician providing the means for death, most often with a prescription for a drug. The patient, not the physician, will ultimately administer the lethal medication.

Piccolo xpress Chemistry Analyzer A compact, portable chemistry analyzer that delivers blood test results quickly.

Pioneer ACO Model A CMS Innovation Center initiative designed to support organizations with experience operating as Accountable Care Organizations (ACOs) or in similar arrangements in providing more coordinated care to beneficiaries at a lower cost to Medicare.

Podiatrists A healthcare professional who provides medical and surgical care for people suffering from foot, ankle, and lower-leg problems and diagnoses illnesses, treats injuries, and performs surgery.

Point-of-service (POS) plans A type of managed care health insurance plan in the United States that combines characteristics of the health maintenance organization (HMO) and the preferred provider organization (PPO).

Point-to-point connections These are used by hospitals and clinics that deliver services directly or outsource specialty services to independent medical service providers by using private high-speed networks.

Poison Prevention Packaging Act of 1970 An act enacted to prevent children from accidentally ingesting substances.

Policy development The creation of comprehensive public health policies based on scientific evidence in service to the public.

Polysomnographic technologist A healthcare professional who performs sleep tests and works with physicians to provide diagnoses of sleep disorders.

Poorhouses Refer **Almshouses**.

Posttraumatic stress disorder A mental disorder that can develop after a person is exposed to a traumatic event, such as sexual assault, warfare, traffic collisions, or other threats on a person's life.

Practice profiling An offshoot of retrospective utilization review, it examines specific provider patterns of practice.

Predictive and asymptomatic testing Testing to identify any gene changes that may increase the likelihood of a person developing a disease.

Preferred provider organizations (PPOs) A type of health plan that contracts with medical providers, such as hospitals and doctors, to create a network of participating providers. You pay less if you use providers that belong to the plan's network. You can use doctors, hospitals, and providers outside of the network for an additional cost.

Pregnancy Discrimination Act of 1978 This act protects female employees who are discriminated against based on pregnancy-related conditions, which constitutes illegal sex discrimination.

Preimplantation genetic diagnosis (PGD) It is used to test embryos for tissue compatibility with their siblings prior to being transplanted into the mother.

Premenstrual dysphoric disorder A severe disorder in which depression and anxiety co-occur with menstruation, impacts between 3% and 5% of women.

Prenatal testing Testing to identify fetuses with potential diseases or conditions.

Prepayment A concept in health insurance coverage in which the individual pays a fixed, predetermined amount.

Presumed consent It means that if a parent does not actively oppose the transplantation, the procedure automatically occurs.

Prevention and Public Health Fund It was established to provide funding for national public health programs.

Price fixing An illegal action as per the Sherman Act of 1890 which prevents consumers from paying a fair price because competitors establish a certain price (by either increasing or lowering prices) among themselves to stabilize the market.

Price information exchange An illegal action as per the Sherman Act of 1890 where exchange of price information between healthcare providers can also be illegal.

Priestly model A model which assumes the doctor will make the best decisions for the patient's health. The patient assumes a very passive role, giving the provider great power in the decision-making process.

Primary care It is often referred to as essential health care and could include health education, counseling, and other preventive services.

Primary care and specialist referral services The services that may involve a primary care or allied health professional providing a consultation with a patient or a specialist assisting the primary care physician in rendering a diagnosis.

Primary care case manager An individual healthcare provider (or groups of providers) that agrees to act as an individual's primary care provider and receives a small monthly payment for helping to coordinate referrals and other medical services.

Primary Care Extension Program (PCEP) A program developed by ACA to educate and provide assistance to primary care providers about preventive medicine.

Primary prevention An intervention or an activity that reduces health risks by protecting healthy individuals from illness or disease before it even occurs.

Privacy rule Is intended to further protect patient's personal medical records and other personal health information maintained by healthcare providers, hospitals, insurance companies, and health plans.

Procreation To produce babies or the process of generating children.

Professional associations Associations that represent healthcare stakeholders like physicians, nurses, hospitals, long-term care facilities, and that guide them regarding their role in the healthcare industry.

Program of All-Inclusive Care for the Elderly (PACE) A comprehensive healthcare delivery system funded by Medicare and Medicaid that focuses on providing community-based care and services to people who otherwise need nursing home levels of care.

Proportionality It is one of the five justification criteria that considers public health intervention against freedom of choice. Where the proportionality of public health intervention outweighs freedom of choice, then the intervention must be warranted.

Proprietary hospitals Also referred to as investor-owned hospitals, these are for-profit institutions and are owned by corporations, individuals, or partnerships.

Prospective payment system A method of reimbursement in which Medicare payment is made based on a predetermined, fixed amount. The payment amount for a particular service is derived based on the classification system of that service.

Prospective reimbursement A method of reimbursement in which Medicare payment is made based on a predetermined, fixed amount based on care criteria for certain conditions, regardless of providers' costs.

Prospective utilization review A review implemented before the service is actually performed by having the procedure authorized by the MCO, having the primary care provider decide to refer the member for the service, or assessing the service based on the clinical guidelines.

Prosthetist A specialist who designs "prostheses" or devices for patients who have limb amputations to replace the limb function.

Provider sponsored organizations (PSOs) Organizations owned or controlled by healthcare provider organizations that are formed to directly contract with purchasers to deliver healthcare services.

Pseudo dementias Also known as false dementias, the conditions develop as a result of medications, drug interactions, poor diet, or heart and gland diseases.

Psychiatric technicians and aides A segment of healthcare workforce who care for people who have mental illness or developmental disabilities. The two occupations are related, but technicians typically provide therapeutic care, and aides help patients in their daily activities.

Psychiatrists Specialty physicians who can provide diagnosis and treatment of mental illness, prescribe medication, and admit patients to hospitals.

Psychologists Healthcare providers who collaborate with physicians, social workers, and others to treat illness and promote overall wellness by a study of the human mind and human behavior.

Psychotropic medications Any drug capable of affecting the mind, emotions, and behavior. Some legal drugs, such as lithium for bipolar disorder, are psychotropic.

Public education It is one of the five justification criteria where public health workers must provide public education to explain their interventions and why the infringement on individual choices is warranted.

Public health It refers to the overall health and safety of the U.S. population achieved by preventing disease, monitoring, regulating, and promoting health through organized efforts, including core functions and essential services by several federal departments and agencies.

Public Health Accreditation Board (PHAB) It was formed as a nonprofit organization dedicated to improving and protecting the health of the public by advancing the quality and performance of tribal, state, local, and territorial public health departments.

Public health educational campaign An educational strategy to inform the community about positive health behavior, targeting those at risk to change or maintain positive health behavior.

Public health functions The responsibility of local health departments to protect and promote health, and prevent disease and injury, which includes child immunization programs, health screenings in schools, community health services, substance abuse programs, and sexually transmitted disease control.

Public health laboratory testing It is the ability to conduct rapid and conventional detection, characterization, confirmatory testing, data reporting, investigative support, and laboratory networking to address actual or potential exposure to all hazards.

Public health preparedness A continuous cycle of planning, organizing, training, equipping, exercising, evaluating, and taking corrective action in an effort to ensure effective coordination during incident response.

Public Health Security and Bioterrorism Preparedness and Response Act An act that provided grants to hospitals and public health organizations to prepare for bioterrorism as a result of the September 11, 2001, attacks.

Public health surveillance and epidemiological investigation It is the ability to create, maintain, support, and strengthen routine surveillance and detection systems and epidemiological investigation processes, as well as to expand these systems and processes in response to incidents of public health significance.

Public hospitals An oldest type of hospital owned by the federal, state, or local government.

Public Plan Option A public health insurance option that would provide health insurance for individuals who could not afford private health insurance premiums.

Public welfare insurance A program based on income for millions of individuals, including children, that provides health care for its enrollees. The primary example of public welfare insurance is Medicaid.

Punitive damages Damages that are intended to punish the defendant.

Q

Quality committee A committee that is responsible for overseeing and monitoring the quality of healthcare services, including patient and environmental safety, within the Medical Center.

Quality improvement committee A committee that is responsible for quality improvement programs.

Quaternary care It is an extension of tertiary care and refers to highly specialized, cutting-edge tertiary care performed in research facilities and highly specialized facilities.

Qui tam A concept used in antitrust law, is Latin for 'he who sues'. A qui tam provision enables individuals to sue providers for fraudulent activity against the federal government, recovering a portion of the funds returned to the government.

R

Radio frequency identification A technology that uses chips that transmit data to receivers. Each of these chips is uniquely identified by a signal indicating where it is located.

Radio psychiatry A technology-based application where radio psychologists and psychiatrists provide advice, information, and referrals to consumers.

Recreational therapists A healthcare professional who provides individualized and group recreational therapy for individuals experiencing limitations in life activities as a result of a disabling condition, illness or disease, aging, or developmental factors.

Registered nurse A trained nurse who has been licensed by a state board after passing the national nursing examination.

Rehabilitation Act of 1973 This law applies to organizations that receive financial assistance from federal organizations, including the U.S. Department of Health and Human Services, and forbids discriminating against individuals with disabilities in terms of employee benefits and job opportunities.

Reinsurance Program A temporary program for employers who provide coverage to retirees over age 55 who are not yet eligible for Medicare. It reimburses the employer 80% of the retiree claims of $50,000–90,000.

Remote Area Medical (RAM) An organization founded in 1985 to develop a mobile, efficient workforce to provide free health care in areas of need worldwide.

Remote patient monitoring A technology also called as home telehealth, which uses devices to remotely collect and send data to a home health agency or a remote diagnostic testing facility (RDTF) for interpretation.

Reproductive cloning The deliberate production of genetically identical individuals.

Research cloning It is a procedure that creates a genetic replica, with a focus on replicating sources for stem cells to replace damaged tissues.

Research genetic testing Testing that focuses on how genes impact disease development.

Residential care facilities Facilities that provide around-the-clock social and personal care to the elderly, children, and others who cannot take care of themselves. Examples of residential care facilities are drug rehabilitation centers, group homes, and assisted-living facilities.

Resource utilization group (RUG) A type of prospective payment system for skilled nursing facilities, used by Medicare, provides for a per diem based on the clinical severity of patients.

Resource-based relative value scales (RBRVSs) It is the physician payment system used by the Centers for Medicare & Medicaid Services (CMS) and most other payers based on the principle that payments for physician services should vary with the resource costs for providing those services and is intended to improve and stabilize the payment system while providing physicians an avenue to continuously improve it.

Respect for autonomy It is one of the five basic values that all healthcare providers should observe which states that decision making may be different and healthcare providers must respect their patients' decisions even if they differ from their own.

Respiratory therapist A healthcare professional who performs basic respiratory care procedures, implements and monitors any respiratory therapy under the supervision of a physician or an advanced-level therapist, and reviews patient data, including tests and previous medical history.

Respite care A program developed to provide systematic relief to those caregivers of chronically ill patients who need a break.

Responder safety and health It is the ability to protect public health agency staff responding to an incident and the ability to support the health and safety needs of hospital and medical facility personnel, if requested.

Retrospective bundled payments Under the Bundled Payments Initiative composed of four broadly defined models of care, which link payments that multiple service beneficiaries receive during an episode of care, Model 2 and 3 follow the arrangement in which actual expenditures are reconciled against a target price for an episode of care.

Retrospective reimbursement A method in which a provider submitted a bill to a health insurance company that automatically reimbursed the provider, which gave no incentive to control costs in health care.

Retrospective utilization review It is an evaluation of services once the services have been provided. This may occur to assess treatment patterns of certain diseases. This type of review may include a financial review to assure accuracy of billing.

Risk plans A type of plan offered by Medicare which pays a premium per member that is based on the member's county of residence. Members could use both in-network and out-of-network providers. The risk plans cover all Medicare services and vision and prescription care.

Robert Wood Johnson Foundation It is the nation's largest philanthropy dedicated solely to health, with a goal to help raise the health of everyone in the United States to the level that a great nation deserves, by placing well-being at the center of every aspect of life.

Robotic checkups Checkup using a device consisting of a mobile cart with a two-way video screen and medical monitoring equipment, programmed to maneuver through healthcare facilities which can make rounds, checking on patients in different rooms and managing their individual charts and vital signs without direct human intervention. This is an innovative method of telemedicine.

Robotic surgery A type of minimally invasive surgery (MIS) that is less invasive than traditional surgery—there are smaller incisions, which reduce the risk of infection, shorten hospital stays, and reduce recuperation times.

Rules and regulations These are designated to control or govern conduct. Instituted by administrative agencies by interpreting common law and statutes.

S

Salaries A type of provider remuneration in Managed Care Organization Payment Plan, in which the provider is actually an employee of the MCO.

Sapien heart valve A life-saving alternative to open-heart surgery for patients who need a new valve but for whom surgery is considered high risk. The valve material is made of bovine tissue attached to a stainless-steel stent, which is expanded by inflating a small balloon in the valve space.

Secondary care It focuses on short-term interventions that may require a specialist's intervention.

Secondary prevention An intervention to stop or slow the progress of risk factors by early screening or treatment of the disease or injury.

Security rule Rules that apply to e-PHI, or electronic patient information, because of the increased use of electronic patient records. They are in place to prevent breach of any patient information.

Self-funded or self-insurance Health insurance programs that are implemented and controlled by the company itself and are administered by employers, who bear the financial risk of providing their own health insurance to their employees.

Self-help organizations These are usually nonprofit and free of charge organizations which provide education and support to caregivers of mentally ill individuals. Often, these organizations are anonymous because of the stigma attached to mental disorders.

Senior centers A center that provides a broad array of services for the older population, including meal and nutrition programs, education, recreational programs, health and wellness programs, transportation services, volunteer opportunities, counseling, and other services.

Service benefit plan A plan in which the employer has a contract with a benefit plan and pays a premium for each of its employees. Employees usually also pay a portion of the premium to the health plan. The health plan contracts with certain providers and facilities to provide services to their beneficiaries at a specified rate and makes payments directly to the providers for their services.

Sexual harassment Is defined as unwelcome sexual conduct that has a negative impact on the employee.

Sherman Act of 1890 Focuses on eliminating monopolies, price fixing, market division, tying, boycotts, and price information exchange in healthcare organizations to protect the consumers.

Sherman Antitrust Act of 1890 The first piece of legislation that ensured fair competition in the marketplace for patients by prohibiting monopolies.

Silent PPOs An unauthorized third-party organization outside the contract between the MCO and the physician that gains access to a discounted rate for services from a physician, hospital, or other healthcare provider without direct authorization from the provider to do so.

Silver Sneakers It is a program created to provide free access to organized exercise at national fitness chains and encouraged the elderly to participate in it.

Single-payer system A national healthcare program to provide universal access to health care to all citizens, where the government pays for the healthcare services.

Small Business Health Options Program (SHOP) A marketplace for small employers, either a business or nonprofit organization, which must have 50 or fewer full-time equivalent employees (FTEs), who want to provide health and dental coverage to their employees—affordably, flexibly, and conveniently.

Social and community networks The external influences on the health of an individual characterized by interactions between groups of people and/or organizations and institutions.

Social insurance Insurance provided by the government at all levels: federal, state, and local. An example of this type of insurance is Medicare.

Social media An electronic communication medium dedicated to community-based input, interaction, content-sharing, and collaboration.

Social regulations A set of rules aimed at restricting behaviors that directly threaten public health, safety, welfare, or well-being.

Social Security Act (SSA) An act enacted to provide for the general welfare of older, retired people by establishing a system of federal old-age benefits, and by enabling several states to make more adequate provision for aged, blind, dependent and crippled children, maternal and child welfare, public health, and the administration of their unemployment.

Social Security Act of 1935 An act to provide for the general welfare by establishing a system of federal old-age benefits, and by enabling several states to make more adequate provision for aged persons, blind persons, dependent and crippled children, maternal and child welfare, public health, and the administration of their unemployment compensation laws.

Social Security Amendments of 1983 A bill passed to reform the Medicare reimbursement of hospitals, to extend the federal supplemental compensation program, and for other purposes.

Socialized health insurance system A national healthcare system where the government mandates financial contributions by both employers and employees, with private providers delivering health care.

Sonography A diagnosis test that uses sound waves to generate images of the body for the assessment and diagnosis of various medical conditions.

Specialists A physician who is certified in an area of specialization after additional years of training and a board certifying or credentialing examination.

Specialty care A result of the primary care evaluation where the primary care provider will coordinate the overall care of the patient by referring to a specialist for additional care.

Specialty maldistribution It refers to an issue in physician supply, with an increasing proportion of specialists to generalists.

Staff model A type of closed-panel HMO which hires physicians to work at a physical location.

Stakeholder An individual or group that has an active interest in an organization or activity. In the healthcare industry, employers outside are also stakeholders because they provide a large percentage of health insurance coverage to individuals nationwide.

Stakeholder management It focuses on the relationship between organizations and all of their constituents, including shareholders, and how management recognizes the different expectations of each group.

Standard of care The level and type of care that a reasonably competent and skilled healthcare professional, with a similar background and in the same medical community, would have provided under the circumstances that led to the alleged malpractice.

State health departments Departments or agencies of the state governments of the United States focused on public health. They monitor communities to identify, diagnose, and investigate health problems and provide education about health issues.

State licensure State governments oversee the licensure of healthcare facilities, including hospitals, with a focus on building codes, sanitation, equipment, and personnel before granting license to operate.

Statutes Laws created by legislative bodies such as the U.S. Congress.

Statutory consent If a patient cannot clinically give consent to a lifesaving medical treatment, it is presumed a reasonable person would give consent to the lifesaving procedure.

Stem cells These are "starter" cells for the development of body tissue that has yet to be formed into specialized tissues for certain parts of the body.

Stewardship model It states that public health officials should achieve the stated health outcomes for the population while minimizing restrictions on people's freedom of choice.

Stop-loss measure A form of reinsurance for self-insured employers that sets a specific amount of limit the employers will have to pay for each person's health care.

Summary of Benefits and Coverage (SBC) It is established by the ACA, which offers consumers the opportunity to easily compare health insurance plans.

Surgeon General The chief health educator of the United States, who provides information on how to improve the health of the U.S. population.

Surgeon technologist A healthcare professional responsible for preparing the operating room by equipping the room with the appropriate sterile supplies and verifying the equipment is working properly.

Surgical assistant A specialized physician's assistant whose main goal is to ensure the surgeon has a safe and sterile environment in which to perform. They determine the appropriate equipment for the procedure, select radiographs for a surgeon's reference, assist in moving the patient, confirm procedures with the surgeon, and assist with the procedure as directed by the surgeon.

Surveillance It is the monitoring of patterns of disease and investigating disease outbreaks to develop public health intervention strategies to combat disease.

T

Take Care Clinic Clinics where licensed healthcare professionals treat patients 18 months and older and can prescribe medications when appropriate.

Task Force on Promoting Resilience in Response to Terrorism An association that produced fact sheets that are intended to provide information to psychologists assisting those target populations impacted by terrorist events.

Tax Equity and Fiscal Responsibility Act (TEFRA) A United States federal law created in order to reduce the budget gap by generating revenue through closure of tax loopholes and introduction of tougher enforcement of tax rules, as opposed to changing marginal income tax rates.

Teaching hospitals A hospital that has one or more graduate resident programs approved by the AMA.

Telebehavioral health Using video conferencing technology, telebehavioral health services allow "real time" visits with a behavioral health specialist in another location who can assist in the evaluation, diagnosis, management, and treatment of health problems.

Telehealth It is the broad term that encompasses the use of IT to deliver education, research, and clinical care.

Telemedicine Refers to the use of information technology to enable healthcare providers to communicate with rural healthcare providers regarding patient care or to communicate directly with patients regarding treatment.

Telephone counseling Any type of psychological service performed over the telephone.

Telesurgery The concept of surgery which combines virtual reality, robots, and medicine, developed by the National Aeronautic and Space Administration (NASA).

Temporary care programs Refer **Respite care**.

Tertiary care It is a complex level of medical care, typically done by surgeons—physicians who perform operations to treat disease, physical problems, and injuries.

Tertiary prevention An intervention to prevent further damage or injury, reduce pain, slow the progression of the disease or injury, prevent the disease or injury from causing further complications, and rehabilitate as much as possible to improve quality of life.

The Joint Commission A private, nonprofit organization that continues to improve the safety and quality of

U.S. health care. It assesses performance improvement and provides accreditation to healthcare organizations.

Therapeutic cloning A procedure that creates a genetic replica of a cell or organism, with a focus on replicating sources for stem cells to replace damaged tissues. It is considered unethical because it involves destroying embryos to obtain healthy stem cells for research.

Third-party payer An insurance company that provides reimbursement to healthcare providers for services rendered to a patient.

Tort A category of wrongful acts, in civil law, which may not have a preexisting contract.

Tort reform It is a contentious political issue. The reform advocates, among other things, procedural limits on the ability to file claims and capping the awards of damages.

Transfusion medicine specialist A specialist in blood banking (SBB) technology who provides routine and specialized tests for blood donor centers, transfusion centers, laboratories, and research centers.

Transplantation It is the general procedure of implanting a functional organ from one person to another.

Treasurer An employee who is responsible for cash management, banking relations, accounts payable, etc.

TRICARE A healthcare program of the United States Department of Defense Military Health System that provides insurance coverage to current and retired members of the U.S. armed forces.

Triple Aim An act that focuses on three goals: improving patient satisfaction, reducing health costs, and improving public health.

Tying An illegal action as per the Sherman Act of 1890 that refers to healthcare providers that will only sell a product to a consumer who will also buy a second product from them.

U

Underinsured People who have insurance but have high deductibles and out-of-pocket expenses compared to their income.

Uniformed Services Employment and Reemployment Rights Act (USERRA) An act that entitles individuals who leave for military service to return to their job.

United Way A civic organization that is active in identifying health risks and implementing community public health programs to target these risks.

Universal healthcare program A type of health care where everyone is provided coverage regardless of their income, race, age, preexisting conditions, gender, or wealth.

Urgent and emergent care centers A care center used for consumers who need medical care but whose situation is not life-threatening.

Usual, customary, and reasonable (UCR) services Medical services for which the amount paid is based on what providers in the area usually charge for the same or similar

medical service that does not exceed the customary fee in that geographic area, and is reasonable based on the circumstances.

Utilization review Evaluation of the necessity, appropriateness, and efficiency of the use of healthcare services, procedures, and facilities.

Utilization review committee A committee that evaluates the necessity, appropriateness, and efficiency of the use of healthcare services, procedures, and facilities and ensures inpatient stays are clinically appropriate.

V

Value-based purchasing (VBP) A demand-side strategy to measure, report, and reward excellence in healthcare delivery.

Visiting nurse agencies An agency that provides medical services in a patient's home; often provided to elderly or disabled individuals or patients who are too weak to come to the hospital or physician's office or have just been released from the hospital.

Visualization A technique where a patient creates a mental image of wellness and recovery. It is used by traditional healthcare providers to treat substance abuse, panic disorders, and stress.

Voluntary commitment It occurs when people commit themselves willingly to receive care. If a person voluntarily commits for treatment, that person can leave of his or her own free will.

Voluntary euthanasia Assisting a patient with ending his or her life at the patient's request.

Voluntary health insurance (VHI) Schemes that range from employer-based for-profit schemes, to small nonprofit schemes such as community-based health insurance in which the decision to join and paying premium is voluntary.

Voluntary hospitals These are hospitals that are privately owned and nonprofit facilities considered voluntary because their financial support is the result of community organizational efforts.

Volunteer management It is the ability to coordinate the identification, recruitment, registration, credential verification, training, and engagement of volunteers to support the jurisdictional public health agency's response to incidents of public health significance.

W

Web-based e-health patient service sites A website that provides direct consumer outreach and services over the Internet.

Women's Health and Cancer Rights Act (WHCRA) An act that helps protect many women with breast cancer who choose to have their breasts rebuilt (reconstructed) after a mastectomy.

Worker Adjustment and Retraining Notification Act of 1989 An act that states employers with 100 employees or more must give their employees 60 days' notice of layoffs and business closings.

Workers' compensation A state-administered program that employers are required to have to cover employees who get sick or injured on the job may receive cash for lost wages, payment for medical treatment, survivor's death benefits, and indemnification for loss of skills.

Working Group on Healthcare Quality A federal interagency that was established to develop national initiatives on quality performance collaborating with other federal agencies to implement the National Quality Strategy developed by the DHHS.

Workplace bullying An ongoing harassing workplace behavior between employees, which results in negative health outcomes for the targeted employees.

X

Xenotransplantation Transfer of organs from one species to another.

Y

Yoga An Indian system that uses breathing techniques, stretching, and meditation to balance the body.

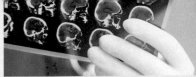

Index